MURTY CLASSICAL
LIBRARY OF INDIA

Sheldon Pollock, General Editor

KALIDASA
THE LINEAGE OF THE RAGHUS

MCLI 38

KALIDASA

कालिदास

THE LINEAGE
OF THE RAGHUS

Edited and translated by
CSABA DEZSŐ, DOMINIC GOODALL,
and HARUNAGA ISAACSON

MURTY CLASSICAL LIBRARY OF INDIA

HARVARD UNIVERSITY PRESS

Cambridge, Massachusetts

London, England

2024

SERIES DESIGN BY M9DESIGN

Library of Congress Cataloging-in-Publication Data

Names: Kālidāsa, author. |
Kālidāsa. Raghuvaṃśa. |
Kālidāsa. Raghuvaṃśa. English (Dezső, Goodall and Isaacson)
| Dezső, Csaba, editor, translator. |
Goodall, Dominic, editor, translator. |
Isaacson, Harunaga, 1965- editor, translator.
Title: The lineage of the Raghus / Kalidasa ;
edited and translated by Csaba Dezső,
Dominic Goodall and Harunaga Isaacson.
Other titles: Murty classical library of India ; 38.
Description: Cambridge, Massachusetts ; London, England :
Harvard University Press, 2024. |
Series: Murty classical library of India ; 38 |
Author's name also appears on the title page in Devanagari script. |
Includes bibliographical references and index. |
Sanskrit (Devanagari script) with English translation.
Identifiers: LCCN 2023003090 |
ISBN 9780674292598 (cloth)
Subjects: LCSH: Suryavamsha dynasty--Early works to 1800--Poetry. |
Suryavamsha dynasty--Early works to 1800--
Poetry--Translations into English. |
Epic poetry, Sanskrit--Early works to 1800. |
Epic poetry, Sanskrit--Early works to 1800--Translations into English.
Classification: LCC PK3796.R3 .D49 2024 |
DDC 891/.21--dc23/eng/20230614
LC record available at https://lccn.loc.gov/2023003090

CONTENTS

INTRODUCTION *ix*

NOTE ON THE TEXT AND TRANSLATION *xxix*

1 Reaching Vasishtha's Ashram *3*

2 Nandini Bestows a Boon *27*

3 Raghu's Birth and Duel with Indra *49*

4 Raghu Conquers the Four Directions *71*

5 Raghu Sends Aja to Bhoja's Court as a Suitor *95*

6 Indumati Chooses a Husband *121*

7 A Wedding and an Ambush *149*

8 Aja's Lament *171*

9 Dasharatha Goes Hunting *197*

10 Rama Descends *225*

11 Rama's Youth *249*

12 Rama, Banished to the Forest, Loses and Recaptures Sita *275*

13 Rama and Sita Return to Ayodhya *303*

14 Sita Rejected *329*

15 Sita Is Swallowed by Her Mother the Earth *357*

16 Ayodhya Abandoned, Then Restored to Glory *385*

17 Atithi, the Perfect King *411*

18 A Catalogue of Kings *433*

19 Agnivarna's Revels *451*

ABBREVIATIONS *469*

NOTES TO THE TEXT *471*

NOTES TO THE TRANSLATION *501*

GLOSSARY *543*

BIBLIOGRAPHY *549*

INDEX *555*

INTRODUCTION

Who Was Kalidasa?

An ignorant and illiterate cowherd, says the tradition.[1]
He aspired to the hand of a princess, the daughter of King
Vikramaditya, and thanks to the grace of the goddess Kali, he
became the greatest Sanskrit poet and playwright of all time.
A murderous courtesan is said to have cut short his life in Sri
Lanka. But such tales cannot be traced back to any time near
Kalidasa's own, and we know a great deal less about him than
we do about Shakespeare, another poet whose life has been
the subject of fevered and largely fruitless speculation, and
to whom Kalidasa is often compared. What is clear, however,
is that, for a millennium and a half, his verses have been read,
recited, and loved wherever Sanskrit has been studied.

Kalidasa's literary style, characterized by harmony,
profundity of sense, and freedom from verbal pyrotechnics,
is traditionally associated with the region of Vidarbha in
central India. But there is no settled consensus about where
and when Kalidasa lived and worked, and various ancient
and modern scholars have claimed him for different regions.
Such claims tend to be based on Kalidasa's supposedly inti-
mate knowledge of the geography and customs of particular
places, as evinced in chapters 4 and 6 of *The Lineage of the
Raghus,* which offer a panoramic sweep across the Indian
subcontinent. Chapter 4 is especially rich in geographical
information, because it describes King Raghu's conquests
in every direction. Conspicuous in the account of those

conquests is the mention of famous trade items associated with the places described, and it is possible that these items steered Kalidasa's description. In other words, it may not be fruitful to worry over the precise order in which Kalidasa presents certain rivers and polities and what this might reveal about where he lived or which places he visited.[2] It seems possible that Kalidasa intended not so much to present exact or relative locations and descriptions of places as to emphasize the richness of all the regions conquered.[3]

Although it may be difficult to pin down Kalidasa on the map, most recent scholarship places him somewhere in central India. The city of Ujjain was evidently important to Kalidasa, since its temple to Shiva Mahakala is mentioned in each of his three great poems. Kalidasa appears to have had a marked devotion to the deity Shiva, who is venerated at the start of *The Lineage of the Raghus* and is generally prominent in Kalidasa's works, which are rich in Shaiva mythology. Indeed, it is Kalidasa who gives the earliest full account for some details of Hindu myth: for example, his golden narration in *Kumārasambhava* of the sequence of events that led to the birth of Shiva's son, the war god Kumara, has largely eclipsed other versions. Relics of those versions have survived, notably in the great epic the *Mahābhārata,* but it is Kalidasa's that lives on in sculptures, paintings, and countless retellings.

A further indication of Kalidasa's Shaiva leanings could be his name, which may be translated as "Servant (*dāsa*) of Kali."[4] The association between the terrible goddess Kali and Shiva is less than certain, though. Kali is not an important deity in surviving sources prior to the fifth century, and the poet's name is an oddity for its time.

Kalidasa's period has been as contested as his provenance. Because of the absence of firmly dated works (or epigraphs) of even distantly comparable style, dating him to before the beginning of the Common Era seems implausible. The earliest dated document that mentions Kalidasa by name is a Sanskrit epigraph from 634 C.E., in which the author, Ravikirti, compares his own prowess with that of the poets Kalidasa and Bharavi.[5] But there are unmistakable parallels to Kalidasa's lines from slightly earlier—in Sanskrit inscriptions from the first quarter of the seventh century in Cambodia, and in a Gupta inscription from the fifth century—that reveal the influence of his writings.[6] Other possible echoes of his turns of phrase appear in later Gupta and Vakataka inscriptions.[7]

Whether or not such similarities in wording demonstrate that the poets who wrote the inscriptional Gupta and Vakataka panegyrics were influenced by Kalidasa, many scholars have long suspected a close connection between our poet and the Gupta dynasty. The plot of Kalidasa's play the *Mālavikāgnimitra* (Malavika and Agnimitra) might mirror the political milieu of the Gupta age, especially the dynastic relationship between the Guptas and their southern neighbors, the Vakatakas.[8] Several scholars have pointed out the close parallels between Samudragupta's Allahabad inscription, dated 350 C.E., and Raghu's world conquest in the fourth chapter of *The Lineage of the Raghus*.[9] In short, a late fourth- or early fifth-century date for the poet's career seems most likely.[10]

An Unusual Literary Epic?

The immense "universal" epics of ancient India—universal because they are known to all, sometimes in a re-creation or translation into another language, and have inspired countless other works—are famously the *Rāmāyaṇa* and the *Mahābhārata. The Lineage of the Raghus* belongs to another, more consciously literary genre, also referred to in translation as "epic" but known in Sanskrit as the *mahākāvya*, "court poem." According to the most famous definition, given by the rhetorician and poet Dandin in his *Kāvyādarśa* (The Mirror of Poetry), composed around the turn of the seventh to the eighth century, such a poem may

> begin with a blessing, a veneration, or a naming of the
> principal theme. It may be drawn from a story in the
> [ancient] epics or it may be some other [story] about
> noble [events and people]. It speaks of the fruition of
> the four aims [of man, namely Piety (*dharma*), Profit
> (*artha*), Pleasure (*kāma*) and Liberation (*mokṣa*)].
> Its hero is clever and noble.[11] It is embellished with
> descriptions of a city, the sea, mountains, the risings
> of the moon and sun, games played in gardens or in
> water, bouts of drinking and feasts of love, separations
> and marriages, the birth of a boy, counsel, embassies,
> campaigns, battles and the hero's ascent to success.
> It should not be too condensed, and it should be
> pervaded with [whatever has been chosen to be
> the predominant] poetic sentiment and with what
> gives expression [to that sentiment]. It should have
> chapters that are not too long, well connected to each

other, and composed in meters that are pleasing to the ear. They should always conclude with a different meter. Such a poem, pleasing to the world and with well-chosen figures of speech, is one that may last until the end of an age.[12]

The Lineage of the Raghus fits this description in all but one particular: there is no single set of protagonists and, hence, no unity of plot, a striking contrast to the other beloved works of this genre. A set of six *mahākāvya*s is usually celebrated: Kalidasa's own *Raghuvaṃśa* and *Kumārasambhava* (The Birth of the War God); the sixth-century *Kirātārjunīya* (Arjuna and the Hunter) by Bharavi; the sixth-century *Rāvaṇavadha* (The Slaying of Ravana) by Bhatti, also called the *Bhaṭṭikāvya*; the seventh-century *Śiśupālavadha* (The Killing of Shishupala) by Magha; and the twelfth-century *Naiṣadhacarita* (The Deeds of Nala) by Shriharsha. *The Lineage of the Raghus* stands out in this list because it has not just one plotline but several. And yet it is, for many, the greatest example of a genre whose "ground rules" it flouts.

Kalidasa's Works

Beside *The Lineage of the Raghus,* five other works are securely attributed to Kalidasa.[13] One is another *mahākāvya*, the *Kumārasambhava* (The Birth of the War God); one is a lyrical "messenger poem," the *Meghadūta* (The Cloud Messenger), in which a forlorn *yakṣa* (a type of demigod) requests of a cloud that it carry a message to his beloved. The other three are dramas: the *Abhijñānaśākuntala* (The Recognition of Shakuntala), whose arrival in Europe in translated form was fêted in literary circles and famously inspired Goethe to add a prologue to his *Faust;* the *Vikramorvaśīya* (Urvashi Won by Valor); and a play about a court intrigue called the *Mālavikāgnimitra* (Malavika and Agnimitra). To this undisputed corpus of six works, some add the *Ṛtusaṃhāra* (Compendium of the Seasons), an anthology of verses celebrating each of the six seasons of Indian poetic convention in turn, but its attribution is doubtful.

Of the three poems, one deals with the world of the gods and no ordinary human figures (*The Birth of the War God*); another with the world of men, although gods often intervene (*The Lineage of the Raghus*), and the last with the world of the semidivine *yakṣas* (*The Cloud Messenger*). Short as it is, *The Cloud Messenger* has a special place; the *yakṣa* separated from his beloved is in a sense an Everyman (the poem begins significantly with the indefinite masculine pronoun *kaścit,* "a certain"). Kalidasa seems deliberately to work in not only the sacred geography of his native north India but also an astonishingly rich range of allusions to all the most important elements of his imaginaire, which gives the poem almost the feeling of a mnemonic encyclopedia. None of his other compositions has been as often commented on or imitated.

The three plays can likewise be seen as each related to a separate sphere: one to the epic *Mahābhārata* (*The Recognition of Shakuntala*), one to ancient Vedic myth (*Urvashi Won by Valor*), and one (*Malavika and Agnimitra*) evoking the world of the court culture (slightly idealized no doubt) that Kalidasa himself must have known, and somewhat similar in tone and content to the *Bṛhatkathā* (The Great Tale, explicitly referred to in *The Cloud Messenger*).[14]

In spite of their seemingly deliberate differences, these six works share a distinctive temper and genius.[15] The nature of that is well-nigh impossible to describe, but words that have come to the minds of many who have read Kalidasa are "tolerance" and "harmony": a kindly tolerance that encompasses all, and a no less universal harmony interweaving and balancing the spheres of heaven and earth, humankind and nature, enjoyment and renunciation, and life and death.[16] We should note, however, that only the first eight chapters of the *Kumārasambhava* are almost universally accepted to be the work of Kalidasa. The subsequent chapters have long been widely suspected to be spurious. The case of *The Lineage of the Raghus* is less clear-cut. Ancient authorities do not question the authenticity of the whole, but some modern commentators have been skeptical about chapters 9 through 19. Even before explicit doubts were raised,[17] there were criticisms of the comparatively humdrum tone of the chapters that overlap with the narration of the *Rāmāyaṇa,* and one scholar, without adverting to the question, has observed the absence in the later chapters of a curious stylistic feature discernible in the first eight chapters, a sort of interlinking of contiguous verses by measured repetition of vocabulary.[18] Nonetheless, the evidence of the oldest manuscript of *The Lineage of the Raghus,*[19] the oldest commentary (that of Vallabhadeva), a number of citations in works from at the latest the early tenth century onward, and echoes too numerous to be ignored in inscriptions in South and South

East Asia from as early as the late sixth century show that these chapters, unlike chapters 9 to 17 of the *Kumārasambhava,* cannot be a late medieval addition. Furthermore, they contain at least occasional flashes—for instance, in the description of a flight over the ocean at the beginning of chapter 13 and of the abandoned city of Ayodhya in chapter 16—of what seems to us the same poetic genius that is more easily recognizable in the earlier part of the work.

There is a body of scholarship surrounding the relative dates of the different parts of Kalidasa's œuvre, but most of it is inevitably speculative and based on personal intuitions and convictions. Some feel that *The Lineage of the Raghus* breathes a cynicism about monarchy as a system of government, which suggests in turn that Kalidasa had matured beyond a youthful enthusiasm for court intrigue, evident in his *Mālavikāgnimitra.*[20] Others attempt close stylistic comparison of stanzas on comparable subject matter in different works. *The Lineage of the Raghus* and the *Kumārasambhava,* for instance, both include descriptions of a wedding—they even share a number of phrases— and it has been argued that the version of the *Kumārasambhava* is more polished and that *The Lineage of the Raghus* is therefore the earlier of the two compositions.[21] One problem with this sort of approach is that the wording of the verses compared—and indeed the wording of all of Kalidasa's surviving writings—is so far from settled. His works have reached us through thousands of premodern manuscript copies written in multiple scripts and spanning fifteen centuries (see Note on the Text and Translation).

Naturally, this transmission is complex, lacunose, and far from univocal.

Although there may be some debate about which works are juvenilia, there is a general agreement that the *Abhijñānaśākuntala,* which incidentally has the most complicated transmission history of them all, is a work of mature genius.

The Plotlines of The Lineage of the Raghus

The Lineage of the Raghus has no unitary plot; instead, it sketches the lives of a series of ancient kings, all ruling in the remote past of a "silver age" when lifetimes lasted tens of thousands of years, usually concentrating on one or two striking episodes. These kings rule a kingdom from their capital city of Ayodhya, in the heart of the Gangetic plain. The first nine chapters cover kings Dilipa, Raghu, Aja, and Dasharatha (until the birth of his son Rama). As we shall see from the stories chosen to highlight their reigns, the first three kings wrestle respectively with what Indian tradition characterizes as the three principal *puruṣārtha*s (aims of man): Dilipa is governed by *dharma* (moral duties); the chief events of Raghu's life concern the handling of *artha* (wealth and policy); Aja's life is one of friendships, familial bonds, love and loss, and he thus embodies the engagement with *kāma* (desires, love).

Chapters 10 through 15 recount the tumultuous lives of Rama and Sita, the central protagonists of Valmiki's *Rāmāyaṇa.* The reigns of Kusha and Atithi, son and grandson respectively of Rama, are recounted in chapters 16 and

17; then follows a long and remarkably unmemorable list of monarchs in chapter 18 before the final portrait of the dissolute and sex-addicted King Agnivarna in chapter 19.

The Reception of The Lineage of the Raghus

More than fifty premodern Sanskrit commentaries on the *Raghuvaṃśa* have survived, and the epic continues to be beloved to Sanskrit readers both because and in spite of its use for well over a thousand years as a schoolroom text.[22]

All sorts of evidence—including plentiful allusions in the politico-religious poetry of royal inscriptions from at the latest the seventh century onward and over the whole area of Sanskritic influence, from what is now Pakistan in the west to Cambodia and Indonesia in the east—shows that *The Lineage of the Raghus* has long been recognized as a masterpiece of Sanskrit literature. Kalidasa's enormous influence upon Sanskrit poetry in general is also ubiquitous: along with Valmiki, the author of the *Rāmāyaṇa,* he is the poet most frequently praised by his successors in the beginnings of their works, and there is hardly any *mahākāvya* after his time that does not contain at least a few echoes.

It is striking, then, that the European reception of *The Lineage of the Raghus* seems not to have been enthusiastic. Unlike Kalidasa's lyrical *Meghadūta* (The Cloud Messenger) or his famous play about Shakuntala, *Abhijñānaśākuntala* (The Recognition of Shakuntala), *The Lineage of the Raghus* received no rapturous encomium by Goethe (that it was translated into a Western language much later than the other two works may be one reason).

European critics (perhaps under the shadow of Aristotle's notions of the unity of action, time, and place) have tended to quibble over the fragmented character of its narrative, with a change of hero every couple of chapters. They have also speculated (as did medieval Indian commentators) about whether the text was really complete in nineteen chapters, because the ending is decidedly surprising, and about whether the last eleven chapters are by Kalidasa at all. And they have commented with disapproval on the perfunctory retelling of the story of Valmiki's *Rāmāyaṇa* in chapters 10 through 14. Some have also wondered whether the poem was intended as a denunciation of the moral failings of the lineage of kings it claims to glorify or a condemnation of the political system they represented, since the narrative begins with a problem of infertility and ends with the last scion of the line still in the womb, after the libidinous father has succumbed to a venereal disease.[23]

But if the poem's completeness is in doubt, if the authenticity of its latter half is questionable, if the main characters keep changing and there is no single plot, if the treatment of Rama in the central section is perfunctory, and if the eulogy of the whole dynasty and many individuals in it seems to ring suspiciously hollow, then what can explain well over a thousand years of extraordinary popularity?

Not all these criticisms are unanswerable. The narration of the central section is light perhaps simply because Kalidasa expected all readers to know Valmiki's *Rāmāyaṇa* already.[24] The absence of a unitary plot does not mean that the plotting is weak: Kalidasa's poem, in fact, often has great narrative drive, but each plotline is contained within one or two chapters. In other words, the work is plot driven but strongly episodic. Some unity, however, is created by focusing on a single patriline through centuries of mythical time. The other supposed weaknesses might also be reckoned as strengths, for they concern aesthetic and moral ambiguities that Kalidasa might well have intended. They arguably create a sort of *sfumato* that requires the receiver to resolve ambivalence into clarity, thus allowing different audiences to hear different ideas. Something like this seems to be remarked upon by a late medieval exegete from Kerala, Arunagirinatha, commenting on a passage where such haziness seems heightened: the scene of Indumati's choice of a husband in chapter 6. As Indumati progresses around a glittering assembly of eligible princes, each of her royal suitors is glowingly described with a stanza or two by the lady who guides her. Several descriptions, as Arunagirinatha observes, are very subtly double-edged, even though no puns are involved: many a vaunted virtue could imply that such a husband might not really suit the bride.[25] The effect is masterfully achieved because, while the expression throughout seems limpidly clear, it is oddly difficult to decide what message each description is intended to convey.

One quality, then, for which Kalidasa may be admired is writing that seems extremely clear but is at the same time rich in possibilities of evocation (*dhvani*). His style, as noted, is traditionally characterized as that of the region of Vidarbha in central India, which was prized for its sweetness and directness, and for eschewing double entendre, which is both common and often elaborate in Sanskrit belles lettres. Another virtue of Kalidasa's writing that tradition has long valued is his choice of perfectly apposite similes (*upamā*), and it is arguable that he most favored this literary figure.

But other than a felicitous style, well-chosen similes, and a capacity for richness achieved partly through what we have called *sfumato,* is there something else that readers loved and that might appeal to readers of the *Raghuvaṃśa* in translation? That authors of royal eulogies through the centuries have drawn more upon the *Raghuvaṃśa* than upon any other poem is natural enough, given that it is about a lineage of kings. But the theme may matter little. For although Kalidasa writes about a world of heroic myth for which the reader's suspension of disbelief is mandatory, it comes alive in large part because he so beautifully describes—or by the lightest of touches contrives to call to mind—universal human emotions. Most famous in this regard is the portrayal of Aja's grief at the loss of his beloved wife, Indumati, in chapter 8. Other strong feelings are also powerfully evinced in other less-celebrated passages: the father's thrill at the conception and birth of his first son, for instance, is skillfully conjured up in chapter 3.

Kalidasa's Sources

Kalidasa drew his material from diverse sources, including the body of Vedic literature, the two epics *Mahābhārata* and *Rāmāyaṇa,* the *Bṛhatkathā,* and probably some early Purana.

His predecessors include Valmiki, the legendary author of the *Rāmāyaṇa,* generally referred to as the "first poet" (*ādikavi*). Valmiki is surely the first among the "ancient seers" whose "gateway of speech" Kalidasa acknowledges having used in *The Lineage of the Raghus*.[26] We must assume that many other unnamed earlier poets, including several close to Kalidasa's time, have been forgotten, along with their works. One illustrious antecedent whom we can identify, although Kalidasa does not name him, is Ashvaghosha, who lived at least three centuries earlier. Ashvaghosha's poetry—honey, as he himself describes it, to make the bitter medicine of the truths of the Buddha's teaching sweet[27]—survives in Sanskrit mainly because of the devotion of Buddhist scribes in Nepal and Central Asia, and it was largely forgotten elsewhere. Numerous phrases in Kalidasa's works unmistakably recall Ashvaghosha's, and some twentieth-century critics have even debated about the direction of influence. It seems clear to us, however, that Ashvaghosha's work is closer to the infancy of the *mahākāvya* genre. Apart from Valmiki, the only predecessors named by Kalidasa (in his play *Mālavikāgnimitra*) are the poets Bhasa, Saumilla, and Kaviputra; however, the works of the last two are lost, and the authenticity of the surviving dramas attributed to the first is the subject of passionate controversy. Kalidasa's well-deserved popularity in later times may have contributed to this loss of nearly all of his predecessors' poems and plays.

Our poet's works also reflect his familiarity with the world of Sanskrit technical literature; they are rich in references to philosophical ideas and, for instance, to details of grammar, law, and statecraft. The last of these deserves brief discussion here. As is to be expected in an epic describing the reigns of kings, many passages in *The Lineage of the Raghus* show the influence of Sanskrit treatises on statecraft, particularly Kautilya's *Arthaśāstra:* for instance, Kalidasa uses technical terms such as "pacifying the territory gained" (*labdhapraśamana*) in 4.14, a topic treated in detail in *Arthaśāstra* 13.5; and "the tactic of reeds" (*vaitasī vṛtti*) in 4.36, mentioned in *Arthaśāstra* 12.1.1.[28] The seventeenth chapter of *The Lineage of the Raghus,* in which Kalidasa describes the exemplary reign of King Atithi, is full of allusions to the science of statecraft. The characteristics of the royal chaplain (*purohita*) and his role in counteracting both divine and human calamities, frequently invoked in *The Lineage of the Raghus,* are also expounded in the *Arthaśāstra.*[29] The topic of vices or addictions (*vyasana*s) and especially womanizing and hunting play an important role in Kalidasa's epic, the latter in the case of Dasharatha (chapter 9), the former in the case of Agnivarna (chapter 19). These vices are also discussed in detail both in the *Arthaśāstra* and in the *Manusmṛti* (Manu's Code of Law).[30] To read *The Lineage of the Raghus* is, among other things, to be introduced, rather broadly and in the most charming way, to the statecraft of the *Arthaśāstra.*

Acknowledgments

Back in 1991, two members of the team, Dominic Goodall and Harunaga Isaacson, began editing the earliest commentary on *The Lineage of the Raghus,* the *Raghupañcikā* by the tenth-century Kashmirian Vallabhadeva. Since the first volume of that edition appeared in 2003, the editing team has been expanded by the addition of Csaba Dezső and Csaba Kiss, whose research was for some years supported by the European Research Council Synergy project Beyond Boundaries: Religion, Region, Language and the State (Grant agreement no. 609823). The work achieved as part of that editing project has been enormously useful to us in preparing this translation.

We should also like to record our gratitude to the countless students and colleagues with whom we have read different parts of *The Lineage of the Raghus* in various universities around the world and in ten intensive Sanskrit reading retreats. Years ago, we began to translate *Raghuvaṃśa* for another series, now defunct, and we are grateful to Sheldon Pollock, first for having proposed its inclusion in the Murty Classical Library of India, second for his patient courtesy in response to each delay, and third and most important, for his hundreds of suggestions for improving the translation and bringing it into line with the editorial policies of the series. We thank also Csaba Kiss, who has helped us with many things, from checking manuscript readings to finding lost files and solving other technical troubles.

We dedicate this book to our parents.

NOTES

1 See, e.g., Jinavijaya 1933: 3–5.
2 In any case, different transmissions give the verses in different sequences and with plentiful variation in wording.
3 If the merchandise was the criterion for the mention of most places or areas that Raghu conquered, then there may be otherwise important polities or areas (perhaps even ones important for Kalidasa) that were not mentioned simply because they were not firmly associated with luxury goods such as nuts, spices, oleoresins, and birchbark (a writing material produced only in

the far northwest; see 4.76). Goods such as flowers or soft fruits might be regarded as luxuries too but are logistically more difficult to trade with over long distances and are not a focus.

4   This is Kali with long vowels, not to be confused with *kali* with short ones, the name of the degenerate age in which we live.

5   See Kielhorn 1902.

6   For the Cambodian echoes, see Kielhorn 1902 and Goodall 2019; on the Gupta inscription (from Mandasor) see Kielhorn 1902 and (independently) Bühler 1890: 69–71.

7   For a broad spread of evidence of Kalidasa's influence on the royal eulogies found in inscriptions, see Sivaramamurti 1944.

8   Bakker 2019: 311ff (elaborating on a remark of Warder).

9   See Ingalls 1976: 16 and Pollock 2006: 241, who contends that Kalidasa actually modeled his account on the Gupta inscription, and thus "the Samudragupta record was released from its immobilization in stone and set free for wide circulation."

10 Verses of a now lost work in which Kalidasa is the hero, called the *Kuntaleśvaradautya*, (Embassy to the Lord of Kuntala) are quoted in Sanskrit works on poetics (cf. Raghavan 1978: 765ff). But the "Lord" in question has been variously identified with Kadamba, Vakataka, and Rashtrakuta kings.

11 It is implicit, not explicit, that only one hero is expected.

12 *Kāvyādarśa* 1.14–19, ed. Böhtlingk 1890.

13 We have included in the bibliography editions with parallel English translations for each: Smith 2005b for the *Kumārasambhava*, Mallinson 2006 for the *Meghadūta*, Vasudeva 2006 for the *Abhijñānaśākuntala*, Narayana Rao and Shulman 2009 for the *Vikramorvaśīya*, Balogh and Somogyi 2009 for the *Mālavikāgnimitra*, and Devadhar 1993 for the *Ṛtusaṃhāra*.

14 The *Bṛhatkathā* is a body of stories interwoven into a multiple-box frame story about a certain Naravahanadatta becoming a magic-wielding wizard (*vidyādhara*). Somewhat like *Orlando Furioso* for the European imagination, it has inspired countless retellings and served as the point of departure for the plots of many works of belles lettres. One such retelling, sadly incomplete, by Budhasvamin, has been translated by Mallinson (2005).

15 This feeling of having sprung from the same mind and sharing the same temper is not the case in the *Compendium of the Seasons*,

although many of its verses are charming, and it is not impossible that a few were written by our poet.

16 For a sympathetic and much fuller attempt to describe Kalidasa's vision, see Ingalls 1976.

17 Perhaps the earliest scholar to call into question the authorship of *Raghuvaṃśa* 9–19 was Kunhan Raja in 1941 and again in 1956.

18 Schubring 1955 refers to this phenomenon as "Verschränkung."

19 What can be read from that fragmentary manuscript has been published by Taticchi (in Gnoli 1962). A range of dates has been proposed. On paleographic grounds, it seems likely to belong to the eighth or ninth century.

20 We have mentioned Ruben 1948 in this regard.

21 See Tubb 1982.

22 Govardhana punningly compares Kalidasa's poetry to love play, in that both give delight even while they are being learned: *sākū tamadhurakomalavilāsinīkaṇṭhakūjitaprāye/ śikṣāsamaye 'pi mude ratilīlākālidāsoktī//* (*Āryāsaptaśatī*, introductory verse 35, in Durgâprasâda and Parab 1895). "Even at the moment when one is first learning them, the play of love and the poetry of Kalidasa both give joy, being full of the passionate, sweet, tender moaning from the throat of a beautiful girl (/being expressive, sweet, tender and like the murmuring from the throat of a beautiful girl)."

23 The title of a monograph from 1948 by the Indologist and Marxist historian Walter Ruben reflects this sort of reaction: "Kalidasa's Raghuvamsha, a Gallery of Ancient Indian Despots" ("Kâlidâsas Raghuvaṃśa, eine Gallerie altindischer Despoten").

24 Another possible justification, offered by Arunagirinatha in his commentary on 12.53, is that the exposition of the *Rāmāyaṇa* is sometimes swift so as not to disturb the dominant poetic mood (*rasa*) of the poem as a whole, namely heroism (*vīra*).

25 In his commentary on 6.67 (which is 6.66 in his numbering), Arunagirinatha, after observing that certain eulogistic statements describing the royal suitors one by one contain criticism intended to repel Indumati (*pratirājavarṇanāni kānicid vākyāni nindāgarbhatvena kanyāvyāvartanaparāṇi*), discusses the passage at some length.

26 *The Lineage of the Raghus* 1.4.

27 See the fine discussion of Ashvaghosha and the professed goals of his poetry in Steiner 2010.

28   See Raghavan 1951, who also refers to previous studies.
29   See Dezső 2020.
30   See Dezső 2014.

NOTE ON THE TEXT
AND TRANSLATION

The *Raghuvaṃśa* has been published countless times over the last two centuries, but the Sanskrit text translated here and printed with the translation on facing pages differs from that of all previous editions. The principal reason is that most editions to date have presented the text as it was known to and commented upon by a medieval scholar called Mallinatha, who lived roughly ten centuries after Kalidasa. Over the course of that intervening millennium, innumerable transmitters of the poem—which was widely admired and used as a textbook example of fine literature—tweaked, corrected, and polished what they regarded as grammatical or factual errors or imperfections of style. It seems also plausible that aspiring poets practiced their skills by producing variants of many verses, some of which found acceptance in one recension or another of the poem.[1] These two phenomena cannot always be clearly distinguished. We find two very different versions of 4.50, for example, one of which refers to the dust of cardamom pods mixed with the detritus of silkworms or spiders. Perhaps this was not to the taste of the majority of medieval transmitters, who prefer a nobler alternative version: "The dust of the cardamom pods that were crushed by the horses rose up and stuck to the temples of elephants in musth, which had a scent similar to theirs." Was an alternative produced in reaction to the perceived unsatisfactoriness of the first version? Or was it by poets honing their craft by devising imitations, and then widely adopted because it also obviated a feature judged to be of questionable taste?

Although the possibility of a partly oral transmission of the text cannot be excluded—even today there are traditional scholars who have memorized the entirety of it—we think that from the time of its composition there must have been a vigorous manuscript transmission. For those who doubt this, we point to the verse of the poem (3.28) that shows how great an importance Kalidasa attributed to the written word for the study and transmission of literature. There must have been hundreds of thousands of manuscripts of the *Raghuvaṃśa* produced over the course of a millennium and a half, or more, perhaps millions.

Among the thousands of extant manuscripts, none survives from Kalidasa's time, but we can return to a state of the text that seems likely to be quite close to Kalidasa's composition by adopting the wording that was commented upon by a much earlier scholiast, the tenth-century Kashmirian writer Vallabhadeva. In a few places, evidence suggests that a variant transmitted by other sources or mentioned by Vallabhadeva as an alternative reading is more likely to be what Kalidasa wrote than the variant that Vallabhadeva actually chose to comment upon. A case in point is 2.42, for which we have two entirely different versions; we have accepted one that is rejected, as far as we are aware, by all editions hitherto printed, as well as by the medieval commentaries that have so far been published.[2] Sometimes these differences in wording make little or no difference to the translations, but we discuss them in notes as and when they do. How do we judge which readings are primary? Each text-critical problem needs to be considered on its own merits and in the light of all evidence that can be found, but we have observed that a verse that contains what later transmitters came to regard as grammatically, rhetorically, or factually problematic tends to be transmitted with variants that do not contain the problem. So, when any verse comes to us in two or more very different versions, we are primed to expect an "error" in what is likely to be the earliest version, an error obviated in other versions, which are therefore likely to be secondary. In some cases, it has taken us many readings to spot the probable catalyst for change, but we have over the years established certain patterns.[3]

In the back of this book we record only the variant readings known to Vallabhadeva and Mallinatha, the earliest and the best-known commentators respectively. Since there are differences in nearly every other verse, we have not cluttered the Sanskrit text with endnote numbers.

More than fifty premodern commentaries in Sanskrit survive, but only a small handful have been edited and printed. We have occasionally referred to those of Arunagirinatha, an insightful fourteenth-century scholar from Kerala; of Jinasamudra, a less original (and justly neglected) Jain author from western India of perhaps the late fifteenth century; of the grammarian Hemadri, perhaps of the same period and clearly different from a celebrated minister and encyclopedist of the same name; and of Shrinatha, whose unpublished commentary is of unknown date and provenance but survives in several northeastern manuscripts, one of which is dated to 1473 C.E.

In accordance with its relatively unenthusiastic reception in Europe, there are curiously few literary translations into European languages of the *Raghuvaṃśa,* arguably the most popular through the ages of all Sanskrit works of belles lettres, and very few are recent. The first one printed was in Latin, a language probably appreciated by fewer readers today than when it appeared in 1832, by "Adolphus Fridericus Stenzler" as an accompaniment to a scholarly edition of the Sanskrit text. It was, in fact, preceded by a translation into Greek by Demetrios Galanos, who died in 1833, but that translation was published posthumously in 1850.

A free-standing English translation in blank pentameter verse by P. de Lacy Johnstone appeared in 1902—an impressive literary achievement, but one that to twenty-first-century sensibilities seems so powerfully redolent of the Edwardian era that the underlying flavors of classical Gupta-period India are often quite drowned out. A similar charge might be leveled at Arthur W. Ryder's 1912 translation into quatrains of two rhyming couplets, which only covers short selected sections of each chapter, and also, although it appeared more than half a century later in 1973, at the blank verse version of Anantapadmanabhan. The most widely used English translations today are schoolroom editions produced in India in the first half of the twentieth century and kept in print by Indian publishing houses in recent decades: those of Kale (1922; multiple reprints, covering chapters 1–10), Karmarkar (1922; multiple reprints), Nandargikar (4th edition of 1971) and Devadhar (1984; multiple reprints). All are in prose, and all accompany annotated editions of the Sanskrit text. Also worth mentioning are the useful translations of Otto Walter of 1914 and of Louis Renou of 1928, into German and French respectively.

In our prose translation we have attempted, while striving for readability, to be as literal as Kale and Nandargikar, but without adding suppletions in brackets. We hope that the result may be read independently.

Of course many of the formal qualities of the poetry cannot be reproduced in translation. Throughout the description of spring in chapter 9, for instance, there is a fixed and relatively elaborate alliterative pattern: the second, third, and fourth syllables of each fourth verse quarter. Also untranslatable, of course, is the local feeling conveyed by the mentions of flora and fauna. In chapter 18, a litany of kings is presented, each described with words that etymologize his name or echo its sound. There we have added endnotes giving the Sanskrit words that playfully comment upon the kings' names.

Another recurrent problem has been how to handle what may seem to be a welter of proper names for the same individual. Some purists opine that such proper names should not be translated at all. Thus the god Shiva, for example, would appear variously as Aṣṭamūrti, Vṛṣabhadhvaja, Śūlabhṛt, Giriśa, Tryambaka, Bhūteśvara, Rudra, Bhūtanātha, Vṛṣāṅka, Maheśvara, Pinākin, and so forth. Indra too would hardly bear the same name twice.

The obvious problem with this strategy is that it perplexes non-Sanskritist readers. Instead of reproducing the whole plethora of untranslated proper names for a single individual, the other evident solution is consistently to translate throughout by "Shiva." But this too is not without problems, for it is a mark of Kalidasa's style that he often carefully chooses from among Sanskrit poetry's rich array of possible kennings for gods, people, and all manner of things, finding expressions that resonate with the particular context in which they are placed. The real and supposed etymologies of all the vocabulary tend to glow rather close beneath the surface of every passage. We have adopted a middle-of-the-road approach: sometimes "translating" rare names with more familiar ones, sometimes reproducing the rare names, sometimes analyzing and translating them and then adding footnotes that identify the persons by their best-known monikers.

The English titles of the chapters are of our own devising but inspired by the characterizations that often appear at the ends of chapters in the medieval commentaries.

1   There are, for instance, two versions of 4.16. For this phenomenon, common in the transmission of *mahākāvya* literature, of what Salomon calls "imitative and interpolated verses," see Salomon 2019: 239ff.
2   The version we accept contains a grammatical form that we know Kalidasa used but that was criticized by grammarians and almost systematically expunged from the *Raghuvaṃśa*. See Goodall 2001.
3   We have discussed such patterns at some length, particularly in Goodall 2001 and 2009.

THE LINEAGE
OF THE RAGHUS

प्रथमः सर्गः

१   वागर्थाविव सम्पृक्तौ वागर्थप्रतिपत्तये ।
    जगतः पितरौ वन्दे पार्वतीपरमेश्वरौ ॥

२   क्व सूर्यप्रभवो वंशः क्व चाल्पविषया मतिः ।
    तितीर्षुर्दुस्तरं मोहादुडुपेनास्मि सागरम् ॥

३   मन्दः कवियशःप्रार्थी गमिष्याम्यवहास्यताम् ।
    प्रांशुलभ्ये फले लोभादुद्बाहुरिव वामनः ॥

४   अथवा कृतवाग्द्वारे वंशे ऽस्मिन्पूर्वसूरिभिः ।
    मणौ वज्रसमुत्कीर्णे सूत्रस्येवास्ति मे गतिः ॥

५   सो ऽहमाजन्मशुद्धानामाफलोदयकर्मणाम् ।
    आसमुद्रक्षितीशानामानाकरथवर्त्मनाम् ॥

६   यथाविधिहुताग्नीनां यथाकामार्चितार्थिनाम् ।
    यथापराधदण्डानां यथाकालप्रबोधिनाम् ॥

CHAPTER 1
Reaching Vasishtha's Ashram

For mastery of word and meaning I venerate the parents 1
of the world, who are entwined together like word and
meaning: Parvati and Parameshvara.[1]

How incommensurate are the lineage arising from the Sun 2
and my mind of little scope! It is folly that makes me
wish to cross an uncrossable ocean on a raft.

A fool who wishes for a poet's fame, I shall become a 3
laughingstock, like a dwarf greedily stretching up his
arms toward a fruit that only the tall can reach.

Or rather, since ancient seers have made a gateway of 4
speech in it, I can enter into this lineage as a thread
enters a jewel bead pierced by a diamond.[2]

Pure from birth, working until the goal is reached, ruling 5
the earth up to the shores of the ocean, the paths of
their chariots ascending to the heavens,

sacrificing according to sacred prescript, honoring 6
suppliants according to their wishes, punishing
according to the crime, rising in accordance with the
hour,

७ त्यागाय सम्भृतार्थानां सत्याय मितभाषिणाम् ।
यशसे विजिगीषूणां प्रजायै गृहमेधिनाम् ॥

८ शैशवेऽभ्यस्तविद्यानां यौवने विषयैषिणाम् ।
वार्द्धके मुनिवृत्तीनां योगेनान्ते तनुत्यजाम् ॥

९ रघूणामन्वयं वक्ष्ये तनुवाग्विभवोऽपि सन् ।
तद्गुणैः कर्णमागत्य चापलाय प्रतारितः ॥

१० तं सन्तः श्रोतुमर्हन्ति सदसद्व्यक्तिहेतवः ।
हेम्नः संलक्ष्यते ह्याग्नौ विशुद्धिः श्यामिकापि वा ॥

११ वैवस्वतो मनुर्नाम माननीयो मनीषिणाम् ।
आसीन्महीक्षितामाद्यः प्रणवश्छन्दसामिव ॥

१२ तदन्वये शुद्धिमति प्रसूतः शुद्धिमत्तरः ।
दिलीप इति राजेन्दुरिन्दुः क्षीरनिधाविव ॥

१३ व्यूढोरस्को वृषस्कन्धः सालप्रांशुर्महाभुजः ।
आत्मकर्मक्षमं देहं क्षात्रो धर्म इवाश्रितः ॥

१४ सर्वातिरिक्तसारेण सर्वतेजोभिभाविना ।
स्थितः सर्वोन्नतेनोर्वीं क्रान्त्वा मेरुरिवात्मना ॥

collecting wealth for the sake of giving it away, restrained   7
    in speech for the sake of truth, wishing to conquer for
    the sake of fame, becoming householders for the sake
    of progeny,

studious in childhood, pursuing the pleasures of the   8
    senses in youth, living as sages in old age, renouncing
    their bodies by yoga at the end:

I shall speak of the lineage of the Raghus, although my   9
    power of speech is slight, impelled to this insolence by
    their virtues, which have reached my ears.

May those good people through whom the difference   10
    between good and bad can be known listen to it;
    for it is in fire that one can see if gold is pure or base.

There was a king called Manu, born of the sun, deserving   11
    respect from the wise. He was the first of kings, as *oṃ*
    is the first of the Vedic mantras.

In his pure lineage was born, even purer, a very moon   12
    among kings, called Dilipa, as the moon was born in
    the ocean of milk.[3]

His chest was broad, his shoulders were like a bull's, he   13
    was tall as a sal tree; it was as if the dharma of warriors
    had assumed a form fit for its tasks.

With his body, whose strength was greater than all others',   14
    which surpassed all other radiances, and which was
    loftier than all others', he stood over the earth like
    Mount Meru.[4]

१५ आकारसदृशप्रज्ञः प्रज्ञया सदृशागमः ।
आगमैः सदृशारम्भः प्रारम्भसदृशोदयः ॥

१६ भीमकान्तैर्नृपगुणैः स बभूवोपजीविनाम् ।
अधृष्यश्चाभिगम्यश्च यादोरत्नैरिवार्णवः ॥

१७ रेखामात्रमपि क्षुण्णादात्मनो वर्त्मनः परम् ।
न व्यतीयुः प्रजास्तस्य नियन्तुर्नेमिवृत्तयः ॥

१८ प्रजानामेव भूत्यर्थं स ताभ्यो बलिमग्रहीत् ।
सहस्रगुणमुत्स्रष्टुमादत्ते हि रसं रविः ॥

१९ सेना परिच्छदस्तस्य द्वयमेवार्थसाधनम् ।
शास्त्रे च व्यापृता बुद्धिर्मौर्वी धनुषि चाततता ॥

२० तस्य संवृतमन्त्रस्य गूढाकारेङ्गितस्य च ।
फलानुमेयाः प्रारम्भाः संस्काराः प्राक्तना इव ॥

२१ जुगोपात्मानमत्रस्तो भेजे धर्ममनातुरः ।
अगृध्नुराददे सो ऽर्थानसक्तः सुखमन्वभूत् ॥

२२ ज्ञाने मौनं क्षमा शक्तौ त्यागे श्लाघाविपर्ययः ।
गुणा गुणानुबन्धित्वात्तस्य सप्रसवा इव ॥

His wisdom matched his form, his learning matched his   15
    wisdom, his undertakings matched his learning, and
    his successes matched his undertakings.

For those who served him he was, with kingly virtues both   16
    frightening and charming, at once unassailable and
    approachable, like the ocean with its monsters and its
    jewels.[5]

The subjects of that charioteer, moving like the rims of   17
    the wheels, did not stray even a hair's breadth outside
    their proper paths.

He levied taxes from the people, but only for their own   18
    prosperity; for the sun draws up moisture only to pour
    it down a thousandfold.

For him the army was no more than a retinue. With   19
    just two things he achieved his aims: his own mind,
    engaged in the shastras, and the hempen string taut
    on his bow.

With his plans kept secret and his face and body betraying   20
    nothing, his actions could only be inferred from their
    results, like the traces of our former deeds.[6]

He protected himself without being afraid, was pious   21
    without being ill, collected wealth without greed, and
    enjoyed pleasures without being attached to them.[7]

With knowledge, silence; with power, patience; with   22
    giving, the opposite of boastfulness—his virtues
    linked thus with other virtues all seemed to have
    begotten offspring.

२३ अनाकृष्टस्य विषयैर्विद्यानां पारदृश्वनः ।
तस्य धर्मरतेरासीद्वृद्धत्वं जरसा विना ॥

२४ प्रजानां विनयाधानाद्रक्षणाद्भरणादपि ।
स पिता पितरस्तासां केवलं जन्महेतवः ॥

२५ स्थित्यै दण्डयतो दण्ड्यान्परिणेतुः प्रसूतये ।
अप्यर्थकामौ तस्यास्तां धर्म एव मनीषिणः ॥

२६ दुदोह गां स यज्ञाय सस्याय मघवा दिवम् ।
सम्पद्विनिमयेनोभौ दधतुर्भुवनद्वयम् ॥

२७ न किलानुययुस्तस्य राजानो रक्षितुर्यशः ।
व्यावृत्ता यत्परस्वेभ्यः श्रुतौ तस्करता स्थिता ॥

२८ द्वेष्यो ऽपि सम्मतः शिष्टस्तस्यार्तस्य यथौषधम् ।
त्याज्यो दुष्टः प्रियो ऽप्यासीदङ्गुष्ठ इवाहिना ॥

२९ तं वेधा विदधे नूनं महाभूतसमाधिना ।
तथा हि सर्वे तस्यासन्परार्थैकफला गुणाः ॥

३० स वेलावप्रवलयां परिखीकृतसागराम् ।
अनन्यशासनामुर्वीं शशासैकपुरीमिव ॥

Not seduced by the objects of the senses, having
 thoroughly mastered all the sciences, fond only of
 Dharma, he was truly mature without yet being old.
   23

By instilling courtesy in his subjects, by protecting and
 supporting them, he was their father; their fathers
 only caused their births.
   24

To maintain order he punished those who deserved
 punishment; to ensure progeny he married; thus both
 politics and pleasure were just Dharma for that wise
 king.[8]
   25

He milked the earth for sacrifice; Indra milked heaven for
 the crops. Together they sustained both worlds by
 reciprocal exchange of wealth.[9]
   26

Other kings, it is said, could not follow the fame of that
 protector, for theft turned away from the property of
 others and remained only in its name.
   27

A man of good conduct, even if an enemy, was welcome to
 him, as is medicine to the sick; a bad man was cut off,
 even if a friend, like a thumb bitten by a snake.
   28

Surely the creator must have created him with the same
 concentration with which he made the elements, for
 all his virtues had as sole fruit the benefit of others.[10]
   29

He governed the earth, which obeyed no other rule, like
 a single citadel, with encircling beaches for ramparts
 and oceans for a moat.
   30

३१ तस्य दाक्षिण्यरूढेन नाम्ना मागधवंशजा ।
पत्नी सुदक्षिणेत्यासीदध्वरस्येव दक्षिणा ॥

३२ कलत्रवन्तमात्मानमवरोधे महत्यपि ।
तया मेने मनस्विन्या लक्ष्या च वसुधाधिपः ॥

३३ तस्यामात्मानुरूपायामात्मजन्मसमुत्सुकः ।
विलम्बितफलैः कालं स निनाय मनोरथैः ॥

३४ गङ्गां भगीरथेनेव पूर्वेषां पावनक्षमाम् ।
ईप्सता सन्ततिं न्यस्ता तेन मन्त्रिषु कोसला ॥

३५ अथाभ्यर्च्य विधातारं प्रयतौ पुत्रकाम्यया ।
तौ दम्पती वसिष्ठस्य गुरोर्जग्मतुराश्रमम् ॥

३६ स्निग्धगम्भीरनिर्घोषमेकं स्यन्दनमाश्रितौ ।
प्रावृषेण्यं पयोवाहं विद्युदैरावताविव ॥

३७ मा भूदाश्रमपीडेति परिमेयपुरःसरौ ।
वशानागौ सगन्धाल्पकलभानुगताविव ॥

३८ सेव्यमानौ सुखस्पर्शैः सालनिर्यासगन्धिभिः ।
पुष्परेणूत्किरैर्वातैराधूतवनराजिभिः ॥

He had a wife born of the lineage of the lords of Magadha, 31
called by a name based on her dexterity, Sudakshina,
just as Sacrifice has Dakshina as his wife.[11]

Although his harem was large, the lord of the earth only 32
thought himself wedded because of this spirited
woman and because of Royal Glory.[12]

Eager for a son born from that wife who matched him, he 33
passed the time in longings that were slow in bearing
fruit.

Yearning for progeny, like Bhagiratha eager to bring down 34
the Ganga, which alone was capable of purifying his
ancestors,[13] Dilipa placed the affairs of Kosala in the
hands of his ministers.

Out of their desire for a son, the couple took on an 35
observance, venerated the creator, and set off for the
ashram of their guru Vasishtha.

Soft and deep was the sound of the chariot in which they 36
sat together, like lightning and a rainbow riding upon
a monsoon cloud.

Lest they cause trouble to the ashram, they traveled with 37
few attendants, like an elephant cow and bull followed
by a few kindred calves.

They were served by the breezes, sweet to the touch, 38
redolent of the sap of sal trees, scattering pollen and
shaking each grove of trees.

३९ पवनस्यानुकूलत्वात्प्रार्थनासिद्धिशंसिनः ।
रजोभिस्तुरगोत्कीर्णैरस्पृष्टालकवेष्टनौ ॥

४० हैयङ्गवीनमादाय घोषवृद्धानुपागतान् ।
नामधेयानि पृच्छन्तौ वन्यानां मार्गशाखिनाम् ॥

४१ सरसीष्वरविन्दानां वीचिविक्षोभशीतलम् ।
आमोदमुपजिघ्रन्तौ स्वनिःश्वासानुकारिणम् ॥

४२ मनोभिरामाः शृण्वन्तौ रथनेमिस्वनोन्मुखैः ।
षड्जसंवादिनीः केका द्विधा भिन्नाः शिखण्डिभिः ॥

४३ परस्पराक्षिसादृश्यमदूरोज्झितवर्त्मसु ।
मृगद्वन्द्वेषु पश्यन्तौ स्यन्दनाबद्धदृष्टिषु ॥

४४ श्रेणिबन्धाद्वितन्वद्भिरस्तम्भां तोरणस्रजम् ।
सारसैः कलनिर्ह्रादैः क्वचिदुन्नमिताननौ ॥

४५ ग्रामेष्वात्मनिसृष्टेषु यूपचिह्नेषु यज्वनाम् ।
अमोघाः प्रतिगृह्णन्ताववध्र्यानुपदमाशिषः ॥

४६ काप्यभिख्या तयोरासीद्व्रजतोः शुद्धवेशयोः ।
हिमनिर्मुक्तयोर्योगे चित्राचन्द्रमसोरिव ॥

Because the wind was propitious, heralding the success   39
of their pleas, their hair and clothing remained
untouched by the dust raised by the horses.

They asked elders of cowherd settlements, who   40
approached them to offer freshly churned butter,
about the names of the wayside forest trees.

They smelled the waft of fragrance from lotus blossoms in   41
the lakes, cooled by the movement of the waves; it was
like their own breath.

They listened to the paired calls—in tune with the first   42
note of the scale—of the peacocks, as they craned
their necks at the sound of the fellies of the wheels.[14]

Each saw the likeness of the other's eyes in the eyes of   43
pairs of deer, who had moved not far from the path
and fixed the chariot with their gaze.

At one point they raised their heads at the sweet   44
susurration of the sarus cranes, who, ranging
themselves in a row, seemed to form a pillarless
triumphal arch.

In the villages they themselves had gifted, which were   45
marked by the sacrificial posts of those engaged in
Vedic sacrifices, the couple received offerings of guest
water, and after that unfailing blessings.

Marvelous was their beauty as they moved along dressed   46
in white, like that of the moon and the bright star
of Virgo when they shake off the frost and move
conjoined.[15]

13

४७ तत्तद्भूमिपतिः पत्न्यै दर्शयन्प्रियदर्शनः ।
अपि लङ्घितमध्वानं बुबुधे न बुधोपमः ॥

४८ स दुष्प्रापयशाः प्रापदाश्रमं श्रान्तवाहनः ।
सायं संयमिनस्तस्य महर्षेर्महिषीसखः ॥

४९ वनान्तरादुपावृत्तैः स्कन्धासक्तसमित्कुशैः ।
अग्निप्रत्युद्गमात्पूतैः पूर्यमाणं तपस्विभिः ॥

५० सेकान्ते मुनिकन्याभिर्विविक्तीकृतवृक्षकम् ।
आश्वासाय विहङ्गानामालवालाम्बुपायिनाम् ॥

५१ आकीर्णमृषिपत्नीनामुटजद्वाररोधिभिः ।
अपत्यैरिव नीवारभागधेयोचितैर्मृगैः ॥

५२ अभ्युद्धृताग्निपिशुनैरतिथीनाश्रमोन्मुखान् ।
पुनानं पवनोद्धूतैर्धूमैराहुतिगन्धिभिः ॥

५३ अथ यन्तारमादिश्य धुर्यान्विश्रमयेति सः ।
तामवारोहयत्पत्नीं रथादवरुरोह च ॥

५४ तस्मै सभ्याः सभार्याय गोप्त्रे गुप्ततमेन्द्रियाः ।
अर्हणामर्हते चक्रुर्मुनयो नयचक्षुषे ॥

14

Pointing out one thing after another to his wife, the   47
    handsome king, who resembled Budha, was not aware
    of the road, even when it lay behind them.[16]

In the evening, their horses weary, the king of matchless   48
    fame, along with his wife, reached the ashram of the
    mighty self-controlled sage.

It was growing crowded with ascetics returning from other   49
    parts of the forest with firewood strapped to their
    shoulders, purified by the sacred fires that went out to
    meet them.[17]

There the sages' daughters distanced themselves from the   50
    trees after watering them, to let the birds that drink
    water from the trenches around them do so at ease.

It was thronged with deer accustomed to their share of   51
    wild rice, blocking the doors to the cottages as though
    they were the children of the sages' wives.

The ashram purified the guests, eager to enter it, with   52
    wisps of smoke that were lifted by the wind and
    scented with oblations, announcing the kindling of
    the fires.

The king instructed the charioteer to rest the horses,   53
    helped his wife to alight, and got down himself from
    the chariot.

The courteous ascetics, who most carefully guarded   54
    their senses, honored the king with his wife—the
    king, worthy of honor, who watched over them, his
    statesmanship the eyes that guided him.

५५ विधेः सायन्तनस्यान्ते स ददर्श तपोनिधिम् ।
अन्वासितमरुन्धत्या स्वाहयेव हविर्भुजम् ॥

५६ तयोर्जगृहतुः पादौ राजा राज्ञी च मागधी ।
तौ गुरुर्गुरुपत्नी च प्रीत्या प्रतिननन्दतुः ॥

५७ आतिथेयस्तमातिथ्यविनीताध्वपरिश्रमम् ।
पप्रच्छ कुशलं राज्ये राज्याश्रममुनिं मुनिः ॥

५८ अथाथर्वनिधेस्तस्य विजितारिपुरः पुरः ।
अर्थ्यामर्थपतिर्वाचमाददे वदतां वरः ॥

५९ उपपन्नं ननु शिवं समस्त्वङ्गेषु यस्य मे ।
दैवीनां मानुषीणां च प्रतिकर्ता त्वमापदाम् ॥

६० तव मन्त्रकृतो मन्त्रैर्दूरात्संयमितारिभिः ।
प्रत्यादिश्यन्त इव मे दृष्टलक्ष्यभिदः शराः ॥

६१ हविरावर्जितं होतस्त्वया विधिवदग्निषु ।
वृष्टिर्भवति सस्यानामवग्रहविशोषिणाम् ॥

६२ पुरुषायुषजीविन्यो निरातङ्का निरीतयः ।
यन्मदीयाः प्रजास्तत्र हेतुस्त्वद्ब्रह्मवर्चसम् ॥

At the end of the evening rites he beheld the treasure store   55
    of ascetic power, attended upon by Arundhati, like
    Fire by Svaha.[18]

The king and his Magadhan queen grasped the feet of   56
    them both, and the guru and his wife affectionately
    greeted them in turn.

Once his guest's weariness from the road had been allayed   57
    by hospitality, the welcoming sage asked the king, a
    sage in the ashram that is his kingdom, about the well-
    being of his realm.

Then the king, conqueror of enemy cities, rich in wealth   58
    and best of orators, spoke this speech rich in meaning,
    before that storehouse of Atharvanic spells.[19]

"Surely only good can come to all the seven components   59
    of my state while you are there to counteract ills
    produced by gods and men![20]

"You create mantras, and mantras can quell enemies at   60
    a distance, eclipsing my arrows, which pierce only
    targets I can see.[21]

"Sacrificer! The ghee that you pour into the fires in   61
    accordance with precept becomes the rain for the
    crops that would dry up in a drought.

"If my subjects live the full lease of a man's life without   62
    fears and without calamities, the cause is the fire of
    your Brahman power.

६३ तदेवं चिन्त्यमानस्य गुरुणा ब्रह्मयोनिना ।
सानुबन्धाः कथं न स्युः सम्पदो मे निरापदः ॥

६४ किं तु वध्वां तवैतस्यामदृष्टसदृशप्रजम् ।
न मामवति सद्वीपा रत्नसूरपि मेदिनी ॥

६५ मत्परं दुर्लभं मत्वा नूनमावर्जितं मया ।
पयः पूर्वे स्वनिःश्वासकदुष्णमुपभुञ्जते ॥

६६ सो ऽहमिज्याविशुद्धात्मा प्रजालोपनिमीलितः ।
प्रकाशश्चान्धकारश्च लोकालोक इवाचलः ॥

६७ लोकान्तरसुखं पुण्यं तपोदानसमुद्भवम् ।
सन्ततिः शुद्धवंश्या तु परत्रेह च शर्मणे ॥

६८ तया हीनं विनेता मां कथं पश्यन्न दूयते ।
सिक्तं स्वयमिव स्नेहाद्वन्ध्यमाश्रमवृक्षकम् ॥

६९ असह्यपीडं भगवन्नृणबन्धमवैहि मे ।
अरुन्तुदमिवालानं नवबद्धस्य दन्तिनः ॥

७० तस्माद्यथा विमुच्येयं संविधातुं तथार्हसि ।
इक्ष्वाकूणां दुरापे ऽर्थे त्वदधीना हि सिद्धयः ॥

18

"So with you thinking of me, my guru born of Brahma, 63
    how could I not experience a constant string of
    successes unmixed with failure?

"But since I have seen no offspring who would resemble 64
    me conceived in your daughter-in-law here, the
    treasure-laden earth with all its continents brings me
    no joy.[22]

"My ancestors must surely worry that the libations I 65
    offer will cease with me, and must be drinking them
    warmed by their sighs.[23]

"Here I am, my soul resplendent with sacrifices, but 66
    shadowed by the absence of offspring: I am light and
    I am dark, like the mountain that separates world
    from nonworld.[24]

"The good karma that comes from asceticism and charity 67
    brings happiness in another world; but offspring of
    one's pure lineage afford blessings both there and
    here.

"How can you, my guide, not be troubled seeing me 68
    deprived of this, like a tree in the ashram you yourself
    lovingly water that remains barren?

"Master, understand what intolerable torment this burden 69
    of debt is to me, like a tethering post that torments a
    newly bound elephant.[25]

"Therefore please find a way that I may be rid of it! When 70
    some object eludes the Ikshvakus, it is in you that
    success reposes."

७१ इति विज्ञापितो राज्ञा ध्यानस्तिमितलोचनः ।
क्षणमात्रमृषिस्तस्थौ सुप्तमीन इव ह्रदः ॥

७२ सो ऽपश्यत्प्रणिधानेन सन्ततिस्तम्भकारणम् ।
भावितात्मा भुवो भर्तुरथैनं प्रत्यबोधयत् ॥

७३ पुरा शक्रमुपस्थाय तवोर्वीं प्रतियास्यतः ।
आसीत्कल्पतरुच्छायासेविनी सुरभिः पथि ॥

७४ इमां देवीमृतुस्नातां स्मृत्वा सपदि सत्वरः ।
प्रदक्षिणक्रियातीतस्तस्याः कोपमजीजनः ॥

७५ अवजानासि मां यस्मादतस्ते न भविष्यति ।
मत्प्रसूतिमनाराध्य प्रजेति त्वा शशाप सा ॥

७६ स शापो न त्वया राजन्न च सारथिना श्रुतः ।
नदत्याकाशगङ्गायाः स्रोतस्युद्दामदिग्गजे ॥

७७ अवैमि तदपध्यानाद्वत्सलापेक्षं मनोरथम् ।
प्रतिबध्नाति हि श्रेयः पूज्यपूजाव्यतिक्रमः ॥

७८ हविषे दीर्घसत्त्रस्य सा चेदानीं प्रचेतसः ।
भुजङ्गपिहितद्वारं पातालमधितिष्ठति ॥

Requested thus by the king, the sage remained for a   71
    moment with eyes unmoving in meditation, like a
    pond in which the fish are sleeping.

Plunged in meditation, by his samadhi he perceived what   72
    was blocking the king's progeny, and replied to him:

"Once when you were returning to earth after serving   73
    Indra, the cow Surabhi was sheltering in the shade of
    the celestial wish-fulfilling tree on your path.

"Remembering that this queen of yours had just bathed   74
    after her menses, you at once hurried on, neglecting
    to walk reverently around Surabhi, and thereby
    provoked her anger.[26]

"She cursed you, saying: 'Since you have shown me   75
    disrespect, you will have no offspring—until you
    propitiate my own!'

"That curse, oh king, neither you nor your charioteer   76
    could hear above the roaring of the stream of the
    celestial Ganga, where the elephants of the quarters
    were playing boisterously.[27]

"I discern that attaining your desire requires efforts   77
    on your part, because you offended her. Failing to
    venerate the venerable is an obstacle to blessings.

"And now she is away in the netherworld to provide ghee   78
    for a long sacrifice of Prachetas; there serpents bar
    the gates.

७९ स त्वमेकान्तरां तस्या मदीयां वत्समातरम् ।
आराधय सपत्नीकः सा वां कामं प्रदास्यति ॥

८० इति वादिन एवास्य होतुराहुतिसाधनम् ।
अनिन्द्या नन्दिनी नाम धेनुराववृते वनात् ॥

८१ ताम्रा ललाटजां राजिं बिभ्रती सासितेतराम् ।
सन्ध्या प्रातिपदेनेव व्यतिभिन्ना हिमांशुना ॥

८२ भुवं कोष्णेन कुण्डोध्री मेध्येनावभृथादपि ।
प्रस्रवेणाभिवर्षन्ती वत्सालोकप्रवर्तिना ॥

८३ रजःकणैः खुरोद्धूतैः स्पृशद्भिर्गात्रमन्तिकात् ।
तीर्थाभिषेकजां शुद्धिमादधाना महीक्षितः ॥

८४ तां पुण्यदर्शनां दृष्ट्वा निमित्तज्ञस्तपोधनः ।
याज्यमाशंसितावन्ध्यप्रार्थनं पुनरब्रवीत् ॥

८५ अदूरवर्तिनीं सिद्धिं राजन्विगणयात्मनः ।
उपस्थितेयं कल्याणी नाम्नि कीर्तित एव यत् ॥

८६ वन्यवृत्तिरिमां शश्वदात्मानुगमनेन गाम् ।
विद्यामभ्यसनेनेव प्रसादयितुमर्हसि ॥

"You and your wife may propitiate this cow of mine, the   79
    mother of a calf, who is her granddaughter. She will
    grant your wish."

Just as the sacrificer was speaking these words, the   80
    blameless cow who provided his fire-offerings
    returned from the forest.

Copper-colored and bearing a white line on her forehead,   81
    she resembled the twilight marked by the crescent
    moon on its first day.

From her pot-like udders, she sprinkled the ground with   82
    trickling warm milk—even purer than the bath after a
    sacrifice—that began to flow at the sight of her calf.

With the specks of dust kicked up by her hooves that   83
    settled on the king's body as she came close, she
    brought him the purification of bathing in a sacred
    ford.

At the sight of the cow, who was pure to behold, the sage, a   84
    reader of auspices, again spoke to the king, for whom
    he offered sacrifices, and whose longed-for wish he
    foresaw would bear fruit:

"You may count upon it, king, that success for you is not   85
    far off, for this auspicious being has appeared as soon
    as her name was uttered.

"Adopting the life of a forest dweller, you must win the   86
    favor of this cow by following her constantly, as you
    would win that of knowledge by constant practice.

८७ प्रस्थितायां प्रतिष्ठेथाः स्थितायां स्थानमाचरेः ।
   निषण्णायां निषीदास्यां पीताम्भसि पिवेरपः ॥

८८ वधूर्भक्तिमती चैनामर्चितामा तपोवनात् ।
   प्रयातां प्रातरन्वेतु सायं प्रत्युद्व्रजेदपि ॥

८९ इत्या प्रसादादस्यास्त्वं परिचर्यापरो भव ।
   अविघ्नमस्तु ते स्थेयाः पितेव धुरि पुत्रिणाम् ॥

९० तथेति प्रतिजग्राह प्रीतिमान्सपरिग्रहः ।
   आदेशं देशकालज्ञः शिष्यः शासितुरानतः ॥

९१ अथ प्रदोषे दोषज्ञः संवेशाय विशां पतिम् ।
   सूनुः सूनृतवाक्स्रष्टुर्विससर्जोर्जितश्रियम् ॥

९२ सत्यामपि तपःसिद्धौ नियमापेक्षया मुनिः ।
   कल्पवित्कल्पयामास वन्यामेवास्य संविधाम् ॥

९३ निर्दिष्टां कुलपतिना स पर्णशाला-
   मध्यास्य प्रयतपरिग्रहद्वितीयः ।
   तच्छिष्याध्ययननिवेदितावसानां
   संविष्टः कुशशयने निशां निनाय ॥

इति रघुवंशे महाकाव्ये प्रथमः सर्गः ॥

"When she sets off, you set off. When she stands still, you 87
stand still. When she sits, you sit. When she drinks
water, you drink water.

"Have your wife accompany her with devotion to the 88
ashram boundary when she sets off, after being
worshiped, at dawn. And have her also receive her
back in the evening.

"In this way, remain intent upon serving her until she 89
shows her favor. May you face no obstacles! Like your
own father, may you long remain foremost among
men blessed with sons!"

"So be it," said the delighted disciple, always aware of 90
the appropriate time and place, as he received these
instructions from his teacher, bowing before him with
his wife.

Then at nightfall, the son of Brahma the creator, ever 91
conscious of possible faults, whose words were
pleasing and true, sent off the glorious king to sleep.

Although endowed with power won from his asceticism, 92
the sage, conscious of ritual rules, only prepared for
him arrangements suited to the forest, in view of the
observance.[28]

Accompanied by his dutiful wife, the king entered the 93
leaf hut assigned by the master of the household, lay
down on a bed of kusa grass, and passed the night, its
end proclaimed by the Vedic chanting of his master's
students.

द्वितीयः सर्गः

१ अथ प्रजानामधिपः प्रभाते जायाप्रतिग्राहितगन्धमाल्याम् ।
   वनाय पीतप्रतिबद्धवत्सां यशोधनो धेनुमृषेर्मुमोच ॥

२ तस्याः खुरन्यासपवित्रपांसुमपांसुलानां धुरि कीर्तनीया ।
   मार्गं मनुष्येश्वरधर्मपत्नी श्रुतेरिवार्थं स्मृतिरन्वगच्छत् ॥

३ निवर्त्य राजा दयितां दयालुस्तां सौरभेयीं सुरभिर्यशोभिः ।
   पयोधरीभूतचतुःसमुद्रां जुगोप गोरूपधरामिवोर्वीम् ॥

४ व्रताय तेनानुचरेण धेनोर्न्यषेधि शेषो ऽप्यनुयायिवर्गः ।
   न चान्यतस्तस्य शरीररक्षा स्ववीर्यगुप्ता हि मनोः प्रसूतिः ॥

५ आस्वादवद्भिः कवलैस्तृणानां कण्डूयनैर्दंशनिवारणैश्च ।
   अव्याहतस्वैरगतैश्च तस्याः सम्राड्रमाराधनतत्परो ऽभूत् ॥

26

CHAPTER 2
Nandini Bestows a Boon

Then, at dawn, the queen gave the sage's cow sweet-smelling unguent and a garland. After the calf had drunk its fill and been tethered, the king, who treasured most his fame, set the cow free to go to the forest.[1]

The sovereign's consort, most praiseworthy of the pure, followed the cow's path—its soil purified by the tread of her hooves—just as sages' lore follows the Vedas' meaning.[2]

But being solicitous of his beloved wife, the king sent her back, and he himself, scented with glory, stayed guarding Nandini—the offspring of sweet-scented Surabhi—as if she were the earth itself, her udders the four oceans.[3]

Since it was his observance to wait upon the cow, he dismissed all remaining attendants. Nor did he look to others to protect his person, for those born in Manu's race are shielded by their own heroic nature.

With tasty mouthfuls of grass, with scratching her, chasing off biting insects, and letting her go wherever she desired unchecked, the king devoted all his care to pleasing her.

६ स्थितः स्थितामुच्चलितः प्रयातां निषेदुषीमासनबन्धधीरः ।
जलाभिलाषी जलमाददानां छायेव तां भूपतिरन्वगच्छत् ॥

७ स न्यस्तचिह्नामपि राजलक्ष्मीं तेजोविशेषानुमितां दधानः ।
आसीदनाविष्कृतदानराजिरन्तर्मदावस्थ इव द्विपेन्द्रः ॥

८ लताप्रतानोद्ग्रथितैः स केशैरधिज्यधन्वा विचचार दावम् ।
रक्षापदेशादुरुहोमधेनोर्व्यान्विनेष्यन्निव दुष्टसत्त्वान् ॥

९ विसृष्टपार्श्वानुचरस्य तस्य पार्श्वद्रुमाः पाशभृता समस्य ।
उदीरयामासुरिवोन्मदानामालोकशब्दं वयसां विरावैः ॥

१० मरुत्प्रयुक्ताश्च मरुत्सखाभं तमर्च्यमारादभिवर्तमानम् ।
अवाकिरन्बाललताः प्रसूनैराचारलाजैरिव पौरकन्याः ॥

११ धनुर्भृतो ऽप्यस्य दयार्द्रभावमाख्यातमन्तःकरणैर्विशङ्कैः ।
विलोकयन्त्यो वपुरापुरक्ष्णां प्रकामविस्तारफलं हरिण्यः ॥

१२ स कीचकैर्मरुतपूर्णरन्ध्रैः कूजद्भिरापादितवंशकृत्यम् ।
शुश्राव कुञ्जेषु यशः स्वमुच्चैरुद्गीयमानं वनदेवताभिः ॥

He stood still when she stood, moved when she moved,   6
remained calmly seated when she sat, sought water
when she took water—the king followed her like a
shadow.

Although he had removed his regalia, a special fieriness   7
revealed the majesty he bore. He was like a lordly
elephant on whom no streak of ichor could be seen,
his state of musth invisible within.[4]

His hair tied up with vine tendrils, strung bow at the   8
ready, he roamed the woods as if meaning to tame the
fierce beasts of the forest, under the guise of guarding
the cow who gave milk for the sage's oblations.

He had dismissed his retinue, but the trees at his side   9
appeared to call out—since he seemed like Varuna
himself—through the cries of excited birds: "Behold
the king!"[5]

And as that king worthy of worship passed close by,   10
shining like fire, the wind's friend, the tender vines
were prompted by the wind to cover him with flowers,
like girls of the city showering down the customary
parched grains.[6]

The deer felt no fear, their hearts sensing that though he   11
carried a bow he was merciful. Gazing at his body,
they reaped at last the reward of having eyes of such
extended length.

He heard the woodland deities loudly singing his fame in   12
the bowers, while the bamboo, their hollows filled by
the wind, acted as softly murmuring flutes.

29

१३ पृक्तस्तुषारैर्वननिर्झराणामनोकहाकम्पनपुष्पगन्धी ।
तमातपक्लान्तमनातपत्रमाचारपूतं पवनः सिषेवे ॥

१४ शशाम वृष्ट्यापि विना दवाग्निरासीद्विशेषात्फलपुष्पवृद्धिः ।
ऊनं न सत्त्वेष्वधिको बबाधे तस्मिन्वनं गोप्तरि गाहमाने ॥

१५ सञ्चारपूतानि दिगन्तराणि कृत्वा दिनान्ते निलयाय गन्तुम् ।
प्रचक्रमे पल्लवरागताम्रा प्रभा पतङ्गस्य मुनेश्च धेनुः ॥

१६ तां देवतापित्रतिथिक्रियार्थमन्वग्ययौ मध्यमलोकपालः ।
बभौ च सा तेन सतां मतेन श्रद्धेव साक्षाद्विधिनोपपन्ना ॥

१७ स पल्वलोत्तीर्णवराहयूथान्यावासवृक्षोन्मुखबर्हिणानि ।
ययौ मृगाध्यासितशाद्वलानि श्यामायमानानि वनानि पश्यन् ॥

१८ आपीनभारोद्वहनप्रयत्नाद्दृष्टिर्गुरुत्वादुरसो नरेन्द्रः ।
उभावलंचक्रतुरञ्जिताभ्यां तपोवनावृत्तिपथं गताभ्याम् ॥

१९ वसिष्ठधेनोरनुयायिनं तमावर्तमानं वनिता वनान्तात् ।
पपौ निमेषालसपक्ष्मपङ्क्तिरुपोषिताभ्यामिव लोचनाभ्याम् ॥

Mixed with the spray of mountain waterfalls and carrying   13
the scent of flowers from shaking the trees, the
purifying wind refreshed him, pure in conduct, when
without parasol and weary from the heat.

Forest fires ceased even without rain, fruits and flowers   14
burst forth in abundance, the stronger beasts stopped
harassing the weak, as that protector plunged deeper
into the woods.

At the close of day, after purifying the quarters by their   15
wanderings, the light of the sun and the sage's cow,
both copper-hued like fresh sprouts, began to wend
their way home.

The protector of the middle world followed the cow, who   16
made rites for gods, ancestors, and guests possible. In
company with him, who was revered by good people,
she shone like faith incarnate attended by incarnate
ritual.[7]

As he walked, he watched the darkening woods, the boars   17
emerging from the waterholes, the peacocks eager for
their roosting trees, the deer settling down on grassy
swards.

Both cow and king beautified the path back to the hermits'   18
grove with their swaying gaits, she from straining to
bear the burden of her udders, and he from the weight
of his chest.

When he returned from the forest following behind   19
Vasishtha's cow, his wife drank him in with eyes that
seemed to have been fasting, her lashes loath to blink.

२० पुरस्कृता वर्त्मनि पार्थिवेन प्रत्युद्गता पार्थिववधूरमपल्या ।
    तदन्तरे सा विरराज धेनुर्दिनक्षपामध्यगतेव सन्ध्या ॥

२१ प्रदक्षिणीकृत्य पयस्विनीं तां सुदक्षिणा साक्षतपात्रहस्ता ।
    प्रणम्य चानर्च विशालमस्याः शृङ्गान्तरं द्वारमिवार्थसिद्धेः ॥

२२ वत्सोत्सुकापि स्तिमिता सपर्यां प्रत्यग्रहीत्सेति ननन्दतुस्तौ ।
    भक्त्योपपन्नेषु हि तद्विधानां प्रसादचिह्नानि पुरःफलानि ॥

२३ गुरोः सदारस्य निपीड्य पादौ समाप्य सान्ध्यं च विधिं दिलीपः ।
    दोहावसाने पुनरेव दोग्ध्रीं भेजे भुजोत्सन्नरिपुर्निषण्णाम् ॥

२४ तामन्तिकन्यस्तबलिप्रदीपामन्वास्य गोष्ठे गृहिणीसहायः ।
    क्रमेण सुप्तामनु संविवेश सुप्तोत्थितां प्रातरनूदतिष्ठत् ॥

२५ इत्थं व्रतं पालयतः प्रजार्थं समं महिष्या महनीयकीर्तेः ।
    सप्त व्यतीयुस्त्रिगुणानि तस्य दिनान्यमित्रोद्धरणोचितस्य ॥

२६ अन्येद्युरात्मानुचरस्य भावं जिज्ञासमाना मुनिहोमधेनुः ।
    गङ्गाप्रपातान्तविरूढशष्पं गौरीगुरोर्गह्वरमाविवेश ॥

Between the king, who followed on her path, and the   20
    king's consort, who rose to receive her, Nandini shone
    like twilight bounded by day and night.

Sudakshina reverently circled the milch cow with a dish   21
    of unhusked rice in her hands, bowed, and made
    offerings to the broad brow between her horns, as if it
    were the gateway to the accomplishment of goals.

The couple rejoiced that, although yearning for her calf,   22
    she stopped and accepted their homage. For signs of
    grace shown by such as she toward devoted suppliants
    portend success.

Dilipa, whose arms had rooted out enemies, touched the   23
    feet of his guru and his guru's wife, completed the
    twilight rite, and waited once more upon the milch
    cow when she lay down after milking.

The protector and his wife set beside her a food offering   24
    and a lamp, and then sat down when she did, retired
    when in due course she slept, and rose in the morning
    when she rose from sleep.

Three weeks went by as the illustrious king, uprooter of   25
    his enemies, followed this observance along with his
    wife for the sake of offspring.

Next day, the cow who provisioned the sage's sacrifices,   26
    wishing to test the mettle of her follower, entered a
    cave of Himalaya, father of Gauri,* where grass had
    taken root beside a cataract of the Ganga.

———

* Parvati.

२७ सा दुष्प्रधर्षा मनसापि हिंस्रैरित्यद्रिशोभाप्रहितेक्षणेन ।
अलक्षिताभ्युत्पतनो नृपेण प्रसह्य सिंहः किल तां चकर्ष ॥

२८ तदीयमाक्रन्दितमार्तसाधोर्गुहानिबद्धप्रतिशब्ददीर्घम् ।
रश्मिष्विवादाय नगेन्द्रदत्तां निवर्तयामास नृपस्य दृष्टिम् ॥

२९ स पाटलायां गवि तस्थिवांसं धनुर्धरः केसरिणं ददर्श ।
अधित्यकायामिव धातुमय्यां रोध्रद्रुमं सानुमतः प्रफुल्तम् ॥

३० ततो मृगेन्द्रस्य मृगेन्द्रगामी वधाय वध्यस्य शरं शरण्यः ।
जाताभिषङ्गो नृपतिर्निषङ्गादुद्धर्तुमैच्छत्प्रसभोद्धृतारिः ॥

३१ वामेतरस्तस्य करः प्रहर्तुर्नखप्रभाभारूषितकङ्कपत्त्रे ।
सक्ताङ्गुलिः सायकपुङ्ख एव चित्रार्पितारम्भ इवावतस्थे ॥

३२ बाहुप्रतिस्तम्भविवृद्धमन्युरभ्यर्णमागस्कृतमस्पृशद्भिः ।
राजा स्वतेजोभिरदह्यतान्तर्भोगीव मन्त्रप्रतिबद्धवीर्यः ॥

३३ तमार्यगृह्यां निगृहीतधेनुर्मनुष्यवाचा मनुवंशकेतुम् ।
विस्मापयन्विस्मितमात्मवृत्तौ भूपालसिंहं निजगाद सिंहः ॥

Thinking that fierce animals would not even dream of   27
  assailing her, he allowed his gaze to be drawn to the
  beauties of the mountain. A lion, its approach unseen
  by the king, overpowered her, it seemed, and dragged
  her in.

The gaze of the king, friend to those in distress, was fixed   28
  on the majestic mountain—until the cow's bellow,
  prolonged by echoing through the cave, wrenched it
  back as if by tugging on reins.

Bow in hand, he beheld the maned beast that had pounced   29
  upon the reddish cow, looking like a *rodhra* tree in
  flower upon a mountain shelf rich with reddish ores.

Then the king, a firm refuge, with a lion's stride, who slew   30
  his enemies with force, felt humiliated and sought
  to draw an arrow from his quiver, to strike dead the
  death-deserving lion.

But as he made to shoot, his right hand stopped   31
  motionless, as if captured in a picture in mid-act, his
  fingers stuck to the flights of the arrow, reddening the
  egret feathers with the gleam of his nails.

His rage mounting at the immobilization of his arm, the   32
  king burned within from his own fieriness, incapable
  as it was of touching the offender right beside him,
  like a serpent whose venomous power is checked by
  mantras and herbs.

The lion who had seized the cow addressed him—friend   33
  to the noble, bright banner in Manu's lineage—in a
  human voice, further astonishing that lion among
  kings, already astonished at his own plight.

३४ अलं महीपाल तव श्रमेण प्रयुक्तमप्यस्त्रमितो वृथा स्यात् ।
न पादपोन्मूलनशक्ति रंहः शिलोच्चये मूर्छति मारुतस्य ॥

३५ कैलासगौरं वृषमारुरुक्षोः पादार्पणानुग्रहपूतपृष्ठम् ।
अवैहि मां किङ्करमष्टमूर्तेः कुम्भोदरं नाम निकुम्भमित्रम् ॥

३६ अमुं पुरः पश्यसि देवदारुं पुत्रीकृतो ऽयं वृषभध्वजेन ।
यो हेमकुम्भस्तननिःसृतानां स्कन्दस्य मातुः पयसां रसज्ञः ॥

३७ कण्डूयमानेन कटं कदाचिद्व्यद्विपेनोन्मथिता त्वगस्य ।
अथैनमद्रेस्तनया शुशोच सेनान्यमालीढमिवासुरास्त्रैः ॥

३८ तदा प्रभृत्येव मतङ्गजानां त्रासार्थमस्मिन्नहमद्रिकुक्षौ ।
व्यापारितः शूलभृता विधाय सिंहत्वमङ्गागतसत्त्ववृत्ति ॥

३९ तस्यालमेषा क्षुधितस्य तृप्त्यै प्रदिष्टकाला परमेश्वरेण ।
उपस्थिता शोणितपारणा मे सुरद्विषश्चान्द्रमसी सुधेव ॥

४० स त्वं निवर्तस्व विहाय लज्जां गुरोर्भवान्दर्शितशिष्यभक्तिः ।
शस्त्रेण रक्ष्यं यदशक्यरक्षं न तद्यशः शस्त्रभृतां क्षिणोति ॥

"Enough of your struggles, oh king! Even if you could use   34
  your weapon on me, it would be in vain. The wind's
  force might be able to uproot trees, but it will fail
  against a rocky outcrop.

"Know that I am the servant of eightfold Shiva: my back is   35
  made pure by the grace of the touch of his foot, placed
  there when he wants to climb upon his bull, white as
  Mount Kailasa. I am Kumbhodara by name, a friend of
  Nikumbha.

"You see this deodar before you? It has been adopted by   36
  Bull-bannered Shiva as a son and knows the taste of
  the milk that flows from the jar-like golden breasts of
  Skanda's mother.

"Once its bark was broken by a forest elephant scratching   37
  its temple lobes, and Parvati grieved as though Skanda
  himself had been grazed by the *asuras'* weapons.

"From that time on, to protect the tree from elephants, I   38
  have been assigned to this mountain cave by trident-
  wielding Śiva, who turned me into a lion feeding on
  creatures that fall into my lap.

"This cow has arrived, her hour appointed by the Supreme   39
  Lord, a breakfast of blood just right to satisfy my
  hunger, as perfect as the moon's nectar for satisfying
  the hunger of the gods' enemy Rahu.

"As for you, you may turn back without shame: you   40
  have shown the devotion a student owes his guru.
  A warrior's fame is not harmed if his sword fails to
  protect what cannot be protected."

४१ इति प्रगल्भं पुरुषाधिराजो मृगाधिराजस्य वचो निशम्य ।
प्रत्याहतास्त्रो गिरिशप्रभावादात्मन्यवज्ञां शिथिलीचकार ॥

४२ प्रत्याह चैनं शरमोक्षवन्ध्यो भयत्रपत्वात्स्वरभेदमात्रैः ।
प्रहीणपूर्वध्वनिनाधिरूढस्तुलामसारेण शरद्घनेन ॥

४३ संरुद्धचेष्टस्य मृगेन्द्र कामं हास्यं वचस्तद्यदहं विवक्षुः ।
अन्तर्गतं प्राणभृतां तु वेद सर्वं भवान्भावमतो ऽभिधास्ये ॥

४४ मान्यः स मे स्थावरजङ्गमानां सर्गस्थितिप्रत्यवहारहेतुः ।
गुरोरपीदं धनमाहिताग्नेर्नश्यत्पुरस्तादनुपेक्षणीयम् ॥

४५ स त्वं मदीयेन शरीरवृत्तिं देहेन निर्वर्तयितुं प्रसीद ।
दिनावसानोत्सुकबालवत्सा विमुच्यतां धेनुरियं महर्षेः ॥

४६ अथान्धकारं गिरिकन्दराणां दंष्ट्रामयूखैः शकलानि कुर्वन् ।
भूयः स भूतेश्वरपार्श्ववर्ती किञ्चिद्विहस्यार्थपतिं बभाषे ॥

४७ एकातपत्रं जगतः प्रभुत्वं नवं वयः कान्तमिदं वपुश्च ।
अल्पस्य हेतोर्बहु हातुमिच्छन् विचारमूढः प्रतिभासि मे त्वम् ॥

४८ भूतानुकम्पा तव चेदियं गौरेका भवेत्स्वस्तिमती त्वदन्ते ।
जीवन्पुनः शश्वदुपप्लवेभ्यः प्रजाः प्रजानाथ पितेव पासि ॥

Hearing these proud words from the king of beasts, the   41
    king of men relaxed the scorn he felt for himself,
    realizing that it was by Shiva's power that his weapon
    had been blocked.

And he replied to him, his voice cracking from shame,   42
    powerless to fire his arrows, like an autumnal wisp of
    cloud no longer able to thunder as before.

"Doubtless what I want to say, lord of beasts, as I stand   43
    here paralyzed, will seem laughable, but since you
    know all the inner thoughts of creatures, I shall speak.

"I must revere the creator, maintainer, and destroyer of all   44
    things that move and do not move. And yet I cannot
    let this property of my guru, who keeps the Vedic
    fires, be destroyed before my eyes.

"Pray use my body for your sustenance. Release this cow,   45
    which belongs to the great sage; her young calf is
    yearning for her now that day is ending."

Thereupon, laughing a little, and splintering the darkness   46
    of the mountain caverns with the shafts of light from
    his fangs, the servant of the lord of spirits spoke to the
    lord of wealth once more:[8]

"Your royal parasol alone is raised, showing your   47
    sovereignty over all the world; your youth is fresh; this
    body of yours is beautiful. You seem to me guileless
    indeed to wish to sacrifice so much for so little![9]

"If compassion for creatures is what moves you, you   48
    would save just this one cow by dying. But if you live,
    lord of men, you can constantly protect your subjects
    from disasters, like a father.

४९ अथैकधेनोरपराधदण्डा-
दुरोः कृषाणुप्रतिमाद्विभेषि ।
शक्यो ऽस्य मन्युर्भवता विनेतुं
गाः कोटिशः स्पर्शयता घटोध्नीः ॥

५० तद्रक्ष कल्याणपरम्पराणां भोक्तारमूर्जस्वलमात्मदेहम् ।
महीतलस्पर्शनमात्रभिन्नमृद्धं हि राज्यं पदमैन्द्रमाहुः ॥

५१ एतावदुक्त्वा विरते मृगेन्द्रे प्रतिस्वनेनास्य गुहागतेन ।
शिलोच्चयो ऽपि क्षितिपालमुच्चैः प्रीत्या तमेवार्थमभाषतेव ॥

५२ तथा समर्थां गिरमूचिवांसं प्रत्याह देवानुचरं दिलीपः ।
धेन्वा तदध्यासनकातराक्ष्या निरीक्ष्यमाणः सुतरां दयालुः ॥

५३ क्षतात्किल त्रायत इत्युदग्रः क्षत्तस्य शब्दो भुवनेषु रूढः ।
राज्येन किं तद्विपरीतवृत्तेः प्राणैरुपाक्रोशमलीमसैर्वा ॥

५४ कथं च शक्यो ऽनुनयो महर्षेर्विश्राणनादन्यपयस्विनीनाम् ।
इमामनूनां सुरभेर्वैहि रुद्रौजसा तु प्रहृतं त्वयास्याम् ॥

५५ सेयं स्वदेहार्पणनिष्क्रयेण न्याय्यं मया मोचयितुं भवत्तः ।
न पारणा स्याद्विहता तवैवं भवेदलुप्तश्च मुनेः क्रियार्थः ॥

"If you fear punishment from your fire-like guru for a   49
    crime against one cow, you can dispel his rage by
    bestowing millions of cows with pot-like udders.

"So keep safe your own powerful body, which will enjoy an   50
    abundance of blessings. For a rich kingdom is Indra's
    heaven itself, they say, except that feet still touch the
    ground."[10]

With this, the lion fell silent, but the mountain, with the 51
    echo resounding in its caves, seemed approvingly
    to repeat out loud the same advice to the earth's
    protector.

The lion had spoken persuasively, and Dilipa responded,   52
    all the more full of pity because the cow was gazing at
    him, her eyes tremulous with fear, while straddled by
    the god's acolyte.

"The warrior's title *kṣattra* has come to be used in every   53
    world in the sense of 'one who protects,' *trāyate,* 'from
    harm,' *kṣatāt.* If my actions belie that, what use would
    my kingdom be to me? What use my very life breath,
    if stained by ignominy?[11]

"And how could I appease the great sage by offering other   54
    milch cows? You should know that this one is the
    equal of Surabhi: it is only because of Rudra's power
    that you have nonetheless been able to attack her.

"Far better to free this cow from you by offering my own   55
    body as ransom. In that way your meal will not be
    spoiled, and the sage's goal, his ritual, will not be lost.

५६ भवानपीदं परवानवैति महान्हि यत्रस्तव देवदारौ ।
स्थातुं नियोक्तुर्यदि शक्यमग्रे विनाश्य रक्ष्यं स्वयमक्षतेन ॥

५७ किमप्यहिंस्यस्तव चेन्मतो ऽहं यशःशरीरे भव मे दयालुः ।
एकान्तविध्वंसिषु मद्विधानां पिण्डेष्वनास्था खलु भौतिकेषु ॥

५८ सम्बन्धमाभाषणपूर्वमाहुर्जातः स नौ सङ्गतयोर्वनान्ते ।
तद्भूतनाथानुग नार्हसि त्वं सम्बन्धिनो मे प्रणयं विहन्तुम् ॥

५९ तथेति गामुक्तवते दिलीपः सद्यः प्रतिस्तम्भविमुक्तबाहुः ।
स न्यस्तशस्त्रं हरये स्वदेहमुपानयत्पिण्डमिवामिषस्य ॥

६० तस्मिन्क्षणे पालयितुः प्रजानामुत्पश्यतः सिंहनिपातमुग्रम् ।
अवाङ्मुखस्योपरि पुष्पवृष्टिः पपात विद्याधरहस्तमुक्ता ॥

६१ उत्तिष्ठ वत्सेत्यमृतायमानं वचो निशम्योत्थितमुत्थितः सन् ।
ददर्श राजा जननीमिव स्वां गामग्रतः प्रस्नविणीं न सिंहम् ॥

६२ तं विस्मितं धेनुरुवाच साधो मायां मयोद्भाव्य परीक्षितो ऽसि ।
ऋषिप्रभावान्मयि नान्तको ऽपि प्रभुः प्रहर्तुं किमुतान्यहिंस्राः ॥

"You know too, since you yourself serve another, taking   56
    great pains to protect this deodar, that one cannot let
    one's charge be destroyed and return to stand before
    one's master unwounded.

"If you still somehow think I should not be harmed, then   57
    take pity on the body of my fame: people like me, as
    you must know, put no trust in lumps of flesh, made
    up of the elements of matter and most certainly
    destined to perish.

"Conversation creates a bond, they say, and this we now   58
    share after meeting in the forest. Therefore, since
    I am thus bound to you, bondsman of the lord of
    creatures,* do not refuse my entreaty!"

"So be it!" said the lion, and at once Dilipa felt his arm   59
    freed from paralysis. He laid down his weapon and
    offered him his body, like a lump of meat.

At that very moment, as the protector of his people lay   60
    face down expecting the lion's cruel pounce, a shower
    of blossoms cast from the hands of *vidyādharas* rained
    down upon him.

Hearing a voice that acted on him like ambrosia and that   61
    said "Rise, my child!" the king rose and saw before
    him not the lion but the cow, flowing with milk, like
    his own mother.

As he stood there astonished, the cow said to him, "This   62
    was an illusion I created to test you, virtuous man.
    Thanks to the sage's power, not even Death can attack
    me, much less other beasts of prey!

———

* Shiva.

६३ भक्त्या गुरौ मय्यनुकम्पया च प्रीतास्मि ते पुत्र वरं वृणीष्व ।
न केवलानां पयसां प्रसूतिमवैहि मां कामदुघां प्रसन्नाम् ॥

६४ ततः समानीय स मानितार्थी हस्तौ स्वहस्तार्जितवीरशब्दः ।
वंशस्य कर्तारमनन्तकीर्तिं सुदक्षिणायां तनयं ययाचे ॥

६५ सन्तानकामाय तथेति कामं राज्ञे प्रतिश्रुत्य पयस्विनी सा ।
दुग्ध्वा पयः पत्त्रपुटे मदीयं पुत्रोपयुङ्क्ष्वेति तमादिदेश ॥

६६ वत्सस्य होमार्थविधेश्च शेषमृषेरनुज्ञामधिगम्य मातः ।
ऊधस्यमिच्छामि तवोपभोक्तुं षष्ठांशमुर्व्या इव रक्षितायाः ॥

६७ इत्थं क्षितीशेन वसिष्ठधेनुर्विज्ञापिता प्रीततरा बभूव ।
तदन्विता हैमवताच्च कुक्षेः प्रत्याययावाश्रममश्रमैव ॥

६८ तस्याः प्रसन्नेन्दुमुखः प्रसादं गुरुर्नृपाणां गुरवे निवेद्य ।
मुखप्रसादानुमितं प्रियायै शशंस वाचा पुनरुक्तयैव ॥

६९ स नन्दिनीस्तन्यमनिन्दितात्मा सद्वत्सलो वत्सनिपीतशेषम् ।
पपौ वसिष्ठेन कृताभ्यनुज्ञः शुद्धं यशो भूय इवावितृष्णः ॥

"I am pleased, my son, by your devotion to your guru and   63
your compassion for me. Choose a boon! Know that I
do not just give milk; when well disposed, I can bestow
anything you wish."

Then the king, who honored suppliants and who had won   64
the title "hero" by his own hands, put those hands
together and requested a son born to Sudakshina who
would establish a dynasty and enjoy glory without
end.

Flowing with milk, the cow agreed to the request of the   65
king who longed for offspring, saying "Granted!" and
instructed him: "Draw my milk into a vessel made of
leaves, my son, and drink it."

"With the sage's permission, I will gladly drink whatever   66
remains of the milk from your udders once your calf
has drunk and the oblations have been made, just as I
take a sixth part of the produce of the earth in return
for my protecting her."[12]

When the king said this, Vasishtha's cow was even more   67
pleased, and returned with him, unwearied, from the
Himalayan cave to the ashram.

His moon-like face serene, the guru of kings announced to   68
his guru the grace she had bestowed, and then made it
known—redundantly, for it could be inferred from the
serenity of his face—to his beloved wife.

With Vasishtha's permission, the blameless king, who felt   69
a parent's affection for the good, took a deep drink
of Nandini's milk after her calf had drunk its fill, as
though he were drinking his bright fame a second
time.[13]

७० प्रातर्यथोक्तव्रतपारणान्ते प्रास्थानिकं स्वस्त्ययनं प्रयुज्य ।
तौ दम्पती स्वां प्रति राजधानीं प्रस्थापयामास वशी वसिष्ठः ॥

७१ प्रदक्षिणीकृत्य हुतं हुताशमनन्तरं भर्तुररुन्धतीं च ।
धेनुं सवत्सां च नृपः प्रतस्थे सन्मङ्गलोदग्रतरानुभावः ॥

७२ श्रोत्राभिरामध्वनिना रथेन स धर्मपत्नीसहितः सहिष्णुः ।
ययावनुद्धातसुखेन मार्गं स्वेनेव पूर्णेन मनोरथेन ॥

७३ तमाहितोत्कण्ठमदर्शनेन प्रजाः प्रजार्थव्रतकर्शिताङ्गम् ।
नेत्रैः पपुस्तृप्तिमनाप्नुवद्भिर्नवोदितं नाथमिवौषधीनाम् ॥

७४ पुरन्दरश्रीः पुरमुत्पताकं प्रविश्य पौरैरभिनन्द्यमानः ।
भुजे भुजङ्गेन्द्रसमानसारे भूयः स भूमेर्धुरमाससञ्ज ॥

७५ अथ नयनसमुत्थं ज्योतिरत्रेरिव द्यौः
सुरसरिदिव तेजो वह्निनिष्ठ्यूतमैशम् ।
नरपतिकुलभूत्यै गर्भमाधत्त राज्ञी
गुरुभिरभिनिविष्टं लोकपालानुभावैः ॥

इति रघुवंशे महाकाव्ये द्वितीयः सर्गः ॥

At dawn, after the ceremonial breaking of fast at the   70
    end of the observance earlier described, the self-
    controlled Vasishtha sent the couple on their way back
    to their royal capital, after pronouncing a blessing for
    the journey.

The king circumambulated the fire, which had received   71
    its oblations, and then Vasishtha and Arundhati, and
    the cow with her calf. Thereupon he set off, auspicious
    auguries brightening his majesty yet further.

The king, who had endured much, progressed along the   72
    road in his chariot, whose rumbling pleased the ears,
    traveling agreeably without jolts, with his consort
    beside him, as though he were propelled by the
    chariot of his own wish, now fulfilled.[14]

His subjects, eager from not having seen him, drank him   73
    in with their eyes without being able to quench their
    thirst; his body had grown lean from his observance
    for attaining offspring, as though he were the newly
    rising moon, the lord of herbs.[15]

Splendid as Indra, he entered his city with its banners   74
    fluttering, was greeted by the city folk, and took
    back into his arms, strong as the lord of serpents, the
    burden of the earth.

Like the sky receiving its light, the moon, from Atri's eye,   75
    like the celestial river receiving the fiery energy of
    Shiva spat forth by Agni, the queen then conceived
    a child imbued with the weighty powers of the gods
    who guard the directions, one that would bring glory
    to that lineage of kings.[16]

तृतीयः सर्गः

१ अथेप्सितं भर्तुरुपस्थितोदयं सखीजनोद्वीक्षणकौमुदीमुखम् ।
   निदानमिक्ष्वाकुकुलस्य सन्ततेः सुदक्षिणा दौहृदलक्षणं दधौ ॥

२ मुखेन सा केतकपत्त्रपाण्डुना कृशाङ्गयष्टिः परिमेयभूषणा ।
   स्थितात्पतारां करुणेन्दुमण्डलां विभातकल्पां रजनीं व्यडम्बयत् ॥

३ तदाननं सेवितमृत्तिकालवं नृपः समाघ्राय न तृप्तिमाययौ ।
   करीव सिक्तं पृषतैः पयोमुचां शुचिव्यपाये वनराजिपल्वलम् ॥

४ दिवं मरुत्वानिव भोक्ष्यते महीं दिगन्तविश्रान्तरथो हि मत्सुतः ।
   अतो ऽभिलाषे प्रथमं तथाविधे मनो बबन्धान्यरसान्विलङ्घ्य सा ॥

५ न मे ह्रिया शंसति किञ्चिदीप्सितं स्पृहावती वस्तुषु केषु मागधी ।
   इति स्म पृच्छत्यतिवेलमादृतः प्रियासखीरुत्तरकोसलेश्वरः ॥

CHAPTER 3
Raghu's Birth and Duel with Indra

Then, as was the dearest wish of her husband, Sudakshina 1
showed the signs of the pregnancy whose happy
issue grew close. It was to be the starting point of the
lineage of the Ikshvaku dynasty, and it was a dawn of
autumn moonlight to the gaze of her friends.[1]

With her face as pale as pandanus leaves, her delicate 2
body gaunt, and wearing only a few ornaments, she
resembled night turning into dawn, when few stars
remain and the disk of the moon is piteously wan.

The king did not tire of breathing in the scent of her 3
mouth, for she had been eating morsels of earth, as
an elephant breathes in the scent of a forest pond
sprinkled with drops from the clouds at summer's
end.[2]

"Just as Indra enjoys the heavens, so will my son the earth, 4
halting his chariot only at the limits of the directions."
That is why her mind fixed first on such a longing,
ignoring other tastes.[3]

"She herself is too embarrassed to tell me what she wants. 5
What things does the princess of Magadha long for?"
In this way the lord of Uttarakosala would time and
again respectfully question his beloved's confidantes.

६ उपेत्य सा दोहददुःखशीलतां यदेव वव्रे तदपश्यदाहृतम् ।
न हीष्टमस्यास्त्रिदिवे ऽपि भूपतेर्बभूव दुष्प्रापमधिज्यधन्वनः ॥

७ दिनेषु गच्छत्सु मधूकपाण्डुरं तदीयमाशाममुखं स्तनद्वयम् ।
समुद्रयोर्वारणदन्तकोशयोर्बभार कान्तिं गवलापिधानयोः ॥

८ क्रमेण निस्तीर्य च दोहदव्यथामुपोढगात्रोपचया रराज सा ।
पुराणपत्त्रापगमादनन्तरं लतेव सन्नद्धमनोज्ञपल्लवा ॥

९ निधानगर्भामिव सागराम्बरां शमीमिवाभ्यन्तरलीनपावकाम् ।
नदीमिवान्तःसलिलां सरस्वतीं नृपः सगर्भां महिषीममन्यत ॥

१० प्रियानुरागस्य मनःसमुन्नतेर्भुजार्जितानां च दिगन्तसम्पदाम् ।
यथाक्रमं पुंसवनादिकाः क्रिया धृतेश्च धीरः सदृशीर्व्यधत्त सः ॥

११ सुरेन्द्रमात्राश्रितगर्भगौरवात् प्रयत्नमुक्तासनया गृहागतः ।
तयोपचाराञ्जलिखिन्नहस्तया ननन्द पारिप्लवनेत्रया नृपः ॥

When she began to suffer from pregnancy cravings,   6
    whatever she wished she saw brought to her, for there
    was nothing in the three worlds she desired that was
    unobtainable for the king, when he strung his bow.⁴

As the days went by, her breasts became dark-tipped and   7
    pale as mahua flowers; they looked as beautiful as
    round ivory boxes with lids of buffalo horn.⁵

Gradually overcoming the discomfort of her pregnancy   8
    cravings, her body became more ample, and she shone
    like a plant that sprouts pleasing new shoots after
    shedding old leaves.

The king thought of his pregnant wife as like the seagirt   9
    earth with treasure within; like the wood of the *śamī*
    tree where fire lies hidden; or like the river Sarasvati,
    whose waters run underground.

Resolute, he performed the rites of passage in due order,   10
    beginning with that which makes the unborn child
    male, in a manner that accorded with his affection
    for his beloved, with his nobility of mind, with the
    treasures won by his arm from every quarter, and with
    his joy.⁶

The king was delighted each time he returned home to   11
    be welcomed by his queen, rising from her seat with
    difficulty—because she was weighed down by the
    parts of the deities of the directions that inhabited
    her womb—and offering guest water with trembling
    cupped hands and quivering eyes.⁷

१२ कुमारभृत्यैः कुशलैरधिष्ठिते भिषग्भिराप्तैरथ गर्भवेश्मनि ।
निरत्ययाय प्रसवाय तस्थुषी बभौ समासन्नफला क्रियेव सा ॥

१३ ग्रहैस्ततः पञ्चभिरुच्चसंश्रयैरसूर्यगैः सूचितभाग्यसम्पदम् ।
असूत पुत्रं समये शचीसमा त्रिसाधना शक्तिरिवार्थमक्षतम् ॥

१४ दिशः प्रसेदुर्मरुतो ववुः शिवाः
प्रदक्षिणार्चिर्हुतमग्निराददे ।
बभूव सर्वं शुभशंसि तत्क्षणं
भवो हि लोकाभ्युदयाय तादृशाम् ॥

१५ अरिष्टशय्यां परितो विसारिणा सुजन्मनस्तस्य निजेन तेजसा ।
निशीथदीपाः सहसा हतत्विषो बभूवुरालेख्यसमर्पिता इव ॥

१६ जनाय शुद्धान्तचराय शंसते कुमारजन्मामृतसम्मिताक्षरम् ।
अदेयमासीत्तयमेव भूपतेः शशिप्रभं छत्त्रमुभे च चामरे ॥

१७ स वीक्ष्य पुत्रस्य चिरात्पिता मुखं निधानकुम्भस्य युवेव दुर्गतः ।
मुदा शरीरे प्रबभूव नात्मनः पयोधिरिन्दूदयमूर्छितो यथा ॥

१८ स जातकर्मण्यखिले तपस्विना तपोवनादेत्य पुरोधसा कृते ।
दिलीपसूनुर्मणिराकरोद्गतः प्रयुक्तसंस्कार इवाधिकं बभौ ॥

In the delivery chamber, which was overseen by doctors   12
    skilled in midwifery, physicians, and trusted friends,
    she remained in readiness for the safe birth of the
    child, like a sacrament about to produce its fruit.[8]

Then, at the perfect moment—the five planets were in the   13
    ascendant and did not join the sun, portending good
    fortune in full measure—the queen, Shachi's equal,
    gave birth to a son, as threefold power gives birth to
    prosperity undiminished.[9]

The horizons brightened; favorable winds blew; the fire   14
    received oblations with its flames turning rightward:
    everything augured well at that moment, for the birth
    of such beings benefits the world.

Around the delivery bed, the auspiciously born baby's   15
    natural radiance spread out and suddenly dimmed the
    night lamps, as if they were captured in a painting.

To the servant from the women's quarters who spoke the   16
    nectar-sweet words that a son was born, there were
    only three things the king was not ready to give: his
    moon-bright parasol and his two yak-tail whisks.[10]

When at long last the father looked upon the face of his   17
    son, like a penniless youth seeing the mouth of a pot of
    treasure, he could not contain himself within his body
    for joy, like the ocean swelling at the rise of the moon.

After the ascetic family priest had come from the penance   18
    grove and performed all the birth rites, Dilipa's son
    shone brighter still, like a jewel from the mine when
    polished.

१९   सुखश्रवा मङ्गलतूर्यनिःस्वनाः प्रमोदनृत्तैः सह वारयोषिताम् ।
न केवलं सद्मनि मागधीपतेः पथि व्यजृम्भन्त दिवौकसामपि ॥

२०   न संयतस्तस्य बभूव रक्षितुर्विमोचयेद्यं सुतजन्महर्षितः ।
ऋणाभिधानात्स्वयमेव केवलं तदा पितॄणां मुमुचे स बन्धनात् ॥

२१   श्रुतस्य यायादयमन्तमर्भकस्तथा परेषां युधि चेति पार्थिवः ।
अवेक्ष्य धातोर्गमनार्थमर्थविच्चकार नाम्ना रघुमात्मसम्भवम् ॥

२२   पितुः प्रयत्नात्स समग्रसम्पदः शुभैः शरीरावयवैर्दिने दिने ।
पुपोष वृद्धिं हरिदश्वदीधितेरनुप्रवेशादिव बालचन्द्रमाः ॥

२३   उमावृषाङ्कौ शरजन्मना यथा यथा जयन्तेन शचीपुरन्दरौ ।
तथा नृपः सा च सुतेन मागधी ननन्दतुस्तत्सदृशेन तत्समौ ॥

२४   रथाङ्गनाम्नोरिव भावबन्धनं बभूव यत्प्रेम परस्परं प्रति ।
विभक्तमप्येकसुते न तत्तयोः परस्परस्योपरि पर्यहीयत ॥

२५   यदाह धात्र्या प्रथमोदितं वचो ययौ तदीयामवलम्ब्य चाङ्गुलिम् ।
अभूच्च नम्रः प्रणिपातशिक्षया पितुर्मुदं तेन ततान सो ऽर्भकः ॥

The booming of auspicious drums, while courtesans   19
    danced joyfully, spread out to delight the ear not only
    at the court of the lord of the Magadhan princess, but
    also in the sky, the path of the celestials.

There were no prisoners for that protector, overjoyed   20
    at the birth of a son, to set free. Instead he freed
    only himself from the fetter, known as "debt," of his
    forefathers.[11]

"May this child reach the end of his studies, and the end 21
    of his enemies in war!" With this in mind, the king, a
    true expert in the meanings of words, named his son
    Raghu, considering its root meaning "reach."[12]

By the efforts of his father, who commanded great   22
    wealth, the boy grew day by day, each part of his body
    auspiciously bright, like the new moon growing day by
    day when infused by the sun's ray.[13]

Like Uma* and Shiva because of Skanda, like Shachi and   23
    Indra because of Jayanta, the king and the princess
    of Magadha, the equals of those parents, rejoiced
    because of their son, the equal of those sons.

Their love for each other, like that of a shelduck pair,   24
    firmly bound their hearts; and although now shared
    with their one and only son, that love did not
    diminish, not for the one nor for the other.[14]

When he spoke the words his nurse had spoken first,   25
    walked hanging on her finger, and bent when he was
    taught to bow, the child brought joy to his father.

———

* Parvati.

२६ तमङ्कमारोप्य शरीरयोगजैः सुखैर्निषिञ्चन्तमिवामृतं त्वचि ।
त्रिभागसम्मीलितलोचनो नृपश्चिरात्सुतस्पर्शरसज्ञतां ययौ ॥

२७ अमंस्त चानेन पराध्र्यजन्मना स्थितेरभेत्ता स्थितिमन्तमन्वयम् ।
स्वमूर्तिभेदेन गुणाग्र्यवृत्तिना पतिः प्रजानामिव सर्गमात्मनः ॥

२८ स वृत्तचूलश्चलकाकपक्षकैरमात्यपुत्रैः सवयोभिरन्वितः ।
लिपेर्यथावद्ग्रहणेन वाङ्मयं नदीमुखेनेव समुद्रमाविशत् ॥

२९ अथोपनीतं विधिवद्द्विपश्चितो विनिन्युरेनं गुरवो गुरुप्रियम् ।
अवन्ध्ययत्नाश्च बभूवुरत्र ते क्रिया हि वस्तूपहिता प्रसीदति ॥

३० धियः समग्रैः स गुणैरुदारधीः क्रमाच्चतस्रश्चतुरर्णवोपमाः ।
ततार विद्याः पवनातिपातिभिर्दिशो हरिद्भिर्हरितामिवेश्वरः ॥

३१ त्वचं स मेध्यां परिधाय रौरवीमशिक्षतास्त्रं पितुरेव मन्त्रवत् ।
प्रयोगसंहाररहस्यवित्तमो बभूव चास्त्रेषु यथा पुरन्दरः ॥

56

When the king set him on his lap, the boy seemed to pour   26
    nectar on his skin through the joys of bodily contact.
    And with eyes one third closed, he savored at long last
    the touch of a son.

A maintainer of stability, he judged that his line had been   27
    made stable by this precious son, a form of himself
    composed of his best qualities, just as Brahma judges
    that his creation is made stable by a form of himself in
    which the highest of the qualities prevail.[15]

He received tonsure and, along with ministers' sons of   28
    the same age, who, like him, wore long, flapping
    sidelocks, he entered the world of literature by way of
    thoroughly learning his letters, as one can enter the
    ocean by way of a river.

Then, when he had received initiation according to   29
    precept, learned gurus educated him, who was dear to
    his gurus. And their efforts were not wasted upon him;
    for actions succeed when directed to fitting objects.

With his excellent qualities of mind, the noble-minded   30
    Raghu traversed one after the other the four ocean-
    like realms of knowledge, as the sun traverses the
    quarters with his chestnut horses that outrun the
    wind.[16]

Donning the pure skin of a black buck, he learned the use   31
    of weaponry with mantras from his father and, like
    Indra, he became especially skilled in the secrets of
    discharging and recalling his weapons.

३२ महोक्षतां वत्सतरः स्पृशन्निव द्विपेन्द्रभावं कलभः श्रयन्निव ।
रघुः क्रमादौवनभिन्नशैशवः पुपोष गम्भीरमनोहरं वपुः ॥

३३ अथास्य गोदानविधेरनन्तरं विवाहदीक्षां निरवर्तयत्प्रभुः ।
नरेन्द्रकन्यास्तमवाप्य सत्पतिं तमोपहं दक्षसुता इवाबभुः ॥

३४ युवा युगव्यायतबाहुरंसलः कवाटवक्षाः परिणद्धकन्धरः ।
वपुष्प्रकर्षादजयद्गुरुं रघुस्तथापि नीचैर्विनयादद‍ृश्यत ॥

३५ अथ प्रजानां चिरमात्मना धृतां नितान्तगुर्वीं लघयिष्यता धुरम् ।
वशीति मत्वा मतिचक्षुषा सुतो नृपेण चक्रे युवराजशब्दभाक् ॥

३६ नरेन्द्रमूलायतनादनन्तरं तदास्पदं श्रीर्युवराजसंज्ञितम् ।
अगच्छदंशेन गुणाभिलाषिणी नवावतारं कमलादिवोत्पलम् ॥

३७ उषर्बुधः सारथिनेव वायुना घनव्यपायेन गभस्तिमानिव ।
बभूव तेनातितरां दुरुत्सहः कटप्रभेदेन करीव पार्थिवः ॥

Like a bullock on the verge of becoming a great bull, like   32
    an elephant calf about to turn into a princely tusker,
    Raghu developed a body both strong and handsome,
    as childhood gradually gave way to youth.

Then, after the rite of donating a cow, the king arranged   33
    his wedding ceremony. The princesses who gained
    him as an excellent husband shone like the daughters
    of Daksha on gaining the gloom-dispelling moon.[17]

As a youth, with arms as long as a yoke, powerful should-   34
    ers, a chest like a door panel, and a thick neck, Raghu
    outshone his father in excellence of form, but none-
    theless, out of good manners, was seen to stand
    less tall.

Then, when the king, who judged by the eye of his mind,   35
    saw that his son was self-controlled, he bestowed on
    him the title of "Young King," intending to lighten the
    extremely weighty burden that he had borne so long
    of governing his subjects.[18]

Desirous of excellence, Majesty next moved partly from   36
    her principal residence, the king, to the one who
    had come to be called the "Young King," Raghu, just
    as beauty partly moves from the lotus to the newly
    opened water lily.[19]

As Fire with his charioteer Wind, as the sun with the   37
    dispersal of the clouds, as a bull elephant with the
    splitting open of his temples, so the king, with Raghu,
    became utterly invincible.[20]

३८ नियुज्य तं मेध्यतुरङ्गरक्षणे धनुर्धरै राजसुतैरनुद्रुतम् ।
अपूर्णमेकेन शतक्रतूपमः शतं क्रतूनामपविघ्नमाप सः ॥

३९ अतः परं तेन मखाय यज्वना तुरङ्गमुत्सृष्टमनर्गलं पुनः ।
धनुर्भृतामग्रत एव रक्षिणां जहार शक्रः किल गूढविग्रहः ॥

४० विषादलुप्तप्रतिपत्ति विस्मितं कुमारसैन्यं सपदि स्थितं च तत् ।
वसिष्ठधेनुश्च यदृच्छयागता श्रुतप्रभावा दृदृशे ऽथ नन्दिनी ॥

४१ तदङ्घ्रिनिःष्यन्दलवेन लोचने प्रमृज्य पुण्येन पुरस्कृतः सताम् ।
अतीन्द्रियेष्वप्युपपन्नदर्शनो बभूव भावेषु दिलीपनन्दनः ॥

४२ स पूर्वतः पर्वतपक्षशातनं ददर्श देवं नरदेवसम्भवः ।
पुनः पुनः सूतनिषिद्धचापलं हरन्तमश्वं रथरश्मिसंयुतम् ॥

४३ शतैस्तमक्षणामनिमेषवृत्तिभिर्हरिं विदित्वा हरिभिश्च वाजिभिः ।
अवोचदेनं गगनस्पृशा रघुः स्वरेण धीरेण निवर्तयन्निव ॥

Dilipa, who resembled the God of a Hundred Sacrifices, charged Raghu and a train of bow-wielding princes with the protection of the sacrificial horse, and attained without hindrance one short of a hundred sacrifices.[21] 38

At that point, so the story goes, Indra made himself invisible and, right in front of the archers protecting it, snatched away the horse, which Dilipa as sacrificer had once again set free to roam unchecked for this sacrifice. 39

The army of princes suddenly stood still, stupefied in their dejection. At that very moment they saw Nandini, Vasishtha's cow, renowned for her powers, arrive by chance. 40

Wiping his eyes with a drop of the sacred liquid that flowed from her body, the son of Dilipa, first among the just, acquired sight even of things that are beyond the senses.[22] 41

The prince, born of a god among men, saw Indra in the east. The god who once severed the mountains' wings was leading away the horse attached to the reins of his chariot, while his charioteer repeatedly checked its frisking.[23] 42

When he realized from his hundreds of unblinking eyes and his chestnut horses that it was Hari, Raghu addressed him in a firm voice that reached the heavens and seemed to stop him in his tracks.[24] 43

४४ मखांशभाजां प्रथमो मनीषिभिस्त्वमेव देवेन्द्र यदा निगद्यसे ।
अजस्रदीक्षाप्रयतस्य मद्गुरोः क्रियाविघाताय कथं प्रवर्तसे ॥

४५ त्रिलोकनाथेन सता मखद्विष-
स्त्वया नियाम्या ननु दिव्यचक्षुषा ।
स चेत्स्वयं कर्मसु धर्मचारिणां
त्वमन्तरायीभवसि च्युतो विधिः ॥

४६ तदङ्गमग्र्यं मघवन्महाक्रतोरमुं तुरङ्गं प्रतिमोक्तुमर्हसि ।
पथः शुचेर्दर्शयितार ईश्वरा मलीमसामाददते न पद्धतिम् ॥

४७ इति प्रगल्भं रघुणा समीरितं वचो निशम्याधिपतिर्दिवौकसाम् ।
निवर्तयामास रथं सविस्मयः प्रचक्रमे च प्रतिवक्तुमुत्तरम् ॥

४८ यथात्थ राजन्यकुमार तत्तथा यशस्तु रक्ष्यं परतो यशोधनैः ।
जगत्प्रकाशं तदशेषमिज्यया भवद्गुरुर्लङ्घयितुं ममोद्यतः ॥

४९ हरिर्ययैकः पुरुषोत्तमः स्मृतो महेश्वरस्त्र्यम्बक एव नापरः ।
तथा विदुर्मा मुनयः शतक्रतुं द्वितीयगामी न हि शब्द एष नः ॥

५० अतो ऽयमश्वः कपिलानुकारिणा पितुस्त्वदीयस्य मयापहारितः ।
अलं प्रयत्नेन तवात्र मा निधाः पदं पदव्यां सगरस्य सन्ततेः ॥

"Lord of the gods, sages count you foremost among those   44
   who enjoy a share of each sacrifice. How then can you
   act to destroy the rite undertaken by my father, who is
   constantly purified by consecration for sacrifices?

"Surely with your celestial vision, you, as lord of the   45
   triple universe, ought to keep in check the enemies
   of sacrifice. If you yourself become an obstacle to the
   rites of the righteous, then ritual is done for!

"Therefore it behooves you, Indra, to release this horse,   46
   an indispensable element of a solemn sacrifice. The
   powerful show the way that is pure; they do not take a
   tainted path."

Hearing the bold words uttered by Raghu, the overlord of   47
   the celestials turned back his chariot astonished and
   began to respond.

"Prince of warriors, what you say is true. But those whose   48
   wealth is their fame must protect that fame from
   others. Mine shines throughout the universe; by
   holding this sacrifice, your father has set out to eclipse
   it all.

"Just as Vishnu alone is remembered as 'The Best of Souls'   49
   and only the three-eyed Śiva as 'The Great Lord,' so
   sages know me to be 'Him of a Hundred Sacrifices.'
   This name of mine applies to no one else.[25]

"That is why, after the manner of Kapila, I took your   50
   father's horse away. Make no further efforts to regain
   it. Do not set foot on the path of Sagara's sons!"[26]

५१ ततः प्रहस्याह पुनः पुरन्दरं व्यपेतभीर्भूमिपुरन्दरात्मजः ।
गृहाण शस्त्रं यदि सर्ग एष ते न खल्वनिर्जित्य रघुं कृती भवान् ॥

५२ स एवमुक्त्वा मघवन्तमुन्मुखः करिष्यमाणः सशरं शरासनम् ।
अतिष्ठदालीढविशेषशोभिना वपुष्प्रकर्षेण विडम्बितेश्वरः ॥

५३ रघोरवष्टम्भमयेन पत्त्रिणा हृदि क्षतो गोत्रभिदप्यमर्षणः ।
नवाम्बुदानीकमुहूर्तलाञ्छने धनुष्यमोघं समधत्त मार्गणम् ॥

५४ नरेन्द्रसूनोः स बृहद्भुजान्तरं प्रविश्य भीमासुरशोणितोचितः ।
पपावनास्वादितपूर्वमाशुगः कुतूहलेनेव मनुष्यशोणितम् ॥

५५ हरेः कुमारो ऽपि कुमारविक्रमः सुरद्विपास्फालनकर्कशाङ्गुलौ ।
भुजे शचीपत्त्रविशेषकाङ्क्षिते स्वनामचिह्नं निचखान सायकम् ॥

५६ जहार चान्येन मयूरलाञ्छनं शरेण शक्रस्य महाशनिध्वजम् ।
चुकोप तस्मै स भृशं सुरश्रियः प्रसह्य केशव्यपरोपणादिव ॥

५७ तयोरुपान्तस्थितसिद्धसैनिकं गरुत्मदाशीविषभीमदर्शनैः ।
बभूव युद्धं तुमुलं जयैषिणोरधोमुखैरूर्ध्वमुखैश्च पत्त्रिभिः ॥

The fearless son of an Indra on earth then laughingly   51
    replied to Indra: "Take up your weapon if such is your
    resolve. You certainly will not succeed without first
    vanquishing Raghu!"

With this, he took his stand, gazing up at Indra to nock an   52
    arrow on his bow and aim, and in the archer's posture
    his magnificent physique was as splendid as Shiva's.[27]

Struck to the heart by Raghu's arrow-like defiance, Indra   53
    too, furious, set an unfailing arrow to his bow, the
    fleeting banner of armies of fresh clouds.[28]

His arrow, used to the blood of fierce *asuras,* entered the   54
    king's son's broad chest and with curiosity, it seemed,
    drank human blood, which it had never tasted before.

For his part the prince, with the valor of Kumara, buried   55
    an arrow inscribed with his name in Indra's arm, its
    fingers roughened from goading the elephant of the
    gods and marked with traces of the leaf designs with
    which he decorated Shachi's face.[29]

And with another arrow he cut down Shakra's great   56
    thunderbolt banner that was marked with a peacock
    ensign. Indra flew into a rage at him, as though he had
    violently cut off the hair of Shri herself, the Fortune of
    the gods.[30]

While their armies of siddhas and soldiers stood by, there   57
    ensued a tumultuous clash between the two vying for
    victory, their arrows shooting upward and downward
    like birds and serpents, a terrifying sight.

५८ अतिप्रबन्धप्रहितास्त्रवृष्टिभिस्तमाश्रयं दुष्प्रसहस्य तेजसः ।
शशाक निर्वापयितुं न वासवः स्वतश्च्युतं वह्निमिवाद्रिरम्बुदः ॥

५९ ततः प्रकोष्ठाद्धरिचन्दनाङ्कितात् प्रमथ्यमानार्णवधीरनादिनीम् ।
रघुः शशाङ्कार्धमुखेन पत्त्रिणा शरासनज्यामलुनाद्द्विडोजसः ॥

६० स चापमुत्सृज्य विवृद्धमत्सरः प्रवासनाय प्रबलस्य विद्विषः ।
महीध्रपक्षव्यपरोपणोद्धृतं स्फुरत्प्रभामण्डलमस्त्रमाददे ॥

६१ रघुर्भृशं वक्षसि तेन ताडितः पपात भूमौ सह सैनिकास्रुभिः ।
निमेषमात्रादवधूय च व्यथां सहोत्थितः सैनिकहर्षनिःस्वनैः ॥

६२ तथापि शस्त्रव्यवहारनिष्ठुरे विपक्षभावे स्थिरमस्य तस्थुषः ।
तुतोष वीर्यातिशयेन वृत्रहा पदं हि सर्वत्र गुणैर्विधीयते ॥

६३ असङ्गमद्रिष्वपि सारवत्तया न मे त्वदन्येन विसोढमायुधम् ।
अवैहि मां प्रीतमृते तुरङ्गमाद्वरं वृणीष्वेति तमाह वृत्रहा ॥

६४ ततो निषङ्गादसमग्रमुद्धृतं सुवर्णपुङ्खद्युतिरञ्जिताङ्गुलिम् ।
दिलीपसूनुः प्रतिसंहरन्निषुं प्रियंवदः प्रत्यवदत्सुरेश्वरम् ॥

Raghu was an abode of fiery power impossible to   58
    withstand, and Vasava could no more extinguish
    him with the shower of weapons he discharged in a
    ceaseless stream than a cloud can extinguish with its
    waters the lightning fire that falls from it.

Then, with an arrow tipped with a blade like the   59
    crescent moon, Raghu cut Indra's bowstring,
    which reverberated loudly as it snapped from his
    sandal-smeared forearm, like the ocean when it was
    churned.[31]

With mounting rage Indra cast aside his bow and took up   60
    the weapon with shining halo that could pride itself
    on having severed the mountains' wings, in order to
    destroy this even mightier enemy.[32]

Struck hard on the chest by this, Raghu fell to the ground,   61
    along with his soldiers' tears; but a moment later,
    throwing off his shock, he rose up, along with his
    soldiers' shouts of joy.

Indra, the slayer of Vritra, was pleased with Raghu's   62
    exceptional heroism as he stood firm in opposition, in
    spite of the dreadful back and forth of weapons; for
    virtues gain a foothold in every heart.

Indra said to him: "No one other than you has withstood   63
    my weapon, so strong that even the mountains were
    not able to resist it. Know that I am pleased: ask for
    anything you wish—except the horse!"

Then the silver-tongued son of Dilipa, pushing back the   64
    arrow that was half drawn out from his quiver, letting
    the gleam of its golden flights color his fingers, replied
    to the leader of the gods.

६५ अमोच्यमश्वं यदि मन्यते प्रभुस्ततः समाप्ते विधिनैव कर्मणि ।
अजस्रदीक्षातनुरद्य मे गुरुः क्रतोरशेषेण फलेन युज्यताम् ॥

६६ यथा च वृत्तान्तमिमं सदोगतस्त्रिलोचनैकांशतया दुरासदः ।
तवैव सन्देशहराद्विषां पतिः शृणोति नाकेश तथा विधीयताम् ॥

६७ तथेति कामं प्रतिशुश्रुवात्रघोर्यथागतं मातलिसारथिर्ययौ ।
नृपस्य नातिप्रमनाः सदोगृहं सुदक्षिणासूनुरपि न्यवर्तत ॥

६८ तमभ्यनन्दत्प्रथमप्रबोधितः प्रजेश्वरः शासनहारिणा हरेः ।
परामृशन्हर्षचलेन पाणिना तदीयमङ्गं कुलिशव्रणाङ्कितम् ॥

६९ इति क्षितीशो नवतिं नवाधिकां महाक्रतूनां महनीयशासनः ।
समारुरुक्षुर्दिवमायुषः क्षये ततान सोपानपरम्परामिव ॥

७० अथ स विषयव्यावृत्तात्मा यथाविधि सूनवे
नृपतिककुदं दत्त्वा यूने सितातपवारणम् ।
मुनिवनतरुच्छायां देव्या तया सह शिश्रिये
गलितवयसामिक्ष्वाकूणामिदं हि कुलव्रतम् ॥

इति रघुवंशे महाकाव्ये तृतीयः सर्गः ॥

"If the lord judges that the horse may not be released,   65
    then, after the ritual has been completed in strict
    accord with procedures, may my father, now
    emaciated from his ceaseless sacrificial consecration,
    be rewarded with the entire fruit of the sacrifice.

"And please arrange, lord of heaven, that the lord of men   66
    hear this news from your own messenger, since in the
    sacrificial hall he is unapproachable, because he has
    become a part of Shiva."[33]

"So be it!" said Indra, acceding to Raghu's wish, and he   67
    left the way he had come with his charioteer Matali.
    For his part, the son of Sudakshina returned, none too
    pleased, to the king's place of sacrifice.

Informed in advance by Indra's messenger, the king   68
    welcomed Raghu and with a hand trembling with
    joy touched his body that had been wounded by the
    thunderbolt.

Thus the king, whose commands were to be honored,   69
    performed ninety-nine great sacrifices—a staircase, it
    almost seemed, for ascending to heaven when his life's
    breath was spent.

Then, as his spirit turned away from sensory pleasures, he   70
    handed over the white parasol, emblem of kingship,
    to his young son in accordance with precept, and with
    his queen sought refuge in the shade of the trees of a
    sages' grove. For such was the family observance of
    the Ikshvakus when their prime had passed.

चतुर्थः सर्गः

१ स राज्यं गुरुणा दत्तं प्रतिपद्यादिकं बभौ ।
   दिनान्ते निहितं तेजः सवित्रेव हुताशनः ॥

२ न्यस्तशस्त्रं दिलीपं च तं च शुश्रूवुषां प्रभुम् ।
   राज्ञामुद्धृतनाराचे हृदि शूलमिवार्पितम् ॥

३ पुरुहूतध्वजस्येव तस्योन्नयनपङ्क्तयः ।
   नवाभ्युत्थानदर्शिन्यो ननन्दुः सप्रजाः प्रजाः ॥

४ सममेव समाक्रान्तं द्वयं द्विरदगामिना ।
   तेन सिंहासनं पित्र्यमखिलं चारिमण्डलम् ॥

५ छायामण्डललक्ष्येण तमदृश्या किल स्वयम् ।
   पद्मा पद्मातपत्रेण भेजे साम्राज्यदीक्षितम् ॥

६ परिकल्पितसान्निध्या काले काले च वन्दिषु ।
   स्तुत्यं स्तुतिभिरर्थ्याभिरुपतस्थे सरस्वती ॥

CHAPTER 4
Raghu Conquers the Four Directions

When Raghu acquired the kingdom bequeathed by his 1
father, he shone even more, as fire becomes brighter
when it receives splendor from the sun at day's end.

To the kings who learned that Dilipa had laid down his 2
weapons and Raghu had become ruler, it seemed as if
no sooner had an arrow been extracted than a spear
had been lodged in their heart.

With rows of upturned eyes, his subjects with their 3
children rejoiced to behold his present elevation, as
when beholding the rise of Indra's banner.[1]

Riding on an elephant, he took control of two things at one 4
and the same time: his father's throne and the circle of
his enemies.

When he was consecrated as king, they say it was Lakshmi 5
herself who, unseen, honored him with a lotus parasol,
its presence made known only by its shadow's disk.[2]

Sarasvati, too, time and again made herself present in the 6
bards and attended upon him, worthy of praise, with
fitting songs of praise.

७ मनुप्रभृतिभिर्मान्यैर्भुक्ता यद्यपि राजभिः ।
तथाप्यनन्यपूर्वेव तस्मिन्नासीद्वसुन्धरा ॥

८ स हि सर्वस्य लोकस्य युक्तदण्डतया मनः ।
आददे नातिशीतोष्णो नभस्वानिव दक्षिणः ॥

९ कामं कमलपत्त्राणां नेत्रे तस्यानुकारिणी ।
चक्षुष्मत्ता तु शास्त्रेण सूक्ष्मकार्यार्थदर्शिना ॥

१० यथा प्रह्लादनाच्चन्द्रः प्रतापात्तपनो यथा ।
तथैव सो ऽभूदन्वर्थो राजा प्रकृतिरञ्जनात् ॥

११ नयविद्भिर्नवे राज्ञि सदसच्चोपदर्शितम् ।
पूर्व एवाभवत्पक्षस्तस्मिन्नाभवदुत्तरः ॥

१२ मन्दोत्कण्ठाः कृतास्तेन गुणाधिकतया गुरौ ।
फलेन सहकारस्य पुष्पोद्गम इव प्रजाः ॥

१३ पञ्चानामपि भूतानामुत्कर्षं पुपुषुर्गुणाः ।
नवे तस्मिन्महीपाले सर्वं नवमिवाभवत् ॥

१४ लब्धप्रशमनस्वस्थमथैनं समुपस्थिता ।
पार्थिवश्रीर्द्वितीयेव शरत्पङ्कजलक्षणा ॥

Earth had been enjoyed by kings of good repute from   7
    Manu onward, but under his reign it seemed as if she
    had never belonged to anyone else.

For by meting out just punishment—neither too harsh nor   8
    too mild, like the southern wind—he won the hearts
    of all the people.

He had eyes like lotus petals, to be sure, but his real eyes   9
    were the sciences, whereby he saw subtler things, his
    stratagems.

The moon got its name because it delights, and the sun its   10
    name because it burns. In just the same way he was
    rightly called "regal" because he regaled his subjects.[3]

Experts in politics showed the new king both what is good   11
    and what is bad. The first alone became his policy, and
    not the second.[4]

He eased the people's nostalgia for his father with his   12
    superior qualities, just as the fruits of the mango allay
    the longing for its blossom.

The qualities of all five elements were intensified: with   13
    him as new protector of the earth, everything seemed
    renewed.[5]

Now, once he had secured the kingdom and was at ease,   14
    Autumn came to wait on him, like a second Royal
    Fortune, recognizable by her lotus flowers.[6]

१५ निर्वृष्टलघुभिर्मेघैः सवितुस्तस्य चोभयोः ।
वर्धिष्णवो दिशां भागाः प्रतापायेव रेचिताः ॥

१६ अधिज्यमायुधं कर्तुं समयो ऽयं रघोरिति ।
स्वं धनुः शङ्कितेनेव संजहे शतमन्युना ॥

१७ पुण्डरीकातपत्रस्तं विकसत्काशचामरः ।
ऋतुर्विडम्बयामास न पुनः प्राप तच्छ्रियम् ॥

१८ प्रसादसुमुखे तस्मिंश्चन्द्रे च विषदप्रभे ।
तदा चक्षुष्मतां प्रीतिरासीत्समरसा द्वयोः ॥

१९ हंसश्रेणिषु तारासु कुमुद्वत्सु च वारिषु ।
विभूतयस्तदीयानां पर्यस्ता यशसामिव ॥

२० इक्षुच्छायानिषादिन्यस्तस्य गोप्तुर्गुणोदयम् ।
आकुमारकथोद्घातं शालिगोप्यो जगुर्यशः ॥

२१ प्रससादोदयादम्भः कुम्भयोनेर्महौजसः ।
रघोस्त्वभिभवाशङ्कि चुक्षुभे द्विषतां मनः ॥

२२ मदोदग्राः ककुद्मन्तः सरितां कूलमुद्रुजाः ।
लीलाखेलमनुप्रापुर्महोक्षास्तस्य विक्रमम् ॥

The heavens' unfolding quarters became emptied of the   15
  now light and rainless clouds, as if to let both sun and
  king spread their fiery energy.

"This is the time for Raghu to string his bow." As if in fear   16
  of this, the god of hundredfold anger laid aside his
  own bow.[7]

With lotuses for parasols and blooming kans grass for   17
  chowries, the season emulated his Royal Glory but
  could not attain it.[8]

At that time, people with eyes to see rejoiced with equal   18
  pleasure in him, his face bright with serenity, and in
  the moon, of spotless radiance.

It seemed as if the riches of his fame had been spread   19
  about among the rows of geese, the stars, and the lily
  ponds.[9]

Seated in the shade of the sugarcane, the women guarding   20
  the crops sang of their protector's glory, sprung
  from his virtues, beginning with the stories of his
  childhood.

When the mighty sage, the pot-born Agastya, rose in the   21
  sky, the waters grew calm. But when Raghu arose, the
  hearts of his enemies, foreseeing defeat, shuddered.[10]

The great humped bulls, wild with rut, showed a valor as   22
  exuberant as his when they tore up the riverbanks.

२३ प्रसवैः सप्तपर्णानां मदगन्धिभिराहताः ।
असूययेव तन्नागाः सप्तधैव प्रसुसुवुः ॥

२४ सरितः कुर्वती गाधाः पथश्चाश्यानकर्दमान् ।
यात्रायै चोदयामास तं शक्तेः प्रथमं शरत् ॥

२५ तस्मै सम्यग्घुतो वह्निर्वाजिनीराजनाविधौ ।
प्रदक्षिणार्चिर्व्याजेन हस्तेनेव जयं ददौ ॥

२६ स गुप्तमूलप्रत्यन्तः शुद्धपार्ष्णिरयान्वितः ।
षड्विधं बलमादाय प्रतस्थे दिग्जिगीषया ॥

२७ अवाकिरन्वयोवृद्धास्तं लाजैः पौरयोषितः ।
पृषतैर्मन्दरोद्धूतैः क्षीरोर्मिय इवाच्युतम् ॥

२८ स ययौ प्रथमं प्राचीं तुल्यः प्राचीनबर्हिषा ।
अहिताननिलोद्धूतैस्तर्जयन्निव केतुभिः ॥

२९ रजोभिः स्यन्दनोद्धूतैर्गजैश्च घनसन्निभैः ।
भुवस्तलमिव व्योम कुर्वन्व्योमेव भूतलम् ॥

३० प्रतापो ऽग्रे ततः शब्दः पुरोगास्तदनन्तरम् ।
ययौ पश्चाद्द्विजानीकं चतुःस्कन्धेव सा चमूः ॥

Touched by the musth-scented flowers of the seven-leaf   23
trees, his elephants, as if out of jealousy, discharged
musth juice through all seven outlets.[11]

Making the rivers fordable and drying out the mud on the   24
roads, Autumn, even before his Power, urged Raghu
to start his campaign.

The sacrificial fire, duly fed at the lustration ceremony of   25
his horses, seemed to be proffering him victory, with
its right-turning flame as hand.

With homeland and frontiers protected, with those at his   26
heels quiet, and with good fortune by his side, he led
his sixfold army out to conquer the world in every
direction.[12]

The city matrons sprinkled him with parched grain, as the   27
waves of the milk ocean sprinkled the never-falling
Vishnu with froth churned up by Mount Mandara.

He was like Prachinabarhis as he marched toward the east,   28
and with his wind-tossed banners he seemed to shake
a menacing finger toward his enemies.[13]

With the dust stirred up by his chariots and with his   29
cloud-like elephants, he seemed to transform sky into
earth and earth into sky.

Reports of his fierceness came first, then the din, then the   30
vanguard, and after them the host of elephants. These
are what seemed to be four parts of Raghu's army.[14]

३१ पुरोगैः कलुषास्तस्य सहप्रस्थायिभिः कृशाः ।
पश्चात्प्रयायिभिः पङ्कं चक्रिरे मार्गनिम्नगाः ॥

३२ मरुपृष्ठान्युदम्भांसि नाव्याः सुप्रतरा नदीः ।
विपिनानि प्रकाशानि शक्तिमत्त्वाञ्चकार सः ॥

३३ स सेनां महतीं कर्षन्पूर्वसागरगामिनीम् ।
बभौ हरजटाभ्रष्टां गङ्गामिव भगीरथः ॥

३४ त्याजितैः फलमुत्खातैर्भग्रैश्च बहुधा नृपैः ।
तस्यासीदुल्बणो मार्गः पादपैरिव दन्तिनः ॥

३५ पौरस्त्यानेवमाक्रामंस्तांस्ताञ्जनपदाञ्जिती ।
प्राप तालीवनश्याममुपकण्ठं महोदधेः ॥

३६ अनम्राणां समुद्धर्तुस्तस्मात्सिन्धुरयादिव ।
आत्मा संरक्षितः सुह्रौर्वृत्तिमाश्रित्य वैतसीम् ॥

३७ वङ्गानुत्खाय तरसा नेता नौसाधनोद्धतान् ।
निचखान जयस्तम्भानगङ्गास्रोतोन्तरेषु सः ॥

३८ आपादपद्मप्रणताः कलमा इव ते रघुम् ।
फलैः संवर्धयामासुरुत्खातप्रतिरोपिताः ॥

His vanguard made the rivers along the way murky;
    those marching with him made them thin; and the
    rearguard turned them to mud.

His power was such that he made deserts flow with water,
    turned navigable rivers into easily fordable ones, and
    made jungles into open clearings.[15]

Leading his great army as it headed toward the eastern
    sea, he resembled Bhagiratha leading the Ganga fallen
    from Shiva's matted hair.[16]

As the path of an elephant is clearly visible from the trees
    stripped of their fruits, or uprooted or broken in
    various ways, his path was clearly visible because of
    the kings forced to hand over their wealth, dethroned,
    or vanquished in various ways.

Thus conquering various eastern countries, he
    triumphantly reached the ocean's shore, dark with
    forests of palm trees.

Like the torrent of a river he uprooted those who would
    not bend: the Suhmas saved themselves by resorting
    to the tactic of reeds.[17]

With force the commander destroyed the Vangas, who
    were proud of their navy, and planted victory columns
    between the streams of the Ganga.[18]

Ousted and then reinstalled, they bowed down to Raghu's
    lotus feet and paid him tribute, as rice gives rich
    harvest when first pulled out and then replanted.

31

32

33

34

35

36

37

38

३९ स तीर्त्वा कपिशां सैन्यैर्बद्धद्विरदसेतुभिः ।
उत्कलादेशितपथः कलिङ्गाभिमुखो ययौ ॥

४० स प्रतापं महेन्द्रस्य मूर्ध्नि तीक्ष्णं न्यवेशयत् ।
अङ्कुशं द्विरदस्येव यन्ता गम्भीरवेदिनः ॥

४१ प्रतिजग्राह कालिङ्गस्तमस्त्रैर्गजसाधनः ।
पक्षच्छेदोद्यतं शक्रं शिलावर्षीव पर्वतः ॥

४२ द्विषां विषह्य काकुत्स्थस्तत्र नाराचदुर्दिनम् ।
सन्मङ्गलस्नात इव प्रतिपेदे जयश्रियम् ॥

४३ वायव्यास्तविनिर्धूतात्पक्षाविद्धादिवोदधेः ।
गजानीकात्स कालिङ्गं तार्क्ष्यः सर्पमिवाददे ॥

४४ ताम्बूलीनां दलैस्तस्य रचितापानभूमयः ।
नारिकेलासवं योधाः शात्रवं च यशः पपुः ॥

४५ गृहीतप्रतिमुक्तस्य स धर्मविजयी नृपः ।
श्रियं महेन्द्रनाथस्य जहार न तु मेदिनीम् ॥

४६ ततो वेलातटेनैव फलवत्पूगमालिना ।
अगस्त्यचरितामाशामनाशास्यजयो ययौ ॥

Then he crossed the Kapisha with his soldiers, who used   39
    elephants to form a bridge, and once the Utkalas had
    shown him the way, he marched on toward Kalinga.[19]

He planted his fierce power on the crest of Mount   40
    Mahendra, as a mahout brings down his sharp goad on
    the head of the thick-skinned sort of elephant.[20]

The king of Kalinga, with his army of elephants, received   41
    him with missiles, like a mountain raining down rocks
    on Indra when he was poised to cut its wings.[21]

Raghu Kakutstha won the glory of victory there after   42
    enduring a downpour of arrows as if receiving an
    auspicious bath.[22]

He scattered the army of elephants with a wind-spell   43
    missile and plucked out the king of Kalinga, as Garuda
    whips the ocean with his wings to fish out a serpent.[23]

His soldiers arranged drinking grounds with betel leaves   44
    and drank coconut toddy, and with it the honor of the
    enemy.[24]

The righteous conqueror first captured and then released   45
    the king of Mahendra, seizing his glory but not his
    land.[25]

The king, who never had to pray for victory, went from   46
    there along the seashore garlanded with areca trees in
    fruit, toward the quarter where Agastya bides.[26]

४७ स सैन्यपरिभोगेन गजदानसुगन्धिना ।
कावेरीं सरितां पत्युः शङ्कनीयामिवाकरोत् ॥

४८ भयोत्सृष्टविभूषाणां तेन केरलयोषिताम् ।
अलकेषु चमूरेणुश्चूर्णप्रतिनिधीकृतः ॥

४९ बलैरध्युषितास्तस्य विजिगीषोर्गताध्वनः ।
हारीतोच्छिष्टमरिचा मलयाद्रेरुपत्यकाः ॥

५० आजानेयखुरक्षुण्णपङ्कैलाक्षेत्रसम्भवम् ।
व्यानशे सपदि व्योम कीटकोशाबिलं रजः ॥

५१ भोगिवेष्टनमार्गेषु चन्दनानां समर्पितम् ।
नास्रंसत्करिणां ग्रैवं त्रिपदीछेदिनामपि ॥

५२ दिशि मन्दायते तेजो दक्षिणस्यां रवेरपि ।
तस्यामेव रघोः पाण्ड्याः प्रतापं न विषेहिरे ॥

५३ ताम्रपर्णीसमेतस्य मुक्तासारं महोदधेः ।
ते निपत्य ददुस्तस्मै यशः स्वमिव सञ्चितम् ॥

He made the ocean, husband of rivers, doubt the 47
    faithfulness of the Kaveri when the revels of his army
    scented her water with elephant musk.[27]

The women of Kerala discarded all adornment out of fear, 48
    but he provided a substitute powder for their hair—
    the dust raised by his army.

When the conqueror had covered some distance, his 49
    troops settled on the slopes of the Malaya mountain,
    scattered with peppercorns half-eaten by green
    pigeons.

The sky was suddenly filled with dust, tainted with the 50
    cocoons of insects, rising from the fields of ripe
    cardamom crushed by the hooves of his purebred
    horses.

Fastened to the sandal trees in grooves left by the windings 51
    of snakes, the elephants' neck chains did not slip even
    when they shifted in their three-footed stance.[28]

Even the sun's heat weakens in the south, yet in just that 52
    quarter the Pandyas could not withstand Raghu's fiery
    power.[29]

They bowed down and gave him the best pearls from 53
    where the sea meets the Tamraparni River, as if
    offering him their own hoarded fame.

५४ स निर्विश्य यथाकामं तटस्वाधीनचन्दनौ ।
स्तनाविव दिशस्तस्याः शैलौ मलयदुर्दुरौ ॥

५५ असह्यविक्रमः सह्यं दूरमुक्तमुदन्वता ।
नितम्बमिव मेदिन्याः स्रस्तांशुकमलङ्घयत् ॥

५६ तस्यानीकैर्विसर्पद्भिरपरान्तजयोद्यतैः ।
रामेषूत्सारितो ऽप्यासीत्सह्यलग्न इवार्णवः ॥

५७ मुरलामारुतोद्धूतमगमत्कैतकं रजः ।
तद्योधवारवाणानामयत्नपटवासताम् ॥

५८ अभ्यभूयत वाहानां रथानां चास्य शिञ्जितैः ।
मर्मरः पवनोद्धूतराजतालीवनध्वनिः ॥

५९ खर्जूरीस्कन्धनद्धानां मदोद्गारसुगन्धिषु ।
कटेषु करिणां पेतुः पुन्नागेभ्यः शिलीमुखाः ॥

६० अवकाशं किलोदन्वांस्त्रामायाभ्यर्थितो ददौ ।
अपरान्तमहीपालव्याजेन राघवे करम् ॥

६१ महेभरदनोत्कीर्णव्यक्तविक्रमलक्षणम् ।
त्रिकूटमेव तत्रोच्चैर्जयस्तम्भं चकार सः ॥

He enjoyed to his heart's content the Malaya and the   54–55
  Durdura mountains, as if they were the breasts of that
  region, who had herself covered them with sandal;
  then, with irresistible prowess, he mounted the Sahya,
  like the hips of earth laid bare by the ocean, as if her
  skirt had fallen away.[30]

When his regiments fanned out in their eagerness to   56
  conquer Aparanta, it seemed as if the ocean, though
  driven back by Parashurama's arrows, were surging
  against the Sahya range.

The pollen of the *ketaki* flowers blown by the breeze from   57
  the Murala River became a serendipitous perfume for
  the soldiers' breastplates.[31]

The rustling sound of the talipot palm forest ruffled by the   58
  wind was drowned out by the clanking of his horses
  and chariots.

The bees flew from the Indian laurels onto the temples,   59
  perfumed by the discharge of musth, of the elephants
  tethered to the trunks of date palms.

According to legend, when Parashurama asked for space,   60
  the ocean gave it to him. In the guise of the king of
  Aparanta, it gave Raghu rich tribute.[32]

There, with the marks of his valor carved out by the tusks   61
  of his mighty elephants, he transformed Mount
  Trikuta itself into a lofty victory column.[33]

६२ पारसीकांस्ततो जेतुं प्रतस्थे स्थलवर्त्मना ।
इन्द्रियारव्यानिव रिपूंस्तत्त्वज्ञानेन संयमी ॥

६३ यवनीमुखपद्मानां सेहे मधुमदं न सः ।
बालातपमिवाब्जानामकालजलदोदयः ॥

६४ सङ्ग्रामस्तुमुलस्तस्य पारसीकाश्वसाधनैः ।
शार्ङ्गकूजितविज्ञेयप्रतियोधो रजस्यभूत् ॥

६५ भल्लापवर्जितैस्तेषां शिरोभिः श्मश्रुलैर्महीम् ।
तस्तार सरघाव्याप्तैः स क्षौद्रपटलैरिव ॥

६६ अपनीतशिरस्त्राणाः शेषास्तं शरणं ययुः ।
प्रणिपातप्रतीकारः संरम्भो हि महात्मनाम् ॥

६७ विनयन्ते स्म तद्योधा मधुभिर्विजयश्रमम् ।
आस्तीर्णाजिनरत्नासु द्राक्षावलयभूमिषु ॥

६८ ततः प्रतस्थे कौबेरीं भास्वानिव रघुर्दिशम् ।
शरैरुस्रैरिवोदीच्यानुद्धरिष्यत्रसानिव ॥

६९ जितानजय्यस्तानेव कृत्वा रथपुरःसरान् ।
महार्णवमिवौर्वाग्निः प्रविवेशोत्तरापथम् ॥

Then he set out by the land route to conquer the Persians, 62
as a self-controlled man sets out to subdue his
enemies, the senses, by knowledge of truth.[34]

Just as an unseasonable swell of clouds will not allow 63
lotuses the morning sunshine, he did not allow the
flush of wine on the lotus faces of Yavana women.[35]

He fought a tumultuous battle with the Persian cavalry, 64
the enemy soldiers recognizable through the dust only
by the twanging of their bows.

He strewed the ground with their bearded heads, severed 65
by sword-blade arrows, as if with honeycombs full of
bees.

Those who survived removed their helmets and 66
surrendered to him. The fury of great men can indeed
be counteracted—but only by submission.

His soldiers allayed their fatigue after the victorious battle 67
with drafts of wine in vineyards where the ground was
spread with the finest deerskins.

Then Raghu set out for the region of Kubera, intending to 68
root out the northerners with his arrows, as the sun
moves north to draw out the waters with its rays.[36]

After defeating them and making them walk before his 69
chariot, the undefeatable Raghu entered the northern
country, as Aurva's fire once entered the ocean.[37]

७० विनीताध्वश्रमास्तस्य वङ्क्षुतीरविवेष्टनैः ।
दुधुवुर्वाजिनः स्कन्धाँल्लग्नकुङ्कुमकेसरान् ॥

७१ तत्र हूनावरोधानां भर्तृषु व्यक्तविक्रमम् ।
कपोलपाटनादेशि बभूव रघुचेष्टितम् ॥

७२ काम्बोजाः समरे वीर्यं तस्य सोढुमनीश्वराः ।
गजालानपरिक्लिष्टैरक्षोटैः सार्धमानताः ॥

७३ तेषां सदश्वभूयिष्ठास्तुङ्गा द्रविणराशयः ।
विविशुस्तं विशां नाथमुदन्वन्तमिवापगाः ॥

७४ ततो गौरीगुरुं शैलमारुरोह ससाधनः ।
वर्धयन्निव तत्कूटानुद्धतैर्धातुरेणुभिः ॥

७५ प्रशंसंस्तुल्यसत्त्वानां सैन्यघोषे ऽप्यसम्भ्रमम् ।
गुहागतानां सिंहानां परिवृत्त्यावलोकितम् ॥

७६ भूर्जेषु मर्मरीभूताः कीचकध्वनिहेतवः ।
गङ्गाशीकरिणो मार्गे मरुतस्तं सिषेविरे ॥

७७ विशश्रमुर्नमेरूणां छायास्वध्यास्य सैनिकाः ।
दृषदो वासितोत्सङ्गा निषण्णमृगनाभिभिः ॥

His horses relieved the fatigue of the road by rolling on 70
the banks of the Vankshu, then shook from their
shoulders the filaments of saffron clinging to them.[38]

Raghu's deeds there, displaying his valor against their 71
husbands, taught the women of the Huns to rend their
cheeks.[39]

The Kambojas, unable to endure his might in battle, 72
bowed down, along with the walnut trees that were
tormented by the chains of his elephants.

Their towering heaps of wealth, enriched with fine horses, 73
streamed toward that lord of the people, like rivers
toward the sea.

Next, he and his army climbed the mountain that is 74
Gauri's father,* seeming to make the peaks higher
with the dust of mineral ores that they raised.[40]

He praised the way the lions in the caves, whose courage 75
matched his own, turned to look at him, unperturbed
even by the army's din.

The winds that rustled among the birch trees, inspiring 76
the bamboos with sound and carrying drops of the
Ganga, refreshed him on the way.

His soldiers rested in the shade of *rudrākṣa* trees, sitting 77
on stones whose tops were scented by the navels of
deer that had lain on them.[41]

---

* Himalaya.

७८ सरलासक्तमातङ्गग्रैवेयोपचितत्विषः ।
आसन्नोषधयो नेतुर्नक्तमस्नेहदीपिकाः ॥

७९ तस्यावासेषु दानार्द्रैर्गण्डभित्तिविघट्टनैः ।
गजवर्ष्म किरातेभ्यः शशंसुर्देवदारवः ॥

८० तत्र जन्यं रघोर्घोरं पर्वतीयैर्गणैरभूत् ।
नाराचक्षेपणीयाश्मनिष्पेषोत्पतितानलः ॥

८१ शरैरुत्सवसङ्केतान्स कृत्वा करदान्कृती ।
जयोदाहरणं बाह्वोर्गापयामास किन्नरान् ॥

८२ परस्परस्य विज्ञातस्तेषूपायनपाणिषु ।
राज्ञा हिमवतः सारो राज्ञः सारो हिमाद्रिणा ॥

८३ तत्राक्षोभ्यं यशोराशिं निवेश्यावरुरोह सः ।
पौलस्त्यतुलितस्याद्रेरादधान इव ह्रियम् ॥

८४ चकम्पे तीर्णलौहित्ये तस्मिन्प्राग्ज्योतिषेश्वरः ।
तद्गजालानतां प्राप्तैः सह कालागुरुद्रुमैः ॥

८५ न प्रसेहे स रुद्धार्कमनभ्रमयदुर्दिनम् ।
रथवंशरजो ऽप्यस्य कुत एव पताकिनीम् ॥

At night, nearby herbs served the commander as lamps   78
　　that needed no oil, their light redoubled by reflection
　　in the neck chains of the elephants tethered to the
　　pines.[42]

At his camps the deodars revealed to forest hunters the   79
　　height of his elephants by the marks, wet with musth
　　juice, they had left from scratching with their temples.

There Raghu fought a fierce battle with hordes of   80
　　mountain tribesmen, where flames shot up when bolts
　　and slingshot stones chafed against each other.

With his arrows the skillful king forced the Utsava-   81
　　sanketas to pay him tribute, prompting the *kinnaras*
　　themselves to sing the victory won by his arms.

When they approached him, offerings in hand, there   82
　　was mutual recognition: the king knew the wealth of
　　Himalaya, and Himalaya the might of the king.[43]

There, before descending, he planted a mound of fame   83
　　that would be unmovable, thereby putting to shame
　　the mountain that was moved by Ravana.[44]

When he crossed the Lauhitya River,* the king of   84
　　Pragjyotisha† trembled, along with the eaglewood
　　trees that were made into tethering posts for Raghu's
　　elephants.

He could not bear even the dust of the succession of   85
　　Raghu's chariots—it blocked the sun and made the
　　cloudless day dark—let alone Raghu's army.

---

* The Brahmaputra River.
† A polity in Kamarupa (now Assam).

८६ तमीशः कामरूपाणामत्याखण्डलविक्रमम् ।
भेजे भिन्नकटैर्नागैरन्यानुपरुरोध यैः ॥

८७ कामरूपेश्वरस्तस्य हेमपीठाधिदेवताम् ।
रत्नपुष्पोपहारेण च्छायामानर्च पादयोः ॥

८८ इति जित्वा दिशो जिष्णुर्न्यवर्तत रथोद्धतम् ।
रजो विश्रमयन्नाज्ञां छत्रशून्येषु मौलिषु ॥

८९ स विश्वजितमाजह्रे क्रतुं सर्वस्वदक्षिणम् ।
आदानं हि विसर्गाय सतां वारिमुचामिव ॥

९० सत्त्रान्ते सचिवसखः पुरस्क्रियाभि-
र्गुर्वीभिः शमितपराजयव्यलीकान् ।
काकुत्स्थश्चिरविरहोत्सुकावरोधान्
राजन्यान्स्वपुरनिवृत्तये ऽनुमेने ॥

९१ ते रेखाध्वजकलशातपत्रचिह्नं
सम्राजश्चरणयुगं प्रसादलभ्यम् ।
प्रस्थानप्रणतिभिरङ्गुलीषु चक्रु-
र्मौलिस्रक्च्युतमकरन्दरेणुगौरम् ॥

इति रघुवंशे महाकाव्ये चतुर्थः सर्गः ॥

The same elephants, with temples splitting in their musth,   86
    that the lord of Kamarupa had once used to lay siege
    to others he now made over to Raghu, whose valor
    exceeded Indra's.

The king of Kamarupa worshiped the shadow of Raghu's   87
    feet, a deity enthroned on a golden footstool, with
    offerings of jewels for flowers.

Having conquered all quarters of the world, the victorious   88
    Raghu returned, letting the dust raised by his chariots
    settle upon other kings' heads no longer covered by
    royal parasols.

He performed the All-Conquering Sacrifice, whose ritual   89
    fee is everything one possesses. Indeed, the virtuous,
    like clouds, take only so that they can give.

At the end of the sacrificial session, Raghu, attended by   90
    his ministers, assuaged the pain of the princes' defeat
    with great gifts of honor and gave them leave to return
    to their own cities, where their wives were pining from
    long separation.

As they bowed down to him in taking leave, the nectar and   91
    pollen falling from the chaplets on their heads gilded
    the toes of the king's feet—feet marked with lines
    forming the signs of banner, urn, and parasol, that
    only those enjoying the king's favor could touch.[45]

पञ्चमः सर्गः

१ तमध्वरे विश्वजिति क्षितीशं निःशेषविश्राणितकोशजातम् ।
   उपात्तविद्यो गुरुदक्षिणार्थी कौत्सः प्रपेदे वरतन्तुशिष्यः ॥

२ स मृण्मये वीतहिरण्मयत्वात्पात्रे निधायार्घ्यमनर्घशीलः ।
   श्रुतप्रकाशं यशसा प्रकाशः प्रत्युज्जगामातिथिमातिथेयः ॥

३ तमर्चयित्वा विधिवद्द्विधिज्ञस्तपोधनं मानधनाग्रयायी ।
   कृताञ्जलिः कृत्यविचारदक्षो विशां पतिर्विष्टरभाजमाह ॥

४ अप्यग्रणीर्मन्त्रकृतामृषीणां कुशाग्रबुद्धे कुशली गुरुस्ते ।
   यतस्त्वया ज्ञानमशेषमाप्तं चैतन्यमुद्ग्रादिव दीक्षितेन ॥

CHAPTER 5
Raghu Sends Aja to Bhoja's Court as a Suitor

When the lord of the earth had given away all his treasures   1
at the All-Conquering Sacrifice, a pupil of Varatantu,
named Kautsa, who had just completed his studies,
approached him seeking a gift for his teacher.

The king of priceless virtue, dazzling with fame, poured   2
the welcoming water into an earthen cup, since no
golden ones were left, and then hospitably rose to
meet his guest, who dazzled with learning.

The lord of the people, first among those whose wealth is   3
honor, knew the etiquette and duly honored Kautsa.
Then, with characteristic discernment in determining
his duties, he cupped his hands in reverence and
addressed him, whose wealth was asceticism, once he
had seated him on a spread of sacred grass.[1]

"Oh you whose mind is sharp like a blade of kusa grass,   4
I hope your teacher, the foremost among sages who
wield mantras, is faring well. You have obtained
comprehensive knowledge from him, as the
consecrated sacrificer obtains consciousness from
Ugra.[2]

५ कायेन वाचा मनसा च तद्यं यद्द्विजिणो धैर्यविपर्ययाय ।
आपाद्यते न व्ययमन्तरायैः कच्चिन्महर्षेस्त्रिविधं तपस्तत् ॥

६ आधारबन्धप्रमुखैः प्रयत्नैः संवर्धितानां सुतनिर्विशेषम् ।
कच्चिन्न वाय्वादिरुपप्लवो वः श्रमच्छिदामाश्रमपादपानाम् ॥

७ क्रियानिमित्तेष्वपि वत्सलत्वादभग्नकामा मुनिभिः कुशेषु ।
तदङ्कशय्याच्युतनाभिनाला कच्चिन्मृगीणामनघा प्रसूतिः ॥

८ निर्वर्त्यते यैर्नियमाभिषेको यतो निवापाञ्जलयः पितृणाम् ।
तान्युच्छषष्टाङ्कितसैकतानि शिवानि वस्तीर्थजलानि कच्चित् ॥

९ नीवारपाकादि कडङ्गरीयैरामृष्यते जानपदैर्न कच्चित् ।
कालोपपन्नातिथिभागधेयं वन्यं शरीरस्थितिसाधनं वः ॥

१० अपि प्रसन्नेन महर्षिणा त्वं सम्यग्विनीयानुमतो गृहाय ।
कालो ह्ययं सङ्क्रमितुं द्वितीयं सर्वोपकारक्षममाश्रमं ते ॥

११ अनुग्रहेणाभिगमस्थितेन
तवार्हतस्तुष्यति मे न चेतः ।
अप्याज्ञया शासितुरात्मना वा
प्राप्तो ऽसि सम्भावयितुं वनान्माम् ॥

"The great sage's threefold ascetic power, stored up by   5
   ascetic practices of body, speech, and mind, and
   capable of disturbing even Indra's composure—I trust
   no obstacles hinder it.³

"The ashram trees that relieve fatigue, which you have   6
   raised like sons, troubling to build troughs around
   them and the like—I trust neither gales nor other
   mishaps have harmed them?

"The does' fawns that sages do not thwart in their hunger   7
   for kusa grass, even though it is needed for rituals,
   and whom they let lie in their laps as soon as they drop
   their umbilical cords—I trust they are safe?

"The holy fords whose water you use to perform your   8
   ritual ablutions and offer in cupped hands to the
   ancestors, and whose sandy banks are dotted with
   a sixth part of the gleanings—I trust they remain
   propitious?

"The wild rice and other forest grains that sustain your   9
   body and that you share when guests chance to
   arrive—I trust they are not grazed on by country
   livestock?

"Has the great sage, now that in his kindness he has   10
   properly trained you, given you permission for a
   household? For now is the time for you to enter the
   second stage of life, the one that is beneficial to all.⁴

"My revered guest's visit is not yet enough to satisfy my 11
   heart. Have you come from the forest to honor me at
   the bidding of your teacher, or of your own accord?"⁵

१२ इत्यर्घ्यपात्रानुमितव्ययस्य रघोरुदारामपि गां निशम्य ।
स्वार्थोपपत्तिं प्रति दुर्बलाशः प्रत्याह कौत्सस्तमपेतकुत्सम् ॥

१३ सर्वत्र नो वार्त्तमवैहि राजन्नाथे कुतस्त्वय्यशुभं प्रजानाम् ।
सूर्ये तपत्यावरणाय दृष्टेः कल्पेत लोकस्य कथं तमिस्रा ॥

१४ भक्तिः प्रतीक्ष्येषु कुलोचिता ते पूर्वान्महाभागतयातिशेषे ।
व्यपेतकालस्त्वहमभ्युपेतस्त्वामर्थिभावादिति मे विषादः ॥

१५ शरीरमात्रेण नरेन्द्र तिष्ठन्नाभासि तीर्थप्रतिपादितर्द्धिः ।
आरण्यकोपात्तफलप्रसूतिः स्तम्बेन नीवार इवावशिष्टः ॥

१६ स्थाने भवानेकनराधिपः सन्नकिञ्चनत्वं मखजं व्यनक्ति ।
पर्यायपीतस्य सुरैर्हिमांशोः कलाक्षयः श्लाघ्यतरो हि वृद्धेः ॥

१७ तदन्यतस्तावदनन्यकार्यो गुर्वर्थमाहर्तुमहं यतिष्ये ।
स्वस्त्यस्तु ते निर्गलिताम्बुगर्भं शरद्घनं नार्दति चातको ऽपि ॥

१८ एतावदुत्त्वा प्रतियातुकामं शिष्यं महर्षेर्नृपतिर्निषिध्य ।
किं वस्तु विद्वन्गुरवे प्रदेयं त्वया कियद्द्वेति तमन्वयुङ्क ॥

When Kautsa heard his words, noble though they were, he   12
    despaired of accomplishing his goal—that Raghu had
    disbursed his wealth could be inferred from the cup
    of welcome. He replied to the king, who was beyond
    reproach:

"Your Majesty, be assured that all is well with us. With   13
    you as our protector, how could any ill befall your
    subjects? When the sun shines, how can darkness
    occlude people's sight?

"As befits your family, you are devoted to those who   14
    deserve regard. Indeed, you even surpass your
    ancestors in magnanimity. But I have come too late to
    make a request of you, and this saddens me.

"As you stand here, lord of men, with nothing left you but   15
    your body, after donating your wealth to the worthy,
    you resemble the wild rice when forest dwellers have
    harvested the grain and only the stem remains.

"Being the sovereign, it is proper that you should   16
    impoverish yourself by sacrifice. For the waning of the
    digits of the moon, as the gods one by one drink it up,
    is more praiseworthy than its waxing.[6]

"So I shall seek the gift for my teacher elsewhere, the sole   17
    task I have to accomplish. Farewell! Even the *cātaka*
    bird does not entreat the autumn cloud once emptied
    of water."[7]

The great sage's pupil said no more and was about to leave   18
    when the king stopped him and asked: "Learned one,
    what and how much should you give to your teacher?"

१९ ततो यथावद्विहिताध्वराय तस्मै समयावेशविवर्जिताय ।
वर्णाश्रमाणां गुरवे स वर्णी विचक्षणः प्रस्तुतमाचचक्षे ॥

२० अवाप्तविद्येन मया महर्षिर्विज्ञापितो ऽभूद्गुरुदक्षिणायै ।
स मे चिरादस्खलितोपचारां तां भक्तिमेवागणयत्पुरस्तात् ॥

२१ निर्बन्धसञ्जातरुषाथ कार्श्यमचिन्तयित्वा गुरुणाहमुक्तः ।
वित्तस्य विद्यापरिसङ्ख्यया मे कोटीश्चतस्रो दश चाहरेति ॥

२२ सो ऽहं सपर्याविधिभाजनेन मत्वा भवन्तं प्रभुशब्दशेषम् ।
अभ्युत्सहे सम्प्रति नोपरोद्धुमल्पेतरत्वाच्छुतनिष्क्रयस्य ॥

२३ इत्थं द्विजेन द्विजराजकान्तिरावेदितो वेदविदां वरेण ।
एनोनिवृत्तेन्द्रियवृत्तिरेनं जगाद भूयो जगदेकनाथः ॥

२४ गुर्वर्थमर्थी श्रुतपारदृश्वा रघोः सकाशादनवाप्तकामः ।
गतो वदन्यान्तरमित्ययं मे मा भूत्परीवादनवावतारः ॥

२५ स त्वं प्रयस्ते महितो मदीये वसंश्चतुर्थो ऽग्निरिवाध्यगारे ।
द्वित्राण्यहान्यर्हसि सोढुमर्हन्यावद्यते साधयितुं त्वदर्थम् ॥

Then the learned student explained matters to the king, 19
    who had duly sacrificed, whom conceit could not
    possess, and who was like a father to those in all social
    classes and stages of life.[8]

"When I completed my studies, I asked the great sage 20
    about a teacher's gift, but he first took the view that
    my long devotion of unfailing service was itself the
    gift.

"Then, when my importunity angered him, my teacher 21
    said to me, making no allowances for my poverty:
    'Bring me fourteen crores, tallying with the number of
    the sciences, in cash.'[9]

"Realizing from the vessel you used for the rite of 22
    welcoming me that all you have left is the title 'lord,'
    I cannot now beleaguer you, for the price of my
    learning is anything but small."

Thus the twice-born, the best of those learned in the Veda, 23
    informed the king, who was lustrous as the moon, king
    of the twice-born. Then the sole lord of the world,
    whose senses had turned away from sin, addressed the
    Brahman again:[10]

"May the unprecedented censure not be laid on me that a 24
    most learned suppliant seeking wealth for his teacher
    had his wish refused by Raghu and went to another,
    more generous donor.

"Respected sir, please tolerate two or three days' stay as 25
    honored guest in my sanctified fire shrine, as if you
    were its fourth fire, while I try to procure what you
    need."[11]

२६ तथेति तस्याविततं प्रतीतः प्रत्यग्रहीत्सङ्करमग्यजन्मा ।
गामात्तसारां रघुरप्यवेक्ष्य निष्क्रष्टुमर्थं चकमे कुबेरात् ॥

२७ वसिष्ठमन्त्रोक्षणजातप्रभावादुदन्वदाकाशमहीधरेषु ।
मरुत्सखस्येव बलाहकस्य गतिर्विजघ्ने न हि तद्रथस्य ॥

२८ अथाधिशिश्ये प्रयतः प्रदोषे रथं रघुः कल्पितमस्त्रगर्भम् ।
सामन्तसम्भावनयैव धीरः कैलासनाथं तरसा जिगीषुः ॥

२९ प्रातः प्रयाणाभिमुखाय तस्मै सविस्मयागन्तुमुदो नियुक्ताः ।
हिरण्मयीं कोशगृहस्य मध्ये वृष्टिं शशंसुः पतितां नभस्तः ॥

३० तं भूपतिर्भास्वरहेमराशिं लब्धं कुबेरादभियास्यमानात् ।
दिदेश कौत्साय समग्रमेव पादं सुमेरोरिव वज्रभिन्नम् ॥

३१ जनस्य साकेतनिवासिनस्तौ द्वावप्यभूतामभिनन्द्यसत्त्वौ ।
गुरुप्रदेयाधिकनिःस्पृहो ऽर्थी नृपो ऽर्थिकामादधिकप्रदश्च ॥

३२ अथोष्ट्रवामीशतहारितार्थं प्रजेश्वरं प्रीतमना मनीषी ।
स्पृशन्करेणानतपूर्वकायं सम्प्रस्थितो वाक्यमुवाच कौत्सः ॥

"So be it," the Brahman said, accepting his sincere   26
  promise. Raghu knew that the treasures of the earth
  had been exhausted, so he set his mind on extracting
  riches from Kubera.

For with the power bestowed by a lustration Vasishtha had   27
  performed with mantras, Raghu's chariot could race
  unhindered over sea, sky, and mountain, as a cloud
  races when befriended by the wind.

Then in the evening the determined Raghu fasted and   28
  went to sleep in the chariot made ready and primed
  with weapons, aiming to defeat the lord of Kailasa by
  force, since he considered him to be a vassal king.[12]

In the morning, just as he was about to set off on   29
  campaign, his officers, amazed and suddenly joyful,
  told him that a shower of gold had fallen from the sky
  right into the middle of his treasury.

The king gave Kautsa all that dazzling heap of gold   30
  received from Kubera, whom he had been about to
  attack—it was like a foothill of Mount Sumeru split off
  by a thunderbolt.[13]

The citizens of Ayodhya found the spirit of both men   31
  worthy of praise: the suppliant who desired no more
  than what he was to give to his teacher, and the king
  who gave more than the suppliant desired.

Then, once the king had the treasure loaded onto a   32
  hundred she-camels, the wise Kautsa was pleased and,
  when he was about to leave, touched the king, who
  bowed at the waist before him, with his hand, saying:

३३ किमत्र चित्रं यदि कामसूर्भूर्वृत्तस्थितस्याधिपतेः प्रजानाम् ।
अचिन्तनीयस्तव तु प्रभावो मनीषितं द्यौरपि येन दुग्धा ॥

३४ आशास्यमन्यत्पुनरुक्तभूतं श्रेयांसि सर्वाण्यधिजग्मुषस्ते ।
पुत्रं लभस्वात्मगुणानुरूपं भवन्तमीड्यो भवतः पितेव ॥

३५ इत्थं प्रयुज्याशिषमग्र्यजन्मा राज्ञे प्रतीयाय गुरोः सकाशम् ।
राजापि लेभे सुतमाशु तस्मादालोकमर्कादिव जीवलोकः ॥

३६ ब्राह्मे मुहूर्ते किल तस्य देवी कुमारकल्पं सुषुवे कुमारम् ।
अतः पिता ब्रह्मण एव नाम्ना तमग्र्यजन्मानमजं चकार ॥

३७ रूपं तदोजस्वि तदेव वीर्यं तदेव नैसर्गिकमुन्नतत्वम् ।
न कारणात्स्वाद्बिभिदे कुमारः प्रवर्तितो दीप इव प्रदीपात् ॥

३८ उपात्तविद्यं विधिवदुरुभ्यस्तं यौवनोद्भेदविशेषकान्तम् ।
श्रीः कामयानापि गुरोरनुज्ञां धीरेव कन्या पितुराचकाङ्ख ॥

३९ अथेश्वरेण क्रथकैशिकानां स्वयंवरार्थं स्वसुरिन्दुमत्याः ।
आप्तः कुमारानयनोत्सुकेन भोजेन दूतो रघवे विसृष्टः ॥

"Why should one be amazed that the earth grants the   33
    wishes of a king who abides by good conduct? But
    your power, which lets you milk all you desire from
    heaven itself, is truly inconceivable.

"To give you any other blessing would be redundant, for   34
    you have already acquired all good things. May you
    obtain a son whose qualities match yours, just as your
    venerable father obtained you!"

Having thus bestowed his blessing on the king, the   35
    Brahman returned to his teacher. Soon after, the king
    obtained a son thanks to him, as the world of living
    beings obtains light from the sun.

His queen gave birth in Brahma's hour, it is said, to a boy   36
    who resembled Kumara, so the father named him, his
    firstborn, Aja, after another of Brahma's names.[14]

The same strong build, the same heroic spirit, the same   37
    inborn loftiness—the boy did not differ from the
    cause that made him, any more than one lamp lit from
    another.

When he duly obtained learning from his teachers and had   38
    grown especially handsome as his youth blossomed,
    Royal Fortune, though yearning for him, still waited
    for his father's permission, as a wise girl awaits her
    father's blessing.

Now, at that time, Bhoja, king of the Krathakaishikas, sent   39
    a trusted envoy to Raghu to announce the husband-
    choosing ceremony of his sister Indumati, because he
    wanted to invite the prince.

४० तं श्लाघ्यसम्बन्धमसौ विचिन्त्य दारक्रियायोग्यदशं च पुत्रम् ।
प्रस्थापयामास ससैन्यमेनमृद्धां विदर्भाधिपराजधानीम् ॥

४१ तस्योपकार्यारचितोपकारा वन्ध्येतरा जानपदोपधाभिः ।
मार्गे निवासा मनुजेन्द्रसूनोर्बभूवुरुद्यानविहारकल्पाः ॥

४२ स नर्मदारोधसि शीकरार्द्रैर्मरुद्भिरानर्तितकेतुमाले ।
निवेशयामास विलङ्घिताध्वा सेनां श्रमोत्फेनवनायुजाश्राम् ॥

४३ अथोपरिष्टाद्भ्रमरैर्भ्रमद्भिः प्राक्सूचितान्तःसलिलप्रवेशः ।
निर्धौतदानामलगण्डभित्तिर्वन्यः सरित्तो गज उन्ममज्ज ॥

४४ अप्यौघविक्षालितगैरिकेण वप्रक्रियामृक्षवतस्तटेषु ।
नीलोर्ध्वलेखाशबलेन शंसन्दन्तद्वयेनाश्मविकुण्ठितेन ॥

४५ स भोगिभोगाधिकपीवरेण हस्तेन तीराभिमुखः सशब्दम् ।
संवेष्टितार्धप्रहितेन दीर्घाश्चिक्षेप वारीपरिघानिवोर्मीन् ॥

४६ कारण्डवोच्छिष्टमृदुप्रतानाः पुलिन्दयोषाम्बुविहारकाञ्चीः ।
कर्षन्स शेवाललता नदीष्णः प्रोहावलग्नास्तटमुत्ससर्प ॥

Raghu considered an alliance with Bhoja desirable, and his   40
son at the right age for marriage. So he sent him off
with a troop of soldiers to the rich capital of the king
of Vidarbha.

The prince's stops along the way resembled outings to   41
the park: flower decorations were arranged in royal
tents, and there were plentiful gifts brought by the
countryfolk.

When he had covered some distance, and the   42
thoroughbred horses of his army were so tired they
were foaming, he ordered his troops to encamp on the
bank of the Narmada, their rows of battle standards
dancing in winds moist with droplets.

Just then a forest elephant emerged from the river; the   43
bees hovering above already betrayed his plunge into
the water, and now his broad temples were washed
clean of the stain of musth.

Although the stream had washed the red chalk off both   44
tusks, they were streaked with dark scratches on their
upper sides and blunted by rocks, which revealed
that he had been playfully butting the slopes of the
Rikshavat mountain.[15]

As he headed toward the bank, he noisily parted the long   45
waves with his trunk, thicker than a great serpent's
coils, which he half furled and then unfurled, as if
breaking the bolts of a stable.

The weed stalks whose tender shoots had been half-eaten   46
by ducks, and which tribal women used as girdles
when they sported in the water, were now pulled along
by the elephant as he climbed the slope.

४७ तस्यैकनागस्य कपोलभित्त्योर्हदावगाहक्षणमात्रशान्ता ।
वन्येतरानेकपदर्शनेन पुनर्दिदीपे मद्दुर्दिनश्रीः ॥

४८ सम्मच्छदक्षीरकटुप्रवाहमसह्यमाघ्राय मदं तदीयम् ।
विलङ्घिताधोरणतीव्रयत्नाः सेनागजेन्द्रा विमुखीबभूवुः ॥

४९ स च्छिन्नबन्धद्रुतयुग्यशून्यं भग्नाक्षपर्यस्तरथं क्षणेन ।
रामापरित्राणविहस्तयोधं सेनानिवेशं तुमुलं चकार ॥

५० तमापतन्तं नृपतेरवध्यो वन्यः करीति श्रुतवान्कुमारः ।
निवर्तयिष्यन्विशिखेन कुम्भे जघान नात्यायतकृष्टशार्ङ्गः ॥

५१ स विद्धमात्रः किल नागरूपमुत्सृज्य तद्विस्मितसैन्यदृष्टः ।
स्फुरत्प्रभामण्डलमध्यवर्ति कान्तं वपुर्व्योमचरं प्रपेदे ॥

५२ अथ प्रभावोपनतैः कुमारं कल्पद्रुमोत्थैरवकीर्य पुष्पैः ।
उवाच वाग्मी दशनप्रभाभिः संवर्धितोरःस्थलतारहारः ॥

५३ मतङ्गशापादवलेपमूलादवाप्तवानस्मि मतङ्गजत्वम् ।
अवैहि गन्धर्वपतेस्तनूजं प्रियंवदं मां प्रियदर्शनस्य ॥

The musth that had briefly disappeared when the rogue   47
    elephant plunged into the water glittered once again
    in a rich shower on his temples as soon as he noticed
    Aja's tamed elephants.

When they caught the smell of his musth, whose bitter   48
    flow was like the sap of the seven-leaf trees, the
    mighty elephants of the army defied their mahouts'
    violent efforts and turned tail.[16]

The horses snapped their reins and vanished in a   49
    stampede; the chariots were overturned, their axles
    broken; the soldiers were unable to protect the
    women: in an instant the beast had caused mayhem in
    the army camp.

It charged at Aja, but the prince had learned that a king is   50
    forbidden to kill a forest elephant. So all he sought to
    do was turn it, and he struck it on its forehead with an
    arrow, without drawing his bow too far back.[17]

They say that as soon as it was shot it shed its elephant   51
    form, and while the soldiers stared in amazement
    it took on a beautiful, celestial body, ringed with a
    quivering halo of light.

Then he showered the prince with flowers of the wish-   52
    fulfilling tree, which he fetched by his divine power,
    and, augmenting the radiant pearl necklace on Aja's
    chest with the luster of his teeth, addressed him
    eloquently:

"I had been turned into an elephant by Matanga's   53
    curse, incurred through my own insolence. Know
    me to be Priyamvada, son of the *gandharva* king
    Priyadarshana.[18]

५४ स चानुनीतः प्रणतेन पश्चान्मया महर्षिर्मृदुतामगच्छत् ।
उष्णत्वमग्यातपसम्प्रयोगाच्छैत्यं हि यत्सा प्रकृतिर्जलस्य ॥

५५ इक्ष्वाकुवंशप्रभवो यदा ते भेत्स्यत्यजः कुम्भमयोमुखेन ।
संयोक्ष्यसे स्वेन पुनर्महिम्ना तदेत्यवोचत्स तपोनिधिर्माम् ॥

५६ स मोचितः शापकलेस्त्वयाहं गतिं प्रपन्नो विहितां विधात्रा ।
प्रतिक्रियां चेद्व्रवतो न कुर्यां व्यर्था हि मे स्यात्स्वपदोपलब्धिः ॥

५७ गान्धर्वमस्त्रं तदितः प्रतीच्छ प्रयोगसंहारविभक्तमन्त्रम् ।
प्रस्वापनं नाम यतः प्रहर्तुर्न चारिहिंसा विजयश्च हस्ते ॥

५८ अलं ह्रिया मां प्रति यन्मुहूर्तं दयापरो ऽभूः प्रहरन्नपि त्वम् ।
तस्मादुपच्छन्दयति प्रयोज्यं मयि त्वया न प्रतिषेधरौक्ष्यम् ॥

५९ तथेत्युपस्पृश्य पयः पवित्रं सोमोद्भवायाः सरितो नृसोमः ।
उदङ्मुखः सो ऽस्त्रविदस्त्रमन्त्रं जग्राह तस्मान्निगृहीतशापात् ॥

६० एवं तयोरध्वनि दैवयोगादासेदुषोः सख्यमचिन्त्यहेतु ।
एको ययौ चैत्ररथप्रदेशान्सौराज्यरम्यानपरो विदर्भान् ॥

"But when I bowed before the sage and besought him, he   54
    was mollified. For water turns hot from contact with
    fire or the heat of the sun, but coolness is its natural
    state.

" 'When Aja, scion of Ikshvaku's lineage, will pierce your   55
    forehead with an arrow,' the ascetic told me, 'you will
    regain your exalted position.'

"Because you have released me from this dread curse,   56
    I have returned to the state the creator ordained
    for me. Were I to fail to reciprocate your favor, the
    recovery of my true condition would be in vain
    indeed.

"So please accept from me a *gāndharva* weapon, which can   57
    be launched and recalled by separate spells. Its name
    is Somniferous; it does not harm the enemy and yet
    ensures victory for whoever wields it.

"You should feel no shame before me. Since even when   58
    you shot me you felt a moment's compassion, do not
    be so cruel now as to refuse me when I beseech you."

"So be it," said that moon among men as he touched pure   59
    water from the moon-born Narmada River. Facing
    north, that master of weapons accepted the weapon
    and its spells from Priyamvada, now freed from the
    curse.[19]

After thus meeting by chance on the road and forming a   60
    friendship so unaccountable, one left for the regions
    of Chaitraratha, the other for the well-ruled realm of
    the Vidarbhans.

६१ तं तस्थिवांसं नगरोपकण्ठे तदागमारूढगुरुप्रहर्षः ।
प्रत्युज्जगाम क्रथकैशिकेन्द्रश्चन्द्रं प्रवृद्धोर्मिरिवोर्मिमाली ॥

६२ प्रवेश्य चैनं पुरमग्रयायी नीचैस्तथोपाचरदर्पितश्रीः ।
मेने यथा तत्र जनः समेतो वैदर्भमागन्तुमजं गृहेशम् ॥

६३ तस्याधिकारिपुरुषैः प्रणतैः प्रदिष्टां
प्राग्द्वारवेदिविनिवेशितहेमकुम्भाम् ।
रम्यां रघुप्रतिनिधिः स नवोपकार्यां
बाल्यात्परामिव दशां मदनो ऽधितस्थौ ॥

६४ तत्र स्वयंवरसमाहृतराजलोकं
कन्याललाम कमनीयमजस्य लिप्सोः ।
भावावबोधकलुषा दयितेव रात्रौ
निद्रा चिरेण नयनाभिमुखीबभूव ॥

६५ तं कर्णभूषणनिपीडितपीवरांसं
शय्योत्तरच्छदविमर्दकृशाङ्गरागम् ।
वैतालिका ललितबन्धमनोहराभिः
प्राबोधयन्नुषसि वाग्भिरुषर्बुधाभम् ॥

६६ रात्रिर्गता मतिमतां वर मुञ्च शय्यां
धात्रा द्विधैव जगतो ननु धूर्विभक्ता ।
यामेकतस्तव बिभर्ति गुरुर्वितन्द्री-
र्यस्या भवानपरधुर्यपदावलम्बी ॥

When Aja was on the outskirts of the city, the king of the   61
 Krathakaishikas, overjoyed by his arrival, came out to
 welcome him, as the wave-wreathed sea surges toward
 the moon when its billows swell.

Leading the way, he brought him into the city and, lending   62
 his own royal glory, humbly waited on him in such
 a way that the assembled crowd thought the king of
 Vidarbha the guest, and Aja the host.

The king's officials bowed and showed Aja to a beautiful   63
 new royal tent, a golden jar upon a dais at its entrance.
 And the prince, the perfect likeness of his father
 Raghu, entered, as Kama enters the age that follows
 childhood.[20]

There at night, with Aja yearning to win that lovely jewel   64
 of a girl for whose husband-choosing ceremony the
 princes had been summoned, sleep came to his eyes
 only after a long time, like a wife aggrieved to learn her
 husband's true feelings.

At daybreak, his fleshy shoulders sore from the press of   65
 his earrings and the unguents on his body rubbed thin
 from the bedsheet's chafing, the bards woke Aja, who
 resembled dusk-waking fire, with verses that beguiled
 with their delightful composition.[21]

"The night has passed, best of the wise; leave your bed.   66
 Surely the creator has divided the burden of the
 world into two: one half is borne by your indefatigable
 father, and the role of bearer of the other is yours.

६७ निद्रावशेन भवता ह्यनवेक्ष्यमाणा
पर्युत्सुकत्वमबला निशि खण्डितेव ।
लक्ष्मीर्विनोदयति येन दिगन्तलम्बी
सो ऽपि त्वदाननरुचं विजहाति चन्द्रः ॥

६८ तद्वल्गुना युगपदुन्मिषितेन तावत्
सद्यः परस्परतुलामधिरोहतां द्वे ।
प्रस्पन्दमानपरुषेतरतारमन्तश्
चक्षुस्तव प्रचलितभ्रमरं च पद्मम् ॥

६९ वृन्तश्लथं हरति पुष्पमनोकहानां
संसृज्यते सरसिजैररुणांशुभिन्नैः ।
स्वाभाविकं परगुणेन विभातवातः
सौगन्ध्यमीप्सुरिव ते मुखमारुतस्य ॥

७० ताम्रोदरेषु पतितं द्रुमपल्लवेषु
निर्धौतहारगुलिकाविषदं हिमाम्भः ।
संलक्ष्यते दशनचन्द्रिकयानुविद्धं
बिम्बोष्ठलब्धपरभागमिव स्मितं ते ॥

७१ यावत्प्रतापनिधिराक्रमते न भानु-
रह्नाय तावदरुणेन तमो निरस्तम् ।
आयोधनाग्रसरतां त्वयि वीर याते
किं वा रिपूंस्तव गुरुः स्वयमुच्छिनत्ति ॥

"Overcome by Sleep, you neglected Royal Glory at night, 67
so she, like a woman jilted for the night, assuaged her
pangs by gazing at the moon—but now that moon too,
sinking below the horizon, is losing the luster that
your face possesses.

"So let these two things open, charmingly, at the same 68
moment, and so come suddenly to resemble each
other: your eye with its delicate pupil trembling in the
middle, and the lotus with a bee fluttering inside.

"Plucking the loose flowers on the trees from their stalks 69
and mingling with the lotuses opened by dawn's light,
the morning breeze seems set on acquiring the natural
fragrance of your breath by borrowing the qualities of
others.

"The dew, white as polished pearls lying sprinkled on the 70
new tree shoots with their reddish hue, recalls your
smile suffused with the moonlight of your teeth and
beautified by the red bimba fruits of your lips.

"Before the sun, that reservoir of heat, has even risen, 71
dawn has quickly dispersed the darkness. Now
that you, our hero, have joined the front ranks of
fighters, should your father be cutting down enemies
himself?[22]

७२ शय्यां जहत्युभयपक्षविनीतनिद्राः
सेनागजा मुखरशृङ्खलकर्षिणस्ते ।
येषां विभान्ति तरुणारुणरागयोगाद्
भिन्नाद्रिगैरिकतटा इव दन्तकोशाः ॥

७३ दीर्घेष्वमी नियमिताः पटमण्डपेषु
निद्रां विधूय वनजाक्ष वनायुजास्ते ।
वक्रोष्मणा मलिनयन्ति पुरोगतानि
लेह्यानि सैन्धवशिलाशकलानि वाहाः ॥

७४ भवति विरलभक्तिर्म्लानपुष्पोपकारः
स्वकिरणपरिवेशोद्भेदशून्याः प्रदीपाः ।
अयमपि च गिरं नस्त्वत्प्रबोधप्रयुक्ता-
मनुवदति शुकस्ते मञ्जुवाक्पञ्जरस्थः ॥

७५ इति स विहृतनिद्रस्तल्पमल्पेतरांसः
सुरगज इव गाङ्गं सैकतं सुप्रतीकः ।
परिजनवनितानां पादयोर्व्यापृतानां
वलयमणिविदष्टप्रच्छदान्तं मुमोच ॥

"Your army elephants are quitting their resting place,
     turning from side to side as they cast off slumber,
     pulling at their noisy chains, their curved tusks,
     touched by the red glow of early morning, shining as if
     they have been splitting mountainsides of red chalk.

"Tethered in long tents, these Vanayu-bred horses of
     yours, lotus-eyed prince, have shaken off sleep and
     now sully with their steaming breath the crystals of
     rock salt set before them to be licked.[23]

"The arrangement of the strew of flowers is loosening as
     its blossoms fade; a nimbus of rays no longer flares up
     around the lamps; and your sweet-voiced parakeet
     here in the cage is repeating the words we are singing
     to wake you up."

Thus shorn of sleep, the broad-shouldered prince left his
     bed, the fringe of its coverlet catching on jewels in
     the bracelets of the servant girls occupied at his feet,
     resembling the celestial elephant Supratika leaving
     the sandy bank of the Ganga.[24]

72

73

74

75

७६ अथ विधिमवसाय्य शास्त्रदृष्टं
दिवसमुखोचितमञ्जिताक्षिपक्ष्मा ।
कुशलविरचितानुरूपवेशः
क्षितिपसमाजमगात्स्वयंवरस्थम् ॥

इति रघुवंशे महाकाव्ये पञ्चमः सर्गः ॥

Then, having completed the ritual taught in the shastras   76
    as fitting for the beginning of the day, curly-lashed
    Aja, helped by skilled valets into his finery, went to
    join the princes assembled for the husband-choosing
    ceremony.

षष्ठः सर्गः

१ स तत्र मञ्चेषु विमानकल्पेष्वाकल्पसम्मूर्छितरूपशोभान् ।
   सिंहासनस्थान्नृपतीनपश्यद्धूपान्प्रयस्तानिव हैमवेदीन् ॥

२ रतेर्गृहीतानुनयेन कामं प्रत्यर्पितस्वाङ्गमिवेश्वरेण ।
   काकुत्स्थमालोकयतां नृपाणां मनो बभूवेन्दुमतीनिराशम् ॥

३ वैदर्भनिर्दिष्टमथो कुमारः क्लृप्तेन सोपानपथेन मञ्चम् ।
   शिलाविभङ्गैर्मृगराजशावस्तुङ्गं नगोत्सङ्गमिवारुरोह ॥

४ पराध्र्यवर्णास्तरणोपपन्नमासेदिवात्रत्नवदासनं सः ।
   भूयिष्ठमासीदुपमेयकान्तिर्मयूरपृष्ठाश्रयिणा गुहेन ॥

५ तासु श्रिया राजपरम्परासु प्रभाविशेषोदयदुर्निरीक्ष्यः ।
   सहस्रधात्मा व्यरुचद्विभक्तः पयोमुचां पङ्क्तिषु विद्युतेव ॥

६ तेषां महार्हासनसंश्रयाणामुदात्तनेपथ्यभृतां स मध्ये ।
   रराज धाम्ना रघुसूनुरेव कल्पद्रुमाणामिव पारिजातः ॥

७ नेत्रव्रजाः पौरजनस्य तस्मिन्विहाय सर्वान्नृपतीन्निपेतुः ।
   मदोत्कटे रेचितपुष्पवृक्षा गन्धद्विपे वन्य इव द्विरेफाः ॥

CHAPTER 6
Indumati Chooses a Husband

There on daises like celestial palaces Aja saw kings on lion   1
    thrones, their physical beauty heightened by their
    apparel, like decorated sacrificial posts upon golden
    altars.

When the kings beheld him, looking like the god of love   2
    with his body restored by Shiva at Rati's entreaty,
    their hearts despaired of gaining Indumati.[1]

The prince then ascended by way of decorated stairs onto   3
    the dais assigned him by the king of Vidarbha, as a lion
    cub ascends to a mountain outcrop by way of stony
    crags.

When seated upon his jeweled couch spread with   4
    precious-colored covers, in beauty he perfectly
    matched Skanda riding on his peacock mount.

Dividing herself a thousandfold, Royal Glory shone forth   5
    through those princely ranks with an intense light
    hard to look at, like lightning through banks of clouds.

Among those men sitting on precious thrones and dressed   6
    in noble robes, the son of Raghu shone in glory, like
    the *pārijāta* among the wishing trees of paradise.

The hosts of eyes of the citizens forsook all the other   7
    kings and fell on him, like bees abandoning the
    flowering trees and falling on a rutting jungle elephant
    streaming with scented musth.

८　अथ स्तुते वन्दिभिरन्वयज्ञैः सोमार्कवंश्ये नरदेवलोके ।
सञ्चारिते चागुरुसारयोनौ धूपे शिखावासितकेतुमाले ॥

९　पुरोपकण्ठोपवनाश्रयाणां शिखण्डिनामुद्धतनृत्तहेतौ ।
प्रध्मातशङ्खे परितो दिगन्तांस्तूर्यस्वने मूर्छति मङ्गलार्थे ॥

१०　मनुष्यवाहूं चतुरन्तयानमास्थाय कन्यापरिवारशोभि ।
विवेश मञ्जान्तरराजमार्गं पतिंवरा कौतुकमिश्रवेशा ॥

११　तस्मिन्विधानातिशये विधातुः कन्यामये नेत्रसहस्रलक्ष्ये ।
निपेतुरन्तःकरणैर्नरेन्द्रा देहैः स्थिताः केवलमासनेषु ॥

१२　तां प्रत्यभिव्यक्तमनोरथानां महीपतीनां प्रणयाग्रदूत्यः ।
प्रवातशोभा इव पादपानां शृङ्गारचेष्टा विविधा बभूवुः ॥

१३　कश्चित्कराभ्यामुपगूढनालमालोलपत्त्राभिहतद्विरेफम् ।
रजोभिरन्तःपरिवेशशोभि लीलारविन्दं भ्रमयां चकार ॥

१४　विस्रस्तमंसादपरो विलासी केयूरकोटिक्षणजातसङ्गम् ।
प्रावारमुत्क्षिप्य यथाप्रदेशं निनाय साचीकृतचारुवक्त्रः ॥

Then, while those kings, descended from the moon or 8
    sun, received the praise of bards who knew their
    ancestries; while incense from the aloe spread and
    scented the rows of battle standards;

while auspicious clarion calls and conches' blasts now 9
    swelled so that each quarter of the sky was filled,
    rousing the peacocks to dance in the parks fringing
    the city's edge;

the bride made her entrance upon a square palanquin 10
    borne by men, bright with a train of virgins, along a
    royal way between the thrones. Dressed in clothes
    adorned with auspicious bridal charms, she was ready
    to choose her lord.

The minds of the princes fell upon that girl—the cynosure 11
    of a thousand eyes, the creator's supreme creation—
    while their bodies alone remained in their seats.

The kings' longing for her became clear, the first 12
    messengers of their affection being the involuntary
    gestures, like the trembling of trees in the wind, that
    betrayed their passion.[2]

One prince twirled a lotus bloom with his hands covering 13
    the stalk, so that its inner space was brightly ringed
    with pollen and the bees were buffeted by whirling
    petals.

Another suitor turned his handsome face to one side and, 14
    when his cloak slipped from his shoulder and caught
    for a moment on a cusp of his armlet, drew it up to its
    proper place.

१५ आकुञ्चिताग्राङ्गुलिना ततो ऽन्यः किञ्चित्समावर्जितनेत्रशोभः ।
रत्नांशुसम्पृक्तनखप्रभेण पादेन हैमं विलिलेख पीठम् ॥

१६ निवेश्य वामं भुजमासनान्ते गाढाङ्गदं पार्श्वनिपीडनेन ।
कश्चिद्द्विवृत्त्रिकभिन्नहारः सुहृत्समाभाषणतत्परो ऽभूत् ॥

१७ विलासिनीविभ्रमदन्तपत्त्रमापाण्डुरं केतकबर्हमन्यः ।
प्रियानितम्बोचितसन्निपातैर्विपाटयामास युवा नखाग्रैः ॥

१८ कुशेशयाताम्रतलेन कश्चित्करेण रेखाध्वजलाञ्छनेन ।
दीप्राङ्गुलीयप्रभयानुविद्धानुदीरयामास सलीलमक्षान् ॥

१९ कश्चिद्यथाभागमवस्थिते ऽपि स्वसन्निवेशव्यतिलङ्घिनीव ।
वज्रांशुगर्भाङ्गुलिरन्भ्रमेकं व्यापारयामास करं किरीटे ॥

२० ततो नृपाणां श्रुतवृत्तवंशा पुंवत्प्रगल्भा प्रतिहाररक्षी ।
प्राक्सन्निकर्षं मगधेश्वरस्य नीत्वा कुमारीमवदत्सुनन्दा ॥

Another, casting down somewhat the light of his eyes   15
    and curling the tip of his toe, began tracing lines with
    his foot on his golden footstool, the rays of its jewels
    blending with those from his nails.

One prince became engrossed in conversation with a   16
    friend, his left arm leaning on the couch's edge so that
    the pressure on his side pressed the bracelet deep
    into his upper arm, and the string of pearls slid askew
    across his twisting upper back.

With the tips of his nails dealing blows fit for a beloved's   17
    hips, one youth was rending into strips a pale
    pandanus petal, the kind that decorates the ears of
    graceful girls.

Another, from a hand with lotus-reddish palm marked   18
    with the outlines of a flagstaff, playfully cast his dice,
    on which light flickered from his bright ring.[3]

Another busied his hand on his diadem, as if it were   19
    slipping down from where he had set it, although
    it rested perfectly in place; and through the gaps
    between his fingers shone the rays of the diamonds
    they wore.

Then Sunanda, the female doorkeeper, bold as a man   20
    in speech and well-versed in princely deeds and
    pedigrees, led the bride first to the king of Magadha
    and said:[4]

२१ असौ शरण्यः शरणोत्सुकानामगाधसत्त्वो मगधप्रतिष्ठः ।
राजा प्रजारञ्जनलब्धवर्णः परन्तपो नाम यथार्थनामा ॥

२२ कामं नृपाः सन्ति सहस्रसङ्ख्या राजन्वतीमाहुरनेन पृथ्वीम् ।
नक्षत्रताराग्रहसङ्कुलापि ज्योतिष्मती चन्द्रमसैव रात्रिः ॥

२३ क्रियाप्रबन्धादयमध्वराणामजस्रमाहूतसहस्रनेत्रः ।
शच्याश्चिरं पाण्डुकपोललम्बान्मन्दारशून्यानलकांश्चकार ॥

२४ अनेन चेदिच्छसि गृह्यमाणं पाणिं वरेण्येन कुरु प्रवेशे ।
प्रासादवातायनसंश्रयाणां नेत्रोत्सवं पुष्पपुराङ्गनानाम् ॥

२५ एवं तयोक्ते तमवेक्ष्य किञ्चिद्विस्रंसिदूर्वाङ्कमधूकमाला ।
ऋजुप्रणामक्रिययैव तन्वी प्रत्यादिदेशैनमभाषमाणा ॥

२६ तां साथ वेत्रग्रहणे नियुक्ता राजान्तरं राजसुतां निनाय ।
समीरणोत्थेव तरङ्गलेखा पद्मान्तरं मानसराजहंसीम् ॥

"This king, a refuge for all who seek protection, a man of 21
fathomless courage, adroit at pleasing his subjects,
has his seat in Magadha; his name, which fits him, is
Parantapa.*

"Granted, there are kings in thousands; but it is because of 22
this one that they speak of the broad earth as having
a true ruler. The night is crowded with stars, planets,
and constellations, but it is only because of the moon
that she is bright.

"He constantly summons thousand-eyed Indra to attend 23
the unbroken sequence of his sacrifices and so makes
Shachi long wear locks that hang lank beside pale
cheeks, devoid of *mandāra* blossoms.[5]

"If you should wish this worthy man to take your hand, 24
then make the eyes of the Flower City's women
feast as they crowd by the mansion windows at your
entrance."[6]

When Sunanda had said this, the slender girl glanced at 25
him and with a stiff bow, which made her wreath of
mahua flowers mixed with *dūrvā* grass slip down a
little, she spurned him without a word.

Next that lady charged with the staff of office led the 26
princess to another prince, as a line of ripples raised
by the wind conveys a regal goose on Lake Manasa to
another lotus blossom.

* Meaning "one who torments his foes."

२७ जगाद चैनामयमङ्गनाथः सुराङ्गनाप्रार्थितयौवनश्रीः ।
विनीतनागः किल सूत्रकारैरैन्द्रं पदं भूमिगतो ऽपि भुङ्क्ते ॥

२८ अनेन पर्यासयताश्रुबिन्दून्मुक्ताफलस्थूलतमान्स्तनेषु ।
प्रत्यर्पिताः शत्रुविलासिनीनामाक्षेपसूत्रेण विनैव हाराः ॥

२९ निसर्गभिन्नास्पदमेकसंस्थमस्मिन्द्वयं श्रीश्च सरस्वती च ।
कान्त्या गिरा सूनृतया च योग्या त्वमेव कल्याणि तयोस्तृतीया ॥

३० अथाङ्गराजादवतार्य चक्षुर्यातीति जन्यानवदत्कुमारी ।
नासौ न काम्यो न च वेद सम्यग्द्रष्टुं न सा भिन्नरुचिर्हि लोकः ॥

३१ ततः परं दुष्प्रसहं परेषां नृपं नियुक्ता प्रतिहारभूमौ ।
निदर्शयामास विशेषकान्तमिन्दुं नवोत्थानमिवेन्दुमत्याः ॥

३२ अवन्तिनाथो ऽयमुदग्रबाहुर्विशालवक्षास्तनुवृत्तमध्यः ।
आरोप्य चक्रभ्रममुष्णतेजास्त्वष्ट्रैव यन्त्रोल्लिखितो विभाति ॥

३३ अस्य प्रयाणेषु समग्रशक्तेरग्रेसरैर्वाजिभिरुद्धतानि ।
कुर्वन्ति सामन्तशिखामणीनां प्रभाप्ररोहास्तमयं रजांसि ॥

And she said to her, "This is the lord of Anga. Celestial   27
    women desire his youthful beauty, and his elephants
    were trained, they say, by the authors of the treatises
    thereon: so even on earth he enjoys the state of Indra.[7]

"When he caused his enemies' wives to shed tears as large   28
    as pearls onto their breasts, he returned them their
    necklaces without the strings to thread them.[8]

"By nature, Shri and Sarasvati live apart, but here in him   29
    the two reside together. Because of your splendor,
    noble lady, and your speech, both true and pleasing,
    you alone are fit to join them as their third."[9]

Then the girl let her gaze fall away from the king of Anga   30
    and told the porters of her palanquin to move on.
    It wasn't that he was not desirable, nor that she was
    unable to judge him rightly: people just have different
    tastes.

The woman appointed to the post of doorkeeper then   31
    pointed out to Indumati another king, invincible
    to foes, who was especially lovely, like a newly risen
    moon.

"This is the lord of Avanti, long-armed, with massive chest   32
    and slender, rounded waist. He dazzles like the sun
    when Vishvakarman mounted him on a wheel and
    lathed him into shape.[10]

"When he goes on campaigns, in command of all his   33
    powers, the horses in the vanguard kick up clouds of
    dust that dim the rays of light from the jewels in the
    diadems of vassal kings.[11]

३४ असौ महाकालनिकेतनस्य चन्द्रार्धमौलेर्निवसन्नदूरे ।
दिवापि जालान्तरचन्द्रिकाणां नारीसखः स्पर्शसुखानि भुङ्क्ते ॥

३५ अनेन यूना सह पार्थिवेन रम्भोरु कच्चिन्मनसो रुचिस्ते ।
सिप्रातरङ्गानिलकम्पितासु विहर्तुमुद्यानपरम्परासु ॥

३६ तस्मिन्नपि द्योतनरूपबिम्बे प्रतापसंशोषितशत्रुपङ्के ।
बबन्ध सा नोत्तमसौकुमार्या कुमुद्वती भानुमतीव भावम् ॥

३७ तामग्रतस्तामरसान्तराभामनूपराजस्य गुणैरनूनाम् ।
विधाय सृष्टिं ललितां विधातुर्जगाद भूयः सुनसां सुनन्दा ॥

३८ सङ्ग्रामनिर्विष्टसहस्रबाहुरष्टादशद्वीपनिखातयूपः ।
अनन्यसाधारणराजशब्दो बभूव योगी किल कार्तवीर्यः ॥

३९ अकार्यचिन्तासमकालमेव प्रादुर्भवंश्चापधरः पुरस्तात् ।
अन्तःशरीरेष्वपि यः प्रजानां प्रत्यादिदेशाविनयं विनेता ॥

४० ज्याबन्धनिःस्पन्दभुजेन यस्य विनिःश्वसद्व्रकपरम्परेण ।
कारागृहे निर्जितवासवेन दशाननेनोषितमा प्रसादात् ॥

"Living not far from the temple of Mahakala, the god 34
  whose crest jewel is the crescent moon, even by day
  he enjoys with his wives the pleasures of the touch of
  moonbeams filtering through the lattices.[12]

"Perhaps, oh girl with plantain-stem-like thighs, your 35
  heart fancies amusing yourself with this young king
  in the strings of gardens quivering in breezes off the
  waves of the Sipra River?"

That king's body seemed ablaze with light, and indeed his 36
  fiery prowess had parched his enemies like mud. She,
  unsurpassed in her delicacy, could no more love him
  than a water lily can love the sun.[13]

Sunanda brought the pretty-nosed girl before the king 37
  of Anupa and spoke again to her—pale like the heart
  of a lotus, lacking no virtue, the loveliest of all the
  creator's works.[14]

"They say there was once a yogi called Kartavirya. He 38
  had a thousand arms, which he used in battle, and
  he planted sacrificial posts on eighteen continents
  and deserved the title 'king' in a way that no one else
  could.

"The very instant his subjects thought of doing something 39
  they should not, this leader appeared before them,
  bow in hand, and checked misconduct even in their
  minds.

"It was in his prison that the demon once languished, 40
  ten-headed Ravana, conqueror of Indra, arms bound
  motionless with bowstring, row of mouths sighing,
  until pardoned.

४१ तस्यान्वये भूपतिरेष जातः प्रदीप इत्यागमवृद्धसेवी ।
येन श्रियः संश्रयदोषरूढं स्वभावलोलेत्ययशः प्रमृष्टम् ॥

४२ आयोधने कृष्णगतिं सहायमवाप्य यः क्षत्रियकालरात्रिम् ।
धारां शितां रामपरश्वधस्य सम्भावयत्युत्पलपत्तसाराम् ॥

४३ अस्याङ्कलक्ष्मीर्भव दीर्घबाहोर्माहिष्मतीवप्रनितम्बकाञ्चीम् ।
प्रासादजालैर्जलवेणिरम्यां रेवां यदि प्रेक्षितुमस्ति कामः ॥

४४ तस्याः प्रकामप्रियदर्शनो ऽपि न स क्षितीशो रुचये बभूव ।
शरत्प्रमृष्टाम्बुधरोपरागः शशीव पर्याप्तकलो नलिन्याः ॥

४५ सा शूरसेनाधिपतिं सुषेणमुद्दिश्य देशान्तरगीतकीर्तिम् ।
आचारशुद्धोभयवंशदीपं शुद्धान्तरक्ष्या जगदे कुमारी ॥

४६ नीपान्वयः पार्थिव एष यज्वा गुणैर्यमाश्रित्य परस्परेण ।
नैसर्गिको ऽप्युत्ससृजे विरोधः सिद्धाश्रमं शान्तिमिवैत्य सत्त्वैः ॥

"It is in his lineage that this king Pradipa was born. He 41
reveres those venerable for learning and has effaced
the ill repute of Royal Fortune that she is naturally
fickle, a charge rooted in the faults of those she
favors.[15]

"Enlisting black-trailed Fire as his ally in battle, he regards 42
the sharpened blade of Parashurama's battle-ax,
a very night of death to Kshatriyas, as having the
strength of a lily petal.

"Become the goddess of Royal Fortune in the lap of this 43
long-armed man if you desire to gaze down from
the latticed windows of his palace at the Reva River,
charming in its spate, a girdle around the buttocks of
the city of Mahishmati."[16]

Although exceptionally handsome, that king was not to 44
her taste, any more than the full moon released in
autumn from the shadows of the clouds is to the taste
of the lotus.[17]

The lady who guards the inner quarters then spoke to the 45
princess about Sushena, king of Shurasena, whose
fame was sung in distant places, and who was a lamp
brightening both his ancestral lines, each pure in
conduct:[18]

"This king, a performer of sacrifices, was born in the Nipa 46
lineage. Flocking to him, the virtues abandon mutual
strife, although natural to them, like beasts who flock
to a peaceful grove of perfected sages.[19]

४७ यस्यात्मदेहे नयनाभिरामा कान्तिर्हिमांशोरिव सन्निविष्टा ।
हर्म्याग्रसंरूढतृणाङ्कुरेषु तेजो ऽविषह्यं रिपुमन्दिरेषु ॥

४८ यस्यावरोधस्तनचन्दनानां प्रक्षालनाद्वारिविहारकाले ।
कलिन्दकन्या मथुरागतापि गङ्गोर्मिसम्पृक्तजलेव भाति ॥

४९ त्रातेन ताक्ष्र्यात्किल कालियेन मणिं विसृष्टं यमुनौकसा यः ।
वक्षःस्थलव्यापिरुचं दधानः सकौस्तुभं ह्रेपयतीव कृष्णम् ॥

५० सम्भाव्य भर्तारममुं युवानं मृदुप्रवालोत्तरपुष्पशय्ये ।
वृन्दावने चैत्ररथादनूने निर्विशयतां सुन्दरि यौवनश्रीः ॥

५१ अध्यास्य चाम्भःपृष्टतोक्षितानि शैलेयनद्धानि शिलातलानि ।
कलापिनां प्रावृषि पश्य नृत्तं कान्तासु गोवर्धनकन्दरासु ॥

५२ नृपं तमावर्तमनोज्ञनाभिः सा व्यत्यगादन्यवधूर्भवित्री ।
महीधरं मार्गवशादुपेतं स्रोतोवहा सागरगामिनीव ॥

५३ अथाङ्गदश्लिष्टभुजं भुजिष्या हेमाङ्गदं नाम कलिङ्गनाथम् ।
आसेदुषी सादितशत्रुपक्षं बालामबालेन्दुमुखीं बभाषे ॥

"His beauty, as lovely to behold as the cool-rayed moon's, 47
 pervades his body; his fiery power pervades his
 enemies' palaces, where grass has taken root and
 sprouted on the rooftop terraces.[20]

"The women of his inner quarters amuse themselves in 48
 the Kalindi's waters, and with the sandal paste washed
 from their breasts it looks as if its streams have mixed
 with the Ganga's waves even there in Mathura.[21]

"The story is told that Kaliya, the serpent dwelling in the 49
 Yamuna, was protected by this king from Garuda and
 rewarded him with a jewel. When Sushena wears that,
 its luster spreading across the expanse of his chest, he
 puts Krishna, with his Kaustubha gem, to shame![22]

"Honor this young man as your husband, lovely girl, 50
 and enjoy the halcyon days of youth upon a couch of
 flowers mixed with tender shoots in Vrindavana, a
 garden not inferior to Chaitraratha.[23]

"And in the monsoon, sit on the flags of stone covered 51
 with moss and sprinkled with drops of water and
 watch the peacocks dance in the lovely caves of Mount
 Govardhana."[24]

Destined to be the wife of another, the girl, her navel deep 52
 and lovely as an eddy, went past that king like a river
 that passes by a mountain in its path as it flows to the
 sea.

They next approached Hemangada, slayer of enemies and 53
 king of Kalinga, whose upper arms were laden with
 metal armbands, and the servant said to the moon-
 faced girl:[25]

५४ असौ महेन्द्राद्रिसमानसारः पतिर्महेन्द्रस्य महोदधेश्च ।
यस्य क्षरत्सैन्यगजच्छलेन यात्रासु यातीव पुरो महेन्द्रः ॥

५५ ज्याघातलेखे सुभुजो भुजाभ्यां बिभर्ति यश्चापभृतां पुरोगः ।
रिपुश्रियः साञ्जनवाष्पसेके वन्दीकृताया इव पद्धती द्वे ॥

५६ यमात्मनः सद्मनि सौधजालैरालोक्यवेलातटपूगमालः ।
मन्द्रध्वनित्याजितयामतूर्यः प्रबोधयत्यर्णव एव सुप्तम् ॥

५७ अनेन सार्धं विहराम्बुराशेस्तीरेषु तालीवनममरेषु ।
अपाकृतस्वेदलवा मरुद्भिर्द्वीपान्तरानीतलवङ्गपुष्पैः ॥

५८ प्रलोभिता सत्यपि सन्ततभ्रूर्विदर्भराजावरजा तयैवम् ।
तस्मादपावर्तत पौरुषेण नीतेव लक्ष्मीः प्रतिकूलदैवात् ॥

५९ अथोन्नसं नागपुरस्य नाथं दौवारिकी देवसरूपमेत्य ।
इतश्चकोराक्षि विलोकयेति नागाङ्गनाभां निजगाद भोज्याम् ॥

"This lord of Mount Mahendra and of the great ocean has 54
the strength of Mount Mahendra. When he goes on
campaigns Mount Mahendra seems to go before him
in the guise of his musth-streaming war elephants.[26]

"This splendid-armed man, foremost among archers, 55
bears scar lines on both forearms from the backlash
of his bowstring, as though they were the traces,
slick with kohl and tears, from the time he made his
enemies' Royal Fortune his captive.

"The ocean itself, whose fringe of areca-nut palms on 56
the shoreline can be seen from his palace windows,
awakens him from sleep when he is home, drowning
out with its deep roar the drum that marks the
watches.

"Enjoy yourself with him by the ocean shore, where 57
thickets of palmyra trees rustle and winds bringing
clove flowers from far-off islands will dry the beads of
perspiration."

Although thus tempted by Sunanda, the younger sister 58
of the king of Vidarbha turned away from him with
furrowed brow, just as Royal Fortune, although
attracted by valor, turns away from a man whose fate
is adverse.

Next the mistress of the gate approached the high-nosed, 59
god-like lord of Nagapura, and said to the princess of
Bhoja's line, who was like a *nāginī* herself, "Look this
way, lady with partridge eyes![27]

६० पाण्ड्यो ऽयमंसार्पितलम्बहारः कूर्म्माङ्गरागो हरिचन्दनेन ।
आभाति बालातपरक्तसानुः सनिर्झरोद्गार इवाद्रिराजः ॥

६१ विन्ध्यस्य संस्तम्भयिता महाद्रेर्निःशेषपीतोज्झितसिन्धुनाथः ।
प्रीत्याश्वमेधावभृथार्द्रमूर्तेः सौस्नातिको यस्य भवत्यगस्त्यः ॥

६२ अस्त्रं हरादाप्तवता दुरापं येनेन्द्रलोकावजयाय दृप्तः ।
पुरा जनस्थानविमर्दशङ्की सन्धाय लङ्काधिपतिः प्रतस्थे ॥

६३ अनेन पाणौ विधिवद्गृहीते महाकुलीनेन महीव गुर्वी ।
रत्नानुविद्धार्णवमेखलाया दिशः सपत्नी भव दक्षिणस्याः ॥

६४ ताम्बूलवल्लीपरिणद्धपूगास्वैलालतालिङ्गितचन्दनासु ।
तमालपत्रास्तरणासु रन्तुं प्रसीद शश्वन्मलयस्थलीषु ॥

६५ इन्दीवरश्यामतनुर्नृपो ऽयं त्वं रोचनागौरशरीरयष्टिः ।
अन्योन्यशोभापरिवृद्धये वां योगस्तडित्तोयदयोरिवास्तु ॥

"This is the Pandya king. With strings of pearls hanging   60
    from his shoulders, his body colored with red sandal
    paste, he looks like the king of mountains bathed
    with waterfalls, promontories reddened by the sun at
    dawn.

"When this king is still wet from his bath at the end of   61
    a horse sacrifice, it is Agastya who, out of affection,
    plays the ritual role of asking 'Have you bathed
    well?'—that same Agastya who once immobilized the
    great Vindhya mountain and drank up the ocean to
    the last drop, then spewed it out.[28]

"Long ago, this man obtained from Shiva a weapon hard   62
    to obtain, so the overweening lord of Lanka, fearing
    the destruction of Janasthana, could only set out
    to conquer Indra's heaven after making peace with
    him.[29]

"Letting this highborn man duly take your hand in   63
    marriage, become honored as Earth herself and
    co-wife too of the southern quarter, whose girdle is
    the jewel-rich sea!

"Consent to take your pleasure day after day on the slopes   64
    of the Malaya strewn with gamboge leaves, where
    betel creepers twine about areca-nut palms, and
    cardamom plants encircle sandalwood trees!

"This king's body is blue-dark, like the water lily; your   65
    slender frame is pale as orpiment: unite, and, like
    lightning and rain clouds, let the beauty of each
    increase the other's!"[30]

६६ स्वसुर्विदर्भाधिपतेस्तदीयो लेभे ऽन्तरं चेतसि नोपदेशः ।
दिवाकरादर्शनबद्धकोशे तारापतेरंशुरिवारविन्दे ॥

६७ सञ्चारिणी दीपशिखेव रात्रौ यं यं व्यतीयाय पतिंवरा सा ।
नरेन्द्रमार्गाट्ट इव प्रपेदे विवर्णभावं स स भूमिपालः ॥

६८ तस्यां रघोः सूनुरुपस्थितायां वृणीत मां नेति समाकुलो ऽभूत् ।
वामेतरः संशयमस्य बाहुः केयूरबन्धोच्छ्वसितैर्नुनोद ॥

६९ तं प्राप्य सर्वावयवानवद्यं न्यवर्ततान्योपगमात्कुमारी ।
न हि प्रफुल्लं सहकारमेत्य वृक्षान्तरं काङ्क्षति षट्पदाली ॥

७० तस्मिन्समावेशितचित्तवृत्तिमिन्दुप्रभामिन्दुमतीमवेत्य ।
प्रचक्रमे वक्तुमनुक्रमज्ञा सुविस्तरं वाक्यमिदं सुनन्दा ॥

७१ इक्ष्वाकुवंश्यः ककुदं नृपाणां ककुत्स्थ इत्याहतलक्षणो ऽभूत् ।
काकुत्स्थशब्दं यत उन्नतेच्छाः श्लाघ्यं दधत्युत्तरकोसलेन्द्राः ॥

७२ महेन्द्रमास्थाय महोक्षरूपं यः संयति प्राप्तपिनाकिलीलः ।
चकार बाणैरसुराङ्गनानां गण्डस्थलीः प्रोषितपत्त्रलेखाः ॥

Her message found no way inside the heart of the king   66
  of Vidarbha's sister, just as the rays of the moon find
  none inside the lotus, which closes its petals when it
  does not see the sun.

Like mansions on the king's highway at night when the   67
  flame of a lamp passes by, the princes paled one
  after another as she passed them in search of her
  bridegroom.[31]

When she came close to the son of Raghu, he became   68
  agitated, thinking, *She will not choose me.* His right arm
  dispelled his doubts by twitching where he wore his
  armbands.[32]

When she reached him, perfect in every part, the princess   69
  no longer wished to approach anyone else. After all, a
  swarm of bees seeks out no other tree once reaching a
  mango in full bloom.

Seeing that the moon-bright Indumati had fixed her   70
  thoughts on him, Sunanda, aware of what was due,
  proceeded to give this detailed account.

"There once was a scion of the Ikshvaku lineage, chief   71
  among kings, named Kakutstha.[33] After him the high-
  minded lords of Uttarakosala bear the worthy epithet
  Kakutstha.

"As playfully as Pinakin,* he rode in battle on Indra, who   72
  took the form of a great bull, and erased with his
  arrows the painted decorations from the cheeks of the
  women of the *asuras.*[34]

---

* Shiva, wielder of the *pināka* bow.

७३ ऐरावणास्फालनविश्लथं यः सङ्घट्टयन्नङ्गदमङ्गदेन ।
उपेयुषः स्वामपि मूर्तिमग्ग्यामर्धासनं गोत्रभिदो ऽधितस्थौ ॥

७४ जातः कुले तस्य किलेन्दुकीर्तेः कुलप्रदीपो नृपतिर्दिलीपः ।
अतिष्ठदेकोनशतक्रतुत्वे शक्राभ्यसूयाविनिवृत्तये यः ॥

७५ यस्मिन्महीं शासति मानिनीनां निद्रां विहारार्धपथे गतानाम् ।
वातो ऽपि नास्रंसयदंशुकानि को लम्बयेदाभरणाय हस्तम् ॥

७६ पुत्रो रघुस्तस्य पदं प्रशास्ति महाक्रतोर्विश्वजितः प्रयोक्ता ।
चतुर्दिगावर्जनसम्भृतां यो मृत्पात्रशेषामकरोद्विभूतिम् ॥

७७ आरूढमद्रीनुदधीन्प्रतीर्णं भुजङ्गमानां वसतिं प्रविष्टम् ।
ऊर्ध्वं गतं यस्य न चानुबन्धि यशः परिच्छेत्तुमियत्तयालम् ॥

७८ असौ कुमारस्तमजो ऽनुजातस्त्रिविष्टपस्येव पतिं जयन्तः ।
गुर्वीं धुरं यो भुवनस्य पित्रा धुर्येण दम्यः सदृशीं बिभर्ति ॥

७९ कुलेन कान्त्या वयसा नवेन गुणैश्च तैस्तैर्विनयप्रधानैः ।
त्वमात्मनस्तुल्यमिमं वृणीष्व रत्नं समागच्छतु काञ्चनेन ॥

"And when the mountain-splitting god had resumed his   73
own highest form, this king occupied half his throne,
his armlet rubbing against Indra's armlet, which
was loosened from goading the celestial elephant
Airavana.

"They say that King Dilipa, a lamp to his lineage, was born   74
in the family of that man of moon-bright fame. He
stopped at one less than a hundred sacrifices to avoid
provoking Indra's jealousy.[35]

"While he was ruling the earth, even the wind dared not   75
disturb the garments of young women who fall asleep
halfway across the park! Who then would lay hands on
their jewelry?[36]

"His son Raghu now rules the kingdom. He performed   76
the great Vishvajit sacrifice and gave away the riches
acquired from conquering the world to the four
horizons, leaving only a clay vessel for himself.[37]

"His fame has scaled mountains, crossed oceans, and   77
entered the underworld where serpents reside, rising
higher, still enduring; none can measure how vast it is.

"This prince, Aja, was born to him, as Jayanta was to Indra,   78
lord of heaven. Together with his father, he bears the
heavy yoke of the world, as the bullock shares the yoke
with the draft ox.

"In birth, beauty, youth, and in his various virtues, self-   79
restraint foremost among them, he is your equal.
Choose him, and let gemstone join with gold!"

८० ततः सुनन्दावचनावसाने लज्जां मृदूकृत्य नरेन्द्रकन्या ।
दृष्ट्या प्रसादामलया कुमारं प्रत्यग्रहीत्संवरणस्रजेव ॥

८१ सा यूनि तस्मिन्नभिलाषबन्धं शशाक शालीनतया न वक्तुम् ।
रोमाञ्चलक्ष्येण स गात्रयष्टिं भित्त्वा निराक्रामदरालकेश्याः ॥

८२ तथागतायां परिहासपूर्वं सख्यां सखी वेत्रधरा बभाषे ।
आर्ये व्रजामो ऽन्यत इत्यथैनां वधूरसूयाकुटिलं ददर्श ॥

८३ सा चूर्णगौरं रघुनन्दनस्य धात्रीकराभ्यां करभोपमोरूः ।
आसञ्जयामास यथाप्रदेशं कण्ठे गुणं मूर्तिमिवानुरागम् ॥

८४ तया स्रजा मङ्गलपुष्पमय्या विशालवक्षःस्थललम्बया सः ।
अमंस्त कण्ठार्पितबाहुपाशां विदर्भराजावरजां वरेण्यः ॥

८५ शशिनमुपगतेयं कौमुदी मेघमुक्तं
जलनिधिमनुरूपं जह्नुकन्यावतीर्णा ।
इति समगुणयोगप्रीतयस्तत्र पौराः
श्रवणकटु नृपाणामेकवाक्यं विवव्रुः ॥

With that, Sunanda concluded her speech. The princess, 80
overcoming her bashfulness, chose the prince with her
gaze bright with joy, as clearly as with the engagement
garland.

Shyness prevented her from expressing the tie of desire 81
she felt toward the young man, but it broke through
in the guise of the fine hairs standing on end on the
curly-haired girl's slender body.

Seeing her in this state, the doorkeeper said teasingly, one 82
friend to another: "Noble lady, let us move on to the
next!" at which the bride looked angrily askance at
her.

The princess, whose thighs were as smoothly tapered 83
as the back of the hand, let her nurse drape on the
shoulders of Raghu's son the engagement garland.
Reddened with powders, it seemed like her own love
endued with form.[38]

With this garland of auspicious flowers hanging down 84
over his broad chest, that most eligible suitor felt as if
the younger sister of the king of Vidarbha had clasped
her arms around his neck.

"This is autumnal moonlight joining the moon released 85
from monsoon clouds! This is Ganga pouring herself
into the ocean, her equal!" So the citizens there,
delighted at the union of two persons of equal merits,
exclaimed in one voice, bitter to the ears of the other
kings.

८६ प्रमुदितवरपक्षमेकतस्तत्क्षितिपतिमण्डलमन्यतो वितानम् ।
उषसि सर इव प्रफुल्लपद्मं कुमुदवनप्रतिपन्ननिद्रमासीत् ॥

इति रघुवंशे महाकाव्ये षष्ठः सर्गः ॥

On one side, the party of the groom, elated; on the other,   86
    the rest, dejected—the assembly of kings was like a
    lake at dawn, when the lotuses unfold and the forest of
    nenuphars re-enters sleep.

१ अथोपयन्ता सदृशेन युक्तां स्कन्देन साक्षादिव देवसेनाम् ।
स्वसारमादाय विदर्भराजः पुरप्रवेशाभिमुखो बभूव ॥

२ सेनानिवेशान्पृथिवीभृतो ऽपि जग्मुर्विभातग्रहमन्दभासः ।
भोज्यां प्रति व्यर्थमनोरथत्वादूपेषु वेशेषु च साभ्यसूयाः ॥

३ सान्निध्ययोगात्किल तत्र शच्याः स्वयंवरक्षोभकृतामभावः ।
काकुत्स्थमुद्दिश्य समत्सरो ऽपि शशाम तेन क्षितिपाललोकः ॥

४ तावत्प्रकीर्णाभिनवोपकारमिन्द्रायुधद्योतनतोरणाङ्कम् ।
वरः स वध्वा सह राजमार्गं प्राप ध्वजच्छायनिवारितोष्णम् ॥

५ ततस्तदालोकनसत्वराणां सौधेषु चामीकरजालवत्सु ।
बभूवुरित्थं पुरसुन्दरीणां त्यक्तान्यकार्याणि विचेष्टितानि ॥

६ आलोकमार्गं सहसा व्रजन्त्या कयाचिदुद्द्रेष्टनवान्तमाल्यः ।
बद्धुं न सम्भावित एव तावत्करेण रुद्धो ऽपि न केशपाशः ॥

CHAPTER 7
A Wedding and an Ambush

Then the king of Vidarbha, taking his sister along with her 1
fitting groom, like Devasena and Skanda in person,
turned to face the city's entrance.[1]

As for the princes, they returned to their camps looking 2
pale as the planets at dawn. The frustration of their
desire for Indumati left them dissatisfied with their
own looks and apparel.

They say that Shachi herself was present there, and 3
hence nothing disturbed the ceremony of choosing a
husband. The princely throng was jealous of Aja but
held their peace.[2]

That groom with his bride reached the royal avenue, which 4
had been strewn with fresh sprays of flowers, marked
with arches bright as rainbows, and shielded from the
heat by the shade of banners.

Then the city's ladies in their whitewashed mansions with 5
golden-latticed windows abandoned all other tasks
and rushed to see the couple, acting in these ways:

As she hurried to the window, one lady's tresses came 6
undone, the garlands slipping from them; she could
not even check them with her hand, let alone tie them
up.[3]

७ प्रासाधिकालम्बितमग्रपादमाक्षिप्य काचिद्द्वरागमेव ।
   उत्सृष्टलीलागतिरा गवाक्षादलक्तकाङ्कां पदवीं ततान ॥

८ विलोचनं दक्षिणमञ्जनेन सम्भाव्य तद्वज्झितवामनेत्रा ।
   तथैव वातायनसन्निकर्षं ययौ शलाकामपरा वहन्ती ॥

९ जालान्तरप्रेषितदृष्टिरन्या प्रस्थानभिन्नां न बबन्ध नीवीम् ।
   नाभिप्रविष्टाभरणप्रभेण हस्तेन तस्थावववलम्ब्य वासः ॥

१० अर्धाचिता सत्वरमुत्थितायाः पदे पदे दुर्निमितं गलन्ती ।
    कस्याश्चिदासीद्रशना तदानीमङ्गुष्ठमूलार्पितसूत्रशेषा ॥

११ तासां मुखैरासवगन्धगर्भैर्व्याप्तान्तराः सान्द्रकुतूहलानाम् ।
    विलोलनेत्रभ्रमरैर्गवाक्षाः सहस्रपत्त्राभरणा इवासन् ॥

१२ ता राघवं दृष्टिभिरापिवन्त्यो नार्यो न जग्मुर्विषयान्तराणि ।
    तदा हि शेषेन्द्रियवृत्तिरासां सर्वात्मना चक्षुरिव प्रविष्टा ॥

१३ स्थाने वृता भूपतिभिः परोक्षैः स्वयंवरं साधुममंस्त बाला ।
    पद्मेव नारायणमन्यथासौ लभेत कान्तं कथमात्मतुल्यम् ॥

१४ परस्परेण स्पृहणीयरूपं न चेदिदं द्वन्द्वमयोजयिष्यत् ।
    अस्मिन्द्वये रूपविधानयत्नः पत्युः प्रजानां वितथो ऽभविष्यत् ॥

Another one had proffered her foot to her maid-in-   7
    waiting, but she withdrew it with the red lac still
    glistening and, abandoning her graceful gait, left a
    lac-stained path to the window.

One lady had just applied collyrium to her right eye, but   8
    leaving the left one unadorned went just like that to
    the lattice, still clutching her eyebrow pencil.

Yet another forgot to tie the knot of her sash, loosened   9
    by her haste, and stood there peering through her
    lattice, holding her dress in place with a hand whose
    ornaments spread glittering rays across her navel.

Another girl got up with such haste that her girdle, half   10
    threaded with gems, unraveling helter-skelter at every
    step, became no more than a bare thread tied to the
    base of her big toe.[4]

Crowded with the wine-scented faces of these madly   11
    curious women, whose eyes flitted like bees, the
    windows seemed to be decorated with lotuses.

Drinking Aja in with their glances, the ladies could   12
    know no other sense objects; for the activity of all
    their other faculties seemed at that moment to have
    entirely entered into their eyes.

"How fitting that the girl, sought by kings she'd never   13
    seen, agreed to a bridegroom choice. How else
    could she have found a beloved who matches her, as
    Lakshmi found Vishnu?[5]

"If the Lord of Creatures had not joined this couple, each   14
    with a beauty the other longs for, then his effort to
    fashion that beauty in them both would have been in
    vain.

१५ रतिस्मरौ नूनमिमावभूतां राज्ञां सहस्रेषु तथा हि बाला ।
गतेयमात्मप्रतिरूपमेनं मनो हि जात्यन्तरसंगतिज्ञम् ॥

१६ इत्युद्गताः पौरवधूमुखेभ्यः शृण्वन्कथाः श्रोत्रसुखाः कुमारः ।
उद्भासितं मङ्गलसंविधाभिः सम्बन्धिनः सद्म समाससाद ॥

१७ ततो ऽवतीर्याशु करेणुकायाः स कामरूपेश्वरदत्तहस्तः ।
वैदर्भनिर्दिष्टमथो विवेश नारीमनांसीव चतुष्कमन्तः ॥

१८ महार्हशय्यासनसंस्थितो ऽसौ सरत्नमर्घ्यं मधुपर्कमिश्रम् ।
भोजोपनीतं च दुगूलयुग्मं जग्राह सार्धं वनिताकटाक्षैः ॥

१९ दुगूलवासाः स वधूसमीपं निन्ये विनीतैरवरोधरक्षैः ।
वेलासकाशं स्फुटफेनराजिर्वैरुदन्वानिव चन्द्रपादैः ॥

२० तत्रार्चितो भोजपतेः पुरोधा हुत्वाग्निमाज्यादिभिरग्निकल्पः ।
तमेव चाधाय विवाहसाक्ष्ये वधूवरौ सङ्गमयां चकार ॥

२१ हस्तेन हस्तं परिगृह्य वध्वाः स राजसूनुः सुतरां बभासे ।
अनन्तराशोकलताप्रवालं प्राप्येव चूतः प्रतिपल्लवेन ॥

"Surely the pair were once Rati and Kama, for the girl, in   15
the midst of thousands of kings, went straight to him,
who so matches herself. Indeed the heart knows the
unions of past births!"

While hearing from the mouths of the ladies of the city   16
such talk, pleasing to his ears, the prince reached his
new kinsman's house, which was brightly decked out
with auspicious decorations.

Then, with the Lord of Kamarupa lending him a hand,   17
he quickly dismounted from his she-elephant and, as
Bhoja showed the way, he stepped into the courtyard,
and into the women's hearts.

Seated upon a precious couch, he received, along with   18
the ladies' sidelong glances, gem-filled guest water,
together with honey, ghee, and curds, as well as a pair
of silken cloths brought by Bhoja.

Dressed in pale silk, he was brought into the presence   19
of the bride by respectful guardians of the inner
quarters, as the foam-fringed sea is brought to the
shore by the beams of the just-risen moon.

There the revered and fire-like chaplain of King Bhoja   20
offered clarified butter and other oblations into the
fire, making it witness to the marriage, and joined
together bride and groom.

The prince shone brightly as he took the bride's hand in   21
his own, as when a mango tree touches with its shoot
the frond of a neighboring *aśoka's* branch.

२२ आसीद्दुरः कण्टकितप्रकोष्ठः स्विन्नाङ्गुलिः संववृते कुमारी ।
तस्मिन्द्वये तत्क्षणमात्मवृत्तिः समं विभक्तेव मनोभवेन ॥

२३ तयोरपाङ्गप्रविचारितानि क्रियासमापत्तिषु कातराणि ।
ह्रीयन्त्रणामानशिरे मनोज्ञामन्योन्यलोलानि विलोचनानि ॥

२४ प्रदक्षिणप्रक्रमणात्कृशानोरुदर्चिषस्तन्मिथुनं बभासे ।
मेरोरिवान्तेषु विवर्तमानमन्योन्यसंसक्तमहस्त्रियामम् ॥

२५ नितम्बगुर्वी गुरुणा प्रयुक्ता वधूर्विधातृप्रतिमेन तेन ।
चकार सा मत्तचकोरनेत्रा लज्जावती लाजविसर्गमग्नौ ॥

२६ हविःशमीपल्लवलाजगन्धी पुण्यः कृशानोरुदियाय धूमः ।
कपोलसंसर्पिशिखः स तस्या मुहूर्तकर्णोत्पलतां प्रपेदे ॥

२७ तदञ्जनक्षोभसमाकुलाक्षं प्रम्लानबीजाङ्कुरकर्णपूरम् ।
वधूमुखं पाटलगण्डलेखमाचारधूमग्रहणाद्बभूव ॥

२८ तौ स्नातकैर्बन्धुमता च राज्ञा पुरन्ध्रिभिश्च क्रमशः प्रयुक्तम् ।
कन्याकुमारौ कनकासनस्थावार्द्राक्षतारोपणमन्वभूताम् ॥

२९ इति स्वसुर्भोजकुलप्रदीपः सम्पाद्य पाणिग्रहणं स राजा ।
महीपतीनां पृथगर्हणार्थं समादिदेशाधिकृतानधिश्रीः ॥

Hairs stood up upon the groom's forearms; sweat 22
    appeared on the fingers of the princess: in that instant
    Kama seemed to divide the workings of his nature
    evenly between the two of them.[6]

The looks of mutual longing they sent forth from the 23
    corners of their eyes turned timid when they reached
    their goal, and became charmingly restrained by
    shyness.

Stepping forth to circumambulate the blazing fire, the 24
    couple shone radiantly, like day and night locked
    together as they circle close around Mount Meru.

When prompted by their Brahma-like guru, the bride 25
    with ample hips bashfully sprinkled parched grain
    into the fire, her eyes smarting red like the eyes of an
    impassioned partridge.[7]

Purifying smoke rose up from the fire, redolent of ghee, 26
    śamī sprouts, and parched grain, its tip curling up
    beside her cheek to become for an instant a lily resting
    there to grace her ear.

As she breathed in the smoke, as custom dictates, the 27
    bride's face changed: her eyes clouded with smudged
    kohl, the barley sprouts adorning her ears drooped,
    and the curves of her cheeks blushed red.

Seated on thrones of gold, the bride and groom were 28
    showered with moistened barley thrown by Vedic
    graduates, by the king with his relatives, and by
    matrons, in due order.

After thus giving away his sister's hand in marriage, that 29
    most splendid king, light of the Bhoja line, ordered his
    officers to honor each of the princes.

३० लिङ्गैर्मुदः संवृतविक्रियास्ते हृदाः प्रसन्ना इव गूढनक्राः ।
वैदर्भमामन्त्र्य ययुस्तदीयां प्रत्यर्प्य पूजामुपदाच्छलेन ॥

३१ भर्तापि तावत्क्रथकैशिकानामनुष्ठितानन्तरजाविवाहः ।
सत्त्वानुरूपं हरणीकृतश्रीः प्रास्थापयद्राघवमन्वगाच्च ॥

३२ तिस्रस्त्रिलोकप्रथितेन सार्धमजेन मार्गे वसतीरुषित्वा ।
तस्मादपावर्तत भोजराजः पर्वात्यये सोम इवोष्णरश्मेः ॥

३३ स राजलोकः कृतपूर्वसंविदुदारसिद्धौ समराक्षलभ्यम् ।
आदास्यमानः प्रमदामिषं तदावृत्य पन्थानमजस्य तस्थौ ॥

३४ प्रमन्यवः प्रागपि कोसलेन्द्रे प्रत्येकमात्तस्वतया बभूवुः ।
अतो नृपाश्चक्षमिरे समेताः स्त्रीरत्नलाभं न तदात्मजस्य ॥

३५ तमुद्वहन्तं पथि भोजकन्यां रुरोध राजन्यगणः स दृप्तः ।
बलिप्रतिष्ठां श्रियमाददानं त्रैविक्रमं पादमिवेन्द्रशत्रुः ॥

Hiding their emotions with outward signs of joy, like   30
  placid lakes that hide crocodiles within, they took
  their leave of the king of Vidarbha, showing him
  honor in turn by the offering of gifts.

Meanwhile the king of the Krathakaishikas, now that   31
  his younger sister's wedding had been performed,
  bestowed wealth upon her as a dowry, in accordance
  with his noble nature, and set Aja on his way,
  accompanying him a while.

King Bhoja remained with Aja—famed throughout the   32
  three worlds—for three staging posts along the way
  and then turned back from him, as the moon turns
  back from the sun when their union on the new-moon
  day is over.

The group of princes had made a pact among themselves   33
  to win that noble prize. Planning to snatch the girl like
  a trophy to be won in the dice game of a battle, they
  occupied the road that Aja would take, and waited.

The king of Kosala had taken the wealth of one after   34
  another, so each already held a grudge against him;
  now, united, the princes could not endure that his son
  Aja should win that jewel of a woman.[8]

The overweening princes blocked him on the way as he   35
  was leading away Indumati as his bride, just as Indra's
  enemy blocked the foot of Vishnu as he took three
  broad strides and carried away Bali's glory.[9]

३६ तस्याः स रक्षार्थमनल्पयोधमादिश्य पित्र्यं सचिवं कुमारः ।
   प्रत्यग्रहीत्पार्थिववाहिनीं तां ज्योतीरथां शोण इवोत्तरङ्गः ॥

३७ पत्तिः पदातिं रथिनं रथेशस्तुरङ्गसादी तुरगाधिरूढम् ।
   यन्ता गजेनाभ्यपतद्गजस्थं तुल्यप्रतिद्वन्द्वि बभूव युद्धम् ॥

३८ नदत्सु तूर्येष्वविभाव्यवाचो नोदीरयन्ति स्म कुलापदेशान् ।
   बाणाक्षरैरेव परस्पराय नामोर्जितं चापभृतः शशंसुः ॥

३९ उत्थापितः संयति रेणुरश्वैः सान्द्रीकृतः स्यन्दननेमिचक्रैः ।
   विस्तारितः कुञ्जरकर्णतालैर्नेत्रक्रमेणोपरुरोध सूर्यम् ॥

४० मत्स्यध्वजा वायुवशाद्विदीर्णैर्मुखैः प्रयुद्धध्वजिनीरजांसि ।
   बभुः पिवन्तः परमार्थमत्स्याः पर्यार्बिलानीव नवोदकानि ॥

४१ रथो रथाङ्गध्वनिनाधिजज्ञे विलोलघण्टाक्वणितेन नागः ।
   स्वभर्तृनामग्रहणाद्बभूव सान्द्रे रजस्यात्मपरावबोधः ॥

The prince directed his hereditary minister, who   36
    commanded numerous soldiers, to protect Indumati
    while he himself received the host of rival kings, just
    as the choppy Shona River receives the waters of the
    Jyotiratha.[10]

Foot soldier fell upon foot soldier, chariot fighter upon   37
    chariot fighter, horseman upon horseman, mahout
    upon mahout—the battle was waged between like and
    like.

While clarions sounded, the archers' voices were   38
    inaudible, so they did not declaim the titles of their
    lineages; instead they announced to each other their
    illustrious names by means of letters written on their
    arrows.[11]

The dust kicked up in battle by the horses, thickened by   39
    the fellies of the chariot wheels and spread out by the
    elephants' flapping ears, blocked out the sun like a
    veil.[12]

Bright were the fish-shaped flags as they drank the dust   40
    from the fighting armies through mouths distended
    by the force of the wind, like real fish drinking the
    turbid waters of fresh rainfall.

In the dense dust, chariots could be recognized only by the   41
    creaking of wheels, elephants by the jangling of their
    lolling bells, and men realized who was with them
    and who against only because each called his master's
    name.

४२ आवृण्वतो लोचनमार्गमाजौ रजोऽन्धकारस्य विजृम्भितस्य ।
शस्त्रक्षताश्वद्विपवीरजन्मा बालारुणो ऽभूदुधिरप्रवाहः ॥

४३ स च्छिन्नमूलः क्षतजेन रेणुस्तस्योपरिष्टात्पवनावधूतः ।
अङ्गारशेषस्य हुताशनस्य पूर्वोत्थितो धूम इवाबभासे ॥

४४ प्रहारमूर्च्छापगमे रथस्था यन्तॄनुपालभ्य विवर्तिताक्षान् ।
यैः सादिता लक्षितपूर्वकेतूंस्तानेव सामर्षतया निजघ्नुः ॥

४५ अप्यर्धमार्गे परबाणलूना धनुर्भृतां हस्तवतां पृषत्काः ।
अवापुरेवात्मजवानुवृत्त्या पूर्वार्धभागैः फलिभिः शरव्यम् ॥

४६ शिलीमुखोत्कृत्तशिरःफलाढ्या च्युतैः शिरस्त्रैश्च्षकोत्तरेव ।
रणक्षितिः शोणितमद्यकुल्या रराज मृत्योरिव पानभूमिः ॥

४७ आधोरणानां गजसन्निपाते शिरांसि चक्रैर्निशितक्षुरान्तैः ।
कृत्तान्यपि श्येननखाग्रकोटिव्यासक्तकेशानि चिरेण पेतुः ॥

४८ पूर्वप्रहर्ता न जघान भूयः प्रतिप्रहाराक्षममश्वसादी ।
तुरङ्गमस्कन्धनिषण्णदेहं प्रत्याश्वसन्तं रिपुमाचकाङ्क्ष ॥

On the battleground, the river of blood that flowed   42
from wounded horses, elephants, and soldiers was
a dawning sun to the gaping darkness of dust that
blocked the field of view.

The dust, cut off from its source by blood and impelled to   43
float above it by the wind, appeared like smoke that
had earlier billowed up from a fire now reduced to
embers.

Chariot fighters who had lost consciousness on being   44
struck recovered and upbraided their charioteers for
turning the horses back, then furiously attacked those
who had struck them, recognizing them by the battle
standards they had seen before.

Though cut in half midway by enemies' shafts, the arrows   45
of the deft bowmen were carried by their impetus and
reached their targets—at least their front halves did,
which bore the arrowheads.

The battlefield was like a drinking den of Death: strewn   46
with fruits that were arrow-severed heads, littered
with cups that were fallen helmets—and the liquor
that flowed on tap was blood.

As elephants clashed, the heads of mahouts were severed   47
by razor-sharp war quoits but took time to fall, for
eagles caught at their hair with the tips of their
sharpened claws.[13]

A horseman who had struck his opponent once, leaving   48
him leaning against his horse's withers and unable to
retaliate, did not strike again, hoping for him to revive.

४९ तनुत्यजां वर्मभृतां विकोशैर्बृहत्सु दन्तेष्वसिभिः पतद्भिः ।
उद्यन्तमग्निं शमयां बभूवुर्गजा विविग्राः करशीकरेण ॥

५० उपान्तयोर्निष्कुषितं विहङ्गैराक्षिप्य तेभ्यः पिशितप्रियापि ।
केयूरकोटिक्षततालुदेशा शिवा भुजच्छेदमपाचकार ॥

५१ कश्चिद्द्विषत्खड्गहृतोत्तमाङ्गं सद्यो विमानप्रभुतामुपेत्य ।
वामाङ्कसंसक्तसुराङ्गनः स्वं नृत्यत्कबन्धं समरे ददर्श ॥

५२ अन्योन्यसूतोन्मथनादभूतां तावेव सूतौ रथिनौ च कौचित् ।
व्यश्वौ गदाव्यायतसम्प्रहारौ भग्नायुधौ बाहुविमर्दनिष्ठौ ॥

५३ परस्परेण क्षतयोः प्रहर्त्रोर्व्युत्क्रान्तवाय्वोः समकालमेव ।
अमर्त्यभावे ऽपि कयोश्चिदेकाप्सरःप्रार्थितयोर्विवादः ॥

५४ व्यूहावुभौ तावितरेतरस्माद्भङ्गं जयं चापतुरव्यवस्थम् ।
पश्चात्पुरोमारुतयोः प्रवृद्धौ पर्यायवृत्त्येव महार्णवोर्मी ॥

५५ परेण भग्ने ऽपि बले महौजा ययावजः प्रत्यरिसैन्यमेव ।
धूमो निवर्त्येत समीरणेन यतो हि कक्षस्तत एव वह्निः ॥

With showers of water from their trunks, frenzied   49
  elephants extinguished the fires that sprang up when
  the unsheathed swords of armored soldiers ready to
  give up their lives clashed against their massive tusks.

A she-jackal had wrested a hunk of arm from birds that   50
  had torn at it from both sides but spat it out, fond of
  flesh though she was, when her palate was spiked by
  the sharp armlet.

One warrior, his head lopped off by an enemy's sword,   51
  suddenly found himself master of a flying palace, a
  celestial lady on his left, looking down upon his own
  torso dancing on the battlefield.[14]

Two chariot warriors, when their charioteers were slain,   52
  became themselves both charioteer and warrior; when
  their horses were slain, they fought a protracted battle
  with their maces; when their weapons broke, they fell
  to with bare arms.

Two soldiers struck each other and simultaneously   53
  breathed their last, but even though now immortals
  they fell to fighting again when both were chosen by
  one and the same celestial beauty.

The arrays of both those armies suffered defeat and won   54
  victory over each other inconclusively, like two great
  ocean waves swelling from tailwind and headwind by
  turns.

Even when his army was routed by his foes, the mighty Aja 55
  still made straight for the enemy: for sure, smoke may
  be turned away by wind, but where there's hay the fire
  will go.

५६ रथी निषङ्गी कवची धनुष्मान्दृप्तं स राजन्यकमेकवीरः ।
विलोडयामास महावराहः कल्पक्षयोद्वृत्तमिवार्णवाम्भः ॥

५७ न दक्षिणं तूणमुखे न वामं व्यापारयन्हस्तमलक्ष्यतासौ ।
आकर्णकृष्टा सकृदस्य योद्धुर्मौर्वीव बाणान्सुषुवे रिपुघ्नान् ॥

५८ स रोषदष्टाधिकलोहितौष्ठैर्व्यक्तोर्ध्वराजीभ्रुकुटीर्वहद्भिः ।
तस्तार गां भल्लनिकृत्तकण्ठैर्हुङ्कारगर्भैर्द्विषतां शिरोभिः ॥

५९ सर्वैर्बलाङ्गैर्द्विरदप्रधानैः सर्वायुधैः कङ्कटभेदिभिश्च ।
सर्वप्रयत्नेन च भूमिपालास्तस्मिन्प्रजह्रुर्युधि सर्व एव ॥

६० सो ऽस्त्रव्रजैश्छन्नरथः परेषां ध्वजाग्रमात्रेण बभूव लक्ष्यः ।
नीहारमग्नोदितपूर्वभागः किञ्चित्प्रकाशेन यथा विवस्वान् ॥

६१ प्रियंवदात्प्राप्तमथ प्रियार्हः प्रायुङ्क्त राजस्वधिराजसूनुः ।
गान्धर्वमस्त्रं कुसुमास्त्रकान्तः प्रस्वापनं स्वप्ननिवृत्तलौल्यः ॥

६२ ततो धनुष्कर्षणमूढहस्तमेकांसपर्यस्तशिरस्त्रजालम् ।
तस्थौ ध्वजस्तम्भनिषण्णदेहं निद्राविधेयं नरदेवसैन्यम् ॥

Equipped with chariot, quiver, cuirass, and bow, fighting alone, he churned up the proud princely army, as the Great Boar churns up the ocean's waters when they swell at the end of an age.[15]   56

He could not be seen to move either his right or his left hand at the mouth of the quiver; when he fought, the bowstring drawn back once to his ear seemed to be birthing the arrows that slew his enemies.[16]   57

He carpeted the ground with his enemies' heads, cut off at the neck with saber-blade arrows, still biting their flushed lips in anger, still clearly furrowing their arched brows, still ringing with their roars.   58

With all their regiments, the bull elephants being the most important; with all their weapons, which could even pierce armor; and with all their strength the princes hurled themselves upon him in the fight, all together.   59

His chariot obscured by their clouds of weapons, Aja could only be discerned by his battle standard's tip, just as the sun, veiled in mist but with its upper part rising out of it, is discerned by a pale glow.[17]   60

Handsome as the flower-arrowed god of love, deserving of every blessing, the son of the king thereupon deployed against the princes the weapon he had received from the *gandharva* Priyamvada—the Somnifer—while free of any thirst for sleep himself.   61

Hands too drowsy to draw the bow, helmets slipping down one shoulder, bodies slumped against a battle standard's pole, the army of princes rested in the thrall of sleep.   62

६३ ततः प्रियोपात्तरसे ऽधरौष्ठे निवेश्य दध्मौ जलजं कुमारः ।
तेन स्वहस्तार्जितमेकवीरः पिवन्यशो मूर्तिमिवाबभासे ॥

६४ शङ्खस्वनाभिज्ञतया निवृत्तास्तं सन्नशत्रुं ददृशुः स्वयोधाः ।
निमीलितानामिव पङ्कजानां मध्ये स्फुरन्तं प्रतिमाशशाङ्कम् ॥

६५ सशोणितैस्तेन शिलीमुखाग्रैर्निक्षेपिताः केतुषु पार्थिवानाम् ।
यशो हृतं संयति राघवेण न जीवितं वः कृपयेति वर्णाः ॥

६६ स चापकोटीनिहितैकबाहुः शिरस्त्रनिष्कर्षणभिन्नमौलिः ।
ललाटबद्धश्रमवारिबिन्दुर्भीतां प्रियामेत्य वचो बभाषे ॥

६७ इतः परानर्भककहार्यशस्तान्वैदर्भि पश्यानुमता मयैतान् ।
एवंविधेनाहवचेष्टितेन त्वं प्रार्थ्यसे हस्तगता ममैभिः ॥

६८ तस्याः प्रतिद्वन्द्विभवाद्विषादात्सद्यो विमुक्तं मुखमाबभासे ।
निःश्वासवाष्पापगमे प्रपन्नः प्रसादमात्मीयमिवात्मदर्शः ॥

६९ हृष्टापि सा ह्रीविजिता न साक्षा-
द्राग्निः सखीनां प्रियमभ्यनन्दत् ।
स्थली नवाम्भःपृषताभिवृष्टा
मयूरकेकाभिरिवाभ्रकालम् ॥

Then, setting a conch against his lower lip, which had now   63
    tasted the sweetness of his beloved, the crown prince
    blew as if, having seized glory with his own hands
    in battle unaided, he was now drinking it in liquid
    form.[18]

Recognizing the sound of the conch, his troops returned   64
    and beheld him with his enemies asleep around him,
    like a reflection of the moon shimmering in water
    surrounded by lotus blossoms that have folded closed.

With bloody arrowheads he had written on the princes'   65
    flags these words: "The scion of the Raghus' line has
    taken your glory in war, but out of pity not your lives!"

Aja approached his frightened wife and, with one arm   66
    leaning on the tip of his bow, hair disheveled from
    removing his helmet, and drops of sweat beading his
    brow, spoke these words:

"Look, princess of Vidarbha—you have my permission—   67
    at those enemies over there: a child could take their
    weapons from them! By such acts of war they hoped
    to win you, but you are in my hands."

Suddenly freed from the despondency brought on by these   68
    rivals, her face shone like a mirror that returns to its
    natural limpidity when the steam of a sigh evaporates.

Euphoric, but overpowered by bashfulness, she showed   69
    her delight in her beloved not directly but through the
    speeches of her friends, just as land when showered
    with drops of fresh rain shows its delight in the
    monsoon through the cries of peacocks.

७० इति शिरसि स वामं पादमाधाय राज्ञाम्
उदवहदनवद्यां तामवद्यादपेतः।
रथतुरगरजोभिस्तस्य रूक्षालकाग्रा
समरविजयलक्ष्मीः सैव मूर्ता बभूव॥

७१ प्रथमपरिगतार्थस्तं रघुः सन्निवृत्तं
विजयिनमभिनन्द्य श्लाघ्यजायासमेतम्।
तदुपहितकुटुम्बश्रीरमादातुमैच्छ-
न्न हि सति कुलधुर्ये सूर्यवंश्या गृहाय॥

इति रघुवंशे महाकाव्ये सप्तमः सर्गः॥

168

Having thus placed his foot upon the princes' heads, the 70
faultless Aja carried away his faultless bride. With
her locks powdered by the dust raised by his chariot's
horses, she looked as if she were the Lakshmi of
Victory in War, incarnate.

Raghu, who had already learned all that had happened, 71
shared Aja's joy when he returned victorious in the
company of his praiseworthy wife. He handed over to
the prince the cares of the household and was eager
to put on bast garments; for, when a son is ready to
support the family, kings of the solar line will not
remain householders.[19]

अष्टमः सर्गः

१ अथ तस्य विवाहकौतुकं ललितं बिभ्रत एव पार्थिवः ।
वसुधामपि हस्तगामिनीमकरोदिन्दुमतीमिवापराम् ॥

२ दुरितैरपि कर्तुमात्मसात्प्रयतन्ते नृपसूनवो हि यत् ।
तदुपस्थितमग्रहीदजः पितुराज्ञेति न भोगतृष्णया ॥

३ अनुभूय वसिष्ठसंभृतैः सलिलैस्तस्य महाभिषेचनम् ।
विशदोच्छ्वसितेन मेदिनी कथयामास कृतार्थतामिव ॥

४ स बभूव दुरासदो ऽरिभिर्गुरुणाथर्वविदा कृतक्रियः ।
पवनाग्निसमागमो ह्ययं सहितं ब्रह्म यदस्लतेजसा ॥

५ रघुमेव निवृत्तयौवनं तममन्यन्त नवेश्वरं प्रजाः ।
स हि तस्य न केवलां श्रियं प्रतिपेदे सकलानुणानपि ॥

६ अधिकं शुशुभे शुभंयुना द्वितयेन द्वयमेव संगतम् ।
पदमृद्धमजेन पैतृकं विनयेनास्य नवं च यौवनम् ॥

७ सदयं बुभुजे महाभुजः सहसोद्वेगमियं व्रजेदिति ।
अचिरोपनतां स मेदिनीं नवपाणिग्रहणां वधूमिव ॥

CHAPTER 8
Aja's Lament

Now while Aja was still wearing the lovely marriage
    thread, the king entrusted to his hands the earth as
    well, as if she were another Indumati.[1]

What some princes will even commit crimes to make their
    own came of itself to him. And Aja accepted it, not
    out of thirst for pleasure, but because his father so
    commanded.

Having experienced Aja's great consecration with water
    brought by Vasishtha, the earth seemed to express her
    contentment with cloud-white sighs.[2]

Consecrated by his guru, who knew the Atharvan spells,
    he became unassailable to his enemies. To yoke
    brahman with the might of arms is to join wind and
    fire.[3]

His subjects looked upon him, their new king, as upon
    Raghu himself restored to youth, for he had inherited
    not only Raghu's glory but all his virtues too.

Two things, united with two other excellent ones, shone
    yet brighter: the lofty station inherited from his
    father, united with Aja, and his own youthfulness,
    united with courtesy.

Strong-armed Aja enjoyed the newly gained earth
    gently, treating her like his newly wedded wife, lest
    vehemence should make her take fright.

1

2

3

4

5

6

7

८ अहमेव मतो ऽस्य भूपतेरिति सर्वः प्रकृतिष्वचिन्तयत् ।
उदधेरिव निम्नगाशतेष्वभवन्नास्य विमानना क्वचित् ॥

९ परुषो न न भूयसा मृदुः पवमानः पृथिवीरुहानिव ।
स पुरस्कृतमध्यमक्रमो नमयामास नृपाननुद्धरन् ॥

१० अथ वीक्ष्य गुणैः प्रतिष्ठितं प्रकृतिष्वात्मजमाभिगामिकैः ।
पदवीं परिणामदेशितां रघुरादत्त वनान्तगामिनीम् ॥

११ गुणवत्स्वधिरोपितश्रियः परिणामे हि दिलीपवंशजाः ।
पदवीं तरुवल्कवाससां यदि वा संयमिनां प्रपेदिरे ॥

१२ तमरण्यसमाश्रयोन्मुखं शिरसा वेष्टनशोभिना सुतः ।
पितरं प्रणिपत्य पादयोरपरित्यागमयाचतात्मनः ॥

१३ रघुरसुमुखस्य तस्य तत् कृतवानीप्सितमात्मजप्रियः ।
न तु सर्प इव त्वचं पुनः प्रतिपेदे व्यपसर्जितां श्रियम् ॥

१४ स बहिः क्षितिपालवेश्मनो निवसन्नावसथे यतिव्रतः ।
समुपास्यत पुत्रभोग्यया सुषयेवाविकृतेन्द्रियः श्रिया ॥

१५ प्रशमस्थितपूर्वपार्थिवं कुलमूर्जस्वलनूतनेश्वरम् ।
नभसा निभृतेन्दुना तुलामुदितार्केण समारुरोह तत् ॥

All of his courtiers thought, *The king holds me alone in high*   8
regard. Like the ocean for his hundreds of rivers, he
had disdain for none.

Neither harsh nor too gentle, but following the middle   9
path, like the wind among trees, he caused other kings
to bow down to him without uprooting them.

When he saw Aja firmly established among his subjects,   10
thanks to the virtues that made him approachable,
Raghu took the path old age dictated that leads to the
forest.[4]

For in old age the scions of Dilipa's line would transfer   11
their royal majesty to worthy sons and take the path of
bark-clad hermits or of ascetics.[5]

When he was about to retire to the forest, his son fell at his   12
feet, with his head resplendent with the kingly turban,
and begged Raghu not to abandon him.

Since his son was dear to him, Raghu accepted this   13
request, made with tear-stained face; but he would
not take back his royal majesty again, like a snake the
skin it has sloughed.

He lived in a dwelling outside the palace, keeping the vows   14
of an ascetic. There Royal Fortune waited on him like
a daughter-in-law, but she was now enjoyed by his son,
and he remained indifferent to her attractions.

The royal family, its old king at peace and its new king   15
bursting with energy, resembled the sky when the
moon is setting and the sun has risen.

१६ यतिपार्थिवलिङ्गधारिणौ दद्दशाते रघुराघवौ जनैः ।
    अपवर्गमहोदयार्थयोर्भुवमंशाविव धर्मयोर्गतौ ॥

१७ समपृच्यत भूपतिर्युवा सचिवैः प्रत्यहमर्थसिद्धये ।
    अपुनर्जननोपपत्तये प्रवयाः संयुयुजे मनीषिभिः ॥

१८ अनुरञ्जयितुं प्रजाः प्रभुर्व्यवहारासनमाददे नवः ।
    अपरः शुचिविष्टराश्रयः परिचेतुं यतते स्म धारणाः ॥

१९ अनयत्प्रभुशक्तिसम्पदा वशमेको नृपतीननन्तरान् ।
    अपरः प्रणिधानयोग्यया मरुतः पञ्च शरीरगोचरान् ॥

२० नयचक्षुरजो दिद्दक्षया पररन्ध्रस्य ततान मण्डले ।
    हृदये समरोपयन्मनः परमं ज्योतिरवेक्षितुं रघुः ॥

२१ अकरोदचिरेश्वरः क्षितौ द्विषदारम्भफलानि भस्मसात् ।
    इतरो दहने स्वकर्मणां ववृते ज्ञानमयेन वह्निना ॥

२२ पणबन्धमुखान्गुणानजः षडुपायुङ्क्त समीक्ष्य तत्फलम् ।
    रघुरध्यगमद्गुणत्रयं प्रकृतिस्थं समलोष्टकाञ्चनः ॥

२३ न नवः प्रभुरा फलोदयात्स्थिरकर्मा विरराम कर्मणः ।
    न च योगविधेर्नवेतरः स्थितधीरा परमार्थदर्शनात् ॥

With Raghu bearing the insignia of an ascetic and Aja   16
those of a king, the people regarded them as partial
incarnations of two dharmas come to earth: one
aiming at final liberation, the other at supreme
lordship.

The young king daily met with his ministers to settle   17
affairs of state; the older one frequented wise men so
that he might never be reborn again.[6]

The new king occupied the seat of judgment to serve his   18
subjects; the other, seated upon a cushion of pure
grass, strove to master the techniques of meditation.

One subdued nearby kings by means of his royal might,   19
the other the body's five breaths by practice of
meditation.[7]

With his eye of statecraft, Aja surveyed the hostile and   20
friendly powers around him, anxious to discern his
enemies' weaknesses; Raghu focused his mind in his
heart in order to perceive the supreme light.[8]

The new lord reduced to ashes the fruits of his foes'   21
endeavors on earth; the other worked to burn up his
own karma with the fire of knowledge.[9]

Aja employed the six "strands of strategy," friendship   22
and the rest, after assessing their outcomes; Raghu
recognized the three "strands of existence" as
undifferentiated within primal matter, and held gold
to be no different from clay.[10]

The new king, steadfast in action, did not cease from   23
action before reaching his goal, while the old king,
steadfast in thought, did not cease from the practice
of yoga before seeing the ultimate truth.[11]

175

२४ इति शत्रुषु चेन्द्रियेषु च प्रतिषिद्धप्रसरेषु जाग्रतौ ।
प्रसितावुदयापवर्गयोरुभयीं सिद्धिमुभाववापतुः ॥

२५ अथ काश्चिदजव्यपेक्षया गमयित्वा समदर्शनः समाः ।
तमसः परमापदव्ययं पुरुषं योगसमाधिना रघुः ॥

२६ श्रुतदेहविसर्जनः पितुश्चिरमसूणि विसृज्य राघवः ।
विततान समं पुरोधसा क्रतुमन्त्यं पृथिवीशतक्रतोः ॥

२७ विदधे च तदौर्ध्वदैहिकं पितृभक्त्या पितृकार्यकल्पवित् ।
न हि तेन पथा तनूत्यजस्तनयावर्जितपिण्डकाङ्क्षिणः ॥

२८ स परार्ध्यगतेरशोच्यतां पितुरुद्दिश्य सदर्थवेदिभिः ।
शमिताधिरधिज्यकार्मुकः कृतवानप्रतिशासनं जगत् ॥

२९ क्षितिरिन्दुमती च भामिनी पतिमासाद्य तमग्र्यपौरुषम् ।
प्रथमा बहुरत्नसूर्भूदपरा वीरमजीजनत्सुतम् ॥

३० दशरश्मिशतोपमद्युतिं यशसा दिक्षु दशस्वपि श्रुतम् ।
दशपूर्वरथं यमाख्यया दशकण्ठारिगुरुं विदुर्बुधाः ॥

176

Thus both remained watchful, the one toward his enemies,   24
    the other toward his senses, holding in check the
    activities of each; assiduous, they both attained
    success in their domains: dominion and liberation.

For Aja's sake Raghu allowed some years to pass, looking   25
    on all things with equanimity. Then, by means of
    yogic meditation, he joined the eternal soul beyond
    darkness.

Upon hearing that he had shed his body, Raghu's son long   26
    shed tears, then arranged, with his chaplain, the final
    sacrifice for his father, who thus became an "Indra of a
    hundred sacrifices" on earth.[12]

And, knowing the procedure for the rituals for the   27
    ancestors, he performed the rites for the deceased out
    of love for his father. For those who quit the body by
    such a path do not need a son's food offerings.

Knowers of truth explained that his father should not be   28
    mourned, since he had reached the ultimate goal. So
    Aja, his grief assuaged, set his string to his bow and
    made the world free of all rival rule.

Once earth and spirited Indumati had obtained him as   29
    their valorous husband, the former brought forth
    abundant gems, and the latter gave birth to a brave
    son,

bright as the ten-hundred-rayed sun, his fame celebrated   30
    in all ten directions, known to the wise by the name
    Dasharatha, "Ten Chariots," father of the foe of
    ten-headed Ravana.

३१ ऋषिदेवगणस्वधाभुजां श्रुतयागप्रसवैः स पार्थिवः ।
अनृणत्वमुपेयिवान्बभौ परिधेर्मुक्त इवोष्णदीधितिः ॥

३२ बलमार्तभयोपशान्तये विदुषां सन्नतये बहु श्रुतम् ।
वसु तस्य न केवलं विभोर्गुणवत्तापि परप्रयोजनम् ॥

३३ स कदाचिदवेक्षितप्रजः सह देव्या विजहार सुप्रजाः ।
नगरोपवने शचीसखो मरुतां पालयितेव नन्दने ॥

३४ अथ रोधसि दक्षिणोदधेः श्रितगोकर्णनिकेतमीश्वरम् ।
उपवीणयितुं मुनिः पथा पवमानस्य जगाम नारदः ॥

३५ कुसुमैर्ग्रथितामपार्थिवैः स्रजमातोद्यशिरोनिवेशिताम् ।
अहरत्किल तस्य वेगवानधिवासस्पृहयेव मारुतः ॥

३६ भ्रमरैः सुमनोनुसारिभिर्विनिकीर्णा परिवादिनी मुनेः ।
ददृशे पवनावलेपजं सृजती वाष्पमिवाञ्जनाबिलम् ॥

३७ अभिभूय विभूतिमार्तवीं पटुगन्धातिशयेन वीरुधाम् ।
स्रगसज्यत सा महीपतेर्दयितोरश्छदकोटिरत्रयोः ॥

३८ क्षणमात्रसखीं सुजातयोः स्तनयोस्तामवलोक्य विह्वला ।
पुनरप्रतिबोधलब्धये निमिमील क्षितिपालसुन्दरी ॥

178

Now that he had discharged his debts to sages, gods, and   31
    ancestors by Vedic study, sacrifices, and offspring, the
    king shone like the sun freed from a ring of haze.

His power was used to allay the fears of those in distress   32
    and his wide learning to honor scholars: not only the
    king's riches but his virtues too were used for the
    benefit of others.

One day the king, his subjects well cared for and his son   33
    thriving, was diverting himself in a garden by the city
    with his queen, like Indra, lord of winds, with Shachi
    in the heavenly garden Nandana.

Just then, the sage Narada was passing by along the path   34
    of the wind to sing and play the vina before Shiva, who
    was staying at his temple in Gokarna on the shore of
    the southern ocean.[13]

There was a garland woven of heavenly flowers tied to the   35
    head of his vina, and a swift wind, they say, snatched it
    away, as if coveting its fragrance.

With the bees that covered it in pursuit of the flowers,   36
    the sage's vina seemed to shed kohl-sullied tears,
    provoked by the rudeness of the wind.[14]

The garland, whose intense perfume overwhelmed the   37
    vernal fragrance of the flowering plants, became
    caught on those two jewels, the tips of the queen's
    breasts.

The king's beloved blenched when she saw that garland,   38
    the fleeting companion of her beautiful breasts, and
    closed her eyes, never to regain consciousness.

३९ सममेव नराधिपेन सा गुरुसम्मोहविलुप्तचेतसा ।
अगमत्सह तैलबिन्दुना नवदीपार्चिरिव क्षितेस्तलम् ॥

४० उभयोः परिपार्श्ववर्तिभिस्तुमुलेनार्तरवेण वेजिताः ।
विहगाः कमलाकराश्रयाः समदुःखा इव तत्र चुक्रुशुः ॥

४१ नृपतेर्व्यजनादिभिस्तमो नुनुदे सा च तथैव संस्थिता ।
प्रतिकारविधानमायुषः सति शेषे हि फलाय कल्पते ॥

४२ प्रतियोजयितव्यवल्कीसमवस्थामथ सत्त्वसम्प्लवात् ।
स निनाय नितान्तवत्सलः परिगृह्योचितमङ्गमङ्गनाम् ॥

४३ पतिरङ्कनिषण्णया तया करणप्रायणभिन्नवर्णया ।
समलक्ष्यत बिभ्रदाबिलां मृगलेखामुषसीव चन्द्रमाः ॥

४४ विललाप स वाष्पगद्गदं सहजामप्यपहाय धीरताम् ।
अभितप्तमयो ऽपि मार्दवं भजते कैव कथा शरीरिषु ॥

४५ कुसुमान्यपि गात्रसङ्गमात्रप्रभवन्त्यायुरपोहितुं यदि ।
न भविष्यति हन्त साधनं किमिवान्यत्प्रहरिष्यतो विधेः ॥

४६ मृदु वस्तु सदैव हिंसितुं मृदुनैवारभते प्रजान्तकः ।
हिमसेकविपत्तिरत्र मे नलिनी पूर्वनिदर्शनक्षमा ॥

She fell to the ground, and the king, who had lost 39
    consciousness from the overwhelming shock, fell
    along with her, just as the flame of a newly lit lamp
    falls along with a splash of oil.[15]

The loud shrieks of their attendants alarmed the birds in 40
    the lotus pond, who cried out as if they shared their
    pain.

The king was brought to by means of fans and such; she, 41
    however, remained unchanged. The use of remedies
    will only help if some span of life remains.

He took her in his arms and raised her with extreme 42
    tenderness onto his lap, her natural place; with her life
    force gone, she resembled a vina with broken strings.[16]

With her resting on his lap, her complexion altered by the 43
    flight of her senses, Aja looked like the moon at dawn,
    when the mark of the deer it bears is dimmed.

His fortitude, inborn though it was, forsook him, and he 44
    began to keen in a voice choked with tears. Even iron
    will melt when heated; what then of embodied souls?

"If even flowers can snatch life away by brushing 45
    against the body, then alas, what cannot become an
    instrument when fate is poised to strike?

"Death always sets out to destroy one delicate thing by 46
    another: the lotus that withers with a sprinkling of
    snow may serve me as first example.

४७ अथवा सुरमाल्यरूपभागशनिर्निर्मित एष कर्मणा ।
यदनेन तरुर्न पातितः क्षपिता तद्विटपाश्रया लता ॥

४८ स्रगियं यदि जीवितापहा हृदये किं निहिता न हन्ति माम् ।
विषमप्यमृतं क्वचिद्भवेदमृतं वा विषमीश्वरेच्छया ॥

४९ कृतवत्यसि नावधीरणामपराद्धे ऽपि यदा चिरं मयि ।
कथमेकपदे निरागसं जनमाभाष्यमिमं न मन्यसे ॥

५० ध्रुवमस्मि शठः शुचिस्मिते विदितः कैतववत्सलस्तव ।
परलोकमसन्निवृत्तये यदनामन्त्र्य गतासि मामितः ॥

५१ दयितां यदि तावदन्वगाद्विनिवृत्तं किमतस्त्वया विना ।
सहतां हतजीवितं मम प्रबलामात्मकृतेन वेदनाम् ॥

५२ सुरतश्रमवारिबिन्दवो न तु तावद्विरमन्ति ते मुखे ।
स्वयमस्तमितास्यहो वत क्षयिणां देहभृतामसारता ॥

५३ मनसापि न विप्रियं मया कृतपूर्वं ननु किं जहासि माम् ।
वत शब्दपतिः क्षितेरहं त्वयि मे भावनिबन्धनं मनः ॥

५४ कुसुमोत्कचितान्वलीमतश्चलयन्भृङ्गरुचस्तवालकान् ।
करभोरु करोति मारुतस्त्वदुपावर्तनशङ्कि मे मनः ॥

"Or could this have been a thunderbolt, created by karma, with the outward form of a heavenly garland? For it spared the tree but destroyed the vine clinging to its branches. 47

"If this garland is deadly, why, when placed on my heart, does it not kill me? Well, even poison may sometimes become nectar, and nectar poison, at God's will. 48

"Since you never spurned me even when I must long have been offending you, why suddenly do you refuse to address me now, when I have done nothing wrong? 49

"Surely you must think that I am false and only pretended to love you, sweet-smiling woman, since without a word to me you left this world for the next, never to return. 50

"If this wretched spirit of mine first went off in pursuit of you, beloved, then why did it return without you? Let it bear this terrible pain, then, which it brought on itself.[17] 51

"Beads of sweat from our lovemaking still start on your face—yet you yourself have slipped away. Ah, how frail are transient embodied souls! 52

"Surely even in thought I have never done anything to displease you! How then can you abandon me? As for Earth, I am her husband in name only; my heart's affections are fixed on you. 53

"When the wind tousles your curls, wreathed in flowers and black as bees, it makes me think, oh you with thighs that taper like the back of my hand, that you are coming back.[18] 54

५५ इदमुच्छ्वसितालकं मुखं तव विश्रान्तकथं दुनोति माम् ।
निशि सुप्तमिवैकपङ्कजं विरताभ्यन्तरषट्पदस्वनम् ॥

५६ तदपोहितुमर्हसि प्रिये प्रतिबोधेन विषादमाशु मे ।
ज्वलितेन गुहागतं तमस्तुहिनाद्रेरिव नक्तमोषधिः ॥

५७ शशिनं पुनरेति शर्वरी दयिता द्वन्द्वचरं पतत्रिणम् ।
इति तौ विरहान्तरक्षमौ कथमत्यन्तगता न मां दहेः ॥

५८ नवपल्लवसंस्तरे ऽपि ते मृदु दूयेत यदङ्गमर्पितम् ।
तदिदं विषहिष्यते कथं तव वामोरु चिताधिरोहणम् ॥

५९ घनचारुनितम्बगोचरा रशनेयं मुखरा तवाधुना ।
गतिविभ्रमसादनीरवा न शुचा नानुमृतेव लक्ष्यते ॥

६० कलमन्यभृतासु भाषितं कलहंसीषु गतं मनोहरम् ।
पृषतासु विलोलमीक्षितं पवनाधूतलतासु विभ्रमाः ॥

६१ त्रिदिवोत्सुकयाप्यवेक्ष्य मां निहिताः सत्यममी गुणास्त्वया ।
विरहे तव मे गुरुव्यथं हृदयं न त्ववलम्बितुं क्षमाः ॥

६२ मिथुनं परिकल्पितं त्वया सहकारः फलिनी च नन्विमौ ।
अविधाय विवाहसत्क्रियामनयोर्गम्यत इत्यसाम्प्रतम् ॥

"This face of yours, framed by windblown strands of hair 55
but no longer speaking—like a solitary lotus asleep
at night when the hum of a bee trapped inside has
ceased—torments me!

"So please, my darling, wake up again and quickly dispel 56
my sorrow, as herbs in Himalayan caves at night dispel
the darkness with their glow.[19]

"Night will rejoin the moon, the shelduck will rejoin her 57
drake; so moon and drake can bear the intervals of
separation. You are gone forever—how could you not
cause me torment?

"How will this tender frame of yours, my dear with lovely 58
thighs, which would suffer even when laid upon a bed
of fresh shoots, endure being placed upon the pyre?

"This tinkling girdle of yours that lies across your firm 59
sweet haunches is noiseless now that your graceful
step has ceased: it truly seems to follow you in death,
from grief.

"It's true that even as you were bound for heaven you 60–61
thought of me and left behind these graces of yours:
your sweet voice you left with the koels, your pleasing
gait with the geese, your darting glances with the deer,
your graceful movements with vines that sway in the
breeze. But in your absence these cannot sustain my
heavy, aching heart.

"Was it not you who arranged for this mango tree and 62
priyaṅgu vine to be united? It is not right that you
should leave without celebrating their marriage rites!

६३ स्मरतेव सशब्दनूपुरं चरणानुग्रहमन्यदुर्लभम् ।
अमुना कुसुमासुवर्षिणा त्वमशोकेन सुगात्रि शोच्यसे ॥

६४ तव निःश्वसितानुकारिभिर्ग्रथितार्धा बकुलैः समं मया ।
असमाप्य विलासमेखलां किमिदं किन्नरकण्ठि सुप्यते ॥

६५ समदुःखसुखः सखीजनः प्रतिपच्चन्द्रनिभो ऽयमात्मजः ।
अहमेकरसस्तथापि ते व्यवसायः प्रतिपत्तिनिष्ठुरः ॥

६६ धृतिरस्तमिता रतिश्च्युता विरतं गेयमृतुर्निरुत्सवः ।
गतमाभरणप्रयोजनं चिरशून्यं शयनीयमद्य मे ॥

६७ गृहिणी सचिवः सखा मिथः प्रियशिष्या ललिते कलाविधौ ।
करुणारहितेन वेधसा हरता त्वां वत किं न मे हृतम् ॥

६८ मदिराक्षि मदाननार्पितं मधु पीत्वा रसवत्कथं नु मे ।
अनुपास्यसि वाष्पदूषितं परलोकोपनतं जलाञ्जलिम् ॥

६९ विभवे ऽपि सति त्वया विना सुखमेतावदजस्य गण्यताम् ।
अहृतस्य विलोभनान्तरैर्मम सर्वे विषयास्त्वदाश्रयाः ॥

७० विलपन्निति कोसलाधिपः करुणार्थग्रथितं प्रियां प्रति ।
अकरोत्पृथिवीरुहानपि स्रुतशाखारसवाष्पदुर्दिनान् ॥

This *aśoka,* remembering the touch of your foot with   63
    its tinkling anklet—an act of grace few other trees
    could receive—is raining down tears of flowers as if
    mourning you, my lovely one.[20]

"We were in the middle of braiding a chain of *bakula*   64
    flowers as sweet-scented as your breath. How could
    you fall asleep before finishing it, my dear wife with a
    kinnarī's voice?[21]

"These confidantes share all your griefs and joys; this son   65
    of ours is like the new moon; you and I feel the same
    mutual love—and yet you have with cruel firmness
    decided to leave!

"For me, from this day on, contentment is gone, pleasure   66
    lost, song silenced. Seasons will have no festivals,
    adornments no purpose—my bed will long be empty!

"Wife, counselor, friend and, in private, beloved pupil   67
    in the sweetest of the arts—in taking you, what has
    merciless Fate not taken from me?

"You used to drink sweet wine right from my mouth,   68
    you with eyes that intoxicate like wine. How will you
    afterward drink the handful of water sullied by my
    tears that will reach you in the next world?[22]

"Though Aja still has wealth, without you his happiness   69
    must be reckoned now to be over. No other attractions
    draw me; all enjoyments depend on you."

So the king of Kosala mourned his beloved with words   70
    shot through with sorrow and made even the trees
    release the sap of their branches in floods of tears.

७१ अथ तस्य कथञ्चिदङ्कृतः स्वजनस्तामपनीय सुन्दरीम् ।
विससर्ज तदन्तमण्डनामनलायागुरुचन्दनैधसे ॥

७२ प्रमदामनु संस्थितः शुचा क्षितिपः सन्निति वाच्यदर्शनात् ।
न चकार शरीरमग्निसात्सह देव्या न तु जीविताशया ॥

७३ अथ तेन दशाहतः परे गुणशेषामपदिश्य सुन्दरीम् ।
विदुषा विधयो महर्द्धयः पुर एवोपवने वितेनिरे ॥

७४ स विवेश पुरीं तया विना क्षणदापायशशाङ्कदर्शनः ।
परिवाहमिवावलोकयन्स्वशुचः पौरवधूमुखासुषु ॥

७५ तमवेक्ष्य मखाय दीक्षितः प्रणिधानादुरुराश्रमाश्रयः ।
अभिषङ्गिणमीश्वरं विशामिति शिष्येण किलान्वबोधयत् ॥

७६ असमाप्तविधिर्यतो मुनिस्तव विद्वानपि तापकारणम् ।
न भवन्तमुपस्थितः स्वयं प्रकृतौ स्थापयितुं कृतस्थितिः ॥

७७ मयि तस्य सुवृत्त वर्तते लघुसन्देशपदा सरस्वती ।
शृणु विश्रुतसत्त्वसार तां हृदि चैनामुपधातुमर्हसि ॥

७८ त्रिषु धामसु शार्ङ्गधन्वनः समतीतं च भवच्च भावि च ।
स हि निष्प्रतिघेन चक्षुषा त्रितयं ज्ञानमयेन पश्यति ॥

Then, with difficulty, his relatives took the beautiful   71
Indumati from his embrace. With the same
ornaments adorning her in death, they consigned her
to the pyre of agarwood and sandal.[23]

It was only in view of censure—at killing himself, in grief,   72
for a woman, while still the world's protector—and
not because he still wanted to live, that Aja did not
burn his own body with the queen.

Then, after the ten-day ceremony, in the same garden   73
outside the city, the learned king performed in lavish
manner the remaining rites for his beautiful wife, of
whom nothing was left but her high renown.

Looking like the moon as night recedes, he entered the city   74
without her, seeing the overflowing of his own grief in
the tears on the faces of the womenfolk.

His guru was away in his ashram, consecrated for a   75
sacrifice, but he apprehended the king's pain through
meditation and, it is said, sent the following message
through a student:

"The sage who himself established the rules of conduct   76
has not yet finished his ritual. That is why, although he
knows the cause of your torment, he does not come in
person to restore you to your natural state.

"I bear the words of his brief message. Hear it, virtuous   77
man, famed for the strength of your purity, and keep it
in your heart.

"For with unimpeded eye of knowledge the sage sees past,   78
present, and future, all three in all three worlds of
bow-wielding Vishnu.[24]

७९ चरतः किल दुश्चरं तपस्तृणबिन्दोः परिशङ्कितः पुरा ।
प्रजिघाय समाधिभेदिनीं हरिरस्मै हरिणीं सुराङ्गनाम् ॥

८० स तपःप्रतिबन्धमन्युना प्रमुखाविष्कृतचारुदर्शनाम् ।
अशपद्द्रव मानुषीति तां शमवेलाप्रलयोर्मिणा मुनिः ॥

८१ भगवन्परवानयं जनः प्रतिकूलाचरणं क्षमस्व मे ।
इति चोपनतां क्षितिस्पृशं कृतवाना सुरमाल्यदर्शनात् ॥

८२ क्रथकैशिकवंशसम्भवा तव भूत्वा महिषी चिराय सा ।
मुनिशापनिवृत्तिकारणं ध्रुवमापाशु यतस्तनुं जहौ ॥

८३ तदलं तदपायचिन्तया विपदुत्पत्तिमतामवस्थिता ।
वसुधेयमवेक्ष्यतां त्वया वसुमत्या हि नृपाः कलत्रिणः ॥

८४ उदये यदवाप्यमुज्झता श्रुतमाविष्कृतमात्मनस्त्वया ।
मनसस्तदुपस्थिते ज्वरे पुनरक्लीवतया प्रकाश्यताम् ॥

८५ रुदता कुत एव सा पुनर्भवता नानुमृतेरवाप्यते ।
परलोकजुषां स्वकर्मभिर्गतयो भिन्नपथाः शरीरिणाम् ॥

"Long ago, it is said, Indra stood in fear of a certain   79
     Trinabindu, who was performing rigorous asceticism.
     And so he sent the celestial nymph Harini to him,
     since she was capable of breaking his meditation.

"In a rage at this obstacle to his austerities—rage like a   80
     diluvial wave bursting the bounds of his calm—the
     sage cursed her for unveiling her beauty before him,
     saying: 'Become a mortal woman!'

"Yet when she bowed to him, saying, 'Blessed lord, this   81
     person before you answers to another. Forgive me for
     my untoward behavior!' he granted that she should
     live on earth only until she should catch sight of a
     celestial garland.

"She took birth in the lineage of the Krathakaishikas;   82
     became your queen for a while; and then it is clear she
     met the thing that ended the sage's curse, after which
     she quickly left her body.

"Stop brooding therefore on her passing: death is a   83
     constant for creatures that take birth! Look to this
     earth, for Earth is the one true wife of kings.

"At your ascent, you showed your wisdom by not giving   84
     way to your feelings. Now that affliction has assailed
     your mind, show the same wisdom again by not being
     unmanly.

"By dying after her you cannot regain her; how could   85
     you possibly do so by weeping? Souls go to their next
     life by different roads, in accordance with their past
     actions.

८६ अपशोकमतः कुटुम्बिनीमनुगृह्णीष्व निवापदत्तिभिः ।
स्वजनासु किलातिसन्ततं दहति प्रेतमिति प्रचक्षते ॥

८७ मरणं प्रकृतिः शरीरिणां विकृतिर्जीवितमुच्यते बुधैः ।
क्षणमप्यवतिष्ठते श्वसन्यदि जन्तुर्ननु लाभवानसौ ॥

८८ अवगच्छति मूढचेतनः प्रियनाशं हृदि शल्यमर्पितम् ।
इतरस्तु तदेव मन्यते कुशलद्वारतया समुद्धृतम् ॥

८९ स्वशरीरशरीरिणावपि स्मृतसंयोगविपर्ययौ यदा ।
विरहः किमिवानुतापयेद्दृढबाह्यौर्विषयैर्विपश्चितम् ॥

९० न पृथग्जनवच्छुचो वशं वशिनामुत्तम गन्तुमर्हसि ।
द्रुमसानुमतोः किमन्तरं यदि वायौ द्वितये ऽपि ते चलाः ॥

९१ स तथेति विनेतुरुदारमतेः प्रतिगृह्य वचो विससर्ज मुनिम् ।
तदलब्धपदं हृदि शोकघने प्रतियातमिवान्तिकमस्य गुरोः ॥

९२ तेनाष्टौ परिगमिताः समाः कथञ्चि-
द्वालत्वादवितथसूनृतेन सूनोः ।
साहृश्यप्रतिकृतिदर्शनैः प्रियायाः
स्वप्नेषु क्षणिकसमागमोत्सवैश्च ॥

"Do not grieve, then, as you succor your wife with the   86
    offerings for the departed. They say the ceaseless flow
    of kinsmen's tears torments the departed.[25]

"Death, say the wise, is the soul's natural state; it is life   87
    that is unnatural. If a creature remains breathing for
    even a moment, then surely he is fortunate.

"The deluded regard the loss of a loved one like a stake   88
    plunged into the heart, but others see it as a stake
    pulled out, since it is a means to salvation.

"When it is taught that even body and soul unite and   89
    separate, tell me, should any sensible person then be
    distressed when losing outward things?

"You are a man of great self-control. Do not give way to   90
    grief like some ordinary person. What difference
    would there be between a tree and a mountain if both
    were to sway in the wind?"

With a word of assent he acknowledged the message of his   91
    high-minded preceptor, and dismissed the sage. But it
    found no place in his grief-laden heart, and returned,
    as it were, to his guru.

The king, a man of true and pleasing speech, somehow   92
    made it through eight years, his son being a child still,
    by gazing at pictures of his beloved or likenesses of
    her in other things, and by fleeting festivals of reunion
    with her in dreams.

९३ तस्य प्रसह्य हृदयं किल शोकशङ्कुः
प्लक्षप्ररोह इव सौधतलं बिभेद ।
प्राणान्तहेतुमपि तं भिषजामसाध्यं
लाभं प्रियानुगमनत्वरया स मेने ॥

९५ सम्यग्विनीतमथ वर्महरं कुमारम्
आदिश्य रक्षणविधौ विधिवत्प्रजानाम् ।
रोगोपसृष्टतनुदुर्वसतिं मुमुक्षुः
प्रायोपवेशनमतिर्नृपतिर्बभूव ॥

९५ तीर्थे तोयव्यतिकरभवे जह्नुकन्यासरय्वोर्
देहत्यागादमरगणनालेख्यमासाद्य सद्यः ।
पूर्वाकाराधिकतररुचा सङ्गतः कान्तयासौ
लीलागारेष्वरमत पुनर्नन्दनाभ्यन्तरेषु ॥

इति रघुवंशे महाकाव्ये ऽष्टमः सर्गः ॥

A stake of grief, it seems, forced its way into his heart and,   93
like a peepal sapling on a mansion roof, slowly cracked
it open. Even though doctors could not cure it, and
it would cause his death, he was eager to follow his
beloved and took it as a blessing.

Then, when the prince was fully educated and could bear   94
armor, the king charged him with protecting his
subjects in accordance with the law, and, longing to
quit the wretched abode of his disease-ridden body,
resolved on a fast unto death.

Abandoning his body at the confluence of the Ganga   95
and the Sarayu, he at once joined the ranks of the
immortals. Reunited with his beloved, now even
more radiant in form than she was before, he took
his pleasure in the pavilions of the celestial garden
Nandana.

नवमः सर्गः

१ पितुरनन्तरमुत्तरकोसलान् समधिगम्य समाधिजितेन्द्रियः ।
   दशरथः प्रशशास महारथो यमवतामवतां च धुरि स्थितः ॥

२ अधिगतं विधिवद्वदपालयत्प्रकृतिमण्डलमात्मकुलोचितम् ।
   अभवदस्य ततो गुणतत्परं सनगरं नगरन्ध्रकरौजसः ॥

३ उभयमेव वदन्ति मनीषिणः समयवर्षितया कृतकर्मणाम् ।
   बलनिषूदनमर्थपतिं च तं श्रमनुदं मनुदण्डधरान्वयम् ॥

४ जनपदे न गदः पदमादधावभिभवः कुत एव सपत्नजः ।
   क्षितिरभूत्फलवत्यजनन्दने शमरते ऽमरतेजसि पार्थिवे ॥

५ दशदिगन्तजिता रघुणा यथा श्रियमपुष्यदजेन ततः परम् ।
   तमधिगम्य तथैव पुनर्बभौ न न महीनमहीनपराक्रमम् ॥

६ समतया वसुवृष्टिविसर्जनैर्नियमनादसतां च नराधिपः ।
   अनुययौ यमपुण्यजनेश्वरौ सवरुणावरुणाग्रसरं रुचा ॥

196

CHAPTER 9
Dasharatha Goes Hunting

After his father's death, Dasharatha inherited and ruled 1
  over Uttarakosala. Conqueror of his senses by
  concentration, and a great chariot warrior, he was
  foremost both among yogins and among protectors.[1]
His valor was like that of Skanda, splitter of mountains. 2
  Because he duly protected what he had inherited, the
  ministers loyal to his family, along with the citizenry,
  devoted themselves to virtue.
Only two beings, say the wise, rain down timely rewards 3
  and thus dispel the weariness of those who work:
  Indra and a king of the lineage of scepter-wielding
  Manu.
Under the rule of Aja's peace-loving son of god-like 4
  splendor, not even disease entered the country, much
  less afflictions caused by the enemy; and the land
  yielded crops.
Just as the earth flourished thanks to Raghu, who 5
  conquered the ten directions, and then thanks to Aja,
  so too, when it had acquired as its king the no less
  valorous Dasharatha, it did not fail to prosper.[2]
That lord of men imitated Yama in evenhandedness, 6
  Kubera in showering wealth, Varuna in punishing
  wrongdoers, and the sun in splendor.

७ न मृगदावरतिर्न दुरोदरं न च शशिप्रतिमाभरणं मधु ।
तमुदयाय न वा नवयौवनाः प्रियतमा यतमानमपाहरन् ॥

८ न कृपणा प्रभवत्यपि वासवे न वितथा परिहासकथास्वपि ।
अपि सपत्नजने न च तेन वागपरुषा परुषाक्षरमीरिता ॥

९ उदयमस्तमयं च रघूद्बहादुभयमानशिरे वसुधाधिपाः ।
स हि निदेशमलङ्घ्यतामभूत्सुहृदयोहृदयः प्रतिगर्जताम् ॥

१० जघननिर्विषयीकृतमेखलाननुचितासुविलुप्तविशेषकान् ।
स रिपुदारगणानकरोद्बलादनलकानलकाधिपविक्रमः ॥

११ अवनिमेकरथेन वरूथिना जितवतः किल तस्य धनुर्भृतः ।
विजयदुन्दुभितां ययुरर्णवा घनरवा नरवाहनसम्पदः ॥

१२ स्फुरितकोटिसहस्रमरीचिना समचिनोत्कुलिशेन हरिर्यशः ।
स धनुषा युधि सायकवर्षिणा स्वनवता नवतामरसाननः ॥

१३ चरणयोर्नखरागसमृद्धिभिर्मुकुटरत्नमरीचिभिरस्पृशन् ।
नृपतयः शतशो मरुतो यथा शतमखं तमखण्डितपौरुषम् ॥

Not the love of game parks, nor gambling, nor wine graced   7
    with the reflected moon, nor beauties in the bloom of
    youth distracted him as he strove for success.

He did not speak cravenly even when Indra wielded his   8
    power; he did not speak falsely even in jest; and being
    free of anger, he did not speak harshly even to his
    adversaries.

Vassal kings experienced both rises and falls under the   9
    chief of the Raghus, for he was kindhearted to those
    who did not flout his orders, but ironhearted toward
    those who talked back.[3]

Girdle chains no longer found place on the hips of his   10
    enemies' wives; the painted ornaments were wiped
    from their cheeks by unfamiliar tears; and their hair
    no longer was perfumed and powdered in locks when
    he, valorous as Kubera, slew their husbands.

The roaring oceans became victory drums for that   11
    bow-wielding king, wealthy as Kubera, once he had
    conquered the earth with his single armored chariot.

Indra amassed his fame with a thunderbolt shooting   12
    thousands of rays from its coruscant points; fresh-
    lotus-faced Dasharatha did so with a resounding bow
    raining down arrows in battle.

His valor unassailable, kings in their hundreds caressed   13
    his feet with the rays of their diadem gems, intensified
    by the red glow of his nails, just as the gods caress the
    feet of Indra.

१४ निववृते स महार्णवरोधसः सचिवकारितबालसुताञ्जलीन् ।
समनुकम्प्य सपत्नपरिग्रहाननलकानलकानवमां पुरीम् ॥

१५ उपगतो ऽपि च मण्डलनाभितामनुचितान्यसितातपवारणः ।
श्रियमवेक्ष्य स रन्ध्रचलामभूदनलसो ऽनलसोमसमद्युतिः ॥

१६ तमलभन्त पतिं पतिदेवताः शिखरिणामिव सागरमापगाः ।
मलयकोसलकेकयशासिनां दुहितरो ऽहितरोपितमार्गणम् ॥

१७ प्रियतमाभिरसौ तिसृभिर्बभौ तिसृभिरेव भुवं सह शक्तिभिः ।
उपगतो विनिनीषुरिव प्रजा हरिहयो ऽरिहयोगविचक्षणः ॥

१८ क्रतुषु तेन विसर्जितमौलिना भुजसमाहृतदिग्वसुना कृताः ।
कनकयूपसमुच्छ्रितिशोभिनो वितमसा तमसासरयूतटाः ॥

१९ अजिनदण्डभृतं कुशमेखलां यतिगिरं मृगशृङ्गपरिग्रहाम् ।
अधिवसंस्तनुमध्वरदीक्षितामसमभासमभासयदीश्वरः ॥

After showing mercy to his enemies' wives when they 14
appeared before him with hair disheveled, their
boys prompted by counselors to fold their hands in
reverence and bow before him, Dasharatha returned
from the ocean's shore to his capital, the equal of
Alaka.

Though become the hub of the circle of kings, with no 15
other presuming to raise the white parasol, he knew
Royal Fortune flees when it finds weakness, so he was
tirelessly active, blazing now like fire and now like the
moon.[4]

The daughters of the kings of Malaya, Kekaya, and Kosala 16
were joined in marriage with him who had slain his
enemies with arrows, like mountain rivers joined with
the ocean, and held their husband a deity.[5]

With his three beloved wives, he seemed like Indra come 17
to earth with his three powers to govern the subjects,
so skilled he was in the means of destroying enemies.[6]

After gathering wealth from every quarter by the strength 18
of his own arms, he shaved his head and, free of all
tamas, beautified the banks of the Tamasa and Sarayu
by erecting gilded sacrificial posts for sacrifices.[7]

He prepared himself for performing the rite, restraining 19
his speech, taking up buckskin, staff, belt of *darbha*
grass, and antelope horn. Then the Lord* entered his
body, causing it to shine with incomparable radiance.[8]

---

* Shiva.

201

२० अवभृथप्रयतो नियतेन्द्रियः सुरसमाजसमाक्रमणोचितः ।
नमयति स्म स केवलमुन्नतं वनमुचे नमुचेररये शिरः ॥

२१ तमपहाय ककुत्स्थकुलोद्वहं पुरुषमात्मभुवं च सतीव्रता ।
नृपतिमन्यमसेवत देवता सकमला कमलाघवमर्थिषु ॥

२२ स किल संयुगमूर्धि सहायतां मघवतः प्रतिपद्य नराधिपः ।
स्वभुजवीर्यमगापयदुच्छ्रितं सुरवधूरवधूतभयाः शरैः ॥

२३ असकृदेव हि तेन तरस्विना हरिहयाग्रसरेण धनुर्भृता ।
दिनकराभिमुखा रणरेणवो रुरुधिरे रुधिरेण सुरद्विषाम् ॥

२४ अथ महेन्द्रसमं कुसुमैर्नवैस्तमिव सेवितुमेकनराधिपम् ।
उपययौ भुजगेन महीभृता समधुरं मधुरञ्जितविक्रमम् ॥

२५ हिमविवर्णितचन्दनपल्लवं विरहयन्मलयाद्रिमुदङ्मुखः ।
विहगयोः कृपयेव शनैर्ययौ रविरहर्विरहध्रुवभेदयोः ॥

२६ कुसुमजन्म ततो नवपल्लवास्तदनु षड्पदकोकिलकूजितम् ।
इति यथाक्रममाविरभून्मधुर्द्धमवतीमवतीर्य वनस्थलीम् ॥

Purified by the final ablution after sacrifice, and   20
    controlling his senses, he could well have stridden into
    the assembly of the gods. He bowed his high head,
    indeed, only before Indra, the enemy of Namuchi.[9]

Aside from Dasharatha, pride of the Kakutsthas, so   21
    generous to suppliants, and the self-born Soul,* what
    other king would she serve, the ever faithful goddess†
    who holds the lotus?

They say that when he lent his aid to Indra in the van of   22
    battle, it was this king who dispelled the fears of the
    celestial ladies with his arrows, leading them to sing of
    the might of his arms.

For often that powerful king, armed with his bow and   23
    fighting in front of Indra, stilled the dust of battle
    billowing up before the sun with the blood of the
    enemies of the gods.

Then spring arrived, as though to serve Indra's equal   24
    with fresh flowers, the one true king, revered for
    valor, bearer of a burden equal to the earth-bearing
    serpent's.‡

As though out of compassion for pairs of shelducks, fated   25
    to part at close of day, the sun moved slowly north,
    quitting Mount Malaya, its sandal sprouts pale with
    dew.[10]

Blossoms came, then fresh sprouts, and then the murmur   26
    of the bees and koels; thus did spring gradually
    appear, entering the tree-clad forest ground.

* Vishnu.
† Lakshmi.
‡ Shesha.

२७ व्रणगुरुप्रमदाधरदुःसहं जघननिर्विषयीकृतमेखलम् ।
न खलु तावदशेषमपोहितुं रविरलं विरलं कृतवान्हिमम् ॥

२८ परभृता मदनक्षतचेतसः प्रियसखी लघुवागिव योषिताम् ।
प्रियतमानकरोत्कलहान्तरे मृदुखरवादुखरवापसमागमान् ॥

२९ अभिनयान्परिचेतुमिवोद्यता मलयमारुतकम्पितपल्लवा ।
अमदयत्सहकारलता मनः सकलिका कलिकामजितामपि ॥

३० नयगुणोपचितामिव भूपतेः सदुपकारफलां श्रियमर्थिनः ।
अभिययुः सरसो मधुसम्भृतां कमलिनीमलिनीरपतत्रिणः ॥

३१ कुसुममेव न केवलमार्तवं नवमशोकतरोः स्मरदीपनम् ।
किसलयप्रसवो ऽपि विलासिनां मदयिता दयिताश्रवणार्पितः ॥

३२ विरचिता मधुनोपवनश्रियामभिनवा इव पत्त्रविशेषकाः ।
मधुलिहां मधुदानविशारदाः कुरवका रवकारणतां ययुः ॥

३३ दशनचन्द्रिकया व्यवभासितं हसितमासवगन्धि मधोरिव ।
बकुलपुष्पमसेव्यत षड्पदैः शुचिरसं चिरसञ्चितमीप्सुभिः ॥

The cold had been unbearable to ladies' lower lips, swollen   27
    with love bites, and had stopped them from wearing
    their girdle chains on their hips. At first the sun was
    not strong enough to dispel it entirely; it could only
    weaken it.[11]

The sweet-voiced koel, like a soft-spoken confidante, made   28
    it easier for women, when separated by quarrels, to
    reunite again with their beloveds whose hearts were
    tormented by love.

As if striving to express itself by gestures, the budding   29
    spray of mango, its sprouts dancing in the breeze from
    the Malaya mountains, bewitched the hearts even of
    those beyond strife and passion.[12]

Just as suppliants flock to the king's wealth, increased by   30
    good policy and benefiting the worthy, so bees and
    waterfowl flocked to the spring-nourished lotuses of
    the lakes.

Not only did the fresh seasonal flowers of the *aśoka* tree   31
    inflame lovers' passions, but so did its profusion of
    young sprigs decking the ears of their sweethearts.

Like fresh leaf designs drawn by Spring upon the cheeks   32
    of the Splendors of the gardens, the amaranths,
    practiced suppliers of nectar to the bees, set them
    a-buzzing.[13]

In quest of its clear, long-stored nectar, bees hovered over   33
    the *bakula's* flowers, which were like the smile of
    Spring, shining with the moonbeam-bright luster of
    teeth and redolent with wine.[14]

३४ सुरभिसङ्गमजं वनमालया नवपलाशमधार्यत भङ्गुरम् ।
रमणदत्तमिवार्द्रनखक्षतं प्रमदया मदयापितलज्जया ॥

३५ सुवदनावदनासवसम्भृतस्तदनुवादिगुणः कुसुमोद्गमः ।
मधुकरैरकरोन्मधुलोलुभैर्बकुलमाकुलमाततभक्तिभिः ॥

३६ ध्वजपटं मदनस्य धनुर्भृतश्छविकरं मुखचूर्णमृतुश्रियः ।
कुसुमकेसररेणुमलिव्रजाः सपवनोपवनोत्थितमन्वयुः ॥

३७ प्रथममन्यभृताभिरुदीरिताः प्रविरला इव मुग्धवधूकथाः ।
सुरभिगन्धिषु शुश्रुविरे गिरः कुसुमितासु मिता वनराजिषु ॥

३८ तिलकमस्तकहर्म्यकृतास्पदैः कुसुममध्वनुषङ्गसुगन्धिभिः ।
कलमगीयत भृङ्गविलासिनां स्मरयुतैरयुतैरबलासखैः ॥

३९ गमयितुं प्रभुरेष सुखेन मां न महतीं वत पान्थवधूजनः ।
इति दयात इवाभवदायता न रजनी रजनीशवती मधौ ॥

४० अनुभवन्नवदोलमृतूत्सवं पटुमपि प्रियकण्ठजिघृक्षया ।
अनयदासनरज्जुपरिग्रहे भुजलतां जलतामबलाजनः ॥

The row of gardens displayed the curved fresh blossoms,　34
　　born of its union with spring, of the flame-of-
　　the-forest, just as a young woman, brazen in her
　　intoxication, will display the fresh nail marks inflicted
　　by her lover.[15]

The blooming of its flowers, provoked by beautiful girls　35
　　sprinkling it with mouthfuls of wine, whose fragrance
　　the flowers echoed, made the *bakula* teem with bees
　　swarming in long trains and eager for nectar.

The swarms of bees followed the pollen rising from the　36
　　breeze-stirred park. Was it the brightening face
　　powder of vernal Glory herself, or the banner of the
　　love god armed with his bow?

The first faint sounds uttered by female koels, like the　37
　　few words of artless brides, were heard among the
　　fragrant rows of gardens in bloom.

Scented from touching the nectar of flowers, scores of　38
　　ardent bumblebees were sweetly serenading atop the
　　tilaka trees, like lovers seated with their beloveds on
　　rooftop terraces.

With the coming of spring, the moonlit night grew　39
　　shorter, as though out of compassion thinking, *These
　　wives of travelers cannot easily endure me if I am long.*

As the women enjoyed the new swings of the spring　40
　　festival, their slender arms, deft though they were,
　　fumbled to grasp the ropes—they hoped to grasp
　　instead their sweethearts around the neck.

४१ त्यजत मानमलं वत विग्रहैर्न पुनरेति गतं चतुरं वयः ।
परभृताभिरितीव निवेदिते स्मरमते ऽरमतेष्टसखो जनः ॥

४२ अनलसान्यभृतानलसान्मनः कमलधूलिमता मरुतेरिता ।
कुसुमभारनताध्वगयोषितामसमशोकमशोकलताकरोत् ॥

४३ लघयति स्म न पत्यपराधजां
न सहकारतरुस्तरुणीधृताम् ।
कुसुमितो ऽलमितो ऽलिभिरुन्मदैः
स्मरसमाधिकरो ऽधिकरोषिताम् ॥

४४ श्रुतिसुखभ्रमरस्वनगीतयः कुसुमकोमलदन्तरुचो बभुः ।
उपवनान्तलताः पवनाहतैः किसलयैः सलयैरिव पाणिभिः ॥

४५ अपतुषारतया विशदप्रभैः सुरतरागपरिश्रमनोदिभिः ।
कुसुमचापमतेजयदंशुभिर्हिमकरो मकरोर्जितकेतनम् ॥

४६ हुतहुताशनदीप्ति वनश्रियः प्रतिनिधिः कनकाभरणस्य यत् ।
युवतयः कुसुमं दधुराहितं तदलके दलकेसरपेशलम् ॥

४७ अलिभिरञ्जनबिन्दुमनोहरैः कुसुमभक्तिनिपातिभिरङ्कितः ।
न खलु शोभयति स्म वनस्थलीं न तिलकस्तिलकः प्रमदामिव ॥

"Give up your pride! Oh stop your quarrels! Once 41
    charming youth has gone, it won't return"—when
    female koels announced, it seemed, this decree of
    love, loving couples embraced each other.

The slender *aśoka* tree with its busy koels, bowed under 42
    its burden of flowers and stirred by a wind laden with
    lotus pollen, burned up the hearts of travelers' wives,
    whose sorrow was like no other.

The mango tree did not fail to lessen the strong anger 43
    young women bore when wronged by their husbands,
    for fully in bloom and swarming with intoxicated bees,
    it made everyone intent on love.

The gardens' branches were alive with the sweet singing of 44
    the drone of bees, their flowers like tender teeth, and
    they glimmered with shoots lifted by the breeze, like
    hands forming the gestures of a dancer.

Kama was already armed with his bow of flowers, and his 45
    fish banner shone bright, but the moon, by removing
    the fatigue of lovemaking with its bright cool rays,
    undimmed by mists, made him stronger yet.

Young women now wore in their hair that flower with 46
    delicate petals and filaments which Vernal Beauty
    wears as golden ornament, lustrous as a fire ablaze
    with oblations.[16]

The *tilaka* tree adorned the woodland indeed, as a *tilaka* 47
    adorns a girl; the bees that crowded it, falling upon its
    display of flowers, added the charm of drops of kohl.[17]

४८ ललितविभ्रमबन्धविचक्षणं सुरभिगन्धपराजितकेसरम् ।
पतिषु निर्विविशुर्मधुमङ्गनाः स्मरसखं रसखण्डनवर्जितम् ॥

४९ शुशुभिरे स्मितचारुतराननाः स्त्रिय इव श्लथशिञ्जितमेखलाः ।
विकचतामरसा गृहदीर्घिका मदकलोदकलोलविहङ्गमाः ॥

५० अमदयन्मधुगन्धसनाथया किसलयाधरसङ्गतया मनः ।
कुसुमसंभृतया नवमालिका स्मितरुचा तरुचारुविलासिनी ॥

५१ अरुणरागनिषेविविभिरंशुकैरलकलब्धपदैश्च यवाङ्कुरैः ।
परभृताविरुतैश्च विलासिनः स्मरबलैरबलैकरसाः कृताः ॥

५२ विषदचन्द्रकरं सुखमारुतं कुसुमितद्रुममुन्मदकोकिलम् ।
तदुपभोगरसं हिमवर्षिणः परमृतोरमृतोपमतां ययौ ॥

५३ अथ यथासुखमार्तवमुत्सवं समनुभूय विलासवतीसखः ।
नरपतिश्चकमे मृगयारतिं स मधुमन्मधुमन्मथसन्निभः ॥

५४ परिचयं चललक्ष्यनिपातने भयरुषोश्च तदिङ्गितवेदनम् ।
श्रमजयात्प्रगुणां च करोत्यसौ तनुमतो ऽनुमतः सचिवैर्ययौ ॥

Women enjoyed wine more fragrant than *bakula* flowers—   48
  wine, that friend of love who taught them to flirt with
  their husbands and allowed nothing to break the
  mood.

The ponds by the houses shone bright, the lotuses in full   49
  bloom, birds chirping sweetly as they bobbed on
  the water—they were like women bright-faced with
  smiles, their girdle chains jangling softly.

A young jasmine vine, the charming consort of a tree,   50
  intoxicated hearts with the brightness of her smile—
  brightness formed by her flowers, lying on the
  lip-shaped sprays, and paired with the fragrance of
  nectar.

Garments dyed safflower red; barley sprouts that found   51
  their place among locks of hair; the calls of female
  koels—all these, divisions of Love's army, caused
  lovers to delight only in their beloveds.

The moonlight brightened; breezes brought delight; trees   52
  blossomed; koels grew frenzied—thus the successor
  of the season of falling snows, a time when all long for
  enjoyment, turned ambrosial.

Now, after enjoying the spring festival at ease in the   53
  company of amorous women, the king, who was at
  once like Vishnu, Spring, and Love, longed for the
  pleasures of hunting.

He set off with his ministers' approval, since the hunt   54
  brings skill in hitting moving targets, teaches how
  they act in fear or anger, and strengthens the body by
  training it to overcome fatigue.[18]

५५ मृगवनोपगमक्षमवेशभृद्द्विपुलकण्ठनिषक्तशरासनः ।
गगनमश्वखुरोद्धतरेणुभिर्नृसविता सवितानमिवाकरोत् ॥

५६ ग्रथितमौलिरसौ वनमालया नवपलाशसवर्णतनुच्छदः ।
तुरगवल्गनचञ्चलकुण्डलो विरुरुचे रुरुचेष्टितभूमिषु ॥

५७ तनुलताविनिवेशितविग्रहा भ्रमरसङ्कमितेक्षणवृत्तयः ।
दहृशुरध्वनि तं वनदेवताः सुनयनं नयनन्दितकोसलम् ॥

५८ श्वगणिवागुरिकैः प्रथमाश्रितं व्यपगतानलदस्यु विवेश सः ।
स्थिरतुरङ्गमभूमि निपानवन्मृगवयोगवयोपचितं वनम् ॥

५९ अथ नभस्य इव त्रिदशायुधं कनकपिङ्गतडिद्गुणसंयुतम् ।
धनुरधिज्यमनाधिरुपाददे नरवरो रवरोषितकेसरी ॥

६० तस्य स्तनप्रणयिभिर्मुहुरेणशावै-
र्व्याहन्यमानहरिणीगमनं पुरस्तात् ।
आविर्बभूव कुशगर्भमुखं मृगाणां
यूथं तदग्रसरगर्वित-कृष्णसारम् ॥

६१ तत्प्रार्थितं जवनवाजिगतेन राज्ञा
तूणीमुखोद्धृतशरेण विशीर्णपङ्क्ति ।
श्यामीचकार वनमातुरदृष्टिपातै-
र्वितेरितोत्पलदलप्रकरैरिवाम्भः ॥

Wearing dress suited to the hunting ground, his bow   55
hanging from his sturdy neck, that sun among men
seemed to darken the sky with a canopy of dust struck
up by his horse's hooves.

His hair bound up with a garland of forest flowers, his   56
jerkin the color of fresh young leaves, and earrings
swaying with the bounds of his horse, he shone bright
in the haunts of the *ruru* deer.[19]

Along the way, the spirits of the forest transferred   57
their bodies into the slender plants and their eye
movements into the bees, and watched the fine-eyed
king who had made Kosala rejoice in his justice.

The king entered the forest already occupied by   58
houndmen and huntsmen, who had kept it clear of
wildfires and poachers. There the ground allowed his
horse firm footing, there were watering holes, and it
was well stocked with deer, birds, and Nilgai.

Then that best of men confidently grasped his strung   59
bow, enraging the lions with its sound, as the month
of Bhadrapada takes up the rainbow with its golden-
yellow string of lightning.[20]

A herd of deer with grass in their mouths appeared in   60
front of him. The movement of the does was impeded
by the fawns straining again and again for the udders;
a proud black buck went in front.

Chased by the king astride his swift horse, with arrows   61
drawn from his quiver, the disbanded herd darkened
the forest with frightened glances, as water is
darkened by the petals of water lilies strewn by the
wind.

६२ लक्ष्यीकृतस्य हरिणस्य हरिप्रभावः
प्रेक्ष्य स्थितां सहचरीं व्यवधाय देहम् ।
आकर्णकृष्टमपि कामितया स धन्वी
बाणं कृपामृदुमनाः प्रतिसञ्जहार ॥

६३ तस्यापरेष्वपि मृगेषु शरान्मुमुक्षोः
कर्णान्तमेत्य बिभिदे निविडो ऽपि मुष्टिः ।
त्रासातिमात्रचटुलैः स्मरयत्सु नेत्रैः
प्रौढप्रियानयनविभ्रमचेष्टि-तानि ॥

६४ उत्तस्थुषः शिशिरपल्वलपङ्कमध्या-
द्मुञ्झाप्ररोहकवलावयवानुकीर्णम् ।
जग्राह स द्रुतवराहकुलस्य मार्गं
सुव्यञ्जमार्द्रपदपङ्क्तिभिरायताभिः ॥

६५ तं वाहनादवनतोत्तरकायमीष-
द्विध्यन्तमुद्धतसटाः प्रतिहन्तुमीषुः ।
नात्मानमस्य विविदुः सहसा वराहा
वृक्षेषु विद्धमिषुभिर्ज-घनाश्रयेषु ॥

६६ तेनातिपातरभसस्य विकृष्य पत्त्री
वन्यस्य नेत्रविवरे महिषस्य मुक्तः ।
निर्भिन्नविग्रहमशोणितलिप्तशल्यस्तं
पातयां प्रथममास पपात पश्चात् ॥

At the sight of the doe shielding the body of the buck he   62
    was targeting, the heart of the bowman great as Indra
    softened with compassion and he unnocked his arrow,
    although he had drawn it to his ear, since he too was
    inclined to love.

Although he tightened his fist and again drew it to his   63
    ear, intending to shoot his arrows at other deer, it
    loosened, for, with their eyes flitting about wildly in
    fear, they reminded him of the graceful movements of
    the eyes of bold mistresses.

He took up the trail of a fleeing sounder of boars that had   64
    emerged from the mud of a cool pond, a trail easily
    discernible from the long spoors of wet hooves and the
    scattered morsels of chewed shoots of nutgrass.

The boars, with bristling hackles, tried to attack him as   65
    he struck at them, his upper body leaning slightly
    forward from his horse. They were not even aware of
    being suddenly pinned at their loins to trees by his
    arrows.

He drew and shot an arrow through the eye socket of a   66
    forest buffalo as it charged him recklessly. The arrow
    first felled the beast, transpiercing its body with tip
    unbloodied, then fell itself to earth.

६७ प्रायो विषाणपरिमोषलघूत्तमाङ्गान्
खड्गांश्चकार नृपतिर्निशितैः क्षुरप्रैः ।
शृङ्गं स दृप्तविनयाधिकृतः परेषाम्
अत्युच्छ्रितं न ममृषे न तु दीर्घमायुः ॥

६८ व्याघ्रानभीरभिमुखोत्पतितानुगुहाभ्यः
फुल्लासनाग्रविटपानिव वातरुग्णान् ।
शिक्षाविशेषलघुहस्ततया निमेषात्
तूणीचकार शरपूरितवक्रन्ध्रान् ॥

६९ निर्घातोग्रैः कुञ्जलीनाञ्जिघांसुर्
ज्यानिर्घोषैः क्षोभयामास सिंहान् ।
नूनं तेषामभ्यसूयापरो ऽसौ
वीर्योदग्रे राजशब्दे मृगाणाम् ॥

७० तान्हत्वा गजकुलबद्धतीव्रवैरान्
काकुत्स्थः कुटिलनखाग्रमुक्तमुक्तान् ।
आत्मानं रणकृतकर्मणां द्विपानाम्
आनृण्यं गतमिव मार्गणैरमंस्त ॥

७१ द्रुतमन्वपतत्क्वचिच्च यूथं
चमराणां शरलग्नवालधीनाम् ।
नृपतीनिव ताञ्जगाम शान्तिं
सितवालव्यजनैर्वियोज्य सद्यः ॥

The king lightened the heads of many rhinos by robbing   67
   them of their horns with razor-sharp arrows. By right
   the chastiser of the arrogant, he could not abide the
   pride of his enemies, yet he did not begrudge them
   living out their lives.[21]

Tigers leaped at him from caves, looking like the wind-   68
   bent outer branches of blooming *asana* trees; the
   fearless Dasharatha instantly transformed them,
   with sleight of hand acquired by special training, into
   quivers by filling their mouths with arrows.[22]

Eager to kill the lions lurking in thickets, he irked them   69
   with the twanging of his bowstring, frightful as
   thunder. No doubt he was jealous of their heroic title,
   "king of beasts."

By killing those sworn enemies of the race of elephants,   70
   who had pearls stuck to the tips of their curved claws,
   Dasharatha reckoned his debt to the elephants who
   had helped him in battle to have been paid off in
   arrows.[23]

In one place he raced up to a herd of yaks whose tails were   71
   entangled among reeds. But after depriving them—as
   he was wont to do with kings—of fly-whisks, their
   white tails, he was at once placated.[24]

७२ अपि तुरगसमीपादुत्पतन्तं मयूरं
न स रुचिरकलापं बाणलक्ष्यीचकार ।
सपदि गतमनस्कश्छिन्नमाल्यानुकीर्णे
रतिविलुलितबन्धे केशपाशे प्रियायाः ॥

७३ तस्य कर्कशविहारसम्भवं स्वेदमाननविलग्नजालकम् ।
आचचाम सतुषारशीकरो भिन्नपल्लवपुटो वनानिलः ॥

७४ इति विस्मृतान्यकरणीयमात्मनः
सचिवावलम्बितधुरं नराधिपम् ।
परिवृद्धरागमनुबन्धसेवया
मृगया जहार चतुरेव कामिनी ॥

७५ स ललितकुसुमप्रवालशय्या
ज्वलितमहौषधिदीपिकासनाथाः ।
नरपतिरतिवाह्यां बभूव
क्वचिदसमेतपरिच्छदस्त्रियामाः ॥

७६ उषसि च गजयूथकर्णतालैः
पटहपटुध्वनिभिर्विनीतनिद्रः ।
अरमत मधुरस्वनानि शृण्वन्
विहगविकूजितवन्दिमङ्गलानि ॥

७७ अथ जातु रुरोर्गृहीतवर्त्मा विपिने पार्श्वचरैरलक्ष्यमाणः ।
श्रमफेनमुचा तपस्विगाढां तमसां प्राप नदीं तुरङ्गमेण ॥

A beautiful-tailed peacock flew up right beside his horse,   72
    but he aimed no arrow at it, for his mind flitted
    suddenly to the tresses of a beloved, disheveled from
    lovemaking and strewn with wisps of her broken
    chaplet.

The woodland breeze, carrying dewdrops and opening the   73
    furled young leaves, sipped away the sweat that had
    beaded on his face from his rough sport.

Hunting, like a skillful mistress, infatuated the king—   74
    he forgot all other duties, transferring the burden of
    kingship to his ministers—but the more he served her,
    the more his passion grew.

King though he was, he spent his nights in the forest,   75
    with no bedding or the like, sleeping wherever he
    chanced to be on beds made from the tender flowers
    and leaves, with wonderful phosphorescent herbs for
    shining lamps around him.

At dawn he was woken by the flapping ears of an elephant   76
    herd resounding like his palace kettledrums, and he
    relished listening to birdsong in the place of the sweet-
    sounding benedictions of his bards.

Then at some point, as he followed the path of a *ruru*   77
    deer in the forest, unobserved by his companions, his
    horse, lathered with effort, brought him to the Tamasa
    River, thronged with ascetics.

७८ कुम्भपूरणभवः पटुरुच्चैरुच्चचार निनदो ऽम्भसि तस्याः ।
तत्र स द्विरदबृंहितशङ्की शब्दपातिनमिषुं विससर्ज ॥

७९ नृपतेः प्रतिषिद्धमेव तत्कृतवान्पङ्क्तिरथो ऽविशङ्क्य यत् ।
अपथे पदमर्पयन्ति हि श्रुतवन्तो ऽपि रजोनिमीलिताः ॥

८० हा तातेति क्रन्दितमाकर्ण्य विषण्णस्
तस्यान्विष्यन्वेतसगूढप्रभवं सः ।
शल्यप्रोतं वीक्ष्य सकुम्भं मुनिपुत्रं
तापादन्तःशल्य इवास क्षितिपो ऽपि ॥

८१ तेनावतीर्य तुरगात्प्रथितान्वयेन
पृष्टान्वयः स जलकुम्भनिषण्णदेहः ।
तस्मै द्विजोत्तरतपस्विसुतं स्खलद्भिर्
आत्मानमक्षरपदैः कथयां बभूव ॥

८२ तच्चोदितश्च तमनुद्धृतशल्यमेव
पित्रोः सकाशमवसन्नदृशोर्निनाय ।
ताभ्यां तथागतमवेत्य तमेकपुत्रम्
अज्ञानतः स्वचरितं नृपतिः शशंस ॥

८३ तौ दम्पती बहु विलप्य शिशोः प्रहर्त्रा
शल्यं निखातमुदहारयतामुरस्तः ।
सो ऽभूत्परासुरथ भूमिपतिं शशाप
हस्तार्पितैर्नयनवारिभिरेव वृद्धः ॥

220

From the waters of that river came the deep, loud sound   78
    of a pot being filled. He took it for the trumpeting of
    an elephant, and shot an arrow that homed in on the
    sound.[25]

What Dasharatha did without misgivings is definitely   79
    forbidden for a king. Even the learned set their feet on
    the wrong path when blinded by passion.[26]

Hearing the cry "Ah, Father!" that came from a spot   80
    hidden among the reeds, the distraught king set out to
    find its source. When he saw a sage's son, with a water
    pot, pierced by the shaft, he too was transpierced, as it
    were, with remorse.

Dismounting from his horse, he declared his lineage   81
    and asked the lineage of the boy, whose body had
    slumped against the pot. Haltingly, in syllables more
    than words, the boy told him that he was the son of a
    Brahman ascetic.[27]

At his urging the king brought him, without removing the   82
    arrow, to his blind parents. He approached them and
    told them of the lamentable state of their only son,
    and that it was he who had caused it, unwittingly.[28]

The couple lamented at length and asked the boy's   83
    attacker to draw the deep-sunk arrow from his chest;
    when he expired, the old man cursed the king, taking
    his tears themselves in his hands to do so.[29]

८४ दिष्टान्तमाप्स्यति भवानपि पुत्रशोकाद्
अन्ते वयस्यहमिवेति तमुक्तवन्तम् ।
आक्रान्तपूर्वमिव मुक्तविषं भुजङ्गं
प्रत्याह कोसलपतिः प्रथमापराद्धः ॥

८५ शापो ऽप्यदृष्टतनयाननपद्मशोभे
सानुग्रहो भगवता मयि पातितो ऽयम् ।
कृष्यां दहन्नपि खलु क्षितिमिन्धनेद्धो
बीजप्ररोहजननीं ज्वलनः करोति ॥

८६ इत्थं गते गतघृणः किमयं विधत्ताम्
अव्यक्तमित्यभिहिते वसुधाधिपेन ।
एधान्हुताशनवतः स मुनिर्ययाचे
पुत्रं परासुमनुगन्तुमनाः सदारः ॥

८७ प्राप्तानुगः सपदि शासनमस्य राजा
सम्पाद्य पातकविलुप्तधृतिर्निवृत्तः ।
अन्तर्निविष्टपदमात्मविनाशहेतुं
शापं दधज्ज्वलनमौर्वमिवाम्बुराशिः ॥

इति रघुवंशे महाकाव्ये नवमः सर्गः ॥

Like a snake spitting out its venom when trod upon, he   84
   said, "You too will meet your end from grief for your
   son in the last part of your life, just as I do." To this the
   king of Kosala, guilty of his first crime, replied:
"This curse Your Eminence has cast upon me contains a   85
   blessing, for I have not yet seen the beautiful lotus-
   like face of a son. Fire blazing with kindling may burn
   a field, indeed, but also makes it fertile for seeds to
   sprout."
"Things having turned out this way; what should I, cruel   86
   wretch that I am, do now?" the king murmured. At
   that, the sage asked him for flaming brands, intending,
   along with his wife, to follow their departed son.[30]
His entourage had now arrived, and the king carried out   87
   the ascetic's command and returned home. But the
   crime he had committed disturbed his calm, and he
   carried the curse that would destroy him, its words
   fixed in his heart, just as the ocean bears the fire of
   Urva within.[31]

दशमः सर्गः

१ पृथिवीं शासतस्तस्य पाकशासनतेजसः ।
   किञ्चिदूनमनूनर्द्धेः शरदामयुतं ययौ ॥

२ न चोपलेभे पूर्वेषामृणनिर्मोक्षसाधनम् ।
   सुताभिधानं स ज्योतिः सद्यः शोकतमोपहम् ॥

३ मनोर्वंशशिरं तस्मिन्ननभिव्यक्तसन्ततिः ।
   निमज्ज्य पुनरुत्थास्यन्नदः शोण इवाभवत् ॥

४ अतिष्ठत्प्रत्ययापेक्षसन्ततिः सुचिरं नृपः ।
   प्राङ्ग्रन्थादनभिव्यक्तरत्नोत्पत्तिरिवार्णवः ॥

५ वामदेवादयस्तस्य सन्तः सन्तानकाङ्क्षिणः ।
   आरेभिरे यतात्मानः पुत्रीयामिष्टिमृत्विजः ॥

६ अस्मिन्नवसरे देवाः पौलस्त्योपप्लुता हरिम् ।
   अभिजग्मुर्निदाघार्ताश्छायावृक्षमिवाध्वगाः ॥

७ ते च प्रापुरुदन्वन्तं बुबुधे चादिपूरुषः ।
   अव्याक्षेपो भविष्यन्त्याः कार्यसिद्धेर्हि लक्षणम् ॥

224

CHAPTER 10
Rama Descends

Nearly ten thousand years passed with Dasharatha ruling 1
the earth with the might of Indra and in the utmost
prosperity.

But he did not obtain that which men call a son, the light 2
that frees one from the debt to the ancestors and
instantly dispels the darkness of grief.[1]

With him the line of Manu, with no succession manifest, 3
had sunk, but only to rise again, like the Shona River.

For a long while the king was like the milk ocean, unable 4
to display its jewels before being churned: his progeny
awaited some catalyst.[2]

Vamadeva and other Vedic priests, worthy and self- 5
disciplined, undertook a sacrifice to enable the king,
eager for offspring, to beget a son.[3]

At that time, the gods were being harassed by Ravana. 6
They approached Vishnu, as travelers oppressed by
summer's heat approach a shady tree.

They reached the ocean just as the Primordial Being 7
awoke. Lack of delay foretells the coming success of
an enterprise.

८ भोगिभोगासनासीनं दष्टशुक्तं दिवौकसः ।
तत्फणामण्डलोदर्चिर्मणिद्योतितविग्रहम् ॥

९ श्रियः पद्मनिषण्णायाः क्षौमान्तरितमेखले ।
अङ्के निक्षिप्तचरणमास्तीर्णकरपल्लवे ॥

१० प्रफुल्लपुण्डरीकाक्षं बालातपनिभांशुकम् ।
दिवसं शारदमिव प्रारम्भसुखदर्शनम् ॥

११ प्रभानुलिप्तश्रीवत्सं लक्ष्मीविभ्रमदर्पणम् ।
कौस्तुभाख्यमपां सारं बिभ्रतं बृहतोरसा ॥

१२ बाहुभिर्विटपाकारैर्हेमाभरणभूषितैः ।
आविर्भूतं पयोमध्यात्पारिजातमिवापरम् ॥

१३ दैत्यस्त्रीगण्डलेखानां मदरागविलोपिभिः ।
आयुधैश्चेतनावद्भिरुदीरितजयस्वनम् ॥

१४ मुक्तशेषविरोधेन कुलिशव्रणलक्ष्मणा ।
उपस्थितं प्राञ्जलिना विनीतेन गरुत्मता ॥

१५ योगनिद्रान्तविषदैः पावनैरवलोकनैः ।
भृग्वादीननुगृह्णन्तं सौखशायितिकानृषीन् ॥

The gods beheld him resting on the couch formed by the
   coils of the serpent, his body irradiated by the blazing
   gems borne upon the circle of its hoods.[4]   8

His feet rested on Lakshmi's lap, where her tendril-soft
   hands were laid, her girdle covered with a fine cloth, as
   she sat upon her lotus.[5]   9

With eyes like awakened lotuses and garment like
   morning sunlight, he was as beautiful to behold at
   the outset of their endeavor as an autumn day at its
   dawning.   10

He wore on his broad chest that treasure of the ocean
   called Kaustubha—a mirror for Lakshmi's graceful
   movements—which flickered beams of light across his
   Shrivatsa.[6]   11

He was like a second *pārijāta* tree, just emerged from the
   milk, with his arms resembling branches adorned with
   golden ornaments.   12

His sentient weapons, causing the flush of wine to drain
   from the cheeks of demons' wives, cheered him on
   with cries of "Victory!"[7]   13

Abandoning his feud with Shesha, Garuda, marked with
   lightning-bolt scars, waited on him respectfully with
   palms placed together.[8]   14

He graced Bhrigu and other sages, gathered to inquire
   whether he had slept well, with his glances, purifying
   and clear at the end of his yogic sleep.[9]   15

१६ प्रणिपत्य सुरास्तस्मै शमयित्रे सुरद्विषाम् ।
अथैनं तुष्टुवुः स्तुत्यमवाङ्मनसगोचरम् ॥

१७ नमो विश्वसृजे पूर्वं विश्वं तदनु बिभ्रते ।
अथ विश्वस्य संहर्त्रे तुभ्यं त्रेधास्थितात्मने ॥

१८ एकः कारणतस्तां तामवस्थां प्रतिपद्यसे ।
नानात्वं रागसंयोगात्स्फटिकस्येव ते स्थितम् ॥

१९ रसान्तराण्येकरसं यथा दिव्यं पयो ऽश्नुते ।
देशे देशे गुणेष्वेवमवस्थास्त्वमविक्रियः ॥

२० अमेयो मितलोकस्त्वमनर्थी प्रार्थितावहः ।
अजितो जिष्णुरत्यन्तमव्यक्तो व्यक्तकारणम् ॥

२१ हृदयस्थमनासन्नमकामं त्वां तपस्विनम् ।
दयालुमनघस्पृष्टं पुराणमजरं विदुः ॥

२२ सर्वज्ञस्त्वमविज्ञातः सर्वयोनिस्त्वमात्मभूः ।
सर्वप्रभुरनीशस्त्वमेकस्त्वं सर्वरूपभाक् ॥

२३ सप्तसामोपगीतं त्वां सप्तार्णवजलेशयम् ।
सप्तार्चिर्मुखमाचख्युः सप्तलोकैकसंश्रयम् ॥

Then the celestials bowed to him, destroyer of the gods' 16
enemies, and praised him, worthy of praise and yet
beyond the reach of speech and mind.

"Hail to you, who first create all things, who then sustain 17
them, and then draw all back in again. Such is your
threefold nature!

"Although one, you take on this or that form depending 18
on your purpose: you vary like a crystal laid beside
different colors.

"Just as the water of heaven, which has only one taste, 19
takes on different flavors when it falls in different
places, so you, while unchangeable, take on different
aspects in accordance with the strands.[10]

"Unmeasurable, you have measured the worlds; without 20
needs, you meet all needs; unconquered, you conquer
without limits; unmanifest, you are the cause of all
that is manifest.

"Present in each heart, yet remote; with nothing to wish 21
for, yet self-denying; compassionate, yet untouched by
suffering; old, yet unaging—thus do they know you.[11]

"All-knowing, you are unknown; source of all, you are self- 22
born; lord of all, you are without master; one, you take
all forms.

"Praised in the seven *sāmans,* reclining on the water of the 23
seven oceans, with seven-flamed fire as your mouth,
you are the sole support of the seven worlds—so they
describe you.[12]

२४ चतुर्वर्गफलं ज्ञानं कालावस्था चतुर्युगा ।
चतुर्वर्णमयो लोकस्त्वत्तः सर्वं चतुर्मुखात् ॥

२५ अजस्य गृह्णतो जन्म निरीहस्य हतद्विषः ।
स्वपतो जागरूकस्य याथात्म्यं वेद कस्तव ॥

२६ अभ्यासनिगृहीतेन मनसा हृदयास्पदम् ।
ज्योतिर्मयं विचिन्वन्ति योगिनस्त्वां विमुक्तये ॥

२७ शब्दादीन्विषयान्भोक्तुं चरितुं दुश्चरं तपः ।
पर्याप्तो ऽसि प्रजाः पातुमौदासीन्येन वर्तितुम् ॥

२८ बहुधाप्यागमैर्भिन्नाः पन्थानः सिद्धिहेतवः ।
त्वय्येव निपतन्त्योघा जाह्नवीया इवार्णवे ॥

२९ त्वदावेशितचित्तानां त्वत्समर्पितकर्मणाम् ।
गतिस्त्वं वीतरागाणामभूयःसन्निवृत्तये ॥

३० प्रत्यक्षो ऽप्यपरिच्छेद्यो मह्यादिर्महिमा तव ।
आप्तवागनुमानाभ्यां साध्यं त्वां प्रति का कथा ॥

३१ केवलं स्मरणेनैव पुनासि पुरुषं यदा ।
अनेन वृत्तयः शेषा निवेदितफलास्त्वयि ॥

"Knowledge, whose fruit is the four goals of life; time,   24
    ordered in four ages; mankind, with its four classes—
    all this comes from your four faces.[13]

"Unborn, you take birth; inactive, you kill your enemies;   25
    while sleeping you are awake: who can know what you
    really are?

"To attain liberation, yogins keeping their minds in check   26
    by practice contemplate you as light located in their
    hearts.

"You are capable of enjoying sense pleasures, sound and   27
    the rest, while at the same time practicing severe
    asceticism; protecting creatures lovingly while at the
    same time remaining aloof.

"Various paths, deriving from countless traditions, lead   28
    to realization; but they all merge in you alone, like the
    many streams of the Ganga entering the ocean.

"Those who let their minds enter you, offer you the fruits   29
    of their actions, and are free of passion reach you
    alone, never again to return.

"Your grandeur consisting in the elements, earth and   30
    the rest, can be directly perceived, but nonetheless
    it cannot be fully grasped. What to say then of you
    yourself, whom only scripture and inference can
    reach?[14]

"If the soul merely thinks of you, you make it pure. By this   31
    we can know the fruits of other actions directed to
    you.

३२ उदधेरिव रत्नानि तेजांसीव विवस्वतः ।
स्तुतिभ्यो व्यतिरिच्यन्ते दूरेण चरितानि ते ॥

३३ अनवाप्तमवाप्तव्यं न ते किञ्चन विद्यते ।
लोकानुग्रह एवैको हेतुस्ते जन्मकर्मणोः ॥

३४ महिमानं यदुत्कीर्त्य तव सङ्क्षिप्यते वचः ।
श्रमेण तदशक्त्या वा न गुणानामियत्तया ॥

३५ इति प्रसादयामासुस्ते सुरास्तमधोक्षजम् ।
भूतार्थव्याहृतिः सा हि न स्तुतिः परमेष्ठिनः ॥

३६ तस्मै कुशलसंप्रश्नव्यञ्जितप्रीतयः सुराः ।
भयमप्रलयोद्वेलादाचरव्युर्नैर्ऋतोदधेः ॥

३७ अथ वेलासमासन्नशैलरन्ध्रानुनादिना ।
स्वरेण भगवानाह परिभूतार्णवध्वनिः ॥

३८ पुराणस्य कवेस्तस्य चतुर्मुखसमीरिता ।
बभूव भारती भव्या चरितार्था चतुष्टयी ॥

३९ बभासे दशनज्योत्स्ना सा विभोर्वदनोद्गता ।
निर्यातशेषा चरणाद्गङ्गेवोर्ध्वप्रसारिणी ॥

232

"Like the gems of the sea, like the rays of the sun, your   32
    deeds are far beyond praise.

"There is nothing for you to obtain that you have not   33
    already obtained. You take birth and act solely to help
    the world.

"It is out of fatigue or impotence that our speech praising   34
    your greatness concludes here, not because your
    virtues have been fully covered."

Thus the gods spoke; and he who is beyond sense   35
    perception was pleased. For they were stating nothing
    but the facts, not flattering the Supreme Lord.[15]

He showed the gods his goodwill by asking after their   36
    welfare. They told him of their fear of Ravana, who
    was like an ocean, but one that floods beyond its
    shores even before the age's end.

Then the Lord spoke, with a voice that surpassed the   37–38
    ocean's roar and that echoed in mountain caverns by
    the shore; and Speech, emerging perfect and fourfold
    from the four mouths of that ancient sage, fulfilled its
    purpose at last.[16]

The moonlight gleam that flashed from the Lord's teeth,   39
    spilling from his mouth, was like the remainder,
    streaming upward, of the Ganga that had once flowed
    forth from his feet.

४० जाने वो रक्षसाक्रान्तावनुभावपराक्रमौ ।
अङ्गिना तमसेवोभौ गुणौ प्रथममध्यमौ ॥

४१ विदितं ताप्यमानं च तेन मे भुवनत्रयम् ।
अकामोपनतेनेव साधोर्हृदयमेनसा ॥

४२ कार्येषु चैककार्यत्वादभ्यर्थ्यो ऽस्मि न वज्रिणा ।
स्वयमेव हि वातो ऽग्रेः सारथ्यं प्रतिपद्यते ॥

४३ स्वासिधारापरिहृतः कामं चक्रस्य तेन मे ।
स्थापितो दशमो मूर्धा लव्यांश इव रक्षसा ॥

४४ स्रष्टुर्वरातिसर्गाच्च मया तस्य दुरात्मनः ।
अत्यारूढं रिपोः सोढं चन्दनेनेव भोगिनः ॥

४५ धातारं तपसा प्रीतं ययाचे स हि राक्षसः ।
दैवात्सर्गादवध्यत्वं मर्त्येष्वास्थापराङ्मुखः ॥

४६ सो ऽहं दाशरथिर्भूत्वा रणभूमेर्बलिक्षमम् ।
करिष्यामि शरैस्तीक्ष्णैस्तच्छिरःकमलोच्चयम् ॥

४७ अचिराद्यज्वभिर्भागं कल्पितं विधिवत्पुनः ।
मायाविभिरनालीढमादास्यध्वे निशाचरैः ॥

"I know that your dignity and power have been eclipsed   40
    by Ravana, just as the first and the middle strands
    of existence are both eclipsed by darkness when it
    predominates.[17]

"And I am also aware that the three worlds are tormented   41
    by him, as the heart of a good man is tormented by sin
    involuntarily committed.

"And Indra need not urge me on in such affairs, for we two   42
    share one task. Does not Wind of itself become the
    charioteer of Fire?

"Surely the *rākṣasa* saved his tenth head from the blade of   43
    his sword, reserving it as an offering for my war quoit
    to reap.[18]

"I have borne the impertinence of that evil enemy, like a   44
    sandal tree a snake's, only because Brahma had given
    him a boon.[19]

"For that *rākṣasa* asked the creator, who was pleased by   45
    his asceticism, that he might be unslayable by any
    divine being, contemptuous as he was of mortals.

"I myself will become the son of Dasharatha and with   46
    sharp arrows make a heap of his lotus-like heads, a
    suitable offering for the battlefield.[20]

"Soon you will again receive the sacrificial share offered   47
    to you by sacrificers, as the Veda prescribes, without
    it being befouled by the spittle of magic-wielding
    rākṣasas.

४८ वैमानिकाः पुण्यकृतस्त्यजन्तु मरुतां पथि ।
पुष्पकालोकसङ्क्षोभं मेघावरणतत्पराः ॥

४९ मोक्ष्यथ स्वर्गवन्दीनां वेणीबन्धानदूषितान् ।
शापयन्त्नितपौलस्त्यबलात्कारकचग्रहैः ॥

५० रावणावग्रहक्क्रान्तमिति वागमृतेन सः ।
अभिवृष्य मरुत्सस्यं कृष्णमेघस्तिरोदधे ॥

५१ पुरुहूतप्रभृतयः सुरकार्योद्यतं सुराः ।
अंशैरनुययुर्विष्णुं पुष्पैर्वायुमिव द्रुमाः ॥

५२ अथ तस्य विशां पत्युरन्ते काम्यस्य कर्मणः ।
पुरुषः प्रबभूवाग्नेर्विस्मयेन सहर्त्विजाम् ॥

५३ हेमपात्रीकृतं दोर्भ्यामाददानः पयश्चरुम् ।
अनुप्रवेशादाद्यस्य पुंसस्तेनापि दुर्वहम् ॥

५४ प्राजापत्योपनीतं तं चरुं प्रत्यग्रहीन्नृपः ।
वृषेव पयसां सारमाविष्कृतमुदन्वता ॥

५५ अनेन कथिता राज्ञो गुणास्तस्यान्यदुर्लभाः ।
विवृत्तिं चकमे तस्मिंस्त्रैलोक्यप्रभवो ऽपि यत् ॥

"Let the gods in their flying palaces, who now try to hide   48
    themselves among the clouds, lose the fear they feel
    on catching sight of the Pushpaka chariot in the air.[21]

"You will untie the braids of the captive ladies of Heaven,   49
    braids unsullied by Ravana's violent grasp, since a
    curse restrains him."[22]

Then, after showering the gods with the nectar of his   50
    speech, crops withered by the drought of Ravana, the
    dark cloud Vishnu disappeared.[23]

Vishnu was ready to do the gods' work. They, with Indra   51
    at their head, accompanied him with portions of
    themselves, as trees enhance a breeze with their
    flowers.

Just then, as King Dasharatha was finishing the sacrifice   52–53
    for attaining his wish, a being emerged from the fire,
    bringing with him the astonishment of the priests.
    He held in his hands a portion of sacrificial gruel in a
    golden vessel, which even he carried with difficulty,
    since the Primal Being* had entered it.

The king accepted the gruel brought by the representative   54
    of Prajapati, resembling as he did so Indra accepting
    the ambrosia presented by the ocean.[24]

That the origin of the three worlds himself had chosen to   55
    incarnate as his son bespeaks the virtues of that king,
    which were beyond the reach of others.

———

* Vishnu.

५६ स तेजो वैष्णवं पत्न्योर्विभेजे चरुसंज्ञितम् ।
द्यावापृथिव्योः प्रत्यग्रं वृषाकपिरिवातपम् ॥

५७ अर्चिता तस्य कौसल्या प्रिया केकयवंशजा ।
अतः सम्भावितां ताभ्यां सुमित्रामैच्छदीश्वरः ॥

५८ ते बहुज्ञस्य चित्तज्ञे पत्न्यौ पत्युर्महीक्षितः ।
चरोरर्धार्धभागेन तामयोजयतामुभे ॥

५९ सा हि प्रणयवत्यासीत्सपत्न्योरुभयोरपि ।
भ्रमरी वारणस्येव मदनिःष्यन्दलेखयोः ॥

६० ताभिर्गर्भः प्रजाभूत्यै दध्रे देवांशसम्भवः ।
सौरीभिरिव नाडीभिरमृताख्याभिरम्मयः ॥

६१ सममापन्नसत्त्वास्ता बभुरापाण्डुरत्विषः ।
अन्तर्गतफलारम्भाः सस्यानामिव सम्पदः ॥

६२ गुप्तं दट्शुरात्मानं सर्वाः स्वप्ने ऽथ वामनैः ।
असित्सरुगदाशार्ङ्गचक्रलाञ्छितमूर्धभिः ॥

६३ हेमपत्तप्रभाजालं गगने च वितन्वता ।
उह्यन्ते स्म सुपर्णेन वेगाकृष्टपयोमुचा ॥

He divided Vishnu's virile power—the so-called gruel—   56
between two wives, as the sun divides its first light
between sky and earth.

The king respected Kausalya; he loved Kaikeyi. Therefore   57–58
he wished Sumitra to be honored by the two of them.
The two wives understood the intention of their wise
husband the king, and each gave her half their own
gruel.

Indeed Sumitra loved both her rival wives, as a bee   59
loves the streams of musth on both cheeks of a bull
elephant.

The queens carried within them the progeny begotten of   60
the portions of god, as the solar rays called Ambrosia
bear the aquatic embryo.[25]

All became pregnant at the same time, and they shone   61
with a pale golden hue, like rich crops with the
promise of harvest within.

Then they dreamed they saw themselves being guarded   62
by dwarves with heads marked by a sword hilt, mace,
bow, and discus;[26]

being carried by Garuda in the sky, spreading the halo of   63
his golden wings and dragging the clouds with him by
his speed;

६४ बिभ्रत्या कौस्तुभन्न्यासं स्तनान्तरविलम्बिनम् ।
पर्युपास्यन्त लक्ष्म्या च पद्मव्यजनहस्तया ॥

६५ कृताभिषेकैर्दिव्यायां त्रिस्रोतसि च सप्तभिः ।
ब्रह्मर्षिभिः परं ब्रह्म गृणद्भिरुपतस्थिरे ॥

६६ ताभ्यस्तथाविधान्स्वप्नाञ्छ्रुत्वा प्रीतो ऽपि पार्थिवः ।
मेने ऽपराद्धमात्मानं गुरुत्वेन जगद्गुरोः ॥

६७ विभक्तात्मा विभुस्तासामेकः कुक्षिष्वनेकधा ।
उवास प्रतिमाचन्द्रः प्रसन्नानामपामिव ॥

६८ अथाग्य्रमहिषी राज्ञः प्रसूतिसमये सती ।
पुत्रं तमोपहं लेभे नक्तं ज्योतिरिवौषधिः ॥

६९ राम इत्यभिरामेण वपुषा यस्य चोदितः ।
नामधेयं गुरुश्चक्रे जगत्प्रथितमङ्गलम् ॥

७० रघुवंशप्रदीपेन तेनाप्रतिमतेजसा ।
शय्यागृहगता दीपाः प्रत्याख्याता इवाभवन् ॥

७१ शय्यागतेन चानेन माता च्छातोदरी बभौ ।
सैकताम्भोजबलिना जाह्नवीव शरत्कृशा ॥

240

being attended upon by Lakshmi, wearing between her 64
breasts the Kaustubha jewel that had been entrusted
to her, and holding a lotus fan in her hand;

and being worshiped by the seven sages who had bathed in 65
the celestial Ganga and who were reciting the sacred
Veda.[27]

Hearing of such dreams as these, the king was pleased. 66
Yet he thought that to become the father of the Father
of all would make him guilty of an offense.[28]

Though one and all-pervading, the Lord divided himself 67
into many and dwelled in their wombs, like the
reflection of the moon divided among patches of clear
water.

Then, when the time of her delivery arrived, the king's 68
faithful chief queen obtained a son who removed all
darkness, as herbs obtain their light at night.[29]

The beauty of the child's body prompted his father to give 69
him the name Rama, one whose auspiciousness is
famed throughout the world.

The lamps in the birthing chamber seemed to be eclipsed 70
by that incomparably bright light of the Raghu
lineage.

With him lying on her bed, his mother, her waist now slim, 71
shone like Ganga grown thin in autumn and bright
with lotus offerings on her bank.

७२ कैकेय्यास्तनयो जज्ञे भरतो नाम वीर्यवान् ।
जनयित्रीमलञ्चक्रे यः प्रश्रय इव श्रियम् ॥

७३ सुतौ लक्ष्मणशत्रुघ्नौ सुमित्रा सुषुवे यमौ ।
सम्यगागमिता विद्या प्रबोधविनयाविव ॥

७४ निर्दोषमभवत्सर्वमाविष्कृतगुणं जगत् ।
अन्वगादिव हि स्वर्गो गां गतं पुरुषोत्तमम् ॥

७५ तस्योदये चतुर्मूर्तेः पौलस्त्यचकितेश्वराः ।
विरजस्कैर्नभस्वद्भिर्दिदिश उच्छ्वसिता इव ॥

७६ कृषाणुरपधूमत्वात्प्रसन्नत्वात्क्षपाकरः ।
रक्षोविप्रकृतावास्तामपविद्धशुचाविव ॥

७७ दशाननकिरीटेभ्यस्तत्क्षणं राक्षसश्रियः ।
मणिव्याजेन पर्यस्ताः पृथिव्यामसुबिन्दवः ॥

७८ पुत्रजन्मप्रवेश्यानां तूर्याणां तस्य पुत्रिणः ।
आरम्भं प्रथमं चक्रुर्देवदुन्दुभयो दिवि ॥

७९ सन्तानकमयी वृष्टिर्भवने तस्य पेतुषी ।
सन्मङ्गलोपकाराणां शोभाद्वैगुण्यमादधे ॥

To Kaikeyi was born a heroic son called Bharata, who   72
was an ornament to his mother, just as humility is an
ornament to wealth.

Sumitra gave birth to twin sons, Lakshmana and   73
Shatrughna, just as properly mastered wisdom gives
birth to understanding and modesty.

The whole world became free of faults, with every virtue   74
on display, for heaven seemed to follow the Supreme
Being when he descended to earth.

When he was born in these four forms, breezes free from   75
dust began to blow, as if the quarters, their guardian
deities terrified of Ravana, were sighing in relief.[30]

The demon had oppressed both fire and the moon, but   76
now both seemed freed from grief—fire because it was
smokeless, the moon because it was clear.

At that moment, the Royal Fortune of the *rākṣasas* shed   77
teardrops on the ground that took the form of pearls
falling from the diadems of ten-headed Ravana.

Of the musical instruments that are to be brought forth at   78
the birth of a son, it was first the drums of the gods in
heaven that began to sound for the king who now had
sons.

The rain of *santānaka* flowers that fell on his palace   79
rendered its auspicious decorations doubly
beautiful.[31]

८० कुमाराः कृतसंस्कारास्ते धात्रीस्तनपायिनः ।
आनन्देनाग्रजेनेव समं ववृधिरे पितुः ॥

८१ स्वाभाविकं विनीतत्वं तेषां विनयकर्मणा ।
मुमूर्छ सहजं तेजो हविषेव हविर्भुजाम् ॥

८२ परस्पराविरुद्धास्ते तद्रघोरनघं कुलम् ।
अलमुद्द्योतयामासुर्देवारण्यमिवर्तवः ॥

८३ समाने ऽपि हि सौभ्रात्रे यथोभौ रामलक्ष्मणौ ।
तथा भरतशत्रुघ्नौ प्रीत्या द्वन्द्वं बभूवतुः ॥

८४ तेषां द्वयोर्द्वयोरैक्यं बिभिदे न कदाचन ।
यथा वायुविभावस्वोर्यथा चन्द्रसमुद्रयोः ॥

८५ ते प्रजानां प्रजानाथास्तेजसा प्रश्रयेण च ।
मनो जह्रुर्निदाघान्ते श्यामार्धा दिवसा इव ॥

८६ स चतुर्धा बभौ व्यस्तः प्रसवः पृथिवीपतेः ।
धर्मार्थकाममोक्षाणामवतार इवाङ्गवान् ॥

८७ गुणैराराधयामासुस्ते गुरुं गुरुवत्सलाः ।
तमेव चतुरन्तेशं रत्नैरिव महार्णवाः ॥

The new-birth rites performed, the princes, suckling at   80
    the breasts of wet nurses, grew together with their
    father's joy, which was like an elder brother to them.

Their natural courtesy grew as they were taught the rules   81
    of conduct, just as the natural blaze of the sacred fires
    increases with offerings of ghee.

Free from mutual strife, they made the Raghu lineage   82
    shine brightly, just as the seasons together brightly
    illuminate the garden of the gods.[32]

Although all were equally good brothers to each other,   83
    still, affection bound Rama and Lakshmana as a pair,
    and likewise Bharata and Shatrughna.

The unity of these two pairs was never broken, like that   84
    between wind and fire, or moon and sea.

The princes captivated the people's hearts with their   85
    energy and gentleness, like the half-darkened days at
    summer's end.[33]

The king's progeny, divided into four, shone like Piety,   86
    Profit, Pleasure, and Liberation incarnate.[34]

Devoted to their father, they pleased him with their   87
    virtues, just as the four vast oceans pleased that same
    lord of the four quarters with gems.

८८ सुरगज इव दन्तैर्भग्नदैत्यासिधारै-
र्नय इव पणबन्धव्यक्तयोगैरुपायैः।
हरिरिव युगदीर्घैर्दोर्भिरंशैस्तदीयैः
पतिरवनिपतीनां तैश्चतुर्भिश्चकाशे॥

इति रघुवंशे महाकाव्ये दशमः सर्गः॥

As Indra's elephant shines with its tusks that blunt the 88
    edges of demons' swords; as Statecraft shines with
    stratagems, whose deployment is manifested in peace
    treaties; as Vishnu shines with his arms long as yoke
    poles, thus shone the king of kings with those four,
    who were portions of Vishnu.[35]

एकादशः सर्गः

१   कौशिकेन स किल क्षितीश्वरो राममध्वरविघातशान्तये ।
    काकपक्षधरमेत्य याचितस्तेजसो हि न वयः समीक्ष्यते ॥

२   कृच्छ्रलब्धमपि लब्धवर्णभाक्तं दिदेश मुनये सलक्ष्मणम् ।
    अप्यसुप्रणयिनां रघोः कुले न व्यहन्यत कदाचिदर्थिता ॥

३   यावदादिशति पार्थिवस्तयोर्निर्गमाय पुरमार्गसत्क्रियाम् ।
    तावदाशु विहिता मरुत्सखैः सा सपुष्पजलवर्षिभिर्घनैः ॥

४   तौ निदेशकरणोद्यतौ पितुर्वन्दितुं चरणयोर्निपेततुः ।
    भूपतेरपि तयोः प्रवत्स्यतोर्नम्रयोरुपरि वाष्पबिन्दवः ॥

५   लक्ष्मणाभिसरमेव राघवं नेतुमैच्छदृषिरित्यतो नृपः ।
    आशिषं प्रयुयुजे न वाहिनीं सा हि रक्षणविधौ तयोः क्षमा ॥

६   तौ पितुर्नयनजेन वारिणा किञ्चिदुक्षितशिखण्डकावुभौ ।
    धन्विनौ तमृषिमन्वगच्छतां पौरदृष्टिकृतमार्गतोरणौ ॥

CHAPTER 11
Rama's Youth

They say that Vishvamitra asked the king to send Rama to   1
  quell the obstacles to his sacrifice. The lad still wore
  earlocks, but where there is valor, age is no concern.

Though he had obtained Rama as son with such difficulty,   2
  the king, ever a patron of the learned, assigned him
  along with Lakshmana to the sage. In Raghu's line,
  suppliants were never refused, even if what they asked
  was life itself.

No sooner had the king ordered that the royal avenue be   3
  decorated for the two of them to leave than it was
  done by wind-befriended clouds spreading rain with
  flowers.

Ready to do his bidding, the two fell at their father's feet to   4
  honor him; as for the king, his teardrops fell on them
  as they bowed low, ready to set off.

The sage wished to take Rama, and Lakshmana was to   5
  accompany him. So the king gave them not an army
  but his blessing, for they needed no more to protect
  them.

With topknots still damp from their father's tears, the two   6
  archers followed the sage. The gazes of the citizens
  formed an arch of honor above them.

७ मातृवर्गचरणस्पृशौ मुनेस्तौ प्रपद्य पदवीं महौजसः ।
रेजतुर्गतिवशप्रवर्तिनौ भास्करस्य मधुमाधवाविव ॥

८ वीचिलोलभुजयोस्तयोर्गतं शैशवाञ्चपलमप्यशोभत ।
तोयदागम इवोद्ध्वभिद्वयोर्नामधेयसदृशं विचेष्टितम् ॥

९ तौ बलातिबलयोः प्रभावतो विद्ययोस्तदुपदिष्टयोः पथि ।
मम्लतुर्न मणिकुट्टिमोचितौ मातृपार्श्वपरिवर्तिनाविव ॥

१० पूर्ववृत्तकथितैः पुराविदः सानुजः पितृसखस्य राघवः ।
उह्यमान इव वाहनोचितः पादचारमपि न व्यभावयत् ॥

११ तौ सरांसि रसवद्भिरम्बुभिः कूजितैः श्रुतिसुखैः पतत्रिणः ।
वायवः सुरभिपुष्परेणुभिश्छायया च जलदाः सिषेविरे ॥

१२ नाम्भसां विकचपद्मशोभिनां वीरुधां फलभृतां न वा तथा ।
दर्शनेन लघुना यथा तयोः प्रीतिमापुरुभयोस्तपस्विनः ॥

१३ तौ सुकेतुसुतया खिलीकृते कौशिकाद्विदितशापया पथि ।
निन्यतुः स्थलनिवेशिताटनी लीलयैव धनुषी अधिज्यताम् ॥

They touched their mothers' feet and then set off upon the   7
path of that effulgent sage, shining bright themselves,
like Madhu and Madhava proceeding in the sway of
the sun's course.[1]

The gait of the two lads, their arms swaying like waves,   8
was beautiful though still childishly impetuous, like
the movement of the Uddhya and Bhidya Rivers at the
onset of the monsoon.[2]

Though they were used to walking on floors of polished   9
gems, by the power of the spells "Strength" and
"Super Strength" that the sage had taught them, the
two remained as fresh on the road as if still walking at
their mothers' side.

Rama and his younger brother were used to being borne in   10
palanquins; but carried, as it were, by stories of deeds
of yore recounted by their father's friend, a treasure
trove of lore, they did not even notice that they had to
keep moving their feet.

The ponds served them with tasty water, the birds with   11
cooing pleasant to the ear, the winds with fragrant
pollen, and the clouds with shade.

Neither the sight of water beautiful with full-blown   12
lotuses nor that of plants bent low with fruit delighted
the ascetics as much as the longed-for sight of the two
princes.

Vishvamitra told them about the curse on Suketu's   13
daughter. Now, on the path she had made desolate,
they planted the points of their bows in the ground
and effortlessly strung them.[3]

१४ ज्यानिनादमथ गृह्णती तयोः प्रादुरास बहुलक्षपाच्छविः ।
ताटका चलकपालकुण्डला कालिकेव निविडा बलाकिनी ॥

१५ वेगविप्रकृतमार्गवृक्षया प्रेतचीवरवसास्वनोग्रया ।
अभ्यभावि भरताग्रजस्तया वात्ययेव पितृकाननोत्थया ॥

१६ उद्यतैकभुजयष्टिमायतीं श्रोणिलम्बपुरुषान्त्रमेखलाम् ।
तां विलोक्य वनितावधे घृणां पत्त्रिणा सह मुमोच राघवः ॥

१७ रामभिन्नहृदया निपेतुषी सा स्वकाननभुवं न केवलम् ।
विष्टपत्रयपराजयस्थिरां रावणश्रियमपि व्यकम्पयत् ॥

१८ यच्चकार विवरं शिलाघने ताटकोरसि स रामसायकः ।
अप्रविष्टविषयस्य रक्षसां द्वारतामगमदन्तकस्य तत् ॥

१९ राममन्मथशरेण ताडिता दुःसहेन हृदये निशाचरी ।
गन्धवद्रुधिरचन्दनोक्षिता जीवितेशवसतिं जगाम सा ॥

Hearing the reverberation of their bow-strings, Tataka   14
    appeared before them, black as a moonless night,
    with her earring-skulls swinging, like a dense bank of
    clouds fringed by egrets.

Bending the trees in her path with the speed of her   15
    onslaught—a horror clad in the rags of corpses,
    reeking of their fat, and with the voice of the dead—
    she fell upon Bharata's elder brother like a whirlwind
    rising from a charnel ground.

Seeing her approaching with one stick-like arm raised,   16
    trailing a girdle of human entrails from her waist,
    Rama released an arrow—along with all inhibition
    about killing a woman.

When she fell, pierced to the heart by Rama, she shook   17
    not only the ground in her charnel forest but even the
    glory of Ravana, well entrenched though it was in all
    three worlds by his victories.

The hole Rama's arrow made in Tataka's stone-hard   18
    chest became a door for Death, who had never before
    entered the realm of *rākṣasas*.

The prowler of the night, struck in her heart by the   19
    unbearable arrow of that love god Rama and spattered
    with the pungent-smelling sandal that was her own
    blood, departed for the house of the lord* who rules
    over lives.[4]

---

* Death.

२० नैर्ऋतघ्नमथ मन्त्रवन्मुनेः प्रापदस्त्रमपदानतोषितात् ।
ज्योतिरिन्धननिपाति भास्करात्सूर्यकान्त इव ताटकान्तकः ॥

२१ स्थाणुदग्धवपुषस्तपोवनं प्राप्य दाशरथिरात्तकार्मुकः ।
विग्रहेण मदनस्य चारुणा सो ऽभवत्प्रतिनिधिर्न कर्मणा ॥

२२ वामनाश्रमपदं ततः परं पावनं श्रुतमृषेरुपेयिवान् ।
उन्मनाः प्रथमजन्मचेष्टितान्यस्मरन्नपि बभूव राघवः ॥

२३ आससाद मुनिरात्मनस्ततः शिष्यवर्गपरिकल्पिताहेणम् ।
बद्धपल्लवपुटाञ्जलिद्रुमं दर्शनोन्मुखमृगं तपोवनम् ॥

२४ तत्र दीक्षितमृषिं ररक्षतुर्विघ्नतो नृपसुतौ शितैः शरैः ।
लोकमन्धतमसात्क्रमोदितौ रश्मिभिः शशिदिवाकराविव ॥

२५ वीक्ष्य वेदिमथ रक्तबिन्दुभिर्बन्धुजीवपृथुभिः प्रदूषिताम् ।
सम्भ्रमो ऽभवदुपोढकर्मणामृत्विजां च्युतविकङ्कतसुचाम् ॥

२६ उन्मुखः सपदि लक्ष्मणाग्रजो बाणमाशयमुखात्समुद्धरन् ।
रक्षसां बलमपश्यदम्बरे गृध्रपक्षपवनेरितध्वजम् ॥

Then Tataka's nemesis Rama received from the sage, 20
    who was pleased by his brave deed, a demon-slaying
    weapon, together with its mantra, as the sunstone
    receives from the sun the blaze that destroys firewood.

Bow in hand, Rama arrived at the penance grove named 21
    after Kama, whose body had been burned there
    by Shiva; his lovely form—though not his deeds—
    brought to mind the god of love.

Soon after, Rama reached the sacred ashram of Vamana, 22
    which he heard about from the sage; there, although
    he did not recall the deeds of his previous birth, his
    mind became full of longing.[5]

Then the sage arrived at his own penance grove. His 23
    disciples welcomed him respectfully, the trees made
    the gesture of greeting by bringing together the
    clusters of their shoots, and the deer strained their
    necks in their eagerness to see him.

The two princes stayed in the ashram, protecting the 24
    consecrated sage from dangers with their sharpened
    arrows, as the sun and moon, rising in turn, protect
    the world from blind darkness with their rays.

One day, just as the officiants were about to begin their 25
    rites, they noticed the altar being defiled by drops of
    blood as large as scarlet mallow blossoms. Gripped by
    fear, they dropped their ladles of *vikankata* wood.

As the elder brother, Rama, was poised to take an arrow 26
    from the mouth of his quiver, he looked up and
    suddenly saw in the sky an army of *rākṣasas,* its
    banners stirred by the beat of vultures' wings.

२७ तत्र यावधिपती मखद्विषां तौ शरव्यमकरोत्स नेतरान् ।
किं महोरगविसर्पिविक्रमो राजिलेषु गरुडः प्रवर्तते ॥

२८ सो ऽस्त्रमुग्रजवमस्त्रकोविदः सन्दधे धनुषि वायुदैवतम् ।
येन शैलगुरुमप्यपाहरत्पाण्डुपत्त्रमिव ताटकासुतम् ॥

२९ यः सुबाहुरिति राक्षसो ऽपरस्तत्र तत्र विससर्प मायया ।
तं क्षुरप्रशकलीकृतं कृती पत्त्रिणां व्यभजदाश्रमाद्द्विहिः ॥

३० इत्यपास्तमखविघ्नयोस्तयोः सांयुगीनमभिनन्द्य विक्रमम् ।
ऋत्विजः कुलपतेर्यथाक्रमं वाग्यतस्य निरवर्तयन्क्रियाः ॥

३१ तौ प्रणामचलकाकपक्षकौ भ्रातराववभृथाप्लुतो मुनिः ।
आशिषामनुपदं समस्पृशद्गर्भपाटिततलेन पाणिना ॥

३२ तं न्यमन्त्रयत सम्भृतक्रतुर्मैथिलः स मिथिलां व्रजन्वशी ।
राघवावपि निनाय बिभ्रतौ तद्धनुःश्रवणजं कुतूहलम् ॥

३३ तैः शिवेषु वसतिर्गताध्वभिः सायमाश्रमतरुष्वगृह्यत ।
येषु दीर्घतपसः परिग्रहो वासवक्षणकलत्रतां ययौ ॥

In that army, he marked as his targets the two leaders   27
of those enemies of sacrifice, no others. Garuda is
belligerent toward mighty serpents, but does he
attack harmless grass snakes?

Master of weaponry, Rama fitted to his bow an arrow of   28
fearsome speed empowered by the wind god that
caused Tataka's son Maricha, heavy as a mountain
though he was, to fall like a wilted leaf.

The other *rākṣasa,* called Subahu, was slinking from place   29
to place by magic stealth. Rama skillfully cut him to
pieces with razor-tipped shafts and scattered him to
the birds outside the ashram.

When the brothers had removed these obstacles to   30
sacrifice, the priests praised their valor in battle and
performed the rites, in due order, for the head of the
ashram, who was bound to silence.

Freshly bathed at the conclusion of the rites, the sage   31
blessed the brothers, and as they bowed, earlocks
quivering, he laid his hand, its palm scarred by the
sacrificial grass, upon their heads.

Janaka, king of Mithila, had prepared a sacrificial rite and   32
invited Vishvamitra. The self-controlled sage set out
for Mithila with the two descendants of Raghu, who
were full of curiosity after hearing about the king's
bow.

After a day's travel, they lodged at nightfall amid the   33
hallowed trees of the very ashram where Gautama's
spouse had briefly been Indra's wife.[6]

३४ प्रत्यपद्यत चिराय यत्पुनश्चारु गौतमवधूः शिला सती ।
स्वं वपुः स किल किल्बिषच्छिदां रामपादरजसामनुग्रहः ॥

३५ राघवान्वितमुपस्थितं मुनिं तं निशम्य जनको जनेश्वरः ।
अर्थकामसहितं सपर्यया देहबद्धमिव धर्ममभ्यगात् ॥

३६ तौ विदेहपुटभेदनौकसां गां गताविव दिवः पुनर्वसू ।
मन्यते स्म पिवतां विलोचनैः पक्ष्मपातमपि वञ्चनां मनः ॥

३७ यूपवत्यवसिते क्रियाविधौ कालवित्कुशिकवंशवर्धनः ।
राममिश्वसनदर्शनोत्सुकं मैथिलाय कथयां बभूव सः ॥

३८ तस्य वीक्ष्य ललितं शिशोर्वपुः पार्थिवः प्रथितवंशजन्मनः ।
स्वं विचिन्त्य च धनुर्दुरानमं पीडितो दुहितृशुल्कसंस्थया ॥

३९ अब्रवीच्च भगवन्मतङ्गजैर्यन्महद्भिरपि कर्म दुष्करम् ।
तत्र नाहमनुमन्तुमुत्सहे मोघवृत्ति कलभस्य चेष्टितम् ॥

४० ह्रेपिता हि बहवो नरेश्वरास्तेन तात धनुषा धनुर्भृतः ।
ज्याविघातकठिनत्वचो भुजान् ये ऽवधूय धिगिति प्रतस्थिरे ॥

४१ प्रत्युवाच तमृषिर्निशम्यतां सारतो ऽयमथवा कृतं गिरा ।
चाप एव भवतो भविष्यति व्यक्तशक्तिरशनिर्गिराविव ॥

By virtue of the dust of Rama's feet, which is said to   34
    destroy all sin, Gautama's wife, who had become a
    stone, regained her lovely form.

When King Janaka learned that the sage was approaching   35
    with the two descendants of Raghu—like Piety
    incarnate attended by Profit and Pleasure—he went
    forth to meet them with reverence.[7]

The townspeople of Videha drank in Rama and   36
    Lakshmana with their eyes, as if the two Punarvasu
    stars had come to earth from heaven, and they
    considered themselves cheated by each blink of their
    eyes.[8]

When the rites beside the sacrificial post had been   37
    concluded, Vishvamitra, champion of Kushika's
    lineage, ever a judge of the right moment, told Janaka
    that Rama was curious to see the bow.

Seeing the delicate body of that highborn boy, and   38
    knowing his bow to be impossible to string, the king
    bitterly regretted setting that task as his daughter's
    bride price.

And he said, "Sage, I cannot let a calf attempt with   39
    fruitless effort a task difficult even for great elephants
    to accomplish.

"Many indeed, Father, are the bow-wielding kings who   40
    have been humbled by this bow and have gone off
    cursing their arms, skin roughened by the bowstring's
    friction."

The sage replied to him, "As for his strength, he . . . But   41
    what need for words! He will show his power directly
    on your bow, like a thunderbolt on a mountain."

४२ इत्थमाप्तवचनात्स पौरुषं काकपक्षकधरे ऽपि राघवे ।
श्रद्दधे त्रिदशगोपमात्रके दाहशक्तिमिव कृष्णवर्त्मनि ॥

४३ आदिदेश गणशो ऽथ पार्श्वगान्कार्मुकाभिहरणाय मैथिलः ।
तैजसस्य धनुषः प्रवृत्तये तोयदानिव सहस्रलोचनः ॥

४४ तत्प्रसुप्तभुजगेन्द्रभीषणं प्रेक्ष्य दाशरथिराददे धनुः ।
विद्रुतक्रतुमृगानुसारिणं येन बाणमसृजद्वृषध्वजः ॥

४५ आततज्यमकरोत्स संसदा विस्मयस्तिमितनेत्रमीक्षितः ।
शैलसारमपि नातियत्नतः पुष्पचापमिव पेलवं स्मरः ॥

४६ भज्यमानमतिमात्रकर्षणात्तत्स्वनेन गगनस्पृशा धनुः ।
भार्गवाय दृढमन्यवे पुनः क्षत्त्रमुद्यतमिव न्यवेदयत् ॥

४७ दृष्टसारमथ रुद्रकार्मुके वीर्यशुल्कमभिनन्द्य मैथिलः ।
राघवाय तनयामयोनिजां स्वां ददौ श्रियमिवामरद्युतिः ॥

४८ प्राहिणोच्च महितं महाद्युतिः कोसलाधिपतये पुरोधसम् ।
भृत्यभावि दुहितृप्रतिग्रहादिष्यतां कुलमिदं निमेरिति ॥

260

The words of so trustworthy a person made him believe   42
in Rama's strength even though the boy still wore
earlocks, as one believes in the power of a fire to burn
even if it is no larger than a mite.⁹

The king of Mithila ordered a multitude of servants to   43
fetch the bow, just as Indra orders the clouds to bring
forth his arc of fiery light.¹⁰

The bow was as menacing as the cosmic serpent coiled in   44
sleep; the bull-bannered Shiva once shot from it an
arrow that hunted down Sacrifice when it had fled in
the guise of a deer. Rama eyed it and lifted it up.¹¹

Watched by the assembly, their eyes frozen in wonder,   45
Rama set the string to it without great effort, even
though it was tough as rock, like Kama stringing his
soft arc of flowers.

From Rama's mighty pull, the bow broke with a   46
thunderclap that reached the heavens, as if to
proclaim to the ever rancorous Parashurama that
Kshatriyas were once again ready for battle.

Janaka rejoiced at Rama's showing his strength upon   47
Rudra's bow and his paying the bride price with this
heroic feat. Radiant as a god, he bestowed upon him
his daughter, born, like Lakshmi herself, from no
womb.¹²

Then the splendid Janaka sent his revered priest to the   48
king of Kosala with this message: "Deign to accept
my daughter and thereby honor my family, descended
from Nimi, as your servants."¹³

४९ अन्वियेष सदृशीं स च सुषां प्राप चैनमनुकूलवाग्द्विजः ।
सद्य एव सुकृतां विपच्यते कल्पवृक्षफलधर्म काङ्क्षितम् ॥

५० तस्य कल्पितपुरस्क्रियाविधेः शुश्रुवान्वचनमग्रजन्मनः ।
उच्चचाल बलभित्सखो वशी सैन्यरेणुमुषितार्कदीधितिः ॥

५१ आससाद मिथिलां स वेष्टयन्पीडितोपवनपादपां बलैः ।
प्रीतिरोधमसहिष्ट सा पुरी स्त्रीव कान्तपरिभोगमायतम् ॥

५२ तौ समेत्य समयस्थितावुभौ भूपती वरुणवासवोपमौ ।
कन्यकातनयकौतुकक्रियां स्वप्रभावसदृशीं वितेनतुः ॥

५३ पार्थिवीमुदवहत्तदग्रजो मध्यमस्तदनुजामथोर्मिलाम् ।
यौ यमावधिगतौ सुमित्रया तौ कुशध्वजसुते सुमध्यमे ॥

५४ ता नराधिपसुता नृपात्मजैस्ते च ताभिरगमन्कृतार्थताम् ।
सो ऽभवद्वरवधूसमागमः प्रत्ययप्रकृतियोगसन्निभः ॥

५५ ते चतुर्थसहितास्त्रयो बभुः सूनवो नववधूपरिग्रहाः ।
सामदानविधिभेदनिग्रहाः सिद्धिमन्त इव तस्य भूपतेः ॥

५६ एवमात्तरतिरात्मसम्भवांस्तान्निवेश्य चतुरो ऽपि तत्र सः ।
अध्वसु त्रिषु विसृष्टमैथिलः स्वां पुरीं दशरथो न्यवर्तत ॥

Just when Dasharatha conceived a desire for a suitable 49
    daughter-in-law the Brahman arrived with his fitting
    words. The desires of men of merit are like wish-
    granting trees—they bear fruit at once.

After hearing the Brahman's words and performing a 50
    rite to honor him, Indra's powerful friend set forth,
    obscuring the sun's rays with his army's dust.

He reached Mithila and surrounded it with his army, 51
    afflicting the trees in its parks. The city tolerated his
    loving clutches, as a woman the long embraces of her
    beloved.[14]

In keeping with convention, the two kings, like Varuna 52
    and Indra, came to an agreement and performed the
    wedding rites of their sons and daughters in a manner
    befitting their majesty.[15]

The eldest son married Sita, the girl from the earth; the 53
    middle son then married her younger sister Urmila;
    the twins born to Sumitra married the slim-waisted
    daughters of Kushadhvaja.[16]

The princesses were contented with the princes, and the 54
    princes with the princesses; this union of brides and
    grooms was like that of stems and suffixes.[17]

The latter three sons of the king, together with that 55
    fourth, now wedded to new brides, resembled the
    kingly stratagems of peace, giving, dissension, and
    force, each wedded to its own success.

Delighted at successfully marrying off all four sons there, 56
    Dasharatha returned to his city, taking leave of the
    king of Mithila, who accompanied him for three
    stages of the journey.

५७ तस्य जातु मरुतः प्रतीपगा वर्त्मनि ध्वजतरुप्रमाथिनः ।
चिक्लिशुर्भृशतया वरूथिनीमुत्तटा इव नदीरयाः स्थलीम् ॥

५८ लक्ष्यते स्म तदनन्तरं रविर्बद्धभीमपरिवेशमण्डलः ।
वैनतेयशमितस्य भोगिनो भोगवेष्टित इव च्युतो मणिः ॥

५९ श्येनपक्षपरिधूसरालका भूरजःसरुधिरार्द्रवाससः ।
अङ्गना इव रजस्वला दिशो नो बभूवुरवलोकनक्षमाः ॥

६० भास्करश्च दिशमध्युवास यां तां श्रिताः प्रतिभयं ववाशिरे ।
क्षत्रशोणितपितृक्रियोचितं चोदयन्त्य इव भार्गवं शिवाः ॥

६१ तत्प्रतीपपवनादि वैकृतं क्षिप्रशान्तमधिकृत्य कृत्यवित् ।
अन्वयुङ्क गुरुमीश्वरः क्षितेः स्वन्तमित्यलघयत्स तद्व्यथाम् ॥

६२ तेजसः सपदि राशिरुत्थितः प्रादुरास किल वाहिनीमुखे ।
यः प्रमृज्य नयनानि सैनिकैर्लक्षणीयपुरुषाकृतिश्चिरात् ॥

६३ पित्र्यमंशमुपवीतलक्षणं मातृकं च धनुरूर्जितं दधत् ।
यः ससोम इव घर्मदीधितिः सद्द्विजिह्व इव चन्दनद्रुमः ॥

६४ येन रोषपरुषात्मनः पितुः शासने स्थितिभिदो ऽपि तस्थुषा ।
वेपमानजननीशिरश्छिदा प्रागजीयत घृणा ततो मही ॥

At one point, headwinds tore at the trees that were his   57
    battle standards and greatly harried his army on the
    way, as the bank-bursting streams of a river harry the
    land.

Then the sun was seen surrounded by a terrifying halo,   58
    resembling the gem of a serpent fallen from its hood
    and encircled by its coils when Garuda had slain it.[18]

The quarters of the sky became unfit to be seen, like   59
    menstruating women, the wings of hawks their
    sullied locks, the red dust from the earth their bloody
    clothes.[19]

Jackals faced the sun and howled horrifically, as though   60
    inciting Parashurama, used as he was to sating his
    ancestors with libations of Kshatriya blood.[20]

The king, who knew his duty, asked his guru whether the   61
    opposing wind and those other portents would soon
    be calmed, and he allayed the king's fears, saying: "All
    will end well."

A mass of light suddenly appeared, they say, rising in front   62
    of the army. The soldiers wiped their eyes and at last
    could make out the shape of a man.

He wore the sacred thread, his paternal sign, and a fiery   63
    bow, the sign of his mother, making him look like
    the sun appearing together with the moon, or a
    sandalwood tree wreathed by a serpent.[21]

This was the man who had obeyed the command of   64
    his implacable father and beheaded his trembling
    mother, breaking with every tradition; the man who
    conquered first pity and then the earth.

६५ अक्षबीजवलयेन निर्बभौ दक्षिणश्रवणसंस्थितेन यः ।
क्षत्रियान्तकरणैकविंशतेर्व्याजपूर्वगणनामिवोद्वहन् ॥

६६ तं पितुर्वधभवेन मन्युना राजवंशनिधनाय दीक्षितम् ।
बालसूनुरवलोक्य भार्गवं विव्यथे दशरथो दशाच्युतः ॥

६७ नाम राम इति तुल्यमात्मजे वर्तमानमहिते च दारुणे ।
हृद्यमस्य भयदायि चाभवद्रत्नजातमिव हारसर्पयोः ॥

६८ अर्घ्यमर्घ्यमिति वादिनं नृपं सो ऽनवेक्ष्य भरताग्रजो यतः ।
क्षत्रकोपदहनार्चिषं ततः सन्दधे दृशमुदग्रतारकाम् ॥

६९ तेन कार्मुकनिविष्टमुष्टिना राघवो विगतभीः पुरोगतः ।
अङ्गुलीविवरचारिणीमिषुं कुर्वता निजगदे युयुत्सुना ॥

७० क्षत्त्रजातमपकारवैरि मे तन्निहत्य बहुशः शमं गतः ।
सुप्तसर्प इव दण्डघट्टनादुद्घतो ऽस्मि तव विक्रमश्रवात् ॥

७१ मैथिलस्य धनुरन्यपार्थिवैस्त्वं किलानमितपूर्वमक्षिणोः ।
यत्रिशम्य भवता समर्थये वीर्यशृङ्गमिव भग्रमात्मनः ॥

With a string of *rudrākṣa* beads dangling from his right   65
ear, he seemed to be secretly tallying his twenty-one
massacres of Kshatriyas.[22]

His sons still children, and he himself declined from his   66
prime, Dasharatha trembled to see Parashurama bent
on destroying the Kshatriya line in rage at his father's
murder.

The name Rama, denoting both his son and this fierce   67
enemy, now became both dear and fearsome to him,
like a gem of the sort found on both a necklace and a
snake.

Ignoring the king as he called out, "Here's water for the   68
guest! water for the guest!" Parashurama fixed his
fierce gaze, eyes aflame with the fire of his anger
against Kshatriyas, on the spot where Bharata's elder
brother stood.

Parashurama clutched one fist around his bow and passed   69
an arrow between his fingers; thirsting for battle, he
addressed Rama.

"All Kshatriyas are my enemies, for the harm they have   70
caused me. I found peace by killing them many times
over, only to be provoked again by hearing of your
valor, like a sleeping snake struck with a stick.

"It seems you have broken the bow of Mithila's king,   71
which other princes never even bent! When I heard
that, I felt as though you had shattered the proud
mountain of my valor.

७२ अन्यदा जयति राम इत्ययं शब्द उच्चरित एव मामगात् ।
व्रीडमावहति मे स साम्प्रतं व्यस्तवृत्तिरुदयोन्मुखे त्वयि ॥

७३ बिभ्रतो ऽस्त्रमचले ऽप्यकुण्ठितं द्वौ रिपू मम मतौ समागसौ ।
धेनुवत्सहरणात्स हेहयस्त्वं च कीर्तिमपहर्तुमुद्यतः ॥

७४ क्षत्रियान्तकरणो ऽपि विक्रमस्तेन मामवति नाजिते त्वयि ।
पावकस्य महिमा स गण्यते कक्ष्यवज्ज्वलति सागरे ऽपि यत् ॥

७५ विद्धि चात्तरसमोजसा हरेरैश्वरं धनुरभाजि यत्त्वया ।
खातमूलमनिलो नदीरयैः पातयत्यपि मृदुस्तटद्रुमम् ॥

७६ तन्मदीयमिदमाततज्यतां नीयतां विजयसाधनं धनुः ।
तिष्ठतु प्रधनमेवमप्यहं तुल्यबाहुतरसा जितस्त्वया ॥

७७ कातरो ऽसि यदि वोद्धतार्चिषा तर्जितः परशुधारया मम ।
ज्याविमर्दकठिनाङ्गुलिर्वृथा बध्यतामभययाचनाञ्जलिः ॥

७८ एवमुक्तवति भीमदर्शिने भार्गवे स्मितविकम्पिताधरः ।
तद्ध्वनुग्रहणमेव राघवः प्रत्यपद्यत समर्थमुत्तरम् ॥

"Once upon a time, when people uttered the name Rama it   72
applied instantly and only to me. Now, with you eager
for eminence, it has become ambiguous and brings me
shame.

"I, who wield a weapon even a mountain could not blunt,   73
consider two enemies to have affronted me equally:
Kartavirya-Arjuna, because he stole the calf from my
father's cow, and you, who are keen to take from me
my fame.[23]

"And so, although my valor has brought death to   74
Kshatriyas, that brings me no cheer so long as you
remain unconquered. A fire is reckoned mighty when
it can blaze even in the ocean as it does in straw.

"Besides, know that this bow of Shiva that you broke had   75
been sapped of its strength by Vishnu's fieriness; even
a soft breeze may bring down a bankside tree whose
roots have been pulled out by a river's rushing force.[24]

"So string this bow of mine, with which I achieved my   76
victories! No need to fight; just doing that, you will
have conquered me by showing a strength of arms to
equal mine.

"But if you are afraid, daunted by the shining blade of my   77
battle-ax, then it was in vain that you roughened your
fingers by the friction of the bowstring. Clasp them
together instead, and beg for my protection!"

To this speech of the fearsome Bhargava, Rama, a smile   78
playing on his lips, deemed it a fitting reply to simply
grasp Parashurama's bow.

७९ पूर्वजन्मधनुषा समागतः सो ऽतिमात्रलघुदर्शनो ऽभवत् ।
केवलो ऽपि सुभगो नवाम्बुदः किं पुनस्त्रिदशचापलाञ्छितः ॥

८० तेन भूमिनिहितैककोटिना कार्मुकं च बलिनाधिरोपितम् ।
निष्प्रभश्च रिपुरास भूभृतां धूमशेष इव धूमकेतनः ॥

८१ तावुभावपि परस्परं स्थितौ वर्धमानपरिहीनतेजसौ ।
पश्यति स्म जनता दिनक्षये पार्वणौ शशिदिवाकराविव ॥

८२ तं कृपामृदुरवेक्ष्य भार्गवं राघवः स्खलितवीर्यमात्मनि ।
स्वं च संहितममोघमाशुगं व्याजहार हरसूनुसन्निभः ॥

८३ न प्रहर्तुमलमस्मि निर्दयं विप्र इत्यभिभवत्यपि त्वयि ।
शंस किं गतिमनेन पत्त्रिणा हन्मि लोकमथ ते मखार्जितम् ॥

८४ प्रत्युवाच तमृषिर्न तत्त्वतस्त्वां न वेद्मि पुरुषं पुरातनम् ।
गां गतस्य तव धाम वैष्णवं कोपितो ह्यसि मया दिदृक्षुणा ॥

८५ भस्मसात्कृतवतः पितृद्विषः पात्रसाच्च वसुधां ससागराम् ।
आहितो जयविपर्ययो ऽपि मे श्लाघ्य एव परमेष्ठिना त्वया ॥

Reunited with the bow that was his in a former birth, he   79
became especially beautiful to look at. The monsoon
cloud is lovely on its own; how much more so when
marked by Indra's bow?

As he set the point of the bow on the ground and, putting   80
forth his strength, strung it, the enemy of the
Kshatriyas dimmed like a fire reduced to smoke.[25]

People watched as the pair stood face to face, one waning   81
in splendor as the other waxed, like sun and moon at
dusk on full-moon day.

Powerful as Skanda, son of Hara, Rama looked with   82
tender compassion at Parashurama, whose valor was
faltering, and looked at his own arrow, which, once set
to the bow, could never fail to hit a mark. And he said,

"Even though you attacked me, I cannot ruthlessly strike   83
you, because you are a Brahman. Tell me whether I
should use this arrow of mine to destroy your power
to move or the heavenly world you have gained by
sacrifice."[26]

The sage answered him, "It is not that I did not know that   84
you are in truth the Primeval Man.* It was because I
wanted to see you, now come down to earth, wield the
power of Vishnu that I provoked your anger.

"I burned my father's enemies to ash; I gave away the   85
earth and oceans to a worthy recipient. Even so, the
opposite of victory, since it is you, the Supreme Being,
who inflict it on me, is something to celebrate.[27]

———

* An epithet for Vishnu.

८६ तद्वृत्तिं गतिमतां वरेप्सितां पुण्यतीर्थगमनाय रक्ष मे ।
पीडयिष्यति न मां खिलीकृता स्वर्गसङ्गतिरभोगलोलुभम् ॥

८७ प्रत्यपद्यत तथेति राघवः प्राङ्मुखश्च विससर्ज सायकम् ।
भार्गवस्य सुकृतो ऽपि सो ऽभवत्स्वर्गमार्गपरिघो दुरत्ययः ॥

८८ राघवो ऽथ चरणौ तपोनिधेः क्षम्यतामिति वदन्समस्पृशत् ।
निर्जितेषु तरसा तरस्विनां शत्रुषु प्रणतिरेव शोभते ॥

८९ राजसत्त्वमवधूय मातृकं पित्र्यमस्मि गमितः शमं यतः ।
नन्वनिन्दितफलो मम त्वया निग्रहो ऽप्ययमनुग्रहीकृतः ॥

९० साधयाम्यहमविघ्नमस्तु ते देवकार्यमुपपादयिष्यतः ।
ऊचिवानिति वचः सलक्ष्मणं लक्ष्मणाग्रजमृषिस्तिरोदधे ॥

९१ तस्मिन्गते विजयिनं परिरभ्य रामं
स्नेहादमन्यत पिता पुनरेव जातम् ।
तस्याभवत्क्षणशुचः परितोषलाभः
कक्षाग्निलङ्घिततरोरिव वृष्टिसेकः ॥

९२ अथ पथि गमयित्वा कॢप्तरम्योपकार्ये
कतिचिदवनिपालः शर्वरीः शर्वकल्पः ।
पुरमविशदयोध्यां मैथिलीदर्शनीनां
कुवलयितगवाक्षां लोचनैरङ्गनानाम् ॥

इति रघुवंशे महाकाव्य एकादशः सर्गः ॥

272

"Therefore, most exalted among all that move, spare my 86
power to move, which I wish to keep so that I may visit
holy places. It will not trouble me if you block my way
to heaven, for I do not yearn for pleasures."

Rama assented and, turning east, released his arrow, 87
which became an insuperable bar to Parashurama's
way to heaven, however many good deeds he
performed.

Then Rama touched the ascetic's feet and asked 88
forgiveness. Gentleness toward enemies defeated by
strength befits the strong.

"Since you have caused me to give up the passionate 89
nature inherited from my mother and to attain the
peaceful temper of my father, even the defeat you
have inflicted upon me has a result of which I do not
disapprove, and has turned into a blessing.

"I shall go now. May nothing obstruct you from carrying 90
out the works of the gods." Having said this to Rama
and his brother Lakshmana, the sage disappeared.

When he had left, Dasharatha affectionately embraced 91
his victorious son, whom he regarded as reborn. The
access of happiness after a moment of grief was to him
like a downpour of rain for a tree engulfed by a forest
fire.

Then that god-like king, after passing several nights on the 92
road in royal tents prepared there, entered the city of
Ayodhya, where the eyes of the women gazing down
on Sita turned the windows into lily ponds.

द्वादशः सर्गः

१ निर्विष्टविषयस्नेहः स दशान्तमुपेयिवान् ।
   आसीदासन्ननिर्वाणः प्रदीपार्चिरिवोषसि ॥

२ तं कर्णमूलमागत्य रामे श्रीर्न्यस्यतामिति ।
   कैकेयीशङ्क्येवाह पलितच्छद्मना जरा ॥

३ सा पौरान्पौरकान्तस्य रामस्याभ्युदयश्रुतिः ।
   प्रत्येकं ह्लादयां चक्रे कुल्येवोद्यानपादपान् ॥

४ तस्याभिषेकसम्भारं कल्पितं क्रूरनिश्चया ।
   दूषयामास कैकेयी शोकोष्णैः पार्थिवासुभिः ॥

५ सा किलाश्वासिता भर्त्रा चण्डी तत्संश्रुतौ वरौ ।
   उज्जगारेन्द्रसिक्ता भूर्बिलमग्नाविवोरगौ ॥

६ तयोश्चतुर्दशैकेन रामप्रव्राजनं समाः ।
   द्वितीयेन सुतस्यैच्छद्वैधव्यैकफलां श्रियम् ॥

CHAPTER 12
Rama, Banished to the Forest, Loses and Recaptures Sita

After exhausting his pleasure in the objects of the senses, Dasharatha approached the final stage; he came close to extinction, like the flame of a lamp at dawn that has used up the oil in its reservoir and come to the end of its wick.[1] 1

It was as if old age, in the guise of white hair, stole up to his ear and, in fear of Kaikeyi, whispered, "Bestow the royal majesty upon Rama." 2

Word of Rama's elevation delighted every citizen—for they loved him dearly—just as a watercourse delights the trees in a garden. 3

With cruel resolve, Kaikeyi caused all that had been made ready for his consecration to be sullied by the king's tears, hot with sorrow.[2] 4

That wrathful woman, so the story goes, when her husband tried to conciliate her, burst out with demands for the two boons he had formerly promised, like the earth, watered by Indra, ejecting a pair of snakes hiding in its holes. 5

With one of these two boons, she wished for Rama's exile for fourteen years; with the other, she wanted royal majesty for her son, which would result only in her widowhood. 6

७ पित्रा दत्तां रुद्त्रामः प्राङ्गृहीं प्रत्यपद्यत ।
पश्चाद्दूनाय गच्छेति तदाज्ञां मुदितो ऽग्रहीत् ॥

८ दधतो मङ्गलक्षौमे चीरे च परिगृह्णतः ।
दद्दृशुर्दुःखितास्तस्य मुखरागं समं जनाः ॥

९ स सीतालक्ष्मणसखः सत्यादुरुमलोपयन् ।
विवेश दण्डकारण्यं प्रत्येकं च सतां मनः ॥

१० राजापि तद्वियोगार्तः स्मृत्वा शापं स्वकर्मजम् ।
शरीरत्यागमात्रेण शुद्धिलाभममन्यत ॥

११ विप्रोषितकुमारं तद्राज्यमस्तमितेश्वरम् ।
रन्ध्रान्वेषणदक्षाणां द्विषामामिषतां ययौ ॥

१२ अथानाथाः प्रकृतयो मातृबन्धुनिवासिनम् ।
मौलैरानाययामासुर्भरतं स्तम्भिताश्रुभिः ॥

१३ श्रुत्वा तथाविधं मृत्युं कैकेयीतनयः पितुः ।
मातुर्न केवलं स्वस्याः श्रियो ऽप्यासीत्पराङ्मुखः ॥

१४ ससैन्यश्चान्वगादग्रामं दर्शितानाश्रमालयैः ।
तस्य पश्यन्ससौमित्रेरुदसुर्वसतिद्रुमान् ॥

276

Earlier, Rama had wept when accepting the earth   7
    bestowed on him by his father; afterward, he joyfully
    obeyed his command: "Go to the forest."

The saddened citizens beheld exactly the same radiance of   8
    face in Rama when he donned bark garments as when
    he wore ceremonious silks.[3]

Because he would not make his father a liar, Rama, with   9
    Sita and Lakshmana at his side, entered the Dandaka
    forest and at the same time the hearts of all good
    people.

But the king suffered from the separation from Rama, and   10
    he remembered the curse that had resulted from his
    own deed. And he thought that only by relinquishing
    his body could he be purified.

Its lord dead and the princes dispersed, the kingdom lay   11
    open to enemies, who excel in seeking out vulnerable
    points, as a morsel for the taking.

Bharata had been staying with his mother's kin; the   12
    people, bereft of their lord, now had him brought by
    the hereditary ministers, who had to hold back their
    tears.

When Kaikeyi's son heard that his father had died, and   13
    in such a way, he became averse not only to his own
    mother but to royal fortune too.

And with an army he set off after Rama, gazing with tears   14
    in his eyes at the trees, pointed out to him by hermits,
    where Rama had sought shelter with Lakshmana.

१५ चित्रकूटाचलस्थं च कथितस्वर्गतिर्गुरोः ।
लक्ष्या निमन्त्रयां चक्रे तमनुच्छिष्टसम्पदा ॥

१६ स हि प्रथमजे तस्मिन्नकृतश्रीपरिग्रहे ।
परिवेत्तारमात्मानं मेने स्वीकरणाद्भुवः ॥

१७ तमशक्यमपाक्रष्टुं निदेशात्स्वर्गिणः पितुः ।
ययाचे पादुके पश्चात्कर्तुं राज्याधिदैवते ॥

१८ स विसृष्टस्तथेत्युक्त्वा भ्रात्रा नैवाविशत्पुरीम् ।
नन्दिग्रामगतस्तस्य राज्यं न्यासमिवाभुनक् ॥

१९ दृढभक्तिरिति ज्येष्ठे राज्यतृष्णापराङ्मुखः ।
मातुः पापस्य भरतः प्रायश्चित्तमिवाकरोत् ॥

२० रामो ऽपि सह वैदेह्या वने वन्येन वर्तयन् ।
चचार सानुजः शान्तो वृद्धेक्ष्वाकुव्रतं युवा ॥

२१ प्रभावस्तम्भितच्छायमाश्रितः स वनस्पतिम् ।
कदाचिदङ्के सीतायाः शिश्ये किञ्चिदिव श्रमात् ॥

२२ ऐन्द्रिः किल नखैस्तस्या विददार स्तनौ द्विजः ।
प्रियोपभोगचिह्नेषु पौरोभाग्यमिवाचरन् ॥

He found Rama living on Mount Chitrakuta, told him that   15
 their father had gone to heaven, and invited him back,
 pleading that the bloom of Royal Majesty was still
 intact.

For accepting the earth when his elder brother had yet   16
 to take the hand of Shri, he knew he would be the
 scoundrel who marries first.

Unable to dissuade him from following the command of   17
 their father, now in heaven, he then asked for Rama's
 sandals, to make them presiding deities over the
 kingdom.

His brother assented, and dismissed him. But Bharata did   18
 not reenter the city. Instead he stayed in the nearby
 village of Nandigrama, from where he ruled the
 kingdom, which he held as if in trust.[4]

It was as if Bharata, firmly devoted to his brother,   19
 renounced all desire for kingship to expiate his
 mother's evil deed.

And Rama, along with Vaidehi* and Lakshmana, subsisted   20
 on what the forest yielded, and thus, though still
 a youth, dispassionately kept the observance the
 Ikshvakus follow when reaching old age.[5]

Once, beneath a tree whose shade was immobilized by his   21
 power, a little tired, he fell asleep on Sita's lap.

The story goes that a bird—who was really Indra's   22
 son—tore at her breasts with its claws, as though
 begrudging the marks of lovemaking left there by her
 beloved.

———

* Sita.

२३ तस्मिन्नास्थदिषीकास्त्रं रामो रामावबोधितः ।
भ्रान्तश्च मुमुचे तस्मादेकनेत्रव्ययेन सः ॥

२४ रामस्त्वासन्नदेशत्वाद्धरतागमनं पुनः ।
आशङ्क्योत्सुकसारङ्गां चित्रकूटस्थलीं जहौ ॥

२५ प्रययावातिथेयेषु वसन्नृषिकुलेषु सः ।
दक्षिणां दिशमृक्षेषु वार्षिकेष्विव भास्करः ॥

२६ बभौ तमनुगच्छन्ती विदेहाधिपतेः सुता ।
प्रतिषिद्धापि कैकेय्या लक्ष्मीरिव गुणोन्मुखी ॥

२७ अनसूयाविसृष्टेन पुण्यगन्धेन काननम् ।
सा चकाराङ्गरागेण पुष्पोल्ललितषड्पदम् ॥

२८ सन्ध्याभ्रकपिशस्तत्र विराधो नाम राक्षसः ।
अतिष्ठन्मार्गमावृत्य रामस्येन्दोरिव ग्रहः ॥

२९ स जहार तयोर्मध्ये मैथिलीं लोकशोषणः ।
नभोनभस्ययोर्वृष्टिमवग्रह इवान्तरे ॥

३० तं विनिष्पिष्य काकुत्स्थौ पुरा दूषयति स्थलीम् ।
गन्धेनाशुचिना चेति वसुधायां निचख्नतुः ॥

Awakened by his beloved, Rama cast a reed weapon at the 23
  crow, and it fluttered about, only to escape by giving
  up one of its eyes.[6]

Suspecting that Bharata would come again, since he 24
  dwelled nearby, Rama left the slopes of Mount
  Chitrakuta and the deer, who would always miss him.

Lodging in the hospitable dwellings of sages, he made his 25
  way south, as the sun does, staying in the houses of the
  rainy-season stars.

Vaidehi shone brightly, following Rama; it looked as if 26
  Royal Glory were following him, in spite of Kaikeyi's
  forbidding her, out of her fondness for his virtues.

The wonderfully fragrant unguent on her body, given to 27
  her by Anasuya,* caused the bees in the forest to leave
  the flowers and fly to her.

There a *rākṣasa* called Viradha appeared, tawny like a 28
  twilight cloud, blocking Rama's path, as Rahu blocks
  the path of the moon.

That world tormentor stole away Maithili† from between 29
  the two brothers, as world-tormenting drought steals
  away the rains between the months of Nabhas and
  Nabhasya.[7]

Those two Kakutsthas‡ crushed Viradha; then, also 30
  because they feared that the foul stench would pollute
  the forest, they buried him in the earth.[8]

* The wife of the sage Atri.
† Sita.
‡ Rama and Lakshmana.

३१ पञ्चवट्यामथो रामः शासनात्कुम्भजन्मनः ।
अनपोढस्थितिस्तस्थौ विन्ध्याद्रिः प्रकृताविव ॥

३२ रावणावरजा तत्र राघवं मदनातुरा ।
अभिपेदे निदाघार्ता व्यालीव मलयद्रुमम् ॥

३३ सा सीतासन्निधावेव तं वव्रे कथितान्वया ।
अत्यारूढो हि नारीणामकालज्ञो मनोभवः ॥

३४ कलत्रवानहं बाले यवीयांसं भजस्व मे ।
इति रामो वृषस्यन्तीं वृषस्कन्धः शशास ताम् ॥

३५ ज्येष्ठाभिगमनात्पूर्वं तेनाप्यनभिनन्दिता ।
साभूद्रामाश्रया भूयो नदीवोभयकूलभाक् ॥

३६ संरम्भं मैथिलीहासः क्षणसौम्यां निनाय ताम् ।
निवातस्तिमितां वेलां चन्द्रोदय इवोदधेः ॥

३७ फलमस्यावहासस्य सद्यः प्राप्स्यसि पश्य माम् ।
मृगीपरिभवो व्याघ्र्यां मृत्यवे हि त्वया कृतः ॥

३८ इत्युक्त्वा मैथिलीं भर्तुरङ्कानि विशतीं भयात् ।
रूपं शूर्पनखा नाम्नः सदृशं प्रत्यपद्यत ॥

At Agastya's command, Rama then remained in 31
Panchavati, unwavering in his conduct, just as
the Vindhya mountain stays in its natural state,
unwavering in its stability, at the same sage's
command.[9]

There Ravana's younger sister,* sick with love, approached 32
Rama, like a snake tormented by the heat approaching
a sandal tree.

She declared her lineage and right in front of Sita asked 33
Rama to marry her. For when women's desire grows
too strong, it knows no bounds of time or place.

"Young lady, I have a wife. Choose my younger brother." 34
Thus bull-shouldered Rama commanded her when
she revealed her desire.

When he too repudiated her, on the grounds that she had 35
approached his elder brother first, she went again to
Rama, like a river tumbling between two banks.

For a moment she had seemed gentle, but now Sita's 36
laughter infuriated her, just as the ocean's swell,
unstirred by the wind, is roiled by the rise of the
moon.

"Look at me! You will soon taste the fruit of your mocking 37
laughter, for you have slighted a tigress the way one
might slight a gazelle, and that must lead to your
death."[10]

Saying this to Maithili, who shrank in terror into her 38
husband's arms, Shurpanakha returned to the form
that matched her name.[11]

———

* Shurpanakha.

३९ लक्ष्मणः प्रथमं श्रुत्वा कोकिलामञ्जुवादिनीम् ।
शिवाघोरस्वनां पश्चादुबुधे विकृतेति ताम् ॥

४० पर्णशालामथ क्षिप्रं विधृतासिः प्रविश्य सः ।
वैरूप्यपुनरुक्तेन भीषणां तामयोजयत् ॥

४१ सा वक्रनखधारिण्या वेणुकर्कशपर्वया ।
अङ्कुशाकारयाङ्गुल्या तानतर्जयदम्बरात् ॥

४२ प्राप्य चाशु जनस्थानं खरादिभ्यस्तथाविधा ।
रामोपक्रममाचख्यौ रक्षःपरिभवं नवम् ॥

४३ मुखावयवलूनां तां नैर्ऋता यत्पुरो दधुः ।
रामाभियायिनां तेषां तदेवाभूदमङ्गलम् ॥

४४ उदायुधानापततस्तान्दूरान्वीक्ष्य राघवः ।
निदधे विजयाशंसां चापे सीतां च लक्ष्मणे ॥

४५ एको दाशरथिः कामं यातुधानाः सहस्रशः ।
ते तु यावन्त एवासंस्तावद्धा दहृशे स तैः ॥

४६ असज्जनेन काकुत्स्थः प्रयुक्तमथ दूषणम् ।
न चक्षमे शुभाचारो ऽसद्दूषणमिवात्मनः ॥

Lakshmana, after first hearing her voice sweet as a koel's   39
   and then howling like a jackal, understood that she
   had transformed herself.

He rushed into the leaf hut and then, with sword drawn,   40
   made the woman more fearsome by redundantly
   disfiguring her.[12]

From the sky, she threatened them with a finger bearing   41
   crooked nails, rough-jointed like a bamboo stem,
   hooked like an elephant goad.

And in this condition, she quickly reached Janasthana and   42
   told Khara* and the others that Rama had inflicted
   fresh humiliation on the *rākṣasas.*

Inauspicious it was indeed for the *rākṣasas* that when they   43
   set out to attack Rama, they placed in the vanguard
   that woman with her mutilated face.

When Rama saw those overweening *rākṣasas* falling upon   44
   him with weapons raised, he entrusted hope of victory
   to his bow and Sita to Lakshmana.

Although Rama was alone and the *rākṣasas* in the   45
   thousands, he seemed to them to be just as numerous
   as they.[13]

Rama would no more tolerate Dushana, put in the   46
   vanguard by the wicked folk, than a virtuous man can
   tolerate a scoundrel defaming him.[14]

---

* Brother of Shurpanakha and Ravana.

४७ तं शरैः प्रतिजग्राह खरत्रिशिरसौ च सः ।
क्रमशस्ते पुनस्तस्य चापात्समविबोद्ययुः ॥

४८ तैस्त्रयाणां शितैर्बाणैर्यथापूर्वविशुद्धिभिः ।
आयुर्देहातिगैः पीतं रुधिरं च पतत्त्रिभिः ॥

४९ तस्मित्रामशरोत्कृत्ते बले महति रक्षसाम् ।
उच्छितं दद‌ृशे ऽन्यत्र कबन्धेभ्यो न किञ्चन ॥

५० सा बाणवर्षिणं रामं योधयित्वा सुरद्विषाम् ।
अप्रबोधाय सुष्वाप गृध्रच्छाये वरूथिनी ॥

५१ राघवास्त्राग्निदग्धानां रावणं प्रति रक्षसाम् ।
तेषां शूर्पनखैवैका दुष्प्रवृत्तिहराभवत् ॥

५२ निग्रहात्स्वसुराप्रानां वधाच्च धनदानुजः ।
रामेण निहितं मेने पदं दशसु मूर्धसु ॥

५३ रक्षसा मृगरूपेण वञ्चयित्वा स राघवौ ।
जहार सीतां पक्षीन्द्रप्रयासक्षणविघ्नितः ॥

५४ तौ सीतान्वेषिणौ गृध्रं लूनपक्षमपश्यताम् ।
प्राणैर्दशरथप्रीतेरनृणं कण्ठवर्तिभिः ॥

He welcomed him, and Khara and Trishiras too,* with 47
arrows shot one after the other yet that seemed to
leave his bow all at once.

Those sharp arrows passed straight through the bodies 48
of the three *rākṣasas* but remained as clean as before;
they drank their lives but left their blood for carrion
birds to drink.

Nothing of the great *rākṣasa* army, cut down by Rama's 49
arrows, could be seen still standing upright except for
headless trunks.[15]

Having provoked Rama, who rained down arrows, to fight, 50
the *rākṣasa* army slept, never to wake again, in the
shade of the vultures.

Shurpanakha alone survived to bring Ravana the bad news 51
that the *rākṣasas* had been destroyed by the fire of
Rama's arrows.

His sister maimed and his kinsmen slain, the younger 52
brother of Kubera† felt as if Rama had trodden upon
all his ten heads at once.

Ravana tricked Rama and Lakshmana with the help of a 53
rākṣasa who transformed himself into a deer, and he
abducted Sita, hindered, but only for a moment, by
the efforts of Jatayus, king of birds.

The two brothers set out searching for Sita and came 54
upon that vulture. His wings lopped off and his life
breaths in his throat, he was freed from his debt for
Dasharatha's friendship.[16]

* Two *rākṣasas*.
† Ravana.

५५ स रावणहृतां ताभ्यां वचसाचष्ट मैथिलीम् ।
आत्मनस्तु महत्कर्म व्रणैरावेद्य संस्थितः ॥

५६ तयोस्तस्मिन्नवीभूतपितृव्यापत्तिदुःखयोः ।
पितरीवाग्निसंस्कारानन्तरा ववृते क्रिया ॥

५७ वधनिर्धौतशापस्य कबन्धस्योपदेशतः ।
मुमूर्छ सख्यं रामस्य समानव्यसने हरौ ॥

५८ स हत्वा वालिनं वीरस्तत्पदे चिरकाङ्क्षिते ।
धातोः स्थान इवादेशं सुग्रीवं संन्यवेशयत् ॥

५९ इतस्ततश्च वैदेहीमन्वेष्टुं भर्तृचोदिताः ।
कपयश्चेरुरार्तस्य रामस्येव मनोरथाः ॥

६० प्रवृत्तावुपलब्धायां तस्याः सम्पातिदर्शनात् ।
मारुतिः सागरं तीर्णः संसारमिव निर्ममः ॥

६१ दृष्टा विचिन्वता तेन लङ्कायां राक्षसीवृता ।
जानकी विषवल्लीभिः परीतेव महौषधिः ॥

६२ तस्यै भर्तुरभिज्ञानमङ्गुलीयं ददौ हरिः ।
प्रत्युद्गतमिवानुष्णैस्तदानन्दासुबिन्दुभिः ॥

Before he died, Jatayus told them by words that Sita had 55
been abducted by Ravana; of his own heroic deeds he
spoke only by his wounds.

Their grief for their father's death renewed, the brothers 56
performed the rites following Jatayus's cremation as
though for their father.

On the advice of Kabandha, whose curse had been lifted 57
by being killed by Rama, he formed a friendship with a
monkey who had suffered the same sorrows as he.[17]

The hero killed Valin and in his place, long coveted, 58
established Sugriva, as one might establish in place of
one verbal root a substitute.[18]

Like the longings of Rama in his torment, the monkeys at 59
the urging of their master roamed hither and yon in
their search for Sita.

After encountering Sampati* and obtaining news of Sita 60
from him, Hanuman crossed the ocean, as a selfless
person may cross samsara.[19]

Searching Lanka, Hanuman found Sita surrounded by 61
rākṣasa women, like a life-giving herb surrounded by
poisonous vines.

The monkey gave her a ring as a token from her husband, 62
at which the cool droplets of her tears of joy seemed to
spring up in welcome.

---

* The brother of Jatayus.

६३ निर्वाप्य प्रियसन्देशैः सीतामक्षवधोद्धुरः ।
स ददाह विभीर्लङ्कां क्षणसोढारिनिग्रहः ॥

६४ प्रत्यभिज्ञानरत्नं च रामायादर्शयत्कृती ।
हृदयं स्वयमायातं वैदेह्या इव मूर्तिमत् ॥

६५ स प्राप हृदयन्यस्तमणिस्पर्शनिमीलितः ।
अपयोधरसंसर्गां प्रियालिङ्गननिर्वृतिम् ॥

६६ श्रुत्वा रामः प्रियोदन्तं मेने तत्सङ्गमोत्सुकः ।
महार्णवपरिक्षेपं लङ्कायाः परिखालघुम् ॥

६७ स प्रतस्थे ऽरिनाशाय हरिसैन्यैरनुद्रुतः ।
न केवलं भुवः पृष्ठे खे ऽपि सम्बाधवर्त्मनि ॥

६८ निविष्टमुदधेः कूले तं प्रपेदे विभीषणः ।
स्नेहाद्राक्षसलक्ष्म्येव बुद्धिमाविश्य चोदितः ॥

६९ तस्मै निशाचरैश्वर्यं प्रतिशुश्राव राघवः ।
काले खलु समारब्धाः फलं बध्नन्ति नीतयः ॥

७० स सेतुं बन्धयामास यो बभौ लवणाम्भसि ।
रसातलादिवोन्मग्नः शेषः स्वप्राय शार्ङ्गिणः ॥

He consoled Sita with messages from her beloved, and   63
then, emboldened by killing Aksha, he fearlessly
burned down Lanka, after enduring enemy captivity
for a mere instant.[20]

And having fulfilled that task, he showed Rama the jewel   64
she had given as a token; it was as if it were Sita's heart
that had taken form and come of its own accord.

With eyes closed at the touch of the jewel pressed against   65
his heart, he felt the bliss of his beloved's embrace, but
without the touch of her breasts.

When Rama heard the news of his beloved, he was so   66
eager to reunite with her that he thought the great
ocean surrounding Lanka as easy to cross as a moat.

He set off to destroy his enemies, followed by monkey   67
soldiers, crowding the pathways not only on the earth
but also in the sky.

When he had encamped on the shore of the ocean,   68
Vibhishana* took refuge with him, as if the *rākṣasas'*
Royal Fortune had entered his thoughts and was
lovingly urging him on.[21]

Rama promised him the kingship of the *rākṣasas;*   69
indeed, policies undertaken at the right moment pay
dividends.

He had a causeway built that gleamed in the salty ocean   70
as if the great snake Shesha had risen from the
underworld of Rasatala for bow-wielding Vishnu to
sleep upon.[22]

---

* Ravana's virtuous brother.

७१ तेनोत्तीर्य पथा लङ्कां रोधयामास पिङ्गलैः ।
द्वितीयं हेमप्राकारं कुर्वद्भिरिव वानरैः ॥

७२ रणः प्रववृते तत्र भीमः प्लवगरक्षसाम् ।
दिग्विजृम्भितकाकुत्स्थपौलस्त्यजयघोषणः ॥

७३ पादपाविद्धपरिघः शिलानिष्पिष्टमुद्गरः ।
अतिशस्त्रनखन्यासः शैलभग्नमतङ्गजः ॥

७४ अथ रामशिरश्छेददर्शनोद्भ्रान्तचेतसम् ।
सीतां मायेति शंसन्ती त्रिजटा समजीवयत् ॥

७५ कामं जीवति मे नाथ इति सा विजहौ शुचम् ।
प्राङ्गत्वा सत्यमस्यान्तं जीवितास्मीति लज्जिता ॥

७६ गरुडापातविश्लेषि मेघनादास्त्रबन्धनम् ।
दाशरथ्योः क्षणक्लेशि स्वप्नवृत्तमिवाभवत् ॥

७७ ततो बिभेद पौलस्त्यः शक्त्या वक्षसि लक्ष्मणम् ।
रामस्त्वनाहतो ऽप्यासीद्विदीर्णहृदयः शुचा ॥

७८ स मारुतसुतानीतमहौषधिहृतव्यथः ।
लङ्कास्त्रीणां पुनश्चक्रे विलापाचार्यकं शरैः ॥

With that as pathway, Rama crossed and besieged Lanka   71
   with his tawny monkeys, who seemed to form a
   further rampart of gold.

A dreadful battle ensued there between the monkeys and   72
   the *rākṣasas,* in which cries of "Victory to Rama" and
   "Victory to Ravana" resounded in all quarters.

Iron bars were crushed by trees; clubs were pulverized   73
   by stones; claws left wounds worse than those of
   weapons; elephants were broken by rocks.

Sita beheld Rama decapitated, and her mind went blank   74
   with terror, but Trijata revived her by revealing that it
   was an illusion.[23]

Naturally she put aside her grief when she knew that her   75
   lord still lived, but she was ashamed that she had
   remained alive when she had thought his death was
   real.

The two sons of Dasharatha were bound by a weapon of   76
   Meghanada,* but it troubled them only for an instant:
   it dissolved upon Garuda's attack, as if it had been a
   dream.[24]

Then Ravana pierced Lakshmana's chest with his spear,   77
   but it was Rama whose heart was rent with grief,
   although he had not been struck.

His suffering allayed by a powerful herb brought by the   78
   son of the wind, Lakshmana, with his arrows, once
   again taught the women of Lanka to weep.[25]

---

* Indrajit, Ravana's son.

७९ नादं स मेघनादस्य धनुश्छेन्द्रायुधप्रभम् ।
मेघस्येव शरत्कालो न किञ्चित्पर्यशेषयत् ॥

८० कुम्भकर्णः कपीन्द्रेण तुल्यावस्थः स्वसुः कृतः ।
रुरोध रामं शृङ्गीव टङ्कच्छिन्नमनःशिलः ॥

८१ अकाले बोधितो भ्रात्रा प्रियस्वप्नो वृथा भवन् ।
रामेषुभिरितीवासौ दीर्घनिद्रां प्रवेशितः ॥

८२ इतराण्यपि रक्षांसि सेतुर्वानरकोटिषु ।
रजांसि समरोत्थानि तच्छोणितनदीष्विव ॥

८३ निर्ययावथ पौलस्त्यः पुनर्युद्धाय मन्दिरात् ।
अरावणमरामं वा जगद्द्येति निश्चितः ॥

८४ रामं पदातिमालोक्य लङ्केशं च वरूथिनम् ।
हरिरथ्यं रथं तस्मै प्रजिघाय पुरन्दरः ॥

८५ तमाधूतध्वजपटं व्योमगङ्गोर्मिवायुभिः ।
देवसूतभुजालम्बी जैत्रमध्यास्त राघवः ॥

८६ मातलिस्तस्य माहेन्द्रमामुमोच तनुच्छदम् ।
यत्रोत्पलदलक्रैव्यमस्त्राण्यापुः सुरद्विषाम् ॥

Lakshmana allowed nothing to remain of the roaring of   79
   Meghanada, nor of his bow, which was like Indra's
   weapon, just as autumn lets no trace remain of the
   cloud's thunder, nor of its rainbow.[26]

Kumbhakarna, reduced by Sugriva to the same state as   80
   his sister, blocked Rama, like a mountain whose red
   arsenic has been cut open by a pickaxe.[27]

As if telling him, "Sluggard, it was a mistake; your brother   81
   woke you too early," Rama's arrows sent him into a
   lasting sleep.[28]

Other *rākṣasas* too disappeared amid the millions of   82
   monkeys, as the dust stirred up by battle disappeared
   into the rivers of their blood.

Then Ravana emerged from his palace again to fight,   83
   for he had resolved, "Today the world will be rid of
   Rama—or Ravana!"

Seeing that Rama was on foot while the lord of Lanka had   84
   an armored chariot, Indra gave Rama a chariot with
   chestnut horses.

Helped up by the charioteer of the gods, Rama mounted   85
   that victorious vehicle, its banner still fluttering in the
   wind coming off the waves of the celestial Ganga.

Matali armed him with Indra's armor: against it, the   86
   weapons of the enemies of the gods became as soft as
   petals of the water lily.

८७ अन्योन्यदर्शनप्राप्तविक्रमावसरं चिरात् ।
रामरावणयोर्वैरं चरितार्थमिवाभवत् ॥

८८ भुजमूर्धोरुबाहुल्यादेको ऽपि धनदानुजः ।
दद्दशे स यथापूर्वं मातृवंश इव स्थितः ॥

८९ जेतारं लोकपालानां स्वमुखैरर्चितेश्वरम् ।
रामस्तुलितकैलासं तमरिं बह्वमन्यत ॥

९० तस्य स्फुरति पौलस्त्यः सीतासंगमशंसिनि ।
निचखानाधिकक्रोधः शरं सव्येतरे भुजे ॥

९१ रावणस्यापि रामास्तं भित्त्वा हृदयमाशुगम् ।
विवेश भुवमाख्यातुमुरगेभ्य इव प्रियम् ॥

९२ वचसेव तयोर्वाक्यमस्त्रमस्त्रेण निघ्नतोः ।
अन्योन्यजयसंरम्भो ववृधे वादिनोरिव ॥

९३ विक्रमव्यतिहारेण सामान्याभूद्द्वयोरपि ।
जयश्रीरन्तरा वेदिर्मत्तवारणयोरिव ॥

९४ कृतप्रतिकृतप्रीतैस्तयोर्मुक्तां सुरासुरैः ।
परस्परशरव्राताः पुष्पवृष्टिं न सेहिरे ॥

Long had there been enmity between Rama and Ravana,   87
  but only now, when it brought them face to face to
  show their valor, did it seem to bear fruit.

Although he was alone, because of the great quantity of   88
  his arms and heads, Ravana appeared as before, as if
  still in the midst of his mother's kinsmen.[29]

Rama held him in high esteem, an enemy who had   89
  vanquished the protectors of the directions, venerated
  Ishvara* with his own heads, and lifted Mount
  Kailasa.[30]

Ravana in a rage buried an arrow in Rama's right arm,   90
  which was already throbbing, presaging his reunion
  with Sita.[31]

And Rama's swift missile pierced Ravana's breast and   91
  plunged into the ground, as though to proclaim its
  welcome news to the serpents.[32]

As the two destroyed missile with missile, the eagerness   92
  of each to vanquish the other grew greater, like two
  debaters refuting words with words.

Taking turns in bold attack, the two shared the splendor of   93
  victory evenly, like two bull elephants evenly battling
  over a mound.

Their arrows swarming back and forth had no mercy   94
  on the showers of blossoms released by the gods
  and *asuras,* who were delighted by their blows and
  counterblows.

---

* Shiva.

९५ अयःशङ्कुचितां रक्षः शतघ्नीमथ शत्रवे ।
हृतां वैवस्वतस्येव कूटशाल्मलिमक्षिपत् ॥

९६ राघवो रथमप्राप्तां तामाशां च सुरद्विषाम् ।
अर्धचन्द्रमुखैर्बाणैश्चिच्छेद कदलीमिव ॥

९७ अमोघं सन्दधे चासौ धनुष्येकधनुर्धरः ।
ब्राह्मास्त्रं प्रियाशोकशल्यनिष्कर्षणौषधम् ॥

९८ तद्द्योम्नि दशधा भिन्नं दद्दशे दीप्तिमन्मुखम् ।
वपुर्महोरगस्येव करालफणमण्डलम् ॥

९९ तेन मन्त्रप्रयुक्तेन निमेषार्धादपातयत् ।
रामो रिपुशिरःपङ्क्तिमज्ञातव्रणवेदनाम् ॥

१०० बालार्कप्रतिमेवाप्सु वीचिभिन्ना पतिष्यतः ।
रराज रक्षःकायस्य कण्ठच्छेदपरम्परा ॥

१०१ मरुतां पश्यतां तस्य शिरांसि पतितान्यपि ।
मनो नातिविशश्वास पुनःसन्धानशङ्किनाम् ॥

१०२ अथ मदगुरुपक्षैर्लोकपालद्विपानाम्
अनुगतमलिवृन्दैर्गण्डभित्तीर्विहाय ।
अविनियमितरत्ने मूर्ध्नि पौलस्त्यशत्रोः
सुरभि सुरविमुक्तं पुष्पवर्षं पपात ॥

Then the *rākṣasa* launched against his enemy the *śataghnī*   95
    weapon, studded with iron spikes, as if it were the
    stolen spiky *śalmali* mace of Yama.[33]

Before it reached his chariot, Rama used his crescent-   96
    moon-headed arrows to slash through it—and
    through the hopes of the enemies of the gods—as if it
    were a plantain stem.[34]

That unique archer set the unfailing weapon of Brahma to   97
    his bow, a remedy for removing the arrow of the grief
    he felt for his beloved.

That weapon was seen to split into ten parts in the sky,   98
    each with a flaming mouth, like the body of a great
    snake with a circle of fearsome hoods.

With that mantra-empowered weapon Rama cut down   99
    the whole row of his enemy's heads in half an instant,
    without their feeling the pain of a wound.

As the *rākṣasa's* body was about to fall to the earth, the   100
    row of its sliced necks shone red like reflections of a
    newly risen sun dispersed in waves.

Though the gods saw that his heads had fallen, their minds   101
    were not yet reassured, since they feared that he might
    put them back in place again.

Then a fragrant rain of flowers released by the gods fell   102
    upon the as yet uncrowned head of Ravana's enemy,
    followed by swarms of bees, who, wings heavy with
    ichor, left the cheeks of the elephants of the gods who
    protect the directions.[35]

१०३ यन्ता हरेः सपदि संहृतकार्मुकज्यम्
आपृच्छ्य राघवमनुष्ठितदेवकार्यम् ।
नामाङ्करावणशराचितकेतुयष्टिम्
ऊर्ध्वं रथं हरिसहस्रयुतं निनाय ॥

१०४ रघुपतिरपि जातवेदोविशुद्धां प्रगृह्य प्रियां
प्रियसुहृदि विभीषणे सङ्क्रम्य श्रियं वैरिणः ।
रविसुतसहितेन तेनानुयातः ससौमित्रिणा
भुजविजितविमानरत्नाधिरूढः प्रतस्थे पुरीम् ॥

इति रघुवंशे महाकाव्ये द्वादशः सर्गः ॥

Rama had accomplished the work of the gods and now
    at once loosened his bowstring. The charioteer of
    Indra took his leave and led the chariot up and away,
    yoked to its thousand horses, its flagstaff studded with
    arrows marked with Ravana's name.   103

The lord of the Raghus took back his beloved after her
    purity had been proved in fire. Then he transferred
    his enemy's sovereignty to his dear friend Vibhishana,
    mounted the wondrous flying palace* that he had won
    by the strength of his arm, and set off for Ayodhya,
    with Vibhishana, Sugriva, and Lakshmana.   104

* Pushpaka.

त्रयोदशः सर्गः

१ अथात्मनः शब्दगुणं गुणज्ञः पदं विमानेन विगाहमानः ।
रत्नाकरं वीक्ष्य मिथः स जायां रामाभिधानो हरिरित्युवाच ॥

२ वैदेहि पश्या मलयाद्विभक्तं मत्सेतुना फेनिलमम्बुराशिम् ।
छायापथेनेव शरत्प्रसन्नमाकाशमाविष्कृततारतारम् ॥

३ गुरोरियियक्षोः कपिलेन पूर्वं रसातलं संक्रमिते तुरङ्गे ।
तदर्थमूर्वीमवदारयद्भिः पूर्वैः किलायं परिवर्धितो नः ॥

४ गर्भं दधत्यर्कमरीचयो ऽस्मादि्द्ववृद्धिमत्राश्नुवते वसूनि ।
अबिन्धनं वह्निमसौ बिभर्ति प्रह्लादनं ज्योतिरजन्यनेन ॥

५ तां तामवस्थां प्रतिपद्यमानं स्थितं दश व्याप्य दिशो महिम्ना ।
विष्णोरिवास्यानवधारणीयमीदृक्तया रूपमियत्तया वा ॥

CHAPTER 13

Rama and Sita
Return to Ayodhya

Then Hari* in the form called Rama plunged with his   1
    flying chariot into his own realm, whose quality is
    sound. And knowing the qualities of all things, he
    spoke in private with his wife while gazing down at
    the ocean.[1]

"Look, Sita, at the foaming brine divided in two by my   2
    bridge that starts from the Malaya mountain. It
    resembles the sky, clear in autumn and with stars
    shining brightly, divided in two by the Milky Way.[2]

"They say that long ago our forebears increased the   3
    ocean's size by tearing up the earth to find their
    father's sacrificial horse, which Kapila had brought
    down to the underworld.[3]

"From the ocean the sun rays conceive a fetus; in it jewels   4
    ever increase; it holds the fire whose fuel is water; the
    light that delights was born in it.[4]

"Its form is changeable, and its grandeur pervades the ten   5
    directions; like that of Vishnu, one cannot delimit its
    kind or quantity.[5]

---

* Vishnu.

६ नाभिप्ररूढाम्बुरुहासनेन संस्तूयमानः प्रथमेन धात्रा ।
अमुं युगान्तोचितयोगनिद्रः संहृत्य लोकान्पुरुषो ऽधिशेते ॥

७ पक्षच्छिदा गोत्रभिदात्तगर्वाः शरण्यमेनं शतशो महीध्राः ।
नृपा इवोपप्लविनः परेभ्यो धर्मोत्तरं मध्यममाश्रयन्ते ॥

८ रसातलादादिभवेन पुंसा भुवः प्रयुक्तोद्द्वहनक्रियायाः ।
अस्याच्छमम्भः प्रलयप्रवृद्धं मुहूर्तवक्राभरणं बभूव ॥

९ मुखार्पणेषु प्रकृतिप्रगल्भाः स्वयं तरङ्गाधरदानदक्षाः ।
अनन्यसामान्यकलत्रवृत्तिः पिवत्यसौ पाययते च सिन्धूः ॥

१० ससत्त्वमादाय सरिन्मुखाम्भः संमीलयन्तो विवृताननत्वम् ।
अमी शिरोभिस्तिमयः सरन्ध्रैरूर्ध्वं वितन्वन्ति जलप्रवाहान् ॥

११ मातङ्गनक्रैः सहसोत्पतद्भिर्भिन्नान्द्विधा पश्य समुद्रफेनान् ।
कपोलसंसर्पितया य एषां व्रजन्ति कर्णक्षणचामरत्वम् ॥

१२ वेलानिलाय प्रसृता भुजङ्गा महोर्मिविस्फूर्जितनिर्विशेषाः ।
सूर्यांशुसम्पर्कसमृद्धरागैर्व्यज्यन्त एते मणिभिः फणस्थैः ॥

"Upon this ocean Vishnu rests after reabsorbing the   6
    worlds and entering the yogic sleep suitable to the
    age's end, while on the lotus growing from his navel
    the primordial creator sits intoning his praise.[6]

"When Indra cuts the wings of the mountains, destroying   7
    their pride, they take refuge by the hundreds in this
    ocean, just as kings tormented by enemies take refuge
    with an impartial, righteous monarch.[7]

"When at the time of universal destruction the ocean's   8
    clear water swelled, it became for a moment an
    ornament on the face of the earth as she was raised
    from the netherworld by the Primeval Person.[8]

"With his lips, the waves, Ocean skillfully kisses his wives,   9
    the rivers, treating them in a way no other husband
    would, both drinking them, naturally bold as they are
    in offering their mouths, and also making them drink.[9]

"These whales swallow the water from the rivers' mouths   10
    filled with living creatures, then close their gaping
    mouths and shoot jets of water upward through the
    blowholes on their heads.

"Look, as the elephant sharks suddenly leap from the   11
    water, the ocean's bubbles are parted in two and,
    gliding along their cheeks, form momentary chowries
    at their ears!

"The serpents, slithering forth to taste the wind from the 12
    shore, are indistinguishable from the billowing waves,
    and can only be identified by the jewels in their hoods
    that sparkle at the touch of the sun's rays.[10]

१३ तवाधरस्पर्धिषु विद्रुमेषु पर्यस्तमेतत्सहसोर्मिवेगात् ।
ऊर्ध्वाङ्कुरप्रोतमुखं कथञ्चित्क्लेशादपक्रामति शङ्खयूथम् ॥

१४ प्रवृत्तमात्रेण पयांसि पातुमावर्तवेगाद्भ्रमता घनेन ।
आभाति भूयिष्ठमितः समुद्रः प्रमथ्यमानो गिरिणेव भूयः ॥

१५ निस्त्रिंशकल्पस्य निधेर्जलानामेषा तमालद्रुमराजिनीला ।
दूरादरालभ्रु विभाति वेला कलङ्करेखामलिनेव धारा ॥

१६ वेलानिलः केतकरेणुभिस्ते सम्भावयत्याननमायताक्षम् ।
मामक्षमं मण्डनकालहानेर्वेत्तीव बिम्बाधरबद्धतृष्णम् ॥

१७ एते वयं सैकतभिन्नशुक्तिपर्यस्तमुक्तापटलं पयोधेः ।
प्राप्ता मुहूर्तेन विमानवेगात्कूलं फलावर्जितपूगमालि ॥

१८ कुरुष्व तावत्करभोरु पश्चान्मार्गे मृगप्रेक्षिणि दृष्टिपातम् ।
एषा हि दूरीभवतः समुद्रात्सकानना निष्पततीव भूमिः ॥

१९ क्वचित्पथा सञ्चरते सुराणां क्वचिद्धनानां मरुतां क्वचिच्च ।
यथाविधो मे मनसो ऽभिलाषः प्रवर्त्तते पश्य तथा विमानम् ॥

"The sudden force of the waves has heaped together conch   13
    shells onto the coral reef, which rivals the hue of your
    lips, and with their mouths caught on the upright
    coral sprouts they can scarcely float away.[11]

"From here that cloud, set spinning by the force of a   14
    maelstrom as soon as it began to drink, very much
    makes the ocean appear as if it were being churned
    again by the mountain.[12]

"My love with curving brows, here the shore, darkened by   15
    a fringe of gamboge trees, makes the sword-like ocean
    appear from afar as if its blade were stained by a line
    of rust.

"The wind from the shore adorns your large-eyed face   16
    with pandanus pollen. Perhaps it knows that I so
    thirst for your lips, like fruits of the scarlet gourd, that
    I cannot bear the time that would be wasted in putting
    on make-up.

"Here we are, thanks to the speed of the flying palace,   17
    arrived in an instant at the ocean's shore, wreathed in
    palms, laden with areca nuts, and with a coverlet of
    pearls scattered across the sand from opened oysters.

"My darling, whose thighs taper like the trunk of an   18
    elephant and whose gaze is like that of a deer, cast
    your eyes now on the path behind us! Here the land
    with its forests seems almost to be bursting forth from
    the ever-receding ocean.

"Look how the flying palace moves as my mind wills   19
    it, now riding the path of the gods, now that of the
    clouds, and now again that of the winds!

२० असौ महेन्द्रद्विपदानगन्धी त्रिमार्गगावीचिविमर्दशीतः ।
आकाशवायुर्दिनयौवनोत्थानाचामति स्वेदलवान्मुखात्ते ॥

२१ करेण वातायननिःसृतेन स्पृष्टस्त्वया चण्डि कुतूहलिन्या ।
आमुञ्चतीवाभरणं द्वितीयमुद्भिन्नविद्युद्बलयो घनस्ते ॥

२२ अमी जनस्थानमपोढविघ्नं मत्वा समारब्धनवोटजानि ।
अध्यासते चीरभृतो यथास्वं चिरोज्झितान्याश्रममण्डलानि ॥

२३ एषा स्थली यत्र विचिन्वता त्वां भ्रष्टं मया नूपुरमेकमुर्व्याम् ।
अदृश्यत त्वच्चरणारविन्दविश्लेषदुःखादिव बद्धमौनम् ॥

२४ त्वं रक्षसा भीरु यतोऽपनीता तं मार्गमेताः कृपया लता मे ।
अदर्शयन्वक्तुमशक्नुवन्त्यः शाखाभिरावर्जितपल्लवाभिः ॥

२५ मृगयश्च दर्भाङ्कुरनिर्व्यपेक्षास्तवागतिज्ञं समबोधयन्माम् ।
व्यापारयन्त्यो दिशि दक्षिणस्यामुत्पक्ष्मराजीनि विलोचनानि ॥

२६ एतद्गिरेर्माल्यवतः पुरस्तादाविर्भवत्यम्बरलेखि शृङ्गम् ।
नवं पयो यत्र घनैर्मया च त्वद्विप्रयोगाश्रु समं विसृष्टम् ॥

"The breeze here in the upper sky, fragrant with the musth   20
    of Indra's elephant and cool from the tumult of the
    Ganga's waves, sips the droplets of midday sweat from
    your face.

"As you stretch out your hand through the window, quick-   21
    tempered lady, the cloud you are so curious to touch
    flashes forth a bracelet of lightning, giving you, it
    seems, a further ornament.

"These bark-clad hermits, realizing Janasthana to be free   22
    of dangers, have returned to occupy the sites of their
    long-abandoned ashrams, each one his own, where
    new cottages are now being built.

"This is the place where I came to search for you and   23
    found an anklet of yours all alone that had fallen to
    the ground, keeping silent as though from grief at
    separation from your lotus foot.

"These vines here took pity on me and, though unable to   24
    speak, used the twisted leaves of their branches to
    show the path the *rākṣasa* took, my frightened lady,
    when carrying you off.

"When I didn't know the way you had gone, the does,   25
    neglecting their mouthfuls of *darbha* shoots, set me
    right by turning their long-lashed eyes toward the
    south.

"Now the peak of Mount Malyavat appears before us,   26
    scratching the sky. It was here, while the clouds
    poured down their fresh water, that I wept tears of
    separation from you.[13]

२७ गन्धाश्व धाराहतपल्वलानां कदम्बमर्धोद्गतकेसरं च ।
स्निग्धाश्व केकाः शिखिनां त्वया मे यस्मिन्विना दुष्प्रसहान्यभूवन् ॥

२८ पूर्वानुभूतं स्मरता च रात्रौ कम्पोत्तरं भीरु तवोपगूढम् ।
गुहाविसारीण्यतिवाहितानि मया कथञ्चिद्धनगर्जितानि ॥

२९ आसारसिक्तक्षितिवाष्पयोगान्मामक्षिणोद्यत्र च भिन्नकोशैः ।
विडम्ब्यमाना नवकन्दलैस्ते विवाहधूमाकुललोचनश्रीः ॥

३० उपान्तवानीरवनोपगूढान्यलक्ष्यपारिप्लवसारसानि ।
दूरावतीर्णा पिवतीव खेदादमूनि पम्पासलिलानि दृष्टिः ॥

३१ अत्राविमुक्तानि रथाङ्गनाम्नामन्योन्यदत्तोत्पलकेसराणि ।
द्वन्द्वानि दूरान्तरवर्तिना ते मया प्रिये सस्पृहमीक्षितानि ॥

३२ इमां तटाशोकलतां च तन्वीं स्तनाभिरामस्तवकावनम्राम् ।
त्वत्प्राप्तिबुद्ध्या परिरिप्समाणः सौमित्रिणा सासुरहं निषिद्धः ॥

३३ अमूर्विमानान्तविलम्बिनीनां श्रुत्वा स्वनं काञ्चनकिङ्किणीनाम् ।
प्रत्युद्व्रजन्तीव खमुत्पतन्त्यो गोदावरीसारसपङ्क्तयस्त्वाम् ॥

"Here the fragrance of the pools pounded by showers, the 27
sight of the *kadamba* flowers with their half-opened
filaments, and the sweet cries of the peacocks were
intolerable to me without you.

"At night I could only barely endure the long-drawn-out 28
rumbling of the clouds echoing through the caves by
remembering your trembling embrace experienced in
the past on such nights.

"And here freshly blossoming banana flowers were 29
touched by steam rising from the rain-soaked earth,
reminding me painfully of the beauty of your eyes
smarting from the smoke from the wedding fire.[14]

"When my gaze reaches the waters of Lake Pampa, whose 30
banks are covered by thickets of reeds and where
wading sarus cranes can just be seen, it drinks them
in, as if exhausted from its long journey from here on
high.

"Here, my beloved, when I was so far separated from you, 31
I gazed full of envy at the united pairs of shelducks
exchanging filaments of the water lily.

"When I made to embrace this *aśoka* tree on the bank— 32
since it was bent over by its blossom clusters lovely as
breasts, I thought I had found you—Lakshmana held
me back with tears in his eyes.

"At the sound of the golden bells that hang from the back 33
of the flying chariot, these lines of sarus cranes from
the Godavari fly up into the sky as if they were coming
to welcome you.[15]

311

३४ एषा त्वया पेलवमध्ययापि घटाम्बुसंवर्धितबालचूता ।
आह्लादयत्युन्मुखकृष्णसारा दृष्टा चिरात्पञ्चवटी मनो मे ॥

३५ अत्रानुगोदं मृगयानिवृत्तस्तरङ्गवातेन विनीतखेदः ।
रहस्त्वदुत्सङ्गनिषण्णमूर्धा स्मरामि वानीरगृहेषु सुप्तम् ॥

३६ भ्रूभेदमात्रेण पदान्मघोनः प्राभ्रंशयद्यो नहुषं प्रमत्तम् ।
तस्याबिलाम्भःपरिशुद्धिहेतोर्भौमो मुनेः स्थानपरिग्रहो ऽयम् ॥

३७ त्रेताग्निधूमाग्रमुदग्रकीर्तेस्तस्येदमाक्रान्तविमानमार्गम् ।
घ्रात्वा हविर्गन्धि रजोविमुक्तः समश्नुते मे लघिमानमात्मा ॥

३८ एतन्मुनेर्मानिनि सातकर्णेः पञ्चाप्सरो नाम विहारवारि ।
आभाति पर्यन्तवनं विदूरान्मेघान्तरालक्ष्यमिवेन्दुबिम्बम् ॥

३९ पुरा स दर्भाङ्कुरमात्रवृत्तिश्चरन्मृगैः सार्धमृषिर्मघोना ।
समाधिभीतेन किलाभिनीतः पञ्चाप्सरोयौवनकूटबन्धम् ॥

४० तस्यायमन्तर्हितसौधभाजः प्रसक्तसङ्गीतमृदङ्गशब्दः ।
वियद्गतः पुष्पकचन्द्रशालाः क्षणं प्रतिश्रुन्मुखराः करोति ॥

"How I delight at the sight, after so long, of Panchavati,   34
with the spotted antelopes gazing up at us. It was here
that you hoisted, though so slender of waist, large
water pots to nourish the mango saplings.

"I remember sleeping here beside the Godavari when I   35
returned from hunting. The breeze off the river's
waves had eased my fatigue, and I laid my head in your
lap, alone in the cane bower.

"This place is the earthly abode of the sage whose mere   36
frown made the arrogant Nahusha fall from Indra's
high station, and who makes the turbid waters clear in
autumn.[16]

"Here is the plume of the smoke from the three fires of   37
that same illustrious sage, just reaching the path
of our flying chariot. Its fragrance, redolent with
oblations, cleanses my soul of its impurities and
makes me feel light.

"Proud lady, this is the pleasure pond called Five   38
Apsarases, belonging to the sage Satakarni.
Surrounded by forests, it looks from afar like the disk
of the moon visible among the clouds.[17]

"Though that sage, long ago, was wont to live only on   39
shoots of *darbha* grass and to graze with the deer,
Indra, fearing the power of his meditation, caught
him, they say, in the snare of the youth of five celestial
beauties.

"The rumble of the drums rising to the sky from the   40
uninterrupted concerts of that sage in his invisible
palace is making the upper decks of our Pushpaka
chariot resound for a moment with echoes.

४१ हविर्भुजामेधवतां चतुर्णां मध्ये ललाटन्तपसप्तसप्तिः ।
असौ तपस्यत्यपरस्तपस्वी नाम्ना सुतीक्ष्णश्चरितेन दान्तः ॥

४२ अमुं सहासप्रहितेक्षणानि व्याजार्धसन्दर्शितमेखलानि ।
नालं विकर्तुं जनितेन्द्रशङ्कं सुराङ्गनाविभ्रमचेष्टितानि ॥

४३ वाचंयमत्वात्प्रणतिं ममैष कम्पेन किञ्चित्प्रतिगृह्य मूर्ध्ना ।
दृष्टिं विमानव्यवधानमुक्ते पुनः सहस्रार्चिषि संनिधत्ते ॥

४४ अदः शरण्यं शरभङ्गनाम्नस्तपोवनं पावनमाहिताग्रेः ।
चिराय सन्तर्प्य समिद्भिरग्निं यो मन्त्रपूतां तनुमप्यहौषीत् ॥

४५ छायाविनीताध्वपरिश्रमेषु भूयिष्ठसम्भाव्यफलेष्वमीषु ।
तस्यातिथीनामधुना सपर्या स्थिता सुपुत्रेष्विव पादपेषु ॥

४६ धारास्वनोद्गारिदरीमुखो ऽसौ शृङ्गाग्रलग्नाम्बुदवप्रपङ्कः ।
बध्नाति मे बन्धुरगात्रि चक्षुर्दृप्तः ककुद्मानिव चित्रकूटः ॥

४७ एषा प्रसन्नस्तिमितप्रवाहा सरिद्विदूरान्तरभावतन्वी ।
मन्दाकिनी भाति नगोपकण्ठे मुक्तावली कण्ठगतेव भूमेः ॥

"Here, in the midst of four well-stoked fires, with the sun,   41
    with its seven steeds, burning his brow from above,
    another ascetic is practicing asceticism—his name
    Sutikshna, 'Fierce,' his behavior self-controlled.

"Celestial ladies with laughing glances contrive on some   42
    pretext to give a glimpse of their girdles, but their
    coquetry cannot disturb that sage, who has awakened
    Indra's anxiety.

"Because of his vow of silence, he returns my greeting   43
    with a slight nod and directs his gaze back again
    toward the thousand-rayed sun, no longer blocked by
    our flying chariot.[18]

"Over there, a haven for the distressed, is the purifying   44
    ashram of Sharabhanga, keeper of the sacrificial fires.
    Having long fed the fire with wood, he offered up his
    own body as well, once cleansed by mantras.

"Now the task of honoring his guests rests with these   45
    trees, as if they were his pious sons. They relieve the
    fatigue of the journey with their shade and are laden
    with fruit ready for picking.

"My shapely wife, there Mount Chitrakuta arrests my   46
    gaze. With the roar of cataracts resounding from the
    mouths of its caves and with clouds clinging to its
    peaks, it resembles a powerful bull, bellowing and
    with mud stuck to its horns from butting against a
    riverbank.

"Here close around the mountain, the Mandakini River, so   47
    slender seen at this distance, its current calm and still,
    shines like a string of pearls upon the earth's neck.

315

४८ अयं स रूढो ऽनुगिरं तमालः तव प्रवालावचयेन यस्य ।
   कर्णार्पितेनाकरवं कपोलमप्रार्थ्यकालागुरुपत्तलेखम् ॥

४९ अनिग्रहत्रासविनीतसत्त्वमपुष्पहिंसाफलबन्धिवृक्षम् ।
   वनं तपःसाधनमेतदत्रेराविष्कृतोद्ग्रतपःप्रभावम् ॥

५० अत्राभिषेकाय तपोधनानां सप्तर्षिहस्तोचितहेमपद्माम् ।
   प्रवर्तयामास किलानसूया त्रिस्रोतसं त्र्यम्बकमौलिमालाम् ॥

५१ वीरासनैर्ध्यानजुषां मुनीनाममी समध्यासितवेदिबन्धाः ।
   निवातनिष्कम्पतया विभान्ति योगाधिरूढा इव शाखिनो ऽपि ॥

५२ त्वया पुरस्तादुपयाचितो यः सो ऽयं वटः श्याम इति प्रतीतः ।
   राशिर्मणीनामिव गारुडानां सपद्मरागः फलितो विभाति ॥

316

"This gamboge tree growing on the mountain's side is the   48
    one from which I once took a sprig of tender leaves
    and raised it to your cheek, so it no longer required the
    decorative design of a leaf of the black aloewood tree.

"This grove, where Atri performs his asceticism, reveals   49
    his extraordinary power: here creatures become
    tamed without fear of chastisement, and the trees
    bear fruit without their flowers being harmed.

"This is where they say that Anasuya caused the Ganga   50
    to descend, the river that garlands the Three-Eyed
    Shiva's hair and from which the seven sages gather
    golden lotuses with their own hands.

"As the sages meditate here in the hero asana, even the   51
    trees rooted in their sacrificial platforms, motionless
    from lack of wind, seem immersed in yoga.[19]

"Here in front of us is the banyan tree you once beseeched,   52
    the one they call Shyama. Covered in fruit, it is like a
    heap of emeralds mixed with rubies.[20]

५३ क्वचित्प्रभालेपिभिरिन्द्रनीलैर्मुक्तामयी यष्टिरिवानुविद्धा ।
अन्यत्र माला सितपङ्कजानामिन्दीवरैरुत्खचितान्तरेव ॥

५४ क्वचित्खगानां प्रियमानसानां कादम्बसंसर्गवतीव पङ्क्तिः ।
अन्यत्र कालागुरुदत्तपत्रा भक्तिर्भुवश्चन्दनकल्पितेव ॥

५५ क्वचित्प्रभा चान्द्रमसी तमोभिश्छायानिलीनैः शवलीकृतेव ।
अन्यत्र शुभ्रा शरदभ्रलेखा रन्ध्रेष्विवालक्ष्यनभःप्रदेशा ॥

५६ क्वचिच्च कृष्णोरगभूषणेव भस्माङ्गरागा तनुरीश्वरस्य ।
पश्यानवद्याङ्गि विभाति गङ्गा भिन्नप्रवाहा यमुनाजलौघैः ॥

५७ समुद्रपत्न्योर्जलसन्निपाते पूतात्मनामत्र किलाभिषेकात् ।
तत्त्वावबोधेन विनापि भूयस्तनुत्यजां नास्ति शरीरबन्धः ॥

५८ पुरं निषादाधिपतेरिदं तद्यस्मिन्मया मौलिमणिं विहाय ।
जटासु बद्धास्वरुदत्सुमन्त्रः कैकेयि कामाः फलितास्तवेति ॥

५९ पयोधरैः पुण्यजनाङ्गनानां निर्विष्टहेमाम्बुजरेणु यस्याः ।
ब्राह्मं सरः कारणमाप्तवाचो बुद्धेरिवाव्यक्तमुदाहरन्ति ॥

"Look, my faultless princess, at the Ganga, its currents   53–56
    interwoven with rivulets from the Yamuna.
    Sometimes it is like a pearl necklace intertwined
    with sparkling sapphires, elsewhere like a garland
    of white lotuses intermingled with dark water lilies;
    sometimes like rows of the white waterbirds that love
    Lake Manasa mixed with ordinary geese; elsewhere
    like a decoration on the ground made of white sandal
    paste with leaves of the dark aloewood tree admixed;
    sometimes like moonlight mottled by patches of
    darkness lurking in shadows; elsewhere like a skein
    of bright autumn cloud that lets in streaks of sky
    through fissures; and sometimes like black serpents
    entwining the ash-smeared pallor of Shiva's body.[21]

"Even souls who have not realized the truth will never be   57
    incarnated again, they say, if they purify themselves at
    this confluence of the two wives of the ocean and then
    give up their bodies here.

"Here is the town of the chief of Nishada hunters, where   58
    I laid my crest jewel aside and tied up my hair to form
    matted locks—so that Sumantra* wept and cried out,
    'O Kaikeyi, your wishes have come true!'

"This is the river† that trustworthy men say springs from   59
    the lake of Brahma—that lake whose golden lotus
    pollen graces the breasts of *yakṣa* women—just as the
    intellect springs from inchoate matter.[22]

---

* King Dasharatha's minister.
† Sarayu.

६० जलानि या तीरनिखातयूपैर्वहत्ययोध्यामनु राजधानीम् ।
    तुरङ्गमेधावभृथावतीर्णैरिक्ष्वाकुभिः पुण्यतरीकृतानि ॥

६१ यां सैकतोत्सङ्गसुखोषितानां प्राज्यैः पयोभिः परिवर्धितानाम् ।
    सामान्यधात्रीमिव मानसं मे सम्भावयत्युत्तरकोसलानाम् ॥

६२ सेयं मदीया जननीव तेन जन्येन राज्ञा सरयूर्वियुक्ता ।
    दूरे ऽपि सन्तं शिशिरानिलैर्मा तरङ्गहस्तैरुपगूहतीव ॥

६३ विरक्तसन्ध्यापरुषं पुरस्ताद्यथा रजः पार्थिवमुज्जिहीते ।
    शङ्के हनूमत्कथितप्रवृत्तिः प्रत्युद्गतो मां भरतः ससैन्यः ॥

६४ अद्धा श्रियं पारितसङ्कराय प्रत्यर्पयिष्यत्यनघां स साधुः ।
    हत्वा निवृत्ताय मृधे खरादीन्संरक्षितां त्वामिव लक्ष्मणो मे ॥

६५ असौ पुरस्कृत्य गुरुं पदातिः पश्चादवस्थापितवाहिनीकः ।
    वृद्धैरमात्यैः सहचीरवासा मामर्घ्यपाणिर्भरतो ऽभ्युपैति ॥

"Her waters flowing past our capital, Ayodhya, have   60
been made all the more pure by the Ikshvaku kings
immersing themselves for their bath at the close of
their horse sacrifices and erecting sacrificial posts on
her banks.

"She has been the single wet nurse, as it were, of all the   61
kings of Uttarakosala. They were reared on the lap of
her sandbanks; they were nourished by the milk of her
copious waters.

"Sarayu here is like my own mother. She has been parted   62
now from my father the king, but appears to be
stretching out her arms—the ripples that cool the
breezes—to embrace me.

"From the dust of the earth rising up ahead, sullied like   63
the reddened dusk, I infer that Bharata has been
informed of my arrival by Hanuman and is coming out
to greet me with his army.

"Now that I have concluded my promised exile, that   64
good man no doubt intends to restore Royal Fortune
inviolate to me, just as you, Lakshmana, protected Sita
and restored her to me when I returned from killing
Khara and other such enemies in battle.

"Here is Bharata, wearing bark garments and   65
accompanied by the aged ministers, approaching
me with the guest offering of water; our guru* walks
before him, while the army has been directed to follow
behind.

———

* Vasishtha.

६६ पित्रा विसृष्टां मदपेक्षया यः श्रियं युवाप्यङ्गतामभोक्ता ।
इयन्ति वर्षाणि नितान्तकष्टमभ्यस्यतीव व्रतमासिधारम् ॥

६७ एतावदुक्तवति दाशरथौ तदीया-
मिच्छां विमानमधिदेवतया विदित्वा ।
ज्योतिष्पथादवततार सविस्मयाभि-
रुद्वीक्षितं प्रकृतिभि-र्भरतानुगाभिः ॥

६८ तस्मात्पुरःसरविभीषणदेशितेन
सेवाविचक्षणहरीश्वरदत्तहस्तः ।
यानादवातरददूरमहीतलेन
मार्गेण भङ्गिरचितस्फटिकेन रामः ॥

६९ इक्ष्वाकुवंशगुरवे प्रयतः प्रणम्य
स भ्रातरं भरतमर्घ्यपरिग्रहान्ते ।
पर्यश्वरस्वजत मूर्धनि चोपजघ्रौ
तद्व्रत्त्यपोढपितृराज्यमहाभिषेके ॥

७० श्मश्रुप्रवृद्धिजनितानननविक्रियांस्तान्
वृक्षान्प्ररोहजटिलानिव मन्त्रिवृद्धान् ।
अन्वग्रहीत्प्रणमतः शुभदृष्टिदानै-
र्वार्तानुयोगमधुराक्षरया च वाचा ॥

"Out of regard for me he practiced all these years what   66
    almost seems the stringent sword-blade vow: not
    enjoying Royal Fortune, given him by our father,
    though he was a young man and she lay right in his
    lap."[23]

When the son of Dasharatha had finished speaking, the   67
    presiding spirit of the flying chariot discerned his
    wishes and brought the chariot down from the sky,
    while the subjects accompanying Bharata stared up in
    astonishment.

Leaning on the arm of the monkey king,* who knew well   68
    how to serve him, Rama descended down a curving
    stairway, not too high off the ground, that was made
    of crystal, with Vibhishana, who had come out in front
    of the others, showing him the way.

Reverently Rama bowed to the guru of the Ikshvakus,†   69
    and after he had accepted the guest water he tearfully
    embraced his brother Bharata, kissing the head that,
    because of Bharata's devotion to him, had rejected
    consecration to the kingship of their father.

With kindly glances and speeches full of sweet words   70
    of inquiry about their well-being he favored the
    ministers as they bowed, their appearances changed
    by the growth of their beards, like trees shaggy with
    new growth.[24]

---

* Sugriva.
† Vasishtha.

७१ दुर्जातबन्धुरयमृक्षहरीश्वरो मे
पौलस्त्य एष समरेषु पुरःप्रहर्ता ।
इत्याहृतेन कथितौ रघुनन्दनेन
व्युत्क्रान्तलक्ष्मणमुभौ भरतो ववन्दे ॥

७२ सौमित्रिणा तदनु संससृजे स चैन-
मुत्थाप्य नम्रशिरसं भृशमालिलिङ्ग ।
रूढेन्द्रजित्प्रहरणव्रणकर्कशेन
क्लिश्यन्निवास्य भुजमध्यमुरःस्थलेन ॥

७३ रामाज्ञया हरिचमूपतयस्तदानीं
कृत्वा मनुष्यवपुरारुरुहुर्गजेन्द्रान् ।
येषु क्षरत्सु बहुधा मदवारिधाराः
शैलाधिरोहणसुखान्युपलेभिरे ते ॥

७४ सानुप्लवः प्रभुरपि क्षणदाचराणां
भेजे रथं दशरथप्रभवानुशिष्टम् ।
मायाविकल्पितविधैरपि यस्तदीयै-
र्न स्यन्दनैस्तुलितकृत्रिमभक्तिशोभः ॥

७५ भूयस्ततो रघुपतिर्विलसत्पताक-
मध्यास्त कामगति सावरजो विमानम् ।
दोषातनं बुधबृहस्पतियोगदृश्य-
स्तारापतिस्तरलविद्युदिवाभ्रकूटम् ॥

"This is the lord of bears and monkeys, a friend to me in   71
adversity, and this is the son of Pulastya, foremost
warrior in battles."[25] Rama introduced these two
respectfully thus, so Bharata passed over Lakshmana
and bowed first to them.

And after that Bharata was reunited with Lakshmana.   72
He bowed his head, but Bharata made him rise and
embraced him tightly, almost hurting his own chest
with his brother's, hardened as that was by the
wounds inflicted by Indrajit's* weapons.

At Rama's command, the chiefs of the monkey army   73
then took on human form and mounted their lordly
elephants, from which cataracts of plentiful musth
cascaded, so that they felt they were savoring the
pleasures of having climbed onto mountains.

The king of the *rākṣasas*† too, at Rama's bidding, took his   74
seat in his chariot with his attendants. The chariots
of the *rākṣasas* had been magically created, but
none could rival this one for the beauty of its artful
construction.

Then Rama took his seat once more, now with his younger   75
brothers, in the flying chariot controlled by his will,
its flags fluttering, just as the lord of the stars takes his
place with Mercury and Jupiter on a bank of evening
clouds while lightning flickers.

* Ravana's son.
† Vibhishana.

७६ तत्रेश्वरेण जगतां प्रलयादिवोर्वीं
वर्षत्ययेन रुचमभ्रगणादिवेन्दोः ।
रामेण मैथिलसुतां दशकण्ठकृच्छ्रा-
दभ्युद्धृतां धृतिमतीं भरतो ववन्दे ॥

७७ लङ्केश्वरप्रणतिभङ्गदृढव्रतं त-
द्वन्द्वं युगं चरणयोर्जनकात्मजायाः ।
ज्येष्ठानुवृत्तिजटिलं च शिरो ऽस्य साधो-
रन्योन्यपावनमभूदुभयं समेत्य ॥

७८ क्रोशार्धं प्रकृतिपुरःसरेण गत्वा
काकुत्स्थः स्तिमितजवेन पुष्पकेण ।
शत्रुघ्नप्रतिविहितोपकार्यमार्यः
साकेतोपवनमुदारमध्युवास ॥

इति रघुवंशे महाकाव्ये त्रयोदशः सर्गः ॥

There Bharata respectfully greeted the steadfast daughter   76
of the king of Mithila,* now rescued by Rama from
Ravana's clutches, like Earth rescued by the lord of all
creatures from the primal deluge, or like moonlight
rescued by autumn from a host of clouds.

Two things sanctified each other when brought together: 77
the revered feet of Janaka's daughter, firm in rejecting
the prostrations of the lord of Lanka, and the head of
that good man, left unkempt out of loyal duty to his
elder brother.

With the citizens walking out in front, the noble   78
descendant of Kakutstha rode the Pushpaka chariot at
reduced speed half a league further, then alighted in
a beautiful park on the outskirts of Ayodhya that had
been fitted out in readiness by Shatrughna.

* Sita.

चतुर्दशः सर्गः

१ प्रत्यागतौ तत्र चिरप्रवासादपश्यतां दाशरथी जनन्यौ ।
   कुमुद्वतीशीतमरीचिलेखे दिवेव रूपान्तरदुर्विभावे ॥

२ उभावुभाभ्यां प्रणतौ नतारी यथाक्रमं विक्रमशोभिनौ तौ ।
   विस्पष्टमस्नान्धतया न दृष्टौ ज्ञातौ सुतस्पर्शसुखोपलम्भात् ॥

३ आनन्दजः शोकजमस्रु वाष्पस्तयोरशीतं शिशिरो बिभेद ।
   गङ्गासरय्वोर्जलमुष्णतप्तं हिमाद्रिनिःष्यन्द इवावतीर्णः ॥

४ ते पुत्रयोर्नैर्ऋतशस्त्रमार्गानार्द्रानिवाङ्गे सदयं स्पृशन्त्यौ ।
   अभीप्सितं क्षत्रकुलाङ्गनानां न वीरसूशब्दमकामयेताम् ॥

५ क्लेशावहा भर्तुरलक्षणाहं सीतेति नाम स्वमुदाहरन्ती ।
   स्वर्गप्रतिष्ठस्य गुरोर्महिष्यावभक्तिभेदेन वधूर्ववन्दे ॥

CHAPTER 14
Sita Rejected

The two sons of Dasharatha returned from their long exile   1
and saw both their mothers there. Their appearance
had changed so much that it was hard even to discern
them, like the night-blooming lily pond and the
moon's crescent by day.[1]

The two had made their enemies bow to them and shone   2
with the signs of their deeds of valor, but now they
bowed in due order to their mothers, whose tears
blinded them so that they could not see the young
men and could recognize them only by the bliss that a
son's touch can bring.

The mothers' cool tears of joy overwhelmed their hot tears   3
of sorrow, as the snow water descending from the
Himalaya overwhelms the summer-heated waters of
the Ganga and the Sarayu.

Full of pity, they touched the scars left on their sons'   4
bodies by the demons' weapons, as if the wounds were
still fresh. And as they did so they felt no desire for
the title of mother of a hero, though Kshatriya women
aspire to it.

Their daughter-in-law paid homage with equal devotion   5
to the two queens of her father-in-law, now in heaven,
uttering her name with the words "I am that ill-fated
Sita, who brought suffering to your husband."

६ उत्तिष्ठ वत्से ननु सानुजो ऽसौ वृत्तेन भर्ता शुचिना तवैव ।
कृच्छ्रं महत्तीर्ण इति प्रियार्हां तामूचतुस्ते प्रियमप्यमिथ्या ॥

७ अथाभिषेकं रघुवंशकेतोः प्रारब्धमानन्दजलैर्जनन्योः ।
निर्वर्तयामासुरमात्यवृद्धास्तीर्थाहृतैः काञ्चनकुम्भतोयैः ॥

८ सरित्समुद्रान्सरसीश्च गत्वा रक्षःकपीन्द्रैरुपपादितानि ।
तस्यापतन्मूर्ध्नि जलानि जिष्णोर्विन्ध्यस्य मेघप्रभवा इवापः ॥

९ तपस्विवेशक्रिययापि तावद्यः प्रेक्षणीयः सुतरां बभूव ।
राजेन्द्रनेपथ्यविधानशोभा तस्योदिता स्यात्पुनरुक्तदोषः ॥

१० स मौलरक्षोहरिमिश्रसैन्यस्तूर्यस्वनानन्दितपौरवर्गान् ।
विवेश सौधोद्गतलाजवर्षामुत्तोरणामन्वयराजधानीम् ॥

११ सौमित्रिणा सावरजेन मन्दमाधूतवालव्यजनो रथस्थः ।
धृतातपत्रो भरतेन भास्वानुपायसङ्घात इव प्रसिद्धः ॥

"Arise, child! Surely it is solely thanks to your pure   6
conduct that your husband and his younger brother
have overcome their great hardships." Thus the two
spoke to her, who deserved everything pleasing, with
words that though pleasing were not false.

Then the consecration of Rama, the banner of the Raghu   7
lineage, which had been begun by the tears of joy
of his two mothers, was completed by the senior
ministers pouring from golden ewers water brought
from sacred places.

The waters, hauled by *rākṣasa* and monkey chieftains from   8
rivers, oceans, and lakes, poured down upon the head
of victorious Rama like the waters of the clouds falling
on the top of Mount Vindhya.

He had already been most lovely when dressed as an   9
ascetic; the splendor now bestowed on him of wearing
the garb of a king of kings seemed mere tautology.

With the hereditary servants, *rākṣasas,* and monkeys all   10
mingling together among his troops and the sound
of drums delighting the citizenry, he entered his
ancestral capital through triumphal arches newly
erected, a rain of parched grain descending on him
from the mansions.

Saumitri* and his younger twin gently fanned radiant   11
Rama in his chariot, while Bharata held the royal
parasol. With them he resembled the celebrated
group of the royal stratagems.[2]

---

* Son of Sumitra; Lakshmana.

१२ प्रासादकालागुरुधूमराजिस्तस्याः पुरो वायुवशेन नुन्ना ।
वनान्निवृत्तेन रघूद्वहेन मुक्ता स्वयं वेणिरिवाबभासे ॥

१३ श्वश्रूजनानुष्ठितचारुवेशां कर्णीरथस्थां रघुवीरपत्नीम् ।
विमानवातायनदृश्यबन्धैः साकेतनार्यो ऽञ्जलैभिः प्रणेमुः ॥

१४ स्फुरत्प्रभामण्डलमानसूर्यं सा बिभ्रती शाश्वतमङ्गरागम् ।
रराज शुद्धेति पुनः स्वपुर्यैं सन्दर्शिता वह्निगतेव भर्त्रा ॥

१५ वेश्मानि रामः परिवर्हयन्ति विश्राण्य सौहार्द्यनिधिः सुहृद्भ्यः ।
वाष्पायमाणो बलिमन्निकेतमालेख्यशेषस्य पितुर्विवेश ॥

१६ कृताञ्जलिस्तत्र यदम्ब सत्यान्नाभ्रशयत स्वर्गफलादुरुन्नः ।
तच्चिन्त्यमानं सुकृतं तवेति जहार लज्जां भरतस्य मातुः ॥

१७ तथा च सुग्रीवविभीषणादीनुपाचरत्कृत्रिमसंविधाभिः ।
सङ्कल्पमात्रोदितसिद्धयस्ते क्रान्ता यथा चेतसि विस्मयेन ॥

Blown by the breeze, a line of eaglewood smoke from the   12
    houses of the city made it seem as if the scion of the
    Raghus had himself loosened its braid on his return
    from the forest.[3]

The wife of the Raghu hero had been dressed beautifully   13
    by her mothers-in-law, and as she rode in a palanquin,
    the women of Saketa* bowed to her, their hands,
    palms joined, visible at the windows of the mansions.

Since she always wore the fragrant unguent given by   14
    Anasuya, which lent her a halo of light, it looked as if
    her husband were showing to the city Sita standing in
    the midst of fire, to prove her purity.[4]

Rama, full of true friendship, gave Sugriva and his other   15
    friends mansions furnished with all they could need.
    Then with tears in his eyes he entered the palace of
    his father, now present only in a portrait but still the
    recipient of daily offerings.

And there, bowing with palms together, he dispelled the   16
    shame of Bharata's mother† with these words: "That
    our father kept his word and was rewarded for that
    with heaven seems upon reflection, Mother, solely
    thanks to you."

And he served Sugriva, Vibhishana, and the rest by   17
    making arrangements for their comfort in such a
    manner that they were astonished, inwardly, to have
    their every need met no sooner than thought of.

---

* Ayodhya.
† Kaikeyi.

१८ सभाजनायोपगतान्सहिष्णुर्मुनीन्पुरस्कृत्य हतस्य शत्रोः ।
शुश्राव तेभ्यः प्रभवादि वृत्तं स्वविक्रमे गौरवमादधानः ॥

१९ प्रतिप्रयातेषु तपोधनेषु सुखादविज्ञातगतार्धमासान् ।
सीतास्वहस्तोपहिताग्र्यपूजात्रक्षःकपीन्द्रान्विससर्ज रामः ॥

२० तच्चात्मचिन्तासुलभं विमानं हृतं सुरारेः सह जीवितेन ।
कैलासनाथोद्वहनाय भूयः पुष्पं दिवः पुष्पकमन्वमंस्त ॥

२१ पितुर्नियोगाद्वनवासमेवं निस्तीर्य रामः प्रतिपन्नराज्यः ।
धर्मार्थकामेषु समां प्रपेदे यथा तथैवावरजेषु वृत्तिम् ॥

२२ सर्वासु मातृष्वतिवत्सलत्वात्स निर्विशेषप्रतिपत्तिरासीत् ।
षडाननापीतपयोधरासु नेता चमूनामिव कृत्तिकासु ॥

२३ तेनार्थवाँल्लोभपराङ्मुखेन तेन घ्नता विघ्नभयं क्रियावान् ।
तेनास लोकः पितृमान्विनेत्रा तेनैव शोकापनुदेन पुत्री ॥

He honored the celestial sages who had come to laud   18
   him and listened as they told the story of the deeds
   from birth onward of the foe he had slain, a tale that
   magnified his own heroism.

After the ascetics had left again, Rama dismissed the   19
   rākṣasa and monkey chieftains, who had enjoyed
   themselves so much that they had not noticed that a
   fortnight had passed. Sita presented them the finest of
   offerings with her own hands.

And the Pushpaka chariot—that adornment of the sky,   20
   which could be summoned by a mere thought—
   which he had taken, along with the *rākṣasa's* life, he
   permitted to return to its place as the vehicle of the
   lord of Kailasa.*

When at last, after passing his time in the forest as his   21
   father had commanded, he had become king, Rama
   acted as impartially toward the goals of man—piety,
   profit, and pleasure—as he did toward his younger
   brothers.

Out of true affection he acted equally toward all his   22
   mothers too, just as the leader of the armies of the
   gods acts toward the Krittikas, from whose breasts he
   drank deeply with all six mouths.[5]

By his aversion to avarice the people became wealthy;   23
   by his warding off danger from obstacles, they could
   perform sacred rites; by his teaching them good
   conduct, they had in him a father; by his dispelling
   sorrow like no one else, they had in him a son.

─────

* Kubera.

२४ स पौरकार्याणि समीक्ष्य काले रेमे विदेहाधिपतेर्दुहित्रा ।
उपासितश्चारु वपुस्तदीयं कृत्वोपभोगोत्सुकयेव लक्ष्म्या ॥

२५ तयोर्यथाप्रार्थितमिन्द्रियार्थानासेदुषोः सद्यसु चित्रवत्सु ।
प्राप्तानि दुःखान्यपि दण्डकेषु सञ्चिन्त्यमानानि सुखीबभूवुः ॥

२६ अथाधिकस्निग्धविलोचनेन मुखेन सीता शरपाण्डुरेण ।
आनन्दयित्री परिणेतुरासीदनक्षरव्यञ्जितदोहदेन ॥

२७ तामङ्कमारोप्य कृशाङ्गयष्टिं वर्णान्तराक्रान्तपयोधराग्राम् ।
विलज्जमानां रहसि प्रतीतः पप्रच्छ रामां रमणोभिलाषम् ॥

२८ सा दष्टनीवारबलीनि हंसैः सम्बद्धवैखानसकन्यकानि ।
इयेष भूयः कुशवन्ति गन्तुं भागीरथीतीरतपोवनानि ॥

२९ तस्यै प्रतिश्रुत्य रघुप्रवीरस्तदीप्सितं पार्श्वचरानुयातः ।
आलोकयिष्यन्मुदितामयोध्यां प्रासादमभ्रंलिहमारुहोह ॥

३० ऋद्धापणं राजपथं स पश्यन्विपाट्यमानां सरयूं च नौभिः ।
विलासिभिश्चाध्युषितानि पौरैः पुरोपकण्ठोपवनानि रेमे ॥

He would look after the townsmen's affairs at the proper   24
    hour, and at the proper hour make love with the
    daughter of the king of Videha. It was as if Lakshmi
    herself had taken on Sita's body and come to him
    eager for pleasure.

The couple enjoyed every pleasure of the senses they   25
    could wish for, and even the sufferings they had
    endured in the Dandaka forests, when they relived
    them through the paintings in their palaces, turned
    into joys.[6]

Then Sita brought joy to her husband by her face, which   26
    became pale as bamboo stalks, with her eyes glittering
    very brightly in it, and thus told, without words, of her
    being pregnant.

Sita's slender body grew even thinner, and her nipples   27
    changed color. The beautiful woman was shy, but
    when they were alone her delighted husband took her
    on his lap and asked what cravings she had.

What she longed for was to visit once more the ashrams   28
    on the bank of the Ganga, rich in sacred kusa grass,
    where geese used to peck at the wild-rice food
    offerings and she had made friends with the daughters
    of forest ascetics.

The Raghu hero promised to fulfill her wish. Then, with   29
    attendants trailing, he ascended to the roof of his
    sky-scraping palace, keen to behold his joy-filled city,
    Ayodhya.[7]

At the sight of the royal highway with shops well-stocked,   30
    the Sarayu crowded with ships, the gardens bordering
    the city occupied by lovers, Rama rejoiced.

३१ स किंवदन्तीं वदतां पुरोगः सुवृत्तमुद्दिश्य विशुद्धवृत्तः ।
सर्पाधिराजोरुभुजो ऽपसर्प पप्रच्छ भद्रं निहतारिभद्रः ॥

३२ निर्बन्धपृष्टः स जगाद सर्वं स्तुवन्ति पौराश्चरितं त्वदीयम् ।
अन्यत्र रक्षोभवनोषितायाः परिग्रहान्मानवदेव देव्याः ॥

३३ कलत्रनिन्दागुरुणा किलैव सत्याहतं कीर्तिविपर्ययेन ।
अयोघनेनाय इवाभितप्तं वैदेहिबन्धोर्हृदयं विदद्रे ॥

३४ किमात्मनिर्वादकथामुपेक्षे जायामदोषामुत सन्त्यजानि ।
इत्येकपक्षाश्रयविक्लवत्वादासीत्स दोलाचलचित्तवृत्तिः ॥

३५ निश्चित्य चानन्यनिवृत्ति वाच्यं त्यागेन पल्याः परिमार्ष्टुमैच्छत् ।
अपि स्वदेहात्किमुतेन्द्रियार्थाद्यशोधनानां हि यशो गरीयः ॥

३६ स सन्निपात्यावरजान्हतौजास्तद्विक्रियादर्शनलुप्तहर्षान् ।
कौलीनमात्माश्रयमाचचक्षे तेभ्यः पुनश्चेदमुवाच वाक्यम् ॥

३७ राजर्षिवंशस्य रविप्रसूतेरुपस्थितः पश्यत कीदृशो ऽयम् ।
मत्तः सदाचारशुचेः कलङ्कः पयोदवाहादिव दर्पणस्य ॥

That foremost speaker, pure in conduct, his arms as   31
    thick as the king of serpents, defeater of even the
    staunchest foe, asked his spy Bhadra what people were
    saying about his own conduct.

At his persistent questioning, the spy replied: "The   32
    citizens praise all your deeds, lord of men—except for
    your taking back the queen after she had lived in the
    rākṣasa's palace."

It is said that the heart of Vaidehi's husband, when struck   33
    by such infamy, made heavier by the calumny of his
    wife, shattered like heated iron when struck by a
    hammer.

Should I disregard this slander about me? Or should I   34
    abandon my wife, innocent though she is? His mind
    swung back and forth, incapable of deciding on either
    course of action.

But once he determined there was no other way to put an   35
    end to the slur, he preferred to erase it by abandoning
    his queen. Fame, to those who treasure it, counts
    for more than even their own bodies, not to speak of
    sense objects.[8]

He summoned his younger brothers. His usual radiance   36
    was gone, and all joy left them when they saw how
    changed he was. He told them of the rumor about
    himself, and added the following:

"See what a stain I have brought to our family, the lineage   37
    of a royal seer, sprung from the Sun, and purified yet
    further by perfect conduct! Just so, a cloud-bearing
    gust of wind may fleck a mirror.

३८ पौरेषु सो ऽहं बहलीभवन्तमपां तर्झेष्विव तैलबिन्दुम् ।
सोढुं न तत्पूर्वमवर्णमीशः स्थलातिगं स्थाणुमिव द्विपेन्द्रः ॥

३९ तस्यापनोदाय फलप्रवृत्तावुपस्थितायामपि निर्व्यपेक्षः ।
त्यक्ष्यामि वैदेहसुतां पुरस्तात्समुद्रनेमिं पितुराज्ञयेव ॥

४० अवैमि चैनामनघेति किन्तु लोकापवादो बलवान्मतो मे ।
छाया हि भूमेः शशिनो मलत्वे निरूपिता शुद्धिमतः प्रजाभिः ॥

४१ रक्षोवधान्तो न च मे प्रयासः स्त्यर्थः स वैरप्रतिमोचनाय ।
अमर्षणः शोणितवाञ्छया किं पदा स्पृशन्तं दशति द्विजिह्वः ॥

४२ तदेष सर्गः करुणार्द्रचित्तैर्न मे भवद्भिः प्रतिषेधनीयः ।
यद्यर्थिता निर्हृतवाच्यशल्यान्प्राणान्मया धारयता चिरं वः ॥

४३ इत्युक्तवन्तं जनकात्मजायां नितान्तरूक्षाभिनिवेशमीशम् ।
न कश्चन भ्रातृषु तत्र शक्तो निषेद्धुमासीदनुवर्तितुं वा ॥

४४ स लक्ष्मणं लक्ष्मणपूर्वजन्मा विलोक्य लोकत्रयगीतकीर्तिः ।
सौम्येति चाभाष्य यथार्थभाषः स्थितं निदेशे पृथगादिदेश ॥

"Such slander without precedent is spreading among the townsmen like a drop of oil upon the waves. I can no more endure it than a great elephant can endure the hitching post it's tethered to for the first time.[9] 38

"To dispel it, I will abandon the daughter of the king of Videha without hesitation, even though the birth of our offspring is imminent, just as I once abandoned the ocean-girt earth at our father's command. 39

"And I do know that she is blameless, but the reproaches of the people weigh heavy on me. For even the shadow of the earth is taken by men as a stain upon the pure moon. 40

"It was not for a woman that I strove to kill the *rākṣasa;* it was retribution for the harm he did me. When a snake, who brooks no wrong, bites the man who steps on him, does it do so out of desire for blood? 41

"So do not, just because compassion softens your hearts, thwart my will: this dart of ill repute must be removed if you wish me to survive." 42

So the king spoke, making the harshest possible resolve against King Janaka's daughter. And on this point none of his brothers could stop him, nor concur with him. 43

The elder brother of Lakshmana, speaker of truth whose fame was sung throughout the three worlds, looked at the ever-obedient Lakshmana and gave him a separate command. "My dear," he addressed him, 44

४५ प्रजावती दोहदशंसिनी ते तपोवनेषु स्पृहयालुरेव ।
स त्वं रथी तद्व्यपदेशनेयां प्रापय्य वाल्मीकिपदं त्यजैनाम् ॥

४६ स शुश्रुवान्मातरि भार्गवेण पितुर्नियोगात्प्रहृतं विशङ्कम् ।
प्रत्यग्रहीदग्रजशासनं तदाज्ञा गुरूणां ह्यविचारणीया ॥

४७ अथानुकूलश्रवणप्रतीतामत्रस्नुभिर्युक्तधुरं तुरङ्गैः ।
रथं सुमन्तुप्रतिपन्नरश्मिमारोप्य वैदेहसुतां प्रतस्थौ ॥

४८ सा नीयमाना रुचिरान्प्रदेशान्प्रियङ्कुरो मे प्रिय इत्यनन्दत् ।
नाबुद्ध कल्पद्रुमतां विहाय जातं तमात्मन्यसिपत्त्रवृक्षम् ॥

४९ जुगूह तस्याः पथि लक्ष्मणो यत्सव्येतरेण स्फुरता तदक्ष्णा ।
आख्यातमस्यै गुरु भावि दुःखमत्यन्तलुप्तप्रियदर्शनेन ॥

५० सा दुर्निमित्तोपगमादि्द्विषादात्सद्यः परिम्लानमुखारविन्दा ।
राज्ञः शिवं सावरजस्य भूयादित्याशशंसे करणैरबाह्यैः ॥

"when your sister-in-law expressed her pregnancy   45
　　longing, it was for the groves of the hermits. So with
　　your chariot take her, on the pretext of fulfilling that
　　longing, to Valmiki's abode—and abandon her there."

Lakshmana had heard that Parashurama had struck his   46
　　mother without scruple when his father ordered it.
　　Now he accepted his older brother's instructions, for
　　the command of an elder is not to be questioned.[10]

The daughter of the king of Videha was delighted at   47
　　hearing such agreeable news. Lakshmana then placed
　　her in his chariot, yoked with horses who never shied,
　　and set off, with Sumantu holding the reins.

As she was being brought to the places she loved, she   48
　　rejoiced that her dear husband was always doing what
　　would please her. Little did she know that he had left
　　off being a wish-fulfilling tree and become instead a
　　sword-leafed tree of torment.[11]

While on the path Lakshmana concealed from her the   49
　　dreadful suffering that lay ahead; but her own right
　　eye, to which the sight of her beloved was utterly lost,
　　revealed it to her by its throbbing.[12]

In despair at this bad omen, her lotus face was suddenly   50
　　drained of color. Inwardly she uttered a prayer: *May
　　all be well with the king and his younger brothers!*

५१ भ्रातुर्नियोगादथ तां वनान्ते साध्वीं सुमित्रातनयो विहास्यन् ।
अवार्यतेवोच्छ्रितवीचिहस्तैर्जह्नोर्दुहित्रा स्थितया पुरस्तात् ॥

५२ रथात्सुमन्तुप्रतिपन्नवाहात्तां भ्रातृजायां पुलिने ऽवतार्य ।
गङ्गां निषादाहृतनौर्विशेषस्ततार सन्धामिव सत्यसन्धः ॥

५३ अथ व्यवस्थापितवाक्कथञ्चित्सौमित्रिरन्तर्गतमश्रुकण्ठः ।
औत्पातिको मेघ इवाश्मवर्षं महीपतेः शासनमुज्जगार ॥

५४ ततो ऽभिषङ्गानिलविप्रविद्धा प्रभ्रश्यमानाभरणप्रसूना ।
स्वमूर्तिलाभप्रकृतिं धरित्रीं लतेव सीता सहसा जगाम ॥

५५ इक्ष्वाकुवंशप्रभवः कथं त्वां त्यजेदकस्मात्प्रथितार्यवृत्तः ।
इति क्षितिः संशयितेव तस्यै ददौ प्रवेशं जननी न तावत् ॥

५६ सा लुप्तसंज्ञा न विवेद दुःखं प्रत्यागतासुः समतप्यतान्तः ।
तस्याः सुमित्रात्मजयत्नलभ्यो मोहादभूत्कष्टतरः प्रबोधः ॥

Then as Sumitra's son was about to follow his brother's   51
    instructions and abandon her, faithful wife though she
    was, in the forest, for a moment it seemed as if Jahnu's
    daughter* herself were standing before him, lifting up
    her waves like hands to stop him.

The charioteer reined in the horses, and Lakshmana   52
    helped his brother's wife climb down from the chariot
    onto the sandy bank. Then, true to his word, he
    reached the farther shore of the Ganga with her on a
    boat brought by a Nishada tribesman—reaching the
    end, as it were, of his promise to his elder brother too.

Then Saumitri, somehow controlling his voice though   53
    his throat was choked with tears, spit out the king's
    command, as a cloud spits forth a rain of stones,
    foretelling some disaster.

Driven by the windblast of this calamity, Sita, her   54
    ornaments dropping from her like flowers, then
    suddenly fell like a creeper to the sustaining earth, the
    source of her own body.[13]

As if she had some doubt, thinking *How could Rama, born*   55
    in the Ikshvaku line and famous for his noble conduct,
    abandon you without cause?, the Earth, though her
    mother, did not let Sita return inside her just then.

Sita lost consciousness and so was not aware of her own   56
    misfortune; but when her life force returned, she
    burned within: her reawakening, brought about by
    the efforts of Sumitra's son, was more painful than her
    stupor.

———

* Ganga.

५७ न चावदह्वर्तुरवर्णमार्या निराकरिष्णोर्वृजनाद्वते ऽपि ।
आत्मानमेव स्थिरदुःखभाजं पुनः पुनर्दुष्कृतिनं निनिन्द ॥

५८ आश्वास्य रामावरजः स सीतामाख्यातवाल्मीकिनिकेतमार्गः ।
निगृह्य मे भर्तृनिदेशरौक्ष्यं देवि क्षमस्वेति बभूव नम्रः ॥

५९ सीता तमुत्थाप्य जगाद वाक्यं प्रीतास्मि ते सौम्य चिराय जीव ।
विडौजसा विष्णुरिवाग्रजेन भ्रात्रा यदित्थं परवानसि त्वम् ॥

६० श्वश्रूजनं सर्वमनुक्रमेण विज्ञापयेः प्रापितमत्प्रणामः ।
प्रजानिषेकं मयि वर्तमानं सूनोरनुध्यायत चेतसेति ॥

६१ वाच्यस्त्वया मद्वचनात्स राजा वह्नौ विशुद्धामपि यत्समक्षम् ।
मां लोकवादश्रवणादहासीः श्रुतस्य किं तत्सदृशं कुलस्य ॥

६२ कल्याणबुद्धेरथ वा तवायं न कामचारो मयि शङ्कनीयः ।
ममैव जन्मान्तरपातकानां विपाकविस्फूर्जथुरप्रसह्यः ॥

६३ उपस्थितां पूर्वमपास्य लक्ष्मीं वनं मया सार्धमसि प्रपन्नः ।
त्वामास्पदं प्राप्य तया तु रोषात्सोढास्मि न त्वद्वने वसन्ती ॥

Although her husband was punishing her for no crime,　57
　　noble Sita spoke not a word of reproach against him;
　　instead she blamed only herself, time and again, as a
　　wrongdoer who should suffer enduring pain.

Rama's younger brother comforted the excellent woman,　58
　　told her the way to Valmiki's ashram, and bowed
　　down before her with the words: "Queen, forgive my
　　harshness in carrying out my brother's command, for
　　I am subject to him."

Sita made him rise and spoke these words: "My dear, I　59
　　am pleased with you—long may you live!—for being
　　so obedient to your elder brother, as Vishnu is to his,
　　Vidaujas.[14]

"Pay my respects to all my mothers-in-law, in due order,　60
　　and then give them this message: 'Remember in your
　　hearts the seed of your son that I carry!'

"And tell the king this from me: 'Was it in keeping with　61
　　your learning or your lineage to abandon me because
　　of rumors that you heard, in spite of Fire proving my
　　purity before your very eyes?

"'Or rather, no one should think that you, benevolent　62
　　as you are, are doing this of your own free will. It is
　　instead the sudden ripening, unbearably painful, of
　　the consequences of my own sins of past lives.

"'Before, when Royal Fortune had come to you, you　63
　　spurned her and went to the forest with me. But now
　　she has taken up her abode in you, and in her fury she
　　cannot endure me living in your palace.

६४ निशाचरोपप्लुतभर्तृकाणां तपस्विनीनां भवतः प्रसादात् ।
भूत्वा शरण्या शरणार्थमन्यं कथं प्रपत्स्ये त्वयि दीप्यमाने ॥

६५ किं वा तवात्यन्तवियोगमोचे कुर्यामपेक्षां हतजीविते ऽस्मिन् ।
स्याद्रक्षणीयं यदि मे न तेजस्त्वदीयमन्तर्गतमन्तरायः ॥

६६ साहं तपः सूर्यनिविष्टदृष्टिरूर्ध्वं प्रसूतेश्चरितुं यतिष्ये ।
भूयो यथा मे जननान्तरेषु त्वमेव भर्ता न च विप्रयोगः ॥

६७ नृपस्य वर्णाश्रमपालनं यत्स एव धर्मो मनुना प्रणीतः ।
निर्वासिताप्येवमतस्त्वयाहं तपस्विसामान्यमवेक्षणीया ॥

६८ तथेति तस्याः प्रतिगृह्य वाचं रामानुजे दृष्टिपथं व्यतीते ।
सा मुक्तकण्ठं व्यसनातिभाराञ्चक्रन्द विग्ना कुररीव भूयः ॥

६९ नृत्तं मयूराः कुसुमानि वृक्षा दर्भानुपात्तान्विजहुर्हरिण्यः ।
तस्याः प्रपन्ने समदुःखभावमत्यन्तमासीद्रुदितं वने ऽपि ॥

७० तामभ्यगच्छद्रुदितानुसारी कविः कुशेध्माहरणाय यातः ।
निषादविद्धाण्डजदर्शनोत्थः श्लोकत्वमापद्यत यस्य शोकः ॥

"'By your grace I was the one to whom the female ascetics   64
came for refuge when their husbands were harassed
by the demons who roam the night. While you are
still living and radiant, how am I now to approach
someone else for refuge?

"'This wretched life of mine is empty if I am to be   65
separated from you forever. I would not care for it at
all, were it not that your energy, now within me, must
be protected, and thus holds me back.

"'As for myself, after giving birth, I shall fix my eyes on the   66
sun and strive to amass ascetic power, so that from
now on you alone may be my husband in lives to come,
and we may never be separated.

"'The king must protect the social classes and stages of   67
life—such is the law decreed by Manu. So even though
you have exiled me in this way, you must still watch
over me, as you do other ascetics.'"15

Rama's younger brother agreed and departed with the   68
message. When he was out of sight, she cried out
again and again with open throat from the excessive
burden of her grief, like a frightened curlew.

The peacocks gave up their dance, the trees their flowers,   69
the does the grass they had started to chew—so great
was the lamentation in the forest too, which suffered
as much as she did.

The poet-seer, whose grief had turned into poetry when   70
he once saw a bird shot by a Nishada, had come out to
gather kusa grass and firewood. Following the sound
of wailing, he came upon her.16

७१ तमश्रुनेत्रावरणं प्रमृज्य सीता विलापाद्विरता ववन्दे ।
तस्यै पुनर्दोहदलिङ्गदर्शी दत्त्वा स पुत्राशिषमित्युवाच ॥

७२ जाने विसृष्टां प्रणिधानतस्त्वां मिथ्यापवादक्षुभितेन भर्त्रा ।
तन्मा व्यथिष्ठा विषयान्तरस्थं प्राप्तासि वैदेहि पितुर्निकेतम् ॥

७३ उत्खातलोकत्रयकण्टके ऽपि सत्यप्रतिज्ञे ऽप्यविकत्थने ऽपि ।
त्वां प्रत्यकस्मात्प्रतिकूलवृत्तावस्त्येव मन्युर्भरताग्रजे मे ॥

७४ तवोरुकीर्तिः श्वशुरः सखा मे सतां भवच्छेदकरः पिता ते ।
धुरि स्थिता त्वं पतिदेवतानां किं तन्न येनासि मयानुकम्प्या ॥

७५ तपस्विसंसर्गविनीतसत्त्वे तपोवने वीतभया वसास्मिन् ।
इतो भविष्यत्यनघप्रसूतेरपत्यसंस्कारमयो विधिस्ते ॥

७६ अशून्यतीरां मुनिसन्निवेशैस्तमोपहन्त्रीं तमसां विगाह्य ।
तत्सैकतोत्सङ्गबलिक्रियाभिः सम्पत्स्यते ते मनसः प्रसादः ॥

Wiping away the tears that blurred her sight, she ceased   71
lamenting and greeted him respectfully. And he,
observing the signs of pregnancy, pronounced the
blessing that she might bear a son and said:

"Through meditation I have come to know that your   72
husband, shocked by calumny, has sent you away. So
do not be agitated, daughter of King Videha, for here
you have reached your father's house, though in a
foreign land.

"Although he has extirpated the demons who plagued   73
all three worlds; although he is true to his promises;
although he never boasts, I am still filled with anger
at Bharata's elder brother for his perverse and
unjustified behavior toward you.

"Your widely famed father-in-law was my friend. Your   74
father leads good people to break the cycle of rebirth.
You yourself stand at the head of wives devoted to
their husbands. So why should I not feel compassion
for you?

"Live here then, free from fear, in this penance grove   75
where mixing with ascetics has tamed all the
creatures. I will perform the rites for your offspring
after your safe delivery.

"The banks of the Tamasa here are lined by the dwellings   76
of sages. Bathe in this river, which removes all ills,
and make offerings on its sandy banks—this will bring
calm to your mind.

७७ पुष्पं फलं चार्तवमाहरन्त्यो बीजं च बालेयमकृष्टरोहि ।
विनोदयिष्यन्ति नवाभिषङ्गामुदारवाचो मुनिकन्यकास्त्वाम् ॥

७८ पयोघटैराश्रमबालवृक्षान्संवर्धयन्ती स्वबलानुरूपैः ।
असंशयं प्राक्तनयोपपत्तेः स्तनन्धयप्रीतिमवाप्स्यसि त्वम् ॥

७९ अनुग्रहप्रत्यभिनन्दिनीं तां वाल्मीकिरादाय दयार्द्रचेताः ।
सायं मृगाध्यासितवेदिपार्श्वं स्वमाश्रमं शान्तसुखं निनाय ॥

८० समर्पयामास च शोकदीनां तदागमप्रीतिषु तापसीषु ।
निर्विष्टसारां पितृभिर्हिमांशोरन्त्यां कलां दर्श इवौषधीषु ॥

८१ ता इङ्गुदीस्नेहकृतप्रदीपमास्तीर्णमेध्याजिनतल्पमन्तः ।
तस्य सपर्यानुपदं दिनान्ते निवासहेतोरुटजं वितेरुः ॥

८२ तत्राभिषेकप्रयता वसन्ती प्रयुक्तपूजा विबुधातिथिभ्यः ।
वन्येन सा वल्कलिनी शरीरं पत्युः प्रजासन्ततये बभार ॥

"The sages' daughters will bring flowers and fruits of the   77
season and wild grains for your offerings, and with
their lofty talk they will divert you even though your
sorrow is still fresh.

"And nourishing the ashram's saplings with water pots   78
suited to your strength, it will surely be as if, even
before your child is born, you are experiencing the
pleasure of having a baby to suckle."

She accepted his kind offer with joy. Valmiki, his heart   79
tender with compassion, took her with him and
brought her to his delightfully peaceful ashram,
arriving at evening, when deer lie down beside the
altars.

And he entrusted the grief-stricken woman to the female   80
ascetics, who were delighted at her coming, as the
new moon day entrusts to the herbs the moon's last
digit, when its essence has been consumed by the
ancestors.[17]

Those women welcomed her with offerings and then, as   81
the day was over, assigned her a leaf cottage to stay in,
in which there was a lamp with *iṅgudī* oil and a ritually
pure antelope hide spread out as bed.[18]

Living there, Sita purified herself with sacred baths,   82
clothed herself in bark garments, made offerings to
gods and visitors, and sustained her body with wild
roots and fruit for the continuation of her husband's
family line.

८३ अपि प्रभुः सानुशयो ऽधुना स्यादित्युत्सुकः शक्रजितो ऽपि हन्ता ।
शशंस सीतापरिदेवनान्तमनुष्ठितं शासनमग्रजाय ॥

८४ बभूव रामः सहसा सवाष्पस्तुषारवर्षीव सहस्यचन्द्रः ।
कौलीनभीतेन गृहान्निरस्त न तेन वैदेहसुता मनस्तः ॥

८५ निगृह्य शोकं स्वयमेव धीमान्वर्णाश्रमावेक्षणजागरूकः ।
सा भ्रातृसाधारणभोगमृद्धं राज्यं रजोरिक्तमनाः शशास ॥

८६ तस्यैकभार्या परिवादभीरोः साध्वीमपि त्यक्तवतो नृपस्य ।
वक्षस्यसङ्घट्टसुखं वसन्ती रेमे सपत्नीरहितेव लक्ष्मीः ॥

८७ सीतां हित्वा दशमुखरिपुर्नोपयेमे यदन्यां
तस्या एव प्रतिकृतिसखो यत्क्रतूनाजहार ।
वृत्तान्तेन श्रवणविषयप्रापिणा तेन भर्तुः
सा दुर्वारव्यथमपि परित्यागदुःखं विषेहे ॥

इति रघुवंशे महाकाव्ये चतुर्दशः सर्गः ॥

As for the slayer of Shakrajit,* wondering whether the king 83
now felt remorse, he informed his elder brother of the
details of the carrying out of his command, including
the lamentations of Sita.

Rama immediately shed tears, like the winter moon 84
pouring down frosty dew. For fear of scandal, he had
banished the daughter of the king of Videha from his
house, but not from his heart.

Being wise, he controlled his grief by himself, remained 85
vigilant in watching over the social classes and stages
of life, and ruled the prosperous kingdom, which he
enjoyed together with his brothers, his mind unsullied
by *rajas*.[19]

Since fear of ill repute had led the king to renounce his 86
sole wife, although she was true to him, Lakshmi now
dwelled on his breast in happiness without conflict, as
if joyfully free of co-wives.

The slayer of ten-headed Ravana did not wed another after 87
leaving Sita; he performed his rituals accompanied by
her in the form of an image. This news of her husband
reached Sita's ears, and thanks to this she could
endure the sorrow of her abandonment, though she
could not suppress the pain it caused.[20]

* Lakshmana.

पञ्चदशः सर्गः

१ कृतसीतापरित्यागः स रत्नाकरमेखलाम् ।
   बुभुजे पृथिवीपालः पृथिवीमेव केवलाम् ॥

२ लवणेन विलुप्तेज्यास्तामिस्रेण तमभ्ययुः ।
   मुनयो यमुनाभाजः शरण्यं शरणार्थिनः ॥

३ अवेक्ष्य रामं ते तत्र न प्रजह्नुः स्वतेजसा ।
   त्राणाभावे हि शापास्ताः कुर्वन्ति तपसो व्ययम् ॥

४ प्रतिशुश्राव काकुत्स्थस्तेभ्यो विघ्नप्रतिक्रियाम् ।
   धर्मसंरक्षणायैव प्रवृत्तिर्भुवि शार्ङ्गिणः ॥

५ ते रामाय वधोपायमाचख्युर्विबुधद्विषः ।
   दुर्जयो लवणः शूली विशूलः प्रार्थ्यतामिति ॥

६ आदिदेशाथ शत्रुघ्नं तेषां क्षेमाय राघवः ।
   करिष्यन्निव नामास्य यथार्थमरिनिग्रहात् ॥

CHAPTER 15

Sita Is Swallowed by Her Mother the Earth

After his rejection of Sita, that protector of the earth   1
    enjoyed only ocean-girdled Earth.

Some sages who dwelled on the banks of the Yamuna had   2
    seen their sacrifices destroyed by a night-roaming
    demon called Lavana. Seeking protection, they came
    to Rama, granter of refuge.

In view of Rama's presence, they did not strike at the   3
    demon with their own power: those whose only
    weapon is the curse expend their ascetic energy only
    when there is no other protection.

The descendant of Kakutstha* promised a remedy to   4
    these problems. Indeed, the interventions on earth of
    Vishnu, holder of the bow, are for protecting dharma.

They told Rama of a means to kill that enemy of   5
    Brahmans: "Armed with his trident, Lavana is
    invincible! Summon him out when he is unarmed."

Rama then assigned Shatrughna the task of protecting the   6
    sages, as though wishing to render his brother's name
    fully meaningful by the slaying of enemies.[1]

---

* Rama.

७ यः कश्चन रघूणां हि परमेकः परन्तपः ।
अपवाद इवोत्सर्गं व्यावर्तयितुमीश्वरः ॥

८ अग्रजेन प्रयुक्ताशीस्ततो दाशरथी रथी ।
ययौ वनस्थलीः पश्यन्पुष्पिताः सुरभीरभीः ॥

९ रामादेशादनपगं सेनाङ्गं तस्य सिद्धये ।
पश्चादध्ययनार्थस्य धातोरधिरिवाभवत् ॥

१० आदिष्टवर्त्मा मुनिभिः स गच्छंस्तपतां वरः ।
विरराज रथपृष्ठैर्बालखिल्यैरिवांशुमान् ॥

११ तस्य मार्गवशादेका बभूव वसतिर्यतः ।
रथस्वनोत्कर्णमृगे वाल्मीकीये तपोवने ॥

१२ तमृषिः पूजयामास कुमारं क्लान्तवाहनम् ।
तपःप्रभावसिद्धाभिर्विषयप्रतिपत्तिभिः ॥

१३ तस्यामेवास्य यामिन्यामन्तर्वत्नी प्रजावती ।
सुतावसूत सम्पन्ना कोशदण्डाविव क्षितिः ॥

१४ सन्तानश्रवणाद्भ्रातुः सौमित्रिः सौमनस्यवान् ।
प्राञ्जलिर्मुनिमामन्त्र्य प्रातर्युक्तरथो ययौ ॥

For any descendant of Raghu is a scourge to enemies   7
    capable of overpowering a foe, just as an exception
    overpowers a general rule.[2]

Then, once his elder brother had pronounced a blessing   8
    over him, that son of Dasharatha* set off fearlessly in
    his chariot, savoring as he went the fragrant tracts of
    forest in flower.

Following Rama's orders, the divisions of the army stuck   9
    close behind him, just as the verbal prefix *adhi* sticks
    to the root *i* when it means "study."[3]

With the sages pointing out the road, that most fiery   10
    Shatrughna went on his way, shining like the Sun with
    the Balakhilyas preceding his chariot.[4]

In the hermitage of Valmiki, where the deer pricked up   11
    their ears at the sound of his chariot, he made one
    staging post, since that was where his path lay.

The sage respectfully received the prince, whose horses   12
    were tired, proffering things for him to enjoy that
    were procured through the power of his asceticism.

That very night his elder brother's pregnant wife gave   13
    birth to two sons, like the rich Earth giving birth to the
    treasury and the army.[5]

Saumitri† was delighted to hear of the birth of his   14
    brother's offspring. At dawn, with palms pressed
    together in reverence, he took leave of the sage, then
    mounted his chariot and set out.

---

* Shatrughna.
† Son of Sumitra; Shatrughna.

१५ स च प्राप मधूपघ्नं कुम्भीनस्याश्च कुक्षिजः ।
वनात्करमिवादाय सत्वराशिमुपस्थितः ॥

१६ धूमधूम्रो वसागन्धी ज्वालाबभ्रुशिरोरुहः ।
क्रव्यादगणपरीवारश्चिताग्निरिव जङ्गमः ॥

१७ अपशूलं तमासाद्य लवणं लक्ष्मणानुजः ।
रुरोध सम्मुखीनो हि जयो रन्ध्रप्रहारिणाम् ॥

१८ नातिपर्याप्तमालोक्य मत्कुक्षेरद्य वेतनम् ।
दिष्ट्या त्वमसि मे धात्रा भीतेनैवोपपादितः ॥

१९ इति सन्तर्ज्य शत्रुघ्नं राक्षसस्तज्जिघांसया ।
प्रांशुमुत्पाटयामास मुस्तास्तम्बमिव द्रुमम् ॥

२० सौमित्रेर्निशितैर्बाणैरन्तरा शकलीकृतः ।
गात्रं पुष्परजः प्राप न शाखी नैर्ऋतेरितः ॥

२१ निशानं स्वस्य शूलस्य रक्षस्तस्मै महोपलम् ।
प्रजिघाय कृतान्तस्य मुष्टिं पृथगिव स्थितम् ॥

२२ ऐन्द्रमस्त्रमुपादाय शत्रुघ्नेन स ताडितः ।
सिकतत्वादपि परां प्रपेदे परमाणुताम् ॥

Just as he reached Madhupaghna, the demon son of   15
   Kumbhinasi also arrived, bringing a heap of animals,
   like tribute gathered from the forest.[6]

Grimy with smoke, reeking of fat, his hair tawny like   16
   flames, surrounded by a throng of flesh-eating
   demons, he was like a walking funeral pyre.

Finding him without his trident, the younger brother of   17
   Lakshmana blocked his way. For victory awaits the
   man who attacks his enemy's weakness.

"The creator must have thought today's ration for my   18
   belly too scant, and out of concern fortunately
   furnished me with you!"

With this menacing taunt, the demon uprooted a huge   19
   tree as though it were just a clump of sedge, eager to
   kill Shatrughna.

The pollen of its flowers reached Shatrughna's body, but   20
   the tree the demon threw did not, since Shatrughna's
   arrows cut it into splinters midway.

The *rākṣasa* took the huge stone used to whet his trident   21
   and threw it at him, as though it were the disembodied
   fist of Death.

Taking a weapon empowered by Indra, Shatrughna   22
   smashed the stone into its tiniest particles, it being
   after all nothing but compacted sand.

२३ तमुपाद्रवदुद्यम्य दक्षिणं दोर्निशाचरः ।
एकताल इवोत्पातपवनप्रेरितो गिरिः ॥

२४ कार्ष्णेन पत्त्रिणा शत्रोः स भिन्नहृदयः पतन् ।
आनिनाय भुवः कम्पं जहाराश्रमवासिनाम् ॥

२५ वयसां पङ्क्तयः पेतुर्हतस्योपरि रक्षसः ।
तत्प्रतिद्वन्द्विनो मूर्ध्नि दिव्याः कुसुमवृष्टयः ॥

२६ स हत्वा लवणं वीरस्तदा मेने महामनाः ।
भ्रातुः सौदर्यमात्मानमिन्द्रजिद्वधशोभिनः ॥

२७ तस्य संस्तूयमानस्य चरितार्थैस्तपस्विभिः ।
शुशुभे विक्रमोदग्रं व्रीडयावनतं शिरः ॥

२८ उपकूलं स कालिन्द्याः पुरं पौरुषभूषणः ।
निर्ममे निर्ममो ऽर्थेषु मथुरां मधुराकृतिः ॥

२९ या सौराज्यप्रकाशाभिर्बभौ पौरविभूतिभिः ।
स्वर्गाभिष्यन्दवमनं कृत्वेवोपनिवेशिता ॥

३० तत्र सौधगतः पश्यन्यमुनां चक्रवाकिनीम् ।
हेमभक्तिमतीं भूमेः प्रवेणीमिव पिप्रिये ॥

The demon rushed at him, raising his right arm as he ran,   23
    looking like a mountain with a single palm tree on it
    being hurled forward by the wind of the final deluge.

As he fell, his heart split by his adversary's iron arrow, the   24
    demon set off a trembling of the earth while ending
    the hermits' own tremblings.

Flocks of carrion birds fell upon the slain demon; and   25
    upon his rival's head flowers rained down from
    heaven.

After slaying Lavana, that noble-minded warrior at   26
    last considered himself truly the twin brother of
    Lakshmana, who was resplendent with his victory
    over Indrajit.

That head borne high in heroism shone yet more   27
    beautifully when he bowed it modestly while the
    ascetics who had attained their desire praised him.

On the bank of the Yamuna River, the handsome   28
    Shatrughna, whose only ornament was his manly
    valor, and who took no excessive pride in his exploits,
    created the city of Mathura.

The city, resplendent with the citizens' riches, which were   29
    even more in evidence because of good governance,
    seemed as though populated by an overflow from
    heaven.

There, as he looked down from his palace roof on the   30
    Yamuna with its ruddy sheldrakes, like a braid of hair
    tricked out with golden ornaments, he felt delight.

३१ सखा दशरथस्याथ जनकस्य च मन्त्रकृत् ।
संचस्कारोभयप्रीत्या मैथिलेयौ यथाविधि ॥

३२ सुतौ कुशलवोन्मृष्टगर्भक्लेदौ तदाख्यया ।
कविः कुशलवावेव चकार किल नामतः ॥

३३ साङ्गं च वेदमध्याप्य किञ्चिदुत्क्रान्तशैशवौ ।
स्वकृतिं गापयामास कविप्रथमपद्धतिम् ॥

३४ इतरे ऽपि रघोर्वंश्यास्त्रयस्त्रेताग्नितेजसः ।
तद्योगात्पतिवत्नीषु पत्नीष्वासन्द्विसूनवः ॥

३५ शत्रुघातिनि शत्रुघ्नः सुबाहौ च बहुश्रुते ।
मथुराविदिशे सून्वोर्निदधे पूर्वजोत्सुकः ॥

३६ भूयस्तपोव्ययो मा भूद्वाल्मीकिरिति सो ऽत्यगात् ।
मैथिलीतनयोद्गीतनिःस्पन्दमृगमाश्रमम् ॥

३७ वशी विवेश चायोध्यां रथ्यासंस्कारशोभिनीम् ।
लवणस्य वधात्पौरैरधिगौरवमीक्षितः ॥

३८ स ददर्श सभामध्ये सभासद्भिरुपासितम् ।
रामं सीतापरित्यागादसामान्यपतिं भुवः ॥

Valmiki, wielder of mantras and friend of Dasharatha and   31
    Janaka, out of affection for them both performed the
    life-cycle rites for the two sons of Sita.

He had the two newborns wiped dry with kusa and *lava*   32
    grass, and so it was, they say, that the poet named the
    two sons Kusha and Lava.[7]

Soon after they had emerged from infancy, he taught them   33
    to recite the Veda and the auxiliary sciences, and he
    had them sing his own composition, the first pathway
    for poets.[8]

The three other brothers born of Raghu's lineage, as   34
    radiant as the three Vedic fires, also each fathered two
    sons on their respective wives, in harmony with Rama.

Eager to rejoin his elder brother, Shatrughna entrusted   35
    the cities of Mathura and Vidisha to his learned sons
    Shatrughatin and Subahu.

Wishing to make no further demands on the ascetic   36
    energy of the sage, he passed Valmiki's ashram by,
    where the deer stood motionless at the sound of Sita's
    sons chanting.[9]

And the self-controlled Shatrughna entered Ayodhya,   37
    resplendent with decorated streets, the citizenry
    gazing at him with respect because of his having slain
    Lavana.

He saw Rama in the middle of the assembly, attended by   38
    his courtiers, now husband of Earth solely, after his
    rejection of Sita.

३९ तमभ्यनन्दत्प्रणतं लवणान्तकमग्रजः ।
कालनेमिवधात्प्रीतस्तुराषाडिव शार्ङ्गिणम् ॥

४० स पृष्टः सर्वतो वार्तामारव्यद्राज्ञे न सन्ततिम् ।
प्रख्यापयिष्यतः काले कवेराद्यस्य शासनात् ॥

४१ अथाकस्मान्मृतं विप्रः पुत्रमप्राप्तयौवनम् ।
अवतार्याङ्कशय्यास्थं द्वारि चक्रन्द भूपतेः ॥

४२ शोचनीयासि वसुधे या त्वं दशरथाच्च्युता ।
रामहस्तमनुप्राप्ता कष्टात्कष्टतरं गता ॥

४३ श्रुत्वा तस्य शुचो हेतुं गोप्ता जिह्राय राघवः ।
न ह्याकालभवो मृत्युरिक्ष्वाकुपदमस्पृशत् ॥

४४ स मुहूर्तं सहस्वेति द्विजमाश्वास्य दुःखितम् ।
यानं सस्मार कौवेरं वैवस्वतजिगीषया ॥

४५ आत्तशस्त्रस्तदध्यास्य प्रस्थितश्च रघूद्वहः ।
उच्चचार पुनश्चास्य गूढरूपा सरस्वती ॥

४६ राजन्प्रजासु ते कश्चिदपचारः प्रवर्तते ।
तमन्विष्य प्रशमयेर्भवितासि ततः कृती ॥

As he bowed down, his elder brother greeted him as the   39
    vanquisher of Lavana, as once the delighted Indra
    greeted Vishnu after the slaughter of Kalanemi.

When questioned, Shatrughna told the king that things   40
    were well in every regard. But he did not mention the
    birth of his sons, in accordance with the command
    of the first poet, who would announce this at the
    appropriate time.

Now, one day a Brahman whose son had died suddenly   41
    in childhood raised a wail at the palace gate, setting
    down the boy from his lap where he lay:

"Oh Earth, we must weep for you now that you have fallen   42
    from the hands of Dasharatha into those of Rama,
    reaching yet greater suffering."

On hearing the cause of his grief, Rama, the protector, felt   43
    shame, since untimely death never touched the realm
    of the Ikshvakus.

Consoling the grieving Brahman with the words "Have   44
    patience for a moment!" he summoned by thought
    the flying chariot of Kubera, with the intention of
    conquering Death.[10]

The scion of the Raghus took his weapons, climbed into it,   45
    and set off, but the goddess of speech, invisible, spoke
    to him:

"Oh king, some misconduct is afoot among your subjects.   46
    You must find it out and stop it; then your aims will be
    accomplished."

४७ इत्याप्तवचनाद्रामो विचेष्यन्वर्णविक्रियाम् ।
दिशः पपात पत्त्रेण वेगनिष्कम्पकेतुना ॥

४८ अथ धूमाभिताम्राक्षं वृक्षशाखावलम्बिनम् ।
ददर्श कंचिदैक्ष्वाकस्तपस्यन्तमधोमुखम् ॥

४९ पृष्टकामान्वयो राज्ञा स किलाचष्ट धूमपः ।
आत्मानं शाम्बुकं नाम शूद्रं सुरपदार्थिनम् ॥

५० तपस्यनधिकारित्वात्प्रजानां तमघावहम् ।
शीर्षच्छेद्यं परिच्छिद्य नियन्ता शस्त्रमाददे ॥

५१ स तद्वक्त्रं हिमक्लिष्टकिञ्जल्कमिव पङ्कजम् ।
ज्योतिष्कणाहतश्मश्रु कण्ठनालादपाहरत् ॥

५२ धृतदण्डः स्वयं राज्ञा लेभे शूद्रः सतां गतिम् ।
तपसा दुश्चरेणापि न स्वमार्गविलङ्घिना ॥

५३ रघुनाथो ऽप्यगस्त्येन मार्गसन्दर्शितात्मना ।
महौजसा संयुयुजे शरत्काल इवामलः ॥

५४ कुम्भयोनिरलङ्कारं तस्मै दिव्यपरिग्रहम् ।
ददौ दत्तं समुद्रेण भीतेनेवात्मनिष्क्रयम् ॥

Following this trustworthy statement, Rama roamed the   47
directions in his vehicle, its flags motionless from the
speed, in order to discover how the social order could
have been violated.

That descendant of the Ikshvakus then saw someone with   48
eyes red from smoke, performing mortifications by
hanging upside down from the branch of a tree.

They say that when asked his lineage and purpose by the   49
king, the man drinking smoke said he was a Shudra
named Shambhuka, and that he aspired to reach the
realm of the gods.

Because the man did not have the right to perform   50
such austerities, he had brought woe thereby upon
the subjects. Determining that he deserved to be
beheaded, the chastiser took up his weapon.

The man's head, like a lotus with stamens withered by   51
frost, Rama severed from the stalk of its neck in such a
way that sparks singed its beard.

Punished in this way by the king himself, that Shudra   52
attained heaven, but not by his own asceticism,
grueling though that was, since that transgressed the
rules of his path in life.

Rama, bright as the season of autumn, was met by the   53
spirited sage Agastya, who showed him the way
back.[11]

The pot-born sage gave him a jewel of heavenly   54
provenance that he had himself received from the
terrified ocean as ransom.[12]

५५ तं दधन्मैथिलीकण्ठनिर्व्यापारेण बाहुना ।
पश्चान्निववृते रामः प्राक्परासुर्द्विजात्मजः ॥

५६ तस्य पूर्वोदितां निन्दां द्विजः पुत्रसमागतः ।
स्तुत्या निवर्तयामास त्रातुर्वैवस्वतादपि ॥

५७ तमध्वराय मुक्ताश्वं रक्षःकपिनरेश्वराः ।
मेघाः सस्यमिवाम्भोभिरभ्यवर्षन्नुपायनैः ॥

५८ दिग्भ्यो निमन्त्रिताश्चैनमभिजग्मुर्महर्षयः ।
न भौमान्येव धिष्ण्यानि हित्वा ज्योतिर्मयान्यपि ॥

५९ उपशल्यनिविष्टैस्तैश्चतुर्द्वारमुखी बभौ ।
अयोध्या सृष्टलोकेव सद्यः पैतामही तनुः ॥

६० श्लाघ्यस्त्यागो ऽपि वैदेह्याः पत्युः प्राग्वंशवासिनः ।
अनन्यजानेर्यस्यासीत्सैव जाया हिरण्मयी ॥

६१ विधेरधिकसम्भारस्ततः प्रववृते मखः ।
आसन्यत्र क्रियाविघ्ना राक्षसा एव रक्षिणः ॥

६२ अथ प्राचेतसोपज्ञं रामायणमितस्ततः ।
मैथिलेयौ कलगिरौ जगतुर्गुरुचोदितौ ॥

Wearing that on his arm, which no longer embraced Sita's   55
    neck, Rama returned, but even before he did the
    Brahman's dead son returned to life.

Reunited with his son, the Brahman turned his earlier   56
    censure into praise of the one who could protect even
    from death.

When he released a horse for the horse sacrifice, *rākṣasas,*   57
    monkeys, and kings showered gifts upon Rama, as the
    clouds shower waters upon the crops.

The great sages who were invited arrived from all   58
    directions, from homes not just on earth but also
    among the stars.

They stayed in the surroundings, so that the city of   59
    Ayodhya with its four gates resembled the body of
    Brahma when he had just emanated creatures.[13]

Even his abandonment of Sita became a cause for praise   60
    when he took residence in the sacrificer's pavilion,
    since he took no other wife but had her alone there as
    his spouse, in golden effigy.

Then the sacrifice began, even more lavish than scripture   61
    prescribes, and with *rākṣasas,* usually its obstacles, as
    its protectors.

Now, the two sweet-voiced sons of Maithili, prompted by   62
    their guru, were singing in various places the saga of
    Rama's deeds that Prachetasa* had composed.

---

* Another name of Valmiki, their guru.

६३ वृत्तं रामस्य वाल्मीकेः कृतिस्तौ किन्नरस्वनौ ।
    किं तद्येन मनो हर्तुमलं स्यातां न शृण्वताम् ॥

६४ रूपे गीते च माधुर्यं तयोस्तज्ज्ञनिवेदितम् ।
    ददर्श सानुजो रामः शुश्राव च कुतूहली ॥

६५ तद्गीतश्रवणैकाग्रा संसदसुमुखी बभौ ।
    हिमनिःष्यन्दिनी प्रातर्निर्वातेव वनस्थली ॥

६६ वयोवेशविसंवादि रामस्य च तयोश्च सा ।
    जनता प्रेक्ष्य साद‍ृश्यं वीक्षापन्ना व्यतिष्ठत ॥

६७ उभयोर्न तथा लोकः प्रावीण्येन विसिष्मिये ।
    नृपतेः प्रीतिदायेषु वीतस्पृहतया यथा ॥

६८ गेये केन विनीतौ वां कस्य वेयं कवेः कृतिः ।
    इति राज्ञा स्वयं पृष्टौ तौ वाल्मीकिमशंसताम् ॥

६९ अथ सावरजो रामः प्राचेतसमुपेयिवान् ।
    दूरीकृत्यात्मनो देहं राज्यमस्मै न्यवेदयत् ॥

७० स तावाख्याय रामस्य मैथिलेयौ तवात्मजौ ।
    कविः कारुणिको वव्रे सीतायाः संपरिग्रहम् ॥

The deeds were Rama's; the composition Valmiki's; the   63
    singers as sweet-voiced as *gandharvas*. How could the
    two fail to charm the hearts of listeners?

Rama and his younger brothers were informed of their   64
    beauty and sweetness of voice by people who knew
    such things, and they came full of eagerness to gaze
    and listen for themselves.

The assembly, absorbed in listening to their singing and   65
    moved to tears, resembled a forest grove at dawn,
    completely still for lack of wind and dripping with
    cool dew.

The crowd there saw how closely Rama and the two boys   66
    resembled each other in all but age and dress, and
    stood lost in wonder.

As much as the people were astonished by the pair's skill in   67
    singing, they were even more so by their indifference
    to the king's affectionate rewards of wealth.

The king himself asked them who taught them singing and   68
    which poet had produced the composition, and they
    replied: Valmiki.

Then Rama, with his younger brothers, approached   69
    the sage Prachetasa and bestowed everything in his
    kingdom on him, excepting only his person.

After telling Rama that the two were Rama's own sons,   70
    born to Maithili, the compassionate seer requested
    that he receive Sita back.

७१ तात शुद्धा समक्षं नः स्नुषा ते जातवेदसि ।
दौरात्म्याद्राक्षसस्तां तु नात्रत्याः श्रद्दधुः प्रजाः ॥

७२ ताः स्वचरित्रमुद्दिश्य प्रत्याययतु मैथिली ।
ततः पुत्रवतीमेनां प्रतिपत्स्ये तवाज्ञया ॥

७३ इति प्रतिश्रुते राज्ञा जानकीमाश्रमान्मुनिः ।
शिष्यैरानाययामास स्वसिद्धिं नियमैरिव ॥

७४ अन्येद्युरथ काकुत्स्थः सन्निपत्य पुरौकसः ।
कविमाह्वाययामास प्रस्तुतप्रतिपत्तये ॥

७५ स्वरसंस्कारवत्येव पुत्राभ्यां सह सीतया ।
ऋचेवोदर्चिषं सूर्यं रामं मुनिरुपस्थितः ॥

७६ काषायपरिवीतेन स्वपादार्पितचक्षुषा ।
अन्वमीयत शुद्धेति शान्तेन वपुषैव सा ॥

७७ जनास्तदालोकपथात्प्रतिसंहृतचक्षुषः ।
तस्थुरुर्वीमुखाः सर्वे फलिता इव शालयः ॥

७८ तां दृष्टिविषये भर्तुर्मुनिरास्थितविष्टरः ।
कुरु निःसंशयं वत्से स्ववृत्ते लोकमित्यशात् ॥

"Father, your daughter-in-law was proved pure in the fire 71
in our presence, but because of the wickedness of
Ravana the people here would not believe her.[14]

"If Maithili can reassure them regarding her conduct, 72
then I will take her back, along with her sons, as you
command."

After the king had made this promise, the sage let his 73
disciples bring her forth from the ashram, just as he let
observances bring forth the success of his goals.

Now, on the next day the descendant of Kakutstha 74
assembled the citizens and called the sage, with the
intention of settling the matter.

The sage approached Rama, who resembled the sun, 75
bringing Sita along with her two sons, resembling
the Savitri mantra with perfect intonation and
enunciation.[15]

Her purity could be inferred already from her body: it was 76
serene, wrapped in saffron robes, her gaze fixed on her
feet.

The people withdrew their gaze from the path of her sight 77
and all stood looking down at the ground, like so many
ripened ears of rice.

The sage sat down on a seat of grass and instructed Sita in 78
the presence of her husband: "My child, convince the
people beyond doubt as to your conduct."

७९ अथ वाल्मीकिशिष्येण पुण्यमावर्जितं पयः ।
आचम्योदीरयामास सीता सत्यां सरस्वतीम् ॥

८० वाङ्मनःकर्मभिः पत्यौ व्यभिचारो यथा न मे ।
तथा विश्वम्भरा देवी मामन्तर्धातुमर्हति ॥

८१ एवमुक्ते तया साध्व्या रन्ध्रं सद्यो ऽभवद्भुवः ।
शातह्रदमिव ज्योतिः प्रभामण्डलमुद्ययौ ॥

८२ तत्र नागफणोत्क्षिप्तसिंहासननिषादिनी ।
समुद्रवसना साक्षात्प्रादुरासीद्वसुन्धरा ॥

८३ सा सीतामङ्कमारोप्य भर्तृप्रणिहितेक्षणाम् ।
मा मेति व्याहरत्येव तस्मिन्पातालमभ्यगात् ॥

८४ रसायां तस्य संरम्भं सीताप्रत्यर्पणैषिणः ।
गुरुर्विधिबलापेक्षी शमयामास धन्विनः ॥

८५ ऋषीन्विसृज्य यज्ञान्ते सुहृदश्च पुरस्कृतान् ।
रामः सीतागतं स्नेहं निदधे तदपत्ययोः ॥

८६ युधाजितश्च सन्देशात्स देशं सिन्धुकूलगम् ।
ददौ दत्तप्रभावाय भरताय भृतप्रजः ॥

Then, taking a sip of the sacred water poured into her 79
    hand by a disciple of Valmiki, Sita uttered these words
    of truth:

"If I have never strayed from my husband in word, 80
    thought, or deed, may the goddess Earth swallow me
    up!"

As soon as the good Sita had spoken these words, an 81
    opening suddenly appeared in the ground and a disk
    of light as bright as lightning rose up.

Inside that disk, the wealth-bearing Earth appeared before 82
    their eyes, seated on a lion throne borne on the hoods
    of a serpent and clothed in the oceans.[16]

With Sita keeping her eyes fixed on her husband, who 83
    cried out "No, don't!" Earth took Sita on her lap and
    descended into the underworld.

Furious with Earth, Rama took up his bow, wanting Sita 84
    brought back, but his guru, knowing the force of fate,
    calmed his rage.

When the sacrifice had been concluded, Rama duly 85
    honored the sages and his friends and dismissed them.
    From then on, he bestowed the love that he felt for
    Sita upon her sons.[17]

Upon receiving a message from Yudhajit, Rama, supporter 86
    of his subjects, assigned to Bharata, to whom he
    granted power, the territory of Yudhajit's that had
    been appropriated by siddhas.[18]

८७ भरतस्तत्र गन्धर्वान्युधि निर्जित्य केवलम् ।
आतोद्यं ग्राहयामास समत्याजयदायुधम् ॥

८८ स तक्षपुष्कलौ पुत्रौ राजधान्योस्तदाख्ययोः ।
अभिषिच्याभिषेकार्हौ रामान्तिकमगात्पुनः ॥

८९ अङ्गदं चन्द्रकेतुं च लक्ष्मणो ऽप्यात्मसम्भवौ ।
शासनाद्रघुनाथस्य चक्रे कारपथेश्वरौ ॥

९० इति रोपितपुत्रास्ते जननीनां जनेश्वराः ।
भर्तृलोकप्रपन्नानां निवापान्विदधुः क्रमात् ॥

९१ उपेत्य मुनिवेशो ऽथ कालः प्रोवाच राघवम् ।
रहःसंवादिनौ पश्येदावां यस्तं त्यजेरिति ॥

९२ तथेति प्रतिपन्नाय विवृतात्मा नृपाय सः ।
आचख्यौ दिवमध्यास्व शासनात्परमेष्ठिनः ॥

९३ विद्वानपि तयोर्द्वाःस्थः समयं लक्ष्मणो ऽभिनत् ।
भीतो दुर्वाससः शापाद्रामसन्दर्शनार्थिनः ॥

९४ स गत्वा सरयूतीरं देहत्यागेन योगवित् ।
चकारावितथां भ्रातुः प्रतिज्ञां पूर्वजन्मनः ॥

Once he had defeated the *gandharvas* there, Bharata   87
forced them to take up only the instruments of music
and to abandon those of war.

After installing his two sons, Taksha and Pushkala, in   88
capital cities bearing their names and anointing them,
as they deserved, as kings, he returned to be with
Rama.[19]

As for Lakshmana, following Rama's command, he   89
appointed his two sons, Angada and Chandraketu, as
overlords of the Karapatha region.[20]

After thus enthroning their sons, those lords of men   90
performed the obsequies of their mothers as they, one
by one, left to join the world where their husband* had
gone.

Now, one day, Death, disguised as a sage, approached   91
Rama and said: "You should give up to me the person
who sees the two of us talking together in private."

The king assented, and then Death revealed his identity   92
and told him: "Go to heaven, in accordance with
Brahma's command!"

Lakshmana, who was standing at the threshold, then   93
broke in on them. He knew their agreement but
was fearful of the curse of Durvasas, who had come
seeking an audience with Rama.[21]

Lakshmana then went to the bank of the Sarayu and   94
ensured that his elder brother's word remained true
by abandoning his body there, for he knew yoga.[22]

---

* Dasharatha.

९५ तस्मिन्नात्मचतुर्भागे प्राङ्नाकमधितस्थुषि ।
राघवः शिथिलं तस्थौ भुवि धर्मस्त्रिपादिव ॥

९६ स निवेश्य कुशावत्यां रिपुनागाङ्कुशं कुशम् ।
श्रावस्त्यां च सतां सूक्तैर्जनितासुलवं लवम् ॥

९७ उदक्प्रतस्थे स्थिरधीः सानुजो ऽग्निपुरःसरः ।
अन्वितः पतिवात्सल्यादृहवर्जमयोध्यया ॥

९८ जगृहुस्तस्य वृत्तज्ञाः पदवीं हरिराक्षसाः ।
कदम्बमुकुलस्थूलैरभिवृष्टां जनास्रुभिः ॥

९९ उपस्थितविमानेन तेन भक्तानुकम्पिना ।
चक्रे त्रिदिवनिःश्रेणिः सरयूरनुयायिनाम् ॥

१०० यद्घोप्रतरकल्पो ऽभूद्द्विमर्दस्तत्र मज्जताम् ।
अतस्तदाख्यया तीर्थं पावनं तद्धि पप्रथे ॥

१०१ स विभुर्विबुधांशेषु प्रतिपन्नात्ममूर्तिषु ।
त्रिदशीभूतपौरार्थं स्वर्गान्तरमकल्पयत् ॥

With a quarter of himself thus reaching heaven before   95
    him, Rama remained standing on earth unsteadily,
    like Dharma with only three feet.[23]

He settled Kusha, a goad to the elephants that were his   96
    enemies, in the city of Kushavati, and Lava, who
    caused teardrops to well up in his listeners' eyes with
    his verses, in the city of Shravasti.[24]

Resolute in mind, Rama set out toward the north,   97
    accompanied by his younger brothers and carrying
    his sacred fires with him. All Ayodhya followed him,
    leaving their homes behind, with the affection a wife
    feels for her husband.[25]

Understanding what he was about, the monkeys and   98
    rākṣasas took the same path, now splashed with
    tears—as large as *kadamba* buds—shed by his people.

A celestial chariot awaited him. Ever compassionate to   99
    those devoted to him, he made the Sarayu River into a
    stairway for his followers to reach heaven.

Because of the mass of people plunging into it, it was   100
    like a ford where cattle cross, and so that sanctifying
    crossing place became well known by the name of
    Gopratara.*

Once the portions of the gods that had become incarnate   101
    had returned to their original forms, the immanent
    lord created another heaven for the citizens of
    Ayodhya, who had become divine.[26]

---

* Meaning "ox ford."

१०२ निर्वर्त्यैषां दशमुखभयच्छेदकार्यं सुराणां
विश्वक्सेनः स्वतनुमविशत्सम्रलोकप्रतिष्ठां ।
लङ्कानाथं पवनतनयं चोभयं स्थापयित्वा
कीर्तिस्तम्भद्वयमिव गिरौ दक्षिणे चोत्तरे च ॥

इति रघुवंशे महाकाव्ये पञ्चदशः सर्गः ॥

Having accomplished the task of those gods, the   102
    extirpation of the threat that was Ravana, and instated
    the Lord of Lanka* and the Son of the Wind on the
    southern and northern mountains like twin pillars
    proclaiming his glory, Vishvaksena now resumed his
    own divine body, the refuge of the seven worlds.[27]

---

* Vibhishana.

षोडशः सर्गः

१ अथेतरे सप्त रघुप्रवीरा ज्येष्ठं पुरोजन्मतया गुणैश्च ।
चक्रुः कुशं रत्नविशेषभाजं सौभ्रात्रमेषां हि कुलानुसारि ॥

२ ते सेतुवार्तागजबन्धमुख्यैरभ्युच्छ्रिताः कर्मभिरप्यवन्ध्यैः ।
अन्योन्यदेशप्रविभागसीमां वेलां समुद्रा इव न व्यतीयुः ॥

३ चतुर्भुजांशप्रभवः स तेषां दानप्रवृत्तेरनुपारतानाम् ।
सुरद्विपानामिव सामयोनिर्भिन्नो ऽछ्छदा विप्रससार वंशः ॥

४ अथार्धरात्रे स्तिमितप्रदीपे शय्यागृहे सुप्तजने विबुद्धः ।
कुशः प्रवासस्थकलत्रवेषामदृष्टपूर्वां वनितामपश्यत् ॥

CHAPTER 16
Ayodhya Abandoned, Then Restored to Glory

Then the seven other heroic descendants of Raghu 1
made Kusha king, the receiver of the very best of
everything. For he was senior in age and virtue, and
then, too, brotherly love ran in their family.[1]

They all increased their power by such useful activities as 2
bridge building, agriculture, and capturing elephants,
but never overstepped the bounds of each other's
lands, like the oceans their shores.

The lineage, arising from the portions of Four-Armed 3
Vishnu, of these kings, who never stopped showing
generosity, spread far and wide, divided into eight
branches, like the family, arising from the *sāmans,*
of the divine elephants, who never stop flowing with
musth.[2]

Once, in his bedchamber at midnight, when the lamps 4
were burning motionlessly and the servants were
asleep, Kusha awoke and saw a woman he had never
seen before, wearing the dress of a wife whose
husband is away from home.

५ सा साधुसाधारणपार्थिवर्द्धेः स्थित्वा पुरस्तात्पुरुहूतभासः ।
जेतुः परेषां जयशब्दपूर्वं तस्याञ्जलिं बन्धुमतो बबन्ध ॥

६ तां सो ऽनपोढार्गलमप्यगारं छायामिवादर्शतलं प्रविष्टाम् ।
सविस्मयो दाशरथेस्तनूजः प्रोवाच पूर्वार्धविसृष्टतल्पः ॥

७ लब्धो ऽन्तरः सावरणे ऽपि गेहे योगप्रभावो न च लक्ष्यते ते ।
बिभर्षि चाकारमनिर्वृतानां मृणालिनी हैममिवोपरागम् ॥

८ का त्वं शुभे कस्य परिग्रहो वा किं वा मदभ्यागमकारणं ते ।
आचक्ष्व मत्वा वशिनां रघूणां मनः परस्त्रीविमुखप्रवृत्ति ॥

९ तमब्रवीत्सा गुरुणा तव द्यां या नीतपौरा स्वपदोन्मुखेन ।
तस्याः पुरः संप्रति वीतनाथां जानीहि राजन्पुरदेवतां माम् ॥

१० वस्वोकसारामभिभूय साहं सौराज्यबद्धोत्सवया विभूत्या ।
समग्रशक्तौ त्वयि सूर्यवंश्ये सति प्रपन्ना करुणामवस्थाम् ॥

"Victory to you!" With these words she put her palms   5
    together and stood before him, that man whose royal
    wealth was shared among the good, whose luster was
    like Indra's, who conquered his enemies, and who had
    many friends and relatives.

Rama's son sat upright in bed and spoke to her in   6
    astonishment, for she had entered the room while the
    door remained bolted, like a reflection entering the
    surface of a mirror.

"You have found your way into this room, even though it is   7
    locked, and yet you don't seem to have yogic powers.
    You look like someone in distress, like a lotus blanched
    by frost.

"Who are you, good woman, and whose wife are you? Why   8
    have you come to see me? Tell me, and rest assured
    that the Raghus are self-controlled and keep their
    thoughts turned away from others' wives."

She said to him, "Know, oh king, that I am the tutelary   9
    deity, now lordless, of that city* whose people were
    taken to heaven by your father when he headed
    toward his own abode.

"I once surpassed Vasvokasara† by the riches displayed   10
    in the festivals that good governance made possible.
    You are a scion of the solar dynasty, and your power
    is unimpaired. And yet I have fallen into this piteous
    state.

---

* Ayodhya.
† Either Indra's or Kubera's city.

११ विशीर्णतल्पाटृशतो निवेशः पर्यस्तशालः प्रभुणा विना मे ।
विडम्बयत्यस्तनिमग्नसूर्यं दिनान्तमुग्रानिलभिन्नमेघम् ॥

१२ निशासु भास्वत्कलनूपुराणां यः संचरो ऽभूदभिसारिकाणाम् ।
नदन्मुखोल्काविचितामिषाभिः स वाह्यते राजपथः शिवाभिः ॥

१३ आस्फालितं यत्प्रमदाकराग्रैर्मृदङ्गधीरध्वनिमन्वगच्छत् ।
वन्यैरिदानीं महिषैस्तदम्भः शृङ्गाहतं क्रोशति दीर्घिकासु ॥

१४ सोपानमार्गेषु च येषु रामा निक्षिप्तवत्यश्चरणान्सरागान् ।
सद्योहतन्यङ्कुभिरस्रदिग्धं व्याघ्रैः पदं तेषु निधीयते मे ॥

१५ चित्रद्विपाः पद्मवनावतीर्णाः करेणुभिर्दत्तमृणालभङ्गाः ।
नखाङ्कुशाघातविभिन्नकुम्भं सरब्धसिंहप्रहृतं वहन्ति ॥

१६ स्तम्भेषु योषित्प्रतियातनानामुद्धान्तवर्णक्रमधूसराणाम् ।
तनूत्तरीयाणि भवन्ति सङ्गान्निर्मोकपट्टाः फणिभिर्विमुक्ताः ॥

१७ कालान्तरश्यामसुधेषु नक्तमितस्ततो रूढतृणाङ्कुरेषु ।
त एव मुक्तागुणशुद्धयो ऽपि हर्म्येषु मूर्छन्ति न चन्द्रपादाः ॥

"Walls and turrets lie shattered in hundreds; stables are   11
    ruined: without a lord, my home resembles the close
    of day when the sun sinks and high winds scatter the
    clouds.

"At night women, their shiny anklets jingling, used to   12
    hurry along the royal highway to meet their lovers.
    Now female jackals roam on the same road, searching
    for prey with the torches of their howling mouths.[3]

"The waters of the ponds used to imitate the *mṛdaṅga's*   13
    deep sound when women slapped them with their
    palms; they now cry out when struck by the horns of
    forest buffaloes.

"Women used to put their feet painted red with lac on the   14
    flights of my steps; now on the same stairs tigers set
    paws smeared with the blood of deer they have just
    killed.

"The elephant bulls portrayed in my frescos lower   15
    themselves into lotus ponds, where their mates offer
    them mouthfuls of stalks; now angry lions attack and
    split their temple lobes with blows of their goad-like
    claws.[4]

"On the statues of beautiful women carved into the   16
    pillars, now gray because of the gradual fading of their
    colors, snakes have sloughed their skins to serve as
    diaphanous coverings for their breasts.

"At night the same rays of moonlight, still pure white   17
    like pearl necklaces, are no longer magnified on the
    rooftops, where the plaster has darkened with time
    and patches of grass have sprouted.

१८ आवर्ज्य शाखाः सदयं च यासां पुष्पाण्युपात्तानि विलासिनीभिः ।
वन्द्यः पुलिन्दैरिव वानरैस्ताः क्लिश्यन्त उद्यानलता मदीयाः ॥

१९ रात्रावनाविष्कृतदीपभासः कान्तामुखश्रीवियुता दिवापि ।
तिरस्क्रियन्ते कृमितन्तुजालैर्विच्छिन्नधूमप्रसरा गवाक्षाः ॥

२० वृक्षेशया यष्टिनिवासभङ्गान्मृदङ्गशब्दापगमादलस्याः ।
प्राप्ता दवोल्काहतशेषबर्हाः क्रीडामयूरा वनबर्हिणत्वम् ॥

२१ बलिक्रियावर्जितसैकतानि स्नानीयसंसर्गमनापनुवन्ति ।
उपान्तवानीरगृहेषु दृष्ट्वा शून्यानि दूये सरयूजलानि ॥

२२ तदर्हसीमां वसतिं विसृज्य मामभ्युपैतुं कुलराजधानीम् ।
हित्वा तनुं कारणमानुषीं तां यथा गुरुस्ते परमात्ममूर्तिम् ॥

२३ तथेति तस्याः प्रणयं प्रतीतः प्रत्यग्रहीत्राग्रहरो रघूणाम् ।
पूरप्यभिव्यक्तमुखप्रसादा शरीरबन्धेन तिरोबभूव ॥

२४ तद्द्भुतं संसदि रात्रिवृत्तं प्रातर्द्विजेभ्यो नृपतिः शशंस ।
श्रुत्वा त एनं कुलराजधान्या साक्षात्पतित्वे वृतमभ्यनन्दन् ॥

"Once playful women gently bent the branches of my
garden vines to pluck their flowers; now those
vines are pestered by monkeys, like captive women
molested by savages.   18

"No lamplight shines in the ox-eye windows at night; by
day the faces of beautiful women do not appear at
them. Incense no longer billows from them; they are
hidden behind the webs of spiders.   19

"The pet peacocks have become wild: they roost in the
trees now that their perches are broken, they do not
dance now that the *mṛdaṅga* drums have fallen silent,
and only a few of their tail feathers are left unscorched
by forest fires.   20

"It grieves me to see the waters of the Sarayu, empty of
lovers among the bowers of the reeds, not mingled
with their bathing unguents, with no rice offerings
placed on her sandbanks.   21

"So leave this place and come to me, your ancestral capital!
Just so your father abandoned the human body he had
assumed for a reason, and took once more the form of
the supreme soul."   22

"So be it," said the foremost of the Raghus, gladly
assenting to her request. As for the city, joy became
visible on her face, and then her physical form
vanished.   23

In the morning, in the assembly, the king told the
Brahmans the wondrous event of the night. They
listened, and congratulated him on being chosen by
his ancestral city in person as her lord.   24

391

२५ कुशावतीं श्रोत्रियसात्स कृत्वा यात्रानुकूले ऽहनि सावरोधः ।
अनुद्रुतो वायुरिवाभ्रवृन्दैः सैन्यैरयोध्याभिमुखः प्रतस्थे ॥

२६ सा केतुमालोपवना बृहद्भिर्विहारशैलानुगतेव नागैः ।
सेना रथोदारगृहा प्रयाणे तस्याभवज्जङ्गमराजधानी ॥

२७ तेनातपत्रामलमण्डलेन प्रस्थापितः पूर्वनिवासभूमिम् ।
बभौ बलौघः शशिनोद्धृतेन वेलामुदन्वानिव नीयमानः ॥

२८ तस्य प्रयातस्य वरूथिनीनां पीडामपर्याप्नुवतीव सोढुम् ।
वसुंधरा विष्णुपदं द्वितीयमध्यारुरोहेव रजश्छलेन ॥

२९ उद्गच्छमाना गमनाय पश्चात्पुरो निवेशे पथि वा नृपस्य ।
सा यत्र सेना ददृषे जनेन तत्रैव सामग्र्यपदं चकार ॥

३० तस्य द्विपानां मदवारिसेकात्खुराभिघाताच्च तुरंगमाणाम् ।
रेणुः प्रपेदे पथि पङ्कभावं पङ्को ऽपि रेणुत्वमियाय नेतुः ॥

३१ मार्गैषिणी सा कटकान्तरेषु वैन्येषु सेना बहुधा विभिन्ना ।
चकार रेवेव महाविरावा बद्धप्रतिश्रुन्ति गुहामुखानि ॥

३२ स धातुभेदारुणयाननेमिः प्रभुः प्रपातध्वनिमिश्रतूर्यः ।
व्यलङ्घयद्विन्ध्यमुपायनानि पश्यन्पुलिन्दैरुपपादितानि ॥

He entrusted Kushavati to Vedic Brahmans and, on a   25
    day favorable to the journey, he and his wives set off
    toward Ayodhya, his armies following behind like a
    bank of clouds following the wind.

On the march, the army became his mobile capital: the   26
    garlands of flags were the gardens, the great elephants
    following in train resembled pleasure hills, and the
    chariots were the lofty palaces.

Leading the flood of his army to their former lands he   27
    resembled, with the circle of the white parasol above
    him, the moon leading the ocean to the shore.

As he marched, the earth seemed unable to endure the   28
    tread of his armies; it appeared to rise up, in the guise
    of dust, to the realm of Vishnu's second step.[5]

As the king's army was preparing to set off, wherever   29
    people glimpsed it, whether behind or in front, in the
    camp or on the path, they felt they must be seeing all
    of it present in that place.

With the king's elephants showering musth, the dust on   30
    the road turned to mud, and with his horses trampling
    it beneath their hooves, the mud turned to dust.

As the army with its many divisions picked its way over   31
    the slopes of the Vindhya range, it filled the mouths of
    the caves with echoes, like the thundering Reva River
    with its many streams.

The king crossed the Vindhya with his chariot wheels   32
    reddened by the crushing of its minerals, the blare of
    his clarions blending with the rumbling of waterfalls,
    glancing, as he passed, at the gifts brought to him by
    tribal huntsmen.

३३ तीर्थे तदीये गजसेतुबन्धात्प्रतीपगामुत्तरतो ऽस्य गङ्गाम् ।
अयत्नवालव्यजनीबभूवुर्हंसा नभोलङ्घनलोलपक्षाः ॥

३४ स पूर्वजानां कपिलेन रोषाद्भस्मावशेषीकृतविग्रहाणाम् ।
सुरालयप्राप्तिनिमित्तमम्भस्त्रैस्रोतसं सोल्ललितं ववन्दे ॥

३५ इत्यध्वनः कैश्चिदहोभिरन्ते कूलं समासाद्य कुशः सरय्वाः ।
वेदिप्रतिष्ठान्विततताध्वराणां यूपानपश्यच्छतशो रघूणाम् ॥

३६ आधूय शाखाः कुसुमद्रुमाणां स्पृष्ट्वा च शीतान्सरयूतरङ्गान् ।
तं क्रान्तसैन्यं कुलराजधान्याः प्रत्युज्जगामोपवनान्तवातः ॥

३७ अथोपशल्ये रिपुमग्रशल्यस्तस्याः पुरः पौरसखः स राजा ।
कुलध्वजस्तानि चलध्वजानि निवेशयामास बली बलानि ॥

३८ तां शिल्पिसंघाः प्रभुणा नियुक्तास्तथागतां संभृतसाधनत्वात् ।
पुनर्नवीचक्रुरपां विसर्गान्मेघा निदाघग्लपितामिवोर्वीम् ॥

३९ ततः सपर्यां सपशूपहारां पुरः पराध्र्यप्रतिमागृहायाः ।
उपोषितैर्वास्तुविधानविद्भिर्निर्वर्तयामास रघुप्रवीरः ॥

And when he crossed the Ganga, dammed by his elephants   33
   and flowing backward, at a ford, the flapping wings of
   the geese flying into the sky spontaneously became his
   chowries.

He worshiped the rippling waters of the Ganga, the path   34
   to the abode of the gods for his ancestors, whose
   bodies Kapila had reduced to ashes out of anger.[6]

At the end of several days of journeying thus, Kusha   35
   reached the bank of the Sarayu. There he saw
   hundreds of sacrificial posts, still on their altars,
   belonging to the Raghus, who sacrificed unceasingly.

A breeze wafting from the gardens of his ancestral capital   36
   shook the branches of blossoming trees, touched the
   cool ripples of the Sarayu, and came to meet him and
   his weary army.

Then that powerful king, the banner of his family, a friend   37
   to his subjects, but who planted arrows in his enemies,
   encamped his troops, with banners fluttering, on the
   outskirts of the city.

With all necessary means at the ready, guilds of craftsmen   38
   employed by the king renovated the city, now fallen
   into such a state of disrepair, just as clouds pouring
   down water renew the earth exhausted by summer's
   heat.

At the behest of the most excellent of the Raghus, experts   39
   in *vāstu* rites, who had duly been fasting, performed
   a ceremony of worship, accompanied by animal
   sacrifice, of the city with its beautiful temples housing
   images.[7]

४० तस्याः स राजोपपदं निशान्तं कामीव कान्ताहृदयं प्रविश्य ।
यथार्हमन्यैरनुजीविलोकं संभावयामास गृहैस्तदीयैः ॥

४१ सा मन्दुरासंश्रयिभिस्तुरंगैः शालागृहस्तम्भगतैश्च नागैः ।
पूराबभासे विपणिस्थपण्या सर्वाङ्गनद्धाभरणेव नारी ॥

४२ वसन्स तस्यां वसतौ रघूणां पुराणशोभामधिरोपितायाम् ।
न मैथिलेयः स्पृहयां बभूव भर्त्रे दिवो नाप्यलकेश्वराय ॥

४३ अथास्य रत्नग्रथितोत्तरीयमेकान्तपाण्डुस्तनलम्बहारम् ।
निःश्वासहार्यांशुकमाजगाम घर्मः प्रियावेशमिवोपदेष्टुम् ॥

४४ अगस्त्यचिह्नादयनात्समीपं दिगुत्तरा भास्वति संनिवृत्ते ।
आनन्दशीतामिव वाष्पवृष्टिं हिमसूतिं हैमवतीं ससर्ज ॥

४५ प्रवृद्धतापो दिवसो ऽतिमात्रमत्यन्तमेव क्षणदा च तन्वी ।
उभौ विरोधक्रियया विभिन्नौ जायापती सानुशयाविवास्ताम् ॥

४६ दिने दिने शेवलवन्त्यधस्तात्सोपानपर्वाणि विमुञ्चदम्भः ।
उद्दण्डपद्मं गृहदीर्घिकाणां नारीनितम्बद्वयसं बभूव ॥

४७ नवेषु सायनतनमल्लिकाया विजृम्भणोद्गन्धिषु कुड्मलेषु ।
प्रत्येकनिक्षिप्तपदः सशब्दं संख्यामिवैषां भ्रमरश्चकार ॥

He entered the royal apartments like a lover entering the   40
heart of his beloved, and then he honored his retainers
with the gift of other houses in the city according to
their merits.

With horses in the stables, elephants at the posts in the   41
stalls, and merchandise in the shops, the city shone
like a woman adorned with jewelry on every limb.

Living in that home of the Raghus, now restored to its   42
former beauty, Sita's son envied neither the lord of
heaven* nor even the master of Alaka.†

Then the hot season arrived, as if to instruct the women   43
dear to him in matters of dress: upper garments
threaded with gemstones, pearl necklaces hanging on
their completely whitened breasts, and fine muslin
cloths that even a sigh could blow away.[8]

When the sun returned from the path marked by Agastya,   44
the northern quarter dripped with the Himalaya's
melting snow, as if she were showering cool tears of
joy.[9]

Like man and wife separated by a quarrel and now filled   45
with remorse, day grew extremely hot and night
utterly wasted away.

Day by day the water in household ponds sank lower on   46
the moss-covered flights of steps, revealing the lotus
stalks, until it only reached up to the women's hips.

Setting foot upon each of the fresh evening jasmine buds   47
that released fragrance as they opened, the bumblebee
seemed to be counting them aloud.

* Indra.
† Kubera.

४८ स्वेदानुविद्धार्द्रनखक्षताङ्कं भूयिष्ठसंदष्टशिखं कपोले ।
च्युतं न कर्णादपि कामिनीनां शिरीषपुष्पं सहसा पपात ॥

४९ यन्त्रप्रवाहैः शिशिरैः परीतान्त्रसेन धौतान्मलयोद्भवस्य ।
शिलाविशेषानधिशाय्य निन्युर्धारागृहेष्वातपमृद्धिमन्तः ॥

५० स्नानार्द्रमुक्तेष्वनुधूपवासं विन्यस्तसायन्तनमल्लिकेषु ।
कामो वसन्तात्ययमन्दवीर्यः केशेषु लेभे बलमङ्गनानाम् ॥

५१ आपिञ्जरा बद्धरजःकणत्वान्मञ्जर्युदारा रुरुचे ऽर्जुनस्य ।
दग्ध्वापि देहं गिरिशेन रोषात्खण्डीकृता ज्येव मनोभ्वस्य ॥

५२ मनोज्ञगन्धं सहकारभङ्गं पुराणशीधुं नवपाटलं च ।
संबध्नता कामिजनेषु दोषाः सर्वे निदाघावधिना प्रमृष्टाः ॥

५३ जनस्य तस्मिन्समये विगाढे बभूवतुर्द्वौ सविशेषकान्तौ ।
तापापनोदक्षमपादसेवौ स चोदयस्थौ नृपतिः शशी च ॥

५४ अथोर्मिलोलोन्मदराजहंसे रोधोलतापुष्पवहे सरय्वाः ।
विहर्तुमिच्छा वनितासखस्य तस्याम्भसि ग्रीष्मसुखे बभूव ॥

The *śirīṣa* flower slipped from women's ears, but its   48
   filaments stuck fast to their cheeks, which bore fresh
   nail wounds slick with sweat, and it did not fall at
   once.[10]

The wealthy spent the hot days in pavilions fitted with   49
   water cascades, where they lay on rare stones washed
   with sandal water and surrounded by cool streams
   spouting from mechanical devices.

Kama had grown weak with the passing of spring but took   50
   strength from women's long tresses, hanging loose
   while still moist from bathing, then perfumed with
   incense and intertwined with evening jasmine.

The lofty flower spikes of the *arjuna* tree, yellowish from   51
   the pollen that crowds them, shone as if they were
   the love god's bowstring torn to shreds by Shiva, still
   furious even after reducing Kama's body to ashes.

The advent of summer brought together mango sprigs, old   52
   wine, and new trumpet flowers, all fragrant, and thus
   made amends to lovers for the pains it caused.

In that severe season people loved two things, both at their   53
   zenith, above all: the king and the moon. Resorting to
   the king's feet dispelled suffering, and resorting to the
   moon's rays dispelled heat.[11]

Now, one day he had a desire to amuse himself with his   54
   wives in the waters of the Sarayu, so pleasant in
   summer. Swans happily bobbed on its waves and
   flowers from the plants on its banks were swept along.

५५ स तीरभूमौ विहितोपकार्यामानायिभिस्तामपकृष्टनक्राम् ।
विगाहितुं श्रीमहिमानुरूपं प्रचक्रमे चक्रधरप्रभावः ॥

५६ सा तीरसोपानपथावतारादन्योन्यकेयूरविघट्टिनीभिः ।
सनूपुरक्षोभपदाभिरासीद्द्विविग्रहंसा सरिदङ्गनाभिः ॥

५७ परस्परक्षेपणतत्पराणां तासां नृपो मज्जनरागदर्शी ।
नौसंश्रयः पार्श्वचरां किरातामुपात्तवालव्यजनां बभाषे ॥

५८ पश्यावरोधैः शतशो मदीयैर्विगाह्यमानो गलिताङ्गरागैः ।
संध्योदयः साभ्र इवैष वर्णं पुष्यत्यनेकं सरयूप्रवाहः ॥

५९ विलुप्तमन्तःपुरसुन्दरीणां यदञ्जनं सोल्ललिताभिरद्भिः ।
तद्वद्धतीभिर्मदरागशोभां विलोचनेषु प्रतिमुक्तमासाम् ॥

६० एता गुरुश्रोणिपयोधरत्वादात्मानमुद्व्रोढुमशक्नुवत्यः ।
गाढाङ्गदैर्बाहुभिरप्सु बालाः क्लेशोत्तरं रागवशात्प्लवन्ते ॥

६१ अमी शिरीषप्रसवावतंसाः पारिप्लवा वारिविहारिणीनाम् ।
प्रभ्रंशिनः स्रोतसि निम्नगायाः शेवाललोलांश्छलयन्ति मीनान् ॥

६२ आसां जलास्फालनतत्पराणां मुक्ताफलस्पर्धिषु शीकरेषु ।
पयोधरोत्सर्पिषु शीर्यमाणाः संलक्ष्यते न च्छिदुरो ऽपि हारः ॥

Fishermen had removed the gharials, and tents had been   55
 set up on the bank, when Kusha, with the might of
 Vishnu, prepared to enter upon the river in a manner
 befitting the greatness of his majesty.

The geese on the river were flustered by the women,   56
 whose armlets rattled against each other as they came
 down the ghats, their anklets shaking at every step.

As the king sat in the boat he beheld the delight of his   57
 wives as they bathed and splashed each other with
 abandon. He said to the Kirata woman who stood at
 his side, chowry in hand,[12]

"Look how the stream of the Sarayu is taking on many   58
 hues, like a cloudy twilight, thanks to my wives
 plunging into it by the hundreds and washing away
 their body makeup.

"The loss of the kohl, rinsed off in the rippling waters,   59
 is offset by the flush of intoxication that those same
 waters have lent the eyes of the ladies of my harem.

"Out of their passion for the sport, these girls, who can   60
 barely stand straight from the weight of their hips and
 breasts, are making their way with difficulty through
 the water, their arms thickly decked with bangles.

"Over there the bobbing *śirīṣa* flower earrings of the   61
 women playing in the water have fallen into the river's
 flow and so deceive the fish, hungry for waterweed.

"So absorbed are the women in splashing water that, as   62
 the pearl-like drops spread on their breasts, they do
 not notice even when their necklaces snap and scatter.

६३ आवर्तशोभा नतनाभिकान्तेर्भङ्ग्यो भ्रुवोर्द्वन्द्वचराः स्तनानाम् ।
जातानि रूपावयवोपमानान्यदूरवर्तीनि विलासिनीनाम् ॥

६४ तीरस्थलीबर्हिभिरुत्कलापैः प्रस्निग्धकेकैरभिनन्द्यमानम् ।
श्रोत्रेषु संमूर्छति रक्तमासां गीतानुगं वारिमृदङ्गवाद्यम् ॥

६५ संदष्टवस्त्रेष्वबलानितम्बेष्विन्दुप्रकाशान्तरितोडुकल्पाः ।
अमी जलापूरितरन्ध्रमार्गा मौनं भजन्ते रशनाकलापाः ॥

६६ एताः करोत्पीडितदण्डधारा हर्षात्सखीभिर्वदनेषु सिक्ताः ।
वक्रेतराग्रैरलकैस्तरुण्यश्चूर्णारुणान्वारिलवान्वमन्ति ॥

६७ उद्बन्धकेशश्च्युतपत्त्ररेखो विश्लेषिमुक्कालतपत्त्रवेष्टः ।
मनोज्ञ एव प्रमदामुखानामम्भोविहाराकुलितो ऽपि वेषः ॥

६८ स नौविमानादवतीर्य रेमे विलोलमाल्यः सह ताभिरप्सु ।
स्कन्धावलग्रोन्नतपद्मिनीकः करेणुभिर्वन्य इव द्विपेन्द्रः ॥

६९ ततो नृपेणाभिगताः स्त्रियस्ता भ्राजिष्णुना सातिशयं विरेजुः ।
प्रागेव मुक्ता नयनाभिरामाः प्राप्येन्द्रनीलं किमुतोन्मयूखम् ॥

"The charming whirlpools are like their beautiful   63
    deep navels, the waves their eyebrows, the pairs of
    cakravāka birds their breasts. Things that can be
    compared to the parts of these beauties here are not
    far to seek.

"The thrilling sound of water beaten like *mṛdaṅga* drums,   64
    which accompanies their singing, fills the ear and is
    greeted by the sweet cries of peacocks standing on the
    bank with tails expanded.[13]

"The women's garments cling tight to their hips, where   65
    the ornaments on their girdle chains have fallen silent,
    their cracks and crevices clogged by water, like stars
    dimmed by the spread of moonlight.

"The tips of the now lank locks of these young women   66
    scatter drops reddened with curcuma as they strike
    up jets of water with their hands, while their friends
    joyfully splash their faces.

"Their hair is undone, their leaf-shaped decorations   67
    smudged, their pearl-string earrings slipped—yet
    even disordered, the embellishments adorning the
    women's faces are a sweet delight!"

He climbed down into the water from his boat, as grand as   68
    a flying chariot, and cavorted with them, his garland
    tossing hither and thither, like a forest tusker with
    his females, an uprooted lotus plant clinging to his
    shoulders.

Those women then shone all the brighter in the company   69
    of the splendid king. Pearls are a lovely sight in
    themselves; how much more so when set beside a
    radiant sapphire?

७० वर्णोदकैः काञ्चनशृङ्गसंस्थैस्तमायताक्ष्यः प्रणयादसिञ्चन् ।
तथागतः सो ऽतिररां बभासे सधातुनिःष्यन्द इवाद्रिराजः ॥

७१ तेनावरोधप्रमदासखेन विगाहमानेन सरिद्वरां ताम् ।
आकाशगङ्गारतिरप्सरोभिर्वृतो मरुत्वाननुयातलीलः ॥

७२ यत्कुम्भयोनेरधिगम्य रामः कुशाय राज्येन समं दिदेश ।
तदस्य जैत्राभरणं विहर्तुरज्ञातपातं सलिले ममज्ज ॥

७३ स्नात्वा यथाकाममसौ सदारस्तीरोपकार्यां गतमात्र एव ।
दिव्येन शून्यं वलयेन बाहुमुपोढनेपथ्यविधिर्ददर्श ॥

७४ जयश्रियः संवननं यतस्तदामुक्तपूर्वं गुरुणा च यस्मात् ।
सेहे ऽस्य न भ्रंशमतो न लोभात्स तुल्यपुष्पाभरणो हि धीरः ॥

७५ ततः समाज्ञापयदाशु सर्वानानायिनस्तद्द्विचये नदीष्णान् ।
वन्ध्यश्रमास्ते सरयूं विगाह्य तमूचुरम्लानमुखप्रसादम् ॥

७६ कृतः प्रयत्नो न च देव लब्धं मग्नं पयस्याभरणोत्तमं ते ।
नागेन लौल्यात्कुमुदेन नूनमुपात्तमन्तर्हृदवासिना तत् ॥

Adoringly, the long-eyed women squirted him with   70
 colored water from golden syringes, so that he shone
 brilliantly, like the king of mountains with its seams of
 ore.

Bathing in that beautiful river with the ladies of his harem,   71
 the king reenacted the amusements that Indra enjoys,
 surrounded by *aparasa*s, in the heavenly Ganga.

While he was thus diverting himself, the victory jewel that   72
 Rama had once received from Agastya and given to
 Kusha along with the kingdom slipped off unnoticed
 into the water.

After bathing to his heart's content with his wives, he   73
 returned to the tent on the bank and saw at once,
 when he was about to be dressed again, that his arm
 was bare of the heavenly armlet.

He could not bear its loss, not because of greed, but   74
 because it was an amulet of victory and his father
 used to wear it. Indeed, for the wise man, flowers and
 ornaments are the same.

He then immediately ordered all the fishermen, who knew   75
 the river well, to search for it. They dove into the
 Sarayu, but their efforts proved vain, and they said to
 him, as he kept his countenance unfazed:

"We have tried hard, Your Majesty, but we could not find   76
 that most excellent ornament of yours that fell in the
 water. Surely the serpent Kumuda, who lives in a pool
 in the river, must have coveted and seized it."

७७ ततः स कृत्वा धनुराततज्यं धनुर्धरः कोपविलोहिताक्षः।
गारुत्मतं तीरगतस्तरस्वी भुजंगनाशाय समादधे ऽस्त्रम्॥

७८ तस्मिन्ह्रदः संहितमात्र एव क्षोभात्समाविद्धतरङ्गहस्तः।
रोधांस्यभिघ्नन्नवपातमग्रः करीव मत्तः परुषं रराास॥

७९ तस्मात्समुद्रादिव मथ्यमानादुद्धृत्तनक्रात्सहसोन्ममज्ज।
लक्ष्म्येव सार्धं सुरराजवृक्षः कन्यां पुरस्कृत्य भुजंगराजः॥

८० विभूषणप्रत्युपहारहस्तमुपस्थितं वीक्ष्य विशां पतिस्तम्॥
सौपर्णमस्त्रं प्रतिसंजहार प्रह्वेष्वनिर्बन्धरुषो हि सन्तः॥

८१ त्रैलोक्यनाथप्रभवं प्रभावात्कुशं द्विषामङ्कुशवस्तु विद्वान्।
मानोन्नतेनाप्यभिनन्द्य मूर्ध्ना सुधावसिक्तं कुमुदो बभाषे॥

८२ अवैमि कार्यान्तरमानुषस्य विष्णोः सुताख्यामपरां तनुं त्वाम्।
सो ऽहं कथं नाम तवाचरेयमाराधनीयस्य धृतेर्विघातम्॥

८३ कराभिघातोत्थितकन्दुकेयमालोक्य बाला तु कुतूहलेन।
ओघात्पतज्ज्योतिरिवान्तरिक्षादादत्त जैत्राभरणं त्वदीयम्॥

That mighty archer, eyes red with anger, then strung   77
his bow, stood at the river's edge, and drew an
arrow empowered by Garuda with the intention of
destroying the serpent.

The moment he set the arrow to his bow, the deep pool   78
let out a raucous roar, like an elephant in musth fallen
into a trap, smashing against the shore with waves
flailing tumultuously like a trunk.

The pool roiled, agitating the crocodiles, when all of a   79
sudden the serpent king emerged with a girl before
him, as once upon a time the tree of Indra emerged
from the ocean with Lakshmi before it.[14]

Seeing him approach holding the ornament in his hand to   80
return it, the king unnocked his Garuda arrow. For the
anger of the good is not unrelenting toward those who
yield.

Realizing from his great power that Kusha was the son of   81
the lord of the three worlds and a goad to his enemies,
Kumuda, although he held his head high with pride,
bowed in greeting and spoke as if sprinkling the king
with ambrosia:

"I understand that you are another embodiment, known   82
by the word 'son,' of Vishnu, who takes human form
to accomplish certain tasks. You are to be venerated.
How could I displease you?

"This girl had launched her ball upward with a blow of   83
her hand, then watched as your ornament of victory
fell down from the surface of the stream, like a comet
falling from the sky, and out of curiosity she picked it
up.

८४ तदेतदाजानुविलम्बिना ते ज्याघातलेखास्थिरलाञ्छनेन ।
भुजेन रक्षापरिघेण भूमेरुपैतु योगं पुनरंसलेन ॥

८५ इमां स्वसारं च यवीयसीं मे कुमुद्वतीं नार्हसि नानुमन्तुम् ।
आत्मापराधं नुदतीं चिराय शुश्रूषया पार्थिव पादयोस्ते ॥

८६ इत्युक्तवानुपहृताभरणं क्षितीशं
श्लाघ्यो भवान्स्वजन इत्यभिभाषितारम् ।
संयोजयां विधिवदास समेतबन्धुः
कन्यामयेन कुमुदः कुलभूषणेन ॥

८७ तस्याः स्पृष्टे मनुजपतिना साहचर्याय हस्ते
मङ्गल्योर्णावलयिनि पुरः पावकस्योच्छिखस्य ।
दिव्यस्तूर्यध्वनिरुदचरद्व्यश्रुवानो दिगन्तान्
गन्धोदग्रं तदनु ववृषुः पुष्पमाश्चर्यमेघाः ॥

८८ इत्थं नागस्त्रिभुवनगुरोरौरसं मैथिलेयं
लब्ध्वा बन्धुं तमपि च कुशः पञ्चमं तक्षकस्य ।
एकः शङ्कामहिवररिपोरत्यजद्वैनतेया-
द्रद्रव्यालामवनिमपरः पौरकान्तः शशास ॥

इति रघुवंशे महाकाव्ये षोडशः सर्गः ॥

"Here it is. Fix it again on that muscular arm of yours—   84
    permanently scarred with lines scored by your
    bowstring and reaching down to your knees—a bolt
    that serves to protect the world.
"And please deign to accept this younger sister of mine,   85
    Kumudvati. She will make amends for her offense by
    serving Your Majesty's feet for years to come."
So saying, he returned the ornament to the king, who   86
    answered, "You are now my esteemed kinsman." Then
    in the company of his relatives, Kumuda united Kusha
    with the girl, his own family jewel, with due ritual.
As the king took her hand, bound with an auspicious   87
    woolen bracelet, to form the conjugal bond in front
    of an upward-flaring fire, a celestial sound of drums
    swelled and filled the directions, while wondrous
    clouds rained richly fragrant flowers.
Thus the serpent obtained Sita's son, the lord of the three   88
    worlds, and Kusha obtained him, the fifth descendant
    of Takshaka, as kinsman. Thereafter the one lost
    his fear of Garuda, enemy of great serpents, and the
    other, beloved of his subjects, ruled the earth, where
    serpents had now become benign.

१ अतिथिं नाम काकुत्स्थात्पुत्रमाप कुमुद्वती ।
   पश्चिमाद्यामिनीयामात्प्रसादमिव चेतना ॥

२ स पितुः पितृमान्वंशं मातुश्चानुपमद्युतिः ।
   अपुनात्सवितेवोभौ मार्गावुत्तरदक्षिणौ ॥

३ तमादौ कुलविद्यानामर्थमर्थविदां वरः ।
   पश्चात्पार्थिवकन्यानां पाणिमग्राहयत्पिता ॥

४ जन्यस्तेनाभिजातेन शूरः शौर्यवता कुशः ।
   अमन्यतैकमात्मानमेकान्तवशिना वशी ॥

५ स किलोचितमिन्द्रस्य साहायकमुपेयिवान् ।
   जघान समरे दैत्यं दुर्जयं तेन चावधि ॥

६ तं स्वसा नागराजस्य कुमुदस्य कुमुद्वती ।
   अन्वगात्कुमुदानन्दं शशाङ्कमिव कौमुदी ॥

७ तयोर्दिवस्पतेरासीदेकः सिंहासनार्धभाक् ।
   द्वितीयापि सखी शच्याः पारिजातांशभागिनी ॥

CHAPTER 17
Atithi, the Perfect King

From Kusha Kumudvati obtained a son named Atithi, as   1
the mind obtains clarity from the last watch of the
night.

Son of an excellent father, he purified the incomparably   2
glorious lineages of both his mother and his father, as
the sun purifies both its northern and southern paths.

His father, most excellent among the learned, had him   3
first receive the teachings of the learned disciplines of
family tradition—and then the hands of princesses.

The heroic, self-controlled father, Kusha, felt himself to   4
be at one with this noble, heroic, and entirely self-
controlled son.

Tradition has it that Kusha allied himself with Indra,   5
as was the custom, and killed in battle the demon
Durjaya, but was himself slain by him.[1]

Kumudvati, sister of the serpent king Kumuda, followed   6
him, as moonlight, the delight of water lilies, follows
the moon.[2]

One of them shared the throne of the Lord of the skies;   7
the other became the confidante of Shachi, enjoying a
share of her celestial *pārijāta* blossoms.[3]

८ तदात्मसम्भवं राज्ये मन्त्रिवृद्धाः समादधुः ।
   स्मरन्तः पश्चिमामाज्ञां भर्तुः सङ्ग्रामयायिनः ॥

९ ते तस्य कल्पयामासुरभिषेकाय शिल्पिभिः ।
   विमानं नवमुद्देदि चतुःस्तम्भप्रतिष्ठितम् ॥

१० तत्रैनं हेमकुम्भेषु सम्भृतैस्तीर्थवारिभिः ।
   उपतस्थुः प्रकृतयो भद्रपीठे निवेश्य तम् ॥

११ नदद्भिः स्निग्धगम्भीरं तूर्यैः प्रहतपुष्करैः ।
   अन्वमीयत कल्याणं तस्याविच्छिन्नसन्तति ॥

१२ दूर्वायवाङ्कुरप्रलक्षत्वगभिन्नपुटोत्तरम् ।
   ज्ञातिवृद्धप्रयुक्तं स भेजे नीराजनाविधिम् ॥

१३ पुरोहितपुरोगास्तं जिष्णुं जैत्रैरथर्वभिः ।
   उपचक्रमिरे पूर्वमभिषेक्तुं द्विजातयः ॥

१४ तस्यौघमहती मूर्ध्नि निपतन्ती व्यरोचत ।
   सशब्दमभिषेकश्रीर्गङ्गेव त्रिपुरद्विषः ॥

१५ स्तूयमानः क्षणे तस्मिन्नलक्ष्यत स वन्दिभिः ।
   प्रवृष्ट इव पर्जन्यः सारङ्गैरभिनन्दितः ॥

The elders among his ministers then put his son Atithi in charge of the kingdom, remembering their master's last command as he set out for battle. 8

For his consecration ceremony, they had craftsmen erect a new high-platformed pavilion framed by four pillars. 9

There his ministers set him on the throne and waited upon him by pouring sacred waters collected in golden ewers. 10

From the deep sonorous rumble of instruments as the drumskins were struck, one could infer the blessings, including an unbroken line of successors, that would accrue to him. 11

He took part in the rite of the lustration of weapons, performed by elderly relatives, which involved kusa grass, barley sprouts, banyan bark, and unbeaten cotton.[4] 12

Brahmans, headed by his family priest, first approached the victorious king, chanting victory-bringing Atharvanic hymns, to shower him in consecration.[5] 13

The glorious stream of consecratory waters as it cascaded noisily over his head in a great flood looked as beautiful as the Ganga cascading over the head of the Enemy of the three cities.[6] 14

At that moment, as his praises were sung by bards, he resembled a rain cloud being joyously greeted by *cātaka* birds.[7] 15

१६ तस्य सन्मन्त्रपूताभिरद्भिः स्नानं प्रतीच्छतः ।
ववृधे वैद्युतस्याग्रेर्वृष्टिसेकादिव द्युतिः ॥

१७ स तावदभिषेकान्ते स्नातकेभ्यो ददौ वसु ।
यावतैषां समाप्येरन्यज्ञाः पर्याप्तदक्षिणाः ॥

१८ ते प्रीतमनसस्तस्मै यामाशिषमुदैरयन् ।
सा तस्य कर्मनिवृत्तैर्दूरं पश्चात्कृता फलैः ॥

१९ बन्धच्छेदं स बद्धानां वधार्हाणामवध्यताम् ।
धुर्याणां च धुरो मोक्षमदोहं चादिशद्गवाम् ॥

२० क्रीडापतत्रिणो ऽप्यस्य पञ्जरस्थाः शुकादयः ।
लब्धमोक्षास्तदादेशाद्यथेष्टगतयो ऽभवन् ॥

२१ ततः कक्ष्यान्तरन्यस्तं गजदन्तासनं शुचि ।
सोत्तरच्छदमध्यास्त नेपथ्यग्रहणाय सः ॥

२२ तं धूपाश्यानकेशान्तं तोयनिर्णिक्तपाणयः ।
आकल्पसाधनैस्तैस्तैरुपासेदुः प्रसाधकाः ॥

२३ ते ऽस्य मुक्तागुणानद्धां मौलिमभ्यन्तरस्रजम् ।
प्रत्यूपुः पद्मरागेण प्रभामण्डलवर्षिणा ॥

His brilliance increased as he received the cleansing flood 16
purified by Vedic mantras, like that of lightning's fire
when drenched by showers of rain.⁸

At the end of the consecration rite, he gave to the Vedic 17
graduates the wealth required to complete their
own sacrifices, including liberal sacrificial gifts for
officiants.

Deeply gratified, they pronounced blessings upon him, 18
but these were far surpassed by the fruits already
determined by his past acts.⁹

He ordered that prisoners should have their bonds cut, 19
that those condemned to death not be executed, that
draft animals be released from their burdens, and that
cows not be milked.

Even his parakeets and other pet birds in their cages were 20
set free at his command, to fly off where they wished.

He then took his seat upon a bright throne of ivory placed 21
in an inner chamber and fitted with a fine covering, in
order to be clothed in his regalia.

Valets who had cleansed their hands with water dried 22
his hair with incense and adorned him with various
accoutrements.

Into his hair, tied back with a string of pearls and 23
intertwined with garlands, they wove a ruby that
rained forth a halo of light.

२४ चन्दनेनाङ्गरागं च मृगनाभिसुगन्धिना ।
समापय्य ततश्चक्रुः पत्रविन्यस्तरोचनम् ॥

२५ आमुक्ताभरणः स्रग्वी हंसचिह्नदुगूलभृत् ।
आसीदतिशयप्रेक्ष्यः स राज्यश्रीवधूवरः ॥

२६ नेपथ्यदर्शिनश्छाया तस्यादर्शे हिरण्मये ।
विरराज नवे सूर्ये मेरौ कल्पतरोरिव ॥

२७ स राजककुदव्यग्रपाणिभिः पार्श्ववर्तिभिः ।
ययावुदीरितालोकाः सुधर्मानवमां सभाम् ॥

२८ वितानसहितं तत्र भेजे पैतृकमासनम् ।
चूडामणिभिरुद्घृष्टपादपीठं महीक्षिताम् ॥

२९ बभौ भूयः कुमारत्वादधिराज्यमवाप्य सः ।
लेखाभावादुपारूढः सामग्र्यमिव चन्द्रमाः ॥

३० शुशुभे तेन चाक्रान्तं मङ्गलायतनं महत् ।
श्रीवत्सलक्षणं वक्षः कौस्तुभेनेव कैशवम् ॥

३१ प्रसन्नमुखरागं तं स्मितपूर्वाभिभाषिणम् ।
मूर्तिमन्तममन्यन्त विश्वासमनुजीविनः ॥

They completed anointing his body using sandal paste   24
    perfumed with musk, and then decorated him with
    leaf designs painted in yellow orpiment.

Decked with jewels, garlanded, and wearing a diaphanous   25
    stole patterned with geese, he was a feast for the eyes,
    a fitting bridegroom for Royal Fortune.

When he gazed at his apparel in a golden mirror, his   26
    reflected form shone like the wish-fulfilling tree
    reflected at sunrise on Mount Meru.

To the accompaniment of cries of "Behold the king!"   27
    Atithi processed into the assembly, in no way inferior
    to that of heaven, his attendants brandishing the
    emblems of royalty.

There he sat down upon the canopied throne of his   28
    forefathers, its footstool rubbed smooth by the crest
    jewels of vassal kings.

Gaining supreme kingship after boyhood gave him a   29
    brighter glow, like the moon grown to fullness from a
    slender digit.

And once he had taken his seat there, the great auspicious   30
    assembly hall shone brightly too, like Vishnu's chest,
    where the Shrivatsa resides, once the Kaustubha gem
    takes its place there.[10]

With his clear complexion and smiling speech, his   31
    dependents thought of him as trustworthiness
    personified.

३२ स पुरं पुरुहूतश्रीः कल्पद्रुमनिभध्वजाम् ।
क्रममाणश्चकार द्यां नागेनैरावणौजसा ॥

३३ तस्यैकस्योच्छ्रितं छत्रं मूर्ध्नि तेनामलत्विषा ।
पूर्वराजवियोगौष्ण्यं कृत्स्नस्य जगतो हृतम् ॥

३४ धूमस्याग्रेः शिखा पश्चादुदयस्यांशवो रवेः ।
सो ऽतीत्य तेजसो वृत्तिं सममेवोत्थितो गुणैः ॥

३५ तं प्रीतिविषदैर्नेत्रैरन्वयुः पौरयोषितः ।
शरत्प्रसन्नैज्र्योतिर्भिर्विभावर्य इवोडुपम् ॥

३६ अयोध्यादेवताश्चैनं प्रयस्तायतनार्चिताः ।
अनुदध्युरनुध्येयं सान्निध्यैः प्रतिमागतैः ॥

३६ यावन्नाशयायते वेदिरभिषेकजलाप्लुता ।
तावदेवास्य वेलान्तं प्रतापः प्राप दुःसहः ॥

३८ वसिष्ठस्य गुरोर्मन्त्राः सायकास्तस्य धन्विनः ।
किं तत्साध्यं यदुभये साधयेयुर्न सङ्गताः ॥

३९ स धर्मज्ञसखः शश्वदर्थिप्रत्यर्थिनोः स्वयम् ।
ददर्श संशयच्छेत्ता व्यवहारानतन्द्रितः ॥

As resplendent as Indra, he circumambulated the city 32
  upon an elephant that had the vigor of Airavana, and
  made it seem like heaven.

Although it was raised above the head of Atithi alone, his 33
  spotless white parasol shielded the whole world from
  the burning pain of the loss of the previous king.

Fire's flames appear after its smoke, the sun's rays appear 34
  after its rising. Atithi, transcending the nature of
  every fiery thing, appeared simultaneously with his
  virtues.

The womenfolk of the city followed him with their eyes 35
  bright with affection, as the nights follow the moon
  with their stars bright in autumn.

The deities of Ayodhya, worshiped in their decorated 36
  temples, also favored him, who was deserving of favor,
  by standing, in their statues, close to him.

The platform flooded by the waters of his consecration 37
  had not had time to dry before the fearsome reports of
  his valor had reached the seashores.

What task could there be that the arrows of that archer 38
  and the mantras of his guru Vasishtha could not
  achieve when the two combined?

A friend to those learned in law, every day he tirelessly 39
  heard disputes between plaintiffs and defendants,
  cutting away doubts.

४० ततः परमभिव्यक्तसौमनस्यनिवेदितैः ।
युयोज पाकाभिमुखैर्भृत्यान्विज्ञापनाफलैः ॥

४१ प्रजास्तदुरुणा नद्यो नभसेव विवर्धिताः ।
तस्मिंस्तु भूयसीं वृद्धिं नभस्ये ता इवाययुः ॥

४२ यदुवाच न तन्मिथ्या यद्ददौ न जहार तत् ।
सो ऽभूद्बद्धव्रतः शत्रूनुत्खाय प्रतिरोपयन् ॥

४३ वयोरूपविभूतीनामेकैकं मदकारणम् ।
तानि तस्मिन्समेतानि न चास्योत्सिषिचे मनः ॥

४४ इत्थं जनितरागासु प्रकृतिष्वनुवासरम् ।
अक्षोभ्यः स तथा ह्यासीदृढमूल इव द्रुमः ॥

४५ अनित्याः शत्रवो बाह्या विप्रकृष्टाश्च यत्तयः ।
अतः स आन्तरान्नित्यान्षड्वर्गमजयद्रिपून् ॥

४६ प्रसादसुमुखे तस्मिंश्चटुलापि स्वभावतः ।
निकषे हेमलेखेव श्रीरासीदनपायिनी ॥

४७ कातर्यं केवला नीतिः शौर्यं चापलचेष्टितम् ।
अतः सिद्धिं समेताभ्यामुभाभ्यामन्वियेष सः ॥

Only thereupon, in accordance with their requests, would   40
he confer upon his servants their due rewards, already
announced by the benevolence made clear by his
bearing.

The people flourished under his father like rivers in the   41
month of Nabhas, but under Atithi they grew in spate
like rivers in the month of Nabhasya.[11]

What he said was never false; what he gave he never   42
took back. But he broke this observance in that he
reinstalled his enemies after uprooting them.[12]

Youth, beauty, and wealth are each a cause of arrogance.   43
He had all of them together, and yet they did not make
his mind overflow with pride.

As the days went by, with his subjects becoming ever   44
fonder of him, he thus became quite unshakable, like a
firmly rooted tree.

The three types of external enemies are both transient   45
and distant, so he vanquished first the six internal
enemies, which are constantly present.[13]

His face remaining serenely bright, Royal Fortune, though   46
naturally fickle, stayed unwavering by his side, like a
streak of gold upon a touchstone.

Statesmanship by itself is cowardice; bravery alone is   47
recklessness. That is why he pursued his goals using
both together.

४८ न तस्य मण्डले राज्ञो न्यस्तप्रणिधिदीधितेः ।
अदृष्टमभवत्किञ्चिद्व्यभ्रस्येव विवस्वतः ॥

४९ रात्रिन्दिनविभागेषु यदादिष्टं महीक्षिताम् ।
तत्सिषेवे नियोगेन स विकल्पपराङ्मुखः ॥

५० मन्त्रः प्रतिदिनं तस्य बभूव सह मन्त्रिभिः ।
न जातु सेव्यमानो ऽपि गुप्तद्वारः स्म सूच्यते ॥

५१ परेषु स्वेषु च क्षिप्रैरविज्ञातपरस्परैः ।
सो ऽपसर्पैर्जजागार यथाकालं स्वपन्नपि ॥

५२ भव्यमुख्याः समारम्भाः प्रत्यवेक्षा निरत्ययाः ।
गर्भशालिसधर्माणास्तस्य गूढं विपेचिरे ॥

५३ अपथेन प्रववृते न जातूपचितो ऽपि सः ।
वृद्धौ नदीमुखेनैव प्रस्थानं लवणाम्भसः ॥

५४ दुर्गाणि दुर्ग्रहाण्यासंस्तस्य रोद्धुरपि द्विषाम् ।
न हि सिंहो गजास्कन्दी भयाद्गिरिगुहाशयः ॥

५५ कामं प्रकृतिवैराग्यं सद्यः शमयितुं क्षमः ।
यस्य कार्यः प्रतीकारः स तत्रैवोपपादयत् ॥

The king sent out spies like rays of light, so that in his 48
sphere there was nothing that remained unseen, just
as nothing remains unseen in the sphere of the sun
when free of clouds.[14]

Free of doubts, he dutifully carried out the various tasks 49
prescribed for kings for each division of the day and
night.

He took counsel every day with his ministers, but no hint 50
of it ever leaked out, even when he was putting it into
action, for every door was kept firmly closed.

He planted spies, unbeknownst to each other, among 51
adversaries and friends alike, and these kept him
vigilant, even though he slept when it was time to do
so.

His undertakings, full of benefits and, because of his 52
watchfulness, without untoward consequences,
ripened unseen, like rice within its husk.

Even as he swelled in power, he never set out on the wrong 53
path. When the ocean swells and starts to move
inland, it is always through the river's mouth.

Though it was he who besieged his enemies, he 54
maintained impregnable fortresses himself. Surely the
lion, attacker of elephants, does not lie in mountain
caves out of fear.

It is true that he was capable of instantly quelling 55
disaffection among his subjects, but he did nothing
that required any such remedial action.

५६ शक्येष्वेवाभवद्यात्रा तस्य शक्तिमतः सतः ।
समीरणसहायो ऽपि नाम्भःप्रार्थी दवानलः ॥

५७ न धर्ममर्थकामाभ्यां बबाधे न च तेन तौ ।
नार्थं कामेन कामं वा सो ऽर्थेन सदृशस्त्रिषु ॥

५८ हीनान्यनुपकर्तॄणि प्रवृद्धानि विकुर्वते ।
तेन मध्यमशक्तीनि मित्राणि स्थापितान्यतः ॥

५९ परात्मनोः परिच्छिद्य शक्त्यादीनां बलाबलम् ।
ययावतिविशिष्टश्चेत्परस्मादास्त सो ऽन्यथा ॥

६० कोशादाश्रयणीयत्वमिति तस्यार्थसङ्ग्रहः ।
अम्बुगर्भो हि जीमूतश्चातकैरभिनन्द्यते ॥

६१ परकर्मापहः सो ऽभूदुद्यतः स्वेषु कर्मसु ।
आवृणोदात्मनो रन्ध्रं रन्ध्रे च प्राहरद्द्विषाम् ॥

६२ वापीष्विव स्रवन्तीषु वनेष्वपवनेष्विव ।
सार्थाः स्वैरं तदीयेषु चेरुर्वेश्मस्विवाद्रिषु ॥

६३ तपो रक्षन्स विघ्नेभ्यस्तस्करेभ्यश्च सम्पदः ।
यथास्वमाश्रमैश्चक्रे वर्णैरिव षडंशभाक् ॥

424

Although he was powerful, he campaigned only against   56
those within the reach of his power. Even when aided
by the wind, a forest blaze does not seek to consume
water.

He never let profit or pleasure harm piety; nor did he let   57
piety harm those two, nor pleasure profit, nor profit
pleasure. All three he treated equally.[15]

Allies who are too lowly are of no use; if too lofty, they act   58
against one's interest. He therefore made those of
middling power his allies.

He first assessed the strengths and weaknesses of his own   59
and his enemy's armies and other resources. If he was
stronger, he attacked; if not, he stayed put.

He accumulated wealth on the grounds that people resort   60
to a king because of his treasury. For it is clouds full of
water that are hailed by *cātaka* birds.

He labored at his works while obstructing those of his   61
enemies. He attacked his enemies at their weak spots
while hiding his own.[16]

Merchants' caravans moved at will along his rivers as   62
though they were no more than ponds, through
his forests as though they were gardens, among his
mountains as though they were houses.

He enjoyed a sixth part in taxes of earnings from those   63
living in ashrams, according to their means, because
he protected their acquisition of ascetic power, just
as he enjoyed the same from the four social classes,
because he protected their wealth from thieves.[17]

६४ खनिभिः सुषुवे रत्नं क्षेत्रैः सस्यं वनैर्गजान् ।
दिदेश वेतनं तस्मै रक्षासट्टशमेव भूः ॥

६५ स बलानां गुणानां च षण्णां षण्मुखविक्रमः ।
बभूव विनियोगज्ञः साधनीयेषु वस्तुषु ॥

६६ इति क्रमात्प्रयुञ्जानो दण्डनीतिं चतुर्विधाम् ।
आ तीर्थादप्रतीघातं स तस्याः फलमानशे ॥

६७ कूटयुद्धविकल्पे ऽपि तस्मिन्सन्मार्गयोधिनि ।
भेजे ऽभिसारिकावृत्तिं जयश्रीर्वीरकामिनी ॥

६८ प्रायः प्रतापभग्नत्वादरीणां तस्य दुर्लभः ।
रणो गन्धद्विपस्येव गन्धभग्रान्यदन्तिनः ॥

६९ प्रवृद्धो हीयते चन्द्रः समुद्रो ऽपि तथाविधः ।
स च तत्समवृत्तिश्च न चाभूत्ताविव क्षयी ॥

७० सन्तस्तस्याभिगमनादत्यन्तमहतः कृशाः ।
उदधेरिव जीमूताः प्रापुर्दातृत्वमर्थिनः ॥

७१ स्तूयमानः स जिह्राय स्तुत्यमेव समाचरन् ।
तथापि पप्रथे तस्य तत्कारिद्वेषिणो यशः ॥

The mines yielded jewels, the fields crops, the forests
elephants. Thus Earth gave him wages commensurate
with the protection he afforded her.   64

Resembling six-faced Kumara in valor, he knew how to
use the six stratagems and the six types of forces to
achieve his goals.[18]   65

Starting with his dealings with high officials, he
methodically deployed the four strategies of
statesmanship and enjoyed their fruits unimpeded.[19]   66

Even when the option of warfare by subterfuge was open
to him, he chose to fight fair, and the Glory of Victory,
who loves heroes, ventured forth herself to tryst with
him.   67

Since reports of his valor usually put his enemies to flight,
battles became hard for him to find, as they are for a
great elephant in musth who puts other elephants to
flight by his scent.   68

The moon grown full will wane again; the ocean is no
different. He waxed as they did, but never dwindled in
the way they do.   69

Virtuous paupers who came to that most noble king as
suppliants became benefactors themselves, like clouds
upon reaching the ocean.   70

He felt embarrassed when praised, but nonetheless did
only what earned him praise—and still his fame as one
disliking those who praised him continued to grow.   71

७२ दुरितं दर्शनेनैव घ्नन्नर्कं चापनुदंस्तमः ।
प्रजाः स तन्त्रयां चक्रे शश्वत्सूर्य इवोदितः ॥

७३ इन्दोरगतयः पद्मे सूर्यस्य कुमुदेंऽशवः ।
गुणास्तस्य विपक्षे ऽपि गुणिनो लेभिरे ऽन्तरम् ॥

७४ पराभिसन्धानपरं यद्यप्यस्य विचेष्टितम् ।
जिगीषोरश्वमेधाय धर्म्यमेव बभूव तत् ॥

७५ एवमुद्यन्प्रभावेण शास्त्रनिर्दिष्टवर्त्मना ।
वृषेव देवो देवानां राजा राज्ञां बभूव सः ॥

७६ पञ्चमं लोकपालानामाहुः साधर्म्ययोगतः ।
भूतानां महतां षष्ठमष्टमं कुलभूभृताम् ॥

७७ दूरापवर्जितच्छत्रैस्तस्याज्ञां शासनार्पिताम् ।
दधुः शिरोभिर्भूपालाः शेषां पौरन्दरीमिव ॥

७८ ऋत्विजः स तथानर्च दक्षिणाभिर्महाक्रतौ ।
यथा साधारणीभूतं नामास्य धनदस्य च ॥

Dispelling evil and dense darkness by his gaze, he 72
    constantly nourished his subjects like the risen sun.[20]

Moonbeams cannot enter the lotus, nor sunbeams the 73
    water lily, but the virtues of that virtuous king found
    their way into the hearts even of his enemies.

Even his actions directed at outwitting his enemies were 74
    perfectly in keeping with Dharma, for it was only for
    the sake of performing a horse sacrifice that he wished
    to conquer.

Thus, rising in power by the path laid down in scriptures, 75
    he became king of kings, as Indra became god of
    gods.[21]

Because he possessed similar qualities, men called him a 76
    fifth protector of the quarters, a sixth element, and an
    eighth great mountain chain.[22]

Other kings cast their royal parasols far aside and carried 77
    his command, in the form of written orders, on their
    heads, like the garland of Indra.[23]

At the end of his great sacrifice, Atithi honored the priests 78
    so generously that people came to treat his name as
    synonymous with Kubera's.

७९ इन्द्राद्दृष्टिर्नियमितगदोद्रेकवृत्तिर्यमो ऽभूद्
यादोनाथः शिवजलपथः कर्मणे नौचराणाम् ।
पूर्वापेक्षी तदनु विदधे कोशवृद्धिं कुवेरस्
तस्मिन्दण्डोपनतचरितं भेजिरे लोकपालाः ॥

इति रघुवंशे महाकाव्ये सप्तदशः सर्गः ॥

Indra sent rain; Yama kept in check the prevalence of   79
    disease; the overlord of the creatures of the deep* kept
    the ocean's paths calm for seafarers to do their work;
    and after that, Kubera swelled the treasury further
    than for his predecessor. In short, with respect to
    Atithi, the very guardians of the directions adopted
    the conduct of those subdued by his forces.[24]

---

* Varuna.

अष्टादशः सर्गः

१ स नैषधस्याधिपतेः सुतायामुत्पादयामास निषिद्धशत्रुः ।
   अनूनसारं निषधान्नगेन्द्रात्पुत्रं यमाहुर्निषधाख्यमेव ॥

२ तेनोरुकार्येण पिता प्रजायै कल्पिष्यमाणेन ननन्द यूना ।
   सुवृष्टियोगादिव जीवलोकः सस्येन सम्पत्तिफलात्मकेन ॥

३ शब्दादि निर्विश्य सुखं चिराय तस्मिन्प्रतिष्ठापितराजशब्दः ।
   कौमुद्वतेयः कुमुदावदातैर्द्यामर्जितां कर्मभिराररोह ॥

४ पौत्रः कुशस्यापि कुशेशयाक्षः ससागरां सागरधीरचेताः ।
   एकातपत्रां भुवमेकवीरः पुरार्गलादीर्घभुजो बुभोज ॥

५ तस्यानलौजास्तनयस्तदन्ते वंशश्रियं प्राप नलाभिधानः ।
   योद्धा नलानीव गजः परेषां बलान्यमृद्नात्रलिनाभवक्रः ॥

432

CHAPTER 18
A Catalogue of Kings

After defeating his enemies, Atithi fathered upon the
    daughter of the king of Nishadha a son whose
    strength was no less than that of Nishadha, the king of
    mountains, and who was named after that mountain.[1]

His father delighted in his young son, who was well suited
    to continue the lineage and who had great deeds
    before him, just as people delight in crops that are
    about to yield ripe grain thanks to good rains.

Kumudvati's son established his son as king and enjoyed
    the pleasures of the senses, music and the rest, for
    a long time before ascending to heaven thanks to
    the good karma, white as water lilies, that he had
    accumulated.[2]

Kusha's grandson too, his eyes like water lilies, his mind
    as deep as the ocean, his arms long as the bars on the
    city's gates, enjoyed the earth with her oceans.[3] He
    was the sole hero to do so, and his royal parasol alone
    was raised over her.

At his death his son, named Nala, who possessed the
    energy of fire, inherited the fortune of their lineage.
    Though his face was as beautiful as a lotus, he crushed
    the armies of his enemies like an elephant crushing
    reeds.[4]

1

2

3

4

5

६ नभश्वरैर्गीतयशाः प्रपेदे नभस्तलश्यामतनुं तनूजम् ।
ख्यातं नभःशब्दमयेन नाम्ना कान्तं नभोमासमिव प्रजानाम् ॥

७ तस्मै विसृज्योत्तरकोसलानां धर्मोत्तरस्तत्प्रभवः प्रभुत्वम् ।
मृगैरजर्यं जरसोपदिष्टमदेहबन्धाय पुनर्बबन्ध ॥

८ तेन द्विपानामिव पुण्डरीको राज्ञामजय्यो ऽजनि पुण्डरीकः ।
शान्ते पितर्याहितपुण्डरीकं यं पुण्डरीकाक्षमिव श्रिता श्रीः ॥

९ स क्षेमधन्वानममोघधन्वा पुत्रं प्रजाक्षेमविधानदक्षम् ।
क्ष्मां लम्भयित्वा क्षमयोपपन्नं वने तपःक्षामतनुः ससाद ॥

१० अनीकिनीनां समरे ऽग्रयायी तस्यापि देवप्रतिमः सुतो ऽभूत् ।
व्यश्रूयतानीकपदावसानं देवादि नाम त्रिदिवे ऽपि यस्य ॥

११ पिता समाराधनतत्परेण पुत्रेण पुत्री स यथैव तेन ।
पुत्रस्तथैवाधिकवत्सलेन स तेन पित्रा पितृमान्बभूव ॥

434

This king, his fame sung by the skygoing *vidyādharas*,   6
    begot a son whose body was dark blue like the surface
    of the sky, known by the name Nabhas, and dear to the
    people as is the month Nabhas.[5]

His father, intent on Dharma, handed over to him the   7
    kingship of Uttarakosala and, as old age taught him,
    bound himself fast to the company of deer in order to
    unbind himself from rebirth.

From Nabhas was born Pundarika, whom other kings   8
    could no more overcome than earthly elephants could
    the celestial elephant Pundarika. After his father had
    attained peace, he performed the Pundarika sacrifice,
    and Royal Fortune came to him as she does to lotus-
    eyed Vishnu.[6]

That king, an unfailing archer, gave the earth into the   9
    hands of his son, Kshemadhanvan, who was patient
    and skilled in bringing about the welfare of his people;
    then, his body emaciated by austerities, he passed
    away in the forest.[7]

And he in turn had a son resembling a god, always leading   10
    the vanguard of his armies in battle, whose name,
    beginning with *deva* and ending with the word *anīka*,
    was bruited even in heaven.[8]

Just as Kshemadhanvan had in him an excellent son, intent   11
    on serving him, so the son, Devanika, had in him an
    excellent, most affectionate father.

१२ पूर्वस्तयोरात्मसमे चिरोढामात्मोद्भवे वर्णचतुष्टयस्य ।
धुरं निधायैकनिधिर्गुणानां जगाम यज्वा यजमानलोकम् ॥

१३ वशी सुतस्तस्य वशंवदत्वात्स्वेषामिवासीद्द्विषतामपीष्टः ।
सकृद्द्विभिन्नानपि हि प्रयुक्तं माधुर्यमीष्टे हरिणाग्रहीतुम् ॥

१४ अहीनगुर्नाम स गां समग्रामहीनबाहुद्रविणः शशास ।
विहीनसंसर्गपराङ्मुखत्वादूवाप्यनर्थैर्व्यसनैर्विहीनः ॥

१५ गुरोः स चानन्तरमन्तरज्ञः पुंसां पुमानाद्य इवावतीर्णः ।
उपक्रमैरस्खलितैश्चतुर्भिश्चतुर्दिगीशश्चतुरो बभूव ॥

१६ तस्मिन्प्रयाते परलोकयात्रां यातर्यरीणां तनयं तदीयम् ।
उच्चैःशिरस्त्वाज्जितपारियात्रं लक्ष्मीः सिषेवे किल पारियात्रम् ॥

१७ तस्माद्बभूवाथ दलाभिधानो दमान्वितः पद्मदलाभदृष्टिः ।
कुन्दान्तदन्तो रिपुदन्तिसिंहः पतिः पृथिव्याः कुलकैरवेन्दुः ॥

१८ तस्याभवत्सूनुरुदात्तशीलः शलः शिलापृष्ठविशालवक्षाः ।
जितारिपक्षो ऽपि शिलीमुखैर्यः शालीनतामम्रजदस्तमानः ॥

The former, after long bearing the burden of protecting 12
the four social classes, placed it upon his son, who
was equal to himself. And then that sacrificer and
sole repository of all virtues went to the world where
sacrificers go.

His son was self-controlled, and so winning in his words 13
that even his adversaries loved him as much as his own
people did. Indeed, even if deer have at first scattered
in alarm, a sweet song can enchant them.

He was called Ahinagu; with ample strength of arm he 14
ruled the entire earth, and since he was averse to
association with base men he remained, even as a
youth, free of vices.[9]

Then, succeeding his father, Ahinagu, who knew men's 15
hearts, became the skillful ruler of the four directions
by the unfailing application of the four strategies.[10]

When that destroyer of his enemies had gone forth on the 16
journey to the next world, Royal Fortune attached
herself, they say, to his son Pariyatra, who held his
head higher than the Pariyatra mountains.[11]

After him Dala ruled the earth, self-disciplined, with 17
eyes like the petals of a lotus and teeth like the tips of
jasmine buds. He was a lion to the elephants who were
his enemies, the moon to the water lilies who were his
relatives.[12]

His son was Shala, noble in his conduct, and with a chest 18
broad as a slab of stone. He would become bashful
when he was praised, even after he had conquered all
his enemies by his arrows.[13]

१९ तमात्मसम्पन्नमनिन्दितात्मा कृत्वा युवानं युवराजमेव ।
सुखानि सो ऽभुङ्क्त सुखोपरोधि वार्तं हि राज्ञामपरुद्धवृत्तम् ॥

२० तं रागवृद्धिष्वपि तृप्तमेव भोगेषु सौभाग्यविशेषभोग्यम् ।
विलासिनीनामरतिक्षमापि जरा वृथा मत्सरिणी जहार ॥

२१ हित्वाथ भोगांस्तपसोत्तमेन त्रिविष्टपं प्राप्नवति क्षितीशे ।
तदात्मजः सागरधीरचेताः शशास पृथ्वीं सकलां नृसोमः ॥

२२ उन्नाभ इत्युद्धृतनामधेयस्तस्यायथार्थो नतनाभिरन्ध्रः ।
आसीत्सुतः पङ्कजनाभकल्पः कृत्स्नस्य नाभिर्नृपमण्डलस्य ॥

२३ ततः परं वज्रधरप्रभावस्तदात्मजः संयति वज्रघोषः ।
बभूव वज्राकरभूषणायाः पतिः पृथिव्याः किल वज्रनाभः ॥

२४ तस्मिन्गते खं सुकृतोपलब्धं तत्सम्भवं खड्गमनर्णवान्ता ।
उत्खातशत्रुं वसुधोपतस्थे रत्नोपहारैरुदितैः खनिभ्यः ॥

२५ तस्यावसाने हरिदश्वधामा पित्र्यं प्रपेदे पदमश्विरूपः ।
वेलातटेषूषितसैनिकाश्वं पुराविदो यं व्युषिताश्वमाहुः ॥

Faultless Dala appointed that son of his, self-possessed   19
    though but a youth, as the Young King, and then could
    enjoy pleasures. For the overburdened life of a king is
    a wretched thing.

While he was still unsated with the objects of enjoyment—   20
    for they only increase desire—and while his beauty
    still made him desirable to lovely young women,
    impotent Old Age, in her jealousy, pointlessly drew
    him away from them.

So King Dala left those enjoyments. And after he had   21
    practiced extreme asceticism and thereby reached
    heaven, his son Shala, an excellent king with mind as
    steadfast as the ocean, ruled the entire earth.

He had a son with the renowned name Unnabha ("With   22
    protruding navel"), whose navel was deep despite the
    name; he was nearly the equal of the Lord with Lotus
    Navel, and was the nave of the entire circle of kings.[14]

And after him, they say, his son, Vajranabha, powerful   23
    as the wielder of the thunderbolt and roaring like
    thunder in battle, became the lord of the earth,
    adorned by the jewel-yielding oceans.[15]

When he had departed to heaven, earned by his good   24
    deeds, Earth, up to the oceans, served his son
    Khankhana, extirpator of his enemies, with offerings
    of jewels from her mines.[16]

When he passed away, his son, radiant as the sun and   25
    handsome as the Ashvins, took his father's place.
    Those learned in the ancient stories call him
    Vyushitashva, for he quartered his soldiers' horses on
    the shores of the oceans.[17]

२६ आराध्य विश्वेश्वरमीश्वरेण तेन क्षितेर्विश्वसमो ऽधिजग्मे ।
पातुं सहो विश्वसहः समग्रां विश्वम्भरामात्मजमूर्तिरात्मा ॥

२७ अंशे हिरण्याक्षरिपोः स जाते हिरण्यनाभे तनये नयज्ञः ।
द्विषामसह्यः सुतरां तरूणां हिरण्यरेता इव सानिलो ऽभूत् ॥

२८ पिता पितृणामनृणस्तमन्ते वयस्यनन्तानि सुखानि लिप्सुः ।
राजानमाजानुविलम्बिबाहुं कृत्वा कृती वल्कधरो बभूव ॥

२९ कौसल्य इत्युत्तरकोसलानां पत्युः पतङ्गान्वयभूषणस्य ।
तस्यौरसः सोमसुतः सुतो ऽभूत्रोत्सवः सोम इव द्वितीयः ॥

३० यशोभिराब्रह्मसभं प्रकाशः स ब्रह्मभूयां गतिमाजगाम ।
ब्रह्मिष्ठमाधाय निजे ऽधिकारे ब्रह्मिष्ठमेव स्वतनुप्रसूतम् ॥

३१ तस्मिन्कुलापीडनिभे विपीडाः सम्यङ्महीं शासति शासनाङ्काम् ।
प्रजाश्चिरं सुप्रजसि प्रजेशे ननन्दुरानन्दजलोक्षिताक्ष्यः ॥

That king worshiped the Lord of All, and obtained his own   26
 self in the form of a son called Vishvasaha, the equal
 of the Vishva gods, well able to protect the whole of
 the all-supporting earth.[18]

When a son called Hiranyanabha, a partial incarnation   27
 of the slayer of Hiranyaksha,* was born to him,
 Vishvasaha, master of politics, became utterly
 unendurable for his enemies, as fire, when joined by
 wind, is unendurable for trees.

The father, Vishvasaha, was thereby freed from his debt   28
 to his forefathers, and in his old age, wishing to obtain
 pleasures that have no end, he made long-armed
 Hiranyanabha the king; thus having completed all his
 duties, he became an ascetic clad in bast garments.

That Hiranyanabha, king of Uttarakosala, ornament to   29
 the lineage of the sun and presser of the *soma* juice for
 sacrifices, had a lawful son called Kausalya, a feast for
 the eyes like a second moon.[19]

Having acquired fame that made him renowned as far   30
 as Brahma's court, Kausalya became one with the
 Absolute after installing Brahmishtha, a son born
 of his own body, learned in the Veda, in his place as
 king.[20]

King Brahmishtha, the crest jewel, so to speak, of his   31
 lineage, had excellent offspring and long ruled the
 earth righteously; his people remained free of troubles
 and rejoiced, the only tears ever clouding their eyes
 being tears of joy.

───

* Vishnu.

३२ तस्य प्रभानिर्जितपुष्यरागं पौष्यां तिथौ पुष्यमसूत पत्नी ।
यस्मिन्नपुष्यन्नुदिते समग्रां पुष्टिं जनाः पुष्य इव द्वितीये ॥

३३ पात्रीकृतात्मा गुरुसेवनेन स्पर्ध्याकृतिः पत्ररथेन्द्रकेतोः ।
तं पुत्रिणां पुष्करपत्रनेत्रः पुत्रः समारोपयदग्रसङ्ख्यम् ॥

३४ महीं महेच्छः परिकीर्य सूनौ मनीषिणे जैमिनये ऽर्पितात्मा ।
तस्मात्स योग्यादधिगम्य योगमजन्मने ऽकल्पत जन्मभीरुः ॥

३५ ततः परं तत्प्रभवः प्रपेदे ध्रुवोपमेयो ध्रुवसन्धिरुर्वीम् ।
यस्मिन्नभूज्ज्यायसि सत्यसन्धे सन्धिर्ध्रुवः सन्नमतां नृपाणाम् ॥

३६ वंशस्थितिं वंशकरेण तेन सम्भाव्य भावी स सखा मघोनः ।
उपस्पृशन्स्पर्शनिवृत्तलौल्यस्त्रिपुष्करेषु त्रिषु शान्तिमाप ॥

३७ सुते शिशावेव सुदर्शनाख्ये दर्शात्ययेन्दुप्रियदर्शिने सः ।
मृगायताक्षो मृगयाविहारी सिंहादवापद्विपदं नृसिंहः ॥

His wife delivered a son called Pushya on the full moon 32
    day of Pushya. He shone brighter than a yellow
    sapphire, and at his birth all the people became
    prosperous in every way, as if he were a second Pushya
    asterism.[21]

That son with eyes like lotus petals rendered his father 33
    the luckiest of fathers, for he made himself worthy by
    serving his father, and his beautiful form was envied
    by the god whose emblem is the king of birds.*

Noble-minded Brahmishtha left the earth to his son and 34
    gave himself as student to the wise sage Jaimini. From
    that most suitable teacher he learned yoga and, fearful
    of rebirth, attained freedom from rebirth.

After Pushya, his son Dhruvasandhi, firm as the pole star 35
    Dhruva, acquired the earth. To that excellent king,
    always true to his word, all other kings bowed down,
    and their alliances held firm.[22]

When Dhruvasandhi had fathered a son and Pushya knew 36
    for certain his lineage would continue, he gave up
    desire for material objects and, soon to be a friend of
    Indra in heaven, bathed thrice in the Three Pushkaras
    and attained peace.[23]

When his son Sudarshana, a delight to behold like the 37
    new moon after the dark fortnight, was still a child,
    Dhruvasandhi, lion among men, with eyes as wide as a
    deer's, was killed by a lion while out hunting deer.[24]

---

* Vishnu, whose emblem is Garuda.

३८ स्वर्गामिनस्तस्य तमैकमत्यादमात्यवर्गः कुलतन्तुमेकम् ।
आनाथ्यदीनाः प्रकृतीरवेक्ष्य साकेतनाथं विधिवच्चकार ॥

३९ नवेन्दुना तन्नभसोपमेयं शावैकसिंहेन च काननेन ।
रघोः कुलं कुड्डलपुष्करेण तोयेन चाप्रौढनरेन्द्रमासीत् ॥

४० लोकेन भावी पितुरेव तुल्यः सम्भावितो मौलपरिग्रहात्सः ।
दृष्टो हि वृण्वन्कलभप्रमाणो ऽप्याशाः पुरोवातमवाप्य मेघः ॥

४१ तं राजवीथ्यामतिहस्तयन्तमाधोरणालम्बितमध्यदेशम् ।
षड्वर्षदेशीयमपि प्रभुत्वात्रैक्षन्त पौराः पितृगौरवेण ॥

४२ कामं न सो ऽकल्पत पैतृकस्य सिंहासनस्य प्रतिपूरणाय ।
तेजोमहिम्ना पुनराचितेन तद्व्याप चामीकरपिञ्जरेण ॥

४३ तस्मादधः किञ्चिदिवावतीर्णावसंस्पृशन्तौ तपनीयपीठम् ।
सालक्तकौ भूपतयः प्रसिद्धैर्ववन्दिरे मौलिभिरस्य पादौ ॥

४४ मणौ महानील इति प्रभावादल्पप्रमाणे ऽपि यथा न मिथ्या ।
शब्दो महाराज इति प्रयुक्तस्तथैव तस्मिन्युयुजे ऽर्भके ऽपि ॥

After he had gone to heaven, his ministers, seeing that   38
    the subjects were miserable without their lord,
    unanimously chose to make Sudarshana, now
    the single remaining strand of his lineage, lord of
    Ayodhya, following due ritual process.

The Raghu lineage with that child as king was like the sky   39
    with the new moon, a forest with a lion cub, or a pond
    with a lotus in bud.

Because the hereditary ministers accepted him, the people   40
    assumed that he would become just like his father. For
    a cloud, even one small as a young elephant, is seen to
    fill the sky to the horizons when catching a favorable
    wind.

As he passed by on an elephant along the royal road, with   41
    the mahout holding him by the waist, the citizens
    looked up to him with the respect they accorded his
    father, even though he was not yet six, because he was
    now their lord.

Of course he could not entirely fill his father's throne, but   42
    he suffused it with the concentrated greatness of his
    fieriness, bright as gold.

Princes bowed down their ornamented heads to his   43
    lac-painted feet, which dangled a little from the
    throne, not quite touching the golden footstool.

Just as the name "great sapphire" can justly be applied   44
    even to a small gem because of its radiance, so the title
    Maharaja was fittingly applied to him even though he
    was still a boy.

४५ पर्यन्तसञ्चारितचामरस्य कपोललीनोभयकाकपक्षात् ।
तस्याननादुच्चरितो ऽववादश्चस्खाल वेलास्विप नार्णवानाम् ॥

४६ निर्वृत्तजाम्बूनदपट्टबन्धे न्यस्तं ललाटे तिलकं दधानः ।
तेनैव शून्यान्यरिसुन्दरीणां मुखानि स स्मेरमुखश्चकार ॥

४७ शिरीषपुष्पोपमसौकुमार्यो विभूषणेनापि ययौ स खेदम् ।
नितान्तगुर्वीमथ चानुभावादूरं धरित्रीया बिभरां चकार ॥

४८ न्यस्ताक्षरामक्षरभूमिकायां कात्स्र्येन गृह्णाति लिपिं न यावत् ।
तावत्फलानि श्रुतवृद्धयोगात्पक्कान्युपायुङ्क स दण्डनीतेः ॥

४९ उरस्यपर्याप्तनिवेशभागा प्रौढीभविष्यन्तमुदीक्षमाणा ।
सञ्जातलज्जेव तमातपत्रच्छायाच्छलेनोपजुगूह लक्ष्मीः ॥

५० अनश्रुवानेन युगोपमानमबद्धमौर्वीकिणलाञ्छनेन ।
अस्पृष्टखड्गत्सरुणापि चासीद्रक्षावती तस्य भुजेन पृथ्वी ॥

५१ न केवलं गच्छति तस्य काले
ययुः शरीरावयवा विवृद्धिम् ।
वंश्या गुणाः खल्वपि लोककान्ताः
प्रारम्भसूक्ष्माः प्रथिमानमापुः ॥

५२ स पूर्वजन्मान्तरदृष्टपाराः स्मरन्निवाक्लेशकरो गुरूणाम् ।
तिस्रस्त्रिवर्गाधिगमस्य मूलं जग्राह विद्याः प्रकृतीश्च पित्र्याः ॥

A boy's sidelocks still clung to his cheeks, but he was   45
    flanked by waving chowries, and his mouth uttered
    commands that were obeyed unfalteringly even up to
    the oceans' shores.

On his forehead, encircled by a golden band, he bore a   46
    tilak, and smilingly deprived the faces of his enemies'
    wives of the same.[25]

Tender as a *śirīṣa* blossom, he was troubled even by   47
    wearing ornaments. And yet his natural authority
    enabled him to bear the extremely heavy yoke of the
    earth.

Even before fully learning his letters, written for him on   48
    a tablet, he enjoyed the ripe fruits of the science of
    governance by mixing with learned elders.

Not finding space enough to settle on his chest, Lakshmi,   49
    as though ashamed, disguised herself as the shade of
    his parasol and thus embraced him, while waiting for
    him to grow to manhood.

His arm, though not yet long as a yoke, still unmarked by   50
    the scars of a bowstring and ignorant of the touch of a
    sword's hilt, protected the earth.

Though they were small to begin with, not only his limbs   51
    but also his ancestral virtues, so dear to the people,
    grew great in the course of time.

He learned the three sciences, the basis for attaining the   52
    three human goals, without causing any trouble to
    his teachers; it was as if, having mastered them in his
    previous lives, he were now just remembering them.
    Likewise, he took up the constituents of the state
    inherited from his father.[26]

५३ व्यूह्य स्थितः किञ्चिदिवोत्तरार्धमुन्नद्धधूजूटो ऽञ्जितसव्यजानुः ।
आकर्णमाकृष्टसबाणधन्वा व्यरोचतास्त्रेषु विनीयमानः ॥

५४ अथ मधु वनितानां नेत्रनिर्वेशपेयं
मनसिजतरुपुष्पं रागबन्धप्रवालम् ।
अकृतकविधि सर्वाङ्गीनमाकल्पजातं
विलसितपदमाद्यं यौवनं स प्रपेदे ॥

५५ प्रतिकृतिरचनाभ्यो दूतसन्दर्शिताभ्यः
समधिकतररूपाः शुद्धसन्तानकामैः ।
अधिविविदुरमात्यैराहृतास्तस्य यूनः
प्रथमपरिगृहीते श्रीभुवौ राजकन्याः ॥

इति रघुवंशे महाकाव्ये ऽष्टादशः सर्गः ॥

When he was being trained in the handling of weapons, he 53
    looked magnificent as he stood with his upper body
    slightly stretched, his hair tied in a topknot, his left
    knee bent, and his bow, with arrow nocked, drawn to
    his ear.

Then he attained youth, a wine for women to quaff with 54
    the cups that are their eyes, a flower upon the tree that
    is Kama, a shoot upon the bough that is the bond of
    affection, a hoard of unaffected adornments for every
    limb, the natural abode of sensuous grace.

The young king had already married Royal Fortune 55
    and the Earth, but both were now superseded by
    princesses brought by his ministers in the hope of
    pure offspring, each more beautiful than the portrait
    that had been shown by go-betweens.

एकोनविंशः सर्गः

१ अग्निवर्णमभिषिच्य राघवः स्वे पदे तनयमग्नितेजसम् ।
शिश्रिये श्रुतवतामपश्चिमः पश्चिमे वयसि नैमिषं वशी ॥

२ तत्र तीर्थसलिलेन दीर्घिकास्तल्पमन्तरितभूमिभिः कुशैः ।
सौधवासमुटजेन विस्मृतः सञ्चिकाय फलनिःस्पृहस्तपः ॥

३ लब्धपालनविधौ न तत्सुतः खेदमाप गुरुणा हि मेदिनी ।
भोक्तुमेव भुजनिर्जितद्विषा न प्रसाधयितुमस्य कल्पिता ॥

४ सो ऽधिकारमधिपः कुलोचितं काश्चन स्वयमवर्तयत्समाः ।
संनिवेश्य सचिवेष्वतः परं स्त्रीविधेयनवयौवनो ऽभवत् ॥

५ कामिनीसहचरस्य कामिनस्तस्य वेश्मसु मृदङ्गनादिषु ।
ऋद्धिमन्तमधिकर्द्धिरुत्तरः पूर्वमुत्सवमपोहदुत्सवः ॥

६ इन्द्रियार्थपरिशून्यमक्षमः सोढुमेकमपि स क्षणान्तरम् ।
अन्तरेव विहरन्दिवानिशं न व्यपैक्षत समुत्सुकाः प्रजाः ॥

CHAPTER 19
Agnivarna's Revels

In his old age, the self-controlled descendant of Raghu, 1
foremost of the learned, inaugurated his fiery son
Agnivarna into his own position and withdrew to the
Naimisha forest.[1]

There the waters of sacred fords made him forget the 2
palace ponds, kusa grass spread on the ground made
him forget his bed, a leaf hut made him forget his
stuccoed palace, and he practiced austerities with no
desire for rewards.

His son had no trouble protecting what he had obtained, 3
for his father had conquered his enemies by his arm
and bequeathed the earth to him only to enjoy, not to
win over.

For some years the king himself performed the duties 4
proper to his family. Then he entrusted them to
his ministers and devoted the prime of his youth to
women.

That lascivious man dallied with lascivious women in 5
palaces resounding with *mṛdaṅga* drums, where each
lavish party was succeeded by another even more
lavish.

He could not bear even a single moment devoid of sensual 6
pleasures. Day and night he caroused indoors and did
not care about his anxious subjects.

७ गौरवाद्यदपि जातु मन्त्रिणां दर्शनं प्रकृतिकाङ्क्षितं ददौ ।
तद्द्वाक्षविवरावलम्बिना केवलेन चरणेन कल्पितम् ॥

८ तं कृतप्रणतयो ऽनुजीविनः कोमलाग्रनखरागरूषितम् ।
भेजिरे नवदिवाकरातपस्पृष्टपङ्कजतुलाधिरोहणम् ॥

९ यौवनोन्नतविलासिनीस्तनक्षोभलोलकमलाश्च दीर्घिकाः ।
गूढमोहनगृहास्तदम्बुभिः स व्यगाहत विगाढमन्मथः ॥

१० तत्र सेकहृतलोचनाञ्जनैर्धौंतरागपरिपाटलाधरैः ।
अङ्गनास्तमधिकं व्यलोभयन्नर्घितप्रकृतिकान्तिभिर्मुखैः ॥

११ घ्राणकान्तमधुगन्धकर्षिणीः पानभूमिरचनाः प्रियासखः ।
अभ्यपद्यत स वासितासखः पुष्पिताः कमलिनीरिव द्विपः ॥

१२ सातिरेकमदगन्धिनं रहस्तेन दत्तमभिलेषुरङ्गनाः ।
ताभिरप्युपहृतं मुखासवं सो ऽपिबद्द्विकुलतुल्यदोहदः ॥

१३ अङ्कमङ्कपरिवर्तनोचिते तस्य निन्यतुरशून्यतामुभे ।
वल्लकी च हृदयंगमस्वना मञ्जुवागपि च वामलोचना ॥

Even when, out of respect for his ministers, he did   7
    occasionally give his subjects the glimpse of him they
    yearned for, he did so by merely dangling one foot
    from the aperture of an ox-eye window.

When they bowed before that foot, which was reddened   8
    by the rosy glow of its delicate nails, his retainers
    resembled lotuses touched by the rays of the morning
    sun.

Filled with intense lust, he dove into the palace ponds,   9
    where the lotuses were set bobbing when buffeted by
    the youthful plump breasts of beauties, and whose
    water features concealed hidden pleasure chambers.[2]

There the women beguiled him even more, with faces of   10
    exquisite natural beauty, the kohl rinsed from their
    eyes and the rouge washed from their still-red lips.

In the company of his paramours, he took to his drinking   11
    pavilions, which drew him in by their fragrant wafts of
    sweet wine, as an elephant takes to blossoming lotus
    ponds in the company of his she-elephants.

The women craved the taste of his mouth, redolent of   12
    wine, which he bestowed on them in private, and he
    too, thirsting like a *bakula* tree, drank the nectar of
    their proffered mouths.[3]

Two things were always occupying his lap, both of them fit   13
    to take their turn there: the lute, whose sounds tugged
    the strings of the heart, and a lovely-eyed girl with a
    melodious voice.

१४ स स्वयं प्रहतपुष्करः कृती लोलमाल्यवलयो हरन्मनः ।
नर्तकीरभिनयातिलङ्घिनीः पार्श्ववर्तिषु गुरुष्वलज्जयत् ॥

१५ चारु नृत्तविगमे च तन्मुखं स्वेदभिन्नतिलकं परिश्रमात् ।
प्रेमदत्तवदनासवं पिबन्नन्वजीवदमरालकेश्वरौ ॥

१६ तस्य सावरणदृष्टसन्धयः काम्यवस्तुषु नवेषु सङ्गिनः ।
वल्लभाभिरुपसृत्य चक्रिरे सामिभुक्तविषयाः समागमाः ॥

१७ अङ्गुलीकिसलयाग्रतर्जनं भ्रूविभङ्गकुटिलं च वीक्षितम् ।
मेखलाभिरसकृच्च बन्धनं वञ्चयन्प्रणयिनीरवाप सः ॥

१८ तेन दूतिविदितं निषेदुषा पृष्ठतः सुरतवाररात्रिषु ।
शुश्रुवे प्रियजनस्य कातरं विप्रलम्भपरिशङ्किनो वचः ॥

१९ लोलमन्यगृहिणीपरिग्रहान्नर्तकीष्वसुलभासु तद्वपुः ।
वर्तते स्म स कथंचिदालिखन्नङ्गुलिक्षरणसन्नवर्तिकः ॥

२० प्रेमगर्वितविपक्षमत्सरादायताच्च मदनान्महीपतिम् ।
निन्युरुत्सवविधिच्छलेन तं देव्य उज्जितरुषः कृतार्थताम् ॥

When he himself, with garlands and bracelets swaying,　　14
　　took the drum and skillfully beat time, he so
　　captivated hearts that the dancing girls forgot their
　　gestures and were embarrassed before their teachers.

At the end of the dance he kissed their pretty faces,　　15
　　with forehead marks smudged by the sweat of their
　　exertions, as they lovingly offered the nectar of their
　　mouths. Thus did he imitate the lifestyle of Indra,
　　king of immortals, and Kubera, king of Alaka.

He always needed new objects to sate his desire, so when　　16
　　his lovers met him, whether in secret or in the open,
　　they made sure to leave him only half satisfied.

When he deceived his concubines, they shook their　　17
　　sprout-like slender fingers at him, glared at him with
　　knitted brows, and more than once tied him up with
　　the chains of their girdles.

On nights when it was their turn to make love, he sat　　18
　　behind his wives, observed only by the messenger
　　girl, and listened to them talk timidly, fearful of
　　separation.[4]

When his other wives detained him and he couldn't reach　　19
　　his dancing girls, he stayed behind restless with desire,
　　attempting to draw their bodies, his pen slipping from
　　sweating fingers.

But because they were jealous of their rivals, who swelled　　20
　　with pride on gaining his affection, and because their
　　love for him was long-standing, his queens put aside
　　their anger and, under the pretext of celebrating a
　　festive ritual, fulfilled his every desire.

२१ प्रातरेत्य परिभोगशोभिना दर्शनेन कृतखण्डनव्यथः ।
प्राञ्जलिः प्रणयिनीः प्रसादयन्सो ऽदुनोद्व्रहणमन्थरः पुनः ॥

२२ स्वप्रकीर्तितविपक्षमङ्गनाः प्रत्यभैत्सुरवदन्त्य एव तम् ।
प्रच्छदान्तगलिताश्रुबिन्दुभिः क्रोधभिन्नवलयैर्विवर्तनैः ॥

२३ कॢप्तपुष्पशयनाँल्लतागृहानेत्य दूतिकृतमार्गदर्शनः ।
अन्वभूत्परिजनाङ्गनारतं सो ऽवरोधभयवेपथूत्तरम् ॥

२४ नाम वल्लभजनस्य ते मया प्राप्य भाग्यमपि तस्य काङ्क्षते ।
लोलुभं बत मनो ममेति तं गोत्रविस्खलितमूचुरङ्गनाः ॥

२५ चूर्णबभ्रु लुलितं स्रगाकुलं छिन्नमेखलमलक्तकाङ्कितम् ।
उत्थितस्य शयनं विलासिनस्तस्य विभ्रमरतान्यपावृणोत् ॥

२६ स स्वयं चरणरागमादधे योषितां न तु तथा समाहितम् ।
लोभ्यमाननयनः श्लथांशुकैर्मेखलागुणपदैर्नितम्बिभिः ॥

२७ चुम्बने विपरिवर्तिताधरं हस्तरोधि रशनाविघट्टने ।
विघ्रितेच्छमपि तस्य सर्वतो मन्मथेन्धनमभूद्धुरतम् ॥

When he returned in the mornings, his very appearance,   21
    which proclaimed the night's enjoyments, caused
    them to feel the pain of betrayal; and when he
    attempted with folded hands to propitiate his wives,
    he offended them again by being listless in his
    embraces.

When in sleep he blurted out the names of their rivals, his   22
    women reproached him without a word, tossing and
    turning away so that their tears fell on the corner of
    the sheet and their bracelets broke in anger.

Messenger girls showed him the way to arbors where beds   23
    strewn with flowers had been prepared. There he
    made love with servant girls, trembling the while from
    fear of discovery by the ladies of his harem.

When he muddled their names, the women would say to   24
    him, "Now that you have given me your beloved's
    name, I want to have her good fortune too! Ah, my
    heart burns with longing!"

Yellowed with sandal powder, rumpled, bestrewn with   25
    garlands, scattered with broken girdle chains, and
    marked with footprints of lac—the bed revealed that
    libertine's sexual games when he left it.

He himself applied the red lac to the feet of women, but   26
    he could not concentrate as he did so, for his eyes
    were waylaid by the sight of their hips, loosely clad in
    chiffon, where their girdle chains hung.

When he kissed them they turned away their lips; when   27
    he tried to untie their girdle chains they held down his
    hands: even when his desires were thwarted on every
    side, lovemaking with his wives fueled his passions.

२८ दर्पणेषु परिभोगदर्शिनीर्नर्मपूर्वमनुपृष्ठसंश्रयः ।
छायया स्मितमनोज्ञया वधूर्हीनिमीलितमुखीश्वकार सः ॥

२९ कण्ठसक्तमृदुबाहुबन्धनं न्यस्तपादतलमग्रपादयोः ।
प्रार्थयन्त शयनोत्थितं प्रियास्तं निशात्ययविसर्गचुम्बनम् ॥

३० प्रेक्ष्य दर्पणतलस्थमात्मनो राजवेशमतिशक्रशोभितम् ।
पिप्रिये स न तथा यथा युवा व्यक्तलक्ष्म परिभोगमण्डनम् ॥

३१ मित्रकृत्यमपदिश्य पार्श्वतः प्रस्थितं तमनवस्थितं प्रियाः ।
विद्म हे शठ पलायनच्छलान्यञ्जसेति रुरुधुः कचग्रहैः ॥

३२ तस्य निर्दयरतिश्रमालसाः कण्ठसूत्रमपविध्य योषितः ।
अध्यशेरत बृहद्भुजान्तरं पीवरस्तनविलुप्तकुङ्कुमम् ॥

३३ संगमाय विनिगूढचारिणं चारदूतिकथितं पुरोगताः ।
वञ्चयिष्यसि न नस्तमोवृतं कामुकेति चकृषुस्तमङ्गनाः ॥

३४ योषितामुडुपतेरिवार्चिषां स्पर्शनिर्वृतिमसावनाप्नुवन् ।
आरुरोह कुमुदाकरोपमां रात्रिजागरपरो दिवाशयः ॥

He would playfully creep up on his wives behind their 28
backs while they were looking in the mirror at the
marks of yesterday's pleasure, and make them close
their eyes in shame on seeing his happily smiling
reflection.

When he rose from his bed at the end of the night, his 29
mistresses clung to his neck with their tender arms,
placed the soles of their feet on his feet, and begged
him for a farewell kiss.

In youth's prime, he was not as delighted when he saw 30
his royal attire, more beautiful than Indra's, reflected
in the mirror as he was on seeing the marks of his
dalliances clearly stamped on his body.

When he grew restless he would leave his mistresses on 31
the pretext of some business for a friend; but they
would catch him by his hair, saying, "We know well
the tricks you use to run away, you cheat!"

Worn out by merciless lovemaking, the women pushed 32
necklaces aside and lay across his broad chest, wiping
the saffron from it with their plump breasts.

When spying messenger girls reported that he was 33
stealing away to a rendezvous, his wives went out
ahead of him and dragged him back, saying, "You're
not deceiving us under cover of darkness, you lecher!"

Thrilling with pleasure at the touch of women, he woke at 34
night and slept by day, as does a lily pond that thrills at
the touch of the moon's rays.

३५ वेणुना दशनपीडिताधरा वीणया नखपदाङ्कितोरवः ।
शिलपकार्य उभयेन वेजितास्तं विजिह्मनयना व्यलोकयन् ॥

३६ अङ्गसत्त्ववचनाश्रयं मिथः स्त्रीषु नृत्तमवधाय दर्शयन् ।
स प्रयोगनिपुणैः प्रयोक्तृभिः संजघर्ष सह मित्रसंनिधौ ॥

३७ अस्यतश्च कुटजार्जुनस्रजस्तस्य नीपरजसाङ्गरागिणः ।
प्रावृषि प्रमदबर्हिणेष्वभूत्कृत्रिमाद्रिषु विहारविभ्रमः ॥

३८ विग्रहाच्च शयने पराङ्मुखीनिनेतुमबलाः स तत्वरे ।
आचकाङ्क्ष घनशब्दविक्लवास्ता विवृत्य विशतीर्भुजान्तरम् ॥

३९ कार्त्तिकीषु च विमानहर्म्यभाग्यामिनीषु ललिताङ्गनासखः ।
अन्वभुङ्क्त सुरतक्लमापहां मेघमुक्तिविषदां स चन्द्रिकाम् ॥

४० सैकतं च सरयूं विवृण्वतीं श्रोणिबिम्बमिव हंसमेखलम् ।
स्वप्रियाविलसितानुकारिणीं सौधजालविवरैर्व्यलोकयत् ॥

When his women played music, they looked at him   35
   askance, for flute and vina both pained them: the one
   because he had bitten their lips; the other because he
   had scored their thighs with his nails.

Skilled as a choreographer, he took the women aside,   36
   attentively showing them how the dance should
   go through movements, feelings, and words, and
   quarreled with the dancing masters in the presence of
   his friends.

During the monsoon, he cavorted on artificial hills where 37
   intoxicated peacocks roamed, wrapping himself
   in garlands of *kuṭaja* and *arjuna* flowers, his body
   smeared with margosa pollen.[5]

He would not bother to placate a woman who turned away   38
   from him in bed in jealous anger; he hoped she would
   be alarmed by a thunderclap and turn back and rush
   into his embrace.

On autumn nights of the month of Karttik he stayed on   39
   the rooftop terraces of his mansions together with his
   lovely wives and relished the moonlight, which, freed
   now from the cover of clouds, allayed the fatigue of
   lovemaking.

And through the lattice windows of his palace he looked   40
   out upon the river Sarayu imitating the flirtatious
   movements of his harem as she revealed her sandy
   bank, like the curve of a hip, girdled with lines of
   geese.

461

४१ ममरैरगुरुधूमगन्धिभिर्व्यक्तहेमरशनैस्तमेकतः ।
जह्रुराग्रथनमोक्षलोलुभं हैमनैर्निवसनैः सुमध्यमाः ॥

४२ अर्पितस्तिमितदीपदीप्तयो गर्भवेश्मसु निवातकुक्षिषु ।
तस्य सर्वसुरतान्तरक्षमाः प्रेक्ष्यतां शिशिररात्रयो ययुः ॥

४३ दक्षिणेन पवनेन संभृतं वीक्ष्य चूतकुसुमं सपल्लवम् ।
अन्वनैषुरवकीर्णविग्रहास्तं दुरुत्सहवियोगमङ्गनाः ॥

४४ काश्चिदङ्कमधिरोप्य दोलयन्प्रेङ्खया परिजनापविद्धया ।
मुक्तरज्जु निबिडं भयच्छलात्कण्ठबन्धनमवाप बाहुभिः ॥

४५ तं पयोधरनिषक्तचन्दनैर्मौक्तिकप्रथितचारुभूषणैः ।
ग्रीष्मवेशविधिभिः सिषेविरे श्रोणिलम्बमणिमेखलाः स्त्रियः ॥

४६ यत्स भग्नसहकारमासवं रक्तपाटलमनारतं पपौ ।
तेन तस्य मधुनिर्गमात्कृशश्चित्तयोनिरभवत्पुनर्नवः ॥

४७ एवमिन्द्रियसुखानि निर्विशन्नन्यकार्यविमुखः स पार्थिवः ।
आत्मलक्षणनिवेदितानृतूनत्यवाहयदनङ्गवाहितः ॥

Women with beautiful waists beguiled him with their   41
    rustling winter garments perfumed by the smoke of
    aloewood, their golden girdle chains partly visible as
    he eagerly untied their sashes.

Winter nights in the windless innermost parts of his   42
    harem were enchanting, offering him the light of
    unwavering lamps and lending themselves to all sorts
    of lovemaking.

When the women saw the blossoms and tender shoots of   43
    the mango brought forth by the southern breeze, they
    could tolerate separation no longer and, setting aside
    all quarrels, reconciled with him.

He would set some women on his lap and swing on a swing   44
    pushed by servants; they would lose hold of the ropes
    and then wrap their arms tightly around his neck in
    feigned terror.

Women in summer garb waited on him, their breasts   45
    spattered with sandal paste, their lovely ornaments
    strung with pearls, jeweled girdle chains hanging from
    their hips.

He was constantly drinking wine with sprigs of crushed   46
    mango and pale red trumpet flowers, and so
    rejuvenated his passion, which had waned with the
    end of spring.

Thus the king let the seasons pass—each with their   47
    distinctive traits—immersed in the pleasures of
    the senses and ignoring all other tasks, for he was
    transported by Kama.

४८ तं प्रमत्तमपि न प्रभावतः शेकुराक्रमितुमन्यपार्थिवाः ।
आमयस्तु रतिरागसंभवो दक्षशाप इव चन्द्रमक्षिणोत् ॥

४९ दृष्टदोषमपि तत्र चात्यजत्सङ्गवस्तु भिषजामनास्पदम् ।
स्वादुभिः स विषयैर्हृतस्ततो दुःखमिन्द्रियगणो हि वार्यते ॥

५० तस्य पाण्डुवदनाल्पभूषणा सावलम्बगमना मृदुस्वना ।
यक्ष्मणापि परिहानिराययौ कामयानसमवस्थया तुलाम् ॥

५१ व्योम पश्चिमकलास्थितेन्दु वा पङ्कशेषमिव घर्मपल्वलम् ।
राज्ञि तत्कुलमभूत्क्षयातुरे वामनार्चिरिव दीपभाजनम् ॥

५२ गूढमेषु दिवसेषु पार्थिवः कर्म साधयति पुत्रजन्मने ।
इत्यदर्शितरुजो ऽस्य मन्त्रिणः शश्वदूचुरघशङ्किनीः प्रजाः ॥

५३ स त्वनेकवनितासखो ऽपि सन्पावनीमनवलोक्य संततिम् ।
वैद्ययत्नपरिभाविनं गदं न प्रदीप इव वायुमत्यगात् ॥

५४ तं गृहोपवन एव संगताः पश्चिमक्रतुविदा पुरोधसा ।
रोगशान्तिमपदिश्य मन्त्रिणः संभृते शिखिनि गूढमादधुः ॥

In spite of his negligence, his might was such that other   48
    kings could not attack him. But his addiction to sex
    brought a sickness that consumed him, as Daksha's
    curse consumed the moon.[6]

Even though he saw the damage wrought, he did not give   49
    up his cravings, for which doctors could do nothing.
    Indeed, it is hard to check the senses when they are
    carried away by sweet pleasures.

Pale-faced, with few ornaments, he could only walk with   50
    assistance and his voice was feeble. He seemed like a
    man stricken by love, although it was consumption
    that caused his emaciation.

With the king wasting away, his dynasty was like the sky   51
    in which only the last digit of the moon remains, like
    a pond in summer reduced to mud, like an oil lamp
    whose flame has shrunk to a point.

To his subjects, who suspected the worst, his ministers   52
    kept saying: "These days the king is conducting
    a secret ritual for the birth of a son." And so they
    concealed his illness.

But the disease defeated his physicians' efforts and,   53
    although he had many wives, he succumbed to it—like
    a lamp flame succumbing to the wind—before he
    could see an offspring that would purify him.

The ministers, together with the royal chaplain, who knew   54
    well the rites for the departed, gathered in the palace
    garden and consigned him in secret to the flames of a
    pyre, under the pretext of performing a ceremony for
    averting disease.

५५ तैः कृतप्रकृतिमुख्यसंग्रहैराशु तस्य सहधर्मचारिणी ।
साधुदृष्टशुभगर्भलक्षणा प्रत्यपद्यत नराधिपश्रियम् ॥

५६ तस्यास्तथाविधनरेन्द्रविपत्तिशोका-
दुष्णैर्विलोचनजलैः प्रथमाभितप्तः ।
निर्वापितः कनककुम्भमुखोज्झितेन
वंशाभिषेकविधिना शिशिरेण गर्भः ॥

५७ तं भावाय प्रसवसमयाकाङ्क्षिणीनां प्रजाना-
मन्तर्गूढं क्षितिरिव बभौ बीजमुष्टिं दधाना ।
मौलैः सार्धं स्थविरसचिवैर्हेमसिंहासनस्था
राज्ञी राज्यं विधिवदशिषद्धर्तुरव्याहताज्ञा ॥

इति रघुवंशे महाकाव्य एकोनविंशः सर्गः ॥

They convened a meeting of the chief officials and quickly   55
    conferred royal majesty on his chief wife, in whom
    the auspicious signs of a pregnancy could be clearly
    discerned.

The child in her womb was first warmed by the hot tears   56
    she shed as she mourned the death of such a king, then
    cooled by the cold waters of royal consecration poured
    from golden ewers, according to family custom.

The queen was refulgent as she bore the child within her   57
    for the prosperity of the subjects, who eagerly awaited
    the moment of the birth, like the earth bearing
    within herself the seeds sown by the sowers. With the
    hereditary senior ministers, she ruled her husband's
    kingdom according to precept from her golden lion
    throne, her decrees unopposed.

ABBREVIATIONS

A	Arunagirnatha's commentary
conj.	conjecture
em.	emendation
H	Hemadri's commentary
J	Jinasamudra's commentary
M	Mallinatha's commentary
V	Vallabhadeva's commentary
vl.	*varia lectio*

NOTES TO THE TEXT

प्रथमः सर्गः

१.३ ॰म्यवहास्यताम्] V, ॰म्युपहास्यताम् M.

१.९ प्रतारितः] V, प्रणोदितः M.

१.१५ प्रारम्भ॰] V, आरम्भ॰ M.

१.१७ क्षुण्णादात्मनो] V, क्षुण्णादा मनोर् M.

१.१९ शास्त्रे च व्यापृता] V, शास्त्रेष्वकुण्ठिता M.

१.२१ सो ऽर्थान्] V, सो ऽर्थम् M.

१.२८ दष्टो ऽङ्गुष्ठ इवाहिना] V, अङ्गुलीवोरगक्षता M.

१.३१ मागध॰] V, मगध॰ M.

१.३४ गङ्गां भगीरथेनेव पूर्वेषां पावनक्षमाम् । ईप्सता सन्ततिं न्यस्ता तेन मन्त्रिषु कोसला] V, सन्तानार्थाय विधये स्वभुजादवतारिता । तेन धूर्जगतो गुर्वी सचिवेषु निचिक्षिपे M.

१.३६ ॰माश्रितौ] V, ॰मास्थितौ M.

१.३७ वशानागौ सगन्धाल्पकलभानुगताविव] V, अनुभावविशेषात्तु सेनापरिवृताविव M. (After 1.37, the order of verses in M is: 38, 42, 43, 44, 39, 41, 45, 40, 46.)

१.४० ॰नुपागतान्] V, ॰नुपस्थितान् M.

१.४५ ॰निसृष्टेषु] V, ॰विसृष्टेषु M. (After 1.48, the order of verses in M is: 49, 52, 50, 51, 52.)

१.४९ स्कन्धासक्तसमित्कुशैः । अग्निप्रत्युद्गमात्पूतैः पूर्यमाणं तपस्विभिः] V, समित्कुशफलाहरैः । पूर्यमाणमहृदयाग्निप्रत्युद्गातैस्तपस्विभिः M.

१.५० ॰कन्याभिर्विविक्तीकृतवृक्षकम् । आश्वासाय] V, ॰कन्याभिस्तत्क्षणोज्झितवृक्षकम् । विश्वासाय M.

१.५१ आकीर्णमृषिपत्नीनामुटजद्वाररोधिभिः । अपत्यैरिव नीवारभागधेयोचितैर्मृगैः] Vvl., आतपात्ययः (आतपापायः V) ॰सङ्क्षिप्तनीवारासु निषादिभिः । मृगैर्वर्तितरोमन्थमुट जाह्नवभूमिषु VM.

१.५२ अभ्युद्धृता॰] V, अभ्युत्थिता॰ M.

१.५३ तामवारोहयत्] V, तामवारोपयत् M.

१.५७ आतिथेयस्तमातिथ्यविनीताध्वपरिश्रमम्] V, तमातिथ्यक्रियाशान्तरथक्षोभपरिश्रमम् M.

१.५९ प्रतिकर्ता] V, प्रतिहर्ता M.

१.६० संयमितारिभिः] V, प्रशमितारिभिः M.

१.६१ वृष्टीभवति] V, वृष्टिर्भवति M.

१.६२ प्रजास्तन्त्र] V, प्रजास्तस्य.

१.६३ तदेवं] V, त्वयैवं M. Before 1.65 M's text includes this verse: नूनं मत्तः परं वंश्याः पिण्डविच्छेददर्शिनः । न प्रकामभुजः श्राद्धे स्वधासंग्रहतत्पराः.

१.६५ पूर्वे स्वनिःश्वासकदुष्णमुपभुञ्जते] V, पूर्वैः स्वनिःश्वासकवोष्णमुपभुज्यते M.

१.६६ प्रकाशश्चान्धकारश्च] V, प्रकाशश्चाप्रकाशश्च M.

१.६७ तु] V, हि M.

१.६८ विनेता] V, विधातर् M.

१.६९ ०बन्धमवैहि] V, ०मन्त्यमवेहि M. नवबद्धस्य] V, अनिर्वाणस्य M.

१.७० तस्माद्यथा विमुच्येयं] V, तस्मान्मुच्ये यथा तात M.

१.७२ सन्ततिं०] V, सन्ततेः M.

१.७३ ०च्छायासेविनी] V, ०च्छायामाश्रिता M.

१.७४ इमां देवीमृतुस्नातां स्मृत्वा सपदि सत्वरः । प्रदक्षिणक्रियातीतस्त्यस्याः कोपमजीजनः] V, धर्मलोपभयाद्राज्ञीमृतुस्नातामिमां स्मरन् । प्रदक्षिणक्रियाहार्यां तस्यां त्वं साधु नाचरः M.

१.७५ त्वा] V, त्वां M.

१.७७ अवैमि तदपध्यानाद्व‍ल्लापेक्षं मनोरथम्] V, ईप्सितं तदवज्ञानाद्विद्धि सार्गलमात्मनः M.

१.७९ स त्वमेकान्तरां तस्या मदीयां वत्समातरम्] V, सुतां तदीयां सुरभेः कृत्वा प्रतिनिधिं शुचिः M. सा वां कामं प्रदास्यति] V, प्रीता कामदुघा हि सा M.

१.८१ ताम्रा ललाटजां राजिं बिभ्रती सासितेतराम् । सन्ध्या प्रतिपदेनेव व्यतिभिन्ना हिमांशुना] V, ललाटोदयमाभुग्नं पल्लवस्निग्धपाटला । बिभ्रती श्वेतरोमाङ्कं सन्ध्येव शशिनं नवम् M.

१.८२ प्रस्रवेना०] V, प्रस्रवेणा० M.

१.८४ तपोधनः] V, तपोनिधिः M.

१.८७ स्थानम्] V, स्थितिम् M.

१.८८ प्रयातां] V, प्रयता M.

द्वितीयः सर्गः

२.५ ०हतस्वैरगतैश्च] V, ०हतैः स्वैरगतैः स M.

२.८ रक्षापदेशाद्गुरुः०] V, रक्षापदेशान्मुनि० M.

२.१३ ०र्वननिर्झराणाम्] V, ०र्गिरिनिर्झराणाम् M. ०कम्पन०] V, ०कम्पित० M.

२.१४ विशेषात्फलं०] V, विशेषा फलं० M.

२.१६ ०क्रियार्थम्] V, ०क्रियार्थाम् M. बभूव] V, बभौ च M.

२.२१ द्वारमिवात्मसिद्धेः] V, द्वारमिवार्थसिद्धेः M.

२.२३ भुजोत्सन्न०] V, भुजोच्छिन्न० M.

२.२५ पालयतः] V, धारयतः M. दिनान्यमित्रोद्धरणो०] V, दिनानि दीनोद्धरणो० M.

२.२८ नगेन्द्रदत्तां] V, नगेन्द्रसक्तां M.

२.२९ रोध्रद्रुमं सानुमतः प्रफुल्तम्] V, लोध्रद्रुमं सानुमतः प्रफुल्लम् M.

२.३१ ०प्रभारूषित०] V, ०प्रभाभूषित० M.

२.३२ ०प्रतिस्तम्भ०] V, ०प्रतिष्टम्भ० M. मन्त्रप्रतिबद्ध०] V, मन्त्रौषधिरुद्ध० M.

२.३३ विस्मापयन्विस्मयमात्मसिद्धौ भूपालसिंहं] V, विस्माययन्विस्मितमात्मवृत्तौ सिंहोरुसत्त्वं M.

२.३५ निकुम्भमित्रम्] VHM, निकुम्भतुल्यम् AJ.

२.३६ ०यं] V, ०सौ M.

२.३८ मतङ्गजानां] V, वनद्विपानां M.

२.४२ प्रत्याह चैनं शरमोक्षवन्यो भयत्रपत्वात्स्वरभेदमाप्तः / प्रहीणपूर्वध्वनिनाधिरूढस्तु-
लामसारेण शरद्घनेन] Vvl., प्रत्यब्रवीच्चैनमिषुप्रयोगे तत्पूर्वसङ्गे वितथप्रयत्नः /
जडीकृतस्त्र्यम्बकवीक्षितेन (॰वीक्षणेन M) वज्रं मुमुक्षन्निव वज्रपाणिः VM.

२.४५ विमुच्यतां] V, विसृज्यतां M.

२.४६ कन्दराणां] V, ॰गह्वराणां M.

२.४७ विचारमुग्धः] V, विचारमूढः M.

२.४९ ॰दण्डाद्] V, ॰चण्डाद् M. कृषाणु॰] V, कृशानु॰ M.

२.५२ तथा समर्था गिरमूचिवांसं प्रत्याह देवानुचरं दिलीपः] V, निशम्य देवानुचरस्य वाचं
मनुष्यदेवः पुनरप्युवाच M. तदध्यासन॰] V, तदध्यासित॰ M.

२.५३ ॰पाक्रोश] V, ॰प्रकोश M.

२.५४ कथं च] V, कथं नु M. विश्राणनादन्य॰] V, विश्राणनाच्चान्य॰ M.

२.५५ न्याय्यं] V, न्याय्या M.

२.५६ नियोक्तुर्यदि] V, नियोक्तुर्न हि M.

२.५८ जातः] V, वृत्तः M.

२.५९ प्रतिस्तम्भ॰] V, प्रतिष्टम्भ॰ M. स न्यस्तशस्त्रं] V, स न्यस्तशस्त्रो M.

२.६५ पुत्रोपयुङ्क्तेति] V, पुत्रोपभुङ्क्तेति M.

२.६७ ॰मश्रमैव] V, ॰मश्रमेण M.

२.६८ मुखप्रसादानुमितं] V, प्रहर्षचिह्नानुमितं M. पुनरुक्तयैव] V, पुनरुक्तयेव M.

२.६९ वत्सनिपीतशेषम्] V, वत्सहुतावशेषम् M. शुद्धं यशो भूय इवावितृप्तः V, शुभ्रं यशो
मूर्तिमिवातितृष्णः M.

२.७१ ॰तरानुभावः] V, ॰तरप्रभावः M.

२.७३ ॰माहितोत्कण्ठम्] V, ॰माहितौत्सुक्यम् M. नवोदितं] V, नवोदयं M.

तृतीयः सर्गः

३.१ दौहृदलक्षणं] V, दौर्हृदलक्षणं M.

३.२ मुखेन सा केतकपत्त्रपाण्डुना कृशाङ्गयष्टिः परिमेयभूषणा / स्थितास्पतारां करुणेन्दुमण्डलां
विभातकल्पां रजनीं व्यडम्बयत्] V, शरीरसादादसमग्रभूषणा मुखेन सालक्ष्यत लोध्रपा
ण्डुना / तनुप्रकाशेन विचेयतारका प्रभातकल्पा शशिनेव शर्वरी M.

३.३ सेवितमृत्तिकालवं नृपः समाघ्राय] V, मृत्सुरभि क्षितीश्वरो रहस्युपाघ्राय M.

३.४ महीं] V, भुवं M. मत्सुतः] V, तत्सुतः M.

३.६ हीष्टमस्यास्त्रिदिवे] V, हीष्टमस्य त्रिदिवे M. बभूव दुष्प्रापमधिज्यधन्वनः] V,
अभूदनासाद्यमधिज्यधन्वनः M.

३.७ मधूककपाण्डुरं तदीयमाश्याममुखं] V, नितान्तपीवरं तदीयमानीलमुखं M.
समुद्रयोर्वारणदन्तकोशयोर्बभार कान्तिं गवलापिधानयोः] V, तिरश्चकार भ्रमराभिलीनयोः
सुजातयोः पङ्कजकोशयोः श्रियम् M.

३.८ उपोढगात्रोपचया] V, प्रचीयमानावयवा M. (3.8 appears after 3.6 in M's
text.)

३.९ सगर्भां] V, ससत्त्वां M.

३.१२ कुमारभृत्यैः कुशलैरधिष्ठिते] V, कुमारभृत्याकुशलैरनुष्ठिते M. गर्भवेश्मनि] V,

गर्भकर्मणि Mvl., गर्भभर्मणि M. निरत्ययाय प्रसवाय तस्थुषी बभौ समासन्नफला क्रियेव
सा] V, पतिः प्रतीतः प्रसवोन्मुखीं प्रियां ददर्श काले दिवमभ्रितामिव M.

३.१३ ०संश्रयैर्] V, ०संस्थितैर् M. ०मक्षतम्] V, ०मक्षयम् M.

३.१४ शिवाः] V, सुखाः M. ०र्हुतमग्नि०] V, ०र्हविरग्नि० M.

३.१७ स वीक्ष्य पुत्रस्य चिरात्पिता नात्मनः मुखं निधानकुम्भस्य युवेव दुर्गतः ।
मुदा शरीरे प्रबभूव नात्मनः पयोधिरिन्दूदयमूर्छितो यथा] V, निवातपद्मस्तिमितेन
चक्षुषा नृपस्य कान्तं पिबतः सुताननम् । महोदधेः पूर इवेन्दुदर्शनादुरुः प्रहर्षः प्रबभूव
नात्मनि M.

३.१८ ०करोद्गतः] V, ०करोद्द्रवः M.

३.१९ ०नृत्तैः] V, ०नृत्यैः M.

३.२० विमोचयेद्यं] V, विसर्जयेद्यं M.

३.२४ परस्परं प्रति] V, परस्पराश्रयम् M. सुते न] V, सुतेन M. पर्यहीयत] V, पर्यचीयत M.

३.२५ यदाह] V, उवाच M.

३.२६ त्रिभाग०] V, उपान्त० M.

३.२७ ०वृत्तिना] V, ०वर्तिना M.

३.३१ प्रयोगसंहाररहस्यवित्तमो बभूव चास्त्रेषु यथा पुरन्दरः] V, न केवलं तदुरुरेकपार्थिवः
क्षितावभूदेकधनुर्धरो ऽपि सः M.

३.३२ गम्भीर०] V, गाम्भीर्य० M.

३.३३ प्रभुः] V, गुरुः M. तमोपहं] V, तमोनुदं M.

३.३५ अथ] V, ततः M. वशीति मत्वा मतिचक्षुषा सुतो] V, निसर्गसंस्कारविनीत इत्यसौ M.

३.३७ उषर्बुधः] V, विभावसुः M. दुरुत्सहः] V, सुदुःसहः M.

३.३८ मेध्यतुरङ्गरक्षणे धनुर्धरैं] V, होमतुरङ्गरक्षणे धनुर्धरं M.

३.३९ अतः] V, ततः M.

३.४२ ०संयुतम्] V, ०संयतम् M.

३.४४ यदा] V, सदा M.

३.४५ सता] V, सदा M. नियाम्या] V, नियम्या M. त्वमन्तरायी०] V, त्वमन्तरायो M.

३.४६ शुचेर्] V, श्रुतेर् M.

३.४८ यथात्थ] V, यदात्थ M. परतो] M, परितो V.

३.५० कपिलानुकारिणा] V, कपिलानुसारिणा M.

३.५१ ततः प्रहस्याह पुनः पुरन्दरं व्यपेतभीर्भूमिपुरन्दरात्मजः] V, ततः प्रहस्यापभयः पुरन्दरं
पुनर्बभाषे तुरगस्य रक्षिता M.

३.५३ मार्गणम्] V, सायकम् M.

३.५४ नरेन्द्रसूनोः] V, दिलीपसूनोः M.

३.५६ मयूरलाञ्छनं] V, मयूरपत्रिणा M.

३.५९ प्रकोष्ठाद्धरिचन्दनाङ्गितात्] V, प्रकोष्ठे हरिचन्दनाङ्गिते M.

३.६० प्रवासनाय] V, प्रणाशनाय M. ०व्यपरोपणोद्धृतं] V, ०व्यपरोपणोचितं M.

३.६१ च व्यथां] V, तद्व्यथां M.

३.६२ स्थिरमस्य] V, चिरमस्य M. गुणैर्विधीयते] V, गुणैर्निधीयते M.

३.६३ वरं वृणीष्वेति तमाह वृत्रहा] V, किमिच्छसीति स्फुटमाह वासवः M.

३.६४ दिलीपसूनुः] V, नरेन्द्रसूनुः M. प्रियंवदः] *em.*, प्रियं वदः V, प्रियंवदं M.

३.६५ मन्यते प्रभुस्] V, मन्यसे प्रभो M. विधिनैव] M, विधिनेव V. ०तनुरद्य मे गुरुः] V, ०प्रयतः स मद्गुरुः M.

३.६६ नाकेश] V, लोकेश M.

३.६८ प्रथमं] V, प्रथमं M. हर्षचलेन] V, हर्षजडेन M.

चतुर्थः सर्गः

In Nandargikar's edition of Mallinatha's commentary verses 8 through 15 of this chapter occur in this sequence: 8, 12, 11, 13 10, 9, 14, 15.

४.९ कमलपत्त्राणां नेत्रे तस्यानुकारिणी] V, कर्णान्तविश्रान्ते विशाले तस्य लोचने M.

४.१५ सवितुस्तस्य चोभयोः । वर्धिष्णवो दिशां भागाः प्रतापायेव रेचिताः] V, मुक्तवर्मा सुदुःसहः । प्रतापस्तस्य भानोश्च युगपद्व्यानशे दिशः M.

४.१६ अधिज्यमायुधं कर्तुं समयो ऽयं रघोरिति । स्वं धनुः शङ्कितेनेव संजहे शतमन्युना] V, वार्षिकं संजहारेन्द्रो धनुर्जैत्रं रघुर्दधौ । प्रजार्थसाधने तौ हि पर्यायोद्यतकार्मुकौ M.

४.२० इक्षुच्छाया०] V, इक्षुच्छाय० M.

४.२१ रघोस्वभिभवाशङ्कि] V, रघोरभिभवाशङ्कि M.

४.३० पुरोगा०] V, पराग० M.

४.३१ पुरोगैः कलुषास्तस्य सहस्रस्थायिभिः कृशाः । पश्चात्प्रयायिभिः पङ्कं चक्रिरे मार्गनिम्नगाः] V, omits M.

४.३५ ०पदाञ्जिती] V, ०पदाञ्जयी M.

४.३७ नौसाधनोद्धतान्] V, नौसाधनोद्यतान् M.

४.३९ कपिशां] M, कयिमां V. ०देशितपथः] V, ०दर्शितपथः M.

४.४३ वायव्यास्त्रविनिर्धूतात्पक्षाविद्धाद्रिवोदधेः । गजानीकात्स कालिङ्गं तार्क्ष्यः सर्पमिवाददे] V, omits M.

४.४४ तस्य] V, तत्र M. यशः पपुः] V, पपुर्यशः M.

४.४५ श्रियं] M, हियं V.

४.४६ अगस्त्यचरिताम्] V, अगस्त्याचरिताम् M.

४.४९ हारीतोच्छिष्टमरिचा] V, मारीचोद्घ्रान्तहारीता M.

४.५० आजानेयखुरक्षुण्णपङ्कैलाक्षेत्रसम्भवम् । व्यानशे सपदि व्योम कीटकोशाबिलं रजः] V, ससज्जुरश्वक्षुण्णानामेलानामुत्पतिष्णवः । तुल्यगन्धिषु मत्तेभकटेषु फलरेणवः M.

४.५१ नास्संसत्] V, नास्रसत् M.

४.५४ तटस्वाधीनचन्दनौ] V, तटेष्वालीनचन्दनौ M. दुर्दुरौ] V, ०दर्दुरौ M.

४.५५ दूरमुक्तम्] V, दूरान्मुक्तम् M.

४.५६ रामेषूत्सारितो] V, रामास्लोत्सारितो M.

४.५७ मुरलामारुतोद्धूत०] M, पुरो यन्मारुतोद्धूत० V.

४.५८ रथानां चास्य शिञ्जितैः] V, चरतां गात्रशिञ्जितैः M. मर्मरः] V, वर्मभिः M.

४.६१ महेभ०] V, मत्तेभ० M.

४.६४ पारसीकाश्च] V, पाश्चात्त्यैरश्च M. ०योधो] V, ०योधे M.

४.६९ जितानजय्यस्तानेव कृत्वा रथपुरःसरान्। महार्णवमिवौर्वाग्निः प्रविवेशोत्तरापथम्] omits M.

४.७० वङ्क्षुतीरविवेष्टनैः] V, सिन्धुतीरविचेष्टनैः M.

४.७१ हूना॰] V, हूणा॰ M. कपोलपाटनादेशि] V, कपोलपाटलादेशि M.

४.७२ वीर्यं तस्य सोढुम्] V, सोढुं तस्य वीर्यम् M.

४.७३ तुङ्गा] V, तुङ्ग॰ M. विविशुस्तं विशां नाथम्] V, उपदा विविशुः शश्वन् M. उदन्वन्तमिवापगाः] V, नोत्सेकाः कोशलेश्वरम् M.

४.७४ ॰रुरोह ससाधनः] V, ॰रुरोहाश्वसाधनः M. ॰द्धृतै॰] V, ॰द्धूतै॰ M.

४.७५ प्रशंसंस्] V, शशंस M. गुहागतानां] V, गुहाशयानां M.

४.७८ ॰ग्रैवेयोपचित॰] V, ॰ग्रैवेयस्फुरित॰ M.

४.७९ तस्यावासेषु दानार्द्रैर्गण्डभित्तिविघट्टनैः] V, तस्योत्सृष्टनिवासेषु कण्ठरज्जुक्षतत्वचः M.

४.८० तत्र जन्यं रघोर्घोरं पर्वतीयैर्गणैरभूत्] M, विमर्दः सह तैस्तत्र पार्वतीयैरभूद्रघोः] V. ॰तानलः] V, ॰तानलम् M.

४.८१ करदान्कृती] V, विरतोत्सवान् M.

४.८२ परस्परस्य] V, परस्परेण M.

४.८३ ॰दधान] M, ॰ददान V.

४.८५ अनभ्रमय॰] V, अधारावर्ष॰ M. रथवंशरजो] V, रथवर्त्मरजो M.

४.८८ विश्रम॰] V, विश्राम॰ M.

४.८९ क्रतुं] V, यज्ञं M.

४.९१ ॰कलशा॰] V, ॰कुलिशा॰ M.

पञ्चमः सर्गः

५.३ कृताञ्जलिः कृत्यविचारदक्षो विशां पतिर्विष्टरभाजमाह] V, विशां पतिर्विष्टरभाजमारात्कृताञ्जलिः कृत्यविदित्युवाच M.

५.४ चैतन्यमुग्रादिव दीक्षितेन] V, लोकेन चैतन्यमिवोष्णरश्मेः M.

५.५ मनसा च तप्तं यद्द्विजिणो धैर्यविपर्ययाय] V, मनसापि शश्वद्यत्सम्भृतं वासवधैर्यलोपि M.

५.८ यतो] V, येभ्यो M.

५.९ ॰भागधेयं] V, ॰कल्प्यभागं M.

५.११ अनुग्रहेणाभिगमस्थितेन तवार्हतस्तुष्यति मे न चेतः] V(probably), तवार्हतो नाभिगमेन तृप्तं मनो नियोगक्रिययोत्सुकं मे M.

५.१२ प्रत्याह कौत्सस्तमपेतकुत्सम्] V, तमित्यवोचद्धुरतन्तुशिष्यः M.

५.१३ ॰वैहि] V, ॰वेहि M.

५.१४ महाभागतयातिशेषे] V, महाभाग तयातिशेषे M. व्यपेतकाल॰] V, व्यतीतकाल॰ M.

५.२० अवाप्तविद्येन] V, समाप्तविद्येन M. चिरादस्खलितो॰] V, चिरायास्खलितो॰ M.

५.२१ ॰रुषाथ कार्श्यम्] V, ॰रुषार्थकार्श्यम् M.

५.२४ वदन्या॰] V, वदान्या॰ M.

५.२५ प्रयस्ते महितो] V, प्रशस्ते महिते M.

५.२६ ॰ग्यजन्मा] V, ॰ग्रजन्मा M.

५.२८ कल्पितमस्त्रगर्भम्] V, कल्पितशस्त्रगर्भम् M.

५.२९ सविस्मयागन्तुमुदो] V, सविस्मयाः कोषगृहे M.

५.३० भास्वर॰] V, भासुर॰ M. समग्रमेव] V, समस्तमेव M.

५.३२ ॰हारितार्थं] V, ॰वाहितार्थं M. मनीषी] V, महर्षिः M. वाक्यमुवाच] V, वाचमुवाच M.

५.३३ ॰र्वृत्त॰] V, ॰र्वृत्ते M. अचिन्तनीयस्तव तु] V, अचिन्तनीयस्तु तव M.

५.३४ भवन्तमीड्यो] V, भवन्तमीड्यं M.

५.३५ ॰मग्रजन्मा] V, ॰मग्रजन्मा M.

५.३६ ब्राह्मे] V, ब्राह्ये M. तमग्रयजन्मानम्] V, तमात्मजन्मानम् M.

५.३८ श्रीः कामयानापि] V, श्रीः साभिलाषापि M.

५.४१ ॰पकार्यार्चितोपकारा] V, ॰पकार्यार्चितोपचारा M. वन्ध्येतरा जानपदोपधाभिः] V, वन्ध्येतरा जानपदोपदाभिः M.

५.४२ शीकरा॰] V, सीकरा॰ M. ॰केतु] V, ॰नक्त॰ M. सेनां श्रमोत्फेनवनायुजाश्वाम्] V, क्रान्तं रजोधूसरकेतु सैन्यम् M.

५.४४ अप्यौघविक्षालितगैरिकेण] V, निःशेषविक्षालितधातुनापि M. ॰लेखा॰] V, ॰रेखा॰ M.

५.४५ स भोगिभोगाधिकपीवरेण हस्तेन तीराभिमुखः सशब्दम् । संवेष्टितार्धप्रहितेन दीर्घाश्चिक्षेप वारीपरिघानिवोर्मीन्] Vv1., संहारविक्षेपलघुक्रियेण हस्तेन तीराभिमुखः सशब्दम्। बभौ स भिन्दन्सहसा (सहसा] V, बृहतस् M) तर्ज्ञान्वार्यर्गलाभङ्ग इव प्रवृत्तः VM.

५.४६ कारण्डवोच्छिष्टमृदुप्रतानाः पुलिन्दयोषाम्बुविहारकाञ्ची। कर्षन्स शेवाललता नदीणः प्रोहावलग्रास्तटमुत्ससर्प] V, शैलोपमः शैवलमञ्जरीणां जालानि कर्षन्नुरसा स पश्चात्। पूर्वं तदुत्पीडितवारिराशिः सरित्प्रवाहस्तटमुत्ससर्प M.

५.४७ हृदा॰] V, जला॰ M.

५.४८ विमुस्वी॰] numerous commentaries, विमुस्वा VM.

५.५३ अवैहि] V, अवेहि M.

५.५५ पुनर्महिम्ना] V, वपुर्महिम्ना M.

५.५६ स मोचितः शापकलेःस्वयाहं गतिं प्रपन्नो विहितां विधात्रा] V, संमोचितः सत्त्ववता त्वयाहं शापाञ्झिरप्रार्थितदर्शनेन M. प्रतिक्रियां] V, प्रतिप्रियं M. व्यर्था] V, वृथा M.

५.५७ गान्धर्वमस्त्रं तदितः प्रतीच्छ] V, संमोहनं नाम सखे ममास्त्रं M. प्रस्वापनं नाम यतः प्रहर्तुर्] V, गान्धर्वमादत्स्व यतः प्रयोक्तुर् M.

५.५९ तस्मात्रिगृहीतशापात्] M, तस्माद्द्विगृहीतशासी V.

५.६३ ॰धिकारि॰] V, ॰धिकार॰ M. ॰हेम॰] V, ॰पूर्ण॰ M. ॰धितस्थौ] V, ॰ध्युवास M.

५.६५ वैतालिका ललितबन्धमनोहराभिः] V, सूतात्मजाः सवयसः प्रथितप्रबोधे M. ॰रुषर्बुधाभम्] V, ॰रुदारवाचः M.

५.६६ जगतो ननु धूर्वि॰] V, ननु धूर्जगतो वि॰ M. यामेक॰] V, यमेक॰ M. वितन्द्रीर्यस्या] V, विनिद्रस्तस्या M.

५.६७ भवता ह्यान॰] V, भवताप्यन॰ M. ॰रुचं] V, ॰रुचिं M.

५.६९ वृन्तशलथं] V, वृन्ताच्छ्लथं M. ॰वातः सौगन्ध्यम्] V, ॰वातसौरभ्यम् M.

५.७० द्रुम॰] V, तरु॰ M. सलक्ष्यते दशनचन्द्रिकयानुविद्धं बिम्बोष्ठलब्धपरभागमिव स्मितं ते] V, आभाति लब्धपरभागतयाधरोष्ठे लीलास्मितं सदशनार्चिरिव त्वदीयम् M.

५.७२ सेनागजा] V, स्तम्बेरमा M.

५.७३ विधूय] V, विहाय M.

५.७४ ०पकारः] V, ०पहारः M.

५.७५ इति स विहृतनिद्रस्तल्पमल्पेतरांसः सुरगज इव गाङ्गं सैकतं सुप्रतीकः । परिजनवनितानां
पादयोर्व्यापृतानां वलयमणिविदष्टप्रच्छदान्तं मुमोच] V, इति विरचितवाग्भिर्वन्दिपुत्रैः
कुमारः सपदि विगतनिद्रस्तल्पमुज्झाञ्चकार । मदपटु निनदद्भिर्बोधितो राजहंसैः सुरगज
इव गाङ्गं सैकतं सुप्रतीकः M.

५.७६ ०नुरूप०] V, ०नुकूल० M.

षष्ठः सर्गः

६.१ स तत्र मञ्चेषु विमानकल्पेष्वाकल्पसम्मूर्छितरूपशोभान् । सिंहासनस्थानृपतीनपश्यद्घूपान्त्र
यस्तानिव हैमवेदीन्] V, स तत्र मञ्चेषु मनोज्ञवेषान्सिंहासनस्थानुपचारवत्सु । वैमानिकानां
मरुतामपश्यदाकृष्टलीलान्त्ररलोकपालान् M.

६.३ अथो] V, असौ M.

६.६ संश्रयाणामुदात्त०] V, संस्थितानामुदार० M.

६.८ शिखावासितकेतुमाले] V, समुत्सर्पति वैजयन्तीः M.

६.९ शिखण्डिनामुद्धतनृत्तहेतौ] V, कलापिनामुद्धतनृत्यहेतौ M.

६.१० चतुरन्तयानमास्थाय] V, चतुरस्रयानमध्यास्य M. कौतुकमिश्रवेशा] V, कूश्रविवाहवेषा
M.

६.११ नेत्रसहस्रलक्ष्ये] V, नेत्रशतैकलक्ष्ये M.

६.१२ प्रवातशोभा] V, प्रवालशोभा M.

६.१३ ०परिवेशशोभि] V, ०परिवेषबन्धि M.

६.१४ केयूरकोटिक्षणजातसङ्गम्] V, रत्नानुविद्धाङ्गदकोटिलग्रम् M. प्रावारमुत्क्षिप्य यथाप्रदेशं
] V, प्रालम्बमुत्कृष्य यथावकाशं M.

६.१५ रत्नांशुसम्पृक्त०] V, तिर्यग्विसंसर्पि० M.

६.१६ भुजमासनान्ते गाढाङ्गदं पार्श्विनिपीडनेन] V, भुजमासनार्धे तत्सन्निवेशादधिकोन्नतांसः
M.

६.१७ ०सन्निपातैर्] V, ०सन्निवेशैर् M.

६.१८ दीप्रा०] V, रत्ना० M. ०दीरयामास] M, ०दारयामास V.

६.१९ ०वेशव्यति०] V, ०वेशाद्व्यति० M.

६.२१ शरणोत्सुकानाम्] V, शरणोन्मुखानाम् M.

६.२२ सन्ति सहस्रसङ्ख्या] V, सन्तु सहस्रशो ऽन्ये M. पृथ्वीम्] V, भूमिम् M.

६.२४ ०संश्रयाणां] V, ०संश्रितानां M.

६.२७ ०नागः] M, ०भागः V.

६.२८ ०माक्षेपसूत्रेण] V, ०मुन्मुच्य सूत्रेण M.

६.३० यातेति जन्यान्] V, याहीति जन्याम् M.

६.३१ परेषां] V, द्विषद्भिर् M. विशेषकान्तम्] V, विशेषदृश्यम् M. ०वेन्दुमत्याः] V,
०वेन्दुमत्यै M.

६.३२ यन्त्रोल्लिखितो] V, यत्नोल्लिखितो M.

६.३३ ०द्धतानि] V, ०त्थितानि M.

६.३४ चन्द्रार्धमौलेर्निवसन्नदूरे । दिवापि जालान्तरचन्द्रिकाणां नारीसखः स्पर्शसुखानि भुङ्क्ते] V,

वसन्तदूरे किल चन्द्रमौलेः । तमिस्रपक्षे ऽपि सह प्रियाभिर्ज्योत्स्नावतो निर्विशति प्रदोषान् M.

६.३६ तस्मिन्नपि द्योतनरूपबिम्बे] V, तस्मिन्नभिद्योतितबन्धुपद्ये M.

६.३७ सुनसां] V, सुदतीं M.

६.३८ ०निर्विष्ट०] M, ०निर्वृत्त० V.

६.४० दशाननेनो०] V, लङ्केश्वरेणो० M.

६.४१ प्रदीप] V, प्रतीप M.

६.४४ प्रकाम०] V, प्रकामं M. ०धरोपरागः] V, ०धरोपरोधः M.

६.४५ देशान्तर०] V, लोकान्तर० M.

६.४७ ०देहे] V, ०गेहे M.

६.४८ मथुरा०] V, मथुरां M. ०सम्मृक्त०] V, ०संसक्त० M.

६.४९ त्रातेन] V, त्रस्तेन M.

६.५१ ०नद्धानि] V, ०गन्धीनि M. नृत्तं] V, नृत्यं M.

६.५३ ०दश्लिष्ट०] V, ०दाश्लिष्ट० M. आसेदुषी] V, आसेदुषीं M.

६.५५ ०लेखे] V, ०रेखे M. रिपुश्रियः] V, रिपुश्रियां M. वन्दीकृताया इव] V, ०वन्दीकृतानामिव M.

६.५६ सौधजालैरालोक्यवेलातटपूगमालः । मन्द्रध्वनित्याजितयामतूर्यः] V, सन्निकृष्टो मन्द्रध्वनित्याजितयामतूर्यः । प्रासादवातायनदृश्यवीचिः M.

६.५८ प्रलोभिता सत्यपि सन्नतभ्रूर्] Vv.l., प्रबोधिताप्याकृतिलोभनीया V, प्रलोभिताप्या-कृतिलोभनीया M. पौरुषेण नीतेव] V, दूरकृष्टा नीत्यैव M.

६.५९ अथोन्नसं नाग०] V, अथोरगारव्यस्य M. नागाङ्गनाभां] V, पूर्वानुशिष्टां M.

६.६१ ०नाथः] V, ०राजः M.

६.६४ ०स्वैला०] V, ०स्वेला० M.

६.६५ ०यं] V, ०सौ M.

६.६६ तारापतेरंशु०] V, नक्षत्रनाथांशु० M.

६.६९ न्यवर्तता०] V, व्यावर्तता० M. प्रफुल्लं] V, प्रफुल्लं M.

६.७० ०वेत्य] V, ०वेश्य M. सुविस्तरं] V, सविस्तरं M.

६.७१ इत्याहत०] em., इत्याहित० VM.

६.७३ ऐरावणा०] V, ऐरावत० M.

६.७४ किलेन्दुकीर्तेः] V, किलेरुकीर्तिः M.

६.७५ मानिनीनां] V, वाणिनीनां M.

६.७६ ०र्दिगावर्जन०] V, ०र्दिगावर्जित० M.

६.७७ प्रतीर्णं] V, वितीर्णं M.

६.७८ पित्रा] M, पित्र्यां V. सदृशीं] V, सदृशं M.

६.७९ ०मिमं] V, ०ममुं M.

६.८० मृदूकृत्य] V, तनूकृत्य M.

६.८२ वेत्रधरा] V, वेत्रभृदा० M.

६.८६ प्रफुल्ल०] V, प्रफुल्ल० M.

सप्तमः सर्गः

७.१ विदर्भराजः] V, विदर्भनाथः M.

७.२ पृथिवीभृतो] V, पृथिवीक्षितो M.

७.४ ॰पकारम्] V, ॰पचारम् M. ॰द्योतन॰] V, ॰द्योतित॰ M.

७.५ ॰सत्वराणां] V, ॰तत्पराणां M.

७.६ न केशपाशः] V, च केशपाशः M.

७.७ प्रासाधिका॰] V, प्रसाधिका॰ M.

७.१० अर्धाचिता] V, अर्धाञ्चिता M. दुर्निमितं] V, दुर्निमिते M.

७.१२ जगुर्वि॰] V, जग्मुर्वि॰ M. तदा हि] V, तथा हि M.

७.१३ बाला] V, भोज्या M.

७.१४ ॰रूपं] V, ॰शोभं M.

७.१५ ॰रूपमेनं] V, ॰रूपमेव M.

७.१७ ततो ऽवतीर्याशु करेणुकायाः स कामरूपेश्वरदत्तहस्तः। वैदर्भनिर्दिष्टमथो विवेश
नारीमनांसीव चतुष्कमन्तः] V, omits M.

७.१८ ॰शय्यासनसंस्थितो] V, ॰सिंहासनसंस्थितो M. दुगूल] V, दुकूल॰ M.

७.१९ दुगूल॰] V, दुकूल॰ M.

७.२१ बभासे] V, चकाशे M.

७.२२ तस्मिन्द्वये तत्क्षणमात्मवृत्तिः समं विभक्तेव मनोभवेन] VM, वृत्तिस्तयोः पाणिसमागमेन
समं विभक्तेव मनोभवस्य Mvl.

७.२३ ॰प्रविचारितानि क्रियासमापत्तिषु कातराणि] V, ॰प्रतिसारितानि क्रियासमापत्तिनि-
वर्तितानि M.

७.२४ बभासे] V, चकासे M. मेरोरिवान्तेषु विवर्तमानम्] V, मेरोरुपान्तेष्विव वर्तमानम् M.

७.२७ ॰क्षोभ] V, ॰क्रेद॰ M.

७.३१ सत्त्वानुरूपं हरणी॰] V, सत्त्वानुरूपाहरणी॰ M.

७.३२ भोजराजः] V, कुण्डिनेशः M.

७.३३ ॰संविदुदारौदारसिद्धौ समराक्षलभ्यम्] V, ॰संविदारम्भसिद्धौ समयोपलभ्यम् M.

७.३५ ॰प्रतिष्ठां] V, ॰प्रदिष्ठां M.

७.३६ ज्योतीरथां] V, भागीरथीं M.

७.३७ गजेना॰] V, गजस्या॰ M.

७.३८ कुलापदेशान्] V, कुलोपदेशान् M. परस्पराय] V, परस्परस्य M.

७.३९ ॰नेमि॰] V, ॰वंश॰ M.

७.४० प्रयुद्धध्वजिनी॰] V, प्रवृद्धध्वजिनी॰ M.

७.४१ ॰धिजज्ञे] V, विजज्ञे M.

७.४४ विवर्तिता] V, निवर्तिता M.

७.४५ पृष्ठ्राः] V, पृषत्काः M. अवापुरेवा॰] V, संप्रापुरेवा॰ M.

७.४६] placed after 7.49 in M.

७.४७ ॰शितक्षुरान्तैः] V, ॰शितैः क्षुराग्रैः M. कृत्तान्यपि] V, हृतान्यपि M.

७.४८ पूर्वप्रहर्ता] V, पूर्वं प्रहर्ता M.

७.५१ ॰हृतोत्तमांगं] V, ॰हृतोत्तमाङ्गः M.

७.५३ ०व्र्युत्क्रान्त०] V, ०रुत्क्रान्त० M.

७.५५ कक्ष्यस्तत] V, कक्षस्तत M.

७.५६ दृशं] V, दृष्टः M. विलोडयामास] V, निवारयामास M.

७.५७ न दक्षिणं तूणमुखे न] V, स दक्षिणं तूणमुखेन M.

७.५८ ०दृष्टाधिकलोहितौष्ठैर्व्यक्तोर्ध्वराजीर्भृ०] V, ०दृष्टाधिकलोहितोष्ठैर्व्यक्तोर्ध्वरेखा भृ० M.

७.६० ०मग्रोदितपूर्वभागः] V, ०मग्रो दिनपूर्वभागः M. यथा विवस्वान्] V, विवस्वतेव M.

७.६१ प्राप्तमथ प्रियार्हः] V, प्राप्तमसौ कुमारः M.

७.६३ ०धरौष्ठे] V, ०धरोष्ठे M.

७.६५ संयति] V, सम्प्रति M.

७.६७ मयैतान्] V, मयासि M.

७.६८ ०वाष्पापगमे] V, ०बाष्पापगमात् M.

७.६९ ०कालम्] V, ०वृन्दम् M.

७.७१ ०कुटुम्बश्रीरमादातुमैच्छन्] V, ०कुटुम्बः शान्तिमार्गोत्सुको ऽभून् M.

अष्टमः सर्गः

८.३ तस्य महा०] V, तेन सहा० M.

८.४ दुरासदो ऽरिभि०] V, दुरासदः परै० M.

८.५ नवेश्वरं] M, नरेश्वरं V.

८.८ मतो ऽस्य भूपते०] V, मतो महीपते० M.

८.९ परुषो न न] V, न खरो न च M. वशयामास] V, नमयामास M.

८.१० अथ वीक्ष्य गुणैः प्रतिष्ठितं प्रकृतिष्वात्मजमाभिगामिकैः । पदवीं परिणामदेशितां रघुरादत्त वनान्तगामिनीम्] V, अथ वीक्ष्य रघुः प्रतिष्ठितं प्रकृतिष्वात्मजमात्मवत्तया । विषयेषु विनाशधर्मसु त्रिदिवस्थेष्वपि निःस्पृहो ऽभवत् M.

८.११ गुणवत्स्वधिरोपित०] V, गुणवत्सुतरोपित० M. यदि वा] V, प्रयताः M.

८.१३ व्यपसर्जितां] V, व्यपवर्जितां M.

८.१४ स बहिः क्षितिपालवेश्मनो निवसन्नावसथे यतिव्रतः] V, स किलाश्रममन्त्यमाश्रितो निवसन्नावसथे पुराद्बहिः M.

८.१५ कुलमूर्जस्वल०] V, कुलमभ्युद्यत० M.

८.१७ समपृच्यत भूपतिर्युवा सचिवैः प्रत्यहमर्थसिद्धये । अपुनर्जननोपपत्तये प्रवयाः संयुयुजे मनीषिभिः] conj., अजिताधिगमाय मन्त्रिभिर्युयुजे नीतिविशारदैरजः । अनपायिपदोपलब्धये रघुराप्तैः समियाय योगिभिः VM.

८.१८ अनुरञ्जयितुं प्रजाः प्रभुर्व्यवहारासनमाददे नवः । अपरः शुचिविष्टराश्रयः परिचेतुं यतते स्म धारणाः] V, नृपतिः प्रकृतीरवेक्षितुं व्यवहारासनमाददे युवा । परिचेतुमुपांशु धारणां कुशपूतं प्रवयास्तु विष्टरम् M.

८.२० नयचक्षुरजो दिदृक्षया पररन्ध्रस्य ततान मण्डले । हृदये समरोपयन्मनः परमं ज्योतिरवेक्षितुं रघुः] V, omits M.

८.२१ इतरो] V, अपरो M.

८.२२ ०ध्यगमद्रुण०] V, ०प्यजयद्रुण० M.

८.२३ स्थितधीरा] V, स्थिरधीरा M.

८.२६ ॰सूणि विसृज्य राघवः। विततान समं पुरोधसा क्रतुमन्त्यं पृथिवीशतक्रतोः] V, ॰श्रूणि विमुच्य राघवः। विदधे विधिमस्य नैष्ठिकं यतिभिः सार्धमनग्निमग्निचित् M.

८.२७ विदधे च] V, अकरोच्च M.

८.३२ न केवलं विभोर्] V, विभोर्न केवलं M. परप्रयोजनम्] V, परप्रयोजना M.

८.३४ मुनिः पथा पवमानस्य जगाम] V, ययौ र्खेरुदगावृत्तिपथेन M.

८.३६ सुमनोनुसारिभिर्विनिकीर्णा] V, कुसुमानुसारिभिः परिकीर्णा M.

८.३७ पटुः] V, मधु॰ M. स्रगसज्यत सा महीपतेर्दयितोरश्छदकोटिरलयोः] V, नृपतेरमरस्रगाप सा दयितोरस्तनकोटिसुस्थितिम् M.

८.३८ पुनरप्रतिबोधलभ्ये निमिमील क्षितिपालसुन्दरी] V, निमिमील नरोत्तमप्रिया हृतचन्द्रा तमसेव कौमुदी M.

८.३९ सममेव नराधिपेन सा गुरुसम्मोहविलुप्तचेतसा। अगमत्सह तैलबिन्दुना नवदीपार्चिरिव क्षितेस्तलम्] V, वपुषा करणोज्झितेन सा निपतन्ती पतिमप्यपातयत्। ननु तैलनिषेक- बिन्दुना सह दीपार्चिरुपैति मेदिनीम् M.

८.४० उभयोः परिपार्श्ववर्तिभिस्तुमुलेना॰] V, उभयोरपि पार्श्ववर्तिनां तुमुलेन॰ M. ॰कराश्रयाः] V, ॰करालयाः M.

८.४१ च] V, तु M.

८.४२ ॰सम्प्लवात्] V, ॰विप्लवात् M.

८.४३ करणप्रायण॰] V, करणापायवि॰ M.

८.४६ मृदु वस्तु सदैव] V, अथ वा मृदु वस्तु M. ॰दर्शनक्षमा] V, ॰दर्शनं मता M.

८.४७ (placed after 8.48 in M) सुरमाल्यरूपभागशनिर्निर्मित एष कर्मणा। यदनेन तरुर्न पातितः] V, मम भाग्यविप्लवादशनिः कल्पित एष वेधसा। यदनेन न पातितस्तरुः M.

८.५० यदनामन्त्य] V, यदनापृच्छ्य M.

८.५१ किमतस्त्वया] V, किमिदं तया M.

८.५२ सुरतश्रमवारिबिन्दवो न तु तावद्धिरमन्ति ते मुखे। स्वयमस्तमितास्यहो वत क्षयिणां देहभृतामसारता] V, सुरतश्रमसंभृतो मुखे घ्रियते स्वेदलवोद्गमे अपि ते। अथ चास्तमिता त्वमात्मना धिगिमां देहभृतामसारताम् M.

८.५३ ननु किं जहासि माम्। वत] V, तव किं जहासि माम्। ननु M. ॰बन्धनं मनः] V, ॰बन्धना रतिः M.

८.५८ तव] V, वद M.

८.५९ घनचारुनितम्बगोचरा रशनेयं मुखरा तवाधुना] V, इयमप्रतिबोधशायिनीं रशना त्वां प्रथमा रहःसखी M.

८.६० ॰हंसीषु गतं मनोरमम्। पृषतासु] V, ॰हंसीषु मदालसं गतम्। पृषतीषु M.

८.६४ ग्रथितार्धा बकुलैः] V, बकुलैरर्धचितां M.

८.६६ चिरशून्यं] V, परिशून्यं M.

८.६७ सखा] V, सखी M. ॰रहितेन वेधसा] V, ॰विमुखेन मृत्युना M. वत] V, वद M.

८.७१ तदन्त॰] V, कृतान्त्य॰ M.

८.७२ क्षितिपः] V, नृपतिः M.

८.७३ सुन्दरीम्] V, भामिनीम् M. वितेनिरे] V, समापिताः M.

८.७५ तमवेक्ष्य मखाय] V, अथ तं सवनाय M. ॰श्रयः] V, ॰श्रितः M. अभिषङ्गिनमीश्वरं विशाम्] V, अभिषङ्गजडं विजिज्ञिवान् M.

८.७६ कृतस्थितिः] V, ततश्रुतम् M.

८.७८ त्रिषु धामसु शार्ङ्गधन्वनः] V, पुरुषस्य पदेष्वजन्मनः M.

८.८० ॰चारुदर्शनाम्] V, ॰चारुविभ्रमाम् M.

८.८१ ॰चरणं] V, ॰चरितं M. सुरमाल्यः] V, सुरपुष्प॰ M.

८.८२ मुनिशापनिवृत्तिकारणं ध्रुवमापाशु यतस्तनुं जहौ] V, उपलब्धवती दिवश्रुतं विवशा शापनिवृत्तिकारणम् M.

८.८३ ॰मवस्थिता] V, ॰मुपस्थिता M.

८.८४ यदवाप्य॰] V, मदवाच्य॰ M. ॰त्मनस्त्वया । मनसस्तदुपस्थिते] V, ॰त्मवत्तया मनसः समुपस्थिते M.

८.८५ नानुमृतेरवाप्यते] V, नानुमृतापि लभ्यते M. भिन्नपथाः शरीरिणाम्] V, भिन्नपथा हि देहिनाम् M.

८.८६ अपशोकमतः] V, अपशोकमनाः M.

८.८८ इतरस्तु] V, स्थिरधीस्तु M.

८.८९ स्मृत॰] V, श्रुत॰ M. कमिवा॰] V, किमिवा॰ M.

८.९० द्रुमसानुमतोः] V, द्रुमसानुमतां M.

८.९१ ॰दारमतिः] V, ॰दारमतेः M.

८.९५ ॰धिकतररुचा] V, ॰धिकचतुरया M.

नवमः सर्गः

There is considerable variation in the order of the verses in the first half of this chapter. In Nandargikar's edition of Mallinatha's commentary, between 16 and 56 they occur in this sequence (other editions of Mallinatha's commentary differ): 16, 19, 20, 21, 22, 23, 24, 17, 18, 25, 26, 27, 35, 28, 30, 31, 32, 33, 36, 38, 45, 49, 50, 40, 46, 47, 48, 51, 52, 39, 37, 41, 42, 54, 55, 56.

९.२ गुणतत्परं] V, गुणवत्तरं M.

९.७ मृगदावरतिर्न] V, मृगयाभिरतिर्न M. ॰यौवनाः] V, ॰यौवना M.

९.८ अपि सपत्नजने न च] V, न च सपत्नजनेष्वपि M. After 9.9, VM have the following expunged verse: अजयदेकरथेन स मेदिनीमुदधिनेमिमिमधिज्यशरासनः । जयमघोषयदस्य हि केवलं गजवती जवतीव्रहया चमूः ॥

९.१० जघननिर्विषयीकृतमेखलाननुचितासुविलुप्तविशेषकान् । स रिपुदारगणानकरोद्बलादनल-कानलकाधिपविक्रमः] V, omits M.

९.१२ स्फुरितकोटिसहस्रमरीचिना समचिनोत्कुलिशेन हरिर्यशः । स धनुषा युधि सायकवर्षिणा] V, शमितपक्षबलः शतकोटिना शिखरिणां कुलिशेन पुरन्दरः । स शरवृष्टिमुचा धनुषा द्विषां M.

९.१५ ०नुचिता०] V, ०नुदिता० M. श्रियमवेक्ष्य स रन्ध्रचलामभूद्] V, अजितमस्ति नृपास्पदमित्यभूद् M.

९.१६ मलय०] V, मगध० M.

९.१८ ०समुच्छ्रिति०] V, ०समुच्छ्रय० M.

९.२० ०प्रयतो] M, ०प्रयतं V.

९.२१ कुलोद्वहं] V, कुलोद्वहं M. सतीव्रता] V, पतीव्रता M.

९.२२ नराधिपः] V, महारथः M.

९.२३ असकृदेव हि तेन] V, असकृदेकरथेन M.

९.२४ महेन्द्रसमं] V, समाववृते M. उपययौ भुजगेन महीभृता] V, यमकुबेरजलेश्वरवज्रिणां M.

९.२५ हिमविवर्णितचन्दनपल्लवं विरहयन्मलयाद्रिमुदद्भुवः। विहगयोः कृपयेव शनैर्ययौ रविरहर्विरहध्रुवभेदयोः] V, जिगमिषुर्घनदाध्युषितां दिशं रथयुजा परिवर्तिततवाहनः। दिनमुखानि रविर्विहमनिग्रहैर्विमलयन्मलयं नगमत्यजत् M.

९.२८ परभृता मदनक्षतचेतसः प्रियसखी लघुवागिव योषिताम्। प्रियतमानकरोत्कलहान्तरे मृदुरवादुरवापसमागमान्] V, omits M.

९.३३ दशनचन्द्रिकया व्यवभासितं हसितमासवगन्धि मधोरिव। बकुलपुष्पमसेव्यत षद्पदैः शुचिरसं चिरसञ्जितमीप्सुभिः] V, omits M.

९.३४ सुरभिसङ्गमजं वनमालया नवपलाशमधार्यत भङ्गरम्। रमणदत्तमिवार्द्रनखक्षतं] V, उपहितं शिशिरापगमश्रिया मुकुलजालमशोभत किंशुके। प्रणयिनीव नखक्षतमण्डनं M.

९.३५ ०मधुलोलुभैर्बकुलमाकुलमाततभक्तिभिः] V, ०मधुलोलुपैर्बकुलमाकुलमायतपङ्क्तिभिः M.

९.३८ तिलकमस्तकहर्म्यकृतास्पदैः कुसुममध्वनुषङ्गसुगन्धिभिः। कलमगीयत भृङ्गविलासिनां स्मरयतैर्युतैरबलासखैः] V, उपचितावयवा शुचिभिः कणैरलिकदम्बकयोगमुपेयुषी। सट्शकान्तिरलक्ष्यत मञ्जरी तिलकजालकजालकमौक्तिकैः M.

९.३९ गमयितुं प्रभुरेष सुखेन मां न महती वत पान्थवधूजनः। इति दयात इवाभवदायता न रजनी रजनीशवती मधौ] V, उपययौ तनुतां मुखखण्डिता हिमकरोदयपाण्डुमुखच्छविः। सट्शमिष्टसमागमनिर्वृतिं वनितयानितया रजनीवधूः M.

९.४० पटुमपि] V, पटुरपि M.

९.४१ स्मरमते ०रमतेष्टसखो जनः] V, स्मरमते रमते स्म वधूजनः M.

९.४२-४३ अनलसान्यभृतानलसमन्मनः कमलधूलिमता मरुतेरिता। कुसुमभारनताध्वगयोषिता मसमशोकमशोकलताकरोत्॥ लघयति स्म न पत्यपराधजां न सहकारतरुस्तरुणीधृताम्। कुसुमितो ०लमितो ०लिखिरुन्मदैः स्मरसमाधिकरो ०धिकरोषिताम्] V, omits M.

९.४५ सुरतराग०] V, सुरतसङ्ग० M.

९.४७ ०भक्ति०] V, ०पङ्क्ति० M.

९.४८ ०र्विशुर्मधु] M, ०र्विशुर्मद० V.

९.५० ०सङ्ततया। कुसुमसंभृतया] conj., मनः। कुसुमचापभृता V, ०सन्ततया मनः। कुसु-मसंभृतया M.

९.५१ ०निषेविभिरंशुकैरलक०] V, ०निषेधिभिरंशुकैः श्रवण० M.

९.५२ विषदचन्द्रकरं सुखमारुतं कुसुमितद्रुममुन्मदकोकिलम् । तदुपभोगरसं हिमवर्षिणः
परमृतोरमृतोपमतां ययौ] V, omits M.

९.५४ तदिङ्गितवेदनम्] V, तदिङ्गितबोधनम् M.

९.५५ सवितान॰] V, स वितान॰ M.

९.५६ नवपलाश॰] V, तरुपलाश॰ M.

९.५८ प्रथमाश्रितं] V, प्रथमास्थितं M.

९.५९ ॰संयुतम्] V, ॰संगतम् M.

९.६१ वनमातुर॰] V, वनमाकुल॰ M. ॰रिवाम्भः] V, ॰रिवार्द्रैः M.

९.६३ निविडो] V, निबिडो M.

९.६४ ॰मध्यादुज्झा॰] V, ॰मध्यान्मुस्ता॰ M. सुव्यञ्जमार्द्रं] V, सुव्यक्तमार्द्रं॰ M.

९.६५ ॰मुद्धूत॰] V, ॰मुद्धूत॰ M.

९.६६ तेनातिपात॰] V, तेनातिघात॰ M. निर्भिन्न॰] V, निर्भिद्य M. ॰शल्य॰] V, ॰पुंख॰ M.

९.६७ ॰मोष॰] V, ॰मोक्ष॰ M.

९.६८ वातरुग्णान्] V, वायुरुग्णान् M.

९.६९ ॰परो ऽसौ] V, ॰परो ऽभूत् M. मृगाणाम्] V, मृगेषु M.

९.७० ॰मुक्तमुक्तान्] V, ॰लग्नमुक्तान् M. द्विपानाम्] V, गजानाम् M.

९.७१ द्रुतमन्वपतत्क्वचिच्च यूथे चमराणां शरलग्नप्रवालधीनाम् । नृपतीनिव ताञ्जगाम शान्तिं
सितवालव्यजनैर्वियोज्य सद्यः] V, चमरान्परितः प्रवर्तिताश्चः क्वचिदाकर्णविकृष्टभल्लवर्षी ।
नृपतीनिव तान्वियोज्य सद्यः सितवालव्यजनैर्जगाम शान्तिम् M.

९.७२ ॰छिन्न॰] V, ॰चित्र॰ M. ॰विलुलितबन्धे] V, ॰विगलितबन्धे M.

९.७५ ॰शय्या] V, ॰शय्यां M. ॰सनाथाः] V, ॰सनाथाम् M. नरपति॰] M, वनरति॰ V.
त्रियामाः] V, त्रियामाम् M.

९.७६ उषसि च] V, उषसि स M. पटहपटु॰] V, पटुपटह॰ M. मधुरस्वनानि] V, मधुराणि
तत्र M.

९.७९ ॰रथो ऽद्विशङ्क्य] V, ॰रथो विलङ्क्य M.

९.८० वीक्ष्य] V, प्रेक्ष्य M.

९.८१ द्विजोत्तर॰] *conj.*, द्विजेतर॰ VM.

९.८२ तच्चोदितश्च] V, तच्चोदितः स M. ॰मवेत्य] V, ॰मुपेत्य M.

९.८४ अन्ते] V, अन्त्ये M. प्रत्याह] V, प्रोवाच M.

९.८६ अव्यक्तमित्यभिहिते] V, वध्यस्तवेत्यभिहितो M.

दशमः सर्गः

१०.३ मनोर्वंशशिखरं तस्मिन्ननभिव्यक्तसन्ततिः । निमज्ज्य पुनरुत्थास्यन्नदः शोण इवाभवत्] V,
omits M.

१०.४ सुचिरं] V, स चिरं M.

१०.५ वामदेवादयस्तस्य] V, ऋष्यशृङ्गादयस्तस्य M. यतात्मानः] V, जितात्मनः M.

१०.६ अस्मिन्] V, तस्मिन् M.

१०.१० प्रफुल्ल॰] V, प्रबुद्ध॰ M.

१०.११ बिभ्रतं] V, बिभ्राणं M.

१०.१२ हेमा॰] V, दिव्या॰ M. आविर्भूतं पयोमध्यात्] V, आविर्भूतमपां मध्ये M.

१०.१३ आयुधैः॰] V, हेतिभिः॰ M.

१०.१५ ॰शायितिकान्] V, ॰शायनिकान् M.

१०.१६ स्तुत्यम॰] M, स्तुत्यमा॰ V.

१०.१८ स्फटिकस्येव ते स्थितम्] V, स्फाटिकस्येव दृश्यते M.

१०.२० प्रार्थितावहः] V, प्रार्थनावहः M. 10.25 placed after 26 in M.

१०.२६ हृदयास्पदम्] V, हृदयाश्रयम् M.

१०.२९ त्वदा॰] V, त्वय्या॰ M.

१०.३१ यदा] V, यतः M.

१०.३२ दूरेण] V, दूराणि M.

१०.३४ सङ्क्षिप्यते] V, संह्रियते M.

१०.३६ ॰प्रीतयः] V, ॰प्रीतये M.

१०.३७ ॰नादिना] V, ॰वादिना M. स्वरेण भगवानाह] V, स्वरेणोवाच भगवान् M.

१०.३८ चतुर्मुख॰] V, वर्णस्थान॰ M. भारती भव्या चरितार्था चतुष्टयी] V, कृतसंस्कारा
चरितार्थैव भारती M.

१०.३९ बभासे] V, बभौ स॰ M. ॰प्रसारिणी] V, ॰प्रवर्तिनी M.

१०.४० अङ्गिना] V, अङ्गिनां M.

१०.४१ ताप्यमानं] V, तप्यमानं M.

१०.४९ मोक्ष्यथ] V, मोक्ष्यध्वे M.

१०.५३ ॰पात्रीकृतं] V, ॰पात्रगतं M. ॰ददानः] V, ॰दधानः M.

१०.५४ तं चरुं] V, तदन्नं M.

१०.५५ विवृत्तिं] V, प्रसूतिं M.

१०.५६ वृषाकपिरिवा॰] V, अहर्पतिरिवा॰ M.

१०.५८ ॰भागेन] V, ॰भागाभ्यां M.

१०.५९ सा हि] V, सापि M.

१०.६१ बभुरा॰] V, रेजुरा॰ M.

१०.६२ स्वप्रेऽथ] V, स्वप्रेषु M. असित्सरु॰] V, जलजासि॰ M. ॰मूर्धभिः] V, ॰मूर्तिभिः M.

१०.६३ हेमपत्त्र॰] V, हेमपक्ष॰ M.

१०.६६ प्रीतो ऽपि] V, प्रीतो हि M. मेने ऽपराद्धम्] V, मेने परार्ध्यं M.

१०.६८ अथाग्र्य॰] V, अथाग्र॰ M.

१०.६९ जगत्प्रथित॰] V, जगत्प्रथम॰ M.

१०.७० शय्या॰] V, रक्षा॰ M. प्रत्याख्याता] V, प्रत्यादिष्टा M.

१०.७१ चानेन माता च्छातोदरी] V, रामेण माता शातोदरी M.

१०.७२ वीर्यवान्] V, शीलवान् M.

१०.७६ कृषाणु॰] V, कृशानु॰ M. क्षपाकरः] V, प्रभाकरः M.

१०.७७ ॰मस्रु॰] V, ॰मश्रु॰ M.

१०.७९ ॰काराणां] V, ॰चाराणां M. शोभाद्वैगुण्यमादधे] V, सैवादिरचनाभवत् M.

१०.८० ॰स्तन॰] V, ॰स्तन्य॰ M.

१०.८५ श्यामार्धा] V, श्यामाभ्रा M.

१०.८६ इवाङ्गवान्] V, इवाङ्गभाक् M.

१०.८८ तैश्चतुर्भिश्चकाशे] V, तैश्चकाशे चतुर्भिः M.

एकादशः सर्गः

११.१ तेजसो हि न] V, तेजसां हि न M.

११.३ विहितं] V, विदधे M.

११.४ वन्दितुं] V, धन्विनौ M.

११.५ ॰भिसरमेव] V, ॰नुचरमेव M. ॰त्यतो] V, ॰त्यसौ M.

११.७ ॰वश॰] V, ॰वशात् M.

११.९ विद्ययोस्तदुपदिष्टयोः पथि] V, विद्ययोः पथि मुनिप्रदिष्टयोः M.

११.१० वाहनोचितः पादचारमपि न व्यभावयत्] M, नाध्वनो ऽन्तरं पादचारगतमप्यलक्षयत्] V.

११.१२ विकचपद्यशोभिनां वीरुधां फलभृतां न वा तथा] V, कमलशोभिनां तथा शाखिनां न च परिश्रमच्छिदाम् M.

११.१५ वेगविप्रकृत॰] V, तीव्रवेगधुत॰ M. ॰वसास्वनोग्रया] V, ॰वसा स्वनोग्रया M.

११.१६ ॰लम्ब॰] V, ॰लम्बि॰ M.

११.१७ राम॰] V, बाण॰ M. (M reverses the order of verses 17 and 18.)

११.२० ॰पदान॰] V, ॰वदान॰ M. (M places 11.21 between 12 and 13.)

११.२३ दर्शनोन्मुख॰] M, दर्शनोत्सुक॰ V.

११.२४ नृपसुतौ शितैः शरैः] V, दशरथात्मजौ शरैः M.

११.२५ उपोढ॰] V, अपोढ M.

११.२६ आशय॰] V, आश्रय॰ M.

११.३४ शिला सती] V, शिलामयी M.

११.३६ विदेहपुटभेदनौकसां] V, विदेहनगरीनिवासिनां M.

११.३९ महद्भिरपि] V, बृहद्भिरपि M.

११.४० ॰निघात॰] V, ॰विघात॰ M. ये ऽवधूय] V, स्वान्विधूय M.

११.४२ इत्थम्] V, एवम् M.

११.४३ आदिदेश] V, व्यादिदेश M.

११.४४ प्रेक्ष्य] V, वीक्ष्य M.

११.४५ पेलवं] V, पेशलं M.

११.४६ तत्स्वनेन गगनस्पृशा] V, तेन वज्रपरुषस्वनं M.

११.४७ स्वां ददौ श्रियमिवामरद्युतिः] V, पार्थिवः श्रियमिव न्यवेदयत् M. After 11.47, M adds: मैथिलः सपदि सत्यसङ्गरो राघवाय तनयामयोनिजाम् । सन्निधौ द्युतिमतस्तपो-निधेरग्निसाक्षिकमिवातिसृष्टवान् ॥

११.४८ दुहित॰] V, दुहितुः M. इष्यतां] V, दिश्यतां M.

११.४९ विपच्यते कल्पवृक्षफलधर्म] V, हि पच्यते कल्पवृक्षफलधर्मि M.

११.५० ॰मग्र॰] V, ॰मग्र॰ M.

११.५३ ॰वहत्तदग्रजो मध्यमस्] V, ॰वहद्रघूद्वहो लक्ष्मणस् M. यौ यमावधिगतौ सुमित्रया] V, यौ तयोरवरजौ वरौजसौ M.

११.५५ ते चतुर्थसहितास्त्रयो बभुः सूनवो नव॰] M, रामभद्रसहिताश्च ते बभुर्भूपतेर्नव V. ॰निग्रहाः] M, ॰विग्रहः V. तस्य भूपतेः] M, सूनवस्त्रयः V.

११.५९ भूरजःसरुधिरार्द्र॰] *conj.* (Śrīnātha), भूयसा सरुधिराभ्र॰ V, सान्ध्यमेघरुधिरार्द्र॰ M.

११.६० ववाशिरे] V, ववासिरे M.

११.६१ क्षिप्रप्रशान्तम्] V, प्रेक्ष्य शान्तिम् M.

११.६३ यः ससोम इव घर्मदीधितिः] M, भार्गवो ऽथ दह्रशे महाद्युतिः V.

११.६६ भार्गवं विव्यथे दशरथो दशाच्युतः] V, भार्गवं स्वां दशां च विषसाद पार्थिवः M.

११.६९ ॰चारिणीमिषुं] V, ॰चारिणं शरं M.

११.७० उद्यतो] V, रोषितो M.

११.७१ ॰क्षिणोः] V, ॰क्षणोः M.

११.७२ जगति] V, जयति M. साम्प्रतं] V, सम्प्रति M.

११.७३ ॰हरणात्स हेहय॰] V, ॰हरणाज्झ हैहय॰ M.

११.७४ यत्] V, यः M.

११.७५ ॰रसम्] V, ॰बलम् M.

११.७६ तन्मदीयमिदमाततज्यतां नीयतां विजयसाधनं धनुः] V, तन्मदीयमिदमायुधं ज्यया सङ्गम्यम्य सशरं विकृष्यताम् M.

११.७७ ज्याविमर्द॰] V, ज्यानिघात॰ M.

११.८० ॰निहितैककोटिना] V, ॰निहितैककोटि तत् M. निष्प्रभश्च रिपुरास भूभृतां धूमशेष इव धूमकेतनः] M, प्राप वर्णविकृतिं च भार्गवो वृष्टिधौत इव वासवध्वजः V.

११.८१ परस्परं] V, परस्पर॰ M. दिनक्षये] V, दिनात्यये M.

११.८३ लोकमथ] V, लोकमुत M.

११.८६ गतिमतां] V, मतिमतां M. स्वर्गसङ्क्रतिर्भोगलोलुभम्] V, स्वर्गपद्धतिर्भोगलोलुपम् M.

११.८८ राघवो ऽथ] V, राघवो ऽपि M. शोभते] V, कीर्तये M.

११.९० वचः] V, ततः M. The order of 11.89 and 11.90 is inverted in V.

११.९१ वृष्टिसेकः] V, वृष्टिपातः M.

द्वादशः सर्गः

१२.५ भर्त्रा चण्डी] V, चण्डी भर्त्रा M. उज्जगारेन्द्र॰] V, उद्ववामेन्द्र॰ M.

१२.६ रामप्रव्राजनं] V, रामं प्रव्राजयत् M.

१२.८ चीरे च परिगृह्णतः] V, वसानस्य च वल्कले M. दुःखितास्तस्य] V, विस्मितास्तस्य M.

१२.१५ चित्रकूटाचलस्थं] V, चित्रकूटवनस्थं M.

१२.१७ ॰दैवते] V, ॰देवते M.

१२.१९ भरतः] V, शुद्ध्यर्थं M.

१२.२२] VM, मृगमांस ततः सीतां रक्षन्तीमातपे शठः । पक्षतुण्डनखाघातैर्बबाधे वायसो बलात् Vvl.

१२.२७ अनुसूयाविसृष्टेन] V, अनुसूयातिसृष्टेन M.

१२.३१ अथो] V, ततो M.

१२.३४ यवीयांसं] V, कनीयांसं M.

१२.३७ अस्यावहासस्य] V, अस्योपहासस्य M. मृगीपरिभवो व्याघ्या] V, मृग्या परिभवो व्याघ्यां M. मृत्यवे हि त्वया कृतः] V, इत्यवेहि त्वया कृतम् M.

१२.३८ अङ्गानि विशतीं] V, अङ्गं निर्विशतीं M.

१२.३९ ०वादिनीम्] V, ०भाषिणीम् M.

१२.४० विधृतासिः] V, विवृतासिः M. ०पुनरुक्तेन] V, ०पौनरुक्त्येन M.

१२.४१ तानतर्जयदम्बरात्] V, तावतर्जयदम्बरे M.

१२.४२ तथाविधा] V, तथाविधम् M.

१२.४५ एवासंस्तावद्धा] V, एवाजौ तावांश्च M.

१२.४६ शुभाचारो ऽसद्दूषणम्] V, शुभाचारः स दूषणम् M.

१२.४८ च] V, तु M.

१२.४९ उच्छ्रितं दद्दशे ऽन्यत्र] V, उत्थितं दद्दशे ऽन्यच्च M.

१२.५१ राघवास्त्राग्निदग्धानां] V, राघवास्त्रविदीर्णानाम् M.

१२.५५ आत्मनस्तु] V, आत्मनः सु० M.

१२.५६ ०दुःखयोः] V, ०शोकयोः M. ०संस्कारानन्तरा ववृते क्रिया] V, ०संस्कारात्परा ववृतिरे क्रियाः M.

१२.५७ ०निर्धौत०] V, ०निर्धूत० M.

१२.६२ हरिः] V, कपिः M. ०नन्दासु०] V, ०नन्दाश्रु० M.

१२.६३ ०वधोद्धुरः] V, ०वधोद्धतः M. विभीर्] V, पुरीं M.

१२.६७ खे ऽपि] V, व्योम्नि M. ०वर्त्मनि] V, ०वर्त्मभिः M. ०विश्य] V, ०दिश्य M.

१२.७० यो बभौ] V, प्लवगैर् M. ०वोन्मग्रः शेषः] V, ०वोन्मग्रं शेषं M.

१२.७३ शैलभग्र०] V, शैलरुद्ध० M.

१२.७४ ०चेतसम्] V, ०चेतनाम् M.

१२.७६ ०विश्लेषि] V, ०विश्लिष्ट० M. क्षणक्लेशि स्वप्रवृत्तम्] V, क्षणक्लेशः स्वप्रवृत्त M.

१२.७८ मारुतसुतानीत०] V, मारुतिसमानीत० M.

१२.८२ सेतुर्] V, पेतुर् M.

१२.८४ हरिरथ्यं] V, हरियुग्यं M.

१२.८६ अस्त्राण्यापुः] M, शस्त्राण्यापुः V.

१२.८७ ०वैरं] V, ०र्युद्धं M.

१२.८८ स यथापूर्वं] V, सो ऽयथापूर्वो M.

१२.८९ तमरिं] V, अरातिं M.

१२.९१ रामास्त्रं भित्त्वा हृदयमाशुगम्] V, रामास्तो भित्त्वा हृदयमाशुगः M.

१२.९२ वचसेव] V, वचसैव M.

१२.९५ ०शल्मलिम्] V, ०शाल्मलिम् M.

१२.९६ सुरद्विषाम्] M, सुरद्विषः V. कदलीमिव] V, कदलीसुखम् M, Vvl.

१२.९७ चासौ] V, चास्मै M.

१२.९९ रामो रिपु०] V, स रावण० M.

१२.१०२ अविनियमितर्ले] V, उपनतमणिबन्धे M.

१२.१०३ ०शराचित०] V, ०शराङ्कित० M. ०युतं] V, ०युजं M.

१२.१०४ सङ्गमव्यं] V, सङ्गमव्य M.

त्रयोदशः सर्गः

१३.२ ॰विष्कृततारतारम्] V, ॰विष्कृतचारुतारम् M.

१३.३ पूर्वं] V, मेध्ये M.

१३.७ ॰गर्वाः] V, ॰गन्धाः M.

१३.८ ॰भरणं] V, ॰वरणं M.

१३.९ ॰दक्षाः] V, ॰दक्षः V.

१३.१० सरिन्मुखा॰] V, नदीमुखा॰ M. विवृताननत्वम्] V, विवृताननत्वात् M.

१३.१२ ॰स्फूर्जित॰] V, ॰स्फूर्जथु॰ M.

१३.१४ भूयिष्ठमितः] भूयिष्ठमयं M.

१३.१५ निस्त्विंशकल्पस्य निधेर्जलानामेषा तमालदुमराजिनीला। दूरादरालभ्रू विभाति वेला कलङ्कलेखामलिनेव धारा] V, दुरादयश्चक्रनिभस्य तन्वी तमालतालीवनराजिनीला। आभाति वेला लवणाम्बुरा॰शोर्धारानिबद्धेव कलङ्कुरेखा M.

१३.१६ ॰यताक्षम्] V, ॰यताक्षि M.

१३.१७ ॰पूगमालि] V, ॰पूगमालम् M.

१३.१८ एषा हि] V, एषा वि॰ M.

१३.१९ मरुतां] V, पततां M.

१३.२० मुखान्ते] V, मुखे ते M.

१३.२१ ॰निःसृतेन] V, ॰लम्बितेन M.

१३.२३ एषा] V, सैषा M.

१३.२७ गन्ध्याश्व] V, गन्धश्च M. कदम्ब॰] V, कादम्ब॰ M. त्वया मे यस्मिन्विना दुष्प्रसहान्यभूवन्] V, बभूवुर्यस्मिन्नसह्यानि विना त्वया मे M.

१३.२८ रात्रौ] V, यत्र M.

१३.२९ च भिन्न॰] V, विभिन्न॰ M. धूमाकुल॰] V, धूमारुण॰ M.

१३.३२ परिरिप्समानः] V, परिरब्धुकामः M. सासुरहं] V, सास्रमहं M.

१३.३३ ॰मानान्तविलम्बिनीनां] V, ॰मानान्तरलम्बिनीनां M.

१३.३४ पेलव॰] V, पेशल॰ M.

१३.३५ सुसम्] V, सुप्नः M.

१३.३६ प्राभ्रंशद्घो नहुषं प्रमत्तम्] V, प्रभ्रंशयां यो नहुषं चकार M.

१३.३७ ॰मुद्रप्रकीर्ते॰] V, ॰मनिन्द्यकीर्ते॰ M.

१३.३८ सातकर्णेः] V, शातकर्णेः M.

१३.३९ किलाभिनीतः] V, किलोपनीतः M.

१३.४० ॰शब्दः] V, ॰घोषः M. वियद्दताः] M, वियद्दताः V.

१३.४३ ॰मुक्ते] V, ॰मुक्तां M. Expunged alternative to 43: एषो ऽक्षमालावलयी मृगाणां कण्डूयितारं कुशसूचिलावम्। सभाजयन्मे भुजमूर्ध्वबाहुः सव्येतरं प्राङ्मतः प्रयुङ्क्ङ् ॥

१३.४८ स रूढो] V, सुजातो M. तव प्रवालावचयेन यस्य] V, प्रवालमादाय सुगन्धि यस्य M. कर्णार्पितेनाकरवं कपोलमप्रार्थ्यकालागुरुपत्तलेखम्] V, यवाङ्कुरापाण्डुकपोलशोभी मयावतंसः परिकल्पितस्ते M.

१३.४९ ॰हिंसाफल॰] V, ॰लिङ्घात्फल॰ M. ॰द्ग्रतपः] V, ॰द्ग्रतर॰ M.

१३.५० ॰हस्तोचित॰] V, ॰हस्तोद्धृत॰ M. किलानसूया] V, किलानुसूया M.

490

१३.५१ ०जुषां मुनीनाम्] V, ०जुषामृषीणाम् M. ०बन्धाः] V, ०मध्याः M.

५३–५६] M, तमिस्रया शुक्लनिशेव रात्र्या कुन्दस्रगिन्दीवरमाल्ययेव । कृत्तिहिरैः कृष्णमृगत्वचेव
भूतिः स्मरारेरिव कण्ठभासा ॥ दृश्यार्धया शारदमेघलेखा निर्धौतनिस्त्रिंशरुचा दिवेव ।
गवाक्षकालागुरुधूमराज्या हर्म्यस्थलालेपसुधा नवेव ॥ तुषारसङ्घातशिला हिमाद्रेर्जात्यञ्जन-
प्रस्तरशोभयेव । पत्त्रिणां मानसगोचराणां श्रेणीव कादम्बविहङ्गपङ्क्त्या ॥ नितान्त-
शुद्धस्फटिकाक्षयोगाद्दैर्दूर्यकान्त्या रशनावलीव । गङ्गा रवेरात्मजया समेत्य पुष्यत्युदारं
परभागमेषा ॥ V.

१३.६० यूपैः] V, यूपा M.

१३.६१ ०सुखोषितानां] V, ०सुखोचितानां M.

१३.६२ दूरे ऽपि सन्तं] V, दूरे वसन्तं M.

१३.६३ ०परुषं] V, ०कपिशं M. यथा] V, यतो M.

१३.६४ पारित०] V, पालित० M.

१३.६६ विसृष्टां] V, निसृष्टां M. नितान्तकष्टम्] V, तया सहोग्रम् M.

१३.६८ ०देशितेन] V, ०दर्शितेन M.

१३.७० ०जनितानननविक्रियांस्तारियांस्तान्वृक्षान्] V, ०जनिताकृतिविक्रियांश्चप्लक्षान् M. ०दृष्टिदानै
०] V, ०दृष्टिपातै० M.

१३.७१ व्युत्कान्त०] V, व्युत्क्रम्य M.

१३.७३ येषु] V, तेषु M.

१३.७४ ०रथं] V, ०रत्नान् M. ०शिष्टम्] V, ०शिष्टः M. ०विकल्पितविधैरपि यस्तदीयै०] V,
०विकल्परचितैरपि ये तदीयै० M. ०शोभः] V, ०शोभाः M.

१३.७५ ०कूटम्] V, ०वृन्दम् M.

१३.७६ ०गणाद्] V, ०घनाद् M. ०कृच्छ्राद्भ्युद्धतां] V, ०कृच्छ्रात्प्रत्युद्धतां M.

चतुर्दशः सर्गः

१४.१ प्रत्यागतौ तत्र चिरप्रवासादपश्यतां दाशरथी जनन्यौ । कुमुद्वतीशीतमरीचिलेखे दिवेव
रूपान्तरदुर्विभावे] V, भर्तुः प्रणाशादथ शोचनीयं दशान्तरं तत्र समं प्रपन्ने| अपश्यतां
दाशरथी जनन्यौ छेदादिवोपघ्नतरोर्वतल्यौ M.

१४.२ नतारी] V, हतारी M.

१४.४ अभीप्सितं] V, अपीप्सितं M.

१४.५ स्वमुदाहरती] V, स्वमुदीरयन्ती M.

१४.१० ०हरिमिश्रसैन्य०] V, ०हरिभिः ससैन्य० M. ०वर्गान्] V, ०वर्गः M.

१४.११ भास्वान्] V, साक्षाद् M. प्रसिद्धः] V, प्रवृद्धः M.

१४.१२ नुन्ना] V, भिन्ना M.

१४.१३ विमान०] V, प्रासाद० M.

१४.१५ सौहार्द०] V, सौहार्द० M.

१४.१८ सहिष्णुर्] V, स दिव्यान् M. ०दधानः] V, ०दधानम् M.

१४.१९ ०हित०] V, ०हृत० M.

१४.२५ सुखीबभूवुः] V, सुखान्यभूवन् M.

१४.२६ ०दोहदेन] M. ०दौहृदेन M.

१४.२८ हंसैः] V, हिंसैः M.

१४.३० विपाट्यमानां] V, विगाह्यमानां M.

१४.३१ निहतारिभद्रः] V, विजितारिभद्रः M.

१४.३३ किलैव सत्याहतं] V, किलैवमभ्याहतं M.

१४.३७ ०वाहादिव] V, ०वातादिव M.

१४.३८ बहली०] V, बहुली० M. ०मीशः स्थलातिगं] V, ०मीशे आलानिकं M.

१४.४० मलत्वे निरूपिता] V, मलत्वेनारोपिता M.

१४.४१ स्त्वर्थः] V, व्यर्थः M. ०वाञ्छया] V, ०काङ्क्षया M.

१४.४२ धारयता] V, धारयितुं M.

१४.४३ तत्र] V, तेषु M.

१४.४४ सोम्येति चाभाष्य यथार्थभाषः] V, सौम्येति चाभाष्य यथार्थभाषी M.

१४.४६ विशङ्कम्] V, द्विषद्वत् M.

१४.४७ सुमन्तुप्रतिपन्न०] V, सुमन्त्रेण गृहीत० M.

१४.५० ०पगमा०] V, ०पगता० M.

१४.५१ भ्रातुर्नियोगादथ तां] V, गुरोर्नियोगाद्वनितां M.

१४.५२ सुमन्तुप्रतिपन्नवाहात्] V, स यन्त्रा निगृहीतवाहात् M.

१४.५३ ०न्तर्गतमश्रुकण्ठः] V, ०न्तर्गतबाष्पकण्ठः M.

१४.५५ प्रथितार्य०] V, पतिरार्य० M.

१४.५७ ०र्वृजनादृते] V, ०र्वृजिनादृते M.

१४.५८ स सीतां] V, सतीं तां M.

१४.५९ सोम्य] V, सौम्य M.

१४.६० विज्ञापयेः] V, विज्ञापय M.

१४.६३ त्वामास्पदं प्राप्य तया तु] V, तदास्पदं प्राप्य तयाति० M.

१४.६४ ०मन्यं] V, ०मन्यां M.

१४.६५ कुर्यामपेक्षां] V, कुर्यामुपेक्षां M.

१४.६६ जननान्तरेषु] V, जननान्तरे ऽपि M.

१४.६९ नृत्तं] V, नृत्यं M.

१४.७१ दत्त्वा स पुत्रा०] V, दाश्चान्सुपुत्रा० M.

१४.७३ प्रतिकूलवृत्ता०] V, कलुषप्रवृत्ता० M.

१४.७४ मयानुकम्प्या] V, ममानुकम्प्या M.

१४.७९ शान्तसुखं] V, शान्तमृगं M.

१४.८० समर्पयामास] V, तामर्पयामास M.

१४.८२ विबुधा०] V, विधिना० M. प्रतस्थौ] V, प्रतस्थे M.

१४.८६ तस्यैक०] V, तामेक० M.

१४.८७ दुर्वारव्यथमपि] V, दुर्वारं कथमपि M.

पञ्चदशः सर्गः

१५.३ तत्र] V, तस्मिन् M.

१५.४ ०रक्षणायैव] V, ०रक्षणार्थैव M.

१५.९ रामादेशादनपगं सेनाङ्ग तस्य सिद्धये] V, रामादेशादनुगता सेना तस्यार्थसिद्धये M.
१५.११ ॰स्वनोत्कर्ण॰] V, ॰स्वनोत्कण्ठ॰ M.
१५.१३ सम्पन्ना] V, सम्पन्नौ M.
१५.१८ ॰मालोक्य] V, ॰मालक्ष्य M. वेतनम्] V, भोजनम् M. भीतेनैवो॰] V, भीतेनेवो॰ M.
१५.२१ निशानं स्वस्य शूलस्य] V, विनाशात्तस्य वृक्षस्य M.
१५.२४ शत्रोः] V, शत्रुः M.
१५.२६ महामनाः] V, महौजसः M.
१५.२८ पुरं] V, पुरीं M.
१५.३१ ॰रथस्याथ] V, ॰रथस्यापि M.
१५.३२ सुतौ] V, स तौ M. 15.33 After his verse, M has an extra one which reads: रामस्य मधुरं वृत्तं गायन्तौ मातुरग्रतः । तद्वियोगव्यथां किञ्चिच्छिथिलीचक्रतुः सुतौ ॥
१५.३७ अधिगौरवमीक्षितः] V, ईक्षितो ऽत्यन्तगौरवम् M.
१५.३८ ॰रुपासितम्] V, ॰रुपस्थितम् M.
१५.४० वार्ताम्] V, वार्तम् M. प्रख्यापयिष्यतः] V, प्रत्यर्पयिष्यतः M.
१५.४१ अथाकस्मान्मृतं विप्रः पुत्रम्] V, अथ जानपदो विप्रः शिशुम् M.
१५.४२ प्राप्ता] V, प्राप्य M.
१५.४५ प्रस्थितश्च] V, प्रस्थितः स M. पुनश्चास्य] V, पुनस्तस्य M.
१५.४७ विचेष्यन्] V, विनेष्यन् M.
१५.४९ पृष्टकामा॰] V, पृष्टनामा॰ M.
१५.५२ धृतदण्डः] V, कृतदण्डः M.
१५.५३ इवामलः] V, इवेन्दुना M.
१५.५४ भीतेनेवा॰] V, पीतेनेवा॰ M.
१५.६० ॰जानेर्यस्यासीत्सैव] V, ॰जाने॰ सैवासीद्यस्माज् M.
१५.६२ कलगिरौ] V, कुशलवौ M.
१५.६४ तज्ज्ञ॰] V, तज्ज्ञैर् M.
१५.६६ तयोश्च सा] V, तयोस्तदा M. वीक्षापन्ना] V, नाक्षिकम्पं M.
१५.६७ ॰दायेषु] V, ॰दानेषु M.
१५.६८ विनितौ वां] VM, विनीतौ वा Vvl., विनीतं वां Vvl. वेयं] V, चेयं M.
१५.६९ दूरीकृत्य] V, उरीकृत्य M.
१५.७० तवात्मजौ] V, तदात्मजौ M.
१५.७२ तवाज्ञया] V, त्वदाज्ञया M.
१५.७४ सन्निपत्य] V, सन्निपात्य M.
१५.७५ ॰स्कारवत्येव पुत्राभ्यां सह] V, ॰स्कारवत्यासौ पुत्राभ्यामथ M.
१५.७७ तस्थुरुर्वीमुखाः] V, तस्थुस्ते ऽवाङ्मुखाः M.
१५.८० विश्वम्भरा देवी] V, विश्वम्भरे देवि M. ॰मर्हति] V, ॰मर्हसि M.
१५.८१ रन्ध्रे सद्यो ऽभवद्] V, रन्ध्रात्सद्योभवाद् M.
१५.८२ ॰निषादिनी] V, ॰निषेदुषी M. ॰वसना] V, ॰रशना M.
१५.८४ रसायां] V, धरायां M.

१५.८६ स देशं सिन्धुकुलगम्] V, स देशं सिन्धुनामकम् M, आत्मकं सिद्धसाद्रतम् Vvl.
दत्तप्रभावाय] M, Vvl., जेतुं सपुत्राय V, दत्तप्रतापाय Vvl. भृतप्रजः] V, धृतप्रजः M.

१५.८९ कारपथे०] V, कारापथे० M.

१५.९० इति रोपित०] V, इत्यारोपित० M.

१५.९६ श्रावस्त्यां च] V, शरावत्यां M.

१५.९८ वृत्तज्ञाः] V, चित्तज्ञाः M. जनासुभिः] V, प्रजाश्रुभिः M.

१५.१०० तद्धि] V, भुवि M.

१५.१०१ पौरार्थं] V, पौराणां M.

१५.१०२ निर्वर्त्यैषां दशमुखभयच्छेद०] V, निवर्त्यैवं दशमुखशिरश्छेद० M. सम्रलोक०]
V, सर्वलोक० M.

षोडशः सर्गः

१६.४ विबुद्धः] V, प्रबुद्धः M.

१६.६ तां सो ऽनपोढा०] V, अथानपोढा० M.

१६.७ लब्धो ऽन्तरः] V, लब्धान्तरा M.

१६.९ गुरुणा तव द्यां] V, गुरुणानवद्या M. राजन्पुरदेवतां V, राजन्नधिदेवतां M.

१६.१० वस्वो०] V, वस्वौ० M.

१६.१३ दीर्घिकासु V, दीर्घिकाणाम् M.

१६.१३. After this verse M. places verse 20.

१६.१४ This is placed after verse 20 in M.

१६.१४ मे] V, ऽद्य M.

१६.१५ ०कुम्भं] V, ०कुम्भाः M.

१६.१६ ०र्द्धान्त०] V, ०ल्कान्त० M. तनूत्तरीयाणि] V, स्तनोत्तरीयाणि M.

१६.१८ वन्द्यः] V, वन्दैः M.

१६.२० This is placed after verse 13 in M.

१६.२१ This is placed after verse 19 in M. ०गृहेषु] V, ०गृहाणि M.

१६.२७ ०नोद्रतेन] V, ०नोदितेन M.

१६.२९ वा नृपस्य] V, च व्रजन्ती M. जनेन] V, नृपस्य M. ०पदं] V, ०मतिं M.

१६.३२ प्रपातं] V, प्रयाण० M.

१६.३४ सोल्ललितं] V, नौलुलितं M.

१६.३६ ०वातः] V, ०वायुः M.

१६.३८ पुनर्नवी०] V, पुरं नवी० M.

१६.३९ निवर्त०] V, निर्वर्त० M.

१६.४० गृहैस्तदीयैः] V, यथाप्रधानम् M.

१६.४२ ०गृह०] V, ०विधि० M.

१६.४३ ०लम्ब०] V, ०लम्बि० M. प्रियावेशम्] V, प्रिया वेशम् M.

१६.४५ ०त्यन्त०] V, ०त्यर्थ० M.

१६.४६ शेवल०] V, शैवल० M.

१६.४७ नवेषु सायन्तनमल्लिकाया] V, वनेषु सायन्तनमल्लिकानां M.

१६.५१ रुरुचे] V, शुशुभे M.

१६.५६ विविग्र॰] V, उद्विग्र॰ M.

१६.५७ परस्परक्षेपण॰] V, परस्पराभ्युक्षण॰ M. पार्श्वचरां किरातम्] V, पार्श्वगतां किरातीम् M.

१६.५९ सोल्लुलिता॰] V, नौलुलिता॰ M.

१६.६१ पारिप्लवा] V, प्रभ्रंशिनो M. प्रभ्रंशिनः] V, पारिप्लवाः M. शेवाल॰] V, शैवाल॰ M.

१६.६३ भुवोर्] V, भुवां M.

१६.६४ प्रस्निग्ध॰] M, प्रसिद्ध॰ V.

१६.६५ ॰कल्पाः] V, ॰तुल्याः M. ॰रन्ध्र॰] V, ॰सूत्र॰ M.

१६.६६ ॰दण्ड॰] V, ॰वारि॰ M. हर्षात्] V, दर्पात् M.

१६.६७ ॰लत॰] V, ॰फल॰ M.

१६.६८ ॰माल्यः] V, ॰हारः M. ॰लग्रोन्नत॰] V, ॰लग्रोद्धृत॰ M.

१६.६९ नृपेणाभिगताः] V, नृपेणानुगताः M.

१६.७० ॰संस्थैः] V, ॰मुक्तैः M.

१६.७५ ॰प्रसादम्] V, ॰प्रसादाः M.

१६.७७ समादधे] V, समाददे M.

१६.७८ रोधांस्यभिन्नव॰] V, रोधांसि निघ्नव॰ M. मत्तः] V, वन्यः M.

१६.८१ द्विषामङ्कुशवस्तु] V, द्विषामङ्कुशमस्त्र॰ M. सुधावसिक्तं] V, मूर्धाभिषिक्तं M.

१६.८३ बाला तु] V, बालाति॰ M. ओघात्] V, जवात् M.

१६.८४ ॰लेखा॰] V, ॰रेखा॰ M.

१६.८६ इत्युक्तवान्] V, इत्यूचिवान् M. इत्यभि॰] V, इत्यनु॰ M.

१६.८७ मङ्गल्यो॰] V, माङ्गल्यो॰ M.

१६.८८ शङ्खामहिवररिपोरत्यजद्वैनतेयाद्रुद्र॰] V, शङ्खां पितृवधरिपोरत्यजद्वैनतेयाच्छान्त॰ M.

सप्तदशः सर्गः

१७.१ पुत्रमाप] V, पुत्रं प्राप M.

१७.४ जन्य॰] V, जात्य॰ M. ॰मेकान्त॰] V, ॰मनेकं M.

१७.५ किलोचितम्] V, कुलोचितम् M.

१७.१० ॰पीठे निवेश्य तम्] V, ॰पीठोपवेशितम् M.

१७.११ तूर्यैः प्रहत॰] V, तूर्यैर् आहत॰ M.

१७.१२ ॰पुटोत्तरम्] V, पटोत्तरम् M. ॰वृद्धप्रयुक्तं] V, ॰वृद्धैः प्रयुक्तान् M. ॰विधिम्] V, ॰विधीन् M.

१७.१५ प्रवृष्ट] V, प्रवृद्ध M.

१७.१६ सन्मन्त्र॰] M, तन्मन्त्र॰ V. ॰पूताभिरद्भिः स्नानं] V, ॰पूताभिः स्नानमद्भिः M.

१७.२२ उपासेदुः] V, उपसेदुः M.

१७.२३ ॰गुणानद्धां मौलिमभ्यन्तरस्रजम्] conj., ॰गुणानद्धां मालामभ्यन्तरस्रजम् V, ॰गुणोन्नद्धं मौलिमन्तर्गतस्रजम् M. ॰वर्षिणा] V, ॰शोभिना M.

१७.२४ पत्त्रविन्यस्तरोचनम्] V, पत्त्रं विनयतरोचनम् M.

१७.२५ दुगूल॰] V, दुकूल॰ M.

१७.२६ विरराज नवे] V, विरराजोदिते M.

१७.२९ लेखा॰] V, रेखा॰ M. 17.29 and 17.30 are transposed in M.

१७.३२ ॰रावणौजसा] V, ॰रावतौजसा .M

१७.३३ ॰गौष्ण्यं] V, ॰गौष्ण्यं M.

१७.३४ धूमस्याग्रे:] V, धूमादग्रे: M. ॰दयस्यांशवो] V, ॰द्यादंशवो M. तेजसो] V, तेजसां M.

१७.३५ इवोड्डुपम्] V, इव ध्रुवम् M.

१७.३२ प्रयस्ता॰] V, प्रशस्ता॰ M.

१७.३९ धर्मज्ञ॰] V, धर्मस्थ॰ M. ॰प्रत्यर्थिनो:] V, ॰प्रत्यर्थिनां M. ॰च्छेत्ता] V, ॰च्छेद्यान् M.

१७.४२ शत्रूनुत्खाय] V, शत्रूनुद्धृत्य M.

१७.४३ समेतानि] V, समस्तानि M. चास्यो॰ V, तस्यो॰ M.

१७.४४ तथाह्वासीद्] V, नवो ऽप्यासीद् M. रूढमूल] V, दृढमूल M.

१७.४५ यत्त्रय:] V, ते यत: M. स आन्तरान्] V, सो ऽभ्यन्तरान् M.

१७.४६ प्रसादसुमुखे तस्मिंश्चटुलापि] V, प्रसादाभिमुखे तस्मिंश्चपलापि M. ॰लेखेव] V, ॰रेखेव M.

१७.४७ चापल॰] V, श्वापद॰ M.

१७.४९ रात्रिन्दिन॰] V, रात्रिंदिव॰ M.

१७.५० न जातु] V, स जातु M. ॰द्वार: स] V, ॰द्वारो न M. 51–55: M has these verses in this order: 51, 54, 52, 53, 55.

१७.५२ प्रत्यवेक्षा॰] V, प्रत्यवेक्ष्या M.

१७.५४ रोढुरपि] M, योद्धुरपि V.

१७.५९ ययावतिविशिष्टश्चेत्] V, ययावेभिर्बलिष्ठश्चेत् M.

१७.६० कोशादाश्रय॰] V, कोशेनाश्रय॰ M.

१७.६१ रन्ध्रे च प्राहरद्द्विषाम्] V, रन्ध्रेषु प्रहरत्रिपून् M. After 17.61, M includes the following two verses: पित्रा संवर्धितो नित्यं कृतास्त्रः सांपरायिकः। तस्य दण्डवतो दण्डः स्वदेहान्न व्यशिष्यत ॥ सर्पस्येव शिरोरत्नं नास्य शक्तित्रयं परः। न चकर्ष परस्मात्तदयस्कान्त इवायसम् ॥

१७.६२ तदीयेषु] V, स्वकीयेषु M.

१७.६३ वर्णैरिव] V, वर्णैरपि M.

१७.६५ बलानां गुणानां] V, गुणानां बलानां M.

१७.६६ दण्डनीतिं] V, राजनीतिं M.

१७.६७ ॰विकल्पे] V, ॰विधिज्ञे M. ॰कामिनी] V, ॰गामिनी M.

१७.६८ ॰भग्रान्य॰] V, ॰भिन्नान्य॰ M.

१७.६९ प्रवृद्धो] V, प्रवृद्धौ M. स च] V, स तु M.

१७.७० ॰त्यन्तमहत:] V, ॰त्यर्थ महत: M.

१७.७१ पप्रथे] V, ववृधे M.

१७.७२ घ्नन्नक्तं चापनुदंस्तम:] V, घ्नंस्तत्त्वार्थेन नुदंस्तम: M.

१७.७५ राजा राज्ञां] V, राज्ञां राजा M.

१७.७७ ॰पाला: शेषां] V, ॰पला: देवा: M.

१७.७८ यथा] V, तथा M.

अष्टादशः सर्गः

१८.१ नैषधस्याधिपतेः] V, नैषधस्यार्थपतेः M.

१८.२ तेनोरुकार्येण] V, तेनोरुवीर्येण M. ॰फलात्मकेन] V, ॰फलोन्मुखेन M.

१८.५ योद्धा नलानीव] V, यो नड्वलानीव M.

१८.६ प्रपेदे] V, स लेभे M.

१८.७ तत्प्रभवः] V, तत्प्रभवे M.

१८.८ ॰हितपुण्डरीकं] V, ॰हृतपुण्डरीका M.

१८.९ ॰क्षामतनुः ससाद] V, क्षान्ततरश्चकार M.

१८.११ ॰वाधिकं॰] V, ॰वात्मज॰ M.

१८.१३ ॰भिन्नानपि] V, ॰विग्रानपि M.

१८.१४ विहीन॰] V, यो हीन॰ M.

१८.१६ यातर्यरीणां] V, जेतर्यरीणां M. 18.17] omits M.

१८.१८ ॰दात्तशीलः शलः शिलापृष्ठ॰] V, ॰दारशीलः शिलः शिलापट्ट॰ M. ॰व्रजदस्तमानः] V, ॰व्रजदीड्घमानः M.

१८.१९ वार्ता हि राज्ञामप॰] V, वृत्तं हि राज्ञामुप॰ M.

१८.२० रागवृद्धिं॰] V, रागबन्धि॰ M. 18.21] omits M.

१८.२२ ॰यथार्थो नत॰] V, ॰यथार्थोन्रत॰ M. आसीत्सुतः] V, सुतो ऽभवत् M.

१८.२३ वज्रनाभः] V, वज्रणाभः M.

१८.२४ खं सुकृतोपलब्धं] V, द्यां सुकृतोपलब्धां M. खड्डन॰] V, शङ्क्रण॰ M.

१८.२६ ॰समो ऽधिजगमे] V, ॰सहो विजज्ञे M. विश्वसहः] V, विश्वसखः M.

१८.२७ अंशे] M, वंशे V.

१८.२८ वल्कधरो] V, वल्कलवान् M.

१८.२९ कौसल्य] V, कौशल्य M.

१८.३० ब्रह्मभूयां] V, ब्रह्मभूयं M.

१८.३१ विपीडाः] V, विपीडां M. ॰जलोक्षिताक्ष्यः] V, ॰जलाविलाक्ष्यः M.

१८.३२ पुष्परागं] V, पुष्पराग॰ M. यस्मिन्न॰] V, तस्मिन्न॰ M. (The sequence of these verses in M is as follows: 31, 33, 36, 32, 34, 35, 37.)

१८.३३ स्पर्ध्याकृतिः] V, स्पष्टाकृतिः M.

१८.३४ स योग्या॰] V, सयोगा॰ M.

१८.३५ सन्नमतां नृपाणां] V, संनमतामरीणाम् M.

१८.३६ त्रिषु शान्तिमाप] V, त्रिदशत्वमाप M.

१८.३८ आनाथ्य॰] V, अनाथ॰ M.

१८.४१ ॰मतिहस्तयन्तम्] V, ॰मधिहस्ति यान्तम् M. ॰मध्यदेशम्] V, ॰मग्यवेशम् M.

१८.४२ पुनराचितेन] V, पुनरावृतात्मा M.

१८.४४ प्रयुक्त॰] V, प्रतीत॰ M.

१८.४५ कपोललीनो॰] V, कपोललोल॰ M. ऽववाद॰] V, विवाद॰ M.

१८.४७ ॰पुष्पोपमसौकुमार्यो विभूषणेनापि ययौ स खेदम्] V, ॰पुष्पाधिकसौकुमार्यः खेदं स यायादपि भूषणेन M. ॰गुर्वीमथ चानु॰] V, ॰गुर्वीमपि सो ऽनु॰ M. चकार] V, बभूव M.

१८.४८ तावत्फलानि श्रुतवृद्ध्योगात्पक्कान्यु॰] V, सर्वाणि तावच्छ्रुतवृद्ध्योगात्फलान्यु॰ M.

१८.५० पृथ्वी] V, भूमिः M.

१८.५१ लोकान्ताः] M, लोकान्तं V.

१८.५३ ॰जूटो॰] V, ॰चूडो॰ M. व्यरोचतास्त्लेषु] V, व्यरोचतास्त्ले स M.

१८.५४ ॰निर्वेशपेयं] V, ॰निर्वेशनीयं M.

१८.५५ दूत॰] V, दूति॰ M.

<h2 style="text-align:center">एकोनविंशः सर्गः</h2>

१९.२ विस्मृतः] M, विस्मरन् V.

१९.४ ॰मधिपः] V, ॰मभिकः M.

१९.८ ॰लाग्र॰] V, ॰लात्म॰ M.

१९.१० ॰र्घित॰] V, ॰र्पित॰ M.

१९.१२ ॰गन्धिनं] V, ॰कारणं M.

१९.१३ मञ्जु॰] V, वल्गु॰ M.

१९.१५ नृत्त॰] V, नृत्य॰ M. ॰वदनासवं] V, ॰वदनानिलः M. ॰न्वजीव॰] V, ॰त्यजीव॰ M.

१९.१९ लोलमन्य॰] V, लौल्यमेत्य M. ॰ङ्गुलि॰] V, ॰ङ्गुली॰ M.

१९.२० महीपतिम्] V, महीक्षितम् M.

१९.२१ , कृत॰] M, हृत॰ V. ॰व्यथः] V, ॰व्यथाः M. ॰दुनोद्ग्रहण॰] V, ॰दुनोत्प्रणय॰ M.

१९.२४ लोलुभं] V, लोलुपं M.

१९.२५ लुलितं] V, लुलित॰ M.

१९.२६ न तु तथा समाहितम्] V, न च तथा समाहितः M.

१९.२८ नर्म॰] M, नम्र॰ V. ॰संश्रयः] V, ॰संस्थितः M.

१९.३० ॰वेशमतिशक्रशोभितम्] V, ॰वेषमतिशक्रशोभिनम् M.

१९.३२ ॰पविध्य] V, ॰पदिश्य M. ॰कुङ्कुमम्] V, ॰चन्दनम् M.

१९.३३ विनिगूढ॰] V, निशि गूढ॰ M. चार॰] M, चौर॰ V. न नस्तमोवृतं] V, कुतस्तमोवृतः M.

१९.३४ ॰वनाप्लुवन्] V, ॰ववाप्लुवन् M.

१९.३५ व्यलोकयन्] V, व्यलोभयन् M.

१९.३६ नृत्तमवधाय] V, नृत्यमुपधाय M.

१९.३७ अस्यतश्च] V, अंसलम्बि॰ V.

१९.३९ च विमान॰] V, सवितान॰ M. ॰क्रमा॰] V, श्रमा॰ M. ॰मुक्तिविषदां] V, ॰मुक्तविशदां M.

१९.४१ ॰धूम॰] V, ॰धूप॰ M. ॰लोलुभं] V, ॰लोलुपं M.

१९.४२ अर्पितस्तिमितदीपदीप्तयो] *em.*, अर्पितस्तिमितदीपदीप्तयो V, अर्पितस्तिमितदीपदृष्टयो M. प्रेक्ष्यतां] V, साक्षितां M.

१९.४३ वीक्ष्य] V, प्रेक्ष्य M. ॰वकीर्ण॰] V, ॰वधूत॰ M.

१९.४४ काश्चिदङ्गमधिरोप्य दोलयन्प्रेङ्ख्या] V, ताः स्वमङ्गमधिरोप्य दोलया प्रेङ्ख्यन् M.

१९.४५ ॰वेश॰] V, ॰वेष॰ M. ॰लम्ब॰] V, ॰लम्बि॰ M. स्त्रियः] V, प्रियाः M.

१९.४६ ॰मनारतं] V, ॰समागमं M.

१९.४९ चात्यजत्] V, सो ऽत्यजत् M. ॰मनास्पदम्] V, ॰मनाश्रवः M. स्वादुभिः स] V,
     स्वादुभिस्तु M. हि वार्यते] V, निवार्यते M.
१९.५० यक्ष्मणापि] V, राजयक्ष्म॰ M.
१९.५२ गूढ॰] V, बाढ॰ M.
१९.५७ भावाय] V, भावार्थ M. बभौ] V, नभो॰ M.

NOTES TO THE TRANSLATION

1 Reaching Vasishtha's Ashram

1   "Word and meaning" alludes to an old characterization of poetry as compositions in which words and meanings have equal importance and are perfectly matched. Parameshvara (*parameśvara*) means "Supreme Lord." The name is used primarily for Shiva.

2   The "ancient seers" are poets such as Valmiki, the author of the *Rāmāyaṇa*.

3   The moon emerged from the milk ocean when it was churned by the gods and *asuras*, using Mount Mandara as churning stick, to obtain ambrosia.

4   Meru is the mountain at the center of the cosmos, which towers above the celestial luminaries. Meru also means "radiances."

5   "Those who served him" can also refer to those who "serve" the ocean, namely fishermen, and so forth. The ocean is thought to be full of treasures.

6   Ethically non-neutral actions leave karmic traces in the soul. These can, at best, be inferred by seeing their fruits when they arise.

7   People often turn to religion only when at death's door.

8   The three aims of man are *dharma* (religious duty), *artha* (prosperity and good policy), and *kāma* (pleasure), with *mokṣa* (liberation) sometimes added as fourth. The king's inflicting punishment belongs to *artha* and his marrying to *kāma*, but since in both he was motivated by a sense of duty, even these became subsumed within *dharma*.

9   The "milking" of the earth is Dilipa's collecting of substances to offer to the gods, thus sustaining heaven; the "milking" of heaven is Indra pouring down rain, which sustains the earth.

10   The elements of earth, water, fire, air, and space have qualities (*guṇa*) from which only others, living beings, benefit. The same word *guṇa* is here used in the sense of Dilipa's virtues. Others benefited from those virtues, so that Dilipa resembles, by a pun, the elements.

11   The name expresses her *dākṣiṇya*, "dexterity," which derives from a word meaning "right" as opposed to "left." *Dakṣiṇā* means the

12 gift that sacrificers give to officiants of sacrifices, and thus the personified Sacrifice has as his wife the personified Dakshina.

12 The king enjoys marriage with the Earth and with Royal Glory.

13 "Which alone was capable of purifying his ancestors" qualifies both the river Ganga and "progeny."

14 The peacocks mistake the sound of chariot wheels for the thunder of monsoon clouds, which sets them dancing.

15 This coincides with the beginning of spring.

16 Budha, the planet Mercury, is the son of the moon, from whom many kings traced their ancestry. The expression translated "who resembled Budha" could also mean "god-like."

17 The sacred fires invisibly go out to welcome those who maintain them whenever they return.

18 The "treasure store" here is Vasishtha, whose wife, Arundhati, is the ideal of a devoted wife, inseparable from her husband, just as Svaha is from her husband, Fire. Svaha is the personification of *svāhā*, an exclamation uttered when oblations are offered into fire.

19 The *Atharva Veda* is the fourth Veda, associated with magical spells. The king's chaplain is often a specialist in the *Atharva Veda*.

20 The seven components of the state are: the king, the ministers, the allies, the treasury, the army, the territory, and the fortresses.

21 The mantras of the Veda are usually held to be eternal. But this may not have been Kalidasa's view; or the mantras here may be non-Vedic.

22 Dilipa regards Vasishtha as his "father," and therefore speaks of his wife as Vasishtha's daughter-in-law.

23 Dilipa's deceased ancestors fear that, if he has no progeny, no one will pour libations to quench their thirst.

24 The Lokaloka is a mountain ridge encircling all oceans and continents, beyond which the sun's rays do not reach.

25 A man has three debts: a debt to the sages, absolved by Vedic study; a debt to the gods, absolved by sacrifice; and a debt to his ancestors, absolved by begetting sons.

26 A man is obliged to have intercourse with his wife after her period.

27 At the extreme point of each cardinal and intermediate direction, an elephant presides.

28 The sage could have prepared luxurious arrangements using his powers, but the king's "observance" required austere forest life.

2 Nandini Bestows a Boon

1   In verse 57 it becomes clear that the king indeed treasures his fame, more than his life.

2   There are usually two levels of scriptural revelation: *śruti,* "that which is heard," which refers to Vedic revelation; and *smṛti,* "that which is remembered," which refers to what sages recall from now lost parts of the Vedic revelation.

3   The idea that glory (*yaśaḥ*) has scent is an old poetic convention.

4   Most elephant bulls in musth produce musth juice that runs from their temples.

5   Dilipa's lordly air and readiness to chastise any evildoer leads the trees to think of him as their tutelary deity, Varuna.

6   The equivalent of confetti.

7   Our world is above underworlds and hells and below heavens (for the triple universe, see 3.6 and n.).

8   Shiva is referred to as the "lord of spirits," because departed spirits inhabit the cremation ground, where Shiva famously dances.

9   The principal emblem of sovereignty is the white parasol. To have a single white parasol means to be a king without rivals.

10 The gods do not blink or sweat, and their feet do not quite touch the ground.

11 *Kṣattra* is a synonym of *kṣatriya,* warrior.

12 Rather than a mere tithe, a tenth of produce, an Indian king, according to Manu, should take a sixth part as tax.

13 Fame or honor (*yaśaḥ*), like laughter, is conceived of as white; the conceit is that his fame had become liquid as milk. To "drink fame" is to "enjoy fame." He was already famous; now appears to be "drinking fame" again in the form of milk. Related conceits occur, for example, in 4.19, 4.44, and 4.53.

14 "By the chariot of his own wish" renders *manorathena,* literally "mind chariot," but that expression has come to mean "desire" or "wish." The king's wish for a son, now fulfilled, could also be qualified as "pleasant to hear" and "happy without hindrance."

15 The expression translated with "his body had grown lean from his observance for attaining offspring" also punningly describes the moon, "whose body is lean from his [monthly] observance [of giving his nectar to the gods] for the sake of [all] creatures."

16 The moon was born from the eye of Atri, one of the mind-born sons of Brahma. The "celestial river" refers to the Ganga, which

flows also in the heavens. According to one of several ancient myths about the birth of the war god Kumara, Shiva and Parvati were interrupted by Agni while making love. Shiva's semen was spilled and received by Agni, who deposited it in the Ganga. A man born to be king partly embodies the gods who guard the directions: Indra (east), Agni (southeast), Yama (south), Nirriti (southwest), Varuna (west), Vayu (northwest), Kubera or Soma (north), and Shiva (northeast).

3 Raghu's Birth and Duel with Indra

1   Moonlight is cooling and pleasing, the autumn moonlight particularly so. The signs of her pregnancy were like the dawning of the autumn moon to her friends.

2   As the next verse explains, Sudakshina had a pregnancy craving for clay/earth, portending that her son will be an "enjoyer of the earth," a common kenning for a king in Sanskrit.

3   In this interpretation the first line records the thought of Sudakshina. But the whole stanza could be read as a statement of the king's thought after smelling the earth in his wife's mouth. Other commentators read "his son" and take the whole verse to be the words of the poet.

4   The cosmos is described as having different numbers of worlds, but most commonly there are thought to be seven (see 10.23 and n.) or three. The three are heaven, our own world, and the nether regions.

5   Not only the color but also the shape of the mahua flowers is suggested, since they resemble breasts. This verse, with its pair of somewhat discordant similes, did not survive into the commonly accepted version of the text. The stanza that has replaced it means, "As the days went by, her dark-tipped breasts became extremely fleshy and eclipsed the beauty of a pair of lotus buds with bees resting upon them."

6   When the pregnancy begins to show, a life-cycle rite called *pumsavana* is performed to ensure that the child is male.

7   Parts of each of the divinities who protect the directions are held to become incarnate in a king; see 2.75 and n.

8   Perhaps there is only one group of medical personnel in the chamber, all skilled, trusted, and specialized in birth and child care. This verse has been transmitted with considerable variation.

504

9   Much has been written about the planetary configuration, which
    we pass over here. Three aspects of a king's power bring wealth to
    a kingdom (*Arthaśāstra* 6.2.33): physical resources (*prabhuśakti*),
    good counsel (*mantraśakti*), and the king's determination (*utsāha-
    śakti*). Since *śakti* is grammatically feminine, these powers can be
    seen as three spouses of the king (9.17).
10 The white parasol and the two yak-tail fly-whisks are emblems of
    kingship. For the parasol, see 2.47 and n.
11 A man is freed from "debt" to his forefathers by producing male
    progeny who will continue the lineage and ensure that offerings
    are made to them even after he passes.
12 The root *raṅgh/ragh,* from which Raghu's name can be derived,
    means "to go, to reach."
13 The moon is emptied of nectar in the darkening fortnight, then
    refilled through a solar ray called *suṣumnā.*
14 Shelducks (*cakravāka*) are said to mate for life and to be inseparable
    (see also 8.57 and 9.25).
15 According to this interpretation of the simile (others are possible),
    Brahma manifests as Vishnu, who maintains the universe. Among
    the three "qualities" or "strands" that pervade the universe,
    namely purity (*sattva*), energy (*rajas*), and ignorance (*tamas*), the
    best of them, *sattva*, predominates in Vishnu. These strands recur
    in 8.22, 10.19, and 10.40.
16 An archaic list of the four realms of knowledge names them as
    philosophy (*ānvīkṣikī*), the Vedas (*trayī*), trade and agriculture
    (*vārttā*), and statecraft (*daṇḍanīti*).
17 On the completion of his studies, the celibate graduate gives a cow
    to his teacher, after which he may marry. Some stars are personified
    as the daughters of Daksha and wives of the moon.
18 The Young King (*yuvarāja*) not only is the heir to a kingdom in an
    ideal Indian state but also shares his father's duties of governance
    and, as we shall see in the next chapter, warfare.
19 The lotus blooms by day and closes at night, ceding to the night-
    blooming water lily. *Śrī* (beauty) thus moves from one to the other
    at dusk and back again at dawn. But *śrī* is also royal splendor or
    "majesty."
20 The temple glands of an elephant in musth (and also in the
    excitement of battle, according to ch. 2 of Trautmann 2015) split
    and pour forth musth fluid.

21 One of Indra's names, Shatakratu, may mean "of a hundred sacrifices." Indra claimed exclusive right to this title. The horse sacrifice (*aśvamedha*) is a prestigious rite that kings boast of performing. Before being sacrificed, the horse roams freely for a year, its right to do so assured by the military might of the sacrificing king, who asserts dominion over all the territory traversed by the horse.

22 According to commentators, the liquid may be urine or milk. But it is sweat in a variant version. Most cattle do not have sweat glands in their skin, but Indian cows (zebu) do.

23 Before Indra cut them off, mountains had wings. Indra is the god who guards the east.

24 Hari here refers to Indra, who once assumed the form of the sage Gautama in order to seduce the sage's wife, Ahalya. Gautama cursed him and turned Ahalya to stone (see 11.34). Indra was covered in a thousand marks of the female genital organ, which turned into eyes. The eyes of gods never blink.

25 Maheshvara literally means simply "Great Lord," but by convention refers only to Shiva.

26 The sixty thousand sons of Sagara, an ancestor of Raghu, dug down into a subterranean paradise to recover a sacrificial horse, whereupon the sage Kapila, being disturbed, incinerated them with the fire of his rage.

27 This alludes to the culminating moment of the story of Shiva destroying the three flying cities of three overweening demons with an arrow.

28 The bow of Indra, god of storms, is the rainbow.

29 Men typically decorated the faces of their loved ones with vegetal motifs using dyes such as gamboge.

30 Shakra is another name for Indra, who is associated with the peacock, perhaps because of his thousand eyes (see 3.43). Fortune (*śrī*), here the Fortune of the gods, is imagined as a lady (compare 3.36 and n.). Raghu here humbles Indra, and so treats her roughly by cutting off her hair.

31 For the churning of the milk ocean, see 1.12 and n.

32 The weapon with which Indra severed the mountains' wings (see 3.42) was the thunderbolt.

33 One of Shiva's eight forms, called Ugra, is held to enter a man engaged in a Vedic sacrifice. See 5.4.

4 Raghu Conquers the Four Directions

1   Following the consecration, the new king circumambulates the town riding an elephant. The banner of Indra was decorated and raised as part of a spring festival, like a maypole. According to some, however, it refers to a royal festival performed to bring the rains.

2   The white lotus of the goddess of wealth, success, and beauty is fancied here to be the white parasol of sovereignty.

3   This translation captures something of the wordplay by being somewhat free. What is actually suggested is that the word meaning "king" (*rājā*) derives from a verbal root meaning "to please" (*rañj*) and the names for moon and sun from the roots *cand* and *tap*.

4   By preferring what is good, he showed himself suited to rule. The wording playfully alludes to the structure of philosophical debate, where one begins with a preliminary view (*pūrvapakṣa*) that is then countered while arguing in favor of the final conclusion. Here, however, Raghu sticks with the first "view."

5   Each of the five elements—earth, water, fire, air, and ether—possesses one distinctive quality, respectively smell, taste, color, touch, and sound.

6   Autumn is the season of military campaigns because roads become dry and passable after the monsoon. Autumn's lotuses recall the lotuses that fortune, when represented as a goddess, holds in each hand.

7   Indra's bow is the rainbow (compare 3.53). The kenning used for Indra (*śatamanyu*) can mean "of a hundred rages" or "of a hundred sins."

8   For the white parasol as a symbol of kingship, see 2.47 and n.

9   For the conventional whiteness of fame, compare 2.69.

10 The sage born from a pot is Agastya, who is identified with Canopus, which in Kalidasa's time in northern India rose in August, at the end of the monsoon.

11 This may be the blackboard tree or the Indian horse chestnut. The seven musth-emitting outlets are the two temporal lobes, the eyes, the nostrils of the trunk, and the penis.

12 "Those at his heels" translates *pārṣni* (literally "heel"), a shortening of the term *pārṣnigraha* ("one who grasps the heel"), which refers to a king governing the region to the rear when the hero sets off on a military campaign. An army consists of six parts: fighters who

are inherited, furnished by guilds, mercenaries, furnished by allies, vanquished enemies, and forest dwellers.

13   Prachinabarhis, "East-Turning Grass," was a king and sage (*rājarṣi*) so called because he covered the ground with east-pointing kusa grass, according to *Viṣṇu Purāṇa* 1.14.4. Several commentators, perhaps stumped by this reference, interpret the name instead as a kenning for Indra, guardian of the east, or for Agni.

14   The army is also literally composed of four divisions: foot soldiers, cavalry, elephant brigade, chariots. The word *pratāpa* can mean "heat" or "valor," but Vallabhadeva often glosses it to mean "news that causes fear in the enemy." For Mallinatha, the four parts are his fieriness, the din, the dust, and "chariots and so forth." But the word for "dust" (*parāga*) could be a corruption of *puroga* ("vanguard"), and we find no other early occurrence of *parāga* in the sense of dust.

15   This suggests the activities of the sappers of the army, since such proceedings are prescribed in 10.2.16 of the most famous ancient work of statecraft, the *Arthaśāstra* (Olivelle 2013).

16   Bhagiratha had done penance to bring Ganga down to earth to save Sagara's sons. The river's fall was softened when it passed through Shiva's hair: see 1.34 and 3.50 and n. The Ganga too heads toward the eastern sea.

17   The Suhmas formed an ancient polity in the Ganges Delta, whose port city was Tamralipta/Damalipta.

18   Raghu is now in the river delta, hence "the streams of the Ganga."

19   The name of this river, presumably in modern-day Odisha, is uncertain. We have chosen the form given in most printed commentaries. Utkala is the country to the north of Kalinga. Both Utkala and Kalinga are sometimes used as names for the modern Indian state of Odisha, on the Bay of Bengal.

20   As in 4.30, the word is *pratāpa*, "news that causes fear in the enemy," according to Vallabhadeva, which in context suggests perhaps a written message on a flag whose staff is jabbed into the earth.

21   For Indra severing the wings of the mountains, see 3.42 and 3.60.

22   Kakutstha was the grandson of Ikshvaku (after whom the solar dynasty of Raghu is sometimes named) and so one of Raghu's forebears.

23   Garuda, the eagle-like mount of Vishnu, is the sworn enemy of

serpents. As often elsewhere (3.31, 5.57, 11.20, 12.23, 12.99), the hero chooses a weapon empowered with a particular mantra, in this case a mantra invoking Vayu, the god of wind.

24 The whiteness of coconut toddy (or juice, which might be intended instead) fits well with the notion of fame (or "honor") being white (cf. 2.69). We suppose that the betel leaves, a precious commodity, were strewn upon the ground to lie upon while drinking, thus emphasizing the abundance of material wealth in the region conquered. (Compare the tethering of the elephants to precious trees, e.g., in 4.51, 4.72, and 4.78, or the horses shaking saffron from their shoulders in 4.70.) This interpretation best fits the word order, but perhaps Kalidasa meant that they used the betel leaves to drink from.

25 "Righteous conqueror" translates *dharmavijayin,* one who conquers others in accordance with Dharma, "morality." He is contrasted in ancient literature on statecraft (*Arthaśāstra* 12.1) with the *lobhavijayin,* "who conquers out of greed," and the *asuravijayin,* "who conquers like an *asura,*" who is callously murderous.

26 For the myth of the sage Agastya (identified with Canopus) moving permanently to the south, see the Glossary. Agastya appears again in 6.61.

27 The Kaveri River rises in the Western Ghats, passes through Tiruchirappalli, and empties into the Bay of Bengal through a broad fertile delta.

28 Vallabhadeva takes *tripadī* as a "three-footed stance," a constantly shifting posture in which the elephant takes his weight off one leg at a time. Others understand it to be a fetter.

29 After the summer solstice, the sun's course moves southward, and by winter its strength is diminished. The Pandyas are the ruling dynasty of the southernmost part of the subcontinent.

30 Sandal trees on the slopes correspond to the sandal paste smeared on women's breasts. The Sahya range being left behind by the ocean, like hips from which a garment has slipped, evokes the myth alluded to in verses 56 and 60. All three names refer to parts of the Western Ghats: Malaya to the southernmost part; Durdura (or Dardura) to the Nilgiri hills south of Mysore; Sahya to the northernmost part.

31 This coastal plant, pandanus, has fragrant pollen and was traded for its many uses.

32 Some commentators understand the contrast to be that the ocean was forced to give tribute to Raghu, or only gave it out of fear. The offerings of the king of Aparanta were riches from the ocean, such as pearls.

33 Kings erected victory columns (compare 4.37), often inscribed with royal eulogies. The poetic fancy is that Raghu's elephant bulls exuberantly butted the mountain, leaving inscription-like tusk marks, thus making the mountain itself a victory column.

34 Some commentators suggest that the land route is easy, and hence the comparison; others say that the sea route would actually be easier, but crossing the sea is forbidden to the twice-born, including Raghu.

35 Raghu killed these women's husbands, so they gave up their enjoyment of wine and mourned. The word *yavana* can mean Greek (Ionian). Kalidasa may be referring to people in the northwest, somewhere in the wake of Alexander's passage, but he could have used the term as a synonym for *pārasīka,* "Persian," as is common in later usage.

36 The sun moves north before the heat of the summer, which dries the earth, and south at the end of the summer, for the southwest monsoon.

37 Aurva (or Urva) was a sage whose anger became fire. He buried it in the ocean, where it took the form of the head of a mare and remains, burning the ocean's waters as fuel until the end of this cycle of creation. Compare 9.87.

38 In most editions it is the Indus rather than the Vankshu (Oxus) that appears here.

39 This reflects a practice of mourning attributed to the Huns in non-Indian sources (Ingalls 1976: 21).

40 The army stirs up mineral dust because mountains are proverbially rich in colorful mineral ores; compare 2.29.

41 *Rudrākṣa* seeds are used for making rosaries. The deer in question must be musk deer.

42 Certain mountain herbs are reputed to glow at night; compare 8.56, 9.75 and 10.68.

43 The Utsavasanketas live in the Himalaya (perhaps Ladakh), and Raghu recognizes the mountain's riches from their tribute; the mountain, scaled by Raghu, recognizes his power.

44 Mount Kailasa is the seat of Shiva and was shamed by being lifted

up by Ravana and shaken while Shiva and Parvati were sitting on it. Himalaya is Kailasa's rival. By placing on top of Himalaya a white mass of his fame, Raghu caused it to further excel and thereby bring further shame on Kailasa. Other interpretations of the verse have been proposed.

45   It is a sign of greatness if these auspicious symbols are discerned within the lines on the feet of a male.

5 Raghu Sends Aja to Bhoja's Court as a Suitor

1   "Asceticism," *tapas,* refers to the stored power accumulated by ascetic practice.

2   Shiva takes eight entities as "bodies" of his that sustain the universe, namely (1) earth, (2) water, (3) fire, (4) air, (5) ether, (6) sun, (7) moon, and (8) the sacrifice or the sacrificer. In this eighth form, Shiva's name is Ugra, hence the allusion here to Ugra entering the sacrificer (see also 9.19).

3   Indra fears that every sage who accumulates ascetic power may be wishing to usurp his place as king of the gods.

4   After living as a celibate student, he is to enter the phase of life of a married householder, which is "of use to everyone" in that it produces the economic surplus on which celibate students, forest dwellers, and renunciants depend.

5   The reading printed in most editions may be the result of a secondary change to make explicit that Raghu is not content just with the honor of this visit, since he longs to fulfill some command of his guest.

6   The moon is filled with nectar from the sun in the brightening fortnight, which the gods drink in the darkening fortnight. See 3.22 and n.

7   The *cātaka* bird is supposed to live on raindrops.

8   The social classes are Brahman, Kshatriya (warrior/king), Vaishya (merchant/tradesman), and Shudra (servant). The four stages of life, mentioned in 5.10 n., are those of celibate student (*brahmacārin*); married householder (*gṛhastha*); forest hermit (*vānaprastha*), who may be accompanied by his wife; and renunciant (*saṃnyāsin*).

9   A conventional number for the sciences is fourteen: the four Vedas, the six auxiliaries to the Veda (the disciplines of phonetics, ritual, grammar, etymology, metrics, and astronomy), and then legends

(*Purāṇa*), epistemology (*Nyāya*), hermeneutics (*Mīmāṃsā*), and religious law (*Dharmaśāstra*).

10 The moon is "king of the twice-born" because Brahma is said to have appointed him king of stars, planets, Brahmans, and plants.

11 There are three sacred fires in a Vedic fire enclosure; the purity and brightness of Varatantu's disciple make him like a fourth Vedic fire.

12 The abode of Kubera, the guardian deity of the northern direction and the god of wealth, is on Mount Kailasa, which could be said to be neighboring Raghu's empire. Fasting and sleeping in the weapon-laden chariot is prescribed on the night before battle in *Arthaśāstra* 10.3.34.

13 Sumeru is the golden mountain at the center of the cosmos, around which the sun revolves.

14 Brahma's hour refers to the last watch of the night, in which dawn occurs. Aja means "unborn."

15 Mount Rikshavat is often identified with the eastern spur of the Vindhya range, which runs along the northern side of the Narmada River.

16 For the "seven-leaf trees" and their pungent smell, see 4.23 and n.

17 The value of forest elephants for the king was immense. It was not economically viable to feed and rear them in captivity. Wild elephants were therefore captured when mature and trained for their roles in war and ceremony (see Trautmann 2015).

18 Matanga is a sage whose name means "moving at will," an epithet often applied to elephants.

19 The transfer of property is solemnized by touching water. There is uncertainty about why Narmada is "moon-born," but several lexicographical works mention the view that the legendary king Pururavas, born of the lunar dynasty, brought the river to earth.

20 Kama, as god of love, is imagined to be physically perfect, but paradoxically, also bodiless, since Shiva in fury burned his physical frame. The disembodied Kama must reside elsewhere, for instance in people's thoughts or, as here, in youthful people. The golden jar is a common auspicious decoration.

21 The sun, as it sets, passes light to the fire (cf. 4.1), so "dusk-waking" is a Vedic kenning for fire.

22 The young crown prince (*yuvarāja*) shares the burden of kingship with his father the king. The son is responsible for conducting

military campaigns. We are to understand dawn and the sun to have the same relationship.

23 The best horses were said to be those bred in the country Vanayu in the northwest.

24 The servant girls are massaging his feet. Mallinatha has a more puritan version of this verse in which there are no servant girls. Supratika is the celestial elephant who guards the northeast.

6 *Indumati Chooses a Husband*

1 When Kama fired an arrow to cause Shiva to fall in love with Parvati, Shiva burnt Kama, who is therefore bodiless or, according to Kalidasa's *Kumarasambhava* (4.42 in Smith 2005b), restored by Shiva upon his marriage to Parvati at Rati's entreaty.

2 We translate *pravataśobha iva* ("like the trembling of trees in the wind") instead of *pravalaśobha iva* ("resembling the beauty of young sprouts"), which is the variant read by later commentators. This second variant does not as clearly parallel the displacement gestures described in the following verses.

3 A flagstaff is an auspicious mark in Indian palmistry.

4 Sunanda, who appears only in this chapter, is the keeper of the door to the inner apartments, but she is also called "servant" (53), "friend" (82), and Indumati's nurse (83).

5 Indra, as king of the gods, is summoned to each sacrifice to receive offerings; his wife, Shachi, is therefore left sadly alone and dresses accordingly, without ornament and without dressing her hair with flowers of the celestial *mandara* tree.

6 Flower City (Pushpapura), then the capital of Magadha, is today Patna in Bihar. At her wedding, she would process into the city with her husband and be observed by all the ladies from their windows. Such a scene is described at the beginning of ch. 7.

7 This reading reflects ancient elephant lore, according to which all elephants descend from a celestial herd caught, with Indra's help, by the king of Anga. The current king of Anga is similar to Indra because heavenly nymphs desire him and sages serve him. Vallabhadeva, whose reading differs in only one letter, must understand "the sages who laid down the rules assigned him his sacrificial share" instead of "his elephants were trained by the authors of the treatises thereon."

8 In mourning, the wives remove their jewelry.

9   Shri is the goddess of wealth and beauty, and Sarasvati is the goddess of language and learning.

10 Samjna, the wife of the sun, could not bear his dazzling brightness, so Vishvakarman, the divine craftsman, trimmed him on a lathe.

11 For the three powers of a king, see 3.13 and n. The vassal kings are perhaps either marching with him or standing about in his wake as he sets off to attack kings who are not yet vassals. Perhaps dust falls on them because they are without their parasols, precisely because they are vassals. The commentator Narayanapandita suggests that they lack parasols, but he assumes that they are the enemies against whom the king of Avanti marches. Uppity minor kings who fail to acknowledge the king of Avanti's sovereignty may indeed be the enemies he is about to attack. But in that case, would they already be without parasols?

12 Mahakala is the name of Shiva in his temple in Ujjayini (modern Ujjain), through which the river Sipra passes.

13 The sun-loving lotus blooms when the sun appears, whereas the water lily, shunning sunlight, blooms when the moon rises (compare 6.44 and 86).

14 Anupa is the name of the district around the city of Mahishmati in today's Madhya Pradesh, sometimes identified with southern Avanti.

15 Since fortunes shift from one king to another, Shri, or Royal Fortune, is fickle. Her faithfulness to this king, however, shows that her fickleness must be the fault of other kings.

16 The Reva River is the Narmada, and Mahishmati is the capital of Anupa.

17 For this convention, see 6.36 and n.

18 Shurasena is the country around Mathura (now in the modern state of Uttar Pradesh), which was its capital.

19 Some kingly virtues, such as martial valor and forbearance, are inimical to each other.

20 The grass takes root on the terraces of his enemies' mansions because they are abandoned, no longer washed white with lime so as to shine bright when bathed in moonlight.

21 The waters of the Kalindi or Yamuna (today's Jumna) are dark, whereas those of the Ganga are light. The two rivers actually meet in Allahabad (Prayag), not Mathura, but the copious pale sandal washing from their breasts makes it seem as though the rivers

had blended in Mathura. Oddly, Mathura is said to be founded by Shatrughna generations later, in 15.28.

22 Before Krishna came to drive him out, the serpent demon Kaliya took refuge from Garuda in the Yamuna. Cobras are said to bear jewels upon their hoods. Kaustubha is the name of a jewel that Vishnu (and his incarnation Krishna) wears on his chest.

23 Vrindavana, near Mathura, is the name of a garden in which Krishna will pass his youth.

24 The name of a mountain near Vrindavana, famously lifted up by Krishna to protect the cowherds and their families from a storm unleashed by Indra.

25 The name Hemangada means "with golden upper armbands."

26 The elephants are like mountains, both because they are massive and because their streams of musth fluid resemble mountain cataracts.

27 Nagapura literally means "city of serpents." The identification is problematic. It might be Uraiyur, a suburb of Tiruchirappalli said to have been the capital of the Cholas; or Madurai, capital of the Pandyas; or somewhere else. In order to resonate with the place name, Indumati is described as being like a *nāginī*, a beautiful denizen of a netherworld paradise capable of taking serpentine or human form. Saying that she has the eyes of a partridge could mean that her eyes are beautiful, but it suggests the convention that the partridge's eyes turn red when they detect poison.

28 This verse glorifies the Pandya king first by implying that he regularly performs the prestigious Vedic horse sacrifice and second by revealing that the fabled sage Agastya is one of his officiants, taking the role of the Brahman who asks formally whether the final ablutions have been satisfactory.

29 The lord of Lanka is the ten-headed Ravana, the demon king who will abduct Rama's wife, Sita, in ch. 12. Janasthana, in the middle of the Dandaka forest, was a demon stronghold.

30 In Sanskrit, words for "blue" also mean "black." Extremely dark skin may thus be compared both to a blue water lily and to rain clouds.

31 Some commentators interpret the rare word translated as "mansions" to refer instead to "watchtowers."

32 Involuntary twitching of muscles on the right side of a man's body portends success.

33 "Standing on a Hump," so called because in a battle he stood on the back of Indra, who had changed himself into a bull; see v. 72.

34 Shiva too, when he fought the demons of the three flying cities, rode upon Indra in the form of a bull. When Kakutstha slew the *asuras,* their women ceased, in mourning, to apply make-up to their faces.

35 See ch. 3, vv. 38–69.

36 In the reading known to Mallinatha, the women are intoxicated. Vallabhadeva assumes they are women who venture out at night for trysts with lovers (*abhisārikā*).

37 See the end of ch. 4 and the beginning of ch. 5.

38 "Whose thighs were as smoothly tapered as the back of the hand," *karabhoru,* with most commentators. (Alternatively, "whose thighs were like the trunk of an elephant.") "Powders" refers to ground turmeric and the like. The doorkeeper Sunanda must have been Indumati's nurse when she was a child.

7 A Wedding and an Ambush

1 Devasena, the name of Skanda's bride, means "Army of the Gods"; she can indeed be regarded as a personification of that army, which Skanda leads.

2 Medieval commentators allude to a tradition in which Shachi, wife of Indra, is present at weddings and quells trouble.

3 This and several following verses are paralleled in Kalidasa's account of the wedding of Shiva and Parvati in *Kumārasambhava* 7 in Smith 2005b. The question of priority remains open.

4 The girl has tied the girdle thread to her big toe to thread beads and jewels through it before tying it around her waist.

5 When Lakshmi emerged from the ocean after it had been churned, she chose Vishnu as her husband by putting a garland on his shoulder.

6 Love manifests equally in both. Some commentators believe that the symptoms typical of men and women have been deliberately interchanged by Kalidasa to emphasize the pervasion of mutual love.

7 The partridge (*cakora*) is identified as *Perdix rufa,* whose eyes appear red. It is not clear to us whether the bird is "passionate" (*matta*) by nature or only in the mating season. Cf. 6.59 and n.

8 This refers to Raghu's victory over all surrounding kings in ch. 4.

9   There are three possible identifications of Indra's enemy:
     Prahlada, Namuchi (also known as Vritra), and Rahu. The *asura*
     Prahlada caught at Vishnu's foot as he was covering the universe
     with three strides. Vritra is the archetypical "enemy of Indra." Rahu
     is the demon who swallows the moon's nectar, causing eclipses.
     Conceived of as a bodiless head, Rahu is shown blocking Vishnu's
     rising foot in ancient sculptures in Mathura and in Badami. The
     Badami sculptures also show another figure clutching the foot that
     is on the ground; this could be Vritra or Namuchi.

10   The Shona River in central India is the second largest of the
     tributaries of the Ganga (after the Yamuna). It is full in the rains,
     but, being wide and shallow, it leaves disconnected pools of water
     during other parts of the year. The Jyotiratha River is unidentified.

11   In other sources too, archers write their names on their arrows.
     Compare *Vikramorvaśīya* 5.7 in Narayana Rao and Shulman 2009.

12   This is the interpretation of Mallinatha; Vallabhadeva understands
     the final phrase to mean that the dust first clouded the eyes, then
     blocked the sun like a cloud. This could mean that it first rose to
     eye level and only blocked out the sun when it rose above that.

13   For war quoits, see Victoria and Albert Museum No. 3462:1 to 8/
     (IS).

14   Celestial ladies (*apsaras*) fly above battles to select dying warriors
     as husbands by casting garlands upon them. At the moment of
     death, a warrior finds himself flying in a celestial palace beside
     the *apsaras* who chose him. Battlefields are often thronged with
     dancing headless corpses (*kabandha*).

15   The Great Boar is the incarnation of Vishnu that raises up and
     rescues the earth from the ocean. There are different accounts of
     when, why, and how this happens, but Kalidasa places the event at
     the end of an age (also in *Kumārasambhava* 6.8 in Smith 2005b).

16   As usual, we follow here the text known to Vallabhadeva. The text
     is faulty in other editions, for most later commentators grappled
     with a corrupt text that was missing the negation in "He could not
     be seen" (see Goodall 2001: 123).

17   The printed commentaries transmit two "improved" readings of
     the second line, which may be translated: "just as the dawn, veiled
     in mist, is revealed by the wanly glowing sun" and "just as the sun
     is discerned by its faint light when the dawn is covered with fog."

18   Kissing is conceived of as drinking the juice of one's beloved's lower

517

lip. Some commentators distort this element of the verse because they are worried about the impropriety of Aja kissing Indumati so soon after the wedding! Glory is white (see 2.69); for the trope of it thickening into something drinkable, see 4.44.

19   We translate *cīram ādātum aicchat* "was eager to put on bast garments" instead of *śāntimārgotsuko 'bhūt* ("became eager to join the path to peace"), which most commentators support. The first reading has Raghu becoming a forest dweller, whereas the second could refer to his becoming a full renunciate: see 8.11 and n. The bast garments imply becoming a forest dweller (*vānaprastha*), not a full renunciant who has internalized the Vedic fires (*sannyāsin*). Elsewhere the Raghus retire from public life to become forest dwellers (e.g., 3.70), or can become full renunciants (see 8.11). See notes on 8.11 and 8.26.

8   Aja's Lament

1   For this celebrated chapter Kalidasa has mainly used the same meter—one with an extra syllable in the second and fourth quarters, giving the effect of a limp or sob—used for his other great lament, that of Rati in the *Kumārasambhava* (Smith 2005b). The meter may be called *viyoginī*, "woman separated from her beloved," a name likely to postdate Kalidasa.

2   Steam rises from the earth, like sighs of contentment, after water has been poured over Aja to consecrate him.

3   The *AtharvaVeda* is famous for its spells, and the king's chaplain was typically an expert in that corpus (see 1.58). *Brahman* is a power of language associated with Brahmans.

4   Mallinatha's Vedantic variant could be translated: "When Raghu saw that his son was well established among his subjects, he became indifferent even toward heavenly enjoyments, which are perishable, because he knew the Self."

5   Some authorities held that kings were not eligible to be full ascetics (*saṃnyāsins*) and could only become forest-dwelling hermits (*vānaprastha*). There is accordingly a variant that removes the optionality; its second line means: "being restrained, they took the path of ascetics clothed in bark." Compare 7.71 and n., 8.14, and 8.26 and n.

6   Most commentators know a different version of this verse (see Goodall 2009: 72): "Aja conferred with his ministers, who were

skilled in politics, to attain what he had not yet conquered. Raghu joined trustworthy yogis to reach the never-waning state."

7   Yogic traditions speak of five principal life breaths: *prāṇa, apāna, vyāna, udāna, samāna.* "Royal might" translates *prabhuśakti,* one of three powers of the king; see note on 3.13.

8   This verse is omitted in most editions. "Hostile and friendly powers around him" translates *maṇḍala,* which refers to the twelve concentric rings of hostile and friendly kingdoms that surround a king (see *Arthaśāstra,* book 6).

9   Kalidasa may have had in mind *Bhagavadgītā* 4.37: "As firewood a kindled fire / Reduces to ashes, Arjuna, / The fire of knowledge all actions / Reduces to ashes even so" (translation in Edgerton 1952: 51).

10   The six "strands (*guṇa*) of statecraft" are friendship, war, marching, halting, seeking alliances, and sowing dissension (*sandhi, vigraha, yāna, sthāna, saṃśraya, dvaidha*). The three "strands (*guṇa*) of existence" are *sattva* (white, "purity"), *rajas* (red, "energy" or "activity"), and *tamas* (black, "darkness" or "inertia"). Raghu contemplates the latter in their still-undifferentiated state, before primal matter evolves into the material universe and the human soul becomes deluded about its distinctness from matter.

11   The mention of the old king being steadfast in thought (*sthitadhīḥ*) perhaps alludes again to the *Bhagavadgītā* (2.54 and 3.56).

12   Raghu's funeral is his hundredth sacrifice, and so, alone among mortals, he attains at his death the status of Indra, god of one hundred sacrifices. In the commonly printed version of this verse, this poignant boast is removed, probably on the grounds that Raghu had become an ascetic after retirement, and an ascetic's last rites must be performed without fire.

13   Narada is famous as a musician and messenger between gods and humans. His interventions often involuntarily cause trouble.

14   Bees are conventionally black as kohl. Cf. 9.47.

15   A freshly lit lamp will be brimming with oil and the wick, being new, will be at its longest. Some part of the wick, along with a flaming drop of oil, is therefore liable to spill from the lamp. This translation reflects the reading known to the earliest commentary. For further discussion of the variant versions of 8.38 and 8.39, see Goodall 2009: 70–71; 67–68.

16   Taking her onto his lap can mean that he embraces her. The

"natural place" is interpreted by Vallabhadeva to mean the left part of his lap, and indeed wives, in sculpture, are often shown sitting on their husband's left thigh. For a discussion of the variant version of this verse, see Goodall 2009: 71.

17   Commentators other than Vallabhadeva instead have a reading in which Indumati is referred to in the third person.

18   For this surprising and ambiguous vocative, compare 6.83.

19   Certain mountain herbs are reputed to glow at night: cf. 4.78, 9.75, and 10.68.

20   "Mourning," *śocyase*, is etymologically related to *aśoka* (literally "griefless"). Some versions have an extra verse before this on the topos of young ladies causing the *aśoka* to blossom by kicking it: "Only because you satisfied its craving is this *aśoka* tree about to blossom: how can I use these flowers, which should decorate your hair, as a funeral wreath?" We suspect that this version was composed later to replace 8.63 or added as a riff on the same theme.

21   *Kinnarī* is the feminine form of *kinnara* (see the Glossary).

22   This alludes to postfunerary libations made for the dead. Cf. 1.65 and 8.86.

23   Mallinatha understands that the garland that killed her is the ornament that adorns her when she is burned. Following Vallabhadeva, we assume that she is burned wearing the adornments she had dressed herself in. Variants here suggest that transmitters attempted to "improve" the text, and it is hard to be certain what Kalidasa intended.

24   The three worlds are heaven, earth, and the nether regions (see note on 3.6), the three places where Vishnu placed his feet (see under "Bali" in the Glossary).

25   The *Yājñavalkyasmṛti* (3.11), an influential treatise on Dharma that is translated in this series (Olivelle 2019), refers to the notion that the tears and mucus of mourning relatives must be drunk by the deceased.

9 Dasharatha Goes Hunting

1   In 9.1–60, devoted to a description of spring, there is a fixed alliterative pattern: the second, third, and fourth syllables of each fourth verse quarter (for this first verse: *ma va tā*) are identical to the fifth, sixth, and seventh syllables respectively (also *ma va tā*).

Our translation cannot replicate this "sound effect," but it carries no narrative significance.

2 A second possible sense of the expression *ahīnaparākramam* ("who was no less valorous") is "who had the valor of the overlord of serpents [Shesha]."

3 The previous verses show Dasharatha in command of himself, while this and the following verse depict him gaining control of external rivals. Some sources add another verse: "Having strung his bow, he conquered the entire ocean-girt earth with his one chariot, for his army, with its elephants and terrifyingly swift horses, served only to proclaim his victory." We suspect it to be a secondary alternative version of verse 11.

4 For the white parasol as symbol of kingship, see 2.47 and n. For the alternating concentric circles of friendly and inimical states surrounding the king, see 8.20 and n. Vallabhadeva explains that the king's radiance was as hot as fire for enemies and as cool as the moon for others. Others take this to be a reference to the king's approachable and awe-inspiring virtues (see 1.16 and 8.10).

5 Kekaya is the kingdom of the father of Kaikeyi, wife of Dasharatha and mother of Bharata, in the northwestern part of the subcontinent. For Malaya and Kosala, see the Glossary.

6 Kings should possess three (grammatically feminine) powers, of authority (*prabhuśakti*), good counsel (*mantraśakti*), and vigor (*utsāhaśakti*); see 3.13 and n. Here, unusually, they are associated with Indra.

7 For *tamas* and the other two strands that are woven together through all that exists, see 3.27 and 8.22.

8 For the notion that one of Shiva's eight forms (that called Ugra) enters the sacrificer, see 5.4 and n.

9 Namuchi is a demon of Vedic mythology about whom little is known other than that he was defeated by Indra. Because of his prolific sacrificial activity, Dasharatha now enjoys a quasi-divine status, which, the poet suggests, is why he bows only to the king of all the gods, namely Indra.

10 For shelducks being paired for life but separated every night, see 3.24 and 8.57.

11 The girdle chains, being made of precious metals, were unbearably cold to the touch and so had been removed in winter.

12 Sages and ascetics are often supposed to be beyond passion.

13 No Sanskrit word corresponds to "cheeks," but lovers mark the cheeks and breasts of their beloveds with leaf-shaped painted designs. Here Kalidasa suggests the fancy that Spring is a man thus painting the cheeks of his several beloveds, the Splendors of the gardens.

14 The petals of the *bakula* flower are white and pointed, like teeth. Perhaps 9.35, also about *bakula* flowers, was composed as an improved alternative to this awkwardly formulated verse.

15 The flame-of-the-forest has large, bright vermilion flowers hooked like sickles, echoing the crescent-shaped nail marks lovers make.

16 The flower is the *karṇikāra*, according to several commentators. Some explain that the ladies' lovers placed the flowers.

17 A *tilaka* is a forehead decoration worn by ladies. For the *tilaka* tree, see 9.38. Bees are like drops of kohl because they are black. Compare 8.36.

18 This verse echoes a recommendation in *Arthaśāstra* 8.3.46.

19 The *ruru* is the swamp deer (not, as usually understood, the blackbuck; see Syed 1992).

20 Bhadrapada is the month corresponding to the second half of August and the first half of September; it marks the end of the monsoon, heralded by rainbows, in the north Indian plains.

21 There is a pun here on the word *śṛṅga*, which means both "horn" and "pride."

22 We are not certain which plant, and whether its color or its form, is intended.

23 A secretion between the lobes of an elephant can solidify and form a jewel-like lump that Sanskrit poetic tradition speaks of as a sort of pearl (see Sarma 1991). Lions, the enemies of elephants, prize these pearls from elephants' temples (see *Kumārasambhava* 1.6 in Smith 2005b).

24 Fly-whisks made of yak tails are emblems of sovereignty (compare 3.16). This version of the verse has Dasharatha unsportingly assailing ungainly yaks who have got caught up in reeds. We suspect that it was displaced by the version known to Mallinatha, which instead presents Dasharatha as dexterously using a particular sort of arrow to snip the yak tails while dashingly driving his horse on.

25 Shooting an unseen (but heard) target is prized as a special skill in archery.

26 Dasharatha's crime was probably seeking to kill a forest elephant (which is prohibited; see 5.50), rather than acting impetuously.

27 Most texts treat him as the son of a non-Brahman ascetic, the difference in reading being minimal (*dvijetara* instead of *dvijottara*). But this seems to be the result of deliberate manipulation of the story to avoid Dasharatha's being guilty of the inexpiable crime of Brahmanicide.

28 The transmission is a mess here. Medieval commentators attest to numerous small but significant textual differences and several interpretations.

29 He uses his tears because certain solemn acts should be accompanied by the pouring of water (compare 5.59 and n.).

30 The ascetic and his wife intend to follow their son onto the pyre. Mallinatha's reading is different: "'Now things have gone this way, what should this cruel person, who deserves to be killed by you, do?' Addressed in this way, the sage asked him for flaming brands..."

31 The sage Urva's fiery fury threatened to destroy the universe, and he hid it in the ocean. This submarine fire will destroy everything at the end of a cycle of existence. Compare 4.69.

10 Rama Descends

1 For the three debts of a twice-born man, see 1.69 and n., and 8.31.

2 Verse 4 might have been produced by a transmitter as an alternative to verse 3, which does not figure in the texts of the printed commentaries except Hemadri, who treats it as spurious.

3 The more famous sage Rishyashringa appears in most versions at this point, instead of Vamadeva.

4 Vishnu rests on the cosmic serpent Shesha in a state of wakeful sleep (*nidrā*) known as *yoganidrā,* and watches over the cosmos (see 10.15).

5 It is not certain in which sequence Lakshmi places her girdle, her hands, Vishnu's feet, and the fine cloth. Most commentators assume that the cloth protects his feet from being chafed by her girdle.

6 The Kaustubha is a jewel worn by Vishnu. The Shrivatsa is a miniature and often non-anthropomorphic form taken by Lakshmi in order to cling to Vishnu's chest (see the Glossary).

7 The weapons and emblems that Vishnu holds in his hands (discus/

war quoit, conch, mace, etc.) are anthropomorphized. They may be shown with their characteristic symbols forming parts of their heads or of their headgear. This notion reappears in 10.62.

8   Garuda, the avian mount of Vishnu and enemy of all serpents, is scarred by thunderbolts because he fought with Indra when stealing the nectar of immortality.

9   Bhrigu is a son of Brahma who is sometimes included among the seven sages identified with Ursa Major (like Vasishtha). A famous descendant of his is Parashurama.

10 For the three strands (*guṇa*) out of which all material existence is woven, see nn. on 3.27 and 8.22. In God as creator, *sattva* predominates; in God as maintainer, *rajas;* in God as destroyer, *tamas.*

11 The point of the contrast between having no desires and yet practicing austerities is clear in an Indian context, since austerities are generally undertaken in order to achieve some aim.

12 The seven *sāmans* are seven important hymns in the *Sāma Veda.* Fire has seven tongues. The worlds are most commonly numbered either as three (as in 3.6 and 10.41) or as seven.

13 For the four goals of life, see 1.25 and n.; for the four classes, beginning with Brahmans, see 5.19 and n. The four ages (*yuga*) are: *kṛta, tretā, dvāpara,* and *kali,* the last being the most degenerate. In some iconographic forms Vishnu may have three or four faces, but these may not have been known to Kalidasa. Vallabhadeva interprets Vishnu as being only figuratively four-faced, either because he "faces in all directions" or because he has four manifestations according to the theological school known as the Pancharatra. One could also understand that Vishnu is here identified with Brahma, who has four faces.

14 The elements are earth, fire, air, water, and ether. In some theologies, God transcends the physical universe, but here Vishnu is manifested through the elements that make up the universe. Knowing God through direct sense perception is widely regarded as impossible. For some philosophical schools, God can be known only through scripture and inference.

15 The attribute translated with "who is beyond sense perception" (*adhokṣajam*) is mysterious and variously interpreted.

16 Other commentators give differing texts here, none of which assigns four faces to Vishnu at this point, but see 10.24 and n. Further, most

take speech to be fourfold by counting four grammatical parts of speech.

17 Three strands pervade all creation in differing proportions (see 3.27, 8.22, 10.19 and nn.). Ravana is like the third, darkness, and dominates over the gods' dignity and power, which are compared with the other two. The word *aṅginā,* "predominant," can also mean "embodied." Thus the second half could also mean: "as though the first and the middle strands of existence were being eclipsed by darkness incarnate."

18 Ten-headed Ravana once put nine of his heads into fire as a sacrifice to Shiva. Although these heads may have been magically restored afterward (as implied by 10.46), Vishnu speaks of the tenth head being kept for himself to cull because he will incarnate himself as Rama, who will slay Ravana.

19 By convention (see 4.51) snakes like to coil around the branches of sandalwood trees.

20 The battlefield is often compared to the sacrificial arena, and the type of sacrifice mentioned, called *bali,* can involve placing on the ground rice balls, to which the heads are implicitly compared.

21 Ravana had seized Kubera's flying chariot, called Pushpaka, and was using it as his own vehicle.

22 A son of Kubera, and thus also a nephew of Ravana, called Nalakubara, whose beloved Rambha had been raped by Ravana, cursed the demon that his head would split if he touched any woman who did not love him.

23 Vishnu is often likened to a rain cloud, because of his dark-skinned forms, notably Krishna, whose name means "blue-black."

24 For the churning of the milk ocean to attain ambrosia, see 1.12 n.

25 There are rays of the sun that conceive an embryo (*garbha*) that becomes the monsoon rain (compare 13.4 and *Rāmāyaṇa* 4.27:3).

26 These are the personified weapons of Vishnu; see 10.13 and n.

27 The seven sages are identified with the stars in Ursa Major.

28 Other than Vallabhadeva, the printed commentators have Dasharatha pleased to hear the dreams and pleased to regard himself as "precious" because of becoming the father of the Father of the universe.

29 For herbs that glow at night, see 4.78, 8.56, and 9.75.

30 All four sons are spoken of here as partial incarnations (*avatāra*) of Vishnu.

31 The *santānaka* is one of the five flowers of Indra's paradise. Its name suggests continuance of lineage (*santāna*).

32 The beauties of all the seasons, without any opposition among them, may be enjoyed simultaneously in the garden of the gods.

33 Summer in north India is brought to an end by the appearance of dark monsoon clouds.

34 These are the four aims of man: *dharma, artha, kāma* and *mokṣa.* Compare 1.25.

35 Indra rides the elephant Airavata, who has four tusks, compared with the four stratagems of statecraft: peace making, giving gifts, sowing dissension, and force.

11 Rama's Youth

1 Madhu and Madhava are the two months of spring, the beginning of the lunar year and the period of the sun's northern progress.

2 An aphorism of Panini (3.1.115) explains their names are derived from verbal roots meaning to break and to leave, but little more is known about these rivers.

3 The *yakṣa* Suketu's daughter was Tataka. Agastya cursed her for troubling him in his hermitage and transformed her into a *rākṣasī.*

4 There is also a second level of meaning: "The night-prowling demoness, struck in her heart by Rama's resistless arrow and smeared with reeking blood, went to the abode of the Lord of lives, [just as] a woman at night, anointed with fragrant red sandal, steals to the house of the Lord of her life, struck in her heart by Kama's arrow." The word *niśācarī* can mean a "night-prowling demoness" and a lovelorn lady who ventures out at night to meet a lover.

5 The Brahman dwarf Vamana was, like Rama, an incarnation of Vishnu. The imperfect recollection by one incarnation of the deeds of a previous one became a *topos* in poetry.

6 This verse and the next allude to Indra seducing Gautama's wife, Ahalya, by taking on the sage's appearance. Gautama turned her into a stone, but allowed that the curse be lifted when Rama's foot should touch her.

7 Piety, Profit, and Pleasure: see 1.25 and n. and 10.86.

8 The Punarvasu stars are Castor and Pollux, the brightest stars in Gemini.

9 The *indragopa* is probably the red velvet mite, whose brilliant color suggests its fieriness.

10 Indra's bow is the rainbow. See 3.53.

11 When Daksha failed to invite Shiva to his sacrifice, Shiva was furious. Sacrifice took the form of a deer and ran away.

12 When plowing, Janaka found his daughter Sita in a furrow, and she is therefore Earth's daughter. Lakshmi emerged from the churning of the milk ocean.

13 Nimi was the first king of Videha and a son of Ikshvaku, from whom the Raghus were also descended.

14 The encamping army damages trees when tethering its animals; compare 4.51 and 4.72.

15 Indra and Varuna are described as kings in Vedic texts, the former as a conquering warrior, the latter as a king who metes out punishment. In the simile, Dasharatha might correspond to Indra and Janaka to Varuna. Indra is the guardian of the east and Varuna of the west. The commentator Hemadri points out that in a marriage ceremony the one giving the bride faces west and the one receiving faces east.

16 Kushadhvaja was the brother of Janaka. In this version known to Vallabhadeva, Dasharatha's middle son, which should be Bharata, marries Urmila, but in Valmiki's *Rāmāyaṇa,* it is Lakshmana who marries Urmila, and the text known to Mallinatha reflects this. Vallabhadeva's text avoids the problem that Lakshmana would be married first and so be a younger brother who commits the offense of marrying before an elder brother. And yet it seems unlikely that the text known to Vallabhadeva is the result of secondary modification, and it is shared by another early commentator, Shrinatha.

17 The simile contains a pun, for the word translated "contented" also means "having meaning." Stems (the Sanskrit word is feminine) and suffixes (the word is masculine) combine to form words, which then convey meaning.

18 Powerful serpents have gems on their hoods.

19 The aspect of the quarters is inauspicious, so they are intolerable to look at, whereas it is taboo to look at a menstruating woman. This follows the reading of the unprinted commentaries of Vaidyashrigarbha and Shrinatha. In Vallabhadeva's text, all the adjectives are puns: "Like intensely menstruating women, whose locks were dusky as hawks' wings, whose bloody clothes were like [reddish] clouds, the quarters were unfit to be seen:

527

their sullied locks were the wings of hawks; their garments were blood-red clouds."

20 Parashurama satisfied his ancestors by wiping out the Kshatriyas twenty-one times at a place near Kurukshetra called Samanta-panchaka. See 11.65.

21 The sacred thread is the sign of Parashurama's paternal Brahman ancestry, for his father was the sage Jamadagni, and the bow is the sign of his maternal Kshatriya ancestry, for his mother, Renuka, was the daughter of King Prasenajit.

22 Rosaries made by stringing together seeds of the *rudrākṣa* tree are used to count repetitions of mantras.

23 Parashurama is renowned for having split Mount Krauncha and for his enmity toward the thousand-armed warrior Kartavirya-Arjuna, which began when Kartavirya stole the calf of the cow belonging to Parashurama's father, Jamadagni.

24 Vishvakarman, the craftsman of the gods, made two bows, one for Vishnu and one for Shiva. Vishnu weakened Shiva's bow by uttering the mantra *hūṃ*. It was Shiva's bow that came to Janaka and that Rama broke in 11.46.

25 This translates the reading known to Mallinatha. In the reading known to Vallabhadeva, perhaps a secondary one that obviates a grammatical difficulty, the image is of a rainbow washed out by the rain.

26 Parashurama had received a magical power to move about rapidly from the sage Kashyapa.

27 Parashurama gave the earth to Kashyapa.

12 Rama, Banished to the Forest, Loses and Recaptures Sita

1 The verse is punning: "After exhausting his pleasure in the objects of the senses" and "that has used up the oil in its reservoir" translate one expression in the Sanskrit, as do "he came close to extinction" and "come to the end of its wick."

2 Kaikeyi is conniving to get Dasharatha to exile Rama to the forest and place the kingdom in the hands of her own son.

3 Bast garments are a mark of forest-dwelling ascetics (see 7.71); here Rama is being exiled to the forest, but his life there will be like theirs (compare 12.20).

4 The village of Nandigrama was near not to the city but to Chitrakuta, where Rama was then staying.

5   For the renunciation of the Ikshvakus in old age, see 8.11.

6   The reed was, as the northern recension of the *Rāmāyaṇa* relates (see Pollock 1986: 487–489 for the history of this passage), empowered with a mantra, and followed the crow wherever it flew. This could be read as a "just-so" story accounting for all crows having only one eye that rolls from one side to another.

7   Drought occasionally occurs between the two months of the rainy season: Nabhas, corresponding to July–August, and Nabhasya, to August–September.

8   The "also" may allude to another factor mentioned in the *Rāmāyaṇa*, that burial was what Viradha requested.

9   The Vindhya mountain raised itself up to rival Mount Meru; Agastya solved the problem on his journey southward by commanding the Vindhya to lower itself again to allow him to pass, and to remain that way until his return north. Agastya remains to this day, however, in the south (Canopus is only visible in southern skies), and the Vindhya is still low. The expressions "unwavering in his conduct" and "unwavering in its stability" both translate the same punning expression.

10   There are various readings here, one of which can mean instead "You, a gazelle, have slighted a tigress, and that is sure to lead to your death."

11   The name *śūrpaṇakhā* means "with nails like winnowing fans."

12   The story was so well known that there was no need to specify that Lakshmana made Shurpanakha "doubly hideous" (more literally: "joined her with a tautologous repetition of ugliness") by cutting off her ears and nose.

13   In their fear, they imagined him to be legion. Some think that it is implied that Rama was instantly everywhere.

14   Dushana was the *rākṣasa* general of Ravana. His name (*dūṣaṇa*) means "defamation."

15   In Sanskrit poetry, headless corpses regularly dance on battlefields.

16   By putting up a fight, Jatayus acquitted himself of a debt of friendship that he owed to Sita's father-in-law, Dasharatha, the story of which is not related.

17   A large portion of the story is abridged in this verse: a demon, Kabandha, revealed himself to be a *gandharva* who had been cursed to bear demonic form; the curse was removed when Rama mortally wounded him. Before dying, Kabandha told Rama that

Sugriva, the monkey prince who, like Rama, had lost his wife and kingdom, would become his ally.

18 Valin was the monkey who had usurped Sugriva's throne. An example of the grammatical substitution is that of the verbal root *as,* "to be," which for many forms is substituted by the stem form *bhū.* The grammatical simile may seem odd to nongrammarians, but it is a famous one, and no alternative has been transmitted. Perhaps it expresses the inevitability of Rama's ignoble intervention—he did not kill Valin in open combat but shot him from a hiding place—which was problematic for many later readers.

19 Hanuman was the strongest of the monkeys and, in later retellings, Rama's greatest devotee.

20 Again, a lot of story is covered here in one terse verse. Aksha, whom Hanuman killed, was the son of Ravana. Hanuman was captured and had his tail set alight, but he escaped and burned the whole of Ravana's city of Lanka by dashing through it trailing his burning tail.

21 The Royal Fortune of the *rākṣasas* belongs to their king, Ravana, but is supposed here to be changing her loyalty and choosing Vibhishana instead, inspiring him to do what is morally and politically wise.

22 Rasatala is an underground paradise full of treasures where magical snake people (*nāgas*) live.

23 The narration is again compressed here. Sita was deluded into thinking that she had seen her husband decapitated in battle, and Trijata, a lady of Ravana's household (sometimes a younger sister), consoled her by explaining that this was an illusion created by Vidyujjihva, a magician demon. See *Rāmāyaṇa* 6.22.

24 This alludes to the immobilization of Rama and Lakshmana and their entire army by poisoned snake arrows that were in fact demons.

25 Hanuman was sent to search for a death-defying herb called *mṛtasañjīvanī.* Unable to identify the herb, he brought the mountain where it grew.

26 Lakshmana kills the son of Ravana, called both Indrajit ("vanquisher of Indra") and Meghanada ("he who roars like thunder"). The arrival of autumn, at the end of the rainy season,

puts an end to the thunder of monsoon clouds and also to Indra's bow, the rainbow (see 4.16).

27 The sleepy giant Kumbhakarna was another brother of Shurpanakha, whose ears and nose were cut off by Lakshmana (see verse 40). Mountains abound in precious minerals, particularly red arsenic. Disfigured and bloody, he stood blocking Rama like a mountain hacked at to reveal traces of red arsenic.

28 Ravana had to waken his brother Kumbhakarna by having a thousand elephants march over his body.

29 Ravana's mother's family, almost all now slain, were *rākṣasas*. Some commentators read *-ūru-* (for *-uru-*) and interpret this verse as referring to Ravana's having many legs.

30 For Ravana's offering nine of his heads into the fire to propitiate Shiva, see 10.43 and n. Once when Ravana's way was blocked by Kailasa, Shiva's mountain home, he picked the mountain up, with Shiva still upon it, and shook it (see 4.83)

31 Body parts throbbing on the right side of a man are taken as harbingers of good things. The left side is auspicious for women.

32 Serpents inhabit subterranean worlds; see 1.78 and 12.70 and n.

33 The hells are governed by Yama, god of death, and one hell is full of spiny silk cotton trees (*śalmali*). Some think the *śataghnī* weapon of Ravana is here compared with such a tree. We instead take *kūṭaśālmali* as the name of a mace wielded by Yama. Ravana might have stolen Yama's weapon as a trophy when he harrowed the hells.

34 Plantain stems are proverbially insubstantial and weak.

35 According to Vallabhadeva, the elephants of the gods who protect the directions had been stolen by Ravana and were tethered nearby. Mallinatha assumes they were in their usual places in the sky.

13 Rama and Sita Return to Ayodhya

1 Each element has a particular property, that of ether being sound. Ether is the realm of Vishnu in his solar aspect.

2 Malaya refers to the ridge of the Western Ghats, which sink down toward the ocean but are not normally considered as meeting it. The ocean is divided by the causeway to Lanka, constructed by the monkeys in order to cross and rescue Sita (see 12.70).

3 Ganga was brought to earth and the netherworlds by Rama's ancestor Bhagiratha; see 1.34 and 3.50.

4   For the monsoon rains being born from a fetus conceived by the ocean in the (grammatically feminine) sun rays, see 10.60 and n. The ocean is furthermore full of jewels, and contains a submarine fire (see 4.69 and n.). The "light that delights" is the moon, which rises from the ocean in the east and was born from the churning of the milk ocean.

5   The sea is as changeable as Vishnu, who has many avatars, one of which is as a dwarf who then morphed into Trivikrama, covering the entire cosmos in three strides.

6   At the end of a cycle of time, Vishnu reclines on the coils of the cosmic serpent floating on top of the ocean of milk; from his navel a lotus grows, upon which Brahma sits intoning the Vedas.

7   Normally only one mountain, called Mainaka, is said to take refuge in the ocean after creation, to escape Indra's wrath. The use of the present and the reference to hundreds of mountains are surprising. We have found no discussion of this problem.

8   The primeval soul is Vishnu, who took the form of a boar (*varāha*) to rescue the earth, in sculpture often figured as a woman, from the waters.

9   A man kisses by "drinking" the woman's lower lip; in Kalidasa's poetry women are almost exclusively receivers rather than givers of kisses (Smith 2005a). The Ocean is unusual in that both he and his wives drink and in that he kisses all his wives simultaneously.

10   Serpents are said to nourish themselves by drinking the wind.

11   The teeth-white conches caught on the lip-red corals suggest a smile.

12   The mountain-like cloud sips the ocean, is set spinning by a whirlpool, and so resembles Mandara (see 4.27).

13   Rama and Lakshmana spent the rainy season after Sita had been abducted on Mount Malyavat.

14   The smoky dark red and teardrop shape of the banana flower account for this comparison.

15   Male sarus cranes hear the tinkling and mistakenly suppose it comes from female cranes.

16   Nahusha attained the position of Indra by his austerities. One day, as he was being borne in a litter by sages, he touched Agastya with his foot, and Agastya's frown caused him to fall to earth as a snake. Turbid waters settle at the onset of autumn, marked by the appearance of Canopus.

17 Satakarni performed penance in a pond for ten thousand years.
The gods sent five celestial beauties (*apsaras*) to seduce him. The
sage constructed an underwater palace and lived there with the
women.

18 All editions include another verse before or after this one, which
covers the same part of the narrative and may be original instead:
"He has one arm constantly raised but is using the other, his right,
with its *rudrākṣa*-bead bracelet, to answer my greeting—the same
arm with which he scratches the deer and cuts the sharp blades of
kusa grass."

19 The "hero asana" (*vīrāsana*) may not be the same as in contemporary
yogic practice. It may refer to more than one type of posture.

20 At the beginning of their forest exile, Sita beseeched this
banyan tree to grant that she would one day see those at home
again.

21 For verses 53 through 56, Vallabhadeva has a different sequence
of verses, but we think it secondary (see Goodall 2009: 69–70).

22 Sankhya philosophers hold that the intellect, which is like a mirror
reflecting incoming sense data to be cognized by the soul, springs
from matter.

23 Some commentators have obfuscated here, for the sword-blade
observance is when a man sleeps naked beside a naked woman
and does not touch her (see Hatley 2016). There may be an actual
sword placed between them.

24 The ministers had been observing a vow (and so had not shaved)
in view of Rama's misfortune.

25 The lord of bears and monkeys is Sugriva, and the son of Pulastya
is Vibhishana.

14 Sita Rejected

1 Other commentators have a different verse: "Then the two sons of
Dasharatha saw their two mothers, both equally in a lamentable
state; they resembled two creepers after the tree they rested on
has been cut down."

2 The royal stratagems are peace, giving, dissension, and force, with
which the four brothers were compared in 11.55.

3 Women whose husbands are away tie their hair in a braid, to be
loosened by their husband on his return. The city is fancied as such
a woman.

4 For the unguent, see 12.27; for the ordeal by fire, see 12.104.

5 The six-headed war god Skanda was nursed by six celestial ladies identified with the six brightest stars of the Pleiades.

6 The paintings depict their adventures in exile. Bhavabhuti's play *Rāma's Last Act* has Lakshmana showing Rama and Sita such pictures.

7 According to some, the city was rejoicing on the occasion of a festival.

8 The second half is intended to express a general truth, but Sita is implicitly alluded to with this reductively unflattering expression.

9 For the pain felt by a newly captured elephant at being tethered, see 1.69.

10 At his father's behest, Parashurama killed his own mother (see 11.64).

11 One hell has trees with sword blades as leaves.

12 A throb on the right side of the body is inauspicious for women; on the left it is inauspicious for men (compare 12.90 and n.).

13 Janaka found Sita in a furrow when plowing (see 11.47 and n.).

14 Vidaujas is a name of Indra. As gods, Indra and Vishnu are children of Aditi. Vishnu may be called Upendra, "younger brother of Indra."

15 As well as being the primordial king, Manu is also known as a lawmaker to whom a law book called the *Manusmṛti* (trans. Olivelle 2005) is attributed.

16 Valmiki witnessed the grief of a crane (*krauñca*) when its mate was shot by a hunter and spontaneously produced a verse in the meter in which he composed this very story as the first poem, the *Rāmāyaṇa*.

17 The moon is lord of herbs, and when depleted, its nectar-like healing energy is transferred into herbs.

18 The *iṅgudī* tree is commonly called *putrañjīva*, "which gives life to sons." The oil of its seeds is used by ascetics.

19 For *rajas* ("energy," "passion"), one of the three strands of existence, but also a word for "dirt," see 3.27, 8.22, and 10.19.

20 The sacrificer in Vedic rituals must be accompanied by his consort.

15 Sita Is Swallowed by Her Mother the Earth

1 Shatrughna's name means "enemy slayer."

2 The simile is drawn from grammar.

3 The root *i* means to "go," but it means "study" with the prefix *adhi*. As in verse 7, the simile underlines the primacy of grammar in Indian traditions of thought. The army follows behind so that Lavana is not forewarned and does not go in search of his trident.

4 Sixty thousand thumb-sized sages called the Balakhilyas surround the chariot of the Sun.

5 Sita gave birth to Rama's two sons, Lava and Kusha, in Valmiki's hermitage.

6 Kumbhinasi is a sister of Ravana and mother of Lavana. Madhupaghna is Lavana's hermitage.

7 Kusa grass is well-known, but *lava* grass is not. Mallinatha takes *lava* to be hair from a cow's tail; Hemadri understands it to be a wisp of sheep's wool "or similar." Others assume that kusa refers to the tips of the blades of grass and *lava* refers to the bases.

8 Valmiki's *Rāmāyaṇa* is the first poem, and the first model for poets to follow. Mallinatha's text has an extra verse here: "As they sang of Rama's sweet deeds in front of their mother, the two sons somewhat lessened the tribulation she felt at being separated from him."

9 Valmiki's stock of energy accumulated through asceticism would be depleted if he had to conjure up royal delicacies to entertain Shatrughna.

10 As mentioned in 14.20, the chariot comes to him as soon as Rama thinks of it.

11 Rama is compared with autumn because that is when Canopus (Agastya) is visible.

12 Agastya once swallowed the entire ocean in order to reveal the *asuras,* who had hidden from the gods there.

13 Brahma, the creator, has four faces.

14 Rama addresses Valmiki as "Father," and so calls Sita Valmiki's daughter-in-law. For the ordeal by fire, see 12.104.

15 A verse from the *Ṛg Veda* called the Savitri mantra is used to venerate the sun. Vedic Sanskrit has accents of pitch.

16 This is probably the thousand-headed serpent Ananta.

17 In the *Rāmāyaṇa,* a horse released by Rama for a sacrifice wanders past Valmiki's hermitage, which leads to the family reunification. The sacrificial context is only alluded to here.

18 Yudhajit is the brother of Kaikeyi and thus Bharata's maternal

uncle. The territory corresponds to Gandhara. Siddhas are the semidivine musicians known as *gandharvas*.

19 These capitals are Takshashila and Pushkalavati, identified respectively with Taxila and Charsadda, both in today's Pakistan.

20 This might be Baghan west of the Indus in Pakistan, but other identifications have been proposed.

21 The irascible sage Durvasas is prone to blighting the lives of those who cross him with curses.

22 By yogic control, Lakshmana allowed his breath to leave his body definitively.

23 Vishnu is conceived as having four natures, here incarnated in Rama and his brothers. Dharma, the moral order of the world, is likened to a bull, who loses a foot each time a new age (*yuga*) begins. In the first of the four ages, in Rama's lifetime, the bull has all four feet.

24 The word for "goad" (*aṅkuśa*) echoes Kusha's name, and the word for "teardrops" (*asrulava*) echoes Lava's. Kushavati is toward the south, in the Vindhya range, while Shravasti (in Mallinatha's text Sharavati) is identified with a site in the southern foothills of the Himalaya, in Uttar Pradesh.

25 The aged can seek death by setting out toward the north. He carries his sacred fires because one who has taken on the obligations of performing Vedic fire rituals must tend them daily.

26 When Vishnu took the forms of the sons of Dasharatha, parts of other gods became incarnate as figures of Rama's entourage.

27 Vishvaksena is another name for Vishnu that means "he who has armies on all sides." The northern mountain, where Vishnu installed Hanuman, is the Himalaya; the southern mountain, where he installed Vibhishana, is Trikuta on Lanka.

16 Ayodhya Abandoned, Then Restored to Glory

1 The seven brothers are Lava, Taksha, Pushkala, Angada, Chandraketu, Shatrughatin, and Subahu.

2 All together, with Kusha, there are eight brothers, and there are eight celestial elephants, one for each direction, who arose from Brahma's hand when he declaimed sāmans (verses of the *Sāma Veda*). The word *dāna* means both "generosity" and "musth."

3 By convention, female jackals emit flames from their mouths. The light helps them find their prey.

4   The painted elephants are so lifelike that the lions now roaming the city mistake them for real animals.

5   The sky is the realm of Vishnu's second step. See "Bali" in Glossary.

6   For this myth, see 3.50.

7   *Vāstu* is a tradition comparable to feng shui. When the function of a site is changed, the spirits that occupy the place must be propitiated.

8   Their breasts are pale because they have applied sandal paste to cool themselves, according to Vallabhadeva.

9   Agastya is associated with the south (see 4.46); the verse refers to the sun's movement northward as summer unfolds. The quarters are commonly personified as women.

10 The proverbially delicate flower of the *śirīṣa* consists of a fan-shaped burst of fragrant white or red filaments, like the flower of the powder-puff tree in appearance.

11 Here the "feet" and the "rays" are punningly expressed by the same word: *pāda*.

12 *Kirāta* is used of communities of hunters. The king's bodyguard is a *kirāta* woman.

13 For peacocks dancing to sounds that suggest thunder, see 1.42 and n. and 6.9.

14 Lakshmi and the wish-fulfilling tree of Indra's paradise emerged from the churning of the milk ocean. The roiling that disturbed the crocodiles applies both to the river's pool and to the ocean.

17 Atithi, the Perfect King

1   Vallabhadeva acknowledges that he does not know a textual source for the story about Durjaya.

2   *Kaumudī* is the Sanskrit word for moonlight, and *kumuda* is Sanskrit for water lilies.

3   Kusha shared the throne of Indra, husband of Shachi.

4   Cotton is used to make amulet wristbands. Mallinatha has a variant that may refer instead to lotus buds or mahua flowers.

5   For the *Atharva Veda* and its connection with family priests, see 1.58 and 8.4.

6   Ganga's fall to earth is broken by the matted locks of Shiva. For Shiva's destruction of three demons' cities, see 3.52 and 6.72.

7   The *cātaka* bird (*sāraṅga*) is said to live off raindrops (see 5.17 and

17.60), but *sāranga* is polysemous, and commentators suggest it may refer here to elephants, deer, peacocks, or bees.

8   Like the submarine fire (see 13.4), lightning was believed to be fueled by water.

9   Alternatively, the blessing was surpassed by the benefit already accrued through his present acts of generosity.

10   For the Shrivatsa, see 10.11 and n.; for the Kaustubha gem, see 6.49 and n.

11   Nabhas and Nabhasya are names of the months corresponding to mid-July to mid-September, the monsoon on the north Indian plains.

12   After defeating enemy sovereigns in battle, he reinstated them as vassal kings.

13   The six internal enemies are the passions: affection, anger, greed, intoxication, pride, joy. The three external ones are enemies within one's family, enemies who are neighbors, and those who have become enemies because of some slight.

14   We follow the commentator Arunagirinatha, but one could understand "He sent out spies like rays of light throughout his realm, and so nothing was invisible to him, as nothing is invisible to the sun on a cloudless day."

15   For the three principal aims of human life, see 1.25 and n., 10.86, and 11.35.

16   After this, Mallinatha's text contains two further verses: "His army was nourished, trained in weaponry, and inured to battle by his father, and thus no different from his own body. His enemy could no more draw from him his threefold power than it could the jewel from the head of a serpent; but he drew those powers from his enemy as a magnet draws iron." For the three powers of a king, see 3.13 and n. The simile implies a three-headed serpent with a jewel in each hood.

17   For the four social classes (*varṇa*), see 15.19 and n.; for the tax of one sixth of produce, 2.66 and n.

18   The four stratagems (see 10.88, 11.55, and 14.11) are alluded to in the next verse; the list of six overlaps (see 8.22 and n.); for the six types of forces, see 4.26 and n.

19   Eighteen types of "high officials" (*tīrtha*) are conventionally listed, including the crown prince, chaplain, ministers, generals, treasurers, provincial rulers, and gatekeepers.

20 Small variations allow different interpretations: his sight, or sight of him, may destroy poverty or sin, and his teaching of truth may destroy ignorance, or he may deter nocturnal crime.

21 Indra attained his status, says the commentator Narayanapandita, by performing one hundred Vedic sacrifices (see 3.49), and so also "by following the path laid down in scriptures."

22 For the five elements (earth, water, fire, air, ether) see 4.13 and n. Indra guards the east, Yama the south, Varuna the west, Kubera the north. Mahendra, Malaya, Sahya, Shuktiman, Riksha, Vindhya, and Pariyatra are the seven great mountain chains.

23 According to Vallabhadeva, after the spring festival, at which a staff of Indra is raised and decorated, the garland is taken down and worn on the king's head.

24 The predecessor referred to, in this interpretation, is Raghu, whom Kubera showered with wealth in 5.29. Alternatively, some understand that Kubera observed what his own predecessors, the other three guardians of the directions, had just done, and then accordingly bestowed his favor.

18 A Catalogue of Kings

1 Names throughout this chapter are playfully echoed in varying ways (alliteration, etymologization, polyptoton, antanaclasis) by the surrounding words, often to underline their suitability. Here the name Nishadha occurs twice and alliterates with *niṣiddha*, translated here as "after defeating."

2 Unlike his predecessors, Kumudvati's son Atithi does not withdraw to the forest for a life of austerity but continues to enjoy the pleasures of kingship, and he consequently attains not liberation but heaven. Kumudvati's name means "possessing water lilies" and is echoed in the verse by the word *kumuda*, "water lily."

3 Kusha's name is echoed here: "water lily" translates *kuśeśaya*, a kenning that literally means "that which lies in water."

4 Nala's name is echoed here: "reeds" (*nala*).

5 In this month the rainy season is at its height, and it is therefore particularly auspicious.

6 Vallabhadeva mentions a sacrifice called *puṇḍarīka* without explaining what it is. Another reading refers instead to Royal Fortune coming to him "holding lotuses." Pundarika is the

elephant who guards the southeast (see 1.76 and n.). *Puṇḍarīkākṣa*
is rendered as "lotus-eyed Vishnu."

7   Kshemadhanvan's name is echoed in this description of him:
     "archer" (*dhanvan*) and "welfare" (*kṣema*).

8   Devanika's name is echoed in this description: "god" (*deva*) and
     "armies" (*anīkinī*).

9   Ahinagu's name is echoed in this description: "ample" (*ahīna*),
     "earth" (*go*), and "base" and "free" both translate instances of
     vihīna.

10   For the four strategies, see 10.88 and n.

11   One of the seven great mountain ranges. Some identify it with the
     western Vindhyas.

12   Dala's name is echoed: "petals" (*dala*).

13   To resonate with Shala's name, this description alliterates:
     "conduct" (*śīla*), "stone" (*śilā*), "bashful" (*śālīna*), and "arrow"
     (*śilīmukha*).

14   Unnabha's name is echoed by the words used to describe him:
     "navel" (*nābhirandhra*), "the Lord with Lotus Navel" (*paṅka-
     janābha*), and "nave" (*nābhi*).

15   Vajranabha's name is played upon: "thunderbolt," "thunder," and
     "jewel" all translate instances of *vajra*.

16   Khankhana's name is echoed here: "heaven" (*kha*) and "mines"
     (*khāni*).

17   The Ashvins, famed for their beauty, are identified with the
     principal stars of Gemini. Vyushitashva's name is explained here
     with "quartered" (*uṣita*) and "horses" (*aśva*).

18   It is an old (Upanishadic) idea that a son is one's self. Vishvasaha's
     name resonates with the words *viśveśvara* ("Lord of All") and
     viśvambharā ("all-supporting earth").

19   Vedic hymns celebrate the preparation of *soma,* possibly a
     hallucinogenic drink, made by pressing a plant whose identity is
     debated.

20   Brahmishtha's name is explained, because *brahmiṣṭha* translates
     to "learned in the Veda" and *brahman* to "the Absolute."

21   The asterism *puṣya* is auspicious particularly for coronation. The
     verse contains further wordplay on Pushya's name, for *puṣyarāga*
     translates to "yellow sapphire" and *puṣṭim apuṣyan* translates to
     "became prosperous."

22   Dhruvasandhi's name is echoed here: "their alliances held firm"

translates the phrase *sandhir dhruvaḥ*.

23 The location of "the Three Pushkaras" is uncertain; perhaps the confluence of the Ganga, Yamuna, and (the invisible) Sarasvati Rivers at Prayag.

24 Sudarshana's name is echoed here: "a delight to behold" translates *priyadarśana* and "dark fortnight" translates *darśa*.

25 The forehead mark is a sign of prosperity and well-being. For women, it indicates that their husbands are alive and living with them. The king has either killed their husbands or chased them off.

26 For the three goals, see 1.25. The three sciences are the Vedas, economics, and politics. The three human constituents of the state are ministers, allies, and the army.

19 Agnivarna's Revels

1 The name Agnivarna means "fire-colored."

2 Hemadri understands this last expression to mean "whose waters concealed their genitals." But chambers could be concealed behind cascades.

3 For the *bakula*, see 9.33 and n.

4 We imagine that the king has sent the messenger girl to inform a given wife that it is her turn, but he creeps in to listen to that wife's conversation, perhaps because he enjoys teasing his wives and observing them in displays of emotion.

5 The *arjuna* tree (mentioned in 16.51) has long filamentous spikes of fragrant white blossom and is associated with spring. The *kuṭaja* shrub produces cymes of small, fragrant, five-petalled flowers that are associated rather with the rains and that are worn in garlands by lovers.

6 Daksha's daughters were married to the moon, but the moon neglected all except Rohini, so Daksha cursed him to waste away.

GLOSSARY

AGASTYA one of two sages, the
other being Vasishtha, born when
the semen of Varuna and Mitra
was stored in a pot; associated
with the south, where he is said
to have gone to teach, because he
is identified with Canopus, a star
visible in southern skies

AGNI god of fire and guardian
of the southeastern direction;
interrupted the lovemaking of
Shiva and Parvati, caught the
semen that spilled, found it too
hot to hold, and deposited it
in the Ganga, where the infant
Kumara was found among reeds
by the Krittikas, or the Pleiades

AIRAVANA (*airāvaṇa*) the name
of Indra's mount, a white
elephant

ALAKA (*alakā*) the mythical city of
Kubera, god of wealth, thought
to be north of Mount Kailasa in
the Himalayas

ANGA (*aṅga*) kingdom in the
eastern part of north India,
neighbor of Magadha; its capital
city was Champa

APARANTA (*aparānta*) name for the
coastal region of western India
now known as North Konkan

ARUNDHATI (*arundhatī*) wife
of the sage Vasishtha and a
byword for uxorial faithfulness;
identified with Alcor in Ursa
Major, the constellation of the
seven sages

ASHVAMEDHA (*aśvamedha,*
horse sacrifice) prestigious
Vedic sacrifice that many kings
boasted of performing after the
horse roamed freely for a year,
protected by the king's military
might

aśoka (free of sorrow) small tree
with prized red flowers that
blossoms only if a beautiful
woman kicks it

asuras (nongods) demonic
opponents of the gods (*suras*)

ATRI one of seven sages who were
mind-born sons of Brahma; the
moon was born from his eye

AVANTI region in central India
split into north and south by the
Vindhyas; its northern capital
was Ujjain and its southern
capital Mahishmati

bakula tree that puts forth
blossoms when sprinkled by
young women with mouthfuls
of wine

BALI demon who held sway
over the universe until Vishnu
approached him disguised as a
Brahman dwarf and begged for
as much land as he could step
over in three strides; Vishnu
swelled and covered earth and
heaven with the first two strides,

and with the third set his foot upon Bali's head, pressing him down into the underworld

BHAGIRATHA (*bhagīratha*) a descendant of King Sagara; beseeched Shiva to bring the Ganga down to the earth so that her waters would wash through the underworld and purify Sagara's ashes

BHOJA king of the Krathakaishikas in Vidarbha and brother of Indumati

BRAHMA (*brahmā*) creator, also god of sacred speech, from whose four faces the four Vedas are said to be uttered

brahman the Absolute, unqualified single reality, also the power of sacrifice and of sacred speech; associated with Brahmans, who ideally study and maintain the Vedas and Vedic ritual

CHAITRARATHA (*caitraratha*) heavenly park belonging to Chitraratha, also known as Kubera; some say it is so called because Chitraratha is the name of the *gandharva* who designed the garden

DAKSHA (*dakṣa*) father of the stars and of Shiva's first wife, Sati; these are sometimes considered to be two different Dakshas

DASHARATHA (*daśaratha,* [having] ten chariots) son of Aja who married three principal wives: Kausalya, mother of Rama; Sumitra, mother of Lakshmana

and Shatrughna; and Kaikeyi, mother of Bharata

dūrvā auspicious grass used in several rituals

elephants of the directions celestial elephants who preside over the cardinal and intermediate directions

gandharva semidivine being associated with music, magic, and mountains

GANGA (*gaṅgā*) the sacred river Ganges; possesses three streams, one in the heavens, one on earth, one in the netherworld; her waters are light in color, unlike the Yamuna, and purificatory; said to have been created in one of Vishnu's three broad strides when he was vanquishing Bali punctured the heavens

GARUDA (*garuḍa*) bird upon whom Vishnu rides; offspring of Vinata, mother of all birds, who was enslaved to her sister, Kadru, mother of all serpents; the enemy of all serpents, including the cosmic serpent Shesha

HANUMAN commander of the monkey army, son of the wind god, and devotee of Rama

IKSHVAKU (*ikṣvāku*) one of Raghu's illustrious forebears; like Raghu's, his name also came to be used as a family name

INDRA god of storms and leader of the gods; prided himself on being the only person to have performed a hundred Vedic sacrifices; tamed the mountains by cutting off their wings

INDUMATI (*indumatī*) sister of Bhoja, princess of Vidarbha, and wife of Aja

JANASTHANA (*janasthāna*) demon stronghold in the middle of the Dandaka forest where Rama, Sita, and Lakshmana spent part of their exile and that Rama purged of *rākṣasas*

JAYANTA son of Indra, born to his wife Shachi

KAMA, KAMADEVA (*kāma, kāmadeva*) god of love and husband of Rati; consumed by the fire from Shiva's third eye and hence disembodied, living only in people's minds; wields a bow of sugarcane strung with bees and flowers as arrows

KAMARUPA (*kāmarūpa*) region identified with what is today Assam, famous for its elephants

KAPILA irascible sage whose anger incinerated the ancestors of Bhagiratha

KARTAVIRYA (*kārtavīrya*) king of the Haihaya dynasty; granted the boon of having a thousand arms by the sage Dattatreya

KAUSTUBHA jewel that arose from the churning of the milk ocean and is worn by Krishna on his chest

kinnara semidivine musical being who inhabits mountain regions; may have birds' feet or a horse's head

KOSALA region in the eastern part of the north Indian plain ruled by the Raghu kings

KRATHAKAISHIKAS (*krathakaiśika*) a people ruled by Bhoja

KRISHNA (*kṛṣṇa,* dark-skinned) most celebrated avatar of Vishnu; spent his childhood in Vrindavana and near Mathura; lived after Rama but is anachronistically alluded to in chapter 6

KUBERA god of wealth, guardian of the northern quarter, and king of the *yakṣas*; resides in the Himalayas, in a beautiful city called Alaka

KUMARA (*kumāra*) six-faced, peacock-riding god of war, also called Skanda

LAKSHMANA (*lakṣmaṇa*) son of Dasharatha and Sumitra and younger brother of Rama

LAKSHMI (*lakṣmī*) goddess of beauty, wealth, and good fortune, also called Shri; wife of Vishnu but also "married" to the king as Royal Fortune personified; *see* SHRIVATSA

LANKA (*laṅkā*) island stronghold of the demon king Ravana, sometimes identified with Sri Lanka

MAGADHA country in eastern north India whose capital was Pataliputra, today Patna, or Pushpapura, "Flower City"

MAHENDRA a peak in the Eastern Ghats

MALAYA mountain range known today as the Western Ghats

MANASA (*mānasa*) Himalayan lake known today as Manasarovar, famous for its purity and for the geese that yearn for it when the plains grow hot

MANU primordial king, son of the sun, and thus the first king of the solar lineage known as the lineage of the Raghus

MATALI (*mātali*) charioteer of Indra

MERU golden mountain at the center of the cosmos, around which the sun and moon circle; its shadow creates the night

NANDANA celestial garden of Indra

NANDINI (*nandinī*) Vasishtha's wish-fulfilling milch cow, descended from the celestial cow Surabhi, who emerged from the churning of the milk ocean by the gods and *asuras*

NARMADA (*narmadā*) river that runs east to west across India, dividing the north from the Deccan

PANCHAVATI (*pañcavatī*) part of the great southern forest where the river Godavari rises

PANDYA (*pāṇḍya*) hereditary king of the southernmost region of the Tamil-speaking south

PARASHURAMA (*paraśurāma*) partial incarnation of Vishnu, an ax-wielding warrior Brahman who aspired to extirpate all Kshatriyas; drove back the ocean to create the land west of the Western Ghats

pārijāta wish-granting tree of Paradise, produced at the churning of the milk ocean and taken possession of by Indra

PARVATI (*pārvatī*, mountain-born) daughter of the Himalaya mountain, spouse of Shiva, and mother of Kumara; also called Gauri (*gaurī*, pale one) and Uma

PUSHPAKA (*puṣpaka*) Kubera's flying palace-cum-chariot captured by Ravana

RAHU (*rāhu*) planetary demon who swallows the moon whenever there is an eclipse; covets the nectar with which the moon is monthly filled

rākṣasa semidivine but demonic creature who consumes human flesh, moves about at night, and destroys the Vedic sacrifices of Brahmans and ascetics; a subject of Ravana

RAMA (*rāma*) (1) son of Dasharatha and husband of Sita; (2) another name of Parashurama

RATI goddess of sexual pleasure and wife of Kamadeva, god of love

RAVANA (*rāvaṇa*) ten-headed *rākṣasa* king of Lanka

REVA (*revā*) another name of the river Narmada, which flows through the Vindhya mountains

RUDRA ancient name of Shiva, thought to mean "the one who howls" *rudrākṣa* (eyes of Rudra) seeds of a tree used as telling beads for rosaries

sal tree prized for its timber; its dried resin is burnt as incense

śamī hardwood tree believed to contain fire and used as the lower of the two sticks to kindle the sacred fire, the upper stick being of ashwattha wood

SARASVATI (*sarasvatī*) (1) goddess of learning, often represented with a lute-like musical instrument called a vina; (2) ancient river, tributary of the Indus, said to flow underground

SARAYU (*sarayū*) river that flows through Ayodhya, capital city of the Raghus; today identified with the Ghaghra

SHACHI (*śacī*) wife of Indra and mother of Jayanta

SHESHA (*śeṣa*) cosmic serpent who feuds with Vishnu's avian mount Garuda and holds up the burden of the earth; his thousand heads have a jewel in each hood and his coils form the bed on which Vishnu lies, upon the milk ocean

SHIVA (*śiva*, the kindly one) supreme god for many Hindus, married to Himalaya's daughter Uma, or Parvati, and father of Kumara

SHRIVATSA (*śrīvatsa*) a whorl of hair on the chest of Vishnu; the form that Lakshmi takes in order to be able to cling to her husband

SIDDHA (perfected being) being who attains supernatural powers (*siddhi*) through knowledge, accumulated ascetic energy, and the propitiation and mastery of mantras

SITA (*sītā*) daughter of king Janaka and wife of Rama

SUMANTU minister and charioteer of Dasharatha and his sons; also called Sumantra

SUMITRA (*sumitrā*) daughter of the king of Malaya and mother of Lakshmana and Shatrughna

SURABHI (fragrant) celestial wish-fulfilling cow, the mother of all cows

TADAKA (*tāḍakā*) daughter of a *yakṣa* called Suketu, transformed into a *rākṣasī* demoness when Agastya cursed her for troubling him in his hermitage

TAMASA (*tamasā*) branch of the Sarayu River that flows through Ayodhya

UTTARAKOSALA northern Kosala, the region around the city of Ayodhya, the capital of the Raghus

VARUNA (*varuṇa*) god of the ocean and of water, also of plants; Guardian of the West; holds a noose to catch and chastise wrongdoers

VASISHTHA (*vasiṣṭha*) son of Brahma and one of the seven great sages of Ursa Major; the family preceptor of the dynasty of the Raghus; *see* AGASTYA

VIDARBHA region in central India ruled by Bhoja

vidyādhara (spell bearer) semidivine being capable of flight; often celestial musicians

VISHNU (*viṣṇu*) ancient Vedic solar deity who incarnates himself, most famously as Krishna and as Rama, whenever the earth is threatened

yakṣa semidivine being associated with trees and ruled by the god of wealth, Kubera

YAMUNA (*yamunā*) river that flows through Mathura; her waters are dark, unlike the Ganga

BIBLIOGRAPHY

Editions and Translations

Anantapadmanabhan, Kavasseri Narayana, trans. 1973. *Raghuvamsam of Kalidasa: An English Version (A Translation of the Original in Verse).* Madras: Ramayana Pub. House.

Devadhar, Chintaman Ramchandra, ed. 1984. *Works of Kālidāsa. Volume II. Poetry.* New Delhi: Motilal Banarsidass.

Galanos, Demetrius and Geôrgios Kozakês Tupaldos, trans. 1850. *Raggou-Bansa : ê genealogia tou Raggou.* En Athenais : Ek tes Typ. G. Chartophylakos. Available at: http://archive.org/details/raggou-bansageneaookali.

Gnoli, Raniero, ed. 1962. *Udbhaṭa's Commentary on the Kāvyālaṃkāra of Bhāmaha, with an Appendix by Margherita Taticchi Including Some Fragments of Kālidāsa's Raghuvaṃśa.* Serie Orientale Roma 27. Rome: Istituto Italiano per il Medio ed Estremo Orientale.

Goodall, Dominic and Harunaga Isaacson, eds. 2003. *The Raghupañcikā of Vallabhadeva: Being the Earliest Commentary on the Raghuvaṃśa of Kālidāsa.* Groningen Oriental Studies 17. Groningen: Forsten.

Jinavijaya, Muni, ed. 1933. *Prabandha cintāmaṇi of Merutuṅgācārya* Singhi Jaina Series 1. Śāntiniketana: Siṅghī Jaina Jñānapīṭha.

Kale, M. R., ed. and trans. 1922. *The Raghuvaṃśa of Kālidāsa: with the Commentary (the Saṃjīvanī) of Mallinātha; Cantos I–X; Edited with a Literal English Translation, Copious Notes in Sanskrit and English, and Various Readings &c. &c.* Bombay: P. S. Rege.

Karmarkar, Raghunātha Dāmodara., ed. and trans. 1922. *The Raghuvaṃśa of Kālidāsa.* Poona: Agashe; Aryabhushan Mudranalaya.

Lacy Johnstone, P. de., trans. 1902. *The Raghuvança; the Story of Raghu's Line.* London: J. M. Dent.

Nandargikar, Gopal Raghunath, ed. and trans. 1971. *The Raghuvamsa of Kalidasa, with the Commentary of Mallinatha, Ed. with a Literal English Tr. with Copious Notes in English Intermixed with Full Extracts, Illucidating the Text, from the Commentaries of Bhatta Hemadri, Charitravardhana, Vallabha, Dinakaramisra, Sumativijaya, Vijayagani, Vijayanandasuris Varacharanasevaka and Dharmameru, with Various Readings Etc., Etc.* 4th ed. Delhi: Motilal Banarsidass.

Renou, Louis, trans. 1928. *Kālidāsa – Le Raghuvaṃça (La lignée des fils du soleil) Poème en XIX chants traduit du sanscrit.* Les joyaux de l'Orient 6. Paris: Paul Geuthner.

Ryder, Arthur W, trans. 1912. *Kalidasa: Translations of Shakuntala, and Other Works.* London & Toronto; New York: J. M. Dent & Sons; E. P. Dutton & Co.

Stenzler, Adolphus Fridericus, ed. and trans. 1832. *Raghuvansa: Kálidásæ Carmen. Sanskrite et Latine.* London: Oriental Translation Fund of Great Britain and Ireland.

Walter, Otto, trans. 1914. *Raghuvamscha oder Raghus Stamm.* München, Leipzig: Hans Sachs-Verlag.

Other Sources

Arthaśāstra. 2013. *King, Governance, and Law in Ancient India: Kauṭilya's Arthaśāstra. A New Annotated Translation.* Translated by Patrick Olivelle. New York: Oxford University Press.

Bakker, Hans Teye. 2019. "A Theatre of Broken Dreams: Vidiśā in the Days of Gupta Hegemony." In *Holy Ground: Where Art and Text Meet.* Gonda Indological Studies 20. Leiden and Boston: Brill, pp. 301–318. https://doi.org/10.1163/9789004412071_015.

Balogh, Dániel and Eszter Somogyi, ed. and trans. 2009. *Málavika and Agni·mitra by Kali·dasa.* Clay Sanskrit Library. New York: New York University Press; JJC Foundation.

Böhtlingk, Otto von, ed. and trans. 1890. *Poetik (Kâvjâdarça): Sanskrit und Deutsch.* Leipzig: H. Haessel.

Bühler, Georg. 1890. "Die indischen Inschriften und das Alter der indischen Kunstpoesie." *Sitzungsberichte der Philosophisch-Historischen Classe der Kaiserlichen Akademie der Wissenschaften* 122 (Abhandlung XI): 1–97.

Devadhar, C. R., ed and trans. 1993. *Rtusamhara of Kalidasa: Edited with Introduction and English Translation.* New Delhi: Motilal Banarsidass.

Dezső, Csaba. 2014. "'We Do Not Fully Understand the Learned Poet's Intention in Not Composing a Twentieth Canto': Addiction as a Structuring Theme in the Raghuvaṃśa." *South Asian Studies* 30, 2: 159–172.

———. 2020. "Not to Worry, Vasiṣṭha Will Sort It Out: The Role of the Purohita in the Raghuvaṃśa." In *Śaivism and the Tantric Traditions: Essays in Honour of Alexis G. J. S. Sanderson,* ed. Dominic Goodall, Shaman Hatley, Harunaga Isaacson, and Srilata Raman. Gonda Indological Studies 22. Leiden and Boston: Brill, pp. 217–233.

Durgâprasâda, Paṇḍit, and Kâśînâth Pâṇḍurang Parab, eds. 1895. *The Âryâ-Saptaśatî of Govardhanâchârya with The Commentary (Vyangyârtha-Dîpanâ) of Ananta-Paṇḍit.* 2nd rev. ed. Kâvyamâlâ 1. Bombay: Tukârâm Jâvajî.

Edgerton, Franklin, ed. and trans. 1952. *The Bhagavad Gītā Translated and Interpreted. Part 1: Text and Translation.* Harvard Oriental Series 38. Cambridge, Mass.: Harvard University Press.

Goodall, Dominic. 2001. "Bhūte 'āha' iti pramādāt: Firm Evidence for the Direction of Change Where Certain Verses of the Raghuvaṃśa Are Variously Transmitted." *Zeitschrift der Deutschen Morgenländischen Gesellschaft* 151: 103–124. https://menadoc.bibliothek.uni-halle.de/dmg/periodical/titleinfo/150843.

———. 2009. "Retracer la transmission des textes littéraires à l'aide des textes «théoriques» de l'Alaṅkāraśāstra ancien: quelques exemples tirés du Raghuvaṃśa." In *Écrire et transmettre en Inde classique,* ed. Gerdi Gerschheimer and Gérard Colas. Études thématiques 23. Paris: École française d'Extrême-Orient, pp. 63–77.

———. 2019. "Nobles, Bureaucrats or Strongmen? On the 'Vassal Kings' or 'Hereditary Governors' of Pre-Angkorian City-States: Two Sanskrit Inscriptions of Vidyāviśeṣa, Seventh-Century Governor of Tamandarapura (K. 1235 and K. 604), and an Inscription of Śivadatta (K. 1150), Previously Considered a Son of Īśānavarman I." *Udaya: Journal of Khmer Studies* 14: 23–85. http://www.yosothor.org/uploads/images/Udaya/Udaya_pdf/Udaya-Yosothor/No-14-2019/05_Goodall_Udaya%2014_Final.pdf.

Hatley, Shaman. 2016. "Erotic Asceticism: The Razor's Edge Observance (*Asidhārāvrata*) and the Early History of Tantric Coital Ritual." *Bulletin of the School of Oriental and African Studies* 79: 329–45.

Ingalls, Daniel H. H. 1976. "Kālidāsa and the Attitudes of the Golden Age." *Journal of the American Oriental Society* 96, 1: 15–26.

Kielhorn, Franz. 1902. "Aihole Inscription of Pulakesin II, Saka-Samvat 556." *Epigraphia Indica* 6: 1–12.

Kunhan Raja, Chittenjoor. 1941. "Studies on Kālidāsa." *Annals of Oriental Research* 5: 17–40.

———. 1956. *Kalidasa: A Cultural Study.* Waltair: Andhra University.

Mahābhārata. 1933–1959. Critically edited in 19 volumes by Vishnu Sitaram Sukthankar, Shripad Krishna Belvalkar, Parashuram Lakshman Vaidya, Franklin Edgerton, Raghu Vira, Shripad Krishna

Belvalkar, Parashuram Lakshman Vaidya, et al. Poona: Bhandarkar Oriental Research Institute.

Mallinson, James, ed. and trans. 2005. *The Emperor of the Sorcerers.* 2 vols. Clay Sanskrit Library. New York: New York University Press; JJC Foundation.

——, ed. and trans. 2006. *Messenger Poems by Kālidāsa, Dhoyī ⓣ Rūpa Gosvāmin.* Clay Sanskrit Library. New York: New York University Press; JJC Foundation.

Narayana Rao, Velcheru and David Dean Shulman, trans. 2009. *How Úrvashi Was Won.* New York: New York University Press; JJC Foundation.

Olivelle, Patrick, ed. and trans. 2005. *Manu's Code of Law: A Critical Edition and Translation of the Mānava-Dharmásāstra.* New York: Oxford University Press.

——, ed. and trans. 2019. *Yajnavalkya: A Treatise on Dharma.* Murty Classical Library of India 20. Cambridge, Mass.: Harvard University Press.

Pathak, M., ed., *The Critical Edition of the Viṣṇupurāṇa.* 2 vols. Vadodara: Oriental Institute, 1997, 1999.

Pollock, Sheldon I., trans. 1986. *The Rāmāyaṇa of Vālmīki. An Epic of Ancient India. Volume II: Ayodhyākāṇḍa. Introduction, Translation, and Annotation.* Princeton Library of Asian Translations. Princeton, N. J.: Princeton University Press.

——. 2006. *The Language of the Gods in the World of Men: Sanskrit, Culture, and Power in Premodern India.* Berkeley: University of California Press.

——, ed. and trans. 2007. *Rama's Last Act.* Clay Sanskrit Library. New York: New York University Press : JJC Foundation.

Raghavan, V. 1951. "Kālidāsa and Kauṭilya." In *Proceedings of the Thirteenth All-India Oriental Conference, Nagpur, 1946,* pp. 102–108.

——. 1978. *Bhoja's Śṛṅgāra Prakāśa.* 3rd ed. Madras: Punarvasu.

Rāmāyaṇa. 2001–2014. *The Vālmīki-Rāmāyaṇa.* Critically edited in 7 volumes by G. H. Bhatt, P. L. Vaidya, Prahlad C. Divanji, Dolarārāya Raṃ. Māṅkaḍa, Gowriprasad Chunilal Jhala, and Umakant Premanand Shah. 3rd ed. Vadodara: Oriental Institute.

Ruben, Walter. 1948. *Kālidāsa's Raghuvaṃśa, eine Gallerie altindischer Despoten = Kālidāsa'nın Raghuvaṃṣa Adlı Eseri.* Ankara: N.p.

Salomon, Richard. 2019. "The Sincerest Form of Flattery: On Imitations of Aśvaghoṣa's Mahākāvyas." *Journal of Indian Philosophy* 47,

2: 327–340. https://doi.org/10.1007/s10781-019-09383-4.

Sarma, Sreeramula Rajeswara. 1991. "Gajamauktika: Poetic Convention and Reality." *Bulletin d'Études Indiennes* 9: 195–202.

Schubring, Walther. 1955. "Jinasena, Mallinātha, Kālidāsa". *Zeitschrift der Deutschen Morgenländischen Gesellschaft* 105: 331–337.

Sivaramamurti, C. 1944. *Epigraphical Echoes of Kālidāsa.* Madras: Thompson.

Smith, David. 2005a. "Kissing in Kāvya, with Special Reference to Kālidāsa's Kumārasambhava." *Cracow Indological Studies* 7: 53–67.

———, ed. and trans. 2005b. *The Birth of Kumara.* Clay Sanskrit Library. New York: New York University Press; JJC Foundation.

Steiner, Roland. 2010. "Truth Under the Guise of Poetry. Aśvaghoṣa's 'Life of the Buddha.'" In *Lives Lived, Lives Imagined: Biography in the Buddhist Traditions,* ed. Linda Covill, Ulrike Roesler, and Sarah Shaw. Boston: Wisdom Publications/The Oxford Centre for Buddhist Studies, pp. 89–121.

Syed, Renate. 1992. "Zur Bedeutung des kṛṣṇasāra (Antilolpe cervicapra) und des ruru (Cervus d. duvauceli) im Alten Indien." *Beiträge des Südasien-Instituts* 2: 93–156.

Trautmann, Thomas R. 2015. *Elephants and Kings: An Environmental History.* Chicago: University of Chicago Press.

Tubb, Gary A. 1982. "The Relative Priority of the Wedding Passages in the Kumārasambhava and the Raghuvaṃśa." *Journal of the American Oriental Society* 102, 2: 309.

Unknown. *Quoit Turban.* Victoria and Albert Museum, London, England. Available at: collections.vam.ac.uk/item/O72384/quoit-turban-unknown/. Accessed 10 October 2022.

Vasudeva, Somadeva, ed. and trans. 2006. *The Recognition of Shakúntala by Kali·dasa.* Clay Sanskrit Library. New York: New York University Press; JJC Foundation.

INDEX

Abhijñānaśākuntala, xiv, xvii–xviii
Aditi, 534n14
Agastya: Nahusha and, 532n16;
    ocean swallowed by, 139, 535n12;
    pot-born, 75, 507n10; as priest,
    139, 515n28; Rama and, 283, 369,
    405; in south, 81, 509n26, 529n9,
    537n9; as star, 75, 397, 507n10,
    529n9, 535n11; Tataka cursed by,
    526n3; Vindhya immobilized by,
    139, 529n9
Agni, 47, 504n16, 508n13
Agnivarna, xviii, xxiii, 451, 541n1
Ahalya, 506n24, 526n6; Gautama's
    wife, 257, 259
Ahinagu, 437, 540n9
Airavana, 143, 419
Airavata, 526n35
Aja: at bride choice, 121, 143;
    consecration or reign of, 171, 173,
    175, 197; grief of, xxi, 177, 181,
    187, 189, 518n2, 518n6; *kāma* as
    goal for, xvii; ladies watch, 149,
    151; name of, 105, 512n14; princes
    attack, 157, 163, 165, 167, 169;
    Priyamvada and 109, 111; son of,
    197; in Vidarbha, 111, 113, 119
Aksha, 291, 530n20
Alaka, 201, 397, 455
Allahabad, xi, 514n21
Ananta, 533n16
Anasuya, 281, 317, 333
Anga, 129, 513n7
Angada, 379, 536n1
Anupa, 131, 514n14, 514n16

Aparanta, 85, 510n32
Arjuna, xiii, 519n9
Arthaśāstra, xxii–xxiii, 508n15,
    509n25, 519n8, 522n18; fasting
    in, 512n12; powers of, 505n9
Arunagirinatha, xx, xxvinn24–25,
    xxxi, 538n14
Arundhati, 17, 47, 502n18
Āryāsaptaśatī, xxvin22
Ashvaghosha, xxii, xxvin27
Ashvins, 439, 540n17
Assam, 91n
Atharva Veda, 17, 171, 413, 502n19,
    518n3, 537n5
Atithi, xvii, xxiii, 411, 419, 421, 429,
    431; consecrated, 413, 417; goes
    to heaven, 433, 539n2
Atri, 47, 281n, 317, 503n16
Aurva, 87, 510n37. *See also* Urva
Avanti, 129, 514n11, 514n14
Ayodhya: abandoned, xvi, 381,
    387; capital, xvii, 321; citizens
    of, 103, 333, 381; deities of, 387,
    419; Kusha returns to, 393; Rama
    returns to, 273, 301, 303, 327;
    Rama surveys, 337; sages arrive
    in, 371; Shatrughna returns to,
    365; Sudarshana as lord of, 445

Badami, 517n9
Baghan, 534n20
Balakhilyas, 359, 535n4
Bali, 157
Bay of Bengal, 508n19, 509n27
Bhadra, 339

Bhagavadgītā, 519n9, 519n11
Bhagiratha, 11, 79, 508n16, 531n3
Bharata: birth of, 243; greets
  Lakshmana, 325; greets Sita,
  327; in Nandigrama, 279; Rama
  and, 277, 281, 321, 323, 331;
  Shatrughna and, 245; Urmila
  and, 527n16; Yudhajit and, 377,
  379, 535n18
Bharavi, xi, xiii
Bhargava, 269
Bhasa, xxii
Bhatti, xiii
Bhaṭṭikāvya, xiii
Bhavabhuti, 534n6
Bhidya River, 251
Bhoja, 105, 107, 153, 155, 157;
  princess of line of, 137. *See also*
  Vidarbha: king of
Bhrigu, 227, 524n9
Bihar, 513n6
Birth of the War God, The. See
  Kumārasambhava
Brahma, 19, 57, 505n15, 512n10,
  536n2; boons given by, 235;
  command of, 379; comparisons
  to, 155; court of, 441; four faces
  of, 371, 524n13, 535n13; hour of,
  105, 512n14; lake of, 319; sons of,
  25, 503n16, 524n9; on Vishnu's
  navel-lotus, 532n6; weapon of,
  299
Brahman power, 17, 518n3
Brahmans, 101, 103, 105, 221, 263,
  271, 391, 512n10, 515n28, 518n3;
  dwarf Vamana, 526n5; enemy
  of, 357; grieving father, 367,
  371; killed, 221, 523n27; king
  consecrated by, 413; Kushavati

entrusted to, 393; as social class,
  511n8, 524n13; Parashurama's
  father, 528n21
Brahmaputra River, 91n
Brahmishtha, 441, 443, 540n20
Bṛhatkathā, xv, xxi, xxvn14
Buddha, xxii
Buddhists, xxii
Budha, 15, 502n16
Budhasvamin, xxvn14

Cambodia, xi, xviii, xxvn6
Central Asia, xxii
Chaitraratha, 111, 135
Chandraketu, 379, 536n1
Charsadda, 536n19
Chitrakuta, Mount, 279, 281, 315,
  528n4
Cholas, 515n27
Cloud Messenger, The. See
  Meghadūta
Compendium of the Seasons. See
  Ṛtusaṃhāra

Daksha, 59, 465, 505n17, 527n11,
  541n6
Dakshina, 11, 502n11
Dala, 437, 439, 540n12
Damalipta, 508n17
Dandaka forest, 277, 337, 515n29
Dandin, xii
Dardura, 509n30
Dasharatha, xvii, 201, 273, 367,
  523n27, 525n28, 527nn15–16;
  birth of, 177; cursed, 221; friends
  of, 287, 365, 529n16; hunts,
  xxiii, 211, 217, 522n24, 523n26;
  Indra and, 203, 521n9; Kaikeyi
  manipulates, 275, 528n2;

minister of, 319n; Parashurama
and, 267; reign of, 197, 199, 225,
521n3; sons of, 235, 237, 263, 293,
329, 533n1, 536n26; wives of,
199, 379, 521n5
Devanika, 435, 540n8
Devasena, 149, 516n1
Dharma, 9, 381, 429, 435, 509n25,
520n25
Dharmaśāstra, 511n9
Dhruva, 443
Dhruvasandhi, 443, 540n22
Dilipa, xvii, 5, 11, 71, 501nn9–10,
502nn22–23, 503n5; cow
protected by, 23, 33, 41, 43;
lineage of, 173; sacrifices of, 61,
143; son of, 53, 61, 67
Durdura, 85, 509n30
Durjaya, 411, 537n1
Durvasas, 379, 536n21
Dushana, 285, 529n14

Five Apsarases, 313

Gandhara, 535n18
Ganga, xvii, 33, 89, 135, 231,
309, 502n13; Anasuya brings
down, 317; ashrams beside,
337; Bhagiratha brings down,
11, 79, 508n16, 531n3; celestial,
21, 241, 295, 405, 503–504n16;
celestial elephants in, 21, 117;
comparisons to, 145, 241, 413;
described, 319; Jahnu's daughter,
345; Kalindi or Yamuna and,
514n21, 541n23; Kumara born
from, 504n16; Sarayu and, 195,
329; tributaries of, 517n10; from
Shiva's hair, 79, 508n16; from

Vishnu's feet, 233; worshiped,
395
Garuda, 239, 293; arrow of, 407;
scarred, 227, 524n8; serpents'
foe, 81, 135, 227, 257, 265, 409,
508n23, 515n22; Vishnu's
emblem, 443n
Gauri, 33, 89
Gautama, 257, 259, 506n24, 526n6
Godavari, 311, 313
Gokarna, 179
Gopratara, 381
Govardhana, xxvin22
Govardhana, Mount, 135
Greeks, 510n35
Guptas, xi, xxvn6, xxvn9, xxxii

Hanuman, 289, 321, 530nn19–20,
530n25, 536n27
Hara, 271
Harini, 191
Hemadri, xxxi, 523n2, 527n15,
535n7, 541n2
Hemangada, 135, 515n25
Himalaya, 91, 510nn43–44, 536n24,
536n27; caves in, 33, 45, 185;
Gauri's father, 33, 89; snowmelt
from, 329, 397
Hiranyaksha, 441
Hiranyanabha, 441

Ikshvaku, 508n22, 527n13
Ikshvaku dynasty, 19, 49, 321, 345,
367; family observance of, 69,
279; guru of, 323; scions of, 111,
141, 369
Indonesia, xviii
Indra, 235, 361, 397n, 411, 521n6,
532n16; Ahalya and, 257, 506n24,

526n6; attire of, 459; banner of, 71, 507n1, 539n23; bow of, 65, 67, 271, 295, 506n28, 507n7, 527n10, 530n26; bull form of, 141, 516n33, 516n34; chariot or charioteer of, 69, 295, 301; comparisons to, 9, 47, 55, 57, 93, 129, 179, 197, 199, 201, 215, 225, 237, 261, 263, 367, 387, 419, 513n7; directional guardian, 504n16, 506n23, 527n15, 539n22; elephant of, 247, 309, 526n35; enemies of, 157, 203, 516–517n9, 521n9; Hari, 61, 506n24; heaven of, 41, 49, 443, 526n31, 537n14; hundred sacrifices of, 143, 177, 506n21, 519n12, 537n21; king or god of gods, 429, 511n3, 513n5, 521n9; mountains' wings cut by, 61, 67, 81, 305, 506n23, 506n32, 532n7; names of, xxxiii, 506n21, 506n30, 507n7, 508n13, 534n14; pleasures of, 405, 455; Raghu fights, 61, 63, 65, 67, 69, 506n30; rain or storm sent by, 9, 275, 431, 501n9, 515n24; Rama outfitted by, 295; sacrifices given to, 127, 513n5; sacrificial horse stolen by, 61, 63, 506n21; sages feared by, 97, 191, 313, 315, 511n3; Shakra, 65, 506n30; son of, 55, 143, 279; thousand-eyed, 127, 506n24; throne shared with, 143, 537n3; thunderbolts of, 199, 524n8; Varuna and, 263, 527n15; Vidaujas, 347, 534n14; wish-granting tree of, 407, 537n14
Indrajit, 293n, 325, 363, 530n26
Indumati, 515n27, 518n18, 520n17;

bride-choice of, xx, xxvin25, 105, 121, 129, 141; death of, xxi, 189; earth as another, 171, 177; servant of, 129, 513n4, 516n38; suitors of, xxvin25, 149, 157, 159
Indus River, 510n38, 536n20
Ishvara, 297. *See also* Shiva

Jahnu, 345
Jaimini, 443
Jains, xxxi
Jamadagni, 528n21
Janaka, 257, 259, 261, 365, 527n12, 527nn15–16, 528n24, 534n13; daughter of, 327, 341
Janasthana, 139, 285, 309, 515n29
Jatayus, 287, 289, 529n16
Jayanta, 55, 143
Jinasamudra, xxxi
Jumna River, 514n21. *See also* Yamuna
Jyotiratha River, 159, 517n10

Kabandha, 289, 529n17
Kadambas, xxvn10
Kaikeyi, 239, 275, 277, 281, 319, 528n2; Bharata's mother, 333, 521n5; brother of, 535n18; father of, 521n5; son of, 243
Kailasa, Mount, 37, 297, 510–511n44, 512n12, 531n30; lord of, 103, 335
Kakutstha, 81, 141, 508n22, 516n34; descendants of, 203, 281, 327, 357, 375
Kalanemi, 367
Kali, ix, x, xxvn4
Kalidasa: date of, xi; evocative language of, xx–xxi; as hero of

now-lost work, xxvn10; influence of, xi, xviii, xxvn7; inscriptional evidence and, xi, xviii, xxvn7, xxvn9; legends about, ix; places known to, ix–x, xxivn3, 510n35; religious views of, x, 502n21; sources of, xxi–xxiii; works of, xiii–xvii

Kalindi, 135, 514n21

Kalinga, 81, 135, 508n19

Kaliya, 135, 515n22

Kama, 113, 155, 209, 449, 463; arrows or bow of, 209, 526n4; bodiless or burnt up, 255, 261, 399, 512n20, 513n1; Rati and, 153

Kamarupa, 91n, 93, 153

Kambojas, 89

Kapila, 63, 303, 395, 506n26

Kapisha, 81

Karapatha, 379

Kartavirya, 131

Kartavirya-Arjuna, 269, 528n23

Kashmirians, xxiii, xxx

Kashyapa, 528nn26–27

Kausalya (1), 239

Kausalya (2), 441

Kaustubha, 135, 227, 241, 417, 515n22, 523n6

Kautilya, xxiii

Kautsa, 95, 99, 103

Kaveri River, 83, 509n27

Kaviputra, xxii

Kāvyādarśa, xii

Kekaya, 201, 521n5

Kerala, xx, xxxi, 83

Khankhana, 439, 540n16

Khara, 285, 287, 321

Kirātārjunīya, xiii

Kiratas, 401

Kosala, 11, 213; king of, 157, 187, 201, 221, 261

Krathakaishikas, 105, 113, 157, 191

Krauncha, Mount, 528n23

Krishna, 135, 515nn22–24, 525n23

Krittikas, 335

Kshatriyas, 329, 513n8; Parashurama and, 133, 261, 265, 267, 269, 271, 528n20, 528n21

Kshemadhanvan, 435, 540n7

Kubera: Alaka's king, 397, 455; brother of, 287; city of, 387n; directional guardian, 504n16, 512n12, 539n22; Pushpaka chariot of, 335, 367, 525n21; region of, 87, 512n12; son of, 525n22; wealth of, 103, 197, 199, 429, 431, 512n12, 539n24

Kumara, x, 65, 105, 427, 504n16

Kumārasambhava, x, xiii, xv, xvi, 513n1, 516n3, 517n15, 518n1, 522n23

Kumbhakarna, 295, 531n27, 531n28

Kumbhinasi, 361, 535n6

Kumbhodara, 37

Kumuda, 405, 407, 409, 411

Kumudvati, 409, 411, 433, 539n2

Kuntaleśvaradautya, xxvn10

Kurukshetra, 528n20

Kusha, 381, 395, 401; birth of, 535n5; grandson of, 433; Indra's ally, 411, 537n3; jewel lost by, 405, 407, 409; marries Kumudvati, 409; name of, 365, 536n24, 539n3; reign of, xvii, 385; son of, 411

Kushadhvaja, 263, 527n16

Kushavati, 381, 393, 536n24

Kushika, 259

Ladakh, 510n43

Lake Manasa, 127, 319

Lake Pampa, 311

Lakshmana: in Bhavabhuti, 534n6; birth of, 243; body abandoned by, 379, 536n22; in Dandaka forest, 277, 279, 281; demons killed by, 293, 355, 530n26; Rama and, 245, 273, 287, 311, 532n13; returns to Ayodhya, 301, 325; Saumitri, 331, 345; Shatrughna's brother, 361, 363; Shurpanakha disfigured by, 285, 529n12, 531n27; Sita and, 321, 341, 343, 345; sons of, 379; Urmila and, 527n16; Videha, 259; Vishvamitra and, 249; wounded, 293, 530n24

Lakshmi, 71, 169, 203n, 447; dreams about, 241; emerges from milk ocean, 407, 516n5, 527n12, 537n14; Sita compared to, 261, 337, 355; Vishnu and, 151, 227, 516n5, 523nn5–6

Lanka, 536n27; causeway to, 291, 531n2; Hanuman burns, 289, 530n20; lords of, 139, 295, 327, 383, 515n29; women of, 293

Lauhitya River, 91

Lava, 365, 381, 535n5, 536n24

Lavana, 357, 363, 365, 367, 535n3, 535n6

Lineage of the Raghus, The. See Raghuvaṃśa

Lokaloka, 502n24

Madhupaghna, 361, 535n6

Madhya Pradesh, 514n14

Madurai, 515n27

Magadha, 513n6; king of, 125, 127; princess or queen from, 11, 17, 49, 55

Magha, xiii

Mahābhārata, x, xii, xiv, xxi

Mahakala, x, 131, 514n12

Mahendra, Mount, 81, 137, 539n22

Mahishmati, 133, 514n14, 514n16

Mainaka, 532n7

Maithili. See Sita: Maithili

Mālavikāgnimitra, xi, xiv, xvi, xxii, xxvn13

Malaya, 83, 85, 139, 203, 205, 303, 509n30, 531n2, 539n22; king of, 201

Mallinatha, 508n14, 517n12, 523n30, 528n25, 531n35; date of, xxix; extra verses in, 535n8, 538n16; flora or fauna in, 522n24, 537n4; Indumati's garland in, 520n23; influence of, xxix, xxxi; Lakshmana and Urmila in, 527n16; variant spellings in, 536n24; Vedantic variant in, 518n4; women in, 513n24, 516n36

Malyavat, Mount, 309, 532n13

Mandakini River, 315

Mandara, Mount, 77, 501n3, 532n12

Mandasor, xxvn6

Manu, 5, 534n15; laws of, xxiii, 349, 503n12, 534n15; lineage of, 27, 35, 73, 197, 225

Maricha, 257

Matanga, 109, 512n18

Mathura, 135, 365, 514n18, 515n23, 517n9; Shatrughna creates, 363, 514n21

Meghadūta, xiii, xviii

Meghanada, 295, 530n26. *See also* Indrajit

Meru, Mount, 5, 155, 417, 501n4, 529n9
Mīmāṃsā, 511n9
Mithila, 257, 261, 263, 267, 327
Murala River, 85
Mysore, 509n30

Nabhas, 435
Nagapura, 137, 515n27
Nahusha, 313, 532n16
Naimisha forest, 451
Naiṣadhacarita, xiii
Nala, 433, 539n4
Nalakubara, 525n22
Namuchi, 203, 517n9, 521n9
Nandana, 179, 195
Nandigrama, 279, 528n4
Nandini, 27, 33, 45, 61
Narada, 179, 519n13
Naravahanadatta, xxvn14
Narayanapandita, 514n11, 537n21
Narmada River, 107, 111, 512n15, 512n19, 514n16
Nepal, xxii
Nikumbha, 37
Nilgai, 213
Nilgiri hills, 509n30
Nimi, 261, 527n13
Nipa, 133
Nirriti, 504n16
Nishada tribe, 319, 345, 349
Nishadha, 433, 539n1
Nyāya, 511n9

Odisha, 508n19
Oxus River, 510n38

Pakistan, xviii, 536nn19–20
Pancharatra, 524n13

Panchavati, 283, 313
Pandyas, 83, 139, 509n29, 515nn27–28
Panini, 526n2
Parantapa, 127
Parashurama, 85, 133, 524n9; Jamadagni's son, 528n21, 528n23; Kartavirya-Arjuna and, 528n23; Kashyapa and, 528nn26–27; Kshatriyas destroyed by, 261, 265, 267, 528n20; mother of, 343, 528n21, 534n10; Mount Krauncha split by, 528n23; Rama and, 267, 269, 271, 273
Pariyatra, 437, 539n22
Parvati, 3, 33n, 37, 55n, 504n16, 510n44, 513n1, 516n3
Patna, 513n6
Persians, 87, 510n35
Prachetas, 21, 373
Prachetasa, 371, 373
Prachinabarhis, 77, 508n13
Pradipa, 133
Pragjyotisha, 91
Prahlada, 517n9
Prajapati, 237
Prasenajit, 528n21
Prayag, 514n21, 541n23
Priyadarshana, 109
Priyamvada, 109, 111, 165
Pulastya, 325, 533n25
Punarvasu, 259, 526n8
Pundarika, 435, 539n6
Puranas, xxi, 508n13, 511n9
Pururavas, 512n19
Pushkala, 379, 536n1
Pushkalavati, 536n19
Pushpaka, 237, 301n, 313, 327, 335, 525n21

Pushya, 443, 540n21

Raghu, xvii, 507n4, 509n32,
510nn33–35, 510n43, 511n44,
511n5, 512n12, 518n4, 519n10,
539n24; All-Conquering Sacrifice
of, 93, 95, 143; ancestors of,
506n26, 508n22; conquests
of, ix, xi, xxivn3, 77, 79, 81, 83,
85, 87, 89, 91, 93, 197, 508n18,
516n8; consecrated and reigns,
69, 71, 73, 75; death or funeral of,
177, 519n12; descendants of, 257,
259, 359, 367, 385, 451; envoy
received by, 105, 107; Indra
battles, 65, 67, 506n30; Kautsa
and, 95, 99, 101, 103; name of,
55, 505n12; retires, 169, 173, 175,
518n19, 518n6, 519n12; sacrificial
horse protected by, 61, 63; son of,
105, 113, 121, 141, 143, 145, 167,
171 (see also Aja); youth of, 57, 59
Raghupañcikā, xxiii
Raghus, 387, 518n19, 527n13; chief
or lord of, 199, 301, 391; foremost
of, 391, 395; home of, 397; lineage
of, 5, 241, 245, 249, 331, 365, 445;
sacrifices of, 395; scion of, 167,
333, 367
Raghuvaṃśa: alternate versions
of, xxix–xxx; commentaries on,
xv, xviii, xxiii, xxix, xxx, xxxi;
compared to other works, xvi,
xviii; criticism of, xviii–xx; date
of, xi; editions of, xxxii; genre of,
xii–xiii; geographical information
in, ix–x; kennings in, xxxiii–xxxiv;
kings in, xvii; manuscripts of,
xxx; memorized, xxx; meters
in, 518n1; plotlines of, xiii, xvii,
xix; Rama story in, xv, xvii, xix,
xxvin24, 530n23; reception of,
xviii–xxi, xxxii; spurious chapters
of, xv; translations of, xxxii–
xxxiii
Rahu, 37, 281, 517n9
Rama, xvii, xix; Agastya gives
jewel to, 369, 405; Ahalya saved
by, 259, 526n6; allows Sita to
return, 373, 375, 377; arrives
in Ayodhya, 323, 325, 327, 329;
Bhagiratha's descendant, 531n3;
Bharata's brother, 253, 267, 351;
Bharata visits in forest, 277;
in Bhavabhuti, 534n6; birth
of, 241; bow broken by, 261,
528n24; compared to autumn,
369, 535n11; consecrated, 331;
Dasharatha's son, 323; Death
speaks with, 379; deer tricks,
287; departs for Ayodhya, 301;
describes sights, 303; exiled,
275, 277, 279, 281, 528nn2–4,
533n24; Hanuman as devotee
of, 530n19; Hari, 303; horse
sacrifice of, 371, 377, 535n17;
illusory, 293; immobilized by
snake arrows, 293, 530n24; as
incarnation, 525n18, 526n5,
536n23, 536n26; Kabandha killed
by, 289, 529n17; Lakshmana and,
245, 293; marries Sita, 263; meets
his sons, 373; in Mithila, 257, 259,
261; on Mount Malyavat, 309,
532n13; multiplied, 285, 529n13;
Parashurama and, 267, 269, 271,
273; Raghu hero or lord, 301, 333,
337; Ravana fights, 295, 297, 299;

Ravana's army fights, 293, 295,
531n27; reigns, 333, 335, 337,
365, 367; returns to heaven, 381;
sages appeal to, 357; Shambhuka
beheaded by, 369; Shurpanakha
and, 283, 285, 287; Sita exiled by,
339, 341, 345, 347, 349, 355; sons
of (see Lava; Kusha); sons sing
story of, 373, 535n8; Tataka killed
by, 253, 255, 526n4; Valin killed
by, 289, 529–530n18; Valmiki
and, 535n14; Vibhishana meets,
291; Vishvamitra and, 249, 251,
255. *See also* Raghuvaṃśa: Rama
story in
Rāmāyaṇa, xii, 525n25, 527n16,
529n8, 530n23, 535n17; northern
recension of, 529n6; as source
for Kalidasa, xxi–xxii; Valmiki
as author of, xviii, xxi,501n2,
534n16, 535n8. *See also*
Raghuvaṃśa: Rama story in
Rambha, 525n22
Rasatala, 291, 530n22
Rashtrakutas, xxvn10
Rati, 121, 153, 513n1, 518n1
Ravana, 253, 383, 525n17, 525n21,
529n14, 530nn20–21, 530n23,
530n26, 531nn28–30, 531n35;
curse restrains, 237, 525n22; gods
or world harassed by, 225, 233,
235, 237, 243; Indra's conqueror,
131, 139; Lakshmana wounded
by, 293; lord of Lanka, 139, 295,
327, 515n29; Mt. Kailasa moved
by, 91, 297, 510n44, 531n30;
Rama fights, 295, 297, 299, 301;
sisters of, 283, 530n23, 535n6 (*see
also* Shurpanakha); Sita abducted

by, 287, 289, 327, 375, 515n29;
ten-headed, 177, 297, 299,
355, 515n29, 525n18, 531n30;
weapons of, 299, 531n33
Rāvaṇavadha, xiii
Ravikirti, xi
Renuka, 528n21
Reva River, 133, 393, 514n16
R̥g Veda, 535n15
Riksha, 539n22
Rikshavat, Mount, 107, 512n15
Rishyashringa, 523n3
Rohini, 541n6
R̥tusaṃhāra, xiv, xxvn15

Sagara, 63, 506n26
Sahya, 85, 509n30, 539n22
Saketa, 333. *See also* Ayodhya
Sāma Veda, 524n12, 536n2
Samantapanchaka, 528n20
Samjna, 514n10
Sampati, 289
Samudragupta, xi, xxvn9
Sankhya, 533n22
Sanskrit, 515n30, 521n13, 537n2;
commentaries in, xviii, xxxi;
"great poems" in, xii; Kalidasa's,
ix, xviii, xx; inscriptions in, xi;
literature in, xviii, xxii, xxxii;
names or kennings in, xxxiii,
504n2; poetic conventions in,
522n23, 529n15; puns in, 527n17,
528n1; similes based on, 527n17;
technical literature in, xxii;
Vedic, 535n15; works on poetics
in, xxvn10
Sarasvati, 71, 129, 514n9
Sarasvati River, 51, 541n23
Sarayu River, 319n, 321, 379, 391,

461; Ganga and, 195, 329; Kusha reaches, 395; Kusha sports in, 399, 401, 405; sacrificial posts beside, 201; ships on, 337; stairway to heaven, 381

Satakarni, 313, 533n17

Saumilla, xxii

Saumitri. *See* Lakshmana; Shatrughna

Savitri, 375, 535n15

Shachi, 65, 127, 149, 411, 513n5, 516n2, 537n3; comparisons to, 53, 55, 179

Shakra. *See* Indra

Shakrajit, 355

Shala, 437, 439, 540n13

Shambhuka, 369

Sharabhanga, 315

Sharavati, 536n24

Shatakratu, 506n21. *See also* Indra: hundred sacrifices of

Shatrughatin, 365, 536n1

Shatrughna: Bharata and, 245; birth of, 243; Dasharatha's son, 359; Mathura built by, 363, 514n21; name of, 357, 534n1; park prepared by, 327; returns to Ayodhya, 365, 367; sages protected by, 357, 359, 361; Saumitri, 359; sons of, 365; Valmiki and, 359, 365, 535n9

Shesha, 203n, 227, 291, 521n2, 523n4

Shiva: as archer, 65, 141; bow of, 261, 269, 528n24; comparisons to, 47, 55, 65, 79, 319; Daksha and, 527n11; demons' cities destroyed by, 506n27, 516n34, 537n6; deodar tree of, 37;

directional guardian, 504n16; eightfold, 37, 506n33, 511n2; Ganga from hair of, 79, 317, 508n16, 537n6; Ishvara, 297; Kailasa as home of, 510n44, 531n30; Kalidasa's devotion to, x; Kumara's birth from, x, 47, 504n16; in *Kumārasambhava*, x, 516n3; lord, lord of creatures, or lord of spirits, 39, 43, 201, 503n8; love god and, 121, 255, 399, 512n20, 513n1; Mahakala, x, 131, 514n12; Maheshvara, 63, 506n25; names of, xxxiii; Parameshvara, 3, 501n1; Pinakin, 141; power of, 39; Ravana and, 139, 297, 525n18, 531n30; Rudra, xxxiii, 41, 261; in sacrificer's body, 69, 201, 506n33, 511n2, 521n8; temples to, x, 179, 514n12; Ugra, 95, 506n33, 511n2, 521n8

Shona River, 159, 225, 517n10

Shravasti, 381, 536n24

Shri, 65, 129, 279, 513n9, 514n15

Shriharsha, xiii

Shrinatha, xxxi, 527n16, 527n19

Shrivatsa, 227, 417, 523n6

Shudras, 369, 511n8

Shuktiman, 539n22

Shurasena, 133, 514n18

Shurpanakha, 283, 285, 287, 529n12, 531n27

Shyama, 317

Sipra River, 131, 514n12

Śiśupālavadha, xiii

Sita, xvii, 273, 291, 297, 335, 531n2, 533n20, 534n8, 535n14; abandoned, 339, 41, 343, 345, 357, 365; abducted, 287, 515n29,

532n13; in Bhavabhuti, 533; citizens doubt, 339, 375, 377; crow attacks, 279, 281; Earth swallows, 377; Hanuman consoles, 291; illusory Rama killed before, 293, 530n23; image of, 355, 371; Janaka finds, 527n12, 534n13; Lakshmana and, 285, 321, 343, 345, 347; lamentations of, 347, 349, 355; Maithili, 281, 283, 327, 371, 373, 375; mothers-in-law greeted by, 329; pregnancy of, 337; purity of, 301, 333, 375; Rama in exile with, 277, 281; Rama marries, 263; Rama recalls, 373, 375; search for, 287, 289; Shurpanakha and, 283; sights pointed out to, 303; sons of, 359, 365, 375, 377, 397, 409, 535n5 (see also Lava; Kusha); Vaidehi, 279, 281, 337, 339, 341, 343, 351, 355; Valmiki welcomes, 349, 351, 353
Skanda, 37, 55, 534n5; comparisons to, 121, 149, 197, 271; Devasena and, 149, 516n1
Soma, 504n16
Sri Lanka, ix
Subahu (1), 257
Subahu (2), 365, 536n1
Sudakshina, 11, 33, 45, 49, 69, 504nn2–3
Sudarshana, 443, 445, 541n24
Sugriva, 295, 301; in Ayodhya, 301, 323, 333; monkey king, 289, 323, 529n17–530n18, 533n25
Suhmas, 79, 508n17
Suketu, 251, 526n3
Sumantra, 319
Sumantu, 343

Sumeru, Mount, 103, 512n13
Sumitra, 239, 243, 263, 345, 359
Sunanda, 125, 127, 131, 137, 141, 145, 513n4, 516n38
Supratika, 117, 513n24
Surabhi, 21, 27, 41
Sushena, 133, 135
Sutikshna, 315
Svaha, 17, 502n18

Taksha, 379, 536n1r
Takshaka, 409
Takshashila, 536n19
Tamasa River, 201, 219, 351
Tamralipta, 508n17
Tamraparni River, 83
Tataka, 253, 255, 257, 526n3
Taxila, 537n19
Three Pushkaras, 443, 541n23
Tiruchirappalli, 509n27, 515n27
Trijata, 293, 530n23
Trikuta, Mount, 85, 536n27
Trinabindu, 191
Trishiras, 287
Trivikrama, 532n5

Uddhya River, 251
Ugra. See Shiva: Ugra
Ujjain, x, 514n12
Ujjayini, 514n12
Uma, 55. See also Parvati
Unnabha, 439, 540n14
Upanishads, 540n18
Urmila, 263, 527n16
Urva, 223, 510n37, 523n31. See also Aurva
Urvashi Won by Valor. See Vikramorvaśīya
Utkala, 81, 508n19

Utsavasanketas, 91, 510n43
Uttarakosala, 49, 141, 197, 321,
    435, 441
Uttar Pradesh, 514n18, 536n24

Vaidehi. *See* Sita
Vaidyashrigarbha, 527n19
Vaishyas, 511n8
Vajranabha, 439, 540n15
Vakatakas, xi, xxvn10
Valin, 289, 529–530n18
Vallabhadeva, 513n7, 516n36,
    517n12, 520n16, 521n4, 537n8,
    539n6; celestial elephants in,
    531n35; festival described
    by, 539n23; date of, xxiii,
    xxx; other commentaries
    differ from, 517n16, 520n17,
    525n28; grammatical
    difficulties resolved by,
    528n25; Indumati's ornaments
    in, 520n23; Kashmirian,
    xxiii, xxx; Lakshmana and
    Urmila in, 527n16; oldest
    commentator, xv, xxxi; puns
    in, 527n19; source not known
    to, 537n1; variants noted by,
    xxx; verse order differs in,
    533n21; Vishnu's faces in,
    524n13; words glossed by,
    508n14, 509n28
Valmiki, xxii, 501n2, 527n16; first
    poet, xviii, xxi, 373, 534n16,
    535n8; hermitage of, 343, 347,
    353, 359, 365, 535n5, 535n17;
    Lava's and Kusha's guru, 365,
    371, 373; Prachetasa, 371, 373;
    Shatrughna and, 359, 365,
    535n9; Sita and, 343, 347, 353,

373, 377, 535n5, 535n14. *See
    also* Rāmāyaṇa
Vamadeva, 225, 523n3
Vamana, 255, 526n5
Vanayu, 117, 513n23
Vangas, 79
Vankshu River, 89, 510n38
Varatantu, 95, 512n11
Varuna, 29, 197, 431n, 503n5;
    directional guardian, 504n16,
    527n15, 539n22; Indra and,
    263, 527n15
Vasava, 67
Vasishtha, 502n22, 524n9; Aja
    consecrated by, 171; Arundhati
    and, 47, 502n18; ashram of, 11;
    cow of, 23, 31, 45, 61 (*see also*
    Nandini); as guru, 11, 45, 321,
    323, 419; mantras of, 103, 419
Vasvokasara, 387
Vayu, 504n16, 509n23
Vedanta, 518n4
Vedas, 27, 155, 225, 393;
    knowledge or study of, 179,
    502n25, 505n16, 511n9,
    540n20, 541n26; mantras
    of, 415, 502n21, 535n15;
    mythology of, 521n9, 527n15;
    recited, 241, 365, 532n6;
    sacrifices or fires prescribed
    by, 235, 365, 506n33, 512n11,
    512n21, 515n28, 518n19,
    534n20, 536n25, 537n21; *soma*
    pressing in, 540n19; *śruti*,
    503n2; those learned in the,
    101, 441, 540n20; Sanskrit of,
    535n15
Vibhishana, 301, 323, 333,
    530n21, 536n27; lord of Lanka,

383; Pulastya's son, 325, 533n25; Rama meets, 291

Vidarbha, ix, xx, 111; king of, 107, 113, 121, 137, 141, 145, 149, 157 (*see also* Bhoja); princess of, 167 (*see also* Indumati)

Vidaujas, 347, 534n14. *See also* Indra

Videha, 259, 527n13; daughter of king of (*see* Sita: Vaidehi)

Vidisha, 365

Vidyujjihva, 530n23

Vikramaditya, ix

Vikramorvaśīya, xiv, 517n11

Vindhya, Mount, 331, 393, 512n15, 536n24, 539n22, 540n11; Agastya and, 139, 283, 529n9

Viradha, 281, 529n8

Vishnu, 203n, 239, 247, 269, 303, 393, 524n14, 531n1; Best of Souls, 63; boar incarnation of, 165, 305, 517n15, 532n8; comparisons to, 77, 151, 157, 211, 347, 367, 417, 435; dark color of, 237, 525n23; dharma protected by, 357; faces of, 524n13, 524n16; Garuda and, 443n, 508n23, 524n8; gods appeal to, 225; human embodiments of, 407; incarnations of, 237, 441, 517n15, 525n18, 525n30, 526n5, 532n5, 536n23, 536n26; Kaustubha of, 417, 515n22, 523n6; Lakshmi and, 151, 516n5, 523nn5–6; lotus-eyed, 435, 539n6; obedience of, 347; portions of, 247, 385; power or

might of, 239, 271, 401; Primal Being, 237, 271, 305, 532n8; rests on ocean, 305, 532n6; rests on Shesha, 291, 523n4, 532n6; *sattva* predominates in, 505n15; Shiva's bow and, 269, 528n24; steps or strides of, 157, 393, 517n9, 520n24, 532n5, 536n5; Upendra, 534n14; Vamana, 255, 526n5; Vishvaksena, 383, 536n27; weapons of, 523n7, 525n26, 528n24; worlds of, 189

Vishvakarman, 129, 514n10, 528n24

Vishvaksena, 383, 536n27

Vishva gods, 441

Vishvamitra, 249, 251, 257, 259

Vishvasaha, 441, 540n18

Viṣṇu Purāṇa, 508n13

Vrindavana, 135, 515nn23–24

Vritra, 67, 517n9

Vyushitashva, 439, 540n17

Western Ghats, 509n27, 509n30, 531n2

Yājñavalkyasmṛti, 520n25

Yama, 431; comparisons to, 197; directional guardian, 504n16, 539n22; mace of, 297, 531n33

Yamuna River, 135, 517n10; Ganga and, 319, 514n21, 541n23; Kaliya in, 135, 515n22; Mathura built near, 363; sages dwelling near, 357

Yavanas, 87, 510n35

Yudhajit, 377, 535n18

ABOUT THE BOOK

Murty Classical Library of India volumes are designed by Rathna Ramanathan and Guglielmo Rossi. Informed by the history of the Indic book and drawing inspiration from polyphonic classical music, the series design is based on the idea of "unity in diversity," celebrating the individuality of each language while bringing them together within a cohesive visual identity.

The Sanskrit text of this book is set in the Murty Sanskrit typeface, commissioned by Harvard University Press and designed by John Hudson and Fiona Ross. The proportions and styling of the characters are in keeping with the typographic tradition established by the renowned Nirnaya Sagar Press, with a deliberate reduction of the typically high degree of stroke modulation. The result is a robust, modern typeface that includes Sanskrit-specific type forms and conjuncts.

The English text is set in Antwerp, designed by Henrik Kubel from A2-TYPE and chosen for its versatility and balance with the Indic typography. The design is a free-spirited amalgamation and interpretation of the archives of type at the Museum Plantin-Moretus in Antwerp.

All the fonts commissioned for the Murty Classical Library of India will be made available, free of charge, for non-commercial use. For more information about the typography and design of the series, please visit http://www.hup.harvard.edu/mcli.

Printed on acid-free paper by Maple Press, York, Pennsylvania.